A CONCISE

ENCYCLOPEDIA

of the

PHILOSOPHY OF RELIGION

OTHER BOOKS IN THE SAME SERIES

RELATED TITLES PUBLISHED BY ONEWORLD

A CONCISE

ENCYCLOPEDIA

of the

PHILOSOPHY OF RELIGION

ANTHONY C. THISELTON

ONEWORLD

OXFORD

A CONCISE ENCYCLOPEDIA OF THE PHILOSOPHY OF RELIGION

Oneworld Publications
(Sales and Editorial)
185 Banbury Road
Oxford OX2 7AR
England
www.oneworld-publications.com

ISBN 1–85168–301–1

Cover design by Design Deluxe
Typeset by LaserScript, Mitcham, UK
Printed and bound in the United Kingdom by Bell & Bain Ltd, Glasgow

Contents

Preface and acknowledgements

Aims, scope and target readership

The following selection of subject entries has been shaped in the light of many years of feedback from my own students. I have asked them what themes, thinkers and problems in philosophy of religion they have found most stimulating or rewarding, and also where they have needed most help, clarification and explanation. Their answers have been both formal and anonymous, and informal and personal.

In addition to the criterion of 'professional competency' in philosophy of religion, I have explored issues where pressing problems arise from arguments for or against belief in God, and from differences between diverse religious traditions. For many, this subject combines academic rigour with personal and practical issues about religious belief. I have aimed to set out the arguments of major religious traditions and the counter-arguments of their critics with fairness and integrity, even if I myself find nothing irrational about belief in God, to express this as a bare minimum.

It is my hope, therefore, that this volume will not only fill a needed gap as a student textbook, but that it will also provide a ready work of reference and explanation for those readers who wish to explore issues of belief for their own sake. To this extent, I admit to writing for the general enquirer as well as for students who seek a clear, useful textbook for essays and examinations.

At what level is this aimed? Most of my own classes in philosophy of religion have been for second-year degree students. However, they have included also first years and final years. Most have been honours students in theology and/or in philosophy, but many have majored in other subjects. I have been sufficiently impressed by the standards of incoming students who have taken philosophy of religion at 'A' level to have no doubt that the following pages will also provide them with a readable textbook. I point out below that the regular use of cross-references will explain virtually every unfamiliar technical term, and will introduce unfamiliar thinkers.

Style, structure and more on level

I have made a particular point of keeping to short paragraphs, and as far as possible to short sentences. Normally all entries except those of less than three hundred words have been divided by the use of sub-headings, so that no reader need feel intimidated by long, unbroken, pages of argument. The sub-headings also provide easy maps of where arguments lead.

This is the first of my eight books (written to date) without substantial footnotes. This is for the purpose of simplicity and clarity. However, those reference books that fail to identify significant sources for major quotations or arguments lack, to my mind, a resource that may prove to be helpful. Where precise sources are appropriate, authors, titles, publishers and page numbers are cited in brackets in the text. This both relieves the reader of having to take everything on trust, and allows the student to follow up important issues independently.

The system of cross-references and of dates of thinkers or other sources is a key feature. These cross-references assist those readers who need instant explanations of terms, or quick information about the further consequences of arguments under consideration. Dates provide appropriate historical contexts for the accurate understanding of thought in the light of the times. Theologians and philosophers often place different weight respectively upon these: they are more frequently emphasized in theology, but their inclusion prejudices no argument. A further chronological chart is added, without any pre-judgements about the importance of what names may feature in it.

Acknowledgements and thanks

Mrs Carol Dakin has typed this manuscript onto disks throughout. I am deeply grateful to her for this magnificent and excellent work. I regularly gave her unclear handwritten material, which she returned promptly, efficiently and with constant good judgement where guesses must have been inevitable. My former secretaries observed that over the years two qualifications for my Professorship and Headship of Department at Nottingham were required for this post: first, to have taught previously in the University of Durham; and second, to have illegible writing. I was duly appointed.

My weakest points of expertise, I concede, relate to the articles on Islamic philosophy, on Hindu philosophy, and on Buddhist philosophy. I am deeply indebted to Dr Hugh Goddard, Reader in Islamic Theology in the University of Nottingham, for advice on the entry on Islamic Philosophy, and related Islamic thinkers. Likewise, I am very grateful to Dr Philip Goodchild, Senior Lecturer in this Department, for advice and correction on Buddhist philosophy. Dr Brian Carr, Reader in the Department of Philosophy at Nottingham, has given me valuable help, for which I thank him warmly, on Hindu philosophy and Hindu thinkers. He is also co-editor of the *Encyclopaedia of Asian Philosophy*.

During the final month before the submission of the manuscript, I was Scholar in Residence for 2002 in Union University, Jackson, Tennessee. I should like to thank Union University, Dr Randall Bush, and his colleagues for giving me every possible facility to complete the manuscript on time, including my sending quantities of faxed handwriting to Mrs Dakin, and edited e-mails to my wife at home. My time at Union University was a very happy one.

Home life often suffers during these undertakings, and my wife Rosemary continued to put up with my working every day into the late evening even though my previous book of some 1,500 pages had made the same relentless demands for several years without any interval between these books. She went the second mile of reading typescripts for errors, checking through disks, typing revisions, and undertaking related tasks. I am so grateful for this forbearance and for her work. As before, Mrs Sheila Rees also undertook some proof-reading at a period of high pressure, and I thank her most warmly.

Finally, I value immensely the encouragement received from colleagues, from one or two close friends, and from some former students, to persevere with yet another book which they generously encouraged me to think was worthwhile, in spite of other wide-ranging professional and church commitments. Their encouragement has been a special and needed gift. Ms Victoria Warner of Oneworld Publications has also been among these encouragers, and I thank her for her patient advice and support.

Anthony C. Thiselton,
Department of Theology,
University of Nottingham
Good Friday, 2002

A

a fortiori

The term denotes an argument that applies 'all the more', or 'with greater force'. In LOGIC, if a given consequence follows from a case that is actually weaker, *a fortiori* that consequence will follow 'from a stronger' (Latin, *a fortiori*) argument. This logical notion has been used since ancient times. Traditionally it features in Rabbi Hillel's seven 'rules of interpretation' concerning what may be inferred from a biblical text.

a posteriori

Beliefs or truths that are established by *a posteriori* arguments or knowledge are derived from evidence, experience, or observation of the world. The term stands in contrast to A PRIORI, which denotes that which is prior to, and independent of, such experience or observation.

A posteriori arguments depend upon empirical evidence, which subsequently confirms or disconfirms what has been asserted as true, or as possibly true. In philosophy of religion the COSMOLOGICAL ARGUMENT for the existence of God characteristically begins with experience or observations about the world, in contrast to the ONTOLOGICAL ARGUMENT, which turns on logical questions about the concept of God.

Clearly what is true merely by definition, or what is entailed entirely by logical reasoning, belongs to the realm of *a priori* argument; while inferences drawn from empirical observations of the everyday world (including the natural sciences) belong to the realm of *a posteriori* argument. (*See also* ANALYTIC STATEMENTS; GOD, ARGUMENTS FOR THE EXISTENCE OF; KANT; EMPIRICISM.)

a priori

The term (Latin) denotes that which is prior to, or independent of, human experience or observation. It therefore stands in contrast to what is argued A POSTERIORI, i.e. from what is confirmed or disconfirmed from subsequent experience or observation. The clearest examples of *a priori* propositions are ANALYTIC STATEMENTS, i.e. those that are true (or those that are justified) on the basis of *a priori* conceptual definition: e.g. 'all bachelors are unmarried', 'all circles are round'. These remain incontestable independently of observations about particular bachelors, or about a circle that I might try to draw.

Thus *a priori* (from first principle) may be applied to arguments or to propositions or statements. However, their logical currency is often either merely formal (true by definition) or negative (the argument or statement does not depend on what is subsequently experienced or observed). In philosophy of religion the ONTOLOGICAL ARGUMENT for the existence of God characteristically operates on the basis of *a priori* reasoning, in contrast to the COSMOLOGICAL ARGUMENT, which utilizes *a posteriori* inferences from our experience of the world. (*See also* GOD, ARGUMENTS FOR THE EXISTENCE OF; KANT.)

Abelard (Abailard), Peter
(1079–1142)

As a major French philosopher and theologian of the twelfth century, Abelard made his chief contribution to LOGIC and ONTOLOGY. In particular he attempted a mediating position between NOMINALISM (the view that UNIVERSALS are merely linguistic signs or names (Latin, *nomen*) for classes or particular entities) and REALISM (universals are realities in themselves).

Each side, Abelard argued, was right in what it affirmed, but wrong in what it denied. Nominalists are right to insist that logic and SEMANTICS operate in the realm of signs and concepts; they do not trade directly in realities themselves. Realists are right, however, to insist that logic and semantics do not merely chase other signs and concepts that never engage with realities, even if they are wrong to confuse the two levels.

Abelard's mediating position is often known as CONCEPTUALISM. He rejects a merely subjectivist account of meaning, as if meaning had no 'controls'. Yet his attacks on naïve realism are even sharper. He insists that logic operates in its own domain. Logical validity is not identical with truth about a state of affairs.

This emerges most forcefully in Abelard's attention to propositions. Propositions are true or false, i.e. the property of being true-or-false belongs to propositional content. In spite of having access

to Latin translations of only some of ARISTOTLE's words (especially to BOETHIUS' translations of his *Categories* and *On Interpretation*), Abelard developed Aristotle's propositional logic in creative ways.

In relation to Christian theology and religion, Abelard rejected any blind appeal to sheer authority as such. His contemporary, Bernard of Clairvaux (1091–1153), denounced him for so exalting reason and logic as to make faith and revelation, in effect, irrelevant. Parallel debates may be observed in ISLAMIC PHILOSOPHY of this period.

It is difficult to argue that Abelard discounted biblical revelation. After all, he produced an *Exposition of the Epistle to the Romans*. However, he rejected any exclusive claim for the authority of the Bible or the Church Fathers, arguing that ancient Greek philosophy was often closer to the New Testament than the Hebrew Bible or Old Testament.

Abelard also emphasized the importance of thinking for oneself. He disagreed with both of his own very different teachers, Roscellinus (himself unorthodox) and William of Champeaux. Like SOCRATES, he saw doubt (rather than certainty) as the path to knowledge through exploration and discovery.

In theology Abelard's accounts of the Trinity and of the atonement have both been severely criticized. He is credited with expounding a theology of the atonement through Jesus Christ which rests upon 'moral influence' or 'example', rather than on any notion of Godward sacrifice as held by ANSELM and Calvin. His attempt to expound Romans 3:19–26 entirely in terms of a demonstration of God's love hardly does justice to this Pauline text.

However, it was for his logic and ontology, rather than for his theology, that Abelard attracted large numbers of students to Paris. From the twelfth to the sixteenth centuries, it has been said, logic occupied the position of privilege and esteem that the nineteenth century recorded to the sciences. Paris became an important centre of philosophy, and the conceptualism of Abelard influenced such figures as ALBERT the Great and Thomas AQUINAS. He constitutes a major influence on mediaeval Western SCHOLASTICISM.

Absolute

In its widest, most popular sense, the Absolute denotes that which is unconditional and complete in itself. It stands in contrast to all that is relative. In the broadest terms it denotes what is unqualified, independent of conditioning influences, and the ground of its own being (ASEITY).

In more technical terms, the word has different nuances within different philosophical traditions. In German IDEALISM, KANT (1724–1804) uses the term to denote what is unconditionally valid. SCHELLING (1775–1854) postulates an Absolute which is that prior ground before selfhood comes to perceive the world or reach self-awareness in terms of subject and object, or spirit and nature. TILLICH (1886–1965) is partially influenced by Schelling in his insistence that God is not an existent being, but is 'Being-itself'.

It is with HEGEL (1770–1831) that the term is most often associated. Hegel rejected Schelling's account, and identified the Absolute as Spirit. As Absolute, Spirit finds self-expression within the world through a DIALECTIC process of logical and historical NECESSITY.

This is because Hegel's Absolute Idea embraces within itself a unity that is also self-differentiating. In his philosophical theology Hegel postulated a coherence with the Christian doctrine of God as Trinity: God is an unqualified unity who has nevertheless expressed self-differentiation in a historical dialectic as Father, Son and Holy Spirit, in successive modes of self-disclosure.

In the English-speaking world BRADLEY (1846–1924) of Oxford argued that differentiation presupposes the reality of the Absolute as wholeness. Diversity is mere appearance; only the whole is real (*Appearance and Reality*, 1893). The Absolute is unconditioned by time or change, for supposedly even time is unreal.

Josiah Royce (1855–1916) represented American IDEALISM. He identified the Absolute both with God and with the spirit of the great, final, 'community of persons'. An organic whole is presupposed by the differences of human experience (*The Conception of God*, 1897).

In identifying the Absolute with God (against Bradley) Royce was returning to the early tradition of Nicholas of Cusa (1401–64). Nicholas argued that God is 'absolutely infinite'. God so clearly transcends whatever is relative and CONTINGENT that God even holds together as the Absolute a 'coincidence of opposites', just as infinity moves similarly beyond characterization in any specific, limited or relative form.

In spite of these technical nuances in Schelling, Hegel, Bradley, Royce and Nicholas, the term *Absolute* is often used more broadly to stand in contrast with all that is relative or conditioned by other agents or forces. Especially in ETHICS the term is used to exclude cultural, historical or social relativism.

While the broader notion of unconditionedness, ultimacy, self-subsistence and aseity retains a place in the philosophy of religion (*see* GOD, CONCEPTS AND 'ATTRIBUTES' OF; ISLAMIC PHILOSOPHY; TRANSCENDENCE) the more technical claims of German and Anglo-American idealism are less prominent today than they were during the nineteenth century. However, in *Ascent to the Absolute* (London: Allen & Unwin, 1970) J.N. Findlay has argued for the unconditional basis of all things.

accident

Used as a technical term in Aristotelian and in SCHOLASTIC philosophy, accident denotes a CONTINGENT quality that happens to inhere in some underlying substance. The 'substance' remains an enduring supportive substratum, while the apparent quality or accident 'happens' (from the Latin *accidere*, to happen).

Traditional Roman Catholic theology utilized the Aristotelian and Thomist distinction to defend the notion of transubstantiation. The underlying substance changed to become the body and blood of Christ, while the observable accidents remained perceptible to the eye as bread and wine.

AQUINAS writes: 'It is through the accidents (*per accidentia*) that we judge the substance (*de substantia*) ... The accidents of the bread ... remain when the substance of the bread (*substantia panis*) is no longer there' but the substance has become the body and blood of Christ under the outward appearance of the 'accidents' of bread and wine (*Summa Theologiae*, III, Qu. 75, art. 5).

Much recent Catholic doctrine, however, does not remain tied to the formulation of Aquinas in the thirteenth century. The Reformers vigorously opposed it. Both traditions today tend to seek a more dynamic understanding of how the death of Christ is 'proclaimed' or 'called actively to mind with effects' in the Lord's Supper or the Eucharist. (*See also* ARISTOTLE.)

actuality

The broadest, mainline meaning of this term is drawn from ARISTOTLE, in whose writings it stands in contrast to potentiality or 'possibility'. Finite entities have potentialities which become actual when they are realized. Aristotle applied actuality to form; potentiality to matter. Thomas AQUINAS developed this further in his FIVE WAYS of argument concerning the existence of God. Potentiality is the basis of his Kinetological Way (argument from motion) in contrast to God's ASEITY.

Existentialist writers, however, apply the contrast between actuality and possibility differently. HEIDEGGER, MARCEL and SARTRE tend to apply 'actuality' for

'things' or objects, and to reserve 'possibility' to denote an existential mode of being distinctive to persons and agents. Sartre contrasts being-in-itself (*être-en-soi*; cf. actuality) with being-for-itself (*être-pour-soi*; cf. possibility). Possibility denotes a mode of existence in which openness to the future may be realized by decision, whereas actuality denotes an 'it' which is 'closed' to such active decision (*see* BUBER; EXISTENTIALISM).

In TELEOLOGICAL contexts actuality denotes the fulfilment or realization of purpose. This brings us back to Aristotle's contrast between the possibilities of matter which find expression in the 'actuality' of form.

agnosticism

At first sight agnosticism is often perceived as being less dogmatic and more open than either THEISM or ATHEISM when applied to the belief-systems of religions. It appears to suspend the acceptance or rejection of belief.

In practice, however, thoroughgoing agnosticism denotes the belief that to know whether a belief-system is true or false is impossible. Such knowledge lies beyond the enquirer (from Greek *a-gnosis*, no knowledge). This amounts, however, to no less dogmatic a position than theism, atheism or the belief-system in question. For it invites the rejoinder called 'the paradox of SCEPTICISM': 'How do I know that I cannot know, if I cannot know whether I know?'

Agnosticism as a world-view or attitude to theism, therefore, differs from the more pragmatic use of the term to denote a suspension of belief about some particular claim to truth. The latter may be deemed more reasonable if it is not a generalized, systematic attitude towards religion or towards the denial of religious truth. Certainly agnosticism must be clearly distinguished from atheism, which raises broader and more fundamental historical and logical issues.

Albert the Great (Albertus Magnus, *c.* 1200/06–80)

Albert taught in the University of Paris (1245–8) and at Cologne (from 1248) in his native Germany. He is known chiefly as the teacher of Thomas AQUINAS, and as a major interpreter of ARISTOTLE to the medieval West.

Albert's method of inference from observation of the CONTINGENT world anticipated the approach that Aquinas developed in his FIVE WAYS. In common with most leading Islamic interpreters of Aristotle, Albert endorsed the argument from motion (or from 'possibility') to a First Mover or Uncaused Cause. He rejected the notion of an infinite chain or caused causes (*see* CAUSE; COSMOLOGICAL ARGUMENT; ISLAMIC PHILOSOPHY).

In addition to his contribution as a commentator on Aristotle, Albert was a Dominican theologian. He produced biblical commentaries, and also a commentary on Peter Lombard's *Sentences*. He regarded scriptural revelation and human reason as complementary.

Albert's drive towards synthesis and the ultimate reconciliation of differences allowed him to combine the dominant influence of Aristotle with diverse elements from PLATO, NEOPLATONISM, and such Islamic philosophers as AL-FARABI. He perceived the world as a created mystic harmony, which emanated from the One as Prime Mover, or the Ground of all Being.

Albert's encyclopaedic drawing together of multiple sources (from the Bible, Aristotle, Plato, Arabic philosophy and the natural sciences of the day) provides a context for the founding of the ancient European universities of the thirteenth century. His belief in the compatibility of revealed scripture with human reason also provides the background to the work of Thomas Aquinas.

algorithm

This term has a broader and a more technical use. More broadly it denotes a formal operation, or following of set steps, in LOGIC or in mathematics, especially when symbolic logical notation rather than everyday language is used (e.g. If x, then y . . .). The use of general, abstract, symbolic notation permits a formula or algorithm to remain strictly in the realm of logic or mathematics without specific reference to the CONTINGENT or empirical world of everyday life.

These set steps or formulae in calculation or in problem-solving may take the form of rules or instructions for operations. The term is derived from the Latin translation of the Arabic name of a logical mathematics of the ninth century.

More technically and narrowly, the term is applied in computation where an understanding of the operation verges on the deterministic or mechanical. Hence, for broader philosophical views of the world, algorithms are perceived as strictly instrumental processes, i.e. as performing specified tasks in logic rather than yielding broader understandings of the world.

altruism

Traditionally the term denotes a selfless concern for the well-being of others (Latin, *alter*, other), in contrast to the self-interests of egoism. The term is narrower than DEONTOLOGY, which denotes an ethic based on moral obligation or duty more generally.

From HOBBES to NIETZSCHE, and most recently in more radical postmodernist writers, doubt has been expressed about the possibility of genuine altruism in human life. Nietzsche and many postmodernists have suggested that this motivation is illusory, and merely disguises the interests of the self under the pretence of caring only for others. IDEOLOGICAL CRITICISM seeks to unmask and to expose these interests.

In many religions, including especially the Christian tradition, a distinction may be made between the practical difficulty of genuine altruism for fallen humanity unaided by divine GRACE and the altruistic love for others that may spring from the grace of renewal by the influence of the Holy Spirit of God. (*See also* POSTMODERNITY.)

analogy

The wider context of the use of analogy in LANGUAGE IN RELIGION is set out in detail under that separate, broader entry. The use of analogy is one of the most important primary linguistic resources for talk of God. It permits an extension of meaning or logical grammar beyond that of everyday uses of language, while retaining everyday language as its vehicle or vocabulary-stock.

Analogy, however, is not the only resource of this kind. The roles of SYMBOL, METAPHOR, MYTH, CONCEPTUAL GRAMMAR, and MODELS AND QUALIFIERS are also considered under LANGUAGE IN RELIGION, as well as under separate entries.

The classical formulation of the use of analogy in talk of God comes from Thomas AQUINAS (1225–74). In thirteenth-century debate analogy was seen as a middle way between equivocal (or ambivalent) language, which applied everyday language to God without genuine currency, and univocal language (i.e. language that conveys the same literal meaning in a one-to-one match). Further, it also offered a middle path between the language of negation (VIA NEGATIVA), as advocated by the German mystic Meister ECKHART (1260–1327), and language that conveyed a positive, determinate, cognitive content.

THE BASIC APPROACH OF THOMAS AQUINAS

Aquinas firmly excludes any suggestion that everyday words can be applied to God with exactly the same meaning as they carry in contexts of everyday life. He writes: 'It seems that no word can be used literally of God' (*Summa Theologiae*, Ia,

Qu. 13, art. 3 (Blackfriars edn, vol. 3, 57)). However, he does not agree with PSEUDO-DIONYSIUS that on this basis 'it would be truer to say that God is not good or wise ... than to say that he is' (ibid.). For analogical uses of language one should steer between over-confident univocal uses and over-reticent insistence on the *via negativa* only.

Moreover, to use analogical language of God is not to equivocate. Language would be equivocal (Latin, *aequivoca*) only if there were no resemblance (Latin, *similitudo*) between how the word is used in everyday language and how it is applied to God (ibid., art. 5 (Blackfriars edn, vol. 3, 63)). 'Wisdom', for example, can be applied to God without undue ambiguity or impropriety, because there is at least some degree of resemblance, however inadequate, between what it is to ascribe wisdom to God and what it is to ascribe wisdom to a human person. Aquinas agrees that this is not 'univocal' in meaning (ibid.).

Aquinas sums up his general view in this way: 'Some words are used neither univocally nor purely equivocally of God and creatures, but analogically, for we cannot speak of God at all except in the language we use of creatures ...' (ibid. (Blackfriars edn, 65)).

CONTROVERSY ABOUT THE BASIS AND NATURE OF ANALOGY IN AQUINAS

Even during the thirteenth century DUNS SCOTUS (*c.* 1266–1308) argued that Aquinas tried to hold together two incompatible views. For when confronted with any claim for a univocal use of language in talk of God, Aquinas emphasized the value of the *via negativa* in excluding even the barest hint of a one-to-one match between language about created beings and language about God. He did not reject the use of negation: God is infinite; God is immortal. However, he insisted that the way of negation could not offer a comprehensive or exhaustive linguistic resource, but played its part only in complementing analogy.

This marks Aquinas off from the mystical tradition of Meister Eckhart, from the approach of the Jewish philosopher MAIMONIDES (1135–1204), from Plotinus (*c.* 205–70) and NEOPLATONISM, Pseudo-Dionysius (*c.* 500) and strands within Eastern Christian theology.

On the other side, however, Duns Scotus questioned the reliability and stable basis of analogical language, believing that it risked making clear and determinate concepts of God and divine action too vague and indeterminate to convey a reliable content. Such concepts as truth, unity and goodness may be applied, he argued, univocally. Otherwise, in what lies knowledge of God?

All the same, Aquinas believed that analogy, rightly applied, could serve to convey cognitive truth about God. He appealed to an analogy of 'attribution' and an analogy of 'proportionality'. A quality or characteristic can be attributed to someone in a derivative sense. A further more radical qualification emerges from proportionality: whatever is analogically common to two or more beings is possessed by each not in the same way but in proportion to its being.

Thus 'God is wise' is not merely an analogy with 'Socrates is wise' or 'Paul the Apostle is wise'; it also entails the proposition that 'wise', as applied to each, carries a meaning that accords with the distinctive being of each.

This, in turn, implies that an analogy of language rests on an analogy of being (*analogia entis*), and it is this aspect that BARTH (1886–1968) attacks as presupposing a Thomistic 'NATURAL THEOLOGY'. Recently, however, Alan J. Torrance has questioned how far this emphasis rests on an interpretation of Aquinas that became dominant through the writings of Thomas Cajetan (1468–1534), Italian cardinal and philosopher (Torrance, *Persons in Communion*, Edinburgh: T & T Clark, 1996, 127–48).

Interpretations of Aquinas on analogy are controversial and too technical for further discussion here. Fundamentally Aquinas appealed to various logical devices to avoid on one side the collapse of analogy into ANTHROPOMORPHISM and on the other a logical grammar that retained no real currency. The problem, however, that he did not fully solve was that of establishing criteria for appropriate uses of analogy.

Aquinas attempted to refine some of the issues by identifying an 'analogy of proportionality' in which an analogy is held formally, but in proportion to the nature of the analogue. Thus human fatherhood has analogies with divine fatherhood, but is also limited in scope because of the finitude and fallenness of human nature. Hence the 'attribution' of analogy is bound up with its proportionality.

KARL BARTH'S CRITIQUE

It is, in effect, the basis of Thomas Aquinas's appeal to the currency of analogy that Karl Barth attacks, rather than the use of analogy as a purely linguistic or semantic tool within the framework of Christian theology. Barth rejects the notion of 'a common denominator' to which God and the created order may 'both be reduced', like species that belong to a common *genus* (Barth, *Church Dogmatics* III: 3, Eng., Edinburgh: T & T Clark, 19, 102).

Thus, while he questions the whole notion of an *analogia entis* as a metaphorical or ontological notion supposedly independent of theology or revelation, Barth is nevertheless willing to allow for a *analogia operationis*, i.e. for its actual operative currency within theology. The basis lies in God's sovereign act of self-disclosure, which is appropriated as an 'analogy of faith'.

Barth's arguments take us beyond the realm of philosophy. Nevertheless, within philosophy of religion there is room to explore the entailments of a theology of God that perceives God as sheer self-gift.

The medieval and traditional notion of *analogia eminentiae*, of working from the lower to the higher, may address issues of intelligibility, provided that it is not transformed into an ontology that transposes the TRANSCENDENCE of God into what Aquinas seeks to avoid, namely a projected anthropomorphic construct.

Philosophical controversy about similarity and difference and theological beliefs about 'the image of God' and the incarnation of the Word in the person of Jesus Christ as person cannot be held apart. Further, the issue of criteria for the valid use of analogy cannot be separated from the wider issues examined under the entry on LANGUAGE IN RELIGION, where these detailed questions emerge in their proper context.

analytic statements

Analytic statements are true A PRIORI, i.e. by virtue of the definition of their concepts or terms, rather than on the basis of states of affairs in the world. The statement 'all bachelors are unmarried' or 'all circles are round' depends on what constitutes the concept of a bachelor or of a circle. It does not depend upon observations about particular bachelors or circles in the world.

KANT used the term 'analytic proposition' for those statements in which the predicate is covertly contained in the subject, e.g. 'six is a number'. While the early work of WITTGENSTEIN treated such statements as purely formal, i.e. in effect as logical tautologies, in his later work Wittgenstein observed that even a formal tautology might perform some additional function in everyday life, e.g. in directing attention to what might otherwise be neglected or unnoticed.

In his work on LOGICAL POSITIVISM, AYER exempted analytical statements from the need for empirical verification, i.e. they could convey logical meaning even if their truth could not be verified by observing states of affairs in the world.

(*See also* EMPIRICISM; ONTOLOGICAL ARGUMENT for the existence of God.)

analytical philosophy

The term serves as a broad and vague title to denote the methods and explorations of those philosophers mainly in the Anglo-American traditions of the twentieth century who seek to clarify the logical forms and sometimes the grammar of CONCEPTS used in philosophy. It characteristically denotes a rigorous examination and clarification of logical forms which might have become obscured by sentences of natural languages.

It is easier to name the specific philosophers with whom the analytical movement is most closely associated than to suggest a list of features. These include: RUSSELL (1872–1970), George E. Moore (1873–1958), AYER (1910–89), and the earlier work of WITTGENSTEIN (1889–1951). However, more broadly the term is sometimes extended to include the 'informal' logical explorations of RYLE (1900–76) and AUSTIN (1911–60), among others, although Austin represents what is more often called 'Ordinary Language' philosophy.

Since 'analysis' is derived from the Greek *analuo*, to loose, or to untie, it is tempting to cite Wittgenstein's aphorism that we should 'look closely at particular cases' and avoid any 'craving for generality' (*The Blue and Brown Books*, Oxford: Blackwell, 1969, 16 and 17). However, in his later work Wittgenstein expressed reservations about the logical atomism that served to break down complex propositions into their most logically primitive building-blocks of meaning (*Philosophical Investigations*, Oxford: Blackwell, 1967, sects. 39–63).

LOGICAL ATOMISM, LANGUAGE GAMES, 'COMMON SENSE' AND LOGIC

Although Russell favoured a more radically analytical method, Wittgenstein was concerned more especially with avoiding those generalizing propositions that removed words and concepts from the settings in everyday life that gave particular cases their logical and linguistic currency. The problem about such grandiose questions as 'What is time?'; 'What is language?' or 'What is a proposition?' is that 'the language-game in which they are to be applied is missing' (ibid., sects. 92 and 96). We must avoid 'super-concepts', such as 'language' or 'world', unless we pay attention to their specificities of contexts-in-life (ibid., 97).

Early in the twentieth century G. E. Moore posed such a question in response to the grandiose metaphysical claims of BRADLEY. If 'time is unreal', why do we take breakfast 'before' lunch? If reality is 'spiritual', are chairs and tables more like us than we may think? Moore wrote 'A Defence of Common Sense' which contained propositions that seemed to conflict with many of the more grandiose claims of philosophers.

Russell shared with Wittgenstein a 'distrust' of the surface grammar of language. His work ‹ on logic provided formal logical devices for re-formulating statements which in ordinary language appeared to make a truth-claim about an entity while the formal logic of the utterance or sentence could be shown not to do so.

Thus in his *Principia Mathematica* (3 vols. 1910–13, with A. N. Whitehead) Russell developed a theory of descriptions that allowed for the logical re-formulation of such sentences as those containing the phrases 'the King of France' or 'a round square' to '*analyze out*' what were strictly not 'referring' expressions at all. In technical terms an 'existential quantifier' could be used in logical notation to separate out whether or not truth-claims about one entity entailed truth-claims about another. (The notation would take some such form as $(Ex) (Fx \ldots).$)

Russell pressed his drive toward analyses to postulate a theory of 'logical atomism' (lectures in 1918, based on earlier work). However, his understanding of the smallest possible components out of which propositions were built differed from that of the early Wittgenstein. Russell linked his theory with a quasi-materialist view of the 'elements' of the world; in Wittgenstein's view these 'atoms' were purely LOGICAL postulates.

'INFORMAL' LOGIC, CONCEPTUAL ELUCIDATION, AND CATEGORY MISTAKES

AYER's exposition of LOGICAL POSITIVISM and the principle of verification is discussed separately. A more constructive version of 'linguistic' philosophy emerged with the work of Ryle. In *The Concept of Mind* (London: Penguin, 1949) he undertook a logical exploration of the relation between language respectively about the mind and the body in the Dualist tradition of DESCARTES, which he called 'the myth of the ghost in the machine' (ibid., 17).

Ryle perceived the Cartesian doctrine as portraying life lived 'through two collateral histories' (ibid., 13). However, logical analysis exposes 'a category-mistake' (ibid., 17), for the logical currency of what is stated about each differs. This 'double-life' theory generates logical puzzles that are illusory. If body and mind 'exist', each 'exists' in a quite different logical sense (ibid., 24). A fresh logical analysis of the vocabulary relating to intellectual action is needed, including exploring dispositions (*see* BELIEF).

In *Dilemmas* (Cambridge: CUP, 1954) Ryle applies these methods of logical analysis to a series of traditional logical puzzles. Thus the phrase 'It was to be' need not express fatalism, as soon as we understand the difference between prospective and retrospective logic, or 'anterior truths and posterior truths' (ibid., 26; 15–35). The paradox of Achilles and the Tortoise, first formulated by Zeno, depends for its force on the difference between the logic employed by an observer and the logic employed by a participant in the race. Only if we confuse logic that applies to 'the total course' with the participant perspective of the runner does the possibility of a 'paradox' emerge (ibid., 36–55). Again, however, this approach is more strictly 'linguistic' philosophy than 'analytical' philosophy.

In his final essay, 'Formal and Informal Logic', Ryle contrasts 'the logic of insulated and single concepts', which often take the centre of the stage in formal logic, with 'the logical dynamics of apparently interfering systems of concepts' (ibid., 125).

In the 1950s a spate of collections of essays (mainly articles from journals) appeared under such titles as *Essays in Conceptual Analysis* (1956) edited by Antony Plew, with contributions from STRAWSON, G. J. Warnock, John Hospers, J. O. Urmson, Stephen Toulmin and others. However, enough has been said to indicate the varied methods and ethos that the umbrella title 'analytical philosophy' serves to denote.

animism

Animism denotes the belief that many instances of natural phenomena (plants, trees, stones) possess 'souls' (Latin, *anima*) or life-spirits. These may then be perceived as quasi-personal and capable of address. In animistic religion these may become objects of reverence or worship.

Two aspects are especially significant for philosophy of religion. First, animism may be said to extend unduly and uncritically the use of ANALOGY and ANTHROPOMORPHISM.

Second, in *Primitive Culture* (1871) Edward B. Tylor argued that all religion originated as primitive animism. However, today it is widely recognized that Tylor's work rests on flawed assumptions. In the first place, primitive religion did not function like a primitive pseudo-science to explain the world. Its function is different, and does not compete with 'science'. In the second place, Tylor was

too heavily influenced by the almost obsessively evolutionary climate of the late nineteenth century. Robert Segal presses both criticisms ('Tylor's Anthropomorphic Theory of Religion', *Religion*, 25, 1995, 25–30). (*See also* EVOLUTION.)

Anselm of Canterbury
(1033–1109)

In philosophy of religion Anselm is most widely known for his formulation of the ONTOLOGICAL ARGUMENT for the existence of God. Anselm sets out this approach in two distinct forms in the *Proslogion* 2–4. However, the title *Proslogion* denotes 'address', and especially in the first formulation, as BARTH among others insists, the supposed 'argument' is an address on the part of a Christian worshipper or believer expressing adoration, praise, and confession of faith to God. The significance of this mode may be stylistic (recalling the style of AUGUSTINE's *Confessions*), but it may significantly shape how the 'argument' is meant to be understood. Moreover it reminds us that Anselm writes primarily as a philosophical theologian, and not simply as a philosopher. He stands in the broad tradition of Christian Platonism.

Anselm is known under three titles. He is sometimes called Anselm of Aosta, since he was born at Aosta in Italy. He is also known as Anselm of Bec, because prior to 1093 he served as a Benedictine monk at Bec in Normandy. However, in 1093 he became the second Norman Archbishop of Canterbury.

In his period at Bec Anselm wrote the two well-known philosophical works *Monologion* (*Soliloquy*, 1078) and *Proslogion* (*Address* (i.e. to God), 1079). The *Monologion* includes Anselm's version of the COSMOLOGICAL ARGUMENT for the existence of God, in which he infers the existence of the Source of all good things, the Supreme Being, from experience of that which is good within the world. The *Proslogion* (sects. 2–4) and the later *Liber*

Apologeticus pro Insipiente include his two versions of the ontological argument for the existence of God. The heart of his first formulation is that God is 'that than which nothing greater can be conceived (*a liquid quo nihil maius cogitari potest)*'.

This gave rise to controversy, even in Anselm's day, represented by the monk Gaunilo's 'reply' to the effect that Anselm's application of maximal greatness to 'God' proved not the existence of God, but something about the status of the *concept* of God. (In more detail, see the entry on the ONTOLOGICAL ARGUMENT, and GOD, ARGUMENTS FOR THE EXISTENCE OF.) This led to a second formulation (*Liber Apologeticus*), the distinctiveness of which has been underlined in modern discussion by HARTSHORNE (*The Logic of Perfection*, La Salle: Open Court, 1962) and more broadly by PLANTINGA (*The Nature of Necessity*, Oxford: Clarendon, 1974). Maximal greatness cannot logically apply to such CONTINGENT examples as those cited by Gaunilo (Gaunilo's island), since these (unlike God) can be 'conceived not to be'.

During his period at Bec, Anselm also wrote treatises *On Truth*, *On Freedom of Choice* and *On the Fall of the Devil* (*De casu diaboli*). This last work is important for the problem of EVIL. Following Augustine, and anticipating Thomas AQUINAS, Anselm viewed evil as a lack, or privation of being. It denotes the absence of good. Injustice is a lack of harmonious justice. The identification of, for example, telling a lie with lack of truthfulness, or corruptibility as lack of perfection enables Anselm to ascribe to God maximal almighty-ness which also excludes the capacity to lie or the capacity for corruption, since these are negatives that detract from maximal flourishing.

The period of nearly twenty years from the *Monologion* (1078) to Anselm's consecration as Archbishop of Canterbury (1093) was one of mainly philosophical production. At Canterbury, however, Anselm produced one of the lasting classics of Christian theology, *Why God Became Man* (*Cur deus homo*, completed in 1098). Anselm argues that atonement for human sin is a matter that concerns God as God, not merely humankind (Book I: 5). Redemption flows from divine grace as gift through the voluntary sacrifice of Christ (ibid.: 8, 9).

Sin, Anselm insists, is not mere failure, but failure to render to God 'what is due' (ibid., 11–15). God's 'honour' is therefore at stake, since loss of honour implies that 'God would seem to fail in governance'. On the analogy of 'satisfying honour', in a medieval feudal system, the greater is the lord, i.e. God, the greater the 'satisfaction' that is 'fitting' (ibid., 19–24; cf. 'maximal greatness' in *Proslogion* 2–4).

Book I, on atonement and satisfaction, leads on to Book II, on the incarnation of God in Christ as an INSTANTIATION of humankind (*homo*, human person, not *vir*, man). If the 'fitting' satisfaction is of infinite value, only God can offer it: 'No-one but God can make the satisfaction'; but it can be a satisfaction on behalf of humankind if it is offered 'only [by] the God-man', Jesus Christ (II: 6–9). This work on the cross is offered not by compulsion, but through the self-consistency of the God who is gracious, just, almighty and self-giving in love (ibid., 18–20).

This work takes its place as one of the major classic models of the atonement. Its importance, not only for theology, but no less for philosophy of religion, lies in its coherence with Anselm's understanding of the 'maximal greatness' and non-contingent ASEITY of God, from the *Monologion* and *Proslogion* (1076–8) to *Cur deus homo* (1098). For a specialist account of his life, see R.W. Southern, *Saint Anselm: A Portrait in a Landscape* (rev. edn, Cambridge: CUP, 1990). Anselm's works appear in various editions.

anthropomorphism

The term denotes the projection of merely human qualities and characteristics onto

God or gods by (often) an undue extension of ANALOGY. Human characteristics may also be projected onto objects, as when a small child describes the operation of vacuum brakes as a train's 'sneezing'. In word history the term is derived from the Greek *anthropos*, humankind, with *morphe*, form.

An over-ready, uncritical use of anthropomorphic imagery may be seen in ANIMISM, in which 'spirit' or 'soul' is read into inanimate objects, thereby endowing them with personal qualities. Edward B. Tylor notoriously ascribed to primitive religion the status of a pseudo-science which explained mechanistic processes by animistic causes. An incisive critique of Tylor has been offered by Robert A. Segal ('Tylor's Anthropomorphic Theory of Religion', *Religion*, 25, 1995, 25–30).

Traditionally philosophical theologians have been wary of attributing emotions to God as anthropomorphic, but the Hebrew Bible, or Christian Old Testament, often does this in spite of its sensitive awareness of divine otherness, or divine TRANSCENDENCE. MOLTMANN insists on the attribution of feeling and suffering to God, provided that this capacity is understood as the result of God's own free, sovereign decision to love in voluntary vulnerability and inter-personal rapport.

HEGEL views anthropomorphism as part of a 'religious' use of language as it is applied to God by means of SYMBOL, MYTH, METAPHOR or 'representation' (*Vorstellung*) in contrast to the purer, more rigorous 'concept' of philosophy (*Begriff*), with its greater critical awareness. A constellation of such issues emerge in the work of TILLICH and in RAMSEY's work on MODELS AND QUALIFIERS.

apologetics

The English term is derived from the Greek *apologia*, defence, or speech of defence. According to Acts 22:1 and 1 Corinthians 9:3, Paul the Apostle offers a reasoned defence to those who seek to criticize him. Traditionally apologetics has come to denote a reasoned defence of a belief-system (characteristically but not exclusively Christian THEISM, or theism in general) in the face of non-theistic, atheistic, or agnostic objections to such beliefs (*see* AGNOSTICISM; ATHEISM).

PLATO offers an account of the *Apology of Socrates*, and Cardinal John Henry Newman (1801–90) wrote *Apologia pro Vita Sua* (1864) in defence of his own religious and theological journey. The name 'the Apologists' usually denotes the Christian writers of the second century who defended the coherence of Christian belief against non-Christian charges of falsity and inconsistency, e.g. Justin's *Apology* to the Emperor Hadrian and Marcus Aurelius.

In the modern era TILLICH (1886–1965) aimed to produce an apologetic or 'answering' theology, in which Christian theology sought to address the questions of philosophers or, more widely, of thinking people. He proposed a 'principle of correlation', whereby questions about reason, being, existence, ambiguity and history were 'answered' by five respective responses concerning revelation, God, Jesus Christ, the Spirit and the kingdom of God. Many have challenged whether these 'correlations' are genuine 'questions' and 'answers', even if, however, as Tillich insists, 'apologetics presupposes common ground, however vague it may be' (*Systematic Theology*, vol. 1, London, Nisbet, 1953, 6).

In many Protestant circles, especially in Barthianism and in PIETISM, the whole enterprise of apologetics is thought to rest too heavily on the persuasive powers of human reason. However, a long theistic and Christian tradition underlines the value of attempts to defend the coherence and REASONABLENESS of religious or Christian belief.

In the philosophy of religion, a theistic presentation of such issues as arguments for the existence of GOD, the currency of LANGUAGE IN RELIGION and issues about the problem of EVIL and the being of God overlap prominently with traditional theistic or Christian apologetics. To argue that a belief-system is not irrational does not necessarily entail an appeal to RATIONALISM. (*See also* LOCKE.)

Aquinas, Thomas (1225–74)

Born into an aristocratic family in the region of Naples, Thomas was educated first in a Benedictine monastery and then at the University of Naples (1239–44). He then became a Dominican friar, and from 1248 to 1254 studied under ALBERT the Great.

At the University of Naples and under Albert, Aquinas was exposed to the full range of philosophical and logical problems formulated and explored by ARISTOTLE, but as a Dominican monk he remained above all a philosophical theologian.

Thomas Aquinas's greatest achievement was his *Summa Theologiae*, begun in 1266. It ranks as one of the greatest theological classics of all time. In the English and Latin edition of the Dominican Blackfriars, commended by Pope Paul VI (1963) it runs to sixty volumes. 'By official appointment the *Summa* provides the framework for Catholic studies in systematic theology and for a classical Christian philosophy' (Preface, vol. 1, xi).

Thomas not only adapted Aristotelian philosophy to the service of Christian theology in the thirteenth century. Building on the earlier work of Islamic philosophers (*see* ISLAMIC PHILOSOPHY) and Albert the Great, he did more than any other single writer to ensure the revival of Aristotle for the medieval period and beyond. He is generally regarded as the leading figure in SCHOLASTIC PHILOSOPHY.

It is unnecessary to include in this entry a detailed account of Thomas's main philosophical themes, since these are described and evaluated in several more specialist entries (*see* ANALOGY; COSMOLOGICAL ARGUMENT for the existence of

God; FIVE WAYS OF THOMAS AQUINAS; GOD, ARGUMENTS FOR THE EXISTENCE OF; LANGUAGE IN RELIGION).

Prior to the commendation of Pope Paul (1963), Pope Leo XIII (1879) urged that Thomist philosophy be made the basis for education in Roman Catholic schools, and Pope Pius XII (1950) identified it as the surest guide to Roman Catholic theology. Thomas's influence, however, spreads far beyond the Catholic tradition, and touches on a multitude of philosophical, theological and ethical questions.

In addition to his magisterial *Summa Theologiae* (1265–72) Aquinas produced *On Being and Essence* (1242–3), *On truth* (1256–9), *Summa contra Gentiles* (1260) ('Gentiles' in the sense of 'unbelievers'), *On Evil* (1263–8), *On Separate Substances* (1271) and up to eighty other works. It would be misleading to emphasize his role as theologian at the expense of recognizing his genuine stature as a philosopher; but equally, he remains a theologian grounded in the Bible and Christian doctrine, alongside his respect for Aristotle and other Greek, Jewish and Islamic philosophers.

SOME LEADING THEMES (DEVELOPED FURTHER IN SEPARATE ENTRIES)

(1) Since for Thomas, Christian revelation and human reason complement each other, any working distinction between theology and philosophy is not clear-cut. For some, knowledge of the existence of God may come in part through drawing reasonable influences A POSTERIORI from the created order. For others, revelation is essential. However, reason can never reach through to grasp such distinctively Christian truths as that of the Incarnation, the Trinity, or the nature of salvation. These demand faith and revealed truth.

(2) Language in religion operates largely through the use of analogy, although the VIA NEGATIONIS, while inadequate

on its own, nevertheless helps to prevent analogy drifting into ANTHRO-POMORPHISM.

(3) Aristotelian philosophy provides an impressive and constructive range of logical and conceptual resources for religion and for life. Aquinas sides with Aristotle against PLATO on several issues, including Plato's notion of Forms. Only 'beings' exist. Aquinas respected the logical and conceptual insights of Arabic and Islamic philosophers as well as those of the Jewish philosopher MAIMONIDES. In effect, in spite of their differences of attitude towards Christian scripture, all shared the same fundamental task, he believed, of formulating a coherent philosophical theology.

(4) In particular Aquinas drew on Aristotle's concepts of potentiality, POSSIBILITY and movement in his exposition of his Five Ways, as well as the contrast between the CONTINGENT and the NECESSARY. The notions of efficient and final CAUSE also constituted a constructive resource for Thomas.

(5) Aquinas also developed the Aristotelian notions of individual substances, of definition by class and sub-category or distinction (*genus et differentia*) and the notion of a hierarchy, or levels, of being. These provide a background for his view of creation, of the nature of good and evil, and of ethics and virtue. The traditional Greek cardinal virtues are supplemented by the 'theological' virtues of faith, hope and love (*Summa Theologiae*, IIa, Qu. 1–35, on the theological virtues; ibid., Qu. 36–43, on providence, justice, courage, temperance and socio-political virtues).

(6) Aquinas is often said to have taken over the STOIC and Aristotelian notion of natural law. All types of law derive from the Divine law (*ius divinum*, ibid., Ia/IIae, Qu. 90–105). However, it may be less misleading to ascribe to him a wider notion of the 'ordered-

ness' of creation and of civil states as that which builds upon, and reflects, the orderedness of the mind of God.

(7) Although Thomas's masterpiece includes most of the topics discussed in a philosophy of religion, Aquinas goes further than this in the scope of his work. His first main part includes such topics as God, language, creation, humankind, will and intelligent mind, providence and the world. The second main part includes issues of ethics and virtue, as we have noted.

Part III includes more distinctively theological doctrines, notably the death and resurrection of Jesus Christ and the sacraments. Yet philosophy is not left behind. His work on the Eucharist or Lord's Supper appeals to the Aristotelian categories of substance and ACCIDENT for what became, from the thirteenth century onwards, the doctrine of transubstantiation (ibid., III, Qu. 75, art. 5, *accidentia ... substantia*). The range of thought is magisterial and monumental, whether or not some sections remain more controversial than others.

Aristotle (384–322 BCE)

Aristotle is widely regarded as among the half-dozen most influential philosophers of Western thought, and as one of the two most important philosophers of the ancient world. He made lasting contributions to LOGIC, to METAPHYSICS and to ETHICS. His metaphysics, or ONTOLOGY, includes what may be called a NATURAL THEOLOGY of God and of the 'ordered' structure of the world. His metaphysics aimed to construct a unified 'science of Being *qua* Being'.

Born in Stagira in Macedonia, Aristotle came to Athens at the age of eighteen, to study at PLATO's Academy for the next twenty years. After Plato's death he travelled to Asia Minor, and returned to

Macedon where Philip appointed him tutor to his son Alexander (Alexander the Great). In 335 BCE he returned to Athens to found his own philosophical school. This he held in the Lyceum or Peripatos, which also came to serve as names for the Aristotelian school. He taught for twelve years until 323 BCE, a year before his death.

In contrast to Plato's theory of Forms (or Ideas), Aristotle began from observations about particular objects or cases, and reasoned A POSTERIORI towards a unified understanding of the world and of reality. In one of the senses of the term 'inductive reasoning', Aristotle followed an inductive method, although he also formulated a rigorous formal DEDUCTIVE logic. His twofold emphasis on the diversity of the world and a unified theory anticipated an approach that would lead in due course to medieval SCHOLASTICISM.

METAPHYSICS AND ONTOLOGY: CAUSE, SUBSTANCE, THE WORLD AND 'GOD'

'Reality', for Aristotle consisted not in Plato's universal, abstract, Forms or Ideas, but in a hierarchy of Being which began with particular objects in the world. Stones, trees, animals and people constitute the building-blocks that instantiate types or species, or 'forms' in Aristotle's own non-Platonic sense of the term.

Aristotle's notion of causality offers a helpful introduction to his metaphysics or ontology. A CAUSE (Greek, *aitía*) may be of four kinds. In the construction of a statue, for example, the material cause (Greek, *hýlē*, matter or material) may be marble or brass. The efficient cause (Greek, *archè tês kineseōs*, commencement of the motion) is the blows of a chisel. The formal cause (Greek, *ousía*, being or substance) is the pattern or distinctive idea in the mind of the sculptor, or a given architectural style. The final cause (Greek, *telos*, end) is the purpose for which the statue is made; the end that it will serve).

This paves the way for understanding both the complexity and plausibility of Aristotle's concept of reality. Substance constitutes a basic, underlying category, to which ATTRIBUTES may be predicated. These modes of existence may be characterized in terms of quantities, qualities, relations, location in space, location in time, and action or being acted upon by another object.

Aristotle inherited from Empedocles the ancient notion that the basic 'elements' which combined to form the material world were earth, water, air and fire, characterized also as hot or cold, wet or dry. This is closer to modern thought than the Greek terms in English translation might suggest. For they represent respectively solid, liquid and gas; and a luminous, incandescent, hot, gas capable of serving as a catalyst or to produce change. Thus the application of fire differentiates the solid, liquid and gaseous state of ice, water and steam.

This state of affairs underlines the point that matter is mutable and exists as 'POSSIBILITY'. Possibility, however, points not to a chain of infinite causal regress, but in due course to an Unmoved Prime Mover (Greek, *prôton kinoun akineton*). This logic is fundamental to most versions of the COSMOLOGICAL ARGUMENT for the existence of God and especially to the first three of the FIVE WAYS of Aquinas.

Aristotle's concept of an 'ordered' world suggested to him that the ontological 'primary existent' is neither merely 'universal' nor a material particular. This cannot be 'matter' (Greek, *hýlē*) as such, because matter is merely potential. The primary existent is the 'form', but not in Plato's sense of an Idea outside the world. Within Aristotle's emphasis on a unifying system of particulars within the world, his 'form' amounts to the full sum of the characteristics of the species to which the particular thing belongs. An apple tree, for example, is defined not in terms of a specific, solitary tree; but as an organism that together with others of its type or species has its own distinctive 'unity of end' as a full life-process in relation to other life-processes.

Behind this, Aristotle infers a Prime Mover who is Unmoved (Greek, *prôton kinoûn akíneton*). This Unmoved Mover is 'Mind' (*noûs*) or 'God'. 'God is perfect . . . is One . . . Therefore the firmament that God sets in motion is one.' Aristotle's universe therefore has a divine 'ordered-ness' and coherence that also embodies diversity, as AUGUSTINE, AQUINAS, and AL-FARABI sought to expound and to underline.

Aristotle sets out this ontology in part in the *Categories* and mainly in the *Metaphysics*, as a First Philosophy. In effect it is almost a natural theology. 'Reality' is a teleological hierarchy of existents, a graduated scale of forms, looking toward the more rational and more complete. This is the Prime Unmoved Mover, who is Mind. (*See* principle of PLENITUDE); TELEOLOGICAL ARGUMENT for the existence of God.)

Aristotle's concept of 'God' is set out in his *Physics*, books VII–VIII, and in *Metaphysics*, book XII. As actuality, not possibility, God is changeless and imma-terial (*On the Heavens*, 279A, 18). God moves in a non-physical way (*Metaphysics*, 1072B, 4). Aristotle anticipates later versions of the COSMOLOGICAL ARGUMENT for the existence of God. However, although God is final and efficient first cause, this is *not* a doctrine of 'creation', since Aristotle perceives the world itself as eternal.

THE LOGICAL SYLLOGISM AND PROPOSITIONAL LOGIC

Many regard Aristotle's work on formal logic as his greatest contribution to philo-sophy. He regarded deductive logic as fundamental, and provided what amounts to the first formulation of a logical syllo-gism in his *Prior Analytics*. Together with his work on the philosophy of language in *On Interpretation* and in *Categories*, this inspired the logical enquiries of ISLAMIC

PHILOSOPHY, for which the syllogism retains primary importance, as well as the Augustinian–Thomist Christian tradition.

In his work on the syllogism Aristotle distinguished between the 'three terms', of which there must not be more than three, in the major and minor premises and the conclusion that must 'necessarily follow'. The 'middle term' is the term that occurs in both premises, and forms a bridge between them. It must not change its meaning through re-definition (*Prior Ana-lytics*, 25B, 32–7). DEFINITION, therefore, occupies no less an important place in Aristotle's logic.

We may illustrate the logical principle with reference to one version of the cosmological argument, which is unmasked by the formal syllogism as involving a strictly invalid step. The syllogism may superficially run as follows:

Major premise:	Every state of affairs has a cause.
Minor premise:	The universe is a state of affairs.
Conclusion:	Therefore the universe has a cause.

On the surface the three terms 'state of affairs', 'world' and 'cause' appear to represent no more than three terms. However, 'cause' and 'state of affairs' in the major premise mean 'caused cause' and 'caused state of affairs'; while in the minor premise the term 'state of affairs' has changed its meaning. Further, if the conclusion alludes to God, 'cause' here denotes 'uncaused cause'. Hence as a formal logical syllogism it breaks down.

The example itself is not drawn from Aristotle, but if logical notation is used to replace the examples, it can be seen that A, B, B_2, C and C_2 amount to at least A, B, C, D. Symbolic or, notational logic thus exposes the fallacy. Aristotle used symbols to represent logical variables, and this transposed arbitrary language into a for-mal logical 'science'.

Definitions are clarified by Aristotle through *genus et differentia*. For example, 'a human being is a rational animal' defines 'human being' through the *genus* of the animal kingdom and the *differentia* of human rationality. Aristotle elaborated further forms of predication: in addition to *genus* and difference, also species, property and ACCIDENT (CONTINGENT rather than necessary predications).

Propositions remain the basic units of Aristotle's formal logic (propositional logic). The standard form, as today, may be represented by the symbols S (subject) and P (predicate). Their relation may be one of affirmation or denial (*Prior Analytics*, 24A, 16). In turn, the affirmation or denial may be universal ('All S ...' or 'No S ...'); or particular ('Some S ...' or 'Some S is not ...'). These four logical forms are (Greek) *schemata* (forms or figures). It would take us beyond the scope of this entry to include Aristotle's explorations of 'necessary' and 'possible' influences (*see* MODAL LOGIC).

TRUTH, 'SCIENCE' AND ETHICS: AN 'ORDERED' WORLD

Aristotle's special attention to propositions and his theory of definitions cohere with his view of truth. This is firmly a correspondence view of truth. A noun (Greek, *onoma*, name) and verb (*rhema*) combine as REFERENTIAL and attributive components to form a proposition, statement or assertion, which either corresponds or fails to correspond with the state of affairs to which it refers, and which it represents.

This exposition in *On Interpretation* specifies the truth-conditions of various types of proposition. However, in *Posterior Analytics* there is a hint of a broader notion of truth and knowledge. 'Scientific knowledge' does not merely concern assertions that certain states of affairs are the case, but more especially explores 'the causes of things' and their explanations. Yet deductions and formal syllogistic logic remain in play, since the principles of 'science' must be necessary, invariant and demonstrable.

Aristotle does not remain in the realm of theory, however. His *Nicomachean Ethics* and *Politics* address issues of decision, ethics and action. The 'good' is 'well-being' (Greek, *eudaimonia*), which transcends mere pleasure, honour, or wealth, but is the fulfilment of that end (*telos*) for which humankind and the world exist. To discuss this requires the use of REASON and the exercise of patience. All structures, including the structures of the world and of human life, are organized for the end for which they exist.

In more concrete terms, choices toward the good, when habituated, become virtues. The four cardinal virtues represent a relative mean between two less constructive extremes: courage (between rashness and cowardice); moderation (between profligacy and apathy); generosity (between extravagance and miserliness); and greatness of soul (between boastfulness and meanness of soul). Hence Aristotle addresses issues of human choice, the will, and character, as well as questions of ontology and logic.

Yet all are woven into a unifying system within which each branch of philosophy plays its part. Aristotle's 'ordered' philosophy reflects his 'ordered' view of the world as a hierarchy of particularities derived from a First Unmoved Mover. Augustine, Islamic philosophy, and Thomas Aquinas draw on this legacy.

aseity

The term denotes an order of being that is 'from itself' (Latin, *a se esse*). It most usually denotes the uniqueness of God, Allah, or a 'Prime Mover', as *ens a se* in contrast to all CONTINGENT, or finite, beings or objects. These, but not God, are dependent on an agency or CAUSE outside themselves.

The ONTOLOGICAL ARGUMENT for the existence of God presupposes that God is a NECESSARY Being in this sense. The COSMOLOGICAL ARGUMENT for God's existence also postulates this different order of Being as a fundamental alternative to the need to assume an infinite or endless chain of caused causes, all of which depend in turn on some external agency or source of causation.

ANSELM's designation of God as *a se* is to be logically distinguished from SPINOZA's notion of a 'self-caused' Being. This concept would fail to meet the criteria for a genuinely necessary Being, as in Anselm and in the third of the FIVE WAYS of Thomas AQUINAS. In the modern era TILLICH maximizes this distinction when he insists that God is 'Being-itself' in contrast to the more reductive assertion that 'God exists'. The latter may risk compromising divine aseity.

atheism

In the broadest terms, atheism denotes the denial of the existence of God. Broadly also, it is to be distinguished from AGNOSTICISM, the belief that to know whether or not God exists is impossible.

PROBLEMS OF DEFINITION: TYPES OF ATHEISM

Many distinguish between atheism as a view of reality or ONTOLOGY (often called 'theoretical atheism') and atheism as a view that no effective difference in life or in the world is entailed in the proposition 'God exists' ('practical atheism').

Another distinction may be drawn between 'avowed' atheism that positively affirms the assertion 'God does not exist', and a broader atheism that negatively denies the existence of a deity or divine beings. LOGICAL POSITIVISM stands somewhere between this second approach and Agnosticism by denying that the assertion 'God exists' has any genuine currency. It merely expresses an emotive attitude or recommends such belief.

There are many examples of 'fringe' atheism. Socrates (*c.* 470–399 BCE) was accused of atheism, but he merely denied the existence of God or the gods in the form such belief took in the 'superstitions' of the state religion of Athens in his time. KANT (1724–1804) affirmed the reality of God as a presupposition behind the categorical moral imperative, freedom and immortality, but denied the personal God who could act within the world-order as 'ecclesial' religion (*Religion within the Limits of Reason*, 1793).

TILLICH (1886–1965) affirmed the reality of God as 'Being-itself' and as 'ultimate concern'. However, he resolutely insists, 'God does not exist. He is Being-itself, beyond essence and existence. Therefore, to argue that God exists is to deny him.' Tillich did not deny the ontological reality of God as the 'Ground of our being', but rejected the ascription of 'existence' to God, as implying that God is merely one existent entity among others (*Systematic Theology*, vol.1, London: Nisbet, 1953, 261).

QUESTIONABLE ASCRIPTIONS OF ATHEISM

While 'practical' atheism goes back into the dawn of history ('The fool says, "There is no God"', Psalm 14:1, i.e. makes no difference in life) 'theoretical' atheism is a more recent phenomenon than is usually widely assumed. Epicurus (341–270 BCE) was not an avowed atheist, for he challenged not the existence of the divine, but the divine nature: might the divine exist within the spaces between worlds, perhaps as atoms?

Most identify the dawn of theoretical, ontological atheism with the second half of the eighteenth century, although some question whether HOBBES (1588–1679) propounded avowed atheism. In *Leviathan* (1651) Hobbes made the pronouncement on religion that is most frequently quoted: 'In these four things, Opinions of ghosts, Ignorance of second causes, Devotion towards what men fear, and Taking of Things Causall for Prognostiques, consisteth the Naturall seed of Religion.'

Nevertheless more than half of *Leviathan* is concerned to defend 'true' religion against the manipulative abuse of religion to promote conflict within the civil order, e.g. between Catholic and Protestant England. Fear and superstition were the causes not of authentic belief in God, but of religious manipulation. God is 'first and eternal cause of all things', and source of 'irresistible power'. Hobbes was not an atheist.

Voltaire (1694–1778) is regularly credited with supposed atheism. He attacked many manifestations of religions and religious authority, including the theodicy of LEIBNIZ. Nevertheless, he perceived evidences of design in the world from which he inferred the existence of a supreme Being, and attacked the atheism of d'Holbach.

TWO INFLUENCES ON THE RISE OF MODERN ATHEISM

The impetus towards 'avowed' atheism derived its force from two occurrences in the late eighteenth century. First, the French ENLIGHTENMENT and French revolution nurtured a mind-set which, in effect, gave an obsessively high place to AUTONOMY. It was not in fact the progress of science as such that turned a tide. Many leading scientists were committed theists, including, for example, NEWTON (1642–1727).

The obsession with 'autonomy' encouraged the view that scientific method could be extended to constitute a self-contained autonomous theory of the world, or world-view: a comprehensive account of all possible knowledge. Thus d'Holbach (Paul von Holbach, 1723–89) published his *Système de la nature* (1770), in which he proposed an entirely mechanistic account of the world as a 'system'. This excluded the need to postulate 'God', and Voltaire denounced its atheism. In England R.B. Shelley would soon make a similar logical jump (1811–12) by claiming that God could not exist because God was incapable of 'visibility'.

The second major factor was KANT's *Critique of Judgement* (1790). Even HUME's *Dialogues of Natural Religion* (1779) had been sceptical rather than atheistic. However, Kant now claimed that the sense of 'order' that had impressed Newton and Voltaire was not 'there' in the universe, but part of our human categories of understanding through which we made sense of the world. They are construals or projections imposed by the human mind.

Each of these two factors encouraged further atheistic arguments. First, the view that natural science provides not simply a method of enquiry but a comprehensive world-view appeared more plausible in the light of developmental and evolutionary theories of the world and human life.

HEGEL (1770–1831) held together a philosophy of progress and evolving history with belief in God, but FEUERBACH and Marx (*see* MARXIST CRITIQUE OF RELIGION) turned this into a humanist or socio-economic principle. DARWIN (1809–82) formulated a theory of natural selection, which others used to attribute biophysical causes to all natural change. SPENCER (1820–1903) applied Darwin's biological principle to issues of selfhood, intelligence and ethics, and was agnostic on the question of God.

Second, Kant's notion of projection was developed by Hegel's pupil Feuerbach (1804–72) to account for 'God' in terms of a human projection of the infinite. The role of projection is developed further by Marx, by NIETZSCHE, and by Freud (*see* FREUD'S CRITIQUE OF RELIGION).

GOD AS A HUMAN PROJECTION? ATHEISM OR 'NON-REALIST' BELIEF?

Feuerbach began his journey with a quasi-theistic world-view, but (in his own words) moved from 'God', through attention to 'reason', to 'humankind'. He concluded that 'God' is a name for humankind's highest aspirations, which are 'projected' upwards and outwards.

These human values are 'objectified', i.e. transposed into an objective entity 'out there' (*see* OBJECT).

Feuerbach's notion of a 'non-objective' God has come to be known as an 'anti-realist' or 'non-realist' concept of God, as advocated in the writings of CUPITT (b. 1934) (*see* NON-REALISM). Feuerbach insisted that by projecting human ideals and human dignity onto this 'God' humanity reduces its own stature.

In response, theists perceive this speculative theory as a reductionist view of God. God has become a mere human construct (discussed under FEUERBACH, below). The I–Thou interpersonal relationship explored by BUBER has been dissolved. Prayer is talking to oneself. Is a non-realist 'God', *God*?

In his work *The German Ideology* (1845–6) Marx (1818–83) draws upon Feuerbach's materialist world-view to serve his own promotion of socio-economic forces as the driving motivation of ideas as well as history. In particular he perceived religion as a repressive, reactionary and oppressive force which threatens the struggle of the working classes for socio-economic emancipation.

'GOD' AS SERVING PARTICULAR 'INTERESTS': NIETZSCHE AND FREUD

The work of Nietzsche (1844–1900) is atheistic. The basic drive of humankind is the 'will to power'. However, religion, and Christianity in particular, promotes a manipulative ascription of power to priests and to hierarchies, while ensuring (like democracy) that the masses are characterized by the 'slave' mentality of humility, mediocrity and self-denial.

Nietzsche anticipates later anti-theists by arguing that religious language relies on 'a mobile army of metaphors' that can be manipulated to serve interests of power. This is worked out especially in *The Twilight of the Idols* (1889) and *The Antichrist* (1895). 'God forgives him who repents' means 'him who submits to the

priest' (*The Antichrist*, aphorism 26 (in *Complete Works*, 18 vols., London: Allen & Unwin, 1909–13, vol. 16, 161)). To experience 'salvation' means 'the world revolves around me' (ibid., 186; aphorism 43).

Freud (1856–1939) always saw human nature in biophysical, neurological terms, as the metaphor that he uses for 'forces' within the self shows (the ego, the super-ego, and the id in its unconscious depths). The problem of neurosis reflects conflicts between these forces deep within the self. However, these can be projected outwards, so that, for example, conflicts between guilt and aspirations of self-worth may be 'objectified' into the face of a fatherly God who both judges and gives grace.

Freud's theories are complex, and the above summary is too simple. He viewed religion as an 'illusion', although he did not go as far as calling it a 'delusion', which is plainly false. Like Nietzsche and Marx, he saw 'God' as performing an instrumental role to serve particular human interests. This conflicts with theistic beliefs in God as a 'Beyond' who is transcendent and the Ground of all being (*see* TRANSCENDENCE).

Atheistic critiques of religions from France, Germany and Austria may seem to be more powerful, at least at an existential level, than Anglo-American accusations about the logical problem entailed in arguments for the existence of God, or the problem of EVIL. What kind of God should we expect to be capable of logical demonstration or observable as an empirical entity?

All the same, the critique of religion as serving power-interests (Nietzsche) or a way of coping with the inner conflicts of neurosis (Freud) need not logically apply to all religion and all claims about belief in God.

Indeed, many theists find Nietzsche and Freud constructive in facilitating the sifting out of inauthentic from authentic truth-claims in religion. Among Christian

theologians, MOLTMANN, Dietrich Bonhoeffer, and Hans Küng have addressed
these issues head-on. RICOEUR, (b.
1913) utilizes Freud's work on self-deception for
HERMENEUTICS, without subscribing to his
non-theist, mechanistic world-view. (*See
also* EMPIRICISM; EXISTENTIALISM; GOD,
ARGUMENTS FOR THE EXISTENCE OF.)

attribute

In the most general terms, an attribute is a
characteristic, feature or trait, ascribed to
a person or object (in word history, Latin,
ad, to, and *tribuere*, to ascribe). In
philosophy the classical exposition of an
attribute emerges in ARISTOTLE. He
divides the world into substances, each
of which can be characterized by its
attributes.

Strictly, Aristotle understands these
attributes to receive their characterization
under the categories of time, place and
relation. In Thomas AQUINAS the term
becomes extended.

In classical THEISM it was long customary to speak of the attributes of God (e.g.
holiness, wisdom, sovereignty, love).
However, many modern theologians
believe that this fails to take due account
either of the TRANSCENDENCE of God as
Other, or of the dynamic purposiveness of
divine action. It risks encouraging the
distorted notion of God as a static object,
even as a mere object of human thought,
rather than as an initiating Thou who is
'Beyond'. (*See also* BUBER; MOLTMANN;
GOD, CONCEPTS AND 'ATTRIBUTES' OF;
TILLICH.)

Augustine of Hippo (354–430)

Together with PLATO, ARISTOTLE and
Thomas AQUINAS, Augustine may be
counted among the four most influential
thinkers who shaped Western philosophy
before the Renaissance. He is widely
viewed as the first great Christian philosopher, and his theology permanently
influenced Catholic and Protestant theology in the West. He produced the largest
body of Christian writings of the first
millennium.

LIFE

Augustine was born in Thagaste, North
Africa, and was educated, and taught
rhetoric, in Carthage. He did not come
formally to Christian faith until the age of
thirty-two. In spite of the influence of his
Christian mother, Monica, he had found
Christianity insufficiently compatible with
reason to be credible. In early years he fell
under the influence of Manichaeanism,
which he found more intellectually acceptable than Christianity. However, disillusion set in. He remained closer to
NEOPLATONISM, even if as a Christian
who viewed the Incarnation as decisively
distinctive of Christian faith.

Augustine taught rhetoric also at Rome
and Milan, and came to Christian faith
(386–7) partly through reading the Bible
(the famous *tolle, lege*, 'take up and read',
which prompted his reading of Romans
13:13–14), and partly through the influence of Ambrose, Bishop of Milan. He
returned to North Africa (388), was
ordained in 391, and was made Bishop
of Hippo in 395 until his death in 430.

WRITINGS

The enormous range and scope of his
writings may invite possible misinterpreta-
tions if specific treatises by Augustine are
cut loose from their context and purposes.
Many of his works attack 'heresies'. Thus
much of his material on EVIL and CREATION
forms part of his polemic against Manichaeanism; many observations on habit,
will, GRACE and the Church form part of
his attacks on the group known as Dona-
tists; and much, but not all, of his work on
FREE WILL and FREEDOM features within
his attacks on a Pelagian notion of freedom
as autonomous free choice.

Probably the least shaped by polemic
are his widely read *Confessions* (397–
400), written in first-person narrative
style, and the later *Enchiridion* (423),
written as a 'little handbook' on Christian

belief and discipleship. The framework chosen is that of the Creed and Lord's Prayer. Also in this late period Augustine produced his classic *City of God* (twenty-two books, 413–26), which addressed pagan interpretations of the fall of Rome to Alaric the Goth in 410. His philosophical theology can be seen in *De Trinitate* (*On the Trinity*, fifteen books, 400–16). Other works include numerous biblical commentaries and doctrinal treatises as well as letters and dialogues.

EARLIER WRITINGS: REASON, TRUTH AND KNOWLEDGE OF GOD IN THE *SOLILOQUIES* (386–7)

The *Soliloquies* reveal an indebtedness to an earlier reading of Cicero's (lost) *Hortensius* for kindling Augustine's early interest in philosophy (consolidated in *Confessions* III: 4 and 7) as a search for wisdom, or 'blessedness'. A passion for intellectual enquiry remains common to philosophy and Christianity, and in his earlier works Augustine sees in this a close affinity in Neoplatonism. The *Soliloquies* are a dialogue between the writer and reason.

Nevertheless, Augustine argues, knowledge of God is unique. It is distinct both from knowledge of the sensual and from mathematical knowledge: 'My question is not *what* you know but *how* you know. Have you any knowledge that resembles knowledge of God?' (ibid., I: 5: 10).

Even in this very early work a perspective emerges which is common to such later Western thinkers as DESCARTES and KIERKEGAARD: the issue of knowing relates to a first-person 'I', whether it be the SUBJECT in Descartes or subjectivity in Kierkegaard. 'It is impossible to show God to a mind vitiated and sick. Only the healthy mind ... will attain vision' (ibid., 6: 12). REASON is the power of the soul to look, but it does not follow that everyone who looks, sees ... 'Virtue ... is perfect reason' (ibid., 6: 13).

Truth, therefore, thereby concerns the will as well as the intellect (ibid., II: 5: 8). Augustine now moves into the area of

Plato, Neoplatonism and PLOTINUS. What the senses perceive of the material world can be deceptive and false. 'Truth is eternal ... truth cannot perish' (ibid., 15: 27, 28). Truth, he then infers, belongs to the realm of 'the soul and God' who are 'immortal' (ibid., 18: 32).

LANGUAGE AND KNOWLEDGE IN *THE TEACHER* (389)

Augustine later expressed dissatisfaction with the *Soliloquies* as simplistic and confused. He develops his EPISTEMOLOGY further in *De Magistro* (*The Teacher*), but this time perceives the importance of issues about the currency of language. Some early sections may offer hostages to WITTGENSTEIN's critique of REFERENTIAL THEORIES of meaning and OSTENSIVE DEFINITION. Yet even here Augustine recognizes that the circularity of explaining signs by other signs may reach firmer ground when we 'carry out action' (ibid., 4: 7).

Anticipating SCHLEIERMACHER and Wittgenstein, Augustine appeals to teaching, learning and training for understanding how we come to know meanings of signs in experience. Indeed, contrary to Wittgenstein's example from Augustine, 'pointing with the finger can indicate nothing but the object pointed out ... I cannot learn the thing ... nor the sign ... I am not interested in the act of pointing' (ibid., 10: 34). However, Augustine does perceive here the notion of 'Universals' as truth presiding over the mind.

EVIL AND FREEDOM IN *ON FREE WILL* (395–6)

De Libero Arbitrio (*On Free Will*) attacks the Manichaean account of the origin of evil. Augustine rejects their metaphysical DUALISM, as if evil were a positive entity at war with God. Evil has its origin in an evil act of will: 'God is not the author of evil' (*On Free Will*, I: 1: 1). Evil stems from a misdirected will behind the evil act (ibid., 5: 7). Contrary to some of his later anti-Pelagian writings, Augustine is here so concerned to emphasize the voluntary nature of evil acts that he portrays 'the rule of human mind' as able to resist the pull to evil (ibid., 10: 20). 'It is in the power of our will to enjoy or to be without ... a good' (ibid., 12: 26).

If God punishes evil deeds, 'that would be unjust unless the will was free not only to live aright but also to sin' (ibid., II: 1: 3). Even divine foreknowledge does not constrain free will. For divine OMNIS-CIENCE means only that 'no future event [is] to escape his knowledge', not the imposition of compulsion to accord with some 'fixed' scenario (ibid., III: 4: 11).

All of this underlines the goodness of God. God's gifts are good, whether or not humankind chooses to misuse them. 'Why did you not use your free will for the purpose for which I gave it to you, that is, to do right?' (ibid., II: 1: 3).

SELFHOOD, SELF-AWARENESS: GOD AND TIME IN THE *CONFESSIONS* (398)

This first-person narrative offers a retrospective interpretation of past moments and key issues from a theological perspective, in which God is addressed as Thou (*see* BUBER). Such first-person style places philosophy in a new key in terms of such issues as SELF, freedom and hedonism, subject and OBJECT, subjectivity and SELF-INVOLVEMENT and the experience of TIME. RYLE has illustrated the differences between 'observer' logic and 'participant' logic not only in such areas, but also in the generating of supposed paradoxes.

Augustine offers a sternly ethical and theological interpretation of the drive of the self for self-gratification and desire. The self is 'narrow' and capable of self-deception (*Confessions*, I: 4: 4; 5: 6). A child learns language to express the desires of the self (Wittgenstein's selective example of ostensive definition comes in ibid., 8: 13). Desire led, in his sixteenth year, to the theft of pears when 'my pleasure was not in what I stole but in the act of stealing' (ibid., II: 9: 17; cf. II: 4: 9; 6: 12).

Books III and IV recount Augustine's interest in philosophy, sparked by Cicero's *Hortensius*, his involvement with the Manichaeans, his study of Aristotle's *Categories*, and his first reflections on time as duration and timeliness (ibid., IV: 6 :11; 8: 13). Books VI and VII trace his journey through serious engagement with Neoplatonism to his eventual openness to the Epistle to the Romans and Scripture. While Platonism is right that 'God is for ever the same', God chooses to become humble and accessible through the bodily enfleshment of Jesus Christ (ibid., VII: 9: 14).

The theme of praise reiterates the privative view of evil. No one can 'find fault with any part of thy creation' (ibid., 14: 20). Yet this language closely parallels Plotinus and Neoplatonism. 'The evil which overtakes us has its source in self-will ... in the desire for self-ownership' (Plotinus, *Enneads*, V: 1: 1). 'The unchangeable was better than the changeable ... The mind somehow knew the unchangeable ... It arrived at that which is' (*Confessions*, VII: 17: 23, where Augustine recalls a visionary experience along Plotinian lines). Nevertheless, his Christian experience of revelation remains rooted in the Incarnation (ibid., 18: 24, 19: 25). His 'full' conversion comes in Book VIII, especially when a child's song (*tolle, lege*) takes him to Romans 13:13 (ibid., VIII: 12: 29).

The character of God is now perceived as transformative: 'Thou hast pierced our heart with thy love' (ibid., IX: 2: 3). Augustine has no philosophical difficulty about the effectiveness of the intercessory PRAYER of his mother Monica on his behalf (ibid., 10: 26), and her passing through death to life shortly after their fulfilment (ibid., 13).

In books X–XII Augustine leaves the events of his life to explore, still in first-person narrative before God as 'Thou', the themes of self-awareness, memory, time, the mode and time (or temporality) of creation and of God as 'Creator of all times' (ibid., XI: 13: 15). In his last Book, form and differentiation are perceived in relation to divine creation.

'In what temporal medium could the unnumbered ages Thou didst not make pass by, since Thou art the Author and Creator of all the ages?' (ibid., 13: 15). 'Thou madest that very time itself, and periods could not pass by *before* Thou madest the whole temporal procession. But if there was no time *before* heaven and earth, how, then, can it be asked "What wast Thou doing then?" For there was no "then" when there was no time' (ibid.).

Wittgenstein's quotation 'What is time?' (ibid., 14: 17) has as its target Augustine's formulation of a generalizing 'super-question' in the abstract. Yet just as Wittgenstein's critique of Augustine's allusion to ostensive definition tells only half of the story, the *Confessions* books XI are more subtle than we might imagine from the quotation.

Augustine raises the issues of time because it appears to raise problems about *creatio ex nihilo*, i.e. the doctrine that God has created all things without resort to 'earlier material'. Yet how can creation have its 'beginning' in and through God if time permits us to ask what was 'before' this beginning?

In practice Augustine shares with Wittgenstein a recognition of the logical muddle imposed by conceiving of time either as a receptacle into which the world was placed, or as a flowing river which permits the application of 'before' and 'after' to all events. Augustine allows that we may speak of 'before' in relation to given sets of events, but not to denote temporal priority before all events.

Human awareness conditions how we perceive time. For the past, the present no longer exists; the future is not yet; the present vanishes in the very moment of our reflection upon it. It is therefore not 'a thing-in-itself', but is present to the mind in memory, attention (strictly 'experience') and expectation (ibid., 20: 26). However, to deny its independent 'existence as an object' does not entail its unreality. The mind is conscious of duration and succession. 'Time ... is nothing else than extension (*distentio*), though I do not know extension of what' (ibid., 26: 33). Hesitantly he wonders whether this *distentio*, or 'stretching' extension, is the mind; yet he concedes that movement and measurement remain applicable to duration.

Augustine has reached as far as the logical tools of the pre-modern era will permit in appreciating the different logical currencies of time in relation to different contexts and questions. He lays a foundation for modern theories of narrative time, as RICOEUR shows through his use of Augustine's distentio in his *Time and Narrative* (Eng. 1984–8).

EVIL, FREEDOM AND GRACE: DEVELOP-
MENTS OF THEMES IN LATER WORKS

In the later period important sources include the *Enchiridion* (423), *On the Trinity* (400–16), the series of anti-Pelagian writings (411–28); and the *City of God* (413–26; already introduced above).

In the later writings Augustine underlines even more heavily the privative view of evil. 'If you try to find the efficient cause of this evil choice, there is none to be found. For nothing causes an evil will' (*City of God*, XII: 6). His exposition (in partial or 'weaker' form) of the principle of PLENITUDE draws on the visual analogy that for light to be seen as light presupposes shadow (ibid., XI: 23).

This is not unrelated to the Neoplatonist and Plotinian view of form as presupposing difference in the process of creation. The 'orderedness' of the created world yields necessary variety and unevenness: 'What is more beautiful than a fire? What is more useful, with its heat, its comfort ...? Yet nothing causes more distress that the burns inflicted by fire' (ibid., XII: 4). The world as such is good, but it contains potential for the possibility of evil when evil choices misuse it.

The theme of structured order, in contrast to the chaotic and contingent, finds coherent expression no less in *On the Trinity*. The Divine Trinity exhibits unity-in-diversity. The Trinity exemplifies Being, Knowledge and Love. God is One; however, God chooses to become visible and knowable in the Incarnate Word, God the Son. Just as in Plotinus, the eternal One who is 'beyond Being' nevertheless reaches expression as Mind (*Nous*), but is both bound into a unity and yet becomes accessible as Soul or life. Against the Arians Augustine insists (with Athanasius) that the Son is co-eternal with the Father, while the Holy Spirit exhibits the potentiality of 'gift' or 'giveableness' (*On the Trinity*, V: 3: 4; and 14: 15; 15: 16).

The anti-Pelagian writings sharpen Augustine's rejection of definitions of human freedom in terms of autonomy or equipoise. Human fallenness yields a habituated bondage which can be redeemed only by divine grace. Hence the emphasis shifts from his earlier work *On Free Will* in such treatises as *On Nature and Grace* (415), *On the Spirit and the Letter* (412) and *On Grace and Free Will* (426–7).

This distinguishes him sharply from KANT: 'ought' does not presuppose 'can' in ethics. The issue is whether the will and its habituated acts are orientated towards self-gratification or towards God. In common with Neoplatonism, this is related to the constraints of the temporal and CONTINGENT as against fulfilment and blessedness in the eternal and the true.

It will thus be seen that Augustine wrestles with a wide range of the philosophical problems that have occupied minds especially in the West over centuries. In some cases, including his work on selfhood, knowledge and time, he moved almost ahead of the pre-modern world. In other cases, the Platonic philosophical frame, within which much of his thinking developed, yielded constraints. Thus many would detect too great a readiness to accept, and to work within, a mind–body dualism, and an over-sharp contrast between the contingent and the universal. Yet his theology served to qualify this. The Incarnation and resurrection of Jesus Christ stood as the rock that separated Christian faith from Neoplatonism.

Austin, John L. (1911–60)

Austin was a leading exponent of 'ANALYTICAL' or 'Ordinary Language' philosophy. He taught at Oxford for most of his life, and practised this method there from 1945 until his death in 1960. His essay 'Other Minds' (1946) introduced the category of PERFORMATIVE UTTERANCES by distinguishing such first-person utterances as 'I promise', 'I warn' from merely descriptive sentences (in *Philosophical Papers*, Oxford: Clarendon, 1961, 44–84, esp. 65–74). His 1955 Harvard lectures on performative utterances are published as *How to Do Things with Words* (Oxford: OUP, 1962; 2nd edn, 1975).

An utterance such as 'I promise' performs an action in the very saying of it: 'by using this formula ... I have bound myself to others, and staked my reputation' (*Philosophical Papers*, 67). Similarly 'I know' also entails giving 'others my word; I give others my authority for saying "S is P"' (ibid.). 'I promise' or 'I know' is 'quite different' from 'he promises' or 'he knows'.

Nevertheless 'the term "performative" will be used in a variety of cognate ways' (*How to Do Things with Words*, 6). Performatives are effective or ineffective, 'operative' or void, rather than true or false. 'We do not speak of a false bet or a false christening' (ibid., 11). Most performatives presuppose accepted conventions and regimes that words are uttered to appropriate persons in appropriate circumstances.

It no longer constitutes an operative performative to say, 'My seconds will call on you' if or where the conventions of duelling are no longer accepted. Would the utterance 'I baptize this infant 2704' constitute an operative act of baptism?

(ibid., 35). Since presuppositions are entailed 'for a certain performative utterance to be happy, certain statements have to be *true*' (Austin's italics, ibid., 45).

Like WITTGENSTEIN, Austin notes the 'asymmetry' in logical terms between first-person uses and third-person uses of such verbs as 'I believe', 'we mourn', 'I give and bequeath', 'I bet', 'I forgive' and 'I promise' (ibid., 63). These cannot be detected, however, by grammar alone.

At the heart of Austin's work lies the destination between '*locutions*' (roughly uttering a sentence with a meaning), '*illocutionary* acts' (which perform acts in the saying of the utterance) and '*perlocutionary* acts' (which perform acts by the saying of the utterance: ibid., 1–10, 114–16).

Perlocutions often, perhaps always, involve the use of quasi-causal power rather than convention. Thus 'I persuade' usually embodies perlocutionary, rather than illocutionary, action. Austin rightly focuses on illocutions as most fertile for philosophy or conceptual clarification. Thus 'I praise', 'I welcome', 'I repent', 'I promise' come within this latter category. These require and repay clarification concerning the conditions for their operative currency or effectiveness.

RELEVANCE TO THE PHILOSOPHY OF RELIGION

The consequences of Austin's work for LANGUAGE IN RELIGION are too numerous to list in a short article. First, he offers a semantic or performative approach to TRUTH. 'It is true' is more like adding my signature than stating a fact.

Second, much religious language is indeed the performing of an action. Sincerely to say 'I repent' constitutes an act of repentance; it is not an attempt to inform God of a state of mind that God may already know. 'We believe' constitutes a declarative act of nailing one's colours to the mast, as well as a declaration of cognitive content. It depends on and exhibits (to use the term employed by D.D. Evans) the logic of self-involvement.

Third, it also entails what WOLTERSTORFF calls 'count-generation'. An utterance may count as the performing of an action, as when the raising of an umpire's finger may count as a declarative verdict.

Fourth, Austin established the huge variety of types of illocutionary acts that language may perform. Verbs such as reckon, grade, assess, rank, rate, may, in the first person, constitute 'verdictives'. 'I command', 'I proclaim', 'I pardon', 'I announce', 'I appoint' may function as 'executives'. 'I promise', 'I covenant', 'I pledge myself', 'I guarantee' are 'commisives'. 'I thank', 'I welcome', 'I bless', 'I curse' are behabitives (ibid., 150–60).

However, post-Austinian critics have offered improved and more coherent clarifications (notably John SEARLE). Further, Austin has been severely criticized for classifying logical force in terms of English verbs. Performatives cannot adequately be grouped in accordance with stereotypical examples or verbs in the English language.

Even so, nothing can detract from the foundation laid by Austin. SEARLE, Wolterstorff, F. Recanati, Daniel Vanderveken and many others have built upon, and modified, his work.

Some American and German writers on biblical HERMENEUTICS (e.g. Robert Funk and Ernst Fuchs) have over-loosely used the term 'performative' to denote any kind of dimension of action or force without taking account of the rigour and care with which Austin distinguishes different types of force and action and their basis-in situations, conventions and life. He has opened a fruitful field for further research.

authority

In the era of ENLIGHTENMENT rationalism the concept of authority appeared to generate conflict, or at least tensions, between some religions or theological doctrines and philosophical enquiry.

Almost all religions entail such notions as the lordship or kingship of God (or of Christ or of a divine figure) who has authority to decree, to require obedience, to commission agents or to forgive sins. On the other hand, philosophical thought has often assumed the importance of the AUTONOMY of the self (with KANT), and accorded it special privilege.

Neither the concept of autonomy nor the concept of authority is as simple as might appear to be the case. If it means anything to call God, Allah, or Christ 'Lord' or 'King', Christians, Jews and Muslims thereby accord to God a *de jure* authority, i.e. an authority of legitimate right. If they accept this authority in practice, this is also a *de facto* authority.

Problems arise, however, when agents or intermediaries, often in the form of sacred writings, clergy or other ecclesial officers, are invoked. What kind and degree of authority are these 'penultimate' writings or persons to be accorded?

WOLTERSTORFF points out that in everyday life we are familiar with the 'delegated authority' of a vice-chairperson or even personal assistant who acts on behalf of a director, chairperson or president (*Divine Discourse*, Cambridge: CUP, 1995, 37–54). Thus sacred texts and apostles may be authorized or 'commissioned *to speak in the name of God*' (ibid., 41 and 51, his italics). Judaism, Christianity, Islam and some other religious traditions view sacred writings as holding effective and justified power if and when they speak as the word of God.

This does not remove from religious communities the freedom and responsibility of interpretation, practical application, and examining issues that arise from the recontextualizing of sacred texts in a later age. In part this entails the discipline of responsible HERMENEUTICS. The notion that sacred texts are to be read like engineering or scientific textbooks is broadly a 'fundamentalist' tradition within several of the major world religions.

Moreover, the ready abuse of appeals to authority has been unmasked with relish by NIETZSCHE (1844–1900) and other philosophical critics. Kant (1724–1804) held to the notion of the absolute authority of the categorical (moral) imperative, but urged that divine authority is not merely one of raw power and threat, since God respects the dignity, responsibility and freedom of human persons.

KIERKEGAARD (1813–55) represents a way of thinking that readily holds together the importance of religious obedience with an insistence that religious faith is not a matter of responding to second-hand inherited doctrines and rules, but of appropriating faith for oneself in personal self-involvement and SUBJECTIVITY. The two emphases are not incompatible.

On the other hand, FREEDOM of enquiry and freedom to respond are not sheer 'autonomy'. TILLICH (1886–1965) argued for a middle path between 'heteronomy' (a law imposed by another from without) and autonomy. To accept as 'a law' only what come from within one's own nature (autonomy) constitutes a denial of the transformative nature of religion, as Dietrich Bonhoeffer so strongly urged. Tillich calls this middle way 'theonomy'.

Freedom of philosophical enquiry denotes not a 'liberty of indifference' as if the enquirer began always A PRIORI with a blank sheet. Freedom of thought allows for a personal integrity that resists the oppression of social, religious, political or secular totalitarianism. Nevertheless it does not preclude a careful assessment of the claims of TRADITIONS and communities in relation to individual consciousness.

GADAMER (1900–2002) perhaps did more than any to rehabilitate the rational basis of respect for authority. In conscious opposition to the complacent individualism of Enlightenment rationalism, Gadamer asserts: 'Authority ... is ultimately based not on the subjection and addiction of reason but on an act of acknowledgement and knowledge ... namely, that the other is superior ... in judgement and might ... It rests ... on an act of reason itself which, aware of its own limitations, trusts to the better insights of others' (*Truth and Method,* 2nd Eng. edn, London: Sheed & Ward, 1989, 279).

Gadamer alludes primarily to what has been tested in historical traditions. However, in religion the principle may apply to prophetic or apostolic witnesses as well as to traditions of wisdom, narrative and sacred teaching. Much of the old, now dated, over-sharp dualism between authority and reason has dissipated with the recognition of the part played by communities and traditions. However, if individual reason is undervalued, the issue reaches a self-contradictory situation of the kind that emerges in more radical versions of POSTMODERNISM. Both authority and reason are placed under radical criticism and undervalued.

autonomy

In the broad, popular sense of the term autonomy denotes freedom from external constraints to set one's own norms or rules of conduct, or in social applications of the word self-determination or self-government. It derives historically from the Greek *auto-*, self, co-joined with *nomos*, law, rule, norm or principle.

A decisive influence in the history and use of the term was KANT (see below). Prior to the eighteenth century the term largely functioned in a communal, social, or institutional context to denote the self-government of a city-state, state or guild.

(1) PLATO (428–348 BCE) expounds the self-supporting autonomy of the city-state in the *Republic*, where it is clear that autonomy does not apply to individuals. This would create anarchy. There has to be law or rule, but as against tyranny, where the criterion is raw power; against democracy, where it is mere popularity; against oligarchy,

where it is wealth and social influence; aristocracy (Greek, *aristos,* best) promotes what is best for society as a whole.

The ideal state in the *Republic* (bks II–V) is ruled by intellectuals who undergo a rigorous philosophical training in order that the rest of the city-state *(hoi polloi,* the many) may be governed in accordance with truth, wisdom and justice. Yet book VI concedes that in practice philosophers are regarded very differently.

(2) LOCKE (1632–1704) represents a transitional point towards the individualism of modernity. In his *Two Treatises on Government* (1689), especially in his *Second Treatise in Civil Government* Locke proposes that the individual has God-given 'rights' to life, liberty and property. However, in effect by an implicit social contract, a power of government must be conditionally assigned to a group of governmental agents to ensure a just distribution of the rights and liberties. 'Pure' autonomy would be anarchy, when sheer might and power deprive individuals of these rights.

(3) KANT (1724–1804) extends autonomy to the will and moral decision of the individual. This is part of his rejection of the compromise with 'freedom' that is imposed by ecclesial and social traditions and authorities which undermine the ethical status of the individual to determine will and action in free, unconditioned, moral decision. A will is 'good' only if it derives its 'law' from itself alone, i.e. in sheer autonomy.

(4) SCHLEIERMACHER (1768–1834) perceived that Kant's TRANSCENDENTAL PHILOSOPHY, or CRITICAL PHILOSOPHY, raised new questions which theology had to address. However, he also perceived that autonomy struck at the heart of religion and religions. For religion is characterized by an immediacy of awareness or feeling of 'utter

dependence' upon God (*schlechthinig Abhängigkeit, The Christian Faith,* 2nd edn, sect. 4).

(5) TILLICH (1886–1965) subjects both 'autonomy' and 'heteronomy' to a forceful critique. If autonomy is to be viewed positively, 'autonomy does not mean the freedom of the individual to be a law to himself' (*Systematic Theology,* vol. I, London: Nisbet, 1953, 93). At best, it denotes 'obedience to the law of reason' (ibid.).

All the same, individual-centred autonomy remains 'shallow', just as heteronomy (law imposed by another) can be oppressive. What is needed is to avoid the 'catastrophe' of autonomy and the 'destructive' impact of heteronomy by rooting both in 'theonomy': the threefold interaction or DIALECTIC between individual reason, social constraint and divine order, provide a balancing 'depth' which one of these alone fails to yield (ibid., 92–96).

(6) Controversy about the status of autonomy has divided the two broad intellectual approaches that might provisionally be described as the modern and the postmodern. Modernity inherits a philosophy of individual capacities and rights inherited through Locke and Kant. POST-MODERNITY inherits from HEGEL, Marx, NIETZSCHE, HEIDEGGER (1889–1976) and FOUCAULT (1926–84) the view that against the enormous power-shaping factors of social and communal forces, individual autonomy is illusory.

(7) Religions, including the Christian religion, tend also to underline the power of the social structures into which the individual is born, and to be less optimistic than secular modernity about the powers of individual reason. Nevertheless, within a context of a doctrine of divine GRACE and of human dependence upon God, they do not share the pessimism of some postmodern thinkers. They do not

agree that the individual is utterly helpless to make responsible decisions which affect his or her own destiny. They do not see humankind as determined decisively or entirely by social history.

Averroes

See IBN RUSHD.

Avicenna

See IBN SINA.

axiom

Axioms are self-evident propositions or principles. They provide a premise or foundation on the basis of which inference may be deduced. ARISTOTLE defined axioms as indemonstrable propositions that cannot be doubted. They are akin to postulates, except that postulates are capable of demonstration. KANT regarded axioms as A PRIORI principles of intuition. PLATO, DESCARTES and LEIBNIZ held the strongest views of axioms as 'innate' to the human mind, but the term may also be used in a less ABSOLUTE sense to denote what is commonly held to be true.

'Axiom' should be distinguished from 'axiom of choice' as a technical term for a mathematical postulate about sets, and also from 'axiology' which explores issues of value. (*See also* DEDUCTION.)

Ayer, (Sir) Alfred Jules (1910–89)

A.J. Ayer became Professor of Mind and Logic at the University of London (1946–59) and subsequently Wykeham Professor of Logic at the University of Oxford (1959–1978). However, he made his name through the publication of *Language, Truth and Logic* (1936), later revised in the light of criticism in a second edition (London: Gollancz, 1946). This established his reputation as the leading British exponent of LOGICAL POSITIVISM.

AYER'S LOGICAL POSITIVISM

Ayer argued that all propositions are either ANALYTIC STATEMENTS, which derive their truth from formal or 'internal' logical validity, or statements about the world which can be verified by observation and experience, i.e. are empirically verifiable. He expounded this as a theory of meaning.

Propositions that are neither analytic nor empirically verifiable, Ayer argued, do not communicate genuinely propositional meaning. It does not make sense to ask whether they are true or false, since all true-or-false propositions fall into one of these two specified categories only.

Propositions about God or about ethics are 'non-sense', since their meaning cannot be tested and demonstrated by the principle of verification. Such statements as 'To steal is wrong' are not true-or-false propositions; they are recommendations concerning the adoption of values or emotive expressions of approval or disapproval.

Ayer defines 'non-sense' as being 'devoid of literal significance' on the ground that the content of a supposed proposition neither meets the criterion of verification nor depends on the validity of internal logical relations within an analytical proposition. In the latter case, 'the validity depends solely on the definitions of the symbols it contains' (*Language, Truth and Logic*, 2nd edn, 78).

RELIGION, ETHICS and METAPHYSICS characteristically employ sentences that purport 'to express a genuine proposition, but ... in fact, express neither a tautology nor an empirical hypothesis' (ibid., 41). Hence they do not match up to the proposed criteria of meaning. Ayer rejects 'the metaphysical thesis that philosophy affords us knowledge of a reality transcending the world of science and common sense' (ibid., 45).

Ayer asserts: 'The criterion which we use to test the genuineness of apparent statements of fact is the criterion of verifiability' (ibid., 48). Until we know how a proposition would be verified, the speaker 'fails to communicate anything' (ibid., 49).

Although he had earlier demanded a principle or criterion of 'verification', Ayer recognized in his 1946 edition that it was sufficient for a proposition to be capable of verification '*in principle*'. Thus, for example, in the era before space travel the proposition 'There are mountains on the far side of the moon' remained verifiable in principle, even in the era when space technology had not reached the point where it could be verified in practice. In principle the proposition was capable of verification, given the appropriate technology.

In his introduction to his 1946 edition Ayer states the point negatively: 'If ... no possible experience could go on to verify it [the proposition], it does not have any factual meaning at all' (ibid., 15).

CRITIQUES OF THE VERIFICATION PRINCIPLE

Logical positivism looks back for its roots to the VIENNA CIRCLE, with its exaggerated respect for the physical or natural sciences and its extreme distaste for metaphysics. First, as many have observed, not only metaphysics and theology, but no less 'every single moral and aesthetic judgement, any judgement of value of any sort, must be regarded as meaningless' (G. J. Warnock, *English Philosophy since 1900*, Oxford: OUP, 1958, 45). This excludes a wide range of discourse which seems to have genuine communicative currency for very many people, above and beyond merely expressing mere personal preferences or emotions.

Second, Ayer is unclear about why he gives such a privileged status to the principle of verification when it fails to meet its own criteria of meaning. For as a proposition it is neither verifiable by observation of the empirical world nor is it an analytic statement. J.L. Evans described its self-defeating status as like that of a weighing-machine trying to weigh itself.

Third, most seriously of all, Ayer purports to be formulating a theory of meaning and language but in practice merely presents a positivist or materialist world-view disguised in linguistic dress. In the end it is no more than raw positivism dressed up as a theory of meaning.

Fourth, in addition to these three weaknesses, logical positivism too readily divides all language into a simplistic dualism. Apart from propositions of logic, language allegedly either describes observable states of affairs (verifiable at least in principle) or expresses emotions, recommendations, approval or disapproval.

However, as virtually the whole of WITTGENSTEIN's later work clearly shows, language and uses of language reflect a 'multiplicity' that is 'not something fixed', but functions with the diversity of a repertoire of tools in a tool-box to operate in many ways (L. Wittgenstein, *Philosophical Investigations*, Oxford: Blackwell, Germ. and Eng., 1967, sects. 11 and 23).

LANGUAGE IN RELIGION uses commands, declarations, promises, PRAYER, decrees, pronouncements, parables, and many genres which are best understood as performing a variety of SPEECH ACTS. To ask which are either verifiable or analytic propositions, and to dismiss the rest as 'non-sense', ignores the genuine operative currency with which such language performs meaningful communicative acts.

AYER'S OTHER WORKS

Although his reputation is most popularly known through his *Language, Truth and Logic*, Ayer also addressed problems concerning EPISTEMOLOGY (the nature of knowledge) in *The Problem of Knowledge* (1956); and issues concerning personal identity, freedom and CAUSATION, and the relation between language and states of affairs in *Thinking and Meaning* (1947) and *Philosophy and Language* (1960).

Heavily influenced by the EMPIRICISM of HUME and the world-view of RUSSELL, Ayer came to represent a confident, 'common-sense', empiricist world-view in the English philosophy of the 1950s. Yet he also recognized the logical limitations and fallibility of many empiricist claims to 'knowledge'.

In *The Problem of Knowledge* Ayer writes: 'Claims to know empirical statements may be upheld by a reference to perception, or to memory, or to testimony, or to historical records, or to scientific laws. But such backing is not always strong enough for knowledge. Whether it is so or not depends upon the circumstances of the particular case' (London: Pelican, 1956, 31). This allusion to the particular case holds together the various approaches associated with Ayer, RYLE and others, which often used to be called 'OXFORD PHILOSOPHY' in the 1950s and early 1960s.

B

Barth, Karl (1886–1968)

Many regard Barth as a towering figure in Christian theology of the twentieth century. A Swiss theologian and pastor, Barth opposed Hitler and Nazism in Germany. From 1935 he was professor at Basle, and is most widely known for his massive work *Church Dogmatics*. Although this was never fully completed, the four main 'Parts' run to some fourteen large volumes in English translation (Edinburgh: T & T Clark, 1956–77).

In the context of philosophy of religion Barth made an impact in several areas. (1) He attacked ENLIGHTENMENT rationalism as a mind-set which exercised reductive and distorting influences on Christian theology, especially in conjunction with LIBERAL THEOLOGY and NATURAL THEOLOGY. (2) He emphasized the part played by REVELATION in knowledge of God, and the infinite qualitative TRANSCENDENCE of God as 'Other'. (3) He drew attention to the nature of ANSELM's formulation of the ONTOLOGICAL ARGUMENT as a confession of faith rather than as a philosophical argument. (4) He questioned the way in which Thomas AQUINAS had formulated the role of ANALOGY in the use of LANGUAGE IN RELIGION.

Nevertheless, some works on philosophy of religion tend not fully to appreciate the subtlety and complexity of Barth's thinking. Thus H.J. Paton portrays him as placing a 'theological veto' on language about God in philosophy of religion (*The Modern Predicament*, London: Allen & Unwin, 1955, 47–58).

Whereas in classical high modernity the paradigm of 'knowing' is that of the active human SUBJECT scrutinizing 'OBJECTS' of knowledge, Barth anticipates the view that 'objective' apprehension is not value-neutral. Rather, it is that which accords with the nature of the enquiry and its 'object'. It is not to be shaped exclusively by the agenda of the human 'subject'. In theology this exploration should be, as far as possible, in accordance with God as 'God'.

BARTH'S CRITIQUE OF ENLIGHTMENT RATIONALISM

Barth does not simply reject all use of 'reason'. His target is the method employed widely in theology in the late nineteenth and early twentieth centuries associated with such thinkers as A. Harnack. In one respect Barth anticipated the post-modern perspective that rational enquiry is seldom value-neutral (*see* POST-MODERNITY). Because of human fallenness, he did not entirely reject FEUERBACH's claim that all too often people project their wishes and ideals onto a 'God' who is merely an idol of their own construction.

Liberal theology, in which Barth had been educated and trained, largely focused on Jesus as a teacher of ethical truths. In Harnack's view, the heart of Christian teaching lay in 'the fatherhood of God, the brotherhood of humankind and the infinite value of a human soul'.

Barth found that this approach cut little ice in his early work as a pastor. It also underestimated human sin, and the outbreak of the First World War (1914–18), even endorsed by some of his German teachers, seemed further to question any optimism about 'progress'. He turned to a repeated and intensive reading of Paul's Epistle to the Romans and discovered what he called 'the Strange New World within the Bible' (1917), in *The Word of God and the Word of Man*, (1924, Eng. 1957, 43).

In 1919 Barth published his groundbreaking *Commentary on Romans*. This emphasized the distance between humanity and the transcendence and grace of God. A second edition (1922) drew more explicitly on KIERKEGAARD. The only valid starting-point is revelation: 'God is known through God and through God alone' (*Church Dogmatics*, II: 1, sect. 27, Eng. 179).

REVELATION, REASON, 'NATURAL THEOLOGY' AND DIVINE TRANSCENDENCE

'Objectivity' in knowing God is determined by revelation in accordance with the nature of the 'Object' of knowledge. Or, conversely, God, not humankind, is the subject who addresses humankind. 'Religion' in the sense of human religiosity may be about discovery and attempting to reach 'upward', but in authentic address God's Word is free, sovereign, and 'from above'. In his earlier work (later modified) Barth had urged that God is 'wholly Other'.

This gave rise to the debate to which Paton alludes. Is there a 'point of contact' (German, *Anknüpfungspunkt*) between God and man? Emil Brunner, Barth's former collaborator, appeared to affirm as much in *God and Man* (1930) and in his work on ethics, although he also emphasizes human guilt and fallenness. This opened their debate about the legitimacy of 'natural theology'.

When Hitler came to power in 1933, Barth led the stand of the Confessing Church in Germany under the theme 'Christ alone; Scripture alone', stated in the Barmen Declaration of May 1934. It was in Rome, in deep concern about the apparent blind eye of the Vatican towards Hitler in 1934 that Barth attacked Brunner in his work *No!* (*Nein!*). By making theology more broadly based than 'Christ and Scripture' wider traditions seemed to leave room for compromise and manipulation.

In *Church Dogmatics* Barth also argues that sin has so marred the image of God in humankind that no 'point of contact' survives (I: 1, 273). Nevertheless, in GRACE and in faith such 'contact' may occur in times and in ways of God's choosing. This is not to demand 'a complete sacrifice of the intellect' (Paton, *The Modern Predicament*, 51), or to 'veto' human language about God by 'theological positivism' parallel with AYER's LOGICAL POSITIVISM (ibid.). It is not 'rejection of reason' (ibid., 49). It is affirmation of the free sovereign choice of God when or whether to speak through human reason or any other means. Barth approves of 'critical' reflection.

BARTH'S REAPPRAISAL OF ANSELM'S ONTOLOGICAL ARGUMENT

Four years earlier Barth wrote *Anselm: Fides Quaerens Intellectum* (*Faith Seeking Understanding*, 1930, 2nd edn, 1958). In his preface to the second edition he states that this study provides a 'vital key' to the *Church Dogmatics*. Anselm does not perceive knowledge of God as a human striving upwards. Hence he does not use A POSTERIORI arguments. Rather, knowing God is a process that begins from, and ends in, God.

This process is not irrational or illogical, but derives from 'inner' necessity rather than external persuasion. Thus its logical coherence serves to mark God as 'Other' and transcendent. God is not part of the empirical world, and cannot be 'discovered' within it. Nevertheless God 'speaks', but 'where and when' God wills (*Church Dogmatics*, I: 1, sect. 4, 120). We do not say 'God by saying "human person" in a loud voice'. As we observed in our introductory remarks for Barth, 'knowledge' must be in accordance with the nature of its object, not imposed by the human subject 'externally'. This is 'objectivity' in Barth's sense.

BARTH'S REFORMULATION OF THE TRADITIONAL VIEW OF ANALOGY

Barth's *Church Dogmatics* covers a huge range of topics: revelation and the Word of God; the doctrine of God, the Trinity, and Christology; creation and humankind (four large volumes in the English translation), yet more on reconciliation and redemption. Yet a constant theme remains 'the Godhead of God ... God is God' (*Church Dogmatics*, IV: 2, sect. 64, 101). Such a God is self-giving. Thus we see glimpses of his self-giving Fatherhood in the derivative concept of human fatherliness.

Because God as Father loves and gives himself, a child of God may 'model his action on what God does'; yet 'he cannot give what God gives ... The divine love and the human are always two different things' (ibid., sect. 68, 778). Thus human qualities may reflect what God reveals through divine actions, but Barth is hesitant to endorse Thomas AQUINAS's exposition of analogy, lest it risks extrapolation 'upwards' in too strongly anthropomorphic terms (*see* ANTHROPOMOPRHISM).

Barth therefore accepts the notion of an 'analogy of *faith*' but rejects 'analogy of *being*'. 'This is not similarity of being, an *analogia entis*. The being of God cannot be compared with that of man (ibid., III:

2, sect. 45, 220). This does not, however, exclude communicative interaction. For in an analogy of relation a human being may address God as 'Thou', rather than subsuming God within an analogy of being by over-ready uses of 'he', 'she', or 'it'. This is not mere description but 'encounter' (ibid., 243–59).

Even among admirers or followers of Barth, some express reservations about whether his insistence on the transcendent otherness of God has perhaps introduced a confusion of categories into the issue of language in religion. As RAMSEY urges, MODELS have an important place, provided that they are qualified with sufficient care, and their validity rigorously assessed.

As a system of Christian theology, Barth's thought cannot be ignored, and it has profoundly influenced later European theology. In the four areas in which it most clearly impinges on philosophy of religion, it offers corrections to some shallow assumptions, but at times may also risk 'talking past', rather than with, some contrary approaches. It remains challenging, if also provocative, on method in theology and in EPISTEMOLOGY.

behaviourism

Some distinguish between behaviourism as a strictly scientific method in psychology and behaviourism as a philosophical or psychological doctrine. The term was introduced in 1913 by J.B. Watson (1878–1958) to denote a view of the self in psychology that abandoned all data derived from introspection or from supposed mental states to account for the self. Rather, he approaches the self wholly and exhaustively in terms of what can be observed (ideally as if under laboratory conditions) concerning the self's behaviour.

Watson's works *Behaviour* (1914) and *Behaviourism* (1924) provide classic expositions of this view. A starting-point concerning the fallibility of introspection is understandable, but Watson effectively perceives the human self as a mechanism the activities of which may be reduced to biophysical, neurological responses to stimuli of an empirical nature only (*see* EMPIRICISM).

This becomes still more pronounced in the work of Watson's fellow American B.F. Skinner (1904–90). Skinner presses Watson's school of psychology into 'radical behaviourism', arguing for the elimination of 'mind' as a philosophical and psychological doctrine.

Skinner argued that the shaping of the self was primarily by 'operant conditioning', which reinforces behaviour patterns through stimulus and response especially through pain and pleasure. In popular thought Pavlov's experiments in Russia with the application of stimulus and response to dogs provides a well-known model of this approach.

While Skinner introduced a level of rigour into his scientific work, to reduce the mind, in effect, to instrumental computation based on neurological processes risks committing what Lovejoy termed 'the paradox of materialism': how can materialism claim a rational basis if 'rationality' means only bioneurological processes or pragmatic success with immediate 'local' enterprises undertaken by the self (*see* PRAGMATISM)?

The philosophical doctrines of Rudolf Carnap (1891–1970) and AYER (1910–89) also offer reductionist views of the self. This is to be distinguished from the more strictly genuine logical analysis of RYLE (1900–76), who avoids 'dogmatic' behaviourism.

Although some regard WITTGENSTEIN's attack on 'private language' as evidence of his sympathy with behaviourism, Wittgenstein attacks only the traditional logic applied to 'mental states'. He seems to deny that he is a behaviourist, and stands aloof from both sides in terms of a doctrine or world-view (cf. *Philosophical Investigations*, Oxford: Blackwell, 1967, sects. 281–317).

belief

BELIEF AND KNOWLEDGE

In everyday life we are familiar with a contrast between belief and knowledge. Life abounds with practical examples of the need to act upon beliefs for which evidence of their validity or truth is less than conclusive. In management theory, the manager who delays action until budget forecasts, opportunities, or the capacities of personnel can be known with exactitude does not function as a competent, efficient manager. Humankind constantly needs to act with a judicious margin of risk.

The issue is whether such a margin of risk is reasonable. CERTAINTY is not secured by mere psychological certainty, as if sheer intensity of conviction could guarantee the truth of a proposition or state of affairs. LOCKE (1632–1704) addressed this issue. 'REASONABLENESS' generates an 'entitlement' to belief; sheer intensity of belief does not.

Locke spoke of 'assurance of faith', but distinguished it from knowledge. Even if I have full 'assurance' of faith, 'I assent to any article of faith, so that I may steadfastly venture my all upon it, [yet] it is still but believing. Bring it to certainty, and it ceases to be faith' (*Works*, 12th edn, London, 1824, III: 274–5). Belief, for Locke, is based on REVELATION. '*Faith* is to assent to any proposition ... upon the credit of the proposer, as coming from God ...' (ibid., IV: xviii, 2). Knowledge, on the other hand, depends on perceptions of the world.

WOLTERSTORFF convincingly argues that book IV of Locke's *Essay Concerning Human Understanding* is Locke's 'centre of gravity'. This seeks to offer 'a theory of entitled [i.e. permitted, responsible] belief ... There are norms for believing ... Beliefs are entitled if they do not violate these norms.' Locke therefore sought to produce a 'regulative ... epistemology ... what we ought to do by way of forming beliefs' (*John Locke and the Ethics of Belief*, Cambridge: CUP, 1996, xv–xvi).

This is a very different account of 'entitlement to believe' from that suggested by W. K. Clifford (1845–79) on 'The Ethics of Belief' in his *Lectures and Essays* (1879). He argues that it is immoral to believe without sufficient evidence. He uses the example of a shipowner who sends people to sea in a ship concerning the seaworthiness of which he has well-founded doubts. Supposedly he persuades himself to 'believe' that a kindly Providence will guard this against mishap. It is 'wrong to believe on insufficient evidence'. In principle Clifford rightly underlines, with Locke, the responsibility and public effects of belief. However, his criteria go beyond Locke's 'reasonableness' to a virtually positivist demand for unambiguous empirical evidence (*see* EMPIRICISM; POSITIVISM).

FAITH AS VOLITIONAL AND EXISTENTIAL? FAITH AS VENTURE

An anti-rationalist tradition within Christian thought flows from KIERKEGAARD (1813–55) to BULTMANN (1884–1976). Kierkegaard blamed AUGUSTINE for confusing faith with belief, and thereby transposing it into an intellectual system of propositions. In Kierkegaard's view faith is a voluntarist act, a venture, in which the person of faith stakes his or her self. This is the meaning of his aphorism 'SUBJECTIVITY is TRUTH'.

Bultmann likewise perceives faith as 'venture' and obedience. His view that historical research into the life of Jesus is misguided as a basis for faith stems from a particular way of interpreting the pietist legacy of nineteenth-century Lutheranism, which sees rational argumentation in support of faith as an 'intellectual work'. Faith is trust in the bare Word of God (*see* PIETISM).

The truth that Kierkegaard and Bultmann seek to convey, but with misleadingly one-sided formulations, is that faith and belief operate with a logic of SELF-INVOLVEMENT. Faith is not value-neutral assent to supposedly value-neutral descriptive propositions. Bultmann uses the ambivalent term 'existential' to convey this point (*see* EXISTENTIALISM).

V. H. Neufeld, *The Earliest Christian Confessions* (Leiden: Brill, 1963) and D. M. High, *Language, Persons and Belief* (New York: OUP, 1967) bring out the theological and philosophical dimensions (respectively) of self-involving creeds and confessions. These are both self-involving or existential (the speaker is nailing his or her colours to the mast) and declarative truth-claims about states of affairs (the speaker is endorsing the proposition, for example, that Jesus of Nazareth was crucified and raised, or that God created the world). Often the self-involving dimension (e.g. living as a responsible steward) presupposes a prepositional truth (e.g. that God created the world).

DISPOSITIONAL ACCOUNTS OF BELIEF

H.H. Price begins his classic work *Belief* (London: Allen & Unwin, 1969) with a recognition that 'I believe' and 'We believe' are PERFORMATIVE UTTERANCES (*see* AUSTIN). A mere descriptive proposition may simply be stated ('*p*') without the preface 'I believe' or 'I know'. The latter pledges the speaker to guarantee or at least to 'stand behind' the utterance as credible. There is a valuational aspect: 'and I attach importance to this'.

Belief, Price urges, is not primarily to be understood as a 'mental state' as such. It may more accurately be viewed as a disposition to respond in certain ways to certain circumstances. Thus I do not cease to 'believe' if I fall asleep or become unconscious. However, I will seek to respond with reasons to the contrary if someone presents to me arguments against my belief, and seek to 'live out' the practical entailments of my beliefs.

Price observes, 'This "spreading" of belief from a proposition to its consequences is one of the most important ways in which such a disposition is occurrently manifested ... Our beliefs are like stable landmarks' (ibid., 293). The disposition presupposed by a declaration of belief 'is a multiform disposition, which is actualized or manifested in many different ways: not only in ... actions and inactions, but also in emotional states such as hope and fear; in feelings of doubt, surprise and confidence', and also in intellectual operations (ibid., 294).

Such an approach goes back not simply or primarily to RYLE but more especially to the later WITTGENSTEIN. 'What does it mean to *believe* ...? What are the consequences of the belief, where it takes us ... The surroundings give it its importance' (*Philosophical Investigations*, Oxford: Blackwell, 1967, I, sects. 578 and 583). 'I believe' is not giving a report on my state of mind. 'Believing ... is a kind of disposition of the believing person ... shown ... by his behaviour' (ibid., II, 191).

Price includes a plausible account of 'half-belief'. How is it that some believers act in certain ways consonant with their beliefs 'on some occasions' but act very differently 'on other occasions' (*Belief*, 305)? The primary cause is that of keeping beliefs 'in a watertight compartment' where they fail to engage with the whole of life (ibid., 311). Sometimes the path to maturity is a gradual one, as a full integration of the self gradually emerges.

All of the above aspects, with the possible exception of Clifford's over-harsh demand for empirical criteria, contribute something of value to our understanding of the conceptual grammar of belief, and of why it is not simply a 'weaker' form of knowledge. Issues of 'entitlement', reasonableness, self-involvement, and the visibility of belief in the public domain all belong to the grammar of belief in RELIGION.

Bergson, Henri Louis (1859–1941)

Bergson's philosophy expounds the primacy of process and change over against the place of static or solid objects in space.

God, he urges, works in and through the process of EVOLUTION. God is a creative, dynamic force, a vital impetus (*élan vital*) for livingness and movement.

In philosophy of religion Bergson calls into question a 'static' THEISM, but offers a way of understanding God in dynamic terms compatible with evolutionary theory. God and humanity act with a creative, purposive, freedom that transcends the model of the machine. His works include *Creative Evolution* (1907) and *Thought and the Moving* (1934).

Bergson's work resonates with that of subsequent thinkers who stress the priority of temporal over spatial categories in biblical theology (e.g. Oscar Cullmann, b. 1902) and in philosophical theology and narrative theory (e.g. RICOEUR, b. 1913). His initial concern with evolution owed much to the influence of SPENCER (1820–1903), but he rejected Spencer's POSITIVISM and mechanistic world-view. 'Duration' is more than 'clock-time' (*Time and Free Will*, 1890).

Bergson's most lasting legacy is his careful critique of DARWIN's theory. He reaches the conclusion that biological evolution, far from substantiating a mechanistic or positivist world-view, transcends it and exposes its inadequacy. This provided an impetus, in turn, for the PROCESS PHILOSOPHY of WHITEHEAD and Pierre Teilhard de Chardin.

Berkeley, George (1685–1753)

Berkeley built upon the philosophy of perception in LOCKE (1632–1704), to seek to establish an idealist METAPHYSICS of 'immaterialism'. He claimed that nothing material exists, but only the ideas that constitute what is perceived. An Irishman, Berkeley was a philosopher and theological teacher, and also became a bishop.

Locke had allowed that observations of solidity, extension, motion and number were sense-impressions (i.e. perceptions mediated through the five senses, including sight, hearing and touch) and were derived from the external world. However, he argued that 'secondary' qualities (e.g. colour, sound, taste) are subject-dependent, or shaped entirely by how the mind perceives them. Berkeley extended Locke's 'secondary' category to include every object of human perception. Existence is co-extensive with perception, for 'to be is to be perceived' (*esse est percipi*).

Berkeley did not assume that all ideas are merely a creation of the human mind. Some ideas force themselves upon us as unwelcome. These originate in sensations or experience perceived through the senses because they are derived from an infinite divine mind.

For those unfamiliar with EMPIRICISM and IDEALISM it may seem initially puzzling that Berkeley was both an empiricist and an idealist. However, the latter rests on the former. As an empiricist Berkeley based his theory of perception on the view that the mind receives sense-impressions through the avenue of the senses, but as an idealist he believes that these impressions enter the mind as ideas.

Nevertheless Berkeley's 'subjective idealism' (his own term was 'immaterialism') is to be distinguished from the German idealism of FICHTE, SCHELLING and HEGEL. They began from different starting-points and asked different questions. Two of the titles of Berkeley's works illustrate his angle of approach: *An Essay Towards a New Theory of Vision* (1709) and *A Treatise Concerning the Principles of Human Knowledge* (1710).

Berkeley's claim in the second work that trees, tables, houses and lead weights are no more than complex collections of 'ideas' does not founder upon the common-sense objection that to kick a stone is to feel its impact through pain (ascribed to Samuel Johnson). For pain itself is a perception, which, in Berkeley's worldview, finds its ground, like all perception, in the mind of God. Berkeley's aim was to produce a serious philosophy that countered the SCEPTICISM of the day.

Boethius, Anicius Manlius Severinus (*c*. 480–525/6)

Boethius is widely regarded as a bridge from the ancient philosophical legacies of ARISTOTLE, the STOICS and NEOPLATONISM, to the medieval Latin writers and SCHOLASTICISM. A Roman patrician of high standing, he was accused of treason and imprisoned. While awaiting execution he composed his work *On the Consolation of Philosophy* (524–5). He attempted to bring together aspects of Hellenistic and Roman philosophy with Christian thought.

One of the most important conceptual influences bequeathed by Boethius for philosophy of religion was his formulation of a logic of ETERNITY. Eternity was not to be conceived of as 'human' time stretched out in both directions. Boethius recognized that it belonged to God. Eternity is a mode of reality that grasped 'the whole' of past, present, and future as a whole.

Eternity constituted most especially God's own mode of existence. This is 'the complete possession all at once (*totum simul*) of an illimitable life'. Although strictly eternity is not 'everlastingness' in the human sense of this term, because God is 'infinite', eternity remains 'illimitable', and in this special, qualified sense 'endless'.

A greater conceptual problem is raised by the use of '*simul*', at once, at the same time. Is it conceivable that the living, dynamic, purposive, God would exclude 'succession' from eternity? Boethius might see this as implicit in *simul,* but what currency remains? Yet the formulation of Boethius has remained the classic formulation in the tradition of classical Christian theism (*see* GOD, CONCEPTS OF).

Further contributions of Boethius include his identification of the Greek term *hypostasis* with 'person'. He also places the transitory evils and sufferings of life in the light of the eternal values of RELIGION and philosophy. This 'relativizing' of EVIL provoked the protest of

DOSTOEVSKY's Ivan, who sought a more existential and less abstract approach to the problem of evil (*see* EXISTENTIALISM). There are themes in Boethius that may owe more to Neoplatonism than to Christian tradition (e.g. on the flight of the soul). For a judicious assessment see H. Chadwick, *Boethius* (Oxford: Clarendon Press, 1981).

Bonaventure (*c*. 1217–74)

Bonaventure (John of Fadanza) developed a philosophy within the framework of Christian faith, which combined elements of NEOPLATONISM with a Christian MYSTICISM that culminated in POST-MORTAL union with God. Philosophy may enhance happiness, provided that it is directed by faith.

Bonaventure studied at the University of Paris, and in 1257 was appointed professor there (with Thomas AQUINAS), but the same year became Bishop of Albano and subsequently Cardinal. He belonged to the Franciscan Order, and published the *Commentary of the Sentences of Peter Lombard* (1250–1), *On the Mystery of the Trinity* (1253–7) and *The Journey of the Mind to God* (1259).

Every person, Bonaventure maintained, has an implicit knowledge or awareness of God. Philosophical and theological reflection may make this explicit, including the A POSTERIORI arguments from the world to a First Cause (*see* COSMOLOGICAL ARGUMENT for the existence of God). ANSLEM'S ONTOLOGICAL ARGUMENT rightly expresses the perfection of God. Mystical contemplation nurtures a less fallible, less CONTINGENT, vision of divine ideas. *The Journey to the Mind of God* traces an ascent of the mind from contemplation of the world to contemplation of God.

Bradley, Francis H. (1846–1924)

Bradley taught at Oxford for most of his life, and did not shrink from viewing philosophy as an exploration of the nature of reality. Surface appearances give rise to contradictions. However, philosophical enquiry should aim at coherence. Behind the partial and ever-shifting lies the ABSOLUTE as the ground of reality.

Bradley shared with HEGEL (1770–1831) the notion of an Absolute revealed in and through the finite, and also the belief that only the 'Whole' is real. This led to some insights, but also to certain incautious utterances. For example, if 'time is unreal', why, G.E. Moore asked, do we usually take breakfast 'before' lunch?

The relation between diversity and an underlying unity is largely the subject of his work *Appearance and Reality* (1893). He also wrote works on ethics, logic and truth. Some called him 'the English Hegel'.

Buber, Martin Mordechai (1878–1965)

In philosophy of religion Buber is most widely known for his relatively short but influential masterpiece *I and Thou* (German, *Ich und Du* [1923], Eng., New York: Scribner, 2nd edn, 1958). This expounds the core of his philosophy of relationality. 'The attitude of man is twofold ... One primary word is the combination *I–Thou*. The other primary word is the combination *I–It* ... For the *I*, the primary word *I–Thou* is a different *I* from that of the primary word *I–It*' (ibid., 3).

In other words, the human self, or the 'I', plays a different role, and is transformed into a different kind of self, depending on whether we construe 'the other' as a mere object of knowledge (I-It), or as an Other who addresses us as subject-to-subject (I-Thou). The latter nurtures reciprocity, dialogue, mutuality and respect for the Other.

Buber was born in Vienna, and, in early years, influenced by the works of KANT as well as drawn to religious mysticism. The influence of Kantian ethics can be seen in his appeal to the I–Thou relation as treating persons as ends rather than as means (or as I–It objects). Equally, God is no mere 'object' of human thought, but One who commands. When he was a student in Berlin, Wilhelm Dilthey also influenced him, and this laid foundations for a hermeneutical understanding of self and the Other.

As a Jew, Buber involved himself in Jewish affairs. He became Professor of Jewish Religion at Frankfurt until Hitler's rise to power in 1933. His earlier work on mystical relations of immediacy gave way to a more dialogical relation with God as Other, and as Thou. In 1938 he left Germany to become Professor of Social Philosophy of Religion in the Hebrew University in Jerusalem, until his retirement in 1951.

The I–It relation is typical of scientific or empirical methods of observation (see EMPIRICISM). However, this attitude never tells the whole story. Persons may be viewed as objects in as far as they bear physical properties in the public world. They may be 'observed' in scientific study. But persons are more than objects or things. A person is a 'Thou' who addresses me, whom I encounter as a subject.

It is fundamental for Buber that the two different attitudes affect the kind of 'I' who I am. To regard all persons and objects in I–It speech and attitude is thereby to remain isolated and self-centred in interpersonal terms. A non-relational 'I' is not fully a human 'I'. Respect for life may even imply an I–Thou relation to certain objects in the world. 'Without It man cannot live. But he who lives with It alone is not a man.'

While human persons are primarily Thou but in certain contexts also It, God is 'the eternal Thou'. God is always Subject who addresses us. God is never an It; never the mere object of observation or reflection. This is why Buber dismisses arguments for the existence of GOD as 'foolish' (cf. KIERKEGAARD's 'shameless affront'). God can never be the object of speculative thought. Personal involvement and openness to be addressed and commended are required.

Speaking 'Thou' and being in encounter with the Other are ontological (see ONTOLOGY): 'reality' appears between persons, or between God and human persons in their address and response, reciprocal listening and respect for the Other. This comes close to the core of HERMENEUTICS. Dilthey, Buber's teacher in Berlin, spoke of understanding the 'I' in the 'Thou', and subsequently RICOEUR would speak of understanding the otherness of the Other, and of Oneself as Another.

Buber develops his philosophy further in *Between Man and Man* (1947), *Eclipse of God* (1952) and other works. There are resonances with other Jewish thinkers on 'the Other', notably Franz Rosenzweig and LEVINAS.

His respect for 'the Other' led Buber to co-found the Yihud movement to promote not only Arab–Israeli understanding, but also the ideal of Israel–Palestine as a bi-national state for Jews and Arabs.

Love is the responsibility of the 'I' for the 'Thou'. Divine love is elective: God 'confronts me ... being chosen and choosing ... in one'. REVELATION of God is not the transmission of ideas about God, but an event in which God speaks. Buber's later work on the Bible stresses relationality and encounter in terms of a hermeneutic of narrative. The Holocaust is a moment when we witness an *Eclipse of God* (1952). 'We await his voice' (*On Judaism* [1952], New York: Shocken, 1972, 225).

Buddhist philosophy

The title 'the Buddha', 'the Enlightened One' is given primarily to the historical founder of Buddhism, Siddhartha Gautama. Estimates of his date of birth vary between 563, *c.* 485 and *c.* 450 BCE He addressed as a main issue how to avoid suffering and dissatisfaction by escaping the cycle of rebirth. Buddhist philosophy, especially in Indian traditions, is largely derived from this concern. It seeks enlightenment based on an understanding of human nature.

ENLIGHTENMENT AND NIRVANA

Indian forms of Buddhist philosophy flourished especially during the early medieval era until the eleventh century. Like some traditions in Graeco-Roman STOICISM, this philosophy seeks to eliminate the ignorance that places too much value on that which causes and nourishes desire, or too much attention on that which invites aversion. Such desires and aversions breed frustration and dissatisfaction.

The Buddha himself refused to address speculative questions about the nature of reality, since these were thought to lead to an attachment to views that were not conducive to Enlightenment. Philosophical questions were first developed in various schools of the Abhidharma, which expanded the early teachings of the Buddha into an analysis of all the elements of experience and their interdependence.

The Buddha's dying words are said to have been: 'I take my leave of you. All the constituents of being are transitory; work out your salvation with diligence.' Central to the early teachings was the view that there is no abiding self apart from the arising of experience, and that transitory experience arises through an interdependent cycle.

The extinction of all unproductive or worldly desires is known as nirvana (Sanskrit, 'blown out'). This is related to the elimination of greed, hatred and delusion. It is a permanent liberation from the cycle of rebirth. Although it is regarded as release, the Buddha pronounced that nothing can be positively predicated about it that is true. In Mahayana Buddhism nirvana is thus regarded as indistinguishable from the cycle of rebirth. The emphasis of 'Enlightenment' is in realizing the emptiness of constituents of existence.

KARMA AND DHARMA

More explicit philosophical investigations emerged in the Yogacara school of Buddhism (fourth century BCE), also within the Mahayana school. The Yogacara school, however, explores the nature of consciousness, perception, knowledge and ONTOLOGY. It concludes that in a nuanced sense consciousness is real only in terms of convention, and is the cause of *karma*. External objects do not exist, but are illusory.

This school produced the most developed and complex theory of perception and EPISTEMOLOGY in Buddhist philosophy. Sacred texts bore such titles as 'Elucidating the Hidden Connections', and a notion of three natures of the self was formulated.

The link between theoretical and practical philosophy is clearest in the concept of *dharma*, a Sanskrit term that covers a range of meanings including 'teaching', 'law', 'custom', 'justice' and 'religion', as well as the order of reality, or even the constituents of that order. Suggesting perhaps certain resonances with Western thought in ARISTOTLE, this is like a principle of 'orderedness' in the world; a cosmic, and perhaps even (loosely) divine, principle. To follow *dharma* is the path to Enlightenment: perhaps also release from *karma* and reaching nirvana.

Buddhist philosophy in most of its forms retains themes of cessation of desire through disengagement from causes of desire in the world, and the further goal of a cessation of ignorance, suffering and death. Yet there are also positive affirmations of a life of 'balance', for example between ascetic self-denial and self-indulgence. These also resonate with Aristotle's ethic of the Mean, just as *dharma* may resonate perhaps with his notion 'orderedness'.

Yet there are also entirely contrary themes. Consciousness is not understood as a stable individual consciousness in the sense held by Aristotle, AUGUSTINE,

AQUINAS, DESCARTES and LOCKE. A philosophy of the transitory and continuous change applies to the SELF, to personhood and to POST-MORTAL EXISTENCE. Instead of RESURRECTION, rebirth may take place in a number of different realms resembling different heavens and hells.

The continuous rise and fall of the being is determined by its *karma*, the results of its intentional actions. Only in 'Pure Land Buddhism' is the goal not nirvana as such, but rebirth in a heavenly realm created by one of the Buddhas, achieved through calling on the Buddha to transfer his merit. (*See also* MYSTICISM; HINDU PHILOSOPHY; NĀGĀRJUNA; NISHIDA; NISHITANI; VIA NEGATIVA.)

Bultmann, Rudolf (1884–1976)

Bultmann exercised a very large influence on mid-twentieth-century Christian theology. His greatest significance for the philosophy of religion lay in his proposals for a programme of DEMYTHOLOGIZING the New Testament, his devaluation of history as a basis for religious faith, his dualist approach to faith and knowledge, and the COGNITIVE or descriptive and existential dimensions of LANGUAGE IN RELIGION (*see* COGNITION; DUALISM; EXISTENTIALISM).

Bultmann studied at Tübingen, Berlin and Marburg, and inherited from his teacher W. Herrmann a Kantian disjunction between fact and value. Relatively early he published his *History of the Synoptic Tradition* (1919, 1921; Eng., 1963), which ascribed various settings and forms to the material of the first three Gospels on the basis of their function in the life of the earliest churches (their *Sitz im Leben*), in contrast to any historical role in recording facts about Jesus.

This material, Bultmann insists, serves such existential functions as proclamation (*kerygma*), pronouncement, or challenge; it did not serve any interest of historical report. In historical terms, Bultmann believed, the sources reveal little more

than that Jesus lived, proclaimed the kingdom of God, called followers to follow him, and was crucified.

Bultmann was not troubled by this, since for him faith cannot rest on historical reconstruction. This would make faith dependent on intellectual success or achievement, which would be equivalent to 'justification by works' in the intellectual sphere. Bultmann's thought is dominated by a nineteenth-century version of Lutheranism, which goes further in this reapplication of justification by GRACE through faith alone than perhaps Luther himself.

On this basis, Bultmann urges, the language of the New Testament must be 'demythologized'. It must be extricated from any hint of serving to describe or to report. It 'must be interpreted ... existentially' ('New Testament and Mythology' [1941], in H.W. Bartsch, ed., *Kerygma and Myth*, vol. 1, London: SPCK, 1964). 'God' is not a 'given' object (*eine Gegebenheit*) within a system of 'knowledge' (*Erkenntnissen*), as the 'mythical' form might seem to imply ('What Does it Mean to Speak to God' [1925], in *Faith and Understanding*, vol. 1, London: SCM, 1969, 60). Hence 'demythologizing' is to remove a 'false stumbling-block' for the reader.

Bultmann rightly seeks to restore the nature of the New Testament as self-involving address and existential challenge. He uses HEIDEGGER's conceptual scheme, which distinguishes the human (*Dasein*, being-there) from the language of mere 'objects'. However, he fails to recognize that these modes of language are not competing alternatives. Often language may address us and challenge us precisely because it also embodies truth-claims about states of affairs.

Bultmann's positive aims are vitiated and flawed by a dualist view of language, and by a neo-Kantian dualism of fact and value. 'Religion', for Bultmann, belongs almost inclusively to the latter category. He also failed sufficiently to recognize the ambiguities and differences embodied in uses of the word 'MYTH'. As a result he oscillates between contradictory uses of the term. Sometimes it denotes analogy; sometimes it denotes a primitive world-view; at other times it denotes an 'objectifying' use of language that needs to be 'de-objectified'. This last reaches the heart of his concerns most closely. (*See also* KANT.)

C

categories

This term is one of the most slippery and variable in philosophical thought, because it has been used in a variety of (often technical) ways by different major thinkers.

ARISTOTLE (384–322 BCE) used the term to denote a list of basic classifications in ONTOLOGY. 'Being' itself could be classified most basically as substance (Greek, *ousia*, being), to which other categories served as ATTRIBUTES, for example, quantity, quality, location in time, location in space, action or being affected by action. These are expounded in his work *Categories*, but the list is extended and developed further in his *Topics*.

KANT (1724–1804) believed that the structures that we perceive and of which we conceive within the everyday ('phenomenal') world are construed and shaped by the human mind. The mind uses reason as a 'regulative' tool to organize the raw data of sense and sensation into an understandable order. We construe categories by means of which everything is understood.

Kant postulated twelve categories, grouped as those of quantity, quality, relation and modality. Thus unity, plurality and totality are categories of quantity. Positive, negative and limited are categories of quality. Substance–ACCIDENT, CAUSE–effect and reciprocity are categories of relation. POSSIBILITY, actuality and NECESSITY or CONTINGENCY are categories of modality. Kant used the term 'categorical imperative' to denote the ABSOLUTE claim of the moral imperative.

HEGEL, Peirce and RUSSELL use different systems of categories. RYLE expounds particular logical clarifications designed to expose 'category mistakes'. In mathematics yet another nuance of the term denotes structures and transformations.

cause, causation

Traditionally a cause has been regarded as the necessary antecedent to an effect. This view was refined by ARISTOTLE (384–322 BCE), who distinguished between four types of causes. DESCARTES (1596–1650) believed that a cause must contain the qualities of the effect that it produces. On the other hand, HUME (1711–76) insisted that causality can never be the object of empirical observation. Hume noted that in strictly empirical terms we see only repeated examples of constant conjunction (*see* EMPIRICISM).

KANT (1724–1804) argued that cause constituted one of the categories by means of which the human mind organizes sense-data or objects of perception into an intelligible and ordered world, alongside the other categories of time and space. In religious contexts some exponents of ISLAMIC PHILOSOPHY together with more deterministic theologians in Christian and other (especially Islamic) traditions seek to relate an Aristotelian theory of causality to the status of God or Allah as General Cause (not merely First Cause), and verge on OCCASIONALISM (*see* DETERMINISM).

Aristotle offers an analysis of cause (Greek, *aitía*) in terms of four sub-categories. In building a house, for example, the material cause (Greek, *hýlē*, matter) would be the wood or stone necessary for its construction. The efficient cause (*archè tês kineseōs*, commencement of the motion) would be the impact of the tools of the builders. The formal cause (*ousía*, being) is the design-pattern or style appropriated by the architect. The final cause (*telos*, end) is the purpose that the house is to serve.

The Greek terms do not correspond exactly with English parallels. Thus *aitía*, cause, itself denotes that which is responsible for a condition, including ground, cause, reason, circumstances or basis. It approaches the modern notion of 'conditions for'. *Hýlē* denotes the stuff or material out of which something is made, i.e. 'material' in both senses of the modern English word. *Ousía* denotes what exists and has substance.

Hume exposes the fallacy that causality is evidenced by strictly empirical observation. All that we can actually observe is constant conjunction. In other words, so-called 'laws' of causality are not themselves based on the method of A POSTER-IORI scientific observation, even if successful prediction places causality at the very top of the scale of probability of explanation.

Kant's insistence that causality is an A PRIORI category of the mind (*see* CATE-GORIES) may find less than uncontroversial acceptance outside firmly Kantian traditions of philosophy. However, Kant was dissatisfied with Hume's account of a

world of perceptions on the ground that it lacked coherence. Moreover, his approach serves as a reminder in philosophy of religion that just as time and space belong to the created order along with human understanding, so caused causal connections and the cause–effect nexus of 'nature' belong to this order. Yet this differs from such metaphysical concepts as that of an Uncaused (or First) Cause (*see* METAPHYSICS).

This difference serves also to question the validity of a logical step within the COSMOLOGICAL ARGUMENT for the existence of God. The meaning of 'cause' in the major premise (caused cause) slides to that of another term in the conclusion (uncaused cause).

Both narrowing and broadening understandings of cause have found expression in the history of ideas. WILLIAM OF OCKHAM tended to narrow Aristotle's fourfold analyses to focus on efficient cause as what we mainly understand by 'cause'. However, in modern scientific discussions the Greek term *aitía* used by Aristotle seems to have regained some of its original scope as that which provides necessary and sufficient conditions for certain effects.

This recalls the formulation of LEIBNIZ (1646–1716) concerning 'the Principle of Sufficient Reason'. Nothing occurs without sufficient reason for the occurrence. This derives in part, at least, from his ONTOLOGY of temporal continuity.

More recent debates focus on how cause (in the sense of a specific cause of a particular event) relates to causality (as a postulate about how a diversity of conditions may produce different types of effects). On one side, 'laws' of causality are understood by some scientists and philosophers in a mechanistic sense, as if to imply a positivist world-view (*see* POSITIVISM). On the other side, 'laws' are regarded as 'progress reports' of an 'open' universe; i.e. generalizations based on CONTINGENT events up to the present. A third group seeks to give due place to 'order' in the world, but may perceive this orderedness either as a 'given' in the world or as a 'given' of the human mind.

certainty and doubt

Many ordinary religious believers imagine that they are 'certain' about a set of beliefs or claims to truth, and that to doubt them would be blameworthy or less 'religious'. Yet in the history of philosophical and religious thought, certainty, in the epistemological sense of claims to knowledge, more readily characterizes those rationalists who seek 'clear and certain' truths (even sometimes empiricist evidentialists) than most religious believers.

Indeed, in the tradition of SOCRATES and the early dialogues of PLATO, the purpose of DIALECTIC was to expose firmly held opinions as subject to doubt, in order to move from opinion (Greek, *doxa*) to knowledge (*epistēmē*). Without the experience of doubt, a person may merely remain secure within entrenched convictions, without testing them or exploring further issues.

PSYCHOLOGICAL, LOGICAL AND EPISTEMOLOGICAL CERTAINTY

LOCKE (1632–1704) explored grounds for reasonable BELIEF. In this process he observed that mere intensity of personal conviction need not entail the validity of what is believed to be the TRUTH. 'Psychological' certainty alone does not constitute grounds for 'entitlement' to believe, if such belief is not reasonable.

Clearly 'I am certain' in a psychological sense needs to be distinguished from a claim to certainty put forward on grounds of logical or epistemological demonstration. The 'certainty' of the truth of an ANALYTIC STATEMENT is that of the logical validity of stating what is simply true on the basis of a definition of terms.

This complexity of the different uses of 'certain' and 'certainty' receives careful elucidation in WITTGENSTEIN's *On Certainty* (Oxford: Blackwell, 1969) written

in draft as one of his last works (1951). Wittgenstein examines the 'common sense' claim of G.E. Moore that some everyday empirical truths are examples of what we can know with certainty.

Wittgenstein questions whether the formula 'I know ...' in such sentences as 'I know that I am a human being', or 'I know that here is a hand ... for it is *my* hand that I'm looking at' serves genuinely to identify an epistemological certainty (ibid., sects. 1, 4, 6, 12, 19).

WITTGENSTEIN'S EXPLORATIONS IN *ON CERTAINTY*

Against Moore's arguments in 'Proof of an External World' (*Proceedings of the British Academy* 25, 1939; repr. in *Philosophical Papers*, 1959) Wittgenstein questions whether 'I know' constitutes a claim to knowledge based on 'evidence'. It is, rather, the kind of belief for which 'grounds for *doubt* are lacking' (*On Certainty*, sect. 4). In genuine claims to knowledge, one could say, 'I thought I knew ...', but not of Moore's examples (ibid., sect. 21).

In summary, Wittgenstein distinguishes three types of utterance about 'certainty'. First, he calls 'subjective certainty' what above (in connection with Locke) we called 'psychological certainty' (ibid., sect. 194). Mere intensity of a feeling of conviction does not necessarily entail its truth. There is no necessary correlation between these, even of degree or probability.

Second, often we say, 'I am certain ...', or 'It is certain that ...', when to doubt the belief or proposition is simply inconceivable. This is a conceptual point that moves beyond mere psychological description of feeling or innerness. In the case of some belief-claims, 'doubt gradually loses its sense' (ibid., sect. 56). We move from 'subjective' to 'objective' certainty 'when a mistake is not possible [because it is] *logically* excluded' (ibid., sect. 194).

Third, some expressions of certainty are to identify 'hinge' propositions. These are convictions that have 'belonged to scaffolding of our thoughts (Every human being has parents)' (ibid., sect. 211). They are like 'the proposition "It is written"' (ibid., sect. 216). They are 'hinges' (sect. 343) on which other propositions turn. For 'all confirmation and disconfirmation ... takes place already within a system' (ibid., sect. 105). What is 'certain' seems to be 'fixed ... removed from traffic' (ibid., sect. 210).

THE STATUS OF DOUBT

This leads Wittgenstein to explore a relation with the logic of doubt. 'The child learns by believing the adult. Doubt comes *after* belief' (ibid., sect. 160, his italics). Doubt (no less than belief) requires grounds for doubting: 'Doesn't one need grounds for doubt?' (ibid., sect. 122).

Wittgenstein comes close here to Locke's notion of 'reasonable' belief: rational suspicion has 'grounds', i.e. 'the reasonable man believes this' (ibid., sect. 323). He is closer to Locke than perhaps he is to DESCARTES: 'One doubts on specific grounds' (ibid., sect. 458). Except for a purely methodological exercise, there needs to be reasonable doubt as well as reasonable belief.

'Negative' activities (doubting, telling a lie) are parasitic upon belief and truth. They, too, are learned linguistic behaviour. They belong to 'systems' of belief and doubt. A belief-system is like a 'nest of propositions'. Individual twigs can be doubted and removed; but if the system is an object of doubt from the first, the nest itself has collapsed, and there is nothing to doubt.

We should not use the word 'doubt' of what had never been established. 'Why is it not possible for me to doubt that I have never been on the moon? And how could I try to doubt it? ... The supposition that perhaps I have been there would strike me as *idle*. Nothing would follow from it' (ibid., sect. 117).

Our earlier allusion to Socrates now assumes a sharper significance. The 'doubt' exposed by Socrates does not serve to promote SCEPTICISM, any more than Wittgenstein's insistence that Moore does not address epistemological certainty forms part of a sceptical attack on knowledge. Quite the reverse is the case. Both Socrates and Wittgenstein see doubt and knowledge in operational terms for daily life.

In the sacred writings of several religious traditions, claims to certainty may be put forward in the ways described above. Constructive methodological doubt is often used to raise exploratory questions through such media as parables, aphorisms, dialogue or questions. In the New Testament Paul asserts the quasi-Socratic maxim: 'If any among you thinks they are wise (Greek, *sophos*) ... let them become a fool (*moros*) on order that they might become wise' (1 Cor. 3:18). A measure of doubt may begin a journey from illusory complacency to wisdom.

Friedrich Waismann examines the grammar of doubt and of questions. Sometimes 'doubt is suppressed but not disarmed' (*Principles of Linguistic Philosophy*, London: Macmillan, 1865, 17). 'The question is the first groping step of the mind in its journeyings that lead to new horizons. The great mind is the great questioner ... Questions lead us on and over the barriers of traditions' (ibid., 405). On the other hand, 'Questions seduce us, too, and lead us astray' (ibid.).

COGNITION, COGNITIVE

Cognition broadly denotes an act or process of knowledge. Cognitive denotes that which involves an act or process of knowing (Greek, *gnôsis*, knowledge). The words occur in three main contexts of thought.

First, in some writers on SELFHOOD and the philosophy of mind, cognition is said to entail, or to presuppose, an act of judgement on the part of the self. To know *x* means that the SUBJECT of cognition knows the OBJECT of cognition '*as x*' (C.A. Campbell, *On Selfhood and Godhood*,

London: Allen & Unwin, 1957, 41, and more broadly 36–72).

Many philosophers argue that cognition involves perception, memory, intuition and judgement. This has implications for the nature of the self and for the formation of CONCEPTS. However, this claim remains controversial, and some empiricists would not ascribe to cognition all of these aspects (*see* EMPIRICISM).

Second, another context of discussion arises from competing (or at least different) claims about cognitive and non-cognitive LANGUAGE IN RELIGION or in ETHICS. Often the terms are used to denote (respectively) language about facts or states of affairs and other modes of linguistic communication.

Here, expressive language that expresses emotions, attitudes or choices is non-cognitive. However, expressions of BELIEF may include both a cognitive and non-cognitive dimension because beliefs usually presuppose, or claim truth about, states of affairs.

In ethics 'non-cognitive' approaches frequently suggest that ethical approval or disapproval is a matter of mere preference, recommendation, convention or personal attitude. But a sharp polarity between fact and value, or between cognitive and non-cognitive, often overlooks more subtle interconnections between the two. This over-neat contrast vitiates otherwise useful explorations in such theologians as BULTMANN and George Lindbeck.

Finally, a third distinct context is that of cognitive psychology especially in infants. It has emerged that conceptual development is often earlier, more complex, and more closely related to abstraction than older empiricist theories might seem to suggest.

Cohen, Hermann (1842–1918)

Cohen was founder of the Marburg school of Neo-Kantian philosophy. The late nineteenth century saw a revival of Kantian

thought in Germany, but Neo-Kantianism tended to go further than KANT himself in questioning the notion of any 'given'. Cohen rejected the role assigned by Kant to the concept of the 'thing-in-itself'. He challenged Kant's assumption that it is necessary to postulate a prior 'givenness' of sensations (*Empfindung*) that precedes thought.

With Paul Natorp (1854–1924) Cohen argued that Kant had confused psychological consciousness (*Bewusstheit*) with 'consciousness' as the ground of knowledge in a purely logical sense (*Bewusstsein*).

Neo-Kantian philosophy made a significant impact on mathematical physics and the sciences of the day. Thus Hermann von Helmholtz and Heinrich Hertz perceived the role played by 'models' (*Bilder*) rather than only ideas or physical data in scientific work. 'Methods of presentation' (*Darstellungen*) are carefully 'constructed' schemes that facilitate knowledge. Natorp declared: 'Objects are not "given"; consciousness forms them.'

In theology, this radical Kantianism decisively influenced BULTMANN, who devalued the possibility of descriptive propositions in RELIGION: 'God' cannot be 'objectively given' (*eine Gegebenheit*).

concept

Almost any attempt to define 'concept' will invite criticism from some quarter. Even among philosophers (e.g. LOCKE, KANT, HEGEL, WITTGENSTEIN) there is a difference of viewpoint and approach, as well as areas of agreement. Further, the term also occurs in different contexts in psychology, SEMANTICS, linguistics, lexicography and LOGIC.

Concept denotes more, but hardly less, than idea. While many reject a mentalist notion of 'inner' speech, in a more cautious and rigorous way the starting-point of Locke (1632–1704) remains initially constructive. He attributed concepts to the human capacity to discuss and to distinguish relations between ideas in the abstract. Thus human beings not only distinguish this book from that book as objects in the material, empirical, CONTINGENT, everyday world, but also the concept 'book' from the concept 'pamphlet' as categories or classes which this book or that pamphlet instantiates.

Relations between ideas, Locke urged, give rise to complex concepts. Kant (1724–1804) drew a distinction between percepts and concepts. Conceptual thought is not merely the perception of objects or ideas but a structural ordering of what is perceived in terms of such CATEGORIES as those of unity, plurality (quantity); positive, negative (quality); substance, cause (relation); and possibility, actuality (*see also* ARISTOTLE). Human imagination provides the *schemata* of quality and causality (and other categories) to make understanding (*Verständnis*) possible.

Hegel (1770–1831) developed this notion of 'critical ordering' further. Concepts are the fruit of critical reflection upon difference and upon differentiation. Concepts (*Begriff*) operate at the level of critical self-conscious awareness, in contrast to pre-conceptual SYMBOLS, or MYTHS, as mere representations (*Vorstellungen*). The task of philosophy is to enhance conceptual awareness critically.

Wittgenstein (1889–1951) tends to use concept not to denote the phonetic or 'physical' properties of language, but the logical grammar of language uses, i.e. how words and sentences are applied (*Philosophical Investigations*, Oxford: Blackwell, 1967, sects. 104–8). Again, we return to the contrast between a logical understanding and its practical instantiation: 'If a person has not yet got the *concepts*, I shall teach him to use the words by means of examples and by practice' (ibid., sect. 208). 'The application is ... a criticism of understanding' (ibid., sect. 146).

This reflects the widely accepted distinction, especially in ANALYTICAL PHILOSOPHY, between words and concepts, sentences and propositions (or statements),

and (in semantics) between token and type. We need not subscribe to a Platonic DUALISM between objects and forms to perceive that these represent two orders of language-users. The first of each pair is grounded in a particular instance of the second of each pair.

As a child learns to use concepts, an awareness of generality, differentiation and categorization emerges that transcends the more elementary observation concerning differences between objects of different spatio-temporal locations. At its minimum, concepts presuppose a method of classification. At a higher level, conceptual analysis becomes the exploration of logical grammar.

conceptualism

The term denotes a mediating position between more extreme forms of REALISM and NOMINALISM in medieval SCHOLASTIC PHILOSOPHY. It is especially associated with the thought of Peter ABELARD (1079–1142).

Nominalists held that UNIVERSALS (concepts, ideas or definitions that transcend all particulars or specific cases, and have universal application) constitute nothing more than linguistic signs or conceptual constructs. Universals are thus not 'real' entities, but only logical or semantic 'names' (Latin, *nomen*). The opposite view is held by realists. Realists believe that universals possess a reality beyond mere thought and language (Latin, *res*, a thing, something of substance). (Realism also carries a second meaning: *see* REALISM)

Between these two extremes a spectrum of intermediate views exists. While PLATO was a realist, ARISTOTLE and Thomas AQUINAS held a moderate or modified realism. WILLIAM OF OCKHAM attacked realism and is generally regarded as a nominalist.

Abelard attempted a middle path, often called CONCEPTUALISM. This is the origin of his celebrated saying that each side is right in what it affirms and wrong in what it denies. Nominalists are right in perceiving the role performed by SEMANTICS, LOGIC and conceptual construction. However, realists are right to insist that reality consists in more than merely signs chasing (or denoting) other signs (see POSTMODERNITY). Reality is not exhausted by human concepts of reality, but concepts do indeed entail logical construal and construction.

It is just arguable that, for the philosophically informed, conceptualism offers a more 'commonsense' approach than either of the two extremes that it seeks to avoid. Although modern critical realism emerged strictly in the context of theories of causality, critical realism shares the view of conceptualism that there is more to reality than 'what is known' in concepts. Both perceive that description and conceptual construction are not entirely value-neutral, but also have some foundation in a reality external to the activity of the mind. (See also NON-REALISM.)

contingency, the contingent

Contingency may be said to apply to objects or to states of affairs or to propositions. The classic example of a contingent proposition in philosophical logic is: 'It is raining.' It might or might not be true, and its truth may be verified or disconfirmed by evidential empirical observation.

Some propositions, however, are NECESSARY. The statement that the sum of the angles of a triangle amount to 180° remains true irrespective of what triangle I draw. This is an example of an ANALYTIC STATEMENT, for it is true by virtue of the logic entailed in the definition of a triangle. In this case we are speaking of logical necessity.

Can the terms 'necessary' and 'contingent' be applied to persons or objects rather to propositions? The COSMOLOGICAL ARGUMENT for the existence of God depends on the distinction between contingent, finite, caused causes within the world and a 'Prime Mover', First Cause, or Being of a different order, who is characterized by necessity and ASEITY.

Under the cosmological argument the view is examined that if the whole of reality is contingent, we may in principle go back in time to a situation in which nothing (that which might not have been) gives rise to nothing. If all of reality is contingent, it appears that we postulate an infinite regress of finite caused causes, with no ground beyond such a chain. Similarly, the ONTOLOGICAL ARGUMENT for the existence of God hinges in part on what kind of necessity we ascribe to God, or to the concept of God.

ARISTOTLE applied 'contingent' to objects and to events, in contrast to Necessary Being in the context of 'possibility' as against actuality. He also applied the term to propositions the truth or falsity of which are contingent. In LEIBNIZ and in Lessing this became modified in terms of a contrast between the contingent truths of history, or 'facts', and the 'eternal' or necessary truths of REASON. In theology this had profound consequences for Christology.

corrigibility

The term denotes the quality of being subject to subsequent correction, or the capacity to be corrected. It stands in contrast to that which is definitive and final.

HERMENEUTICS poses a dilemma for many religious people. For many, a sacred text is perceived as definitive, but it is usually recognized that communities of interpretation are fallible. Hermeneutical theory since SCHLEIERMACHER has broadly underlined the progressive nature of hermeneutical understanding as a deepening process. Earlier understanding may be more partial (in both senses of the word) than later 'divinatory' and critical reappraisals and rereadings. Each act of understanding is corrigible in the light of subsequent engagements with the text, or with that which is to be understood.

Historical understanding and pragmatic theories of knowledge also point to the corrigibility of progressive levels of apprehending truth. The main dilemma of PRAGMATISM is that what may seem to be justified to a community as a claim to truth may undergo substantial change and revision as history moves on.

Martin Luther's emphasis on the clarity (*claritas*) of scripture was arguably a functional use of the term rather than a claim to 'final' understanding. His opposition to Erasmus provides the context for this Reformation discussion. Erasmus argued that since all biblical interpretation was corrigible, frequently inaction is advisable in the face of uncertainty. Luther insisted that scripture is always sufficiently clear for the next necessary step of action to be taken.

cosmological argument for the existence of God

ARGUMENT FROM OUR EXPERIENCE OF THE WORLD (*A POSTERIORI*)

The cosmological argument for the existence of God begins with A POSTERIORI arguments from the nature of the world, in contrast to the ONTOLOGICAL ARGUMENT, which begins with an A PRIORI analysis of a CONCEPT, namely that of God (*see* GOD, ARGUMENTS FOR THE EXISTENCE OF).

The use of the cosmological argument is not restricted to Christian theism. Formulations can be found in PLATO and ARISTOTLE among the Greeks; in Islamic philosophers such as AL-KINDI, AL-GHAZALI and IBN SINA; and in Judaism (e.g. MAIMONIDES) as well as in Christian theism (briefly in ANSELM but most especially in Thomas AQUINAS). The most notable opponent of the argument was KANT.

FORMULATIONS IN PLATO AND IN ARISTOTLE

Plato (428–348 BCE) discusses good and evil, and in particular change and changelessness, in the *Laws*. In *Laws* X he argues that motion within the world presupposes some source of motion which is itself self-moving and is not set in motion by some eternal agent or cause. This unmoved mover does not belong to realm of the finite or CONTINGENT. It belongs to the realm of soul, spirit, the gods or God.

Aristotle (384–322 BCE) also distinguishes between potentiality and actuality, and offers a careful analysis of the nature of CAUSE and causation. These two innovative and distinctive themes in his philosophy come together in his formulation of the cosmological argument.

On cause, Aristotle distinguishes between efficient cause (in the example of a marble sculpture, the hammer and chisel); final cause (the purpose for which the sculpture is formed); the material cause (the potential of marble as matter) and the formal cause (the potential structure and proportionality of the sculpture seen in terms of style or pattern).

The causal agency that brings the potential into actuality cannot, Aristotle argues, presuppose an infinite chain of potentiality that never springs from, nor ends in, the actual. Otherwise the entire process is merely contingent or possible rather than actual. Hence there is an actual, unmoved, originating Prime Mover.

'If there is nothing eternal, there can be no becoming ... The last member of the series [i.e. of causes and effects] must be ungenerated ... since nothing can come from nothing' (*Metaphysics*, 999b). The Prime Mover is 'NECESSARY'. The argument is *a posteriori* because everything in the world, according to Aristotle, points beyond itself to that upon which it depends.

FORMULATIONS IN ISLAMIC PHILOSOPHY

Al-Kindi (*c.* 813–*c.* 871) and al-Ghazali (1058–1111) reflect a revival of interest in Aristotle in medieval ISLAMIC PHILOSOPHY. These two writers write within the *kalam* tradition of Islam, which shares with Aristotle (and later Thomas Aquinas) the view that an infinite regress of caused causes is impossible. The logical reason is that if such a chain were postulated, the whole of reality, or the universe, in principle may never have come to be. The reason in philosophical theology is that the universe is finite, and has a beginning. It is contingent, not 'necessary'.

This *kalam* argument reflects the distinction already advocated by Plato and Aristotle that only an intelligence, an unmoved originating Mover, can possess the status of a necessary Being. This is One who is self-generated, or is characterized by ASEITY (Latin, *a se*, of itself).

Ibn Sina (Avicenna, 980–1037) and IBN RUSHD (Averroes, 1126–98) did even more to lead to a revival of Aristotle's thought in twelfth-century Europe. Ibn Sina stressed the importance of REASON. A study of the world reveals that contingent objects or agents are finite entities for the existence of which a reason can be postulated. However, contingent beings do not constitute an infinite regress of caused causes.

Contingent beings end in a necessary Being. The difference from the *kalam* tradition of al-Kindi and al-Ghazali lies in the exclusive dependence of their argument on logical inferences from the world without postulating any temporal dimension. It does not require or presuppose the notion of 'the beginning' of the universe.

Ibn Rushd aimed to integrate Aristotelian philosophy with his Islamic theology. He is even more explicitly distanced from the *kalam* tradition in claiming that both God and the world are eternal. Nevertheless, the world remains an effect of God's power, created from eternity. Hence he presses radically the distinction between logical and temporal arguments: the world is eternal but caused; God is eternal and uncaused, since God is God's own ground, unlike the world, and is a 'necessary' Being.

The emphasis thus falls upon the logical status of the One who controls all things. This comes close to the heart of the ontological argument, but strictly remains *a posteriori*.

A MIDDLE WAY: MOSES MAIMONIDES (1135–1204)

This Spanish-born Jewish philosopher engaged directly with the two versions of the Islamic formulations represented respectively by the *kalam* tradition (Al-Kindi and al-Ghazali) and the arguments of Ibn Rushd and Ibn Sina. On one side, the *kalam* tradition not only postulated a beginning to the world, but a version of OCCASIONALISM, i.e. that God is the only true causal agent of every event. Maimonides argued that this reduces the regularities of nature to an arbitrary view of providence.

On the other hand, Maimonides firmly rejected the view of Ibn Sina and Ibn Rushd that the universe had no beginning, since this flatly contradicts the biblical accounts of creation in Genesis, and is also rationally implausible and unnecessary. In Christian theology Thomas AQUINAS also follows this middle way.

ANSELM AND THOMAS AQUINAS

Anselm (1033–1109) is best known in philosophy of religion for his two formulations of the ontological argument for the existence of God, and in Christian theology for his *Why God Became Man*. However, in the *Monologion* (*Soliloquy* or *Meditation*) Anselm argues from the existence of 'good things' in the world to the existence of the source of all good. In particular, 'all that exists exists through a nature or essence that exists *through itself* (*per se*)' (*Monologion*, 13). This is the argument from the contingent to the necessary.

A fuller discussion of the FIVE WAYS of Thomas Aquinas (1225–74) is set out under that entry, which need not be replicated. We may summarize certain selected features. The First Way takes up Aristotle's arguments from the phenomenon of potentiality. It is usually called the kinetological argument, i.e. an argument from 'movement'. It argues to a Prime Mover. However, the Latin *motus* is broader than 'motion'. Hence the argument that all potential, or moving, objects presuppose what set them in motion is not wholly discredited by Newton's law of motion and inertia.

The Second Way begins from the phenomenon of efficient cause, and reflects the earlier arguments from Aristotle. It comes close to the Islamic *kalam* argument. Appeal to originating causes has bequeathed the title 'the aetiological argument' to this Second Way. However, we also noted Thomas's endorsement of the critique of the *kalam* tradition by Maimonides.

The Third Way is the cosmological argument in the most specific sense of the term. If we look around us at the contingency of all finite events in this finite world, we are forced 'to postulate something which is of itself necessary' (*ponere aliquid quod est per se necessarium*) (*Summa Theologiae*, Ia, Qu. 3, art. 3). It is based 'on what need not be (*ex possibile* [the contingent]) and on what must be (*necessario*)'. Aseity is self-groundedness.

On details and replies see entry under Five Ways, where the Fourth and Fifth Ways are also considered. Thomas appeals to the argument of Paul the Apostle in Romans 1 that the Being of God may be inferred from the works of God as Creator. This does not provide demonstrable proof of what God is, but has rational force for the question that God is.

CLARKE'S ADVOCACY AND CRITIQUES FROM HUME, KANT AND MILL

Samuel Clarke (1675–1729) defends the cosmological argument even in the light of NEWTON's formulation of laws of motion, gravity and inertia. In his work *A Discourse Concerning Natural Religion* (1705) Clarke argues that even if we postulate an endless chain of causes ''tis manifest *the whole* cannot be necessary',

since all are 'dependent' entities: only that which of itself is non-contingent and necessary.

Locke (1632–1704), Newton himself (1642–1727) and Leibniz (1646–1716) all defend such an argument. Newton's observations about motion do not in the end dissolve the logical gap between contingent caused causes, and a necessary uncaused cause.

HUME (1711–76) challenges the assumption that the argument can offer an *a posteriori* inference from empirical observation. We like to think that we observe cause and effect, but strictly in empirical terms all that we can observe is 'contiguity', or 'constant conjunction'. What leads us to connect two continguous events as cause and effect is merely habit or custom: that is our usual experience. We experience a succession of impressions; we do not experience the unifying framework that we term 'CAUSATION'. 'Upon examination ... the necessity of a cause is fallacious and sophistical' (Hume, *A Treatise of Human Nature*, 1739 (Critical edn Oxford: OUP, 1978, 79–94)).

KANT (1724–1804) pressed this attack further. Why should everything have a cause? Notions such as 'cause' (together with space and time) are merely 'regulative' principles in terms of which the human mind comes to order the world. Hence virtually every stage of the cosmological argument falls under this critique.

MILL (1806–73) saw value in the TELEOLOGICAL ARGUMENT from purpose or design, but in common with Hume saw no reason to reject the possibility of an infinite regress of caused causes the exclusion of which lies at the heart of the cosmological argument. This rejection of an infinite series may reflect 'our' experience, Mill concedes, but why should it be true of all experience at any time? It is our own minds that demand a resting place.

MORE RECENT DEBATES

Virtually all aspects of the debate continue to receive logical exploration. Thus, for example, W.I. Craig has revived consideration of the *kalam* tradition within Islamic philosophy concerning the finite history of the world (*The Cosmological Argument from Plato to Leibniz*, London: Macmillan, 1980). J.L. Mackie has attacked virtually every aspect of the argument (*The Miracle of Theism*, Oxford: OUP, 1982). G.E.M. Anscombe asks whether Hume's claims about causation apply to every kind of cause in all possible situations ('"Whatever has a beginning of Existence must have a cause": Hume's Argument Exposed', *Analysis*, 34, 1974; repr. in G.E.M. Anscombe, *Collected Philosophical Papers*, 3 vols., Minneapolis: University of Minnesota Press, vol. 1).

Some have sought to find new support or new criticisms in modern post-Newtonian physics, including the work of Hoyle and discussions of 'steady state' theory, 'the Big Bang', and the second law of thermodynamics and principle of entropy. This merely shifts the ground to what kind of cause introduces conditions adequate for matter to exist.

Such discussions also tend to expose a fallacy of a purely logical nature if the traditional version of the argument is expressed in the form of a logical SYLLOGISM as follows: (1) major premise: every state of affairs has a cause; (2) minor premise: the world is a state of affairs; (3) conclusion: therefore the world has a cause. This fails because in a syllogism the terms of the three propositions must retain the same meaning. But in this major premise, 'cause' means 'caused cause', while in this conclusion (unless it refers to an infinite regress) 'cause' denotes 'uncaused cause'. This is a different logical term.

Most recent and contemporary discussion, therefore, focuses on the issue at the heart of the argument, present in Aristotle and stated in Thomas's Third Way, namely the relation between contingent being and necessary Being. We may set aside the criticism that necessarily can be applied

only to propositions that assert logical or mathematical necessity.

In the present context necessary Being relates to aseity. Is it more reasonable to postulate a contingent universe which might or might not have been (at any time whatever, but nevertheless is), or a contingent universe the ground of which is a Being who does not share this quality of contingency, but is of a different order? For most theists, the issue amounts not to 'proof', but at the very least to 'reasonable' belief.

counterfactuals

The term denotes conditionals in which the antecedent, or protasis, is false. An example might be: 'If America were as small as England, I would travel to visit you.' Since the hypothetical condition is false, what is the truth-status of the utterance?

Since in formal LOGIC the inferential 'if *p*, then *q*' lies at the heart of logical calculus, logicians explore the differences of status between factual, open, unfulfilled, and contrary-to-fact conditionals. Some also allude to the ambivalent status of counterfactuals in discussions of the OMNISCIENCE of God. The projection of contrary-to-fact conditional scenarios raises problems of its own in this area of discussion.

creation

Three main approaches to concepts of divine creation of the universe invite comparison. The traditional Hebrew–Christian–Islamic theistic view is that of *creatio ex nihilo*, creation out of nothing, in the sense that God used no pre-existing materials. A second view draws on NEO-PLATONISM and on some traditions of HINDU PHILOSOPHY. The world is seen as an 'emanation' of or from God (PLO-TINUS, *c.* 205–70), or as 'the body' of God (RĀMĀNUJA, *c.* 1017–1137).

A third view presupposes that TIME is infinite, and therefore (with ARISTOTLE,

384–322 BCE) that the world is eternal. Nevertheless, Aristotle infers from the distinction between POSSIBILITY and actuality that a Prime Mover imparts motion to the world as a Changeless Unmoved Mover or First CAUSE.

CREATIO EX NIHILO IN WESTERN THEISM

In the Hebrew–Christian tradition God's creation of the world from nothing is expressed implicitly in the Bible in Genesis 1:2, but explicitly first in 2 Maccabees 7:28; cf. Romans 4:17; Hebrews 11:3; 2 Baruch 21:4; 48:8. The Genesis account alludes in onomatopoeia to the chaos 'without form and void' (Hebrew, *tohu wabhohu* 'shapeless and without content', Gen. 1:2). In Hellenistic Judaism this is accommodated to Greek philosophy as unformed primal matter (Wis. 11:17), as later in Justin (*Apology*, I: 10:2).

If, as PANNENBERG states, the original point was 'simply that the world did not exist before', very soon in early Christian theology it functioned 'to exclude the dualistic idea of an eternal antithesis to God's creative activity' (*Systematic Theology*, vol. 2, Edinburgh: T & T Clark, 1994, 14).

No less important in the biblical accounts is the repeated act of differentiation. 'God separated light from darkness' (Gen. 1:4); 'separated water ... under the firmament ... above the firmament' (1:7); 'to separate the day from the night' (1:14); 'created ... according to their kinds' (1:21). HEGEL (1770–1831) is among those who associate 'form' with differentiation, while the reality of 'difference' is a point of disagreement between Śaṅkārā and Rāmānuja in Hindu philosophy.

Finally, in the Hebrew–Christian–Islamic tradition of THEISM, the acts and action of God call attention to a causal relation of dependency and origin; less, indeed very much less, on the 'how' of cosmological processes. These accounts have a quite different purpose from 'scientific' accounts of cosmological 'origins'.

Even if cosmology is to be traced to a 'big bang' or a cosmic explosion, or to subatomic conditions, this would still leave open the philosophical and theological question of 'Whence?' and 'Why?', rather than 'How?' (*see* SCIENCE AND RELIGION). Proposals for DEMYTHOLOGIZATION may well underestimate the role of states of affairs and description, but at least they have the merit of placing the emphasis on theology and relationship rather than cosmology.

It was left in general to later theology to formulate in more detail than the scriptural sources the continuing work of God in preservation and in providence, apart from scattered texts (e.g. Colossians 1:15–17). Thomas AQUINAS devotes part of book III of the *Summa Contra Gentiles* (ch. 64–77) to the subject of providence including God's use of 'secondary causes' (ch. 77). BARTH speaks of God's 'holding humankind from the abyss of non-being'. In JEWISH and ISLAMIC PHILOSOPHY this theme is implicit in ascribing God the attributes of Life, Power, Wisdom and Will.

CREATION THROUGH DIVINE EMANATIONS

Plotinus sought to remain faithful to PLATO's philosophy, but his Neoplatonism also embodies elements from Aristotle and the STOICS. God is indeed above or beyond the CONTINGENT world, and is ABSOLUTE, transcendent and One. This TRANSCENDENCE is preserved by a 'bridge' of intermediary agencies, who derive their being from God by emanation. Second-century gnosticism postulates a broadly similar notion to bridge a sharp DUALISM. Such intermediaries as *Sophia* play a key role in divine action, by descending into the world.

In Hindu philosophy the tradition of 'modified' or 'qualified' MONISM (the Visistadvaita school) represented especially by Rāmānuja, understands the world as the 'body' of the Supreme Being. This stands in contrast to the monism of

Śaṅkara (788–820), for whom creation itself is an illusion based upon lack of knowledge (*veda*). In as far as creation exists, for both schools it is perceived (in reality or illusion) as part of a cyclical process of rebirth and reincarnation. Whereas Genesis pronounces creation 'good ', in Hindu philosophy it is more truly a source of imperfection, constraint and pain, as also in several Greek traditions.

In Jewish philosophy, MAIMONIDES (1135–1204) was aware of the differences between the biblical account of *creatio ex nihilo* and the Platonic and Aristotelian traditions. In formal terms he adopts the first, but interpreters express reserve about whether he accepted one of these rather than another.

In Islamic philosophy, AL-KINDI (*c.* 813–*c.*871) firmly stressed creation *ex nihilo*, but he also believed that this was compatible with 'the One' of Neoplatonism, and with Aristotle's Prime Mover. By contrast, AL-GHAZALI (1058–1111) firmly accepted the Qur'an's emphasis upon creation *ex nihilo*, and saw this as excluding both a Neoplatonist and Aristotelian view of creation. His view of providence perhaps leans towards OCCASIONALISM. AL-FARABI (875–950) borders on an emanationist view (see below).

ARISTOTLE AND KANT: WOULD 'INFINITE TIME' IMPLY THE ETERNITY OF THE WORLD?

Aristotle argues that the world could have no beginning – for every 'now' logically implies a 'before', *ad infinitum*. Hence he does not have a theistic view of creation in the usual sense. However, if time measures change, and change is eternal, motion presupposes the causal agency of a Prime Mover. In this sense a Supreme Being may be the Ground of Form within the world, since without the Prime Mover, everything would remain in a state of formless potentiality.

Against al-Kindi, in Islamic philosophy al-Farabi believed and taught that the world is eternal. His defence of this view in relation to the sovereign transcendence of Allah is that reality (including the world) for ever flows from God as the Source of all being.

Aquinas believed that it was reasonable to believe in the ETERNITY of the world, but that faith taught a doctrine of creation *ex nihilo*. However, is the notion that every 'now' implies a 'before' a good reason for postulating the infinity of time and the eternity of the world?

KANT (1724–1804) formulates this issue as his first antinomy. The problem may be explained more clearly with reference to space. Try to imagine the end or edge of space! Each time the attempt is made, we need to fence off the piece of further space the other side of the edge or boundary. Is this because space is infinite? Or is it not, rather, because human beings always think in spatial CATEGORIES? Might it not be the same with time? Does this not simply tell us that, in AUGUSTINE's words, space and time were created along with the universe (*cum tempore*, not *in tempore*)?

critical philosophy

The most widely accepted use of this term is to denote the philosophical method of KANT (1724–1804). In contrast to the traditions of RATIONALISM and EMPIRICISM, Kant sought to re-establish the role of REASON by offering a critique of its scope and status.

The issues are set out in the entry TRANSCENDENTAL PHILOSOPHY. Rather than asking simply 'What do we know?', Kant asked, 'What conditions must obtain for the very possibility of knowledge?' The term 'critical' reflects the three titles of Kant's major works: *Critique of Pure Reason* (1781, revised 1787); *Critique of Practical Reason* (1788); and *Critique of Judgement* (1790). Critical philosophy dates from this period.

A little-used meaning of the term originated with C.D. Broad (1887–1971).

Broad reserved the term to denote the 'ordinary-language' REALISM of G.E. Moore and RUSSELL, in contrast to the 'speculative' philosophy of METAPHYSICS or IDEALISM. The term should also be distinguished from critical realism and from critical theory.

critical realism

See REALISM.

Cupitt, Don (b. 1934)

Don Cupitt's work in philosophy of religion develops continuously, but may broadly be identified as emerging in three stages. The groundwork for what would eventually emerge as a non-realist view of God was laid out in works reflecting Kantian and Kierkegaardian themes (1968–79). The 'middle period' gave Cupitt some notoriety in Britain as an 'Atheist' Anglican priest, with the publication of Taking Leave of God (1980) and subsequent works (1980–85). Third, from Life-Lines (1986) and thereafter Cupitt has become involved in POSTMODERNISM and moves continuously in his interests.

Cupitt served as a curate in Salford near Manchester, but from 1962 has spent his entire life in Cambridge, mainly as lecturer in philosophy of religion and Dean of Emmanuel College. From the early years he endorsed NIETZSCHE's maxim that there are no 'givens', only 'interpretations'.

The Leap of Reason (1976) took up PLATO's allegory of the cave. However, whereas for Plato the shadows point to a greater reality of Forms, of which they are mere CONTINGENT or empirical copies, Cupitt's cave is closed, and its inhabitants live on the basis of 'as if ...'. They must make a 'leap' (since there is no opening) about how they are to construe or construct data. In effect, Cupitt offers a critique of the limits of reason, in the tradition of KANT and KIERKEGAARD.

Cupitt's middle period draws on the stock-in-trade of philosophy of religion lectures to promote the claims of FEUERBACH and FREUD about the reductionism not of ATHEISM but of RELIGION. He endorses their critique about religion's encouraging infantile dependency, or diminishing human dignity, at least in its traditional theistic forms. By exposing 'God' as a human projection, Cupitt aims to rehabilitate 'AUTONOMY' and to de-objectify the notion of God. God is not a Being 'out there' (see NON-REALISM).

During this period Cupitt gave a series of talks on British television under the title The Sea of Faith, which was immediately published (1984). He presented such figures as Kant, Kierkegaard, Feuerbach, Freud and WITTGENSTEIN in such a way as to make them appear partners who would support his own enterprise. Sympathizers subsequently formed a 'Sea of Faith Network' (from 1989).

From the late 1980s, Cupitt seems to have had second thoughts about the possibility of human 'autonomy' in the light of a postmodern rhetoric of selfhood. He writes, 'There is no substantial individual self' (Life-Lines, London: SCM, 1986, 198). In Radicals and the Future of the Church (London: SCM, 1989) he observes: 'We are anarchists ... we love mobility' (112). He even promotes 'manipulative' rhetoric and deceit (ibid., 111) on the ground that literary theory exposes the 'illusion' of 'absolute integrity' as a MYTH (ibid., 107).

The period of the later works combines postmodernity, social constructivism and radicalism and attacks, alike, the conservative and the liberal in religion. Literalism has 'collapsed' under the impact of postmodernist assessments of the self.

Cupitt's following is less marked among academic theologians and philosophers than among clergy and laypeople who are disenchanted with established, institutional, orthodox religion. The style of his work has changed from argument to rhetoric, in accordance with his postmodern re-appraisal of REASON.

Most of Cupitt's writings are, in effect and loosely, works of philosophy of religion. However, they presuppose a view of reason found more frequently in critical theory than in most university departments of philosophy. They appear to promote pluralism; but in practice promote a single voice, even if that one voice is 'always on the move'.

D

Darwin, Charles Robert
(1809–82)

Darwin formulated a theory of EVOLU-
TION on the basis of postulating a process
of selection by natural processes of random changes in biological species. He
himself spoke of 'descent with modification', but this became known as evolution
by natural selection.

Two aspects of his thought identify the
core of Darwin's distinctive influence.
First, he stressed that those mechanisms
of change that proved to be useful for
survival were not those of purposive or
designed adaptation. Amidst the random
variables of biological life, some changes
led to degeneration and extinction.
Others, equally the product of mere
chance, had useful consequences which
assisted survival and flourishing, sometimes in ways that might not have been
predicted. Survival and reproduction is a
competitive struggle for existence, pro-
geny and flourishing, although it was
SPENCER (1820–1903) who popularized
the term 'the survival of the fittest'.

Second, Darwin formulated a biological theory, which he sought to demonstrate in empirical terms. Thus, after his
degree at Cambridge, he undertook the
five-year voyage in the *Beagle* to amass
data relating to various life-forms at
different stages of development in different environments.

Darwin published *The Origin of Species* in 1859, and *The Descent of Man* in
1871, among other works. Massive controversy was stirred at the time not only by
the suggestion that explanations in terms
of design or teleology could be replaced by
those of natural, chance processes, but
also by his insistence that the emergence of
humankind depended on the same chance
mechanisms.

Darwin's theories paved the way for
ethical theories based on evolution, and
for formulations of BEHAVIOURISM. T.H.
Huxley (1825–95) argued that human
beings are biomechanistic systems in
whom 'consciousness' is merely an epiphenomenal or derivative byproduct. (*See
also* EMPIRICISM; TELEOLOGICAL ARGU-
MENT; SCIENCE AND RELIGION).

deduction, deductive reasoning

Deduction denotes the logical reasoning in
which a conclusion necessarily follows
from the premises, especially but not
exclusively reasoning from the general to
the particular. The process is fundamental
for the logical theory of ARISTOTLE
(384–322 BCE). Deduction may follow by
inference from a series of propositions in

sequence, from which in the final stage the conclusion is deduced.

The notion that deduction strictly defines inference from the general to the particular reflects its conventional contrast with inductive reasoning. In this latter case reasoning begins with particular cases and seeks to establish a general principle. However, more strictly deductive logic need not begin with the general or axiomatic, as long as the conclusion follows necessarily from the antecedent proposition as a valid inference. (*See also* AXIOM; LOGIC.)

definition

Definitions remain important not only for avoiding misunderstanding and for sustaining clarity, but also for ensuring validity in certain operations of LOGIC. If a logical term is used in more than one way, this may undermine the validity of the argument.

Traditionally, as in the philosophy of ARISTOTLE (384–322 BCE), definitions operated on the basis of genus and difference. 'A human being' is defined as 'a rational animal' on the basis of the genus shared with the animal kingdom, with the *differentia* of 'rationality' in the case of humankind. The definition seeks to identify a common species or genus of a given type, but also specifies what is distinctive to the sub-type or to the particular.

For Aristotle this process was closely bound up with a correspondence theory of TRUTH. A definition signifies the 'essence' of what is to be defined, and is therefore true or false. However, such a view may lose ground in the light of issues raised by NOMINALISM, with the recognition that relations between language and meaning rest upon convention, which may change.

That which is to be defined, the *definiendum*, may relate to the terms in which it is defined (the *definiens*) in several ways.

Stipulative definitions state the proposal of a speaker or writer to define a word in a particular way. These are linguistic actions of assigning meaning for the purpose of a specific discourse or debate. There is no guarantee that the definition will be accepted, still less that others will accept it subsequently, unless it proves useful for future purposes.

OSTENSIVE DEFINITION is discussed in an entry under its name. WITTGENSTEIN and Friedrich Waismann argue that ostensive definitions, for example 'This is a pencil' (as I point to it), presuppose a prior linguistic training or competency, and function only in limited ways with limited effects. This type of definition may work with 'This is Jack' (in an appropriate context), but 'What about such words as "yes" and "no", "can" and "may", "true" and "false"? These need to be explained in a different manner' (Waismann, *Principles of Linguistic Philosophy*, London: Mac-Millan, 1965, 94). The same principle applies to the word 'God'.

Persuasive definitions are the stock-in-trade of propagandist rhetoric, mass advertising and manipulation in politics or religion. In first-century Corinth the church evidently defined 'spiritual' (Greek, *pneumatikos*) in such a way as to link approval and self-affirmation with their own attributes. Paul the Apostle responded by redefining 'spiritual' as that which pertains to the work of the Holy Spirit (*hagion pneûma*). He could address them as 'spiritual people' when they were characterized by 'jealousy and quarrelling' (1 Corinthians 3:1–3). Politicians regularly define 'moving forwards' in terms of what they are advocating, while advertisers define 'what everyone loves' along similar lines. Both are examples of persuasive definition.

Wittgenstein and John Searle demonstrate the importance of contextual definition. How we define the words 'exact' or 'inexact', Wittgenstein observes, will depend on whether we are measuring distances in astronomy (between stars) or distances in joinery (between a dowling and a socket). RUSSELL observes that this becomes highly sensitive in recursive definitions, i.e. when a definition used in one context is reapplied and reused in another.

Dictionaries regularly use lexical definitions, which define one word or set of words in terms of another. These become less productive if such definition becomes circular, although specialists in theoretical linguistics insist that some degree of circularity in intra-linguistic definition is unavoidable. The habit of giving a 'medical explanation' by using a Greek term (as the professional name for the condition in question) may be useful only if both conversation partners presuppose the same linguistic 'background' of medical competency.

The subject is almost without limit, because different contextual situations in language render certain methods of definition more constructive than others, or also more seductive than others. If we emphasize only the growth and fluidity of language, we may become daunted by a postmodern, Derridean desire endlessly to 'defer' indeterminate meaning. If we remain in the realm of purely formal logic or REFERENTIAL language, we may expect a greater stability than living language can provide. There is room for middle ground. (*See also* DERRIDA; POSTMO-DERNISM.)

deism

In the sixteenth century the term was sometimes used to denote belief in God (Latin, *Deus*, God) in contrast to ATHE-ISM. However, this was quickly overtaken by a more important meaning. In the seventeenth and eighteenth centuries deism postulated a view of God that stood in contrast to THEISM (Greek, *Theos*, God). Whereas theists believe in God's active agency within the world, deism denotes a rationalist concept of God as the Source of Creation who remains above and beyond it, but is not immanent within it (*see* IMMANENCE).

In keeping the mechanistic models of ENLIGHTENMENT RATIONALISM, deists saw the universe in terms of a mechanism which God had set going, but in which God had no need to intervene. If the mechanism had been made well, it needed no correction or modification. 'Miracles' belonged to a naïve view of the world (according to deists), since God leaves the universe to run as a well-made self-regulating machine.

In ancient philosophy ARISTOTLE anticipates a deist view of God by insisting that God is above, beyond, and separated from material, CONTINGENT and changing, finite things (*Metaphysics*, bk XII). Conversely, God is not immanent within the world. This latter notion belongs in unqualified form to PANTHEISM, and with qualifications also to theism.

It is no accident that deism flourished in the era of rationalism. John Henry Newman describes the eighteenth century in England as the Age of Reason, when love grows cold. The nineteenth century would replace such rationalism, especially in Germany, with Romanticism, which nourished an organic, rather than mechanistic, model of God's relation to the world. Thomas Carlyle scathingly criticized the deist God as 'an absentee God, sitting idle, ever since the first Sabbath, at the outside of his universe, and seeing it go' (*Sartor Resartus*, 1834, bk II, ch. 7).

Many trace the origins of deism to the writings of Lord Edward Herbert of Cherbury (1583–1643). Herbert enunciated five principles which later were known by some as the five articles of deism: (1) God exists; (2) as Supreme Being, God is worthy of worship; (3) piety and virtue characterize religion; (4) repentance expiates sin; and (5) justice demands reward or punishment in POST-MORTAL EXISTENCE. These are universal, rational 'common notions' (*communes notitiae*) of 'natural' religion (*On Truth*, 1624). This prepares the ground for a NATURAL THEOLOGY without the necessity of 'special' revelation. Reason leads on to faith.

In the eighteenth century a more radical form of deism was promoted by Matthew Tindal (1653–1733). Tindal, like Herbert, was an English deist, educated at Oxford. He saw religion as eternal and universal. The title of his work *Christianity as Old as Creation* (1730) expounds even Christianity as an eternal, timeless 'natural' religion, which is not dependent on special revelation, but only upon universal reason and morality.

John Toland (1670–1722) sums up the deist outlook in the title of his book *Christianity not Mysterious* (1696). He insists that Christianity is fully compatible with reason, and indeed need be based only on rational reflection.

During this period deism was mainly an English phenomenon, although in France Voltaire (1694–1778) was also influenced by the English deists, and Toland was of Irish descent. These writers reflect the rationalist and mechanistic spirit of the age.

The movement paved the way for rationalist assumptions in German biblical criticism nearly a century later. In England, however, the deists were highly controversial. A counter-movement of reaction against a purely rational account of religion emerged in the PIETISM of the Wesleyan revivals. Pietism expressed a belief in, and longing for, the immediacy of a God who is not remote, but is active in human life.

demythologizing, demythologization

This term is associated closely with the work of BULTMANN (1884–1976). His seminal essay on demythologizing the New Testament (1941) proposed not the elimination of myth but its reinterpretation in existential terms (*see* EXISTENTIALISM).

Bultmann defines MYTH in three ways, which may well be incompatible with each other. First, myth is 'the use of imagery [*die Vorstellungsweise*, mode of representation]

to express the other worldly in terms of this world, and the divine in terms of human life' ('New Testament and Mythology' [1941], in H.W. Bartsch, ed., *Kerygma and Myth*, vol. 1, London: SPCK, 1964, 141; German, vol. 1, 23). This verges on the straightforward use of ANALOGY, as when God is spoken of as 'high' or as 'sending' a word or 'God's Son'.

Second, Bultmann regards myth as the explanatory pseudo-science of a primitive, pre-scientific, view of the world. 'The cosmology [*das Weltbild*, picture of the world] of the New Testament is essentially mythical in character. The world is a three-storeyed structure, with earth in the centre, the heaven above, and ... the underworld' (ibid., 1; German, 15). Here appeal to the agency of demons or to the intervention of God may be perceived as 'causal' explanations for ills or for rescue from ill, supposedly equivalent in function to 'scientific' causes such as a virus or aspirin in the modern world.

Third, and most important for Bultmann, myth presents in descriptive or 'objective' guises a form or content which is intended not to describe but to address, to challenge, to involve, or to transform. 'The real purpose of myth is not to present an objective picture of the world (*ein objectives Weltbild*) ... but to express man's understanding of himself in the world in which he lives' (ibid., 10; German, 23). Part of this understanding derives from his collaboration with the Jewish scholar Hans Jonas, but even more from his Kantian and Neo-Kantian background (*see* KANT).

The first and third definitions seem incompatible, as R.W. Hepburn argued. Analogy cannot be discarded; it is essential (*see* LANGUAGE IN RELIGION). However, it is intelligible to seek to replace language that is appropriate for the description of objects by language that calls the reader to respond by confession, change, affirmation or other self-involving attitudes.

It is here that Bultmann draws on HEIDEGGER, who was also his colleague at Marburg. God is not an 'object' about whom discourse occurs; rather, discourse flows from being addressed by God. God is 'wholly "Beyond"' (*der schlechthin Jenseitige: Faith and Understanding*, vol. 1, London: SCM, 1969, 46; German, 14). Hence he draws on Heidegger's conceptuality (*Begrifflichkeit*) to find ways of avoiding 'objectifying' language about God or human persons.

The aim is understandable, but it is false to suppose that existential or self-involving language can operate effectively if it is disengaged from other language that conveys cognitive truth. Thus the PERFORMATIVE illocutionary act 'I forgive you' depends on the state of affairs that the speaker has authority to forgive sins. This point is well made by AUSTIN and others.

Proposals about demythologizing may in some cases recover 'the point' about language in sacred texts. For example, most language about the End functions to call to accountability or to reassure; it is not usually a map of the sequence of end-events. However, the programme of demythologizing bases too much on a false linguistic dualism between description and evaluation or expression. Thereby it tends to neglect the importance of history and the public world, and to ignore the multi-layered, multi-functional character of language in religion.

deontology

The term denotes an understanding of ETHICS in which an ethics of duty or obligation is primary. The agent of moral decision and moral action is motivated by a duty to do what is right, in contrast to consequentialism, or an ethic based on the calculation of optimum consequences. The issues surrounding deontology are discussed in detail in the long entry on ethics. (*See also* BELIEF; KANT.)

Derrida, Jacques (b. 1930)

Derrida, philosopher and literary theorist, born in Algeria and educated in Paris, is one of the most influential and notoriously controversial postmodernist thinkers. He is closely associated with 'deconstruction', a particular approach for undermining and transforming both texts and traditional Western metaphysical systems of thought. His greatest influence is among American literary theorists.

Deconstruction, as Derrida understands it, is not mere demolition: it is an 'enigma' (*Psyché*, Paris: Galilée, 1987, 391); but it involves exposing pseudo-stabilities in texts that presuppose an over-ready 'presence' of entities or determinacies of language.

In his key works of 1967, especially *Grammotology* and *Speech and Phenomena*, Derrida reveals the influence of NIETZSCHE (1844–1900), FREUD (1856–1939), Edmund Husserl (1859–1938) and the later HEIDEGGER (1889–1976). The illusion of stable language, he argues, rests on being centred on words as entities ('logocentrism'). By contrast, he appeals to Ferdinand de Saussure's linguistics for the view that it is the differences between what this or that sign denotes on which meanings hinge.

De Saussure illustrated the point with colour-words (*see* SEMANTICS). The semantic scope of 'red' is greater if its 'difference' marks it off from 'yellow' than if it marks it off from 'orange'. But all this depends on a prior system of signs (French, *la langue*), from which the act or performance of sign selection for use (*la parole*) is taken. Derrida proposes that because this system is also variable, changing and interactive, signs are 'indeterminate'. Meaning is 'deferred'. Prior meaning stands 'under erasure' (*sous rature*).

Hence 'difference' (French, *différence*) yields 'deferment' (Fr. *différance*). However, ARISTOTLE's LOGIC and Western METAPHYSICS, Derrida insists, is 'logocentric', and misleadingly conveys a stability that invites decentring through 'deconstruction'. Post-modern and Freudian suspicion of human consciousness leaves the variable sign-system, without the human subject, as that which generates meaning.

Critics of Derrida argue that he neglects the role of the human subject in making choices about language uses. He subordinates *la parole* to *la langue*, the abstract system. He reduces literary language to a 'play' of indeterminate signs, and reduces propositional logic to 'performances' of roles or to mere semiotic operations. (*See also* POSTMODERNISM.)

Descartes, René (1596–1650)

It is difficult to exaggerate the impact of Descartes on the history of philosophy. Many date the beginning of the modern era from his work. He initiated a new rationalist philosophical method, in contrast to the prevailing tradition of A POSTERIORI argument, which had dominated most philosophical systems from ARISTOTLE to Thomas AQUINAS.

In an early debate with Chandoux in Paris in 1628, Descartes attacked the view that science could be based only on probabilities. He insisted that knowledge could be based on absolute CERTAINTY. He approached the sciences not primarily in terms of drawing inferences from empirical observation, but as a distinguished mathematician seeking logical 'clear' ideas.

In 1637 Decartes published his famous *Discourse on Method*, which was to serve, in effect, as a preface or prolegomena to a work on mathematics and the physical world. This contained three scientific treatises. Although *Discourse on Method* addressed foundational issues for his approach to EPISTEMOLOGY, his major work was to follow four years later, namely *Meditations on First Philosophy* (1641), together with a series of six or seven *Objections* and *Replies to Objections*. In

1644 he expounded his *Principles of Philosophy*, which, he believed, showed that he did not contradict Aristotle. Finally, *The Passions of the Soul* appeared in 1649, a year before his death.

Descartes was a French philosopher, who wrote in French. Jesuit teaching, for which he always retained a respect, influenced his education. For a period of years he also studied mathematics in Holland, and from 1649 gave philosophical instruction to the Queen of Sweden in Stockholm. By 1619 he was already speaking of his aim 'to finish … an absolutely new science'.

THE ARGUMENT IN *DISCOURSE ON METHOD*

The full title is *Discourse on the Method of Properly Conducting One's Reason and in Seeking the Truth in the Sciences*. In part 1, Descartes reflects on the multiplicity and diversity of human opinions, which offer 'little basis … for certainty' (*Discourse on Method*, London: Penguin, 1968, 33). Theology (on the basis of REVELATION) and mathematics alone yield 'certain' TRUTHS. In the case of other disciplines, 'nothing solid could have been built on such a shifting foundation' (ibid., 32).

In part 2, Descartes explains his aim: 'I seek … to reform my own thoughts and to build upon a foundation that is wholly my own' (ibid., 38). He seeks to know of objects 'clearly and distinctly' (ibid. 43). Knowledge is also 'ordered' and interrelated. To achieve this, however, it may be necessary to 'demolish an old house' (ibid., 50).

Descartes introduces his famous '*cogito, ergo sum*' ('I think, therefore I am') near the beginning of part 4 (ibid., 53). He is searching for truth that is 'absolutely indubitable'. That he is consciously aware of 'thinking' is 'so certain and so evident that the sceptics were not capable of shaking it' (ibid., 53–4).

Now, upon this certain foundation, Descartes can begin to build the new 'house' of a new system of established truths. This is done in the second half of part 4 and in part 5. He believed that he could establish the existence of distinctive human souls. To doubt this, he observes, is the worst kind of SCEPTICISM, next 'after the error of those who deny the existence of God' (ibid., 76).

Descartes concludes in part 6 by expressing the hope 'that those who use only their pure natural reason' will be able better to judge his claims than 'those who believe only the books of the ancients' (ibid., 91).

SOME CONSEQUENCES

This brief work lays down Cartesian 'method' for a new kind of approach. *En route* it appears to disparage tradition and is clearly individualistic. It also places the SELF of the knowing SUBJECT at the centre of the epistemological task.

Yet Descartes retains the aim of refuting sceptics by this method, and he does not intend to erode theological 'revelation'. He has begun a new era. Difficulties for THEISM or for RELIGIONS may more readily come from those who apply his method without the limits that he carefully defines. GADAMER exempts him from including all knowledge under methodological doubt (H.G. Gadamer, *Truth and Method*, London: Sheed & Ward, 2nd edn, 1989, 279).

THE *MEDITATIONS* AND OTHER WORKS: CERTAINTY, GOD AND THE SELF

In his second *Meditation* Descartes modifies his promotion of methodological doubt by stating, 'once in a life-time' we must 'demolish everything and start again right from the foundations' (*Meditations*, La Salle: Open Court, 1901, II, 31). Then, 'there remains nothing but what is indubitable' (ibid.). This does not imply a constant dismantling of tradition. Moreover, as Gadamer observes, he exempts 'God' and moral values from this process (*Truth and Method*, 279).

Some criticize Descartes for also arguing that 'God' is a clear, distinct and indubitable idea, which God himself has placed within the mind. God is 'infinite, external, immutable, all-powerful, by which I myself and everything else ... have been created'. There is 'nothing that I should know more easily' than God, except for human prejudice (*Meditation*, V, 81).

The idea of God is so perfect that it could not have originated with any agency other than God. Descartes formulates his own version of the ONTOLOGICAL ARGUMENT for God's existence. 'I cannot conceive of God without existence ... Existence can no more be separated from the essence of God than the fact that the sum of its three angles is equal to two right-hand triangles can be separated from the essence of a triangle' (ibid., 78).

Nevertheless Descartes' treatment of 'existence' as a predicate at once provided a hostage for KANT's critique of the LOGIC of this argument. Similarly, Descartes' notion of CAUSE as potentially carrying its range of effects within it also raised critical questions about both the ontological and COSMOLOGICAL ARGUMENTS for God's existence.

The further argument that mind is a substance whose 'essence' is thought alone, while body is a substance the 'essence' of which is extension alone, yet again brought its own problems. How does mind relate to body, and body to mind? Are we not on the brink of Cartesian DUALISM?

Descartes did not doubt that a relation operates, especially in attitudes or emotions that involve both mind and body, such as love, desire, joy and sorrow. All the same, the dualism of thought and extension leaves a sufficiently quasi-dualist view to invite RYLE's parody of the Cartesian 'myth' of the ghost in the machine. Today most approaches are less dualistic, certainly less individualistic, and probably less centred on the self or subject for an account of epistemology. (*See also* EMPIRICISM; OBJECT; RATIONALISM.)

determinism

At its simplest, determinism denotes the belief that whatever occurs is determined by antecedent CAUSES or conditions. It appears that the future is already fixed. SPINOZA (1632–77) believed that a lack of causal determination is an illusion. Everything 'necessarily' follows from the divine nature, which is also the 'All'.

Some approaches rest upon logical arguments about the relation between a true proposition and a proposition with the same content uttered at a different time in the past or in the future. Some theological arguments rest upon a notion of predestination that places more weight upon divine decree than the nature of the end destiny that such language generally promises. Similarly, other versions of determinism view history as an irreversible mechanical process. Still others believe that determinism is entailed by divine OMNISCIENCE.

'Soft' determinism leaves room for compatibilism (see FREEDOM; FREE WILL). Extreme or 'hard' determinism allows only for incompatibilist views, and sometimes invites OCCASIONALISM. While some insist that actions can be 'mine' only if I freely choose to do them, (rather than to do other alternatives), J.L. Mackie and some others hold that action can be both 'free' and predictable.

Whether quantum theory, Heisenberg's uncertainty principle and other developments in post-Einsteinian physics provide new directions for this debate is still a matter of controversy. However, they do seriously question the older mechanistic models on which earlier eighteenth-century determinism was based. The minimum that needs to be said is that divine omniscience provides no necessary argument for determinism, and that the human consciousness that certain actions are freely 'mine' has moral consequences for accountability that cannot be brushed aside. (See also LOGIC; SCIENCE AND RELIGION.)

dialectic

Dialectic denotes a largely exploratory rather than demonstrative use of logical processes, especially those that involve contradiction, opposition or paradox, to take us beyond an initial assumption or opinion. The term is used in Greek philosophy, but probably the most widely known modern example is that of proceeding from a thesis, through a contrary antithesis, to a 'higher' synthesis. This was first formulated in modern terms by FICHTE (1762–1814), and developed by HEGEL (1770–1831), Fichte's successor at Berlin.

Hegel postulated a dialectical process that 'raises' (German, erheben) the finite and assimilates or 'sublates' it (aufheben) into the 'higher'. Hegel distinctively postulates a parallel historical and logical dialectic whereby what begins in radical historical finitude and particularity emerges as Absolute Spirit (Geist) unfolding itself into the Whole, which constitutes Reason, Reality and God as ABSOLUTE. MARX (1818–3) replaced Hegel's Mind or Spirit by a dialect of socio-economic forces. This system is known as dialectical MATERIALSIM.

The term 'dialectic', however, first emerges in ancient Greek philosophy. ARISTOTLE attributed the origins of dialectic to Zeno of Elea (490–430 BCE). Zeno defended the view of reality as a changeless entity, as propounded by Parmenides, by postulating a series of paradoxes concerning space and motion.

The most famous is that of Achilles and the Tortoise. If Achilles starts to run a race from a given distance behind the tortoise, Achilles can never (supposedly) catch it up, for if the distance between them is successively halved, the successive divisions never reach zero (see RYLE). Hence Zeno concluded that the notions of succession and division are arguably illusory.

In the thought of SOCRATES (470–399 BCE) and PLATO (428–348 BCE) dialectic becomes a logical method of exposing false opinion and initiating constructive exploration especially through conversation (Greek, *dialektos*, debate) and questioning. However, Aristotle (384–322 BCE) prefers the logic of demonstration and non-contradiction. Indeed henceforward, with exceptions, until Fichte it begins to carry the nuance of 'sophistry', as later represented by the Second Sophistic of the first century CE. KANT (1724–1804) also viewed it in a negative light.

Dialectic also serves the heart of KIERKEGAARD's work (1813–55) as facilitating his method of 'indirect communication'. By presenting oppositions and paradoxes (even by opposing his own work through the device of pseudonymous authorship), he aimed to provoke his readers to active engagement, to participation and decision, rather than mere passive assent or disagreement. This facilitated 'venture' as the way of faith, and 'SUBJECTIVITY' as the 'how' (rather than the 'what' of truth.

In the second half of the twentieth century 'the logic of question and answer' became increasingly important in HERMENEUTICS. The issue was made prominent especially thorough the work of GADAMER (1900–2002), who states that his work on hermeneutics owes much to his earlier work on Plato. Gadamer also draws on R.G. Collingwood for this 'logic of question and answer'.

Dostoevsky, (Dostoyesvsky, Dostoevskii), Fédor Mikhailovich (1821–81)

Dostoevsky is well known as the writer of profound philosophical and social novels. His major works include *Crime and Punishment* (1866), *The Idiot* (1868–9), *The Possessed* (1871–2) and especially *The Brothers Karamazov* (1879–80).

It may seem surprising that while Dostoevsky inspired religious writers in Russia (notably Nikolai Berdiaev and Sergei Bulgakov), some in the West,

including Camus, viewed him as an antitheist existentialist. The reason probably lies in his creative use of 'polyphonic' voices in several of his novels (*see* EXISTENTIALISM).

This 'polyphonic' feature was noted in 1929 by the Russian literary theorist Mikhail Mikhailovich Bakhtin (1895–1975). The mystery of God and the complexity of human life cannot be conveyed simply through the lips of a single narrator or a single character. Such complexity requires a more subtle harmonic interplay between the different 'voices' of diverse characters representing different viewpoints.

In this respect Dostoevsky follows KIERKEGAARD's method of 'indirect' communication. This also takes account of an existentialist concern with the individual, the CONTINGENT, the concrete, the particular, or human 'being-there' (cf. HEIDEGGER's *Dasein*).

From the first Dostoevsky offered a critique of social oppression (*Poor Folk*, 1846), as well as expressing a disenchantment with the POSITIVISM or MATERIALISM of FEUERBACH (*Notes from the Underground*, 1864; and *Crime and Punishment*). In contrast to MILL's utilitarian ETHICS, Dostoevsky portrays Prince Myshkin in *The Idiot* as the 'saintly fool' of Russian religious tradition, which resonates with some sayings of Jesus. 'Goodness' entails a kind of 'powerlessness', whatever the consequences.

In *The Brothers Karamazov*, a polyphonic dialogue arises in the face of the problem of evil. The 'voices' come from Ivan, who expresses angry protest, the Christian Alesha (Alyosha) and the church elder Zosima. Dostoevsky's own personal life was marked by too much suffering and tragedy to offer any glib, simplistic 'answer'. His father was murdered by serfs; his mother died when he was fifteen; he was imprisoned for supposed subversion; was condemned to death and reprieved only at the very last moment; and put to forced labour in Siberia.

Ivan rejects the suffering of one tortured child for the sake of some 'higher harmony' (as AQUINAS or LEIBNIZ might have expressed it): 'it is not worth the tears of that one tortured child' (*The Brothers Karamazov*, New York: Norton 1974, 226).

Yet has not Ivan's very 'rebellion' presupposed his compassion? If all were for ever well, what room could there be for compassion or active concern for the other? Only dialogue, in the very process, can dare to address these issues, as the writer of the book of Job was well aware.

No single label can sum up the complexity of Dostoevsky's thought. He may be called an existentialist, but he also seeks a fresh, independent and constructive exploration of Christian truth and ethics. This takes place broadly within the frame of the Russian Orthodox tradition.

Dostoevsky, however, was never satisfied with merely second-hand ideas. He was a creative and powerful thinker, whose novels yield incisive insights into philosophical and social issues. He never lost sight of the concrete in the universal, yet believed in that which is 'beyond' the finite and tragic also.

doubt

See CERTANTY AND DOUBT.

dualism

This term may generate confusion because in philosophy of religion it may denote several different types of radical opposition between two contrasting principles, qualities or agents. It may denote, for example, the sharp opposition between good and evil in Manichaeanism (*see* AUGUSTINE) or in gnosticism; a parallel opposition between Yin and Yan in Taoism (in Chinese religion); or the contrast between the realm of Ideas (or Forms) and objects in the material or CONTINGENT world in PLATO. The dualism of mind and body is attributed especially to DESCARTES.

'METAPHYSICAL' DUALISM

Metaphysical dualism is a theory of the nature of reality that splits all reality into two independent orders or qualities of being. ZOROASTRIANISM (according to the Gāthās, *c.* 1200–1000 BCE revealed through Zoroaster, or Zarathustra) held the view that the Creator of the world (Ahura Mazdā, also known as Ormazd) was opposed by a power of EVIL, personified as Angra Mainyu, the hostile Spirit. The former (the Creator) represents light, life, law, order, truth and goodness. The latter (the hostile Spirit) represents darkness, death, chaos, falsehood and evil.

The world provides a stage for the battle between these two sets of opposed forces. However, since the forces of evil also represent and reflect negativity and are viewed as ultimately parasitic upon the good, it may be argued that Zoroastrianism offers only a relative dualism, not an absolute metaphysical dualism (*see* METAPHYSICS).

In more relative terms, Jewish and Christian apocalyptic verges on a dualism of cosmic conflict between the forces of evil and God as sovereign and good. The world may fall prey to domination by evil forces, but ultimately God and the good will triumph over them, and such vehicles of evil remain God's finite creatures.

A more thoroughgoing dualism can be found in second-century and third-century gnosticism, in which 'God' is opposed by the Maker of the Material World, or the 'Demiurge'. Marcion (*c.* 80–165) identified the Demiurge with the Jewish God of the Old Testament in opposition to the God of Christ and the New Testament, but such a dualism was condemned by the Church Fathers as heresy, and as false.

MIND–BODY DUALISM AND METAPHYSICAL DUALISM

Plato (428–348 BCE) laid the foundations of mind–body dualism by his metaphysical dualism between the realm of Ideas (which supposedly was universal, abstract, and the source and measure of truth) and the material, contingent realm of approximate representations or copies. The 'soul' belongs to the realm of Ideas, and is immortal; the body belongs to the imperfect, contingent, finite realm of material objects. The former is correlated with the 'changeless' and permanent; the latter with change and decay.

Such an extreme of dualist principles was largely avoided by ARISTOTLE, who integrated form and matter in a different way. His definition of 'form' was different from Plato's. Even NEOPLATONISM softened dualism by postulating 'emanations' of the divine which in effect served as bridges between the two realms.

Descartes (1596–1650), however, re-established a sharper dualism between the 'certainties' of the realm of logic, mathematics, reason and ideas and the uncertainties that beset and characterize the material and contingent world. This is related to the difference between mind and body.

Body is extended in space (as *res extensa*), and is conditioned by time and change. Mind is not 'extended', but 'thinking' (as *res cogitans*). This relates to a metaphysical dualism also: 'reality' consists of thought and extension.

Because he saw mind as rooted in a different order of reality from that of body, Descartes saw body and mind as logically independent of each other, although he did allow for some causal interdependence of the kind that in our own day is often thought of as a psychosomatic relationship (Greek, *psyche*, soul or life; *soma*, body or bodily mode of existence).

'Thinking', Descartes wrote, is 'an attitude of the soul ... This alone is inseparable from me ... I am, precisely speaking, only a thinking thing (*res cogitans*), that is, a mind (*mens sive animus*) ... or reason' (Descartes, *The Meditations*, La Salle: Open Court, 1910; 1988, II, 33). There is a relation of logical independence between mind and body, although causal dependence permits such

phenomena as illness or pain to affect the mind.

All the same, 'body' amounts to a merely instrumental tool for transmitting information to the mind through signals, and conversely for obeying the directives of the mind in the public world. This gives rise, in turn, to a dualist EPISTEMOLOGY, or dualist theory of knowledge. Intellectual, logical and mathematical ideas arise in the mind; perceptions of the world emerge through the senses. It is not difficult to see why the certainty of Descartes' ideas of God cohered, in his judgement, with the A PRIORI method of the ONTOLOGICAL ARGUMENT, rather than A POSTERIORI observations of the empirical world.

CRITIQUE OR NEAR-PARODY?

While the philosophical IDEALISM of the nineteenth century found relatively little difficulty with a relative mind–body dualism, this approach lost ground in the twentieth century with more rounded accounts of SELFHOOD. In biblical scholarship there was also a clear recognition that mind and body in the sacred writings of the main Judaeo-Christian religions denoted modes of being and modes of action of a single self rather than a composite dual entity.

RYLE (1900–76) attacked 'Cartesian dualism' in *The Concept of Mind* (London: Hutchinson, 1949). He parodies the view of Descartes as promulgating the myth of 'the ghost in the machine'. In particular he attacks the 'dogma' of Cartesian dualism that 'there occur physical processes and mental processes ... and mental causes of corporeal movements', like a pilot controlling an aircraft with levers and wires (in the pre-electronic era) (ibid., 21–4).

Ryle perceives this as a 'category mistake' (ibid., 17–24) since it treats mental phenomena as 'processes' to be regarded in the same way as physical phenomena. 'Mental happenings' are not 'events', Ryle urges, but adverbial ways of describing how physical life in the public domain is ordered. He parodies 'Cartesianism' (the legacy of Descartes) for presenting the self as one who 'lives through two collateral histories ... The first is public; the second, private' (ibid., 13). The truth is that 'mental' language usually denotes a 'complex of dispositions', not a 'happening' (ibid., 33).

Ryle's method of approach was associated in the public mind with 'ANALYTICAL' or 'OXFORD' PHILOSOPHY. Without doubt his incisive exposure of confused uses of language through neglect of logical or conceptual grammar brought a new clarity and precision to language about the self. Nevertheless, Stuart Hampshire is not alone in asking whether Ryle tries to prove 'too much' ('Critical Review', in O.P. Wood, ed., *Ryle*, London: Macmillan, 1971, 17–44).

Language that relates to the mind need be neither (with Descartes) construed in over-dualistic terms nor (with Ryle) reduced, in effect, to denote adverbial modes of human behaviour. The latter almost verges on BEHAVIOURISM, although like the later WITTGENSTEIN Ryle avoids an explicitly materialist view of the self as a metaphysical theory. (*See also* LOGIC; POST-MORTAL EXISTENCE.)

Duns Scotus, John (c. 1266–1308)

Duns Scotus was one of the most original and powerful thinkers of medieval SCHOLASTICISM. Born in Scotland, he taught at Oxford, Paris and Cologne, and was a priest of the Franciscan order. He brought together in a distinctive way the COSMOLOGICAL, TELEOLOGICAL and ONTOLOGICAL ARGUMENTS for the existence of God. Many see him as a key link in scholasticism between Thomas AQUINAS (c. 1225–74) and WILLIAM OF OCKHAM (c. 1287–1349).

The writings of Duns Scotus include the expected commentaries on ARISTOTLE

(384–322 BCE) and Peter Lombard, but his contributions to METAPHYSICS, theology, EPISTEMOLOGY and ETHICS were distinctive and highly technical. He engaged with, and endorsed, much of the work of IBN SINA (Avicenna, 980–1037), especially a realist understanding of essence and Being.

Scotus was a realist on the issue of UNIVERSALS. He conceded that these were derived from SEMANTICS, but that they nevertheless rested on the basis of the 'thisness' (Latin, *haecceitas*) of individual, distinct entities. 'Formal distinction' applied still as an objective distinction to inseparable entities, and Scotus sought to apply this to the Christian doctrine of the Trinity. William of Ockham rejected this extended theological application.

The reality of Being provides a universal foundation for knowledge of God. Scotus endorses arguments about the CONTINGENCY of the world, in contrast to which God, as transcendent Prime Mover, acts as efficient CAUSE in CREATION. This paves the way for an integrated approach to the argument for the existence of GOD.

Duns Scotus defends the cosmological argument: God is Efficient Cause and First Cause. He complements this by appealing to the role of Final Cause, as well as Efficient Cause in support of the teleological argument. Yet the very contrast between the First, Efficient, and Final Uncaused Cause and the contingent world supports, in turn, the LOGIC of the ontological argument. For how could such a Being be conceived except in terms of perfection? Thus the arguments embody an integrated logic.

The realist epistemology of Scotus disallows a disjunction between a universal CONCEPT and the sum of a composite 'quidditative' (or 'what-ness'-quality) uniqueness that characterizes God as transcendent Being. (*See also* FIVE WAYS; OBJECT; REALISM; TRANSCENDENCE.)

E

Eckhart, Meister Johannes (1260–1327)

Eckhart, German preacher and mystic, taught in Paris, and was influenced especially by ALBERT the Great and by Thomas AQUINAS. His spiritual writings include the *Book of Divine Consolation* (*c.* 1320). Eckhart's mysticism finds expression in such utterances as 'All things are a mere nothing.' He speaks of the 'emptiness' that the soul may attain, which 'gives birth to God'.

Eckhart's philosophical significance lies in part in his exploration of union-and-difference in relation to God. He drew on the mystical traditions of NEOPLATONISM and PLOTINUS. Human persons are characterized by mere 'is-ness' in their relation to God as divine fulness of Being.

The experience of 'desert' and 'emptiness' belongs to the tradition of Christian MYSTICISM and mystical writers. Eckhart was nevertheless condemned as heretical by the Cologne Inquisition of 1327. All the same, his influence on such figures as Nicholas of Cusa and Martin Luther cannot be doubted. (*See also* VIA NEGATIVA.)

empiricism

At its simplest, empiricism denotes the view that all knowledge comes through 'experience' (cf. Greek, *émpeiros*; also *empeirikós*, experienced). Usually the term more specifically denotes the view that knowledge is derived primarily from sense-data perceived or experienced through the five senses (sight, hearing, taste, touch, smell).

In practice empiricism in EPISTEMOLOGY stands in contrast to RATIONALISM and to CRITICAL PHILOSOPHY. Rationalists identify the primary source of knowledge as the human mind in rational reflection. Some versions of rationalism postulate the existence of 'innate ideas' within the SELF. By contrast, LOCKE (1632–1704) rejected the theory of innate ideas, arguing that human beings begin with a blank sheet, a *tabula rasa*, on which experience writes data.

KANT (1724–1804) sought to change the terms of the debate by expounding his more complex critical philosophy, especially in contrast with the empiricism of HUME (1711–76). Kant subjected to radical criticism both the scope and limits of REASON and the status of empirical observation. Neither is as straightforward as pre-Kantian empiricists and rationalists might suggest.

Locke was an empiricist, but recognized that 'experience' itself represents an amalgam of sensation and reflection. What is 'experienced' is more than raw sense-data. The invention of the microscope, for example, showed that what was 'really there' in the world, to be observed, depended at least in part on how and by whom it was observed. Changes of light affect how we 'see' colours; indeed, what colours we see. Hence Locke distinguished between primary givens, such as solidity, extension, movement and numbers and secondary qualities such as colours, sounds and taste.

ANCIENT AND MEDIEVAL EMPIRICISM

Prior to Locke and the late seventeenth century, empiricism took the form of an emphasis upon A POSTERIORI observation, in contrast to A PRIORI logical explorations. Democritus (460–370 BCE) formulated an early version of empiricism by arguing that perception is a physical process occurring by means of 'images' mediated through the five senses. Epicurus (341–270 BCE) developed this approach further. WILLIAM OF OCKHAM (c. 1287–1349) represents a broadly empiricist approach in the medieval period. His advocacy of NOMINALISM on the ground that general concepts arise from language rather than reality led to his emphasizing so-called objective knowledge of particular substances and qualities.

Thomas AQUINAS (1225–74) is often described as broadly 'empiricist', but he does not hold a consistently empiricist theory of knowledge. This would not entirely cohere with his work on knowledge of God. However, the source of CONCEPTS which we employ analogically to speak of God is our experience of the world. He attributes to ARISTOTLE (although the specific source is not clear) the maxim 'There is nothing in the intellect which was not previously in the senses,' and endorses this maxim.

This 'limited' empiricism has led a number of philosophers to distinguish between 'epistemological empiricism' (Democritus, William of Ockham, Hume and AYER), and 'conceptual empiricism'

(Aquinas and others) that appeals to the role of sense-experience for the grounding of intelligible language. Locke might be placed in either category, for he addresses epistemology, but has a carefully balanced agenda.

THE SEVENTEENTH CENTURY: JOHN LOCKE

LOCKE has an altogether more sophisticated approach. Although (as has been noted above) he believed that knowledge enters the mind through the senses as if the mind were a *tabula rasa,* or blank sheet, Locke acknowledges the relativities of how we observe what we observe, and addresses the wider issue of 'reasonable' belief. He seeks to enquire into 'the certainty and extent of human knowledge' including 'the grounds and degrees of belief ... and assent'.

Locke attacks the rationalist theory of 'innate ideas' in book I of his *Essay Concerning Human Understanding* (1690). He comments, 'When men have found some general propositions that could not be doubted, it was a short and easy way to conclude them innate' (I: 1, 5). This 'concluding', Locke suggests, is unfortunate because it tends to put an end to enquiry concerning doubt. Locke's own agenda is both to curb the undue pretensions of illusory claims to CERTAINTY, and to show the possibility of genuinely reasonable belief. Both are relevant to the prevalence of rationalism and English DEISM.

Where knowledge is knowledge of external 'OBJECTS', this knowledge is mediated through 'sensation' and sense-data. Perception of our own ideas, however, depends upon 'reflection'. Locke suggests the analogy of a window that filters light into a dark room (ibid.: II: 11: 27). Ideas are then combined, so that 'from a few simple ideas' can be generated a reservoire 'inexhaustible and truly infinite' (ibid.: ch. 7, 10).

Locke, therefore, does not expect the exhaustive, unqualified, 'demonstration' sought by rationalists or by 'extreme' empiricists. Numerous criteria may determine degrees of probability and the reasonableness of beliefs. Empirical observations provide one of these multiple criteria. Locke's empiricism is sometimes called that of 'English common sense'. More detailed discussion occurs under the entry on Locke.

THE EIGHTEENTH CENTURY: BERKELEY AND HUME

Bishop George BERKELEY (1685–1753) built upon Locke's empiricism. All the same, Berkeley is known chiefly as an idealist. In his own language, Berkeley sought to promote 'immaterialism', as a philosophical defence of THEISM. Yet how can empiricism embrace IDEALISM?

In the case of Locke, Berkeley and Hume, the answer to the question, 'How do we know?' is formulated in empiricist terms. We know through sense-impressions, even if reflection is also involved. The answer to the question 'What do we know?' includes sensory experiences for Locke, but is more significantly ideas of what we perceive. Hence the second question may be answered in idealist terms.

Berkeley reviewed Locke's distinction between primary and secondary qualities. He concluded that perceptions are fundamental not only for apprehending colour, taste and sound, but for solidity, motion, number and all objects of knowledge. If everything depends on perception, 'to be is to be perceived' (*esse est percipi*). This need not imply that the world is a construct of the human mind. There is a 'givenness' about those ideas that is uncontrived, since they may seem at times unwelcome. Indeed, behind them Berkeley sees 'the Divine Mind'.

Hume agreed with Locke and Berkeley that 'experience' is a combination of sense-impressions and ideas. However, he reversed the flow of Berkeley's thought: ideas are derivative from sense-experience. Sense-impressions 'enter with most force ... By *ideas* I mean that faint images of

these in thinking' (*Treatise of Human Nature*, 1739, I: I: 1).

'Nothing is ever present to the mind but perceptions' (ibid.: II: 6). Hume's view of CAUSE and causality illustrates the difference between actual observation (only constant conjunction or contiguity can be observed) and the construal of what is observed by ideas (the principle of causality). In the end, Hume believes only habit and convention transpose these ideas into systems of belief. But the only point of reference remains that of sense-impressions derived from raw sense-data.

Hume was an 'extreme' empiricist. He could not endorse Locke's notion of 'reasonable' belief, for reason is merely the slave of the passions; it operates only instrumentally. He rejected Berkeley's metaphysical idealism, for ideas are untrustworthy copies of sense-impressions. He was sceptical about the self; for the self is merely a bundle of perceptions. Thus, as he concedes, his empiricism leads to a modified scepticism, and verges on POSITIVISM.

THE TWENTIETH CENTURY

Among those modern writers who explicitly own a kinship with the empiricism of Hume, one of the most widely known writers is AYER (1910–89). Ayer's LOGICAL POSITIVISM is discussed under other entries (*see* LANGUAGE IN RELIGION). Ayers' promotion of a positivist worldview under the guise of a theory of language and meaning neither enhances nor diminishes its status as 'extreme' or 'radical' empiricism. It is close to Hume, and distant from Locke. In addition to *Language, Truth and Logic* (2nd edn, 1946), Ayer published *Foundations of Empirical Knowledge* (1940) and *The Problem of Knowledge* (1956).

William James (1842–1910) has been associated with the name 'radical empiricist', but this relates mainly to his formulation of criteria for his PRAGMATISM. His maxims, also cited and endorsed by RORTY, that 'the TRUE is only expedient in our way of thinking, just as the right is only the expedient in the way of our behaving', owes more to pragmatism than to empiricism.

RUSSELL (1872–1970) argues that 'knowledge by acquaintance' is more certain than 'knowledge by description'. Nevertheless, his philosophical thought is too complex to provide a model of empiricist philosophy as such.

This sketch confirms that even within the narrower compass of 'the British empiricists' Locke, Berkeley and Hume, there is no single, easy, definition that can cover very diverse examples of empiricist philosophies. Almost always we need to ask: 'Empiricist – in what sense?' Locke writes as an empiricist with constructive questions for theists about BELIEF; Hume suggests a more reserved, at times sceptical, view of knowledge and selfhood. (*See also* METAPHYSICS; POSITIVISM; SCIENCE AND RELIGION.)

Enlightenment

Immanuel KANT (1724–1804) formulated a classic definition of 'the Enlightenment' (German, *Aufklärung*) as 'man's exodus from his self-incurred tutelage ... [by learning] to use your own understanding'. This throwing off of dependency in second-hand authorities and traditions was based on a confidence in the power of human REASON, an optimistic view of human progress, and an agenda that questioned inherited political and religious structures and values.

Many trace Enlightenment RATIONALISM to the methodological role of doubt proposed by DESCARTES (1596–1650) in his quest for clear and certain knowledge. Helmut Thielicke and many theologians trace a line from Descartes to Lessing, but this approach is less readily adopted among philosophers. Descartes spoke of applying this method 'once in a life-time', and exempted ETHICS and knowledge of God.

ENLIGHTENMENT THOUGHT IN ENGLAND

The Enlightenment reflected different emphases in England, France and

Germany, as well as differences of historical timing. In England seventeenth- and eighteenth-century DEISM exercised a substantial influence on subsequent thought. LOCKE (1632–1704) combined EMPIRICISM with a moderate emphasis on 'reasonableness' of BELIEF, and this both encouraged individual responsibility in beliefs and remained fully compatible with THEISM. In order to avoid replication of material, readers are referred to the entry on deism for earlier English Enlightenment thought.

ENLIGHTENMENT THOUGHT IN FRANCE

In France, Enlightenment thought was more explicitly anti-establishment in matters of RELIGION and in politics. The eighteenth-century Encyclopaedists worked on material edited by Denis Diderot (1713–84). Diderot was influenced by Locke's empiricism, but moved far beyond Locke towards a view of the world that bordered on MATERIALISM. The thirty-five-volume *Encyclopaedia*, which included articles on history, philosophy, religion, and political theory, finally appeared in 1780.

Voltaire (1694–1778; pen-name of François-Marie Arouet) was influenced by NEWTON and by Locke. He shared their concern for empirical method, but arrived at more sceptical results. Newton applied the constancy and universality of rational 'laws' to the natural world, but remained a theist. Voltaire drew elements of SCEPTICISM from Michel de Montaigne (1533–92). They rejected theological dogma and philosophical METAPHYSICS.

Voltaire's humanism is based upon recognition of the fallibility of rationalist and empirical knowledge. Hence his political philosophy stressed tolerance and AUTONOMY. He retained belief in a good God, even if not in all the doctrinal and institutional commitments of the religion of his day.

Voltaire's position differs from that of the two French Enlightenment materialist philosophers, La Mettrie (1709–51) and Paul-Henri-Dietrich d'Holbach (1723–1789). The title of La Mattrie's work *Man the Machine* (1747) exemplifies the extension of Newton's empirical scientific method (appropriate to study of the natural world) to the study of humanity and a philosophical world-view.

Similarly, d'Holbach, one of the Encyclopaedists, published a materialist *System of Nature* (1770) from which Voltaire explicitly distanced his own views. D'Holbach derived all reality from motion and matter, and repudiated any metaphysical systems of thought. His *Christianity Unveiled* (1756) attacked Christianity, REVELATION, and theism as the product of MYTH and mythologization. 'Science' offers liberation from all this.

It is a matter of debate whether we should include Jean Jacques Rousseau (1712–78) as a thinker of the French Enlightenment. He was a man of feeling rather than an arid rationalist. He did not attack religion, although he looks for a religion without priests or temples. It is 'the people' who are sovereign, through 'the will of all' (*volonté de tous*) or 'the general will' (*volonté générale*). His call for liberty and equality influenced Robespierre, but he was not an advocate of revolution, and in his *Social Contract* (1762) private rights had to be yielded for the good of all. Like Voltaire, he dissociated himself from d'Holbach and the Encyclopaedists.

ENLIGHTENMENT THOUGHT IN GERMANY

The beginnings of the German Enlightenment are in general later than those in England, although Christian Wolff (1679–1754) drew on the rationalism of LEIBNIZ for his concepts of religion and philosophy. Samuel Reimarus (1694–1768), whose 'Wolffenbüttel Fragments' were published after his death by G.E. Lessing in 1774–7, took up the threads of an earlier English deism. This included a rejection of miracles and notions of the supernatural. Lessing (1729–81) also represents Enlightenment rationalism. There is an 'ugly ditch' between reason and the historical (empirical) reconstructions of mere probability, at most.

The Jewish philosopher MENDELSSOHN (1729–86) was a friend of Lessing and a follower of Wolff's rationalism. He believed that human reason could lay the foundations for belief in God, and natural religion. Mendelssohn represents 'the Jewish Enlightenment', but arguably in Germany it led to the broader, more diffused development of Reform Judaism.

Kant marks a distinctive moment of transition in Germany. On one side, he stresses autonomy, the decision of the human will, freedom and progress. These are core values of the Enlightenment. On the other side his work on the limits of reason, especially in *The Critique of Pure Reason* (1781, rev. 1787), does not present reason as the sovereign arbiter of the deists, or Enlightenment rationalism. Further, the relegation of 'order' in the world to a regulative principle of the human mind in his *Critique of Judgement* (1790) does not promote the kind of 'natural religion' found among some Enlightenment thinkers.

In spite of FICHTE and HEGEL, the age of ROMANTICISM would soon overtake the Enlightenment era after Kant. Further, by the mid-twentieth century a certain positive revaluation of TRADITION would be explored by such hermeneutical writers as GADAMER (1900–2002), and a reappraisal of reason take place through postmodern perspectives.

In theology, rather than in philosophy, a reappraisal of the influence of Descartes is also important. Descartes, arguably, did not wish to establish the kind of doubt often ascribed to Enlightenment understandings of theism. (*See* also CERTAINTY AND DOUBT; HERMENEUTICS; POSTMODERNISM; SCIENCE and RELIGION; POSITIVISM.) This entry is intended to be read in conjunction with that on rationalism.

epistemology

Epistemology embraces a variety of theories of knowledge (Greek, *epistémé*. It constitutes a core sub-discipline within philosophy, alongside ONTOLOGY, ETHICS, LOGIC and other subject-specific areas such as philosophy of language. It includes issues concerning the sources, limits and nature of knowledge, and modes of knowing.

Special sets of issues within epistemology include BELIEF, SCEPTICISM and criteria for the justification of, or warrants for, belief. However, the three main streams of tradition at the heart of epistemology present the respective claims of EMPIRICISM, RATIONALISM and CRITICAL or TRANSCENDENTAL PHILOSOPHY.

EMPIRICIST, RATIONALIST AND TRANSCENDENTAL APPROACHES

Empiricism investigates how knowledge derives from the sensory world outside the mind, how it is conveyed through the senses, and how it becomes processed as the OBJECT of perception, or as ideas or reflection involving acts of COGNITION.

LOCKE (1632–1704), BERKELEY (1685–1753) and HUME (1711–1776) represent the major early modern empiricists. Locke and Berkeley accord greater place to reasonableness and to ideas, whereas Hume emphasizes perception. Their method is that of observation and A POSTERIORI inference.

Rationalism ascribes the starting-point for knowledge to A PRIORI ideas, often regarded as innate ideas. Logical truth and the method of introspection provide a foundation for deductive inferences, rather than the less certain and fallible findings of sense-data gathered by observation of the CONTINGENT world.

DESCARTES (1596–1650), SPINOZA (1632–77) and LEIBNIZ (1646–1716) are the major early modern rationalists. Descartes sought to find 'clear and distinct' ideas which could not be doubted. Hence he began from the epistemological premise

cogito, ergo sum, 'I am [conscious of] thinking; therefore I exist.'

Critical philosophy emerged in KANT's *Critique of Pure Reason* (1781). Kant saw the need to raise TRANSCENDENTAL questions about knowledge, prior to addressing the traditional agenda. Hence he asked: 'What are the necessary conditions for the *possibility* of knowledge?' How is it *possible* to know? This must be addressed before we ask how we know, or what we know. It entails exploring the nature of knowledge and the limits of reason.

To explore the limits of reason is a constructive rather than a negative exercise. For scepticism may arise out of a sense of disillusion generated by over-high expectations of what reason might achieve. Locke, on the nature and grounds of reasonable belief, and Kant, on the limits of 'pure reason', both serve constructive rather than sceptical goals.

The details of this classic three-sided debate are considered more fully under the entries on empiricism, rationalism, critical philosophy, Kant and other individual thinkers within the empiricist and rationalist traditions.

THE JUSTIFICATION OF BELIEF

WOLTERSTORFF argues convincingly that Locke introduced an ethical dimension into the 'reasonableness' of belief, or 'entitlement' to believe, especially in book IV of his *Essay Concerning Human Understanding* (Wolterstorff, *John Locke and the Ethics of Belief*, Cambridge: CUP, 1996).

W. K. Clifford (1845–79) radicalized Locke's concern by formulating a more brittle and inflexible ethical criterion for the justification of belief. He uses the analogy of a ship-owner who sends emigrants to sea in a ship which he knows is unseaworthy, but salves his conscience with the thought that Providence will care for the ship if necessary. His belief that it is in order to send the ship to sea is immoral because it flies in the face of empirical evidence. Clifford's criterion in his *Lectures and Essays* (1879) has come to be known as Evidentialism, and in effect views belief as justified only when it may be grounded in virtually foolproof empirical evidence.

Roderick Chisholm has defended deontological (or ethically obligated) notions of justification for belief, although William P. Alston refuses to identify 'what is epistemically good', in the sense of maximizing rationality and TRUTH with an ethics of obligation. Foundationalists distinguished the justification of 'basic' beliefs from those beliefs that are derivative from these.

THE QUESTIONING OF EPISTEMOLOGY

POSTMODERNISM has tended to encourage pragmatic criteria of belief. The American tradition of PRAGMATISM that can be traced from William James (1842–1910) through John Dewey (1859–1952) to its post-modern radical extreme in RORTY (b. 1931) argues that in effect epistemology as theory is dead. It has given way to HERMENEUTICS 'as a way of coping' (*Philosophy and the Mirror of Nature*, Princeton: Princeton University Press, 1979, 356; and 315–56). Rorty not only quotes and endorses William James's view that 'the True' is 'only the expedient in ... thinking', but adds that there is no such task as 'getting reality right' because 'there is no Way the World Is' (*Truth and Progress*, Cambridge: CUP, 1998, 21 and 25).

Almost needless to say, however, Rorty's own pragmatic, postmodernist claims demand exploration from that area of epistemology that addresses scepticism. In spite of Rorty's claims that this misses his point, it is relevant to compare his views with those that come to light in the history of scepticism since ancient Greek philosophy. We may also question whether his appeal to hermeneutics in practice turns hermeneutics upside down. (*See also* FOUNDATIONALISM).

eternity

Almost all theists draw a contrast between the change and decay observable in the created order and the Being of God as 'eternal', or not limited by the passing of time. Nevertheless the word 'eternal' may denote at least three different ways of understanding the point at issue.

In the tradition of Parmenides, PLATO, and *advaita* (non-dualist) HINDU PHILOSOPHY, many regard eternity as timelessness, or Being without change. Some, by contrast, regard eternity as embodying temporal sequence, but without limits of beginning or end. Others follow the classic formulation of BOETHIUS (*c.* 480–525) that eternity denotes 'the complete possession all at once (Latin, *totum simul*) of illimitable life'.

Each approach brings its own problems. If eternity denotes timelessness, how can God (or any being beyond this world order) experience duration, periodicy, sequence or progression? If eternity denotes time 'pulled out' infinitely at each end, does this not entail God's being conditioned by time, rather than Creator of time? If eternity denotes *totum simul*, might this not be understood to impose a static mode of being onto God, who then cannot act, or interact, purposively as a living and promissory God?

ETERNITY AS TIMELESSNESS

This approach has a long tradition in Eastern and in Western philosophy. It largely rests upon inferences drawn from a theology of CREATION. AUGUSTINE (354–430) laid down a valid theological axiom when he declared, 'God created the world *with* time (*cum tempore*) not *in* time (*in tempore*).' A moment's reflection on the correlative roles of time and space as CATEGORIES interwoven in the created order adds weight to this, especially in the light of post-Einsteinian notions of space-time.

We know from the theory of relativity that time accelerates or decelerates depending on the direction of spatial motion of an object at extreme velocity. Yet few would claim that space was 'there' before God created the heavens and the earth, except for the minority who believe in the eternity of the world.

In ancient Greek philosophical traditions, Parmenides of Elea (fl. 510–492 BCE) assigned change and motion to the realm of mere 'appearance'. Reality was 'being', not 'becoming'. Plato (428–348 BCE) separated a timeless, changeless realm of eternal Ideas or Forms from a CONTINGENT, temporal, changing, empirical world which had the status only of a replicated or approximate copy of the non-temporal and eternal.

Among Eastern philosophical traditions, Śaṅkārā (788–820) and the 'non-dualist' Hindu philosophy of Advaita Vedanta held that cycles of rebirth and reincarnation, along with 'difference', stood in contrast with ultimate reality as uncharacterizable and undifferentiated *brahman*. Distinction and difference, along with temporal change, belonged to the world of illusion or deception (*māyā*). If *brahman–ātman* is One and without inner differentiation, nothing can change: ultimate reality is timeless and eternal.

This sits uneasily with Hebrew–Christian biblical traditions, however, where God is conceived of in more personal and purposive terms. The living God of Hebrew and Christian scripture is a God who makes promises. (Ex. 12:25; Deut. 1:11, 6:3, 10:9, Hebrew, *dabhar*, 'speak', but contextually, 'promise'); waits, (Isa. 30:18, Hebrew, *chakah*); foreknows, (Rom. 8:29, 11:2, Greek, *proginosko*); and even reconsiders and revises plans of action (Judg. 2:18; Jer. 15:6, Hebrew, *nacham*). Further, even allowing for the more objective, less mentalist meaning of 'remember' in Hebrew, what are we to make of dozens of allusions to God's remembering (*zakar*) God's covenant (Gen. 9:15, 16); or individuals (Gen. 8:1, 19:29; Ex. 32:13); or pledges or promises (Neh.

1:8); past sins (Ps.25:7) or past mercies (Ps. 98:3).

While some references may be anthropomorphic or metaphorical, these verbs seem to play too great a part in disclosures of the nature of God to yield an exhaustive explanation of this kind (*see* ANTHROPOMORPHISM; METAPHOR). Richard SWINBURNE regularly calls attention to such passages in various philosophical contexts. It seems too simple and too general (like a Wittgensteinian 'super-concept') to characterize God's eternity as 'timelessness'.

Nevertheless some have defended this view in recent philosophical thought. Paul Helm argues that it remains fully compatible with an understanding of creation and of OMNISCIENCE, citing also the earlier tradition of ANSELM (1033–1109) 'that timelessness is among the greatness-making or perfection-making properties of God' (*Eternal God: A Study of God without Time*, Oxford: Clarendon, 1988, 11). Nelson Pike similarly understands this as a 'value-making' property (*God and Timelessness*, London: Routledge, 1970, 137). Helm relates this to divine IMMUTABILITY, and argues that it offers 'a metaphysical underpinning for God's functioning as a biblical God' (*Eternal God*, 21).

ETERNITY AS INFINITELY EXTENDED TIME?

The widespread unease shared by many at the identification of 'eternal' with 'timeless' finds a focus in the doubt about whether or how an event in the life of a 'timeless' Being may 'relate ... to any temporal entity or event' (E. Stump and N. Kretzmann, 'Eternity', *Journal of Philosophy*, 78, 1981, 429–58). The dilemma appears to be: a 'timeless' God may seem unable fully to engage in the temporal drama of God's world; a God 'infinitely extended' in time seems to share too much in the contingent qualities of what God has created.

Richard Swinburne defends the 'common sense' understanding of eternity as lack of temporal beginning and end, but not lack of duration. God pre-exists creation, but also: 'There was no time at which he did not exist ... He is backwardly eternal' (*The Coherence of Theism*, [1977] Oxford: Clarendon, 1988, 211). God 'exists at any other nameable time ... will go on existing for ever ... he is forwardly eternal' (ibid.). Swinburne argues that this view is entirely 'coherent', and Anthony Kenny shares a similar view.

THE *TOTUM SIMUL* VIEW OF BOETHIUS: A POSSIBLE MODIFICATION?

Augustine speaks of God as 'the supreme hub of causes' (*summus causarum cardo*: On the Trinity, III: 9: 16). Henry Chadwick comments, 'Boethius suggests, therefore, that as time is to eternity, so the circle is to the centre ... God looks out on the world and arranges what is best for each individual ... For us, events fall into past, present, and future time. God is outside time. For him the knowledge of temporal events is an eternal knowledge in the sense that all is a simultaneous present' (*Boethius*, Oxford: Clarendon, 1981, 242 and 246).

Boethius contextualizes his concept of eternity then, within a doctrine of divine providence and governance and the problem of divine omniscience (see entry on omniscience for details). God's infinite awareness comprehends all at once what from a human standpoint is spread out in TIME as past, present and future.

Thomas AQUINAS (1225–74) endorses and develops this view. He declares, 'The notion of eternity follows immutability, as the notion of time follows movement ... Eternity is nothing else but God Himself ... His eternity includes all times, and not as if He Himself were altered through present, past, and future' (*Summa Theologiae*, Ia, Qu. 10, art. 2).

In contemporary Christian theology, however, the concept of divine immutability has undergone some criticism and modification. It is arguably a simplistic concept of 'perfect' if we argue that what is 'perfect' at Time One is the same as what is 'perfect' at Time Two. Indeed the Epistle to the Hebrews appears to imply that *teleiosis*, being mature or perfect, denotes a developing process (Heb. 2:10; 5:9). These issues are expanded in the entry on immutability.

Can a 'perfect' God act in ongoing, dynamic, purposive ways which express God's own nature, whether we conceive of this as occurring 'within' this-worldly time, or in a 'non-human' sphere, such as 'after' the general resurrection? To express it in a different way, does the heavenly or eschatological realm in the biblical writings seem more akin to a *crescendo* of glory than to a constant, static, everlasting *fortissimo*? Can God no longer do 'new' things, as the God of Abraham, Isaac and Jacob, without thereby forfeiting 'perfection'?

The simple distinction between eternity and time is inadequate. In everyday life we distinguish between astronomical time, clock time, human time, narrative time, opportune time, the timing that reflects a sociology of power and so on. The issue is not whether God is conditioned by time. God is the Creator of time. However, creaturely human time-as-we-know-it is to be distinguished from that temporality from which is derived the very possibility of sequence, tempo, duration, periodicy and opportune time. (We may note that in HEIDEGGER *Zeitlichkeit* (temporality) is the condition for the possibility of time).

Perhaps it is logically possible to retain the basic contrast between human time and 'eternity' as that which characterizes God (as in Boethius), but with some accommodation to notions of progressive action and newness which are also necessary to the nature of the God in Western THEISM and the Bible. (*See also* GOD, CONCEPTS AND ATTRIBUTES OF.)

ethics

Ethics may be defined as the study of concepts and criteria of individual and social human actions, attitudes and behaviour in so far as these are deemed right or wrong, or good or bad. Ethics formulates systems of value, of the good, or of the right in so far as these are, or can be, instantiated in human lives or in social groups.

TYPES OF ETHICAL THEORY

Those systems that focus mainly on criteria or goals of 'right' or 'rightness' generally explore issues of duty and obligation. Theories of necessary obligation without regard to consequences are also known as DEONTOLOGY. Those systems that focus mainly on criteria or goals of 'good' or 'the good' generally explore beneficial consequences. These may include self-realization, or utilitarianism, seeking the greatest good for the greatest number. However, utilitarianism may also be subsumed within a theory of the right.

Many deny that any objective criteria can be found for establishing principles of right conduct or the widest good. Subjective theories of ethics often reduce the ethical to a mere expression of preference, or of approval or disapproval (see AYER; RORTY). Such theories are sometimes also called non-cognitive; but the latter term is broader since it may also denote intuitionist theories.

Ethical intuitionism reflects the view that 'good' cannot be defined by referring to other concepts and to rational arguments. G.E. Moore (1873–1958) held this view. 'Good' is a quality that cannot be analysed, but is simply intuited. Like the colour 'yellow', it is supposedly 'simple' and not known through analysing arguments. To equate 'good' with some other quality is to commit 'the naturalistic fallacy'.

Since these issues bring us into the realm of ANALYTICAL PHILOSOPHY and logical grammar (see LOGIC), the study of conceptual problems in ethics, without

necessarily exploring issues of ethical validity, sometimes called 'meta-ethics', has arisen. R.M. Hare (b. 1919) and P.H. Nowell-Smith (b. 1914) undertake such explorations.

ANCIENT GREEK PHILOSOPHY

The era of the pre-Socratic Sophist philosophers included Protagoras (c. 490–420 BCE), widely known for his maxim 'Man is the measure of all things' (*Fragment* 1). All ethical criteria are subjective matters of convention: what is lawful in Athens may be unlawful in Megara. Gorgias (late fifth century BCE) also extends his metaphysical SCEPTICISM to ethics.

By contrast, SOCRATES, PLATO and ARISTOTLE expound a view of virtue. For Socrates, the acquisition of virtue begins with knowledge. Further, virtue has social implications, and transcends mere individualism. Plato bases his ethics on ONTOLOGY, especially upon the ABSOLUTE 'Form' of the Good, from which good in the CONTINGENT world is derivative. His four 'cardinal virtues' are wisdom, courage, moderation and patience.

Aristotle approaches ethics in terms of teleology and a theory of virtue. Well-being (Greek, *eudaimonia*) lies not in pleasure, honour or wealth, but in the fulfilment of the purpose for which humankind exists, which expresses true human nature. In effect, this is explicated as 'the exercise of reason according to virtue' (Greek, *aretē*). Thus ethical norms are not external to humankind, but entail *self-realization*. At the same time, Aristotle's doctrine of the balanced 'mean' ensures that attention be given to will, habit and consequences for others.

MODERN THOUGHT FROM HOBBES TO KANT

HOBBES (1588–1679) argued that power is the chief regulating principle in ethical judgements. 'Good' denotes little more than the heightening of vitality in the self-gratification that is made possible through power. Yet the application of reason to this situation of universal self-interest results in a recognition of the need of civil law to impose an 'orderedness' through social contract. Hence a state of nature is replaced by a variety of social contracts, and power is passed to a monarch.

If Hobbes had denied the possibility of disinterested action, Joseph Butler (1692–1752) explored the threefold relation and balance between 'self-love', 'benevolence' and 'conscience'. Although the interpretation of these is debated, the first denotes regard to one's interests and well-being; the second, a regard for others motivated by affection; the third, in Butler's words, reflection by which human persons 'approve and disapprove their own actions'. Conscience is to 'preside and govern', but proves to be congruent with self-love and benevolence because of a divine providential ordering of the world.

In the context of philosophy of religion, while it may be more precarious to argue from ethics or moral obligation to God (see MORAL ARGUMENT for the existence of God), the different stances of Hobbes and Bishop Butler reveal the difference that a theistic foundation may make to the formulation of ethical theory. However, critics of Butler ask whether the weight that he places on conscience can account for the differing value systems found in the modern world.

HUME (1711–76) regarded 'the good' exclusively in terms of consequences. However, these consequences are defined in terms of 'all things either directly pleasant or indirectly conducive to pleasure, whether in their owners or in other men'. This is a kind of subjective utilitarianism or Hedonism, but it is not egoism. Hume was unable to offer an 'objective' basis for ethics, since he regarded the SELF as, in effect, a bundle of sensations and emotions served by reason only instrumentally: 'reason is the slave of the passions'.

An entirely opposite approach is adopted by KANT (1724–1804). In formulating his TRANSCENDENTAL PHILOSOPHY Kant places moral obligation on the footing of an Absolute. It is the 'categorical imperative' that comes from beyond the world of the empirical and CONTINGENT that is ordered and construed by the human mind. 'Ought' expresses the relation of objective moral law to the human will.

'Good' is not a functional, relative or abstract quality. Only 'the good will' can be called 'good', when it is directed by the moral law. The emphasis moves from consequences (Hume) to motive. What makes the good will 'good' is not what consequences it brings about, but its recognition of moral duty alone. The laws of ethical obligation apply to all universally; hence they constitute a categorical imperative. This is the approach of deontology.

This may be instantiated through the application of a general moral law: 'So act as to treat humanity in every case as an end.' Other human persons are not 'means' to the end of our own happiness.

The early Romantics, Johann Schiller (1759–1805) and Friedrich Jacobi (1743–1819) were quick to criticize this resolute deontology of will as joyless and divorced from goodness guided by love. Schiller parodied Kantian ethics in satirical verse:

'Willingly serve I my friends; but I
    do it, alas, with affection.
Hence I am cursed with the doubt,
    virtue I have not attained.'
'This is your only recourse: you
    must stubbornly seek to abhor
    them;
Then you can do with disgust that
    which the law may enjoin.'

Arguably, the more purely love guides, the less consciously is 'good' done through duty.

UTILITARIAN ETHICS: BENTHAM AND MILL

Jeremy Bentham (1748–1832) returned to Hume's emphasis on pleasure and pain: 'Man's only object is to seek pleasure and to shun pain.' He is, in effect, the founder of modern utilitarianism: ethical action aimed at the consequence of producing 'the greatest good' (acquisition of pleasure and avoidance of pain) 'for the greatest number'. This maximizes the principle on a social scale.

Bentham explored a theory of government that would achieve this as far as possible by using potential punishment as deterrents, and reward for facilitating social happiness.

However, the calculation of 'greatest' is problematic. Bentham took account of the intensity, duration, certainty, purity and extent of pleasure and pain. Yet what weight is to be given to each in relation to other, and how do we weigh intense pleasure for the few against diffused pleasure for the many?

A further difficulty arises from our inability to know precisely what consequences will follow from a given act. Bentham recognizes the fallibility of such calculation, and even defines 'vice' as 'a miscalculation of chances'. Many ethicists would view this as hugely understated. Is the notion of evil simply illusory?

MILL (1806–73) also promoted ethical utilitarianism, but also attributed to a person of 'properly cultivated moral nature' the motivation of a feeling of unity with fellow human beings. He was more optimistic than Bentham about an individual's willingness to sacrifice happiness as an ethical obligation if this gains happiness for a greater number.

Mill did not resolve the problems that face utilitarianism, however, in calculating the greatest happiness of the greatest number. BRADLEY, among others, criticizes the very logic of 'multiplying' happiness by replicating the same experience of a given level by the number of such experiences. It remains 'this' experience, even if it is replicated.

EVOLUTIONARY ETHICS: HERBERT SPENCER (1820–1903)

SPENCER defined conduct as 'good' in so far as it served to promote 'the contin-uous adjustment' by which an organism (or a person) adapts itself to its environment. 'Bad' conduct hinders such adjustment.

Harmony with one's surroundings and environment brings pleasure; pain is a sign of maladjustment. In effect, Spencer had a utilitarian ethic. Since adaptation is always in process and never perfect, the good is not absolute but a relative preponderance over maladjustment and pain.

Evolutionary development works from the simple to the more complex or 'higher'. At the complex level of the emergence of human life, ethical goals entail co-operation to continue to adapt A happier race will be produced. Spencer, it seems, coined the explicit phrase 'the survival of the fittest'. If there is 'duty', it is to be defined in these terms.

Spencer attempted to apply DARWIN'S biological theories of EVOLUTION to other areas of human life. Yet he left unanswered questions about the human agent's initiative in adapting the environment to human benefit, rather than more passively seeking to 'fit' contexts of nature. Can this provide adequate ground for a system of ethics, especially when 'complexity' and 'higher' forms of life are defined in quasi-mechanistic terms? The routine problems of utilitarianism still face this theory.

VOCABULARY AND CONCEPTS OF ETHICS

Many of the above approaches could be identified as placing emphasis on one side on motive and intention (with Kant), or on the other side on consequences (with Hume and Bentham). Both emphases bring their own problems.

Motive and intention have often been dismissed as matters of psychologistic 'mental states', the currency of which can be determined only in the light of public behaviour. However, intentions may also be defined in terms of what is willed, and what is reflected upon as an object of will. Motive may be rational and COGNITIVE: it arises from the thought of a desirable end.

Aristotle and Thomas AQUINAS explicate will in terms of habit or habituated qualities of will, namely as virtues. In recent thought G.E.M. Anscombe (1919–2001) and especially Alasdair MacIntyre (b. 1929) have proposed a return to ethical explorations based on a more serious and rigorous account of virtue-ethics. This includes continuity of habits of will and continuities of moral traditions.

We have noted difficulties about the calculation of possible consequences. A narrower view, hedonism, holds that the goal of ethical action is that of seeking *pleasure* for the self or for the greatest number. A broader view, consequentialism, holds that any beneficial consequence offers a criterion of ethical action. Nevertheless, the notion of calculating 'units of benefit' seems impossible. It is also impossible to propose a criterion of what some term an 'interpersonal utility comparison' to rank people affected.

In addition to these problems, hedonism (seeking pleasure) may founder on the paradox identified by Aristotle. Pleasure, he argued, emerges only as the by-product of ethical action, just as running produces the bloom on the athlete's cheek. Henry Sidgwick (1838–1900) similarly argued that 'the best way to get pleasure is to forget it', although he urged a modified utilitarianism based on ethical principles.

Charles Stevenson (1908–79) rejects the view that differences of ethical criteria and action arise from differences of cognitive BELIEF. Rather, they reflect prior differences of attitude. Although ethical assertions may embody cognitive statements, the language of ethics is, he urged, primarily non-cognitive, expressing preferences, emotions, approval or disapproval and rhetorical re-valuations or definitions.

This resonates closely with emotive, non-cognitive theories of LANGUAGE IN RELIGION. Hence this approach finds support from Ayer (1910–89), and in post-modern pragmatism from Rorty (b. 1931).

Yet there are other conceptual understandings of ethics. John Rawls (b. 1921) reformulates in terms of a more liberal tradition the notion of justice as 'fairness'. R.M. Hare argues that 'prescriptive' ethics invokes universal principles that apply to classes of similar cases for the status of moral imperatives. To do to others what we wish them to do to us is both universalizable and applicable as a prescriptive rule. Alasdair MacIntyre (above) returns in part to an Aristotelian–Thomist tradition of 'virtue', but in the context of late twentieth-century relativism.

FURTHER ISSUES FOR DEBATE

Sometimes the notion that ethical norms are to be transposed into subjective expressions of 'preference' or 'approval' are dressed up either as theories of language (as in Charles Stevenson and Ayer), or as entailments of a postmodern world-view (as in Rorty).

However, since ethical relativism goes back at least to Protagoras, it is more likely that this approach is simply a correlate of a materialist or positivist world-view. If nothing is normative, stable or absolute except economic or military power, we should not expect to find any grounding for a normative ethic.

Even consequentialist and hedonist theories, however, seem to imply a need for ethical rules or constraints. For in his insistence that self-gratification or pleasure yields a criterion of ethics, Hobbes is forced to recognize that only the constraints of government, ideally of monarchy, can prevent disintegration into anarchy. Only 'civilization' and political power can rescue humankind from a primitive level in which life is 'nasty, brutish, and short'.

Many who reject Kant's notion of the 'categorical imperative' nevertheless recognize the force of his maxim about treating fellow humans as 'ends', and not reducing them to mere 'means' to secure one's own goals and interests. This coheres with notions of personhood as a Thou or 'Other' in BUBER, MARCEL and LEVINAS.

'Orderedness' in the world finds a prominent place in the Aristotelian tradition, and is developed by AUGUSTINE and Aquinas. It leads on to positive and constructive traditions concerning virtue. The potential of 'virtue' ethics is explored, we noted, by MacIntyre.

Whereas non-religious systems of ethics often overlap with those of RELIGION, in many cases the motivation and basis is different. Most non-religious philosophical theories formulate autonomous value-systems that are, in effect, free-standing. By contrast, Christian ethics, for example, constitutes a response, to divine GRACE and the gospel. Given this difference, points of overlapping content also emerge. (*See also* METAPHYSICS; OBJECT; POSITIVISM; POSTMODERNITY; SUBJECT.)

evil

How can the reality and extent of evil and suffering in the world be compatible with belief in God as omnipotent and as perfectly good? How or why did evil originate?

FORMULATIONS OF THE PROBLEM

Formulations of the problem of evil predate even the rise of Christianity and of Islam, although the Hebrew Bible (also the Christian Old Testament) expresses the problem in the book of Job. In the most widely quoted and used formulation of the problem, HUME (1711 –76) alludes to the awareness of the issues in the ancient Greek philosophy of EPICURUS (341–270 BCE).

Hume writes: 'Epicurus' old questions are not yet answered. Is he [God] willing to prevent evil, but not able? Then he is impotent. Is he able, but not willing? Then

he is malevolent. Is he both able and willing? Whence, then, is evil?' (*Dialogues Concerning Natural Religion* [1779], New York: Harper, 1948, pt. X, 66).

Within theistic traditions the most influential classic expositions of the issues include especially those of AUGUSTINE (354–430) and Thomas AQUINAS (1225–74). This is the case, even if Terence W. Tilley argues that Augustine does not present a formal THEODICY. Their arguments turn on three focal points: (1) In what sense is evil an independent or positive entity, or is it primarily absence of good? (2) What logic is involved in calling God 'perfectly good'? (3) What is entailed in ascribing to God 'omnipotence' or 'Almighty-ness'?

Hume similarly portrays the traditional Christian theist 'Cleanthes' in his *Dialogues* as affirming the Almighty-ness of God, God's OMNISCIENCE and God's perfect goodness, which acts as a foil for Hume's own argument through the lips of 'Philo'. Philo argues that if all three of the propositions asserted by Cleanthes were true, evil would not exist. Yet evil does exist. Hence not less than one of these propositions is false or problematic. Alternatively, the problem dissolves if God does not exist.

The work of Hume illustrates a shift in perceptions of the nature of the problem in the eighteenth century. Up to the rationalist ENLIGHTENMENT, in theistic traditions the main challenge presented by the problem of evil was to defend the coherence of THEISM, as a matter of understanding. After the Enlightenment, with the rise of a more widespread ATHEISM, the problem of evil challenges the existence of a sovereign and good God as a matter of credibility. Both challenges remain today.

DIFFERING MODES OF RESPONSE: LOGICAL RELATIONS BETWEEN THE THREE FOCAL THEMES

Responses to the problem of evil may be divided into (a) those that mainly address issues of logic and logical coherence; and (b) those that bring more practical or existential attitudes to the problem. We first consider the logical issues.

Three broad strategies may be employed to try to soften the tensions or alleged inconsistencies generated by the simultaneous assertion of the sovereignty of God, the perfect goodness of God and the reality of evil. Expressed crudely, each of these three foci of discussion may be qualified, modified or eroded in such a way as to dissolve tension between them.

(A) Is God Sovereign and Omnipotent? At very least it must be pointed out that to call God 'Almighty' does not entail God's performing logically self-contradictory acts. It is not an issue of sovereignty to ask whether God can create a stone so heavy that God cannot lift it, or whether God can divide odd numbers in half to leave two sets of integers (*see* OMNIPOTENCE for details). However, this carries us only the part of the way.

MILL (1806–73) and subsequently the American philosopher Edgar S. Brightman (1884–1952) speak of God as 'finite' and 'constrained'. Divine sovereignty cannot, they urge, overrule human freedom. Affirming God's 'finitude', Brightman asserts that God has to work with evil-as-given, to which he gives the name 'dysteleological surd'.

Some types of evil ('surds') remain resistant to divine purpose (*The Problem of God*, 1930; *A Philosophy of Religion*, 1940). Mill saw 'God' as like an artist limited by his medium (*Three Essays on Religion*, 1875). However, such a view is not readily held by such traditional Christian writers as Augustine and Aquinas, and not by most theists. It also contradicts doctrines of God in Judaism and Islam.

In recent thought Peter Geach and Gijsbert van den Brink have perhaps softened some misleading logical entailments of sheer 'omnipotence' by preferring

to use the term 'Almighty' (van den Brink, *Almighty God*, Kampen: Pharos, 1993). On the other hand, SWINBURNE (b. 1934) defends the traditional use of 'omnipotent' (*The Coherence of Theism*, Oxford: Clarendon, 1977, 149–61).

(B) Does 'perfect goodness' belong to God? Bradley (1846–1924) regarded God as the ABSOLUTE, in the tradition of HEGEL. If God is identified with Reality-as-a-Whole and with 'the Wholeness of the True', Bradley rejects the possibility of ascribing moral character to God. Divine will operates from the inner necessity of its nature, not from moral criteria, especially as human persons perceive these.

Most mainline theists will readily acknowledge the need for caution in judging how divine goodness relates to human kindness. HICK urges that God wants humans to be holy, not simply happy (*Evil and the God of Love*, 2nd edn, London: Macmillan, 1977). BARTH insists that love on the part of God is not mere benevolence, but embodies election and covenant, and therefore also 'jealousy, wrath and judgement, God is also holy' (*Church Dogmatics*, III: 3, 351).

(C) Is evil real or illusory? What role does it play? If it can be argued that evil is mere appearance or illusion rather than reality, the problem becomes dissolved. Hinayana Buddhism tends to view evil, in the sense of suffering, as a necessary part of life. To come to terms with it is to experience liberation, which leads to nirvana (*see* BUDDHIST PHILOSOPHY).

In the quasi-PANTHEISM of SPINOZA (1632–77) neither God nor the world could have been other than they are. Among 'practical' religious approaches to the problem WEIL (1909–43) in her last years affirmed a mystical acceptance of God's world in which the beauty of the storm at sea cannot but risk shipwreck by its very nature. God wants creation '*to find itself good*' (*Gateway to God* [1939], 1974).

Hick approaches the problem of evil in the world by seeing it as providing an arena for the growth of human maturity or 'soul-making' (the phrase is borrowed from Keats). He urges that we look not to the past, blaming the Fall for the origin of evil, but to the future. God seeks the maturity and holiness of humankind, but this presupposes the need for struggle, or at least awareness or encounter with evil.

Yet this still might be said to suggest an unacceptably 'utilitarian' role for evil (*see* the criticism from David Griffin in the Hick entry). Is it acceptable that such extremes of human suffering have to provide the price for this goal that God, not humankind, has freely chosen as the goal?

The tradition of Augustine and Aquinas, from which Hick often distances himself, insists that evil is not an existent 'thing' in its own right, and certainly not a 'thing' created by God. God created only the possibility of evil, which human beings make actual by their choice and fallenness.

'Evil is the absence of a good' (Aquinas, *Summa Theologiae*, Ia, Qu. 49, art. 1). 'Evil has no positive nature, but is loss of a good' (Augustine, *City of God*, XI; 9). 'Evil denotes the absence of good ... Thus privation of sight is called blindness' (Aquinas, *Summa Theologiae*, Ia, Qu. 5, art. 48). This 'privative' (negative) view of evil forms a major strand in the traditional Augustinian–Thomist approach to the problem of evil.

CLASSIC EXPOSITIONS OF THE 'LOGICAL COHERENCE' RESPONSE IN AUGUSTINE AND AQUINAS

(A) Origins of evil in creaturely will and choice, not in God. Evil, Augustine insists, was not created by God, but arises from 'a wilful turning of the self in desire from the highest good'. 'The defection (*defectio*) of the will is evil' (*City of God*, XII: 7). God therefore created only the possibility of evil by permitting created beings to make choices and to direct their wills for better or for worse.

Ought God to have granted this free choice? This allows creatures freely to choose God, but if their character becomes evil, their choices cannot but become evil (*On Free Will*, II: 1). In his *Confessions* Augustine traces in terms of autobiographical narrative that 'self-will' generates evil; evil is 'borne of self-interest which generates conflict and competitiveness'. Even a child has 'a wish to be obeyed' (*Confessions*, I: 6: 8). Augustine has embarked on an argument which has come to be known as the FREE-WILL DEFENCE.

Aquinas argues that God bestowed freedom to angels and to human beings as a gift, 'for free choice expresses human dignity' (*Summa Theologiae*, Ia, Qu. 59, art. 3). Freedom from sin is 'true' freedom. If 'freedom' were merely an illusion, exhortations, commands and prohibitions would be 'in vain' (ibid., Qu. 83, art. 1). Only by GRACE can their freedom become positive.

(B) The 'privative' view of evil. This subject was introduced above. Evil is a falling from the best. 'Each single created thing is good ... as a whole they are very good ... What, after all, is anything we call evil except the privation of good?' (Augustine, *Enchiridion*. ch. 3). The Latin *deprivatio* is paralleled elsewhere by *negatio*, *corruptio* and *defectus* (negation, degeneration, defect). Evil is not 'a thing' that God has created.

Evil is a parasitic upon the good. For example, telling a lie achieves its end only if truth is normally presupposed. 'Evil is not a positive substance' (*City of God*, XI: 11).

Aquinas also argues that 'If all evil were prevented, much good would be absent ... A lion would cease to live if there were no slaying of animals' (*Summa Theologiae*, Ia, Qu. 49, art. 2). Creation would be reduced to dull uniformity if there were no 'grades of goodness' (ibid, Qu. 48, art. 2).

(C) The principle of plenitude. The principle of creation was 'difference':

'God *divided* day from night, light from darkness, earth from water' (Gen. 1: 4, 7; cited by Aquinas, ibid. Qu. 47, art. 1). 'The Divine Artist produces complexity, diversity, hierarchy, inequality' (ibid. art. 2) 'Difference' transforms formless chaos into order. Strictly in formal terms the 'principle of PLENITUDE' suggests that every genuine possibility is actualized.

In everyday life we use analogies about the 'tapestry' of life and history to account for unexplained darkness or sorrow as part of a wider many-coloured whole. Augustine writes: 'What is more beautiful than a fire? What is more useful with its heat and comfort ...? Yet nothing can cause more distress than the burns inflicted by fire' (*City of God*, XII: 4).

Hick, however, attacks this view as an 'aesthetic' response to the problem of evil, which places the ordered differentiation of the universe above the well-being of human persons. 'The traditional analogy was based upon the visual arts ... contrasts arising from ... the dark ... the beauty of the whole' (*Evil and the God of Love*, 192; see 170–98).

Hick attributes this approach to an over-concern about 'orderedness' in NEO-PLATONISM and ARISTOTLE, but it is also a biblical theme in Genesis, Leviticus, 1 Corinthians and elsewhere. (For further details, *see* the entries on Hick, LEIBNIZ and PLENITUDE.)

(D) Criticisms and developments of the Augustinian–Thomist view. To trace even the outlines of the debate would over-extend this single entry. Hence some of the major criticisms are discussed in other entries.

The most fundamental and far-ranging of these is the criticism of A. Flew and J. L. Mackie that 'God' could in principle have created free beings who always choose to do what is right. We might be able to predict with CERTAINTY, for example, that Mary would marry Tom, yet they could at the same time do this freely.

Many, including PLANTINGA and Swinburne, provide counter-replies to this claim. Would such a prediction be necessary and certain? If we are speaking of God and the possibility of evil, certainty and necessity would have to be of this kind. However, if such could be imagined, would FREEDOM still be 'freedom', and would human persons still be 'humans'? Swinburne places several issues in the context of omniscience and its logic.

Hick's alternative account is drawn in part, he argues, from Irenaeus and from SCHLEIERMACHER on the image of God and the Fall. Schleiermacher comes close to viewing the 'Fall' as a loss of naïve innocence that signals an acquisition of positive maturity. Hick suggests that this anticipates his own view that to focus on the future goal of divine providence rather on a 'mythological' Fall in the past provides a more satisfactory way forward.

We have not distinguished here between moral evil and natural disasters that cause suffering. Traditionally there have been many diverse responses to such phenomena as animal pain or destructive floods. That pain forms part of a learning process for avoiding destructive situations and forces may advance the argument. Yet we still face the problem of seemingly disproportionate pain. Some theologians allude to cosmic dimensions of the Fall, while others dismiss this as a SYMBOL for structural evil.

A more theoretical criticism concerns the alleged extent to which Augustine draws on Neoplatonism, and Aquinas draws on Aristotle. However, origins of ideas are less relevant than their validity, and these claims, at least for Augustine, are often exaggerated.

'PRACTICAL' OR EXISTENTIAL RESPONSES TO THE PROBLEM OF EVIL

Vincent Brümmer points out that to present to someone the Augustinian–Thomist approach in a time of affliction would be to exhibit 'moral insensitivity'

(*Speaking of a Personal God*, Cambridge: CUP, 1992, 128–51). He concedes that this approach remains fundamental to retain as a background of understanding in more normal times. However, in moments of crisis, as well as in mature thought, practical and existential approaches may offer more to those who are in the process of experiencing evil.

(A) Mystical resonances: Meister Eckhart (1260–1327) **and Simone Weil** (1909–43). ECKHART emphasizes the fullness of God's being. The human self is to empty itself like a desert, to become 'full' of God. Protest on behalf of the self is therefore excluded. Although God is 'good', because God is beyond speech God is also 'beyond' goodness. 'If my life is God's being, God's existence must be my existence ... my "is-ness"'.

Eckhart is content to let 'what-is' disclose itself. The heart of his concern is for 'letting-go' and 'letting-be'; a letting-go of the interests of the self and a letting-be of things as they are.

Although she was well equipped to lecture in philosophy in Paris, Weil chose to experience 'affliction' that 'crushed the spirit' by factory work and in wartime sacrifice and self-deprivation. In her last years she wrote of the need to 'consent' to the world as it is. The sea is 'no less beautiful' because ships are sometimes wrecked because it is what it is. Weil suggests that 'God is not satisfied with finding his creation good, but rather wants it to find itself good'. Evil is not illusory, however (*see* 'The Love of God and Affliction', in S. Weil, *Waiting on God* (London: Routledge & Kegan Paul, 1951), 63–78; also 'Love of the Order of the World', ibid., 97–116). Simone Weil died in wartime London of malnutrition and tuberculosis in 1943 at the age of thirty-four.

(B) Suffering God? Wiesel, Camus and Moltmann. The Jewish novelist Elie Wiesel survived the Holocaust and narrated his experiences in his autobiographical work *Night*. A central episode is that of a young Jewish boy who was hanged at Auschwitz in front of thousands who were compelled to file past the bodies of the child and two adults hanged with him. The child's torment lasted longer than that of the adults, prompting a spectator to exclaim: 'Where is God now?' Wiesel felt a voice within him reply, 'He is hanging here on this gallows.'

Wiesel's narrative may be understood as a reply of protest, implying (with NIETZSCHE) the death of God: God does not exist in such a world. If this is its meaning, it is akin to the 'protest' response of the Algerian existentialist atheist Albert Camus (1913–60). Camus also interprets DOSTOEVSKY's *The Brothers Karamazov* as a protest against theism. Humankind devises its values from human solidarity, not from such external values as 'God' (but *see* Dostoevsky).

The Christian theologian MOLTMANN (b. 1926) expounds a theology of God who co-suffers with the prisoner, the oppressed, the tortured. His answer 'God is hanging on the gallows' offers a profoundly Christian post-Auschwitz theodicy. On the cross God co-suffers with Christ as Trinity, in solidarity with all that is ugly or shameful. Thereby it becomes possible to enter a new world of promise and new creation, inaugurated by RESURRECTION and hope.

AN ATTACK ON 'THEODICY': TILLEY

In *The Evils of Theodicy* (Washington, DC: Georgetown University Press, 1991) Terrence W. Tilley substitutes an approach based on SPEECH ACTS of confession, narrative, prayer, lament, commitment, or declaration for the abstract third-person propositional discourses usually called 'theodicy'.

Tilley argues that 'theodicy' is a modern notion 'initiated in the seventeenth century (coined by Leibniz in 1710). This 'dry, measured, cool, calm, abstract' discourse threatens to marginalize all other more constructive approaches (ibid., 2).

Tilley easily shows that the Hebrew–Christian classic source, the book of Job, does not belong to this theoretical genre. It embodies accusation, lament, reproach, confession, declaration and so on. These are speech acts that transcend mere propositional content. More distinctively Tilley contextualizes Augustine's varied writings. The *Confessions*, for example, are acts of confession. Perhaps only the *Enchiridion* is instruction through propositions; but it remains an exposition, not a 'defence' of belief in God. 'It is not an argument but an instruction' (ibid., 121).

Boethius, Tilley continues, offers a therapeutic medicine against the poisons of falsehood. He redirects the mind-set of his reader, but this is not a 'theodicy'. He helps the reader to overcome a self-dramatizing grief and despair, to be freed to contemplate the Good (ibid., 152). Again, this is a speech act, not an argument.

THE DEVICE OF POLYPHONIC VOICES

It is agreed for the most part that while traditional logical theodicies and more recent 'practical' responses may soften aspects of the problem of evil, no single approach can solve it. In the end, as Plantinga asserts, it does not follow logically that if God has reasons for permitting evil, humankind should assume that we therefore know what the reasons are.

At the same time, we may be open to hints and clues. These may require processes of exploration and listening, and the preferred mode of genre for sustained to-and-fro questioning is a dialogue between 'voices'. To explore possible scenarios these voices may belong to fictional narrative.

Dostoevsky's *The Brothers Karamazov* may be understood in this way. There is no indication that Dostoevsky himself wished to use Ivan Karamazov as his mouthpiece, or indeed that Ivan expresses a merely

negative response of protest. He does, however, underline that a single, simple appeal to 'the higher harmony' is not good enough.

The dialogues of Alyosha, the priory monk, Dimitri, the debauchee, Ivan, the supposed rebel, and Father Zozima, the priest, move through paradox and complexity, dark and light, evil and compassion. 'We are each responsible to all for all.' Dostoevsky commends neither atheism nor passive assent to Russian Orthodoxy. It is through the dynamic wrestling that a form of theistic belief and value may perhaps emerge.

MORE RECENT ADVOCATES OF THE BROADLY AUGUSTINIAN–THOMIST APPROACH

A popular but well-argued version of the traditional approach has been the small but influential non-technical book by C.S. Lewis, *The Problem of Pain* (1940). Lewis discusses the extent to which God's self-consistency brings logical constraints to God's freedom. What kind of world would it be if God repeatedly intervened to make a wooden beam become soft every time we chose to hit someone with it, but let it maintain its hardness as long as it was used for buildings and furniture? What would it be if God made air refuse to vibrate whenever we speak a lie? (ibid., 21).

God is good, Lewis affirms, but that does not mean that God is content with humanity as humans are. God's 'goodness' is not simply human goodness. However, if 'goodness' bore no relation whatever to what we conceive of as 'goodness', we might as well worship the devil.

Evil is real, Lewis adds, but we should not assume that every individual, as an individual, experiences all the combined corporate weight of every evil in every time and place. Lewis thus addresses in popular modern form the traditional three foci of divine sovereignty, divine goodness and the nature of evil, as expounded more philosophically in the Augustinian–Thomist tradition.

In more technical philosophical terms the free-will defence has been attacked by A. Flew and J.L. Mackie, and defended by Plantinga and Swinburne. Swinburne provides sophisticated discussions of God's omniscience as well as God's omnipotence and OMNIPRESENCE.

God is entirely free to act in sovereignty, Swinburne argues, provided that we recall that 'a perfectly free person can only perform an action if he believes that there is no overriding reason for refraining from doing it' (*The Coherence of Theism*, 158–59). To apply Plantinga's caveat to Swinburne's arguments, there may be reasons why God refrains from certain actions, but there are no grounds for assuming that if we do not know them they do not exist. (*See also* EXISTENTIALISM.)

evolution, theory of

'Evolution' may be used in a number of distinct senses. It does not necessarily denote the particular version of evolutionary theory formulated by DARWIN (1809–82). However, in widespread usage the term most often denotes the theory that he expounds in *The Origin of Species* (1859), although greater tensions with theistic BELIEF probably emerge from his later work *The Descent of Man* (1871).

THE STATUS AND IMPLICATIONS OF DARWIN'S THEORY

Darwin claimed that his theory depended on inferences from empirical observations of data concerning different life-forms at different stages of development in different environments. A large amount of empirical data was collected during the five-year voyage of 'The Beagle'.

It is difficult to assess whether the key point of the theory, namely that these changes were purely random variables is genuinely demanded by nothing other than empirical observation and deduction: at very least a measure of inductive reasoning and degree of probability is

entailed. Darwin argued that these random variables lead either to degeneration and extinction or to survival and enhancement.

In place of 'design' or 'purpose' the criterion of usefulness for survival and flourishing moved a species forward in securing the best provision for its future.

Historically controversy became heated because on one side sacred texts were interpreted as if they offered competing theories of 'how' creation emerged, while on the Darwinian side empirical method became transposed into a world-view offering competing answers to the question 'Why?' (The distinction between these two agendas is identified under SCIENCE AND RELIGION)

Yet the most significant protest against Darwin arose from his later work *The Descent of Man*, in which Darwin explicitly stated that humankind had evolved through the same naturalistic random processes as those of more primitive biological life-forms, and was descended from them. It is arguable that a certain narrowness and brittleness on both sides about the incapacity of empirical data to arbitrate on the uniqueness of human personhood as bearing the divine image added confusion rather than light.

CONDITIONS FOR TELEOLOGY: THE POTENTIAL FOR ACTUAL ORDER

Darwin's publications appeared to many to explode the 'Why?' explanation of purpose behind the empirical data of the world. The Psalmist could say that God 'filled every living thing with plenteousness' only because starving creatures died or became extinct. PALEY could say that the eye was designed (like a watch) as a mechanism for sight only because he was unaware that creatures who could not see had once lived and perished.

Yet this is too hasty. TENNANT in his *Philosophical Theology* (2 vols., Cambridge: CUP, 1930) and W.R. Matthews in *The Purpose of God* argued that 'gradualness of construction is in itself no proof of the absence of ... design' (Tennant, *Philosophical Theology*, vol. 2, 84). Design may be seen in the provision of necessary conditions for the emergence of designed effects by whatever route.

Today philosophers and physicists confirm the issue of how many 'lucky accidents' have to occur for the hypothesis of sheer randomness to seem to verge on the unreasonable. Tennant anticipated these kinds of phrases in 1930: 'Lucky accidents and co-incidences bewilderingly accumulate' until the idea of purpose may seem no more unreasonable than a 'groundless contingency' (ibid., 79, 92, 93).

John Polkinghorne and SWINBURNE review this kind of argument in the light of more recent knowledge. 'Lucky accidents' mount up. If the force of gravity were slightly stronger, all stars would be blue giants; if a little weaker, red dwarfs. There is an infinitesimal, small balance between 'the competing effect of explosive expansion and gravitational contraction ... at the very earliest epoch ... (...10\–43 sec. after the big bang) ... a deviation of one part in 10 to the sixtieth' (Polkinghorne, *Science and Creation*, Boston: New Science Library, 1989, 22).

Swinburne compares the potential for 'temporal order' (regularities of succession) and 'spatial order' (regularities of co-presence) with the more mechanistic understandings of 'order' or 'design' that shaped the thought of Paley and his generation (*The Existence of God*, Oxford: OUP, 1979, 36). Even if Darwin's theories seem to explode 'design' as Paley conceived of it, 'evolution' as empirical observation and hypothesis does not exclude design as an ultimate principle in response to the question 'Why?'

THE DEBATE AFTER DARWIN

Yet after Darwin many empiricist 'scientific' thinkers attempted to promote a world-view based on Darwinian theory. T.H. Huxley (1825–95) argued for an entirely mechanistic view of humankind.

'Consciousness' is merely a derivation 'epiphenomenon' or by-product thrown up by increasing 'complexity' in the evolutionary process. It is a short step to the BEHAVIOURISM of Watson and Skinner.

SPENCER (1820–1903) applied the notion of optimum adaptation to environment to an ethical goal of pleasure. Pleasure is a sign of effective adaptation; pain is a symptom of maladjustment. Co-operation may be necessary because of evolutionary complexity.

Richard Dawkins represents this naturalistic perspective today. 'The only watchmaker in nature is the blind forces of physics, albeit deployed in a very special way ... It does not plan for the future ... It is a *blind* watchmaker' (*The Blind Watchmaker*, New York: Norton, 1986, 5).

All the same, have Huxley, Spencer and Dawkins taken full account of what may be inferred from empirical data, or from scientific method, alone? There is a metaphysical 'add-on', namely that we can slide into assuming that the data of biology or physics provide a comprehensive explanation of the whole of reality, of all that is, and that the 'level' of explanation in question includes 'why' as well as 'how'.

It is as if a physicist explained to a musical audience that the sound-waves presented on an oscilloscope exhaustively explained 'the whole of reality' in a symphony performance. The musical forms, the will and mood of the composer, the joy or tragedy of the changing harmonies in major or minor key, are not 'there', so they cannot be 'real'. A musical audience would be inclined to think that such an explanation 'misses the point' of the concert, however accurate it may be at its own level of explanation (On 'levels' see J. Polkinghorne, *The Way the World is*, London: Triangle, 1987, 17). (*See also* CREATION; EMPIRICISM; MATERIALISM; METAPHYSICS; TELEOLOGICAL ARGUMENT; THEISM; POSITIVISM.)

existence

Complex problems are raised by the seemingly common-sense notion of 'existence'. Much depends on the context of argument.

Traditional arguments for the existence of GOD serve to defend the validity of the BELIEF that God is ontologically real rather than a fictitious or functional projection or cipher of the human mind. However, TILLICH (1886–1965) vigorously insists that 'to argue that God exists is to deny him' (*Systematic Theology*, 3 vols. London: Nisbet, 1953, vol. 1, 227). God is, rather, 'the creative ground of essence and existence. The ground of being cannot be found within the totality of beings' (ibid.).

The contrast between essence and existence reveals another problematic facet of 'existence'. Those who follow PLATO in elevating a sphere of Forms, Ideas or Essences 'above' everyday existence associate existence with mere CONTINGENCY and transitions. On the other hand, existentialist writers from KIERKEGAARD (1813–55) to SARTRE (1905–80) perceive 'existence' as the concrete stuff of practical life, while 'essence' remains a theoretical, remote, hypothesis, or at best a merely logical entity.

Logical questions about whether mathematical numbers or UNIVERSALS 'exist' raise issues in the debate between realists and nominalists. Further, in the ONTOLOGICAL ARGUMENT for the existence of God, both sides of the debate address the issue of whether 'existence' constitutes a predicate or attribute, or adds nothing to a proposition about the entity that is said to 'exist'. This set in train a complex logical discussion from DESCARTES (1596–1650) to RUSSELL (1872–1970) and beyond. Russell's theory of descriptions 'brackets' the phrase 'and it exists' into a QUANTIFIER or prefix which removes it from the normal force of the proposition, and assigns a non-referential or non-predicating role to it.

HICK constructively suggests that part of the functional currency of 'exist' is that the attribution of existence 'makes a difference'. Yet even HEIDEGGER (1889–1976), who speaks of 'existentialia', prefers to speak of an 'existent' human being as *Dasein* (being-there), in contrast to the bare existence of objects in the world. (*See also* EXISTENTIALISM; LOGIC; NOMINALISM; ONTOLOGY, REALISM.)

existentialism

SOME BASIC THEMES

The basic themes that characterize existentialist writings include an emphasis upon the individual rather than the crowd (or tradition or community); and the role of active personal engagement and decision for life and for TRUTH, as against passive assent to systems or doctrines. They include most especially an insistence upon starting from concrete human situations ('existence') as against pretentious speculations about truth as universal or abstract ('essence').

These themes can be found in Kierkegaard (1815–55), who is often regarded as the first 'existentialist' thinker. However, Kierkegaard chose as his epitaph 'That Individual', and viewed with distaste any notion of founding a 'school of thought'.

Truth, Kierkegaard stressed, is not handed down at second hand. Authentic truth is that which the individual encounters through wrestling, exploration, struggle, decision and venture at first hand. We encounter truth not by observing or speculating about what is abstract as passive spectators, but through first-hand engagement and participation as active human subjects or agents. In this sense 'SUBJECTIVITY' becomes the 'truth' (*Concluding Unscientific Postscript* [1846] Princeton: Princeton University Press, 1941, 306).

Just as Kierkegaard wrote as an individualistic Christian Protestant with no love for the Church, so NIETZSCHE (1844–1900) represents the atheistic and antitheistic side of existentialist writings. He claimed that 'will to power' is the most fundamental drive in human persons. 'God' and 'RELIGION' are to be unmasked as manipulative devices which emerged only to serve the power-interests of priests or those who could work the system. His work was to 'philosophize with a hammer'.

Nietzsche's suspicion of REASON and of METAPHYSICS as merely instrumental devices to serve the power-interests of the individual brings him close to the themes of other existentialist writers. All claims to arrive at a rational understanding of essences, or of reality-as-a-whole, are illusory, and produced by more basic pre-rational drivers. Since 'God is dead', there is no universal value or ethics. Each person must seek his or her own interests and the 'values' that serve these.

FURTHER THEMES IN
KIERKEGAARD, NIETZSCHE AND
DOSTOEVSKY

Kierkegaard's journey of independent decisions against convention and against expected 'ETHICS' is traced as a vehicle of faith and obedience in his *Fear and Trembling* (1843). His analogy between the story of Adam's 'hiding' from God among the trees of the garden and the 'evasion' of 'being hidden in the crowd' to avoid an address from God (*Purity of Heart is to Will One Thing*, London: Collins, 1961, 163) explicitly finds a place in the existentialist theology of BULTMANN (1884–1976).

The very notion of 'Christendom' as the multitude of those who have given notional assent to an abstract system of doctrine in which they have no active stake is an illusion that verges on blasphemy. Kierkegaard places the blame for such a misapprehension initially upon AUGUSTINE (354–430), for allegedly transposing personal 'faith' into intellectual 'belief'. He also blames HEGEL (1770–1831) for equating Christian faith with an abstract, universal 'system'.

Against Hegel, Kierkegaard reminds us of the sheer finitude of human 'existence'. If truth could be viewed 'theocentrically', Hegel might have a point; but 'I am only a poor, existing, human being' (*Concluding Unscientific Postscript*, 190). He would follow the fashion of admiring the System 'if only I could set eyes on it' (ibid., 97). As it is, humans in this finite situatedness as 'mere' individuals can only venture, choose and obey.

Nietzsche turns these themes upside down. There is no universal or 'theocentric' system or word-view. However, in Nietzsche this does not imply a call for faith. It merely unmasks the illusory basis of THEISM, God and Christianity. God is 'dead'; therefore humankind is free to choose its own destiny and identity. 'The death of God' reflects the unmasking of the cultural crisis at the end of the nineteenth century, which gives way to 'nihilism' (*Thus Spake Zarathustra*, 1883–5).

While such relativism and nihilism feature in *The Gay Science* (1882) and other works, Nietzsche's most violent antitheist attacks emerge in *Twilight of the Idols* (1889) and especially in *The Antichrist* (1895). If rational philosophy and religion are 'fictions' and 'lies', what starting-point (or end) can there be except human situatedness and human will? This leads to a 're-valuation of all values'. Inherited value-systems are deconstructed under 'the hammer'.

DOSTOEVSKY (1821–81) retained his Christian faith, nurtured in Russian Orthodox traditions, but sorely tried and tested in a series of personal tragedies not of his own making. He begins the great tradition of the existentialist literary philosophical novel.

Dostoevsky's experiences of life were too brutal and too contradictory to permit either a bland second-hand theism or merely an ATHEISM of protest, even if his *The Brothers Karamazov* (1879–80) has sometimes been interpreted as atheistic protest (with Albert Camus, 1913–60).

By using at least three or more 'voices' in this profound novel, Dostoevsky shows that 'solutions' to the problem of evil cannot take the form of a single, neatly packaged system, but require address from various angles of finite human life. Among those often called 'existentialists', his work stands as more subtle and sophisticated than is usually allowed for.

'HUMAN BEING' IN HEIDEGGER AND IN JASPERS

Although he rejected the designation 'existentialist', HEIDEGGER (1889–1976) began from the human situation of 'being-there' (*Dasein*) in his earlier period of *Being and Time* (1927) which he characterized as *Existenz*, and to which he applied the German adjective *existentiell* and the noun 'existentiality' (ibid., Introduction, I, sect. 4).

Ontological enquiry concerns Being (*Sein*) but this can be approached only by 'ONTIC' questions, i.e. questions about concrete, human, existent beings in their finite 'thrown-ness' (German, *geworfen*) into the world, their 'facticity' (German, *Faktizität*) (ibid., pt I, ch. 5: Eng. Oxford: Blackwell, 1973, 174 (also Albany, NY: SUNY, 1996)). 'Facticity' is more than 'factuality': it denotes historically finite 'situatedness' in time, place and 'world'. Heidegger entitles this section 'The Existential Constitution of the "There"' (ibid.).

In relation to religious thought Heidegger's work underlines at least two key points. First, we cannot adequately philosophize about humankind, SELFHOOD or personal agency by drawing only on categories of substance observation as if we were concerned only with objects of description. The substantival categories of ARISTOTLE and LOCKE are more appropriate to objects. Participatory language that begins from an EXISTENTIAL 'there' or 'here' of the human situation takes us further.

Second, all human interpretation of life and phenomena rests upon a HERMENEUTIC of understanding. This takes place within the horizon of TIME and operates through the principle of the hermeneutical circle. We begin with finite, corrigible, provisional working assumptions, but these become steadily corrected and filled out (even if they remain provisional) by further dialogue with that which we seek to understand. This circle is thus not 'a vicious one' that is to be avoided: 'The "circle" in understanding belongs to the structure of meaning' (ibid., I: 5, sect. 32, 194–5).

Against PLATO, Heidegger insists, 'The "essence" of *Dasein* (being-there) lies in its existence' (ibid., 42). There is no ideal realm of universal essences. We explore '*existentialia*'. Human anxiety, care, fallenness, guilt and the anticipation of death tell us more than substantival 'categories' that are more appropriate for the description of value-neutral 'objects' of the natural sciences.

Yet Heidegger cannot move beyond 'the human' to 'God'. Indeed, in spite of his aim eventually to produce a philosophy of Being, or ONTOLOGY, in his later work on 'Being', philosophy tends to merge into the more visionary, pre-conceptual disclosures of art and poetry. Here he moves beyond existentialism, but explicitly gives up the project of ontology.

JASPERS (1883–1969) wrote not only as one well-versed in the history of philosophy, but also as one qualified professionally in medicine and in psychiatry. He wrote on selfhood, historicality (human situatedness within a historical time and place), identity and self-transcendence, i.e. the TRANSCENDENCE of the everyday self in particular revelatory experiences.

Like Heidegger, Jaspers explores what it is for the individual, as an individual, to face suffering, loss, guilt, isolation or imminent death. The most extreme of these experiences he calls 'limit-situations', or boundary-situations. When a human person is 'on the edge', second-hand, conventional assumptions often become stripped away as illusions. The individual finds what is authentic truth for him or for her.

Although for Jaspers ontology began as 'the fusion of all modes of thought aglow with being', such ontology 'is rent' (*Philosophy* [1931], Eng. 3 vols., Chicago: University of Chicago Press, 1969–71, vol. 3, 143). In existential terms, the 'encompassing' reality of the world can be reached only indirectly through 'polyvalent' or multi-functional, multi-layered language, which expresses the individual disclosures experienced by individuals.

This pluriformity of language, meaning and truth prevents Jaspers from identifying too closely with any specific religious tradition, whether Catholic or Protestant. However, he values 'religion' as a liberating and often authentic truth. 'Freedom and God are inseparable', even if the term 'freedom' is often abused and widely misunderstood. In the light of both, I can 'be myself' (*The Way of Wisdom*, 1950).

INDIVIDUALITY AND PERSONHOOD
IN MARCEL AND SARTRE, AND
EXISTENTIALIST ATTITUDES TO
RELIGION

To include both MARCEL (1889–1973) and SARTRE (1905–1980) is to see at once that 'existentialism' is represented at every point on the Christian–theist–agnostic–atheist spectrum. Kierkegaard was a Protestant pietist; Nietzsche, an aggressive anti-theist; Dostoevsky, an independent-minded Russian Orthodox Christian; Heidegger thought that the question of God could not be convincingly addressed; Jaspers valued 'religion', but not claims for any one tradition against another; Marcel was a convert to Roman Catholic faith (in 1929); and Sartre remained an atheist existentialist, although from around 1958 he turned increasingly to Marxist political thought. His existentialist axiom 'Man makes himself' recalls a Nietzschean emphasis on individual will to power without reference or recourse to God.

Like Jaspers and Heidegger, Marcel rejected the term 'existentialist', although he is also credited with coining the word. The reason why he is widely regarded as an existentialist thinker, however, lies in his emphatic and powerful emphasis on personhood. Persons are not things. They are not 'statistics' for the sociologist; they are not mere 'cases' for doctors, for psychiatrists or for pastoral care; they are not 'numbers' in a register or on a rota.

Marcel calls attention to the dignity and sacredness of persons-in-relation-to-Being, and in relation to one another. Here he differs from Kierkegaard, Nietzsche, Heidegger and Sartre: persons are truly persons in relation to other persons. In the language of BUBER, a person becomes a person when he or she addresses another as 'Thou'.

In an incisive analysis of twentieth-century society in the West, Marcel sees the reduction of 'persons' to instrumental roles as de-personalizing them by eroding away their capacities, as active agents, to love, to hope and to wonder. Life becomes a journey without a goal. 'Technomania' leads to 'technolatry', as if natural science offers the only way of knowing; the only path to reality. Technology has its value for humanity, but only in its proper place.

These themes are summed up in the titles of several of Marcel's books: *Being and Having* (1935); *The Philosophy of Existence* (1949); *The Mystery of Being* (1950); *Men Against Humanity* (1951); and *The Existential Background of Human Dignity* (1963).

SARTRE is widely regarded as the most prominent of the French existentialists. He became a member of the Underground during the Nazi occupation, and some of his philosophical themes through novels and literature reflect fear, suffering and dread. This aspect reveals the influence of Heidegger, as well as personal experience in war.

Sartre's emphasis upon the existential in contrast to the universal and abstract finds expression in his aphorism 'Existence precedes essence'. He expounds this as meaning: 'that man first of all exists, encounters himself, surges up in the world – and defines himself afterwards ... There is no human nature, because there is no God to have a conception of it ... Man is nothing else than what he makes of himself' (*Existentialism and Humanism* [1946]; Eng., London and New York: Philosophical Library, 1948, 28).

No value-system or 'essence' can be derived from God. For Sartre endorses Nietzsche's declaration in *Thus Spake Zarathustra* that 'God is dead'. Hence the individual creates the rules that shape his or her own decisions and identity. With Kierkegaard and with Nietzsche, Sartre stresses the role of active decision as against passive assent. Convention leads away from authenticity.

Like Heidegger, Buber and Marcel, Sartre distinguishes sharply between the modes of being of persons and of things. An 'object' is complete, finished, and self-contained; it is 'being-in-itself' (*être-en-soi*). A person is always in process of making and shaping themselves as a self and an identity; a person is 'being-for-itself' (*être-pour-soi*).

Dread and nausea arise when the individual is placed under pressure by society or a group by imposing upon that individual an already pre-shaped, mapped out, 'closed' future, which is not of the individual's own making (*see* the entry on Kierkegaard). This submerges that 'being-for-itself' (*être-pour-soi*) into a viscous, sticky slime that engulfs, drowns and destroys it. Conversely, being-for-itself (*être-pour-soi*) is the negation of being-in-itself (*Being and Nothingness* [1943], 4th edn, Eng., New York: Citadel, 1966, 55–81 and 535–46).

POSTSCRIPT: EXISTENTIALISM IN JEWISH AND CHRISTIAN THEOLOGY

This area is discussed under separate entries, especially those on Buber and Bultmann. In the case of Buber, it would not be accurate simply to call him an 'existentialist' thinker. For although he shares (e.g. especially with Marcel) a strong emphasis on the I–Thou dimension of the personal (in contrast to I–it language of 'objects'), Buber's thought has features that move beyond existentialism.

BULTMANN is concerned to utilize a way of using language that does not 'objectify' either God, humankind or divine or human action, but uses existential modes of expression. This gives rise to his programme of DEMYTHOLOGIZING the New Testament.

TILLICH is often described as an existential thinker. However, while he formulates 'existential' questions, Tillich's identification of GOD as 'Being-itself' and his concern for ontology renders this designation questionable as a description of his thought as a whole. (*See also* CORRIGIBILITY; OBJECT; PIETISM.)

F

fallibilism

Fallibilism should not be confused with CORRIGIBILITY. Fallibilism denotes the view that a class or system of BELIEFS is not only open to correction and revision, but also that virtually any set of beliefs or propositions falls short of CERTAINTY. Radical or extreme fallibilism attributes uncertainty to every belief: modified or relative fallibilism exempts such propositions as those of LOGIC or ANALYTIC STATEMENTS.

Both forms of fallibilism reject a 'strong' form of FOUNDATIONALISM which regards primary or fundamental propositions as certain. The enterprise of DESCARTES (1596–1650) and his requirement for 'clear and certain knowledge', in contrast to what is 'obscure and confused' (in *The Meditations*, 1641), would be rejected.

Fallibilism is often associated especially with Charles S. Peirce (1839–1914). Peirce combined logical and semiotic theory to evolve his own version of PRAGMATISM. Part of a pragmatic approach entails the view that claims to truth may be justified in relation to given stages or situations. No system of claims to truth can be complete; hence there remains a provisionality and corrigibility

Given that self-interest and a sense of exploration or journey are never left behind, absolute certainty cannot be found in the midst of this process. Peirce comes close to the more popular notion of 'fallibility' as being unable to guarantee lack of error.

falsification, falsifiability

This entry presupposes a familiarity with the principle of verification, or verifiability, expounded in the entries on AYER and (more briefly) LOGICAL POSITIVISM. Falsifiability, likewise, developed in two different contexts: that of Vienna, although there more in terms of the philosophy of SCIENCE than the VIENNA CIRCLE; and that of English EMPIRICISM, led by Ayer, and (on falsifiability) John Wisdom and Antony Flew.

In Vienna, Karl Popper (1902–94) argued that in science falsification was a more constructive criterion of meaning and TRUTH than verification. To be true-or-false and meaningful, propositions must be capable of disproof by negative instances. 'Confirmation' merely replicates, more narrowly, discoveries of the past. 'Falsifiability' permits a process of exploration, conjecture and hypothesis, which remains open to rational criticism and the elimination of error (Popper, *The Logic of Scientific Discovery*, 1934).

This principle operates in parallel with the axiom in SEMANTICS and linguistics that meaning often derives its currency from what it excludes. It is less closely tied to a positivist or strictly empiricist worldview to ask of LANGUAGE IN RELIGION, 'What does this assertion exclude or negate?' It serves to filter out purely self-affirming understandings of such an utterance as 'God is on our side', from a use of the statement which would permit counter-evidence.

In the English context John Wisdom expounded 'The Parable of the Invisible Gardener'. If two people disagree about whether in a jungle a less 'wild' area suggests the activity of a gardener, one strategy would be to want to make observations. If such a gardener never appears, the 'believer' may insist that this is because the supposed gardener is invisible. A series of tests now takes place, which reveal that the gardener is also inaudible, intangible and odourless. The 'unbeliever' now responds: 'So what does your assertion that there is a gardener amount to, if nothing whatever can count against it?'

HICK points out that this constructively challenges those who use language in religion to identify its cutting edge. If God 'exists', 'exists' must somehow 'make a difference'. If we cannot specify what would count against an assertion, what is it asserting? (See also POSITIVISM.)

al-Farabi (Abu Nasr, 875–950)

Like AL-KINDI, al-Farabi taught in Baghdad, and wrote at length on ARISTOTLE. He produced commentaries on Aristotle's works. In contrast to al-Kindi, however, he praised the virtues of philosophy even above revelation in the Islamic tradition.

Religious truth is expressed through symbols and images, and these may be relative to human situations and societies. The higher activity of philosophy brings conceptual precision and rigour to the mind, and brings an awareness of the conditions necessary for strict logical demonstration. It is difficult to avoid

comparing the later Western contrast drawn by HEGEL (1770–1831) between the use of 'representations' (Vorstellungen) in religion and critical concepts (Begriff) in philosophy.

Because in Islamic philosophy Aristotle was often called 'the First Teacher', al-Farabi's close adherence to Aristotle invited the widespread designation of him as 'the Second Teacher'. However, he also studied and expounded the works of PLATO, including the production of commentaries on the Republic and the Laws.

His view of the relativity of religious expressions has led to the assumption that he supported the Shi'ite sect or tradition within Islam; but he avoided giving any offence to the more dominant Sunnite traditions. He was careful to stress the affinity between the core understandings of Allah in the Qur'an as One, as the First, as the source from whom all creation proceeds; and Aristotelian, Platonic and Plotinian notions of a hierarchy of Being.

Nevertheless against al-Kindi, al-Farabi believed and taught that the world is eternal, without beginning and without end. He attempted to hold this together with Islamic theology by arguing that reality (including the world) flows continually from God as Source of all levels of Being. Whether this synthesis can be genuinely held together is controversial and doubtful. Such a synthesis was strongly opposed by al-Ghazali. A helpful resource is I.R. Netton, Al-Farabi and his School (London: Routledge, 1992). (See also AQUINAS; ISLAMIC PHILOSOPHY.)

Feuerbach, Ludwig (1804–72)

Feuerbach is the founding figure of the movement that interprets God as a projection of the human mind. RELIGION in general projects the 'infinity' of human consciousness and the highest human values onto a figure 'out there'. The Christian religion, Feuerbach proposed, projected a Trinitarian God from the 'infinite' capacity of human reason, human will and human love.

Although KANT (1724–1804) had earlier utilized the notion of projection, Feuerbach first formulated this approach as an explicitly anti-theistic, materialist (some would say non-realist) system of thought, which very heavily influenced the anti-theist accounts of the origins of religion of both MARX (1818–83) and FREUD (1856–1939). Feuerbach studied under, and was influenced by, HEGEL (1770–1831). His published works included *Thoughts on Death and Immortality* (1830), *The Essence of Christianity* (1841) and *The Essence of Religion* (1845).

GOD, REALM AND HUMANKIND

Feuerbach studied theology in Heidelberg, and in Berlin where Hegel taught. However, he became disenchanted with Hegel's identification of DIALECTIC and REASON with the ABSOLUTE as Absolute Spirit, or God. Hegel's own school of disciples split apart into more theological or idealist 'right-wing' Hegelians, and the more materialist 'young left-wing' Hegelians such as D.F. Strauss (1808–74), Bruno Bauer (1809–82) and Feuerbach, who rejected Hegel's principle of IDEALISM or Absolute Spirit (*Geist*).

Hegel had attempted to wrestle with the problem of how universal reason, mind or spirit was concretized in the dialectic of history, and, at another level, LOGIC. Feuerbach and Marx attempted to 'demystify' this dialectical process in radically more concrete terms, as human (Feuerbach) or socio-economic (Marx) forces. The aphorism that Feuerbach and Marx turned Hegel upside-down is widely cited; in their view they put Hegel's feet on the ground.

Feuerbach began his critique of German (and Western) idealism (the primacy of ideas) with *Thoughts on Death and Immortality*, even before Hegel's death. Because, like Marx, he suspected 'ideas'

and rational coherence as such, his works often embody 'aphorisms' rather than elaborate arguments. For the same reason NIETZSCHE would follow the same method in many works. One such aphorism is: 'Humanity is what it eats.' Feuerbach sums up his journey from theology to philosophy; and then from Hegelian idealism to humanistic MATERIALISM in the eloquent aphorism: 'God was my first thought; reason, my second; humankind my third and last thought.'

Many of Feuerbach's aphorisms were explicitly anti-theistic: 'Faith does not solve difficult problems; it only pushes them aside'; (satirical comment on 'Faith moves mountains'); 'Religion once reigned as lord of the head; but its realm is now restricted to the pit of the stomach' (probably aimed at SCHLEIERMACHER). 'What distinguishes the Christian from other honorable people? At most a pious face and parted hair' ('Epigrams' in *Thoughts on Death and Immortality*, Berkeley: University of California, 1980, 189, 191, 205); 'Three things I would not like to be: an old hag, a hack in the academy, and finally a pietist' (ibid., 216); 'Sin came into the world with Christianity' (ibid., 224).

Feuerbach found his studies at Berlin under Schleiermacher 'odious to the point of death'. Schleiermacher taught that the heart of religion was an immediate sense of utter dependence upon God. Christian theology, Feuerbach claimed, simply masked the true human origin of religious belief. It deified a 'God' at the expense of reducing humanity to the unworthy and the finite. 'God' is a mere hypostatization or OBJECTIFICATION of human needs (i.e. needs projected 'out there' onto a 'Being' as 'real' entities).

FEUERBACH'S *ESSENCE OF CHRISTIANITY* (1841)

Theology, then, must be transposed back into 'anthropology', i.e. into the study of humankind. 'God' is not a transcendent reality ('REALISM'), but a product of projected human aspirations ('NON-REA-LISM'). The status of God is not 'objective'.

In reaction against PIETISM and against Schleiermacher, Feuerbach rejected the entire notion of the 'dependence' of a finite humanity upon an infinite God: 'The interest I feel in God's existence is one with the interest I feel in my own existence.' Feuerbach shared with Hegel, with Marx and with Nietzsche the view that critical thought should be liberating: 'God' is to be unmasked as 'a dream of the human mind'.

Feuerbach was assisted in his project by Hegel's questionable maxim that whereas philosophy employed the critical CONCEPT (*Begriff*), religions merely used 'images' (*Vorstellungen*) as proximate, uncritical ways of seeking to express what sometimes lay beyond accurate expression. Thus such an image as 'God is love' may well be a 'religious' but deceptive way of celebrating the infinite power of love. However, this infinity remains a capacity of human nature; it need not be relegated to 'God', as if humanity were incapable of such power and infinite worth by its own nature.

'Religion' becomes a designed celebration of humanness, in which infinite human consciousness becomes transposed into a finite consciousness of the infinite beyond humanity. Humanity's wish-fulfilments result in 'THEISM'. 'Religion is consciousness of the infinite'; but this disguises a human consciousness 'not finite ... but *infinite* ...' (*The Essence of Christianity*, New York: Harper, 1957, 2).

Like Marx, Friedrich Engels and Nietzsche, Feuerbach saw all this as a philosophy of liberation with social and political consequences for the future. The new gospel is true humanism: love of humankind; the unreduced dignity of humankind; faith and trust in unaided humankind only. On the basis of an uncompromisingly materialist view of reality, humankind would not be side-tracked from infinite progress by its own infinite capacities.

CRITIQUE AND ASSESSMENTS

A first problem, which also besets the theories of Freud, is the status of wish-fulfilment for issues of truth and reality. It is entirely the case that merely to wish for something does not bring it into being. Wishes do not amount to claims to truth. Yet the reverse is also the case. It is not true that something cannot exist merely because we also wish and hope for it to exist. In actuality, the status of human wishes remains irrelevant to the ontological status of God, one way or the other. Feuerbach would need to demonstrate that wishes, or projections of God, constitute the exclusive and exhaustive grounds for ascribing ontological reality to God, without remainder.

Further, as BARTH and Dietrich Bonhoeffer insist, a 'God' who accords with human wishes hardly corresponds with the God of the Jewish, Christian or Islamic scriptures. In particular, Bonhoeffer adds, a God who is 'wished for' is not the God of the cross of Jesus Christ: 'If it is I who say where God will be, I will always find there a God who in some way corresponds to me, is agreeable to me'; but the true God 'says where He will be ... That place is the cross of the Christ' (*Meditating on the Word*, Cambridge, MA: Cowley, 1986, 45). The Beatitudes in Matthew 5 do not declare 'Blessed are the powerful', but 'Blessed are the poor ... the pure in heart' (*The Cost of Discipleship*, London: SCM, 1959, 93–176). MOLTMANN similarly defines Christian discipleship as following 'the Way of Jesus Christ' (*The Way of Jesus Christ*, London: SCM, 1990, 210).

A second major problem arises from Feuerbach's claims about the 'infinity' of human consciousness. Hans Küng observes, 'A real infinity of the human being or of the human species and its power ... cannot be accepted without question,' especially since in other contexts Feuerbach infers that reality itself is finite. 'Nowhere did Feuerbach substantiate such an infinity of the human powers ... which would then have no limits ... he assumes it: it appears to be a pure postulate' (*Does God Exist?* London: Collins/Fount, 1980, 206).

Third, it hardly corresponds to the facts to claim with Feuerbach (and with Nietzsche) that religion diminishes the stature of humanity. This is why Moltmann, for example, insists that the gift of the Holy Spirit constitutes 'a universal affirmation' in the face of Nietzsche's claims that the Christian religion is 'world-denying' (*The Spirit of Life: A Universal Affirmation*, London: SCM, 1992, throughout). Courage, venture, loyalty and respect for the other are hallmarks of authentic religion, even if Feuerbach and Nietzsche can readily point to nineteenth-century and earlier historical distortions and abuses of religion.

Barth strongly argues that true humanness is discovered in relation to God. The Jewish philosopher BUBER sees religion as offering a paradigm or model for relating to 'the Other' as a 'Thou' in interpersonal terms of respect, listening and understanding, rather than as an instrumental 'it' in relation to the self. Does 'religion' genuinely and necessarily detract from, and diminish, what is good or noble in human endeavour?

As a critique of idolatrous or manipulative religion, however, Feuerbach's thought contributes a necessary critical dimension to the philosophy of religion. Alternative recounts of the 'origins' of religion to those of classical theism require serious respect and examination.

Fichte, Johann Gottlieb
(1762–1814)

Fichte not only confessed himself an unqualified admirer of KANT, but also, in spite of Kant's apparent indifference to the ideas of the young Fichte at their meeting in 1790, set himself to extend Kant's philosophy a step further. When his name was omitted from his first work (*An Attempt at a Critique of All Revelation*, 1792) and it was mistakenly attributed to Kant, Fichte's reputation as a philosopher was assured.

Fichte became a Professor at Jena in 1794 at the age of thirty-two, with the support of Kant and of Goethe. Developing Kant's notion of the categorical moral imperative, Fichte saw ethics and 'practical reason' as the frame within which religion was to be understood. God remains a principle or presupposition for ethics, rather than a personal Being. 'God' is, in effect, a name for moral order.

At the foundation of the University of Berlin in 1810, Fichte became Dean of the Faculty of Philosophy, when SCHLEIERMACHER became Professor of Theology. Pressing Kant's *Critique of Judgement* radically further than Kant, Fichte saw even the notion of 'necessity' in the world as the creation and projection of human consciousness. SCHELLING described Fichte's thought as 'subjective IDEALISM' (as against his own 'objective' idealism) since the world assumes the status of that which the human mind posits as an act of judgement.

Fichte explored the concept of the 'I' as the principle of this Idealism. Supposed OBJECTIVITY is derived from the SUBJECTIVITY of human ideas as the condition for the possibility of any knowledge. Hence it would not be inappropriate to describe his philosophy as transcendental idealism; for TRANSCENDENTAL PHILOSOPHY (initiated by Kant) asks about the conditions under which knowledge or reason is possible at all.

The most creative theme in Fichte occurs also in HEGEL and in Schleiermacher, in spite of their large differences. SELFHOOD emerges as an intersubjective Phenomenon: the self emerges as 'I' only in relation to other finite rational subjects. This is a turning-point in the history of ideas, which is widely, if still insufficiently, taken for granted today. However, Fichte is often regarded first and foremost as the founder of German idealism.

fideism

The term is generally used pejoratively to denote the view that a given system of religious BELIEFS cannot be tested by any criterion external to itself, including that of rational assessment.

This view has been attributed to Tertullian (*c.* 160–225) and to KIERKEGAARD (1813–55). It is possible that the term was first coined in a positive sense by the French protestant theologian Auguste Sabatier (1839–1901) to denote an emphasis on religious feelings and a relative indifference towards RATIONALISM or the constraints of REASON.

Controversially the term has also been applied to the theology of BARTH (1886–1968) on the ground mainly of his rejection of NATURAL THEOLOGY, and his principle that 'God is known by God alone'. However, his emphasis on the critical function of theology and the complexity of his thought give grounds for hesitation.

Similarly, some claim that WITTGENSTEIN'S view of LANGUAGE GAMES and his hostility to 'theory' rather than description provides grounds for fideistic belief. However, his language games are not self-contained or autonomous, and it is doubtful whether this is more than a possible but one-sided interpretation of his thought.

A variant meaning of the term arises from the condemnation of 'fideism' by Pope Gregory XVI in 1840, against the quasi-mystical thought of Louis Bautain (1796–1867). Bautain rejected rational argument as a basis for belief, on the ground that faith and feeling alone are adequate for knowledge of God. (See AUTONOMY; MYSTICISM; REASONABLENESS).

Five Ways of Thomas Aquinas

These have been introduced under GOD, ARGUMENTS FOR THE EXISTENCE OF, which provides a broader introduction to this subject. We noted there his statement

that 'there are five ways in which one can prove that there is a God' (Latin, *Dicendum quod Deum esse quinque viis probari potest*, in *Summa Theologiae,* Ia, Qu. 2, art. 3).

The five 'ways' operate as A POSTERIORI arguments from our experience of the everyday world. The first three constitute, in effect, different, versions of the COSMOLOGICAL ARGUMENT for the existence of God. The fourth way argues from gradations or degrees of being, to the notion of a 'superlative', or ultimate, who is God. The fifth way argues from the 'ordered' or purposive character of the world to an intelligent creator or designer whom we call God. Thus the fifth way constitutes a version of the TELEOLOGICAL ARGUMENT for the existence of God.

THE FIRST WAY

The first way is variously described as the argument from change or movement (*motus*) within the world, but in view of AQUINAS'S conscious revival of Aristotelian thought may more accurately be regarded as an argument from potentiality. The Latin *motus* is broader than 'movement'. The traditional name, the kinetological argument, simply reflects the Greek word for motion, from which our term 'kinetic energy' is also derived. Whatever is in motion, or in a process of change, within the world, has been set in motion by something else. Thus, for example, wood has the potentiality to become heated and to burn to ash, but it is fire that causes this to occur. The actuality (*in actu*) of burning cannot at the very same time (*simul*) be the potentiality (*in potentia*). 'We must stop somewhere, otherwise there will be no first cause of the change, and as a result no subsequent causes.' This first cause of change or movement is 'not itself changed by anything, and this is what everybody understands by God' (*Summa Theologiae,* Blackfriars edn, 15, Ia, Qu. 2, art. 3).

In his earlier work *Summa contra Gentiles* Aquinas appeals in more detail

to ARISTOTLE (*Physics*, H 241b–242b) for
reasons why an infinite series of CON-
TINGENT CAUSES cannot be postulated. In
the pre-modern world this argument
seemed to carry perhaps the most weight
of the five, but it has been argued in
recent times that NEWTON's law concerning motion 'wrecks the argument of the
First Way ... Uniform motion of a body
can be explained by the principle of
inertia in terms of a body's own previous
motion without appeal to any other
agent' (A. Kenny, *The Five Ways*, London: Routledge, 1969, 28). Further,
BERGSON (1859–1941) and WHITEHEAD
(1861–1947) argue philosophically that
process is fundamental both to the world
and to God, and in Christian theology
MOLTMANN (b. 1926) argues that the
ongoing living God of the Bible is not
simply the static 'changeless' God of
philosophical theism.

THE SECOND WAY

This rests on an exploration of the relation
between cause and effect. Strictly Aquinas
appeals to efficient cause, as against
formal or final cause, and this is sometimes known as the aetiological argument
(from Greek *aitía*, cause). Aetiology often
seeks causes 'behind' effects, characteristically to do with origins. For Aquinas 'a
series of causes must ... stop somewhere'
(*Summa Theologiae*, Ia, Qu. 3, art. 3):
'*Non est possibile quod ... procedatur in
infinitum.*' Therefore we are forced to
suppose 'some first cause, to which everyone gives the name God (*aliquam causam
efficientem primam, quam omnes Deum
nominant*)'.

As first cause, God does not only
initiate causal processes, but also keeps
them in being. In BARTH's language, God
holds his creation 'from the abyss of non-
being' (*Church Dogmatics*, I: 1, Edinburgh: T & T Clark, 1975, 388). The
rejection of an infinite chain of caused
causes closely parallels the argument of
the Islamic philosopher IBN SINA (or
Avicenna, 980–1037).

On whether an infinite chain of causes
can be plausible see the entry on the
cosmological argument. One dilemma that
emerges is that if 'God' as first cause is
conceived of as the beginning or end of the
chain of caused causes, God appears to be
located conceptually 'within' the world; if
God is 'above' the causal chain, how does
God's agency operate and have we now
also changed the meaning of 'cause'?
Further, from an empiricist standpoint
HUME (1711–76) argued that what we
observe is not efficient cause but only
constant conjunctions of events.

From the standpoint of CRITICAL PHI-
LOSOPHY, KANT (1724–1804) viewed
cause–effect as structural categories
imposed on what we observe in order that
the human mind can order what it
perceives by means of intelligible concepts. 'CATEGORIES' derive from human
judgements. They are 'regulative', not
'constitutive' of the world itself. Recently,
Anthony Kenny has argued that the
second way involves 'equivocation
between "first = earlier" and "first =
unprecedented" to show that this series
[of causes] cannot be an infinite one' (*The
Five Ways*, 44).

THE THIRD WAY

The argument depends on the distinction
between possible or contingent and NECES-
SARY objects, persons or states of affairs. In
the language of Aquinas, 'the third way is
based on what need not be (Latin, *ex
possibili*) and on what must be (*necessario*)'. If every object or event were
contingent (i.e. might or might not be or
have been), or subject to generation and to
corruption, we could in principle go back
far enough in time to reach a state of affairs
in which nothing existed. However, the
totality of all that exists cannot be of this
kind, for if this entailed the non-existence
of everything at any point, however
remote, nothing could subsequently have
come into existence. 'One is forced, therefore, to suppose something which must be
of itself (*ponere aliquid quod est per se*

necessarium)'. Such a thing (God) necessarily exists 'of itself' (Latin *a se esse* gives rise to the philosophical notion of ASEITY (i.e. having its own necessary ground).

The distinctions between the first three ways are fine. The first hinges on potentiality to become; the second, also on efficient cause to maintain in being; the third concerns all contingent, possible, or finite being as a whole. Kenny argues that their apparent failure lies in the extent to which they are rooted in the conceptual assumptions of the medieval cosmology of the day.

All the same, by the beginning of the modern era some thinkers were still developing these arguments. Samuel Clarke (1675–1729) focuses especially on a re-formulation of this third way. He considers the status of '*all* things that are or ever were in the universe ... The whole cannot be necessary'. Hence he postulates 'one immutable and independent being' (*A Discourse Concerning Natural Religion*, 1705). More recently Richard Taylor (b. 1919) has argued that whatever the argument might appear to claim about an act of creation, the heart of the matter is to expose the issue of dependence on the part of finite or contingent being (*Metaphysics*, 3rd edn Englewood Cliffs, NJ: Prentice Hall, 1983). In contrast to the phenomenon of dependence in the world, it is not irrational to conceive of a Being who is dependent on nothing other than itself. On the other hand MILL (1806–73) insisted that an infinite regress of finite causes is more reasonable than the notion of a 'first' cause.

THE FOURTH WAY

This also begins (*a posteriori*) from our experience of the everyday world. In everyday experience we come across degrees of beauty, degrees of intelligence, degrees of truth, degrees of size or weight. The argument is based 'on the gradation found in things (*ex gradibus qui in rebus inveniuntur*)'. This is often called the henological argument.

PLATO believed that relative degrees of gradation or attributes in the world pointed to a 'superlative' or perfect Form or Idea. However, for Artistotle things rather than Ideas or Forms exist, and Aquinas follows the logic of Aristotle to argue that the superlative 'highest degree' to which other things approximate (*appropinquant*) in varying degrees is 'therefore something that is the truest and best ... and most in being (*igitur aliquid quod est maxim verissimum et optimum et ... maxime ens*)'. 'This we call God.'

This argument brings us at once into the complexities of an ancient logical debate about the status of UNIVERSALS (derived especially from Plato's realm of Ideas). By contrast, NOMINALISM perceives these not as real entities, but as names or semantic constructs used to denote classes rather than particulars. The debate between nominalists and realists became acute in the Middle Ages.

WITTGENSTEIN (1889–1951) suggests that Platonic Forms and Ideas (cf. Aquinas's superlatives) may constitute paradigm cases of what makes the quality or attribute what it is. Many believe that the formulation of Aquinas owes too much to Plato's theory, in spite of his normally Aristotelian sympathies. It has been argued that so great is his debt here to ANSELM'S prior notion of God as Universal that this fourth way constitutes a (disguised?) version of the A PRIORI ontological argument, even though Aquinas begins with degrees of attributes within the world.

Many theists regard the fourth way as failing to provide an argument for divine existence, but as underlining both continuities and contrasts between the character of God and certain related qualities found within the everyday world. Other theists, however, question whether the 'bottom up' use of analogy does adequate justice to the transcendence or otherness of God, from whom human qualities in a fallen world are both derivative and for the most part flawed (see ANALOGY; LANGUAGE IN RELIGION).

THE FIFTH WAY

This is the version of the teleological argument for the existence of God advocated by Aquinas. It is 'based on the guidedness (or governance) of things in the world (ex gubernatione rerum)'. Aquinas believed that events and states of affairs within the world do not occur by chance or accident (non a casu), 'but tend to a goal (sed ex intentione perveniunt ad finem)'. Hence, just as a purposive occurrence such as the flight of an arrow presupposes an archer, so everything in nature (omnes res naturales) is directed to its goal (ordinantur ad finem) by someone with understanding.

Aquinas appeals to Augustine for his view of God's 'ordering' the world in sovereign goodness (Enchiridion, XI). 'Nature (natura) works for a determinate end at the direction of a higher agent', whom Aquinas identifies both as 'God' and as 'the first of all causes ... unchangeable and self-necessary' (immobile et per se necessariium).

The validity of this approach is discussed below in the entry on the teleological argument. The three most problematic general factors arise from Hume's empiricist critique of causality (on which this argument still rests); on KANT's notion that 'order' is seen to be an organizing or regulative category constructed or construed by the human mind; and the developmental BEHAVIOURISM of which DARWIN's theory of evolution is the most influential popular example.

More specifically to Aquinas is his notion of 'natural law', drawn in part from Aristotle and the STOIC notion of ius naturale. Aquinas expounds his notion of law as 'an ordinance of practical reason' in which 'the whole universe is governed by the divine reason ... the eternal law ... natural law' in Summa Theologiae, Ia/Iiae, Qu. 90–1, esp. Qu. 91, arts. 1–3 (Blackfriars edn, vol. 28). The difficulties of this

specific tradition should not, however, detract from the teleological argument as reformulated by more recent writers. Again we allude to Kenny's claim that many of their limitations, even failures, arise from their rootedness in the medieval cosmology of the day. They represent a significant stage in an ongoing debate about the status of the three main arguments for the existence of God, which has not yet reached a definitive conclusion. (See also EMPIRICISM; POSSIBILITY; REALISM; THEISM.)

Foucault, Michel (1926–84)

Foucault, French postmodernist and philosopher, believed that systems of knowledge served, and were served by, systems of power. He was particularly concerned with systems of bureaucratic and social control, or 'regimes'. He calls in question the 'innocence' of 'thinking' in DESCARTES: 'I think' already operates within a pre-given situatedness that belongs to an 'order of things', with its power and control (The Order of Things, New York: Random House, 1970, 324; French, Les mots et les choses, 1966).

The way in which social control shapes concepts is illustrated in Foucault's A History of Madness (1961) translated into English as Madness and Civilization (1965). In classical Greece and Rome, madness was perceived as 'unreason'. Most 'mad' people were treated as irrational animals; a few were regarded as 'inspired'. By the nineteenth century madness was perceived as a mental illness, and asylums were initially intended as places of sanctuary. In Marxist regimes in the Eastern bloc, 'madness' was attributed to those whose views deviated from supposed public norms of 'reality', namely dissidents.

In his middle period Foucault published Discipline and Punish (1975; English, 1977). 'Surveillance' is the power-tool of the prison service, the police, the army, hospital authorities. Manipulation may be disguised by 'the smiling face in the white coat', but privileged information gives power for control. There is no room for negotiation, for bureaucrats hold all the cards.

The late period concludes with *The History of Sexuality* (3 vols., 1976–84). Individuals, Foucault argued, are controlled in part by self-perception and self-scrutiny, but these are distorted perceptions inherited from society. A comparison with Greek and Roman sexuality reveals the socially CONTINGENT nature of sexual CONCEPTS. These are masked as 'unsurpassable' by those whose power-interests cohere with them.

Much of Foucault's work reveals the influence of NIETZSCHE (1844–1900). This is strengthened with a rhetoric of POSTMODERNITY and a theory of social constructionism. All the same, Foucault takes his place alongside the 'masters of suspicion' (MARX, Nietzsche and FREUD), in identifying a false innocence in much traditional EPISTEMOLOGY, and its individualism.

foundationalism

The proper context of the word is that of epistemic justification, or issues in the justification of BELIEF. Foundationalists see a belief-system as like a building that rests upon a set of 'basic' or 'foundational' beliefs. These are self-evident or self-justifying. Hence other 'non-basic' beliefs will be justified beliefs (or 'entitled' beliefs) if they may be inferred from, or are otherwise supported by, these basic, foundational beliefs. The belief-system will, in effect, take the form of a tiered hierarchy.

TWO TYPES OF FOUNDATIONALISM?

DESCARTES (1596–1650) provides a model for foundationalist RATIONALISM. He sought TRUTH that is 'absolutely indubitable'; 'truth so certain that sceptics were not capable of shaking it' (*Discourse on Method*, pt IV, 53–4). This begins from the

'self-evident' knowledge that Descartes is aware of himself thinking (*cogito*, ibid., 53), on the basis of which it is also demonstrable that he exists (*ergo sum*, ibid.).

By contrast, human opinions offer 'little basis for certainty' (ibid., I, 33). Descartes in fact uses the very metaphors of 'foundation' and 'house'. 'Once in a lifetime' we must demolish the house and 'start right from the foundations' (*Meditations*, La Salle: Open Court, 1901, II, 31). In principle belief in God is also 'an indubitable idea', although this may be clouded by human prejudice (*Meditations*, V).

Descartes is foundationalist in the full sense of the term. However, is his the only possible kind of foundationalism?

PLANTINGA (b. 1932) and WOLTERSTORFF (b. 1932) see Descartes as a 'classical', 'narrow', or 'strong' foundationalist. Plantinga points out that 'Reformed EPISTEMOLOGY' arose as a response to the challenge of evidentialism, i.e. the demand that BELIEF is supported or warranted by demonstrable evidence. Otherwise, it was claimed, it is not 'reasonable' or 'entitled' belief. Theists in the Reformed tradition argue that if theistic belief has itself to be 'based upon' some prior evidential or rational datum, belief in God has been redefined as other than 'basic' for the theist.

Hence Plantinga proposes a 'softer' or 'broader foundationalism' that postulates not prior or 'basic' beliefs of demonstrable certainty but a 'basic' belief in God which retains rationality or 'REASONABLENESS' on its own ground. WOLTERSTORFF was earlier perhaps less committed to speaking positively of foundationalism, but by the 1990s expressed strong sympathy with the broader 'foundationalism' of LOCKE (1632–1704). Wolterstorff 'had attacked' classical foundationalism, but subsequently observed: 'Our attack remained too superficial' (*John Locke and the Ethics of Belief*, Cambridge: CUP, 1996, xi). He adds, 'In Locke's foundationalism there is revealed, more clearly than in Descartes, that depth for which I was looking' (ibid.).

In spite of differences of emphasis between Plantinga and Wolterstorff, both might very broadly be described as 'broad', 'soft', or perhaps 'quasi'-foundationalists. They avoid the supposed 'demonstrable certainties' of either RATIONALISM (which implies a NATURAL THEOLOGY) or of empirical evidentialism. Both of the latter would impose a 'basicality' more foundational than theistic belief. Nevertheless they reject the claim that belief in God is groundless or irrational.

ANTI-FOUNDATIONALISM AND NON-FOUNDATIONALISM

It might seem surprising that Plantinga and Wolterstorff seek so carefully to rescue a version of foundationalism, until we note what 'anti-foundationalism' and 'non-foundationalism' usually denote in America. Anti-foundationalism is too often taken to imply either FIDEISM, relativism or a rejection of epistemology, often on the basis of POSTMODERNISM. Some promote a 'narrative theology' which transposes ontological and epistemological truth-claims about God into narratives about theistic communities.

This kind of shift is as far from traditional THEISM as 'hard' or 'classical' foundationalism is in the opposite direction. In Britain regret is sometimes expressed that these terms are used so widely, and often in dubious contexts, in America. Yet, given their prevalence, it is valuable to have precision from Plantinga and Wolterstorff, and their attempts at what looks like a necessary middle ground for rational theists.

It is not clear, however, what we might conclusively infer from Plantinga's discussion of criteria for 'basicality'. While he rejects the rationality of a hypothetical belief in 'the Great Pumpkin', he defends the theist's 'reasonable belief', but 'not ... on the basis of other propositions' (A.

Plantinga and N. Wolterstorff, eds., *Faith and Rationality*, Notre Dame: University of Notre Dame, 1983).

While a 'coherence' view of TRUTH would normally not readily find room even for 'soft' foundationalism, other models have also been suggested. WITTGENSTEIN'S model of the 'nest of propositions' may allow for a 'basic' interweaving, to which more things could be added. The nest collapses if too much is taken away. A 'soft' coherence dimension holds it together, supported by the basic materials with which it began.

Yet too much should not be read from a metaphor or simile. It is worth recalling that Descartes' house and foundations also remain a metaphor. The tendency to use this terminology to force a heated polemic over epistemic justification may at times distract participants from the actual job in hand. To debate the status of natural theology or the grounds for reasonable BELIEF is the prior objective, and perhaps may not require these labels. (*See also* CERTAINTY AND DOUBT; REVELATION; SCEPTICISM.)

freedom

Freedom is defined and understood differently, sometimes by different thinkers, sometimes in different universes of discourse. Freedom generally denotes the capacity to act without external compulsion, constraint or coercion. Yet this does not address the question of whether a given individual, unfettered by external coercion, is also free to choose any course of action unfettered by internal constraints upon that individual's will to choose.

Larger philosophical issues are raised by the relation between freedom and DETERMINISM. Most people are likely to accept responsibility for an action only if they believe that they could have acted otherwise. Yet some hold a determinist view that whatever occurs is determined by a chain of antecedent CAUSES or conditions. 'Hard' determinists who believe that determinism excludes freedom are often designated as 'incompatabilists'.

By contrast, 'compatabilists' argue that sufficient freedom of action to give currency to moral responsibility does not exclude every kind of determinism. Yet often determinism erodes the concept of freedom to some such concept (among some compatibilists) as 'free to choose in accordance with the agent's desires or character'. AUGUSTINE (354–430) sees no reason to 'think our free will is opposed to God's foreknowledge' (*On Free Will*, III: 4: 10).

CONCEPTS OF FREEDOM

In practice, at least three distinct concepts of freedom are held. The liberty of indifference denotes the view that an agent is free to choose either of two or more alternative courses of action, in effect in virtual equilibrium. Augustine ascribes such a freedom to humankind before the Fall, but argues that the presence of sin in the world suggests a need to modify this definition. Meanwhile, 'it is a sufficient reason why [humankind] ought to have been given it [freedom], because without it humankind could not live aright' (*ibid.*, II: 1: 3). Pelagius (*c.* 360–*c.* 420) believed that all persons possess this freedom of equilibrium.

Liberty of choice (sometimes called liberty of spontaneity) denotes the freedom to express the agent's choice, desire, will or character, even if internal habits, predispositions or concerns shape the nature of this choice. This view is compatible with notions of AUTONOMY: the emphasis is upon self-direction. AQUINAS writes, 'Man has free choice, or otherwise counsels, exhortations, commands ... would be in vain' (*Summa Theologiae,* Ia, Qu. 83, art. 1).

The relation between character, habit, will, wish and desire makes this complex. An agent may make a 'free' choice, and observe, 'I was not "myself" when I decided to do that.' Do circumstances that encourage action 'out of character' constitute an external constraint?

In theology and ETHICS freedom is often defined in terms of freedom to do the good, in contrast to that which proves harmful or self-destructive. Augustine defines as the 'purpose for which God gave free will' as 'in order to do right' (*On Free Will*, II: 1: 3). Aquinas declares that GRACE enables choice; sin restricts choice (*Summa Theologiae*, Ia, Qu. 83, arts. 2–4).

free-will defence

The free-will defence provides a response to issues that arise from the problem of EVIL, and finds classic expression in AUGUSTINE (340–430) and Thomas AQUINAS (1225–74). Evil, these theologians argue, is not the responsibility of God, for it originates in 'a wilful turning of the self in desire from the highest good ... It is the evil will which causes the evil act ...' (Augustine, *City of God*, XII. 6).

God gave free will to humankind as a gift to provide the possibility of doing right. However, by definition such free will thereby also permits the possibility (but not necessarily also the actuality) of evil choice. 'God's gifts are good gifts', but humankind may choose to misuse them for purposes for which they were not given. 'God compels no-one to sin ... Our will would not be "will" unless it were in our power' (*On Free Will*, III: 3: 8).

Over the years, many, including especially PLANTINGA, have supported and developed the free-will defence argument. Yet J.L. Mackie insists, 'All forms of the free will defence fail' (*The Miracle of Theism*, Oxford: Clarendon, 1982, 176). Mackie notes that reluctance to accept DETERMINISM often arises from the belief that if my actions were 'predictable' they would seem not 'to stem *from* my will', but to 'be mediated *through* it' (ibid., 169).

Such an assumption, Mackie argues, is mistaken. An action is not '*more* mine' if no causes that could make it predictable can be identified (ibid.). For example, a couple may freely reach 'their own' decision to marry each other, yet all of

their close friends could have predicted
what would occur. For God to create
Adam and Eve was 'a hell of a risk',
Mackie observes, when divine foreknowledge would tell what (at least) might
occur, and a more restricted 'freedom'
could have ensured conditions for 'right
action' with less risk (ibid., 162–76).

Nevertheless, others reject the notion
of 'freedom' that would be entailed if 'all
people freely to choose to do the right'.
Perhaps the analysis of 'concepts' of freedom (above) does not go far enough.
Colin Gunton argues that the 'freedom'
given by God as gift entails 'space between
God and the world whereby God, by his
action, enables the world to be truly itself',
but in terms of 'personal integrity' for
human agents that 'gives due place to the
other'. For 'freedom' is most constructively defined 'as for and (deriving) from
the other' (God and Freedom, Edinburgh:
T & T Clark, 1995, 132, 133).

HICK and Vincent Brümmer also retain
a personal, or interpersonal, focus in this
context, while Hick explores the related
concept of 'epistemic distance' (Hick, Evil
and the God of Love, London: Macmillan,
1966 and 1977; Brümmer, Speaking of a
Personal God, Cambridge: CUP, 1992,
128–51). Brümmer believes that attacks
upon the free-will defence are misplaced
when they fail to see 'that the free-will
defence is based on the love of God rather
than the supposed intrinsic value of
human freedom and responsibility' (ibid.,
144). (See also SWINBURNE.)

Freud's critique of religion

Sigmund Freud (1856–1939) developed the
theory and medical practice of psychoanalysis in Vienna, which centred on probing
beneath consciousness and more shallow
explanations of human behaviour to pre-
conscious and unconscious drives and conflicts. These seemed to offer more probing
explanations for human desires and actions.

Pre-conscious drives are construed by
Freud in naturalistic or, in effect,

mechanistic terms. He criticizes the view
that people 'make[s] the forces of nature
... into persons ... [even] into gods' (The
Future of an Illusion, London: Hogarth
Press, 1962, 13).

Freud was led to psychoanalysis through
a study of hysteria. In particular he
explored the effects of hypnosis on this
condition. His first main work was published co-jointly with J. Breuer under the
title Studies in Hysteria (1895). This was
soon followed by The Interpretation of
Dreams (1899). Here Freud postulated that
what rises to expression in dreams provides
a mid-point of access to unconscious desires
and conflicts through the interpretation or
hermeneutical process of 'unscrambling'
what a person recounts as 'the dream'.

The dream-as-dreamed, however ('the
dream-thoughts'), is transposed by the
human mind into the 'dream-as-remem-
bered' ('the dream-content'). This serves
to hide the true desires or conflicts that
may become exposed in the dream.
Thereby they are hidden both from the
self and from the psychiatrist.

Hence the dream-content may be a
'condensation' of the dream-thoughts. It
may be edited to make it 'brief, meagre,
and laconic', and may embody 'displace-
ments' of sequences and images for the
purpose of disguise. 'Psychoanalysis' seeks
to recover the deeper 'text' below the
dream-content, or dream-as-recounted.

NEUROSIS, DISGUISE, AND PSYCHOAN-
ALYSIS: THE EGO AND THE ID

In an incisive appreciation and critique
of Freud, RICOEUR points out that Freud
evolves, in an effect, a hermeneutics of
suspicion (Freud and Philosophy: An
Essay in Interpretation, New Haven:
Yale, 1970). Freud takes psychological
data that are capable of being interpreted at a number of levels, in a number
of ways, and sometimes many times over
(technically, 'overdetermined texts') and
seeks to get to the bottom of what is
really being 'said' (the sub-text, or deep
text).

The problem, from the point of view of THEISM or RELIGION, is that Freud regards these drives or disguised motivativations as purely 'forces', or the product of forces. Such psychological processes as repression, displacement or the investing of energies in another are regarded as bio-physical forces. Hence Freud borrows such a term as 'cathexis' from economics to denote 'investing' sexual energy in another person.

On the other side, Freud convincingly exposes the 'opaqueness' of human consciousness, even to the self. The self is driven by drives and desires that it seeks to hide and to disguise even from itself. This raises no difficulty for theism or for religion. The Hebrew scriptures and Paul the Apostle concur that the human heart deceives both itself and others about its motives and intentions (Jer. 17:9; Rom. 7:11; 1 Cor. 4:4, 5). Freud saw the unconscious as 'the centre of resistance of truth'.

Why should the unconscious constitute a mechanism of disguise and deceit? This emerges in Freud's middle and later works, including *Totem and Taboo* (1912–13), *The Ego and the Id* (1923) and *The Future of an Illusion* (1927). The 'superego' acts as a censor or moral judge that reflects the expectations of society (in childhood years, of parents and teachers). The 'id' is the source of the drives of the libido into the psyche. It energizes the self especially through sexual energy and desire.

The third factor within the self is the 'ego', the rational, conscious self that is torn by conflict and by pressure, on one side to obey the directions of the superego as censor and judge; on the other side, by the powerful drives of the id to seek satisfaction for the sexual energies and drives that power it.

When this conflict becomes sufficiently acute to cause discomfort and potential damage, this condition is one of 'neurosis'. The person needs treatment and therapy as a 'neurotic' patient. Although it may be healthy to 'suppress' (i.e. to channel, control or sublimate) desires that are unacceptable to society, the 'repression' of such desires and drives (i.e. pressing them down into pre-conscious depths until they are hidden from self-awareness) causes damaging neurosis.

Psychoanalysis uses the interpretation of dreams, explorations of early childhood 'memories', and 'free association', to trigger unconscious 'give-aways'. These produce awareness of disguises and conflicts. This process may be painful; but only if the source of neurosis and its condition are recognized can the neurotic conflict of opposing forces that saps the energies of the self begin therapeutic resolution.

Without such psychoanalytical therapy the repressed content of the mind festers away, preventing sublimation (or creative re-channelling) of these frustrated desires into more fruitful goals pursued by a united self. Looking to his early work on hysteria, Freud diagnoses hysteria as a frequent effect of the emotional shock produced by a collision between deeply repressed wishes within the self.

RELIGION AS A 'UNIVERSAL OBSESSIONAL NEUROSIS OF HUMANKIND'?

All of the above considerations set the stage for understanding the nature of Freud's critique of religion. Religions, especially theism, provide a mechanism, Freud claims, for projecting the inner conflicts of neurosis upwards and outwards away from the self.

This cannot offer a 'final' or authentic solution, because in Freud's view religion tries to solve a problem of disguise by means of the even deeper disguise that projects inner states into a god-figure. This occurs in religious MYTHS and stories. However, if religion appears to 'comfort' some, this is because it may soften, or seem superficially to soften, the neurotic conflict that would otherwise be unbearable.

By initial over-simplification (qualified below) we might say that in infancy the

human person may project upwards or
outwards on one side the sanctions and
discipline represented by the figure of the
father-parent, and on the other side the
father-figure's love and protection. The
father's affirmation of both the superego
and also in part certain desires for the
gratification of the self (food, protection,
comfort, security) are projected onto a
'God' of judgement and grace. The father
who gazes into the cradle is magnified into
infinity as 'God'.

However, Freud's hypotheses are more
complex than this. In accordance with the
intellectual fashions of the late nineteenth
and early twentieth centuries, Freud draws
heavily on developmental and evolutionary theories of the human race and of the
individual. 'Religion' is associated with
the 'infantile' stage of human person, and
also with the stage of totem and taboo in
the evolution of the human race. Each of
these draws upon 'myth'.

In relation to the infant Freud appeals
to the Oedipus myth, in which the 'hero'
of the myth directs sexual desire (unconsciously) to his mother, and kills the father
who stands in his way. The father-figure is
ambivalent: on one side, a source of help
and love; on the other, a threat to
independence and self-gratification. Submission and rebellion struggle. Hence the
projection of the 'God-figure' permits
'forgiveness' for sexual and self-centred
desires and gives help and grace, while the
'worshipper' regresses into childhood
dependency.

RELIGION, INFANTILE REGRESSION
AND HUMAN MATURITY

In his earliest writings Freud allowed
himself to speculate about repressed memories of pre-pubertal sexual assaults by
fathers, which gave rise to hysteria until
psychoanalysis yielded the 'cathartic dis-
charge' of the disguised, buried conflict-
traumas. He later abandoned this theory,
but remained convinced that psychic
energy arose primarily from sexual desire.
Life-force is Eros. His theories demand the

recognition of infantile sexuality. 'The
Oedipus complex' denotes sexual feelings
toward the parent of the opposite sex.

Freud also elaborated a corporate
socio-historical theory at the level of the
human race rather than the individual. He
acknowledged that he was attracted by the
theories of DARWIN and SPENCER on
EVOLUTION. Further, the works of E.B.
Tylor on cultural anthropology, W.
Robertson Smith on totemism and J.G.
Frazer on 'primitive' religion provided
fertile soil for Freud's theories. In 1907
Freud argued that religious rites are
similar to neurotic obsessive actions,
working this out in *Totem and Taboo*.

The 'totem' animal protects the primitive tribe or group; on the other side
murder and incest constitute the main
prohibited 'taboos'. This appeared to
Freud to offer an ethnological parallel to
the duality and conflict of the infantile
Oedipus myth and Oedipus complex.

The strength and power of human
wishes may generate 'illusion', but not
'delusion' (difference explained below). If
religion utilizes such illusion to soften the
conflicts of neurosis, the price that is paid
is the tendency towards infantile regression. This may include 'longing for a
father ... [as] defence against childish
helplessness' (*The Future of an Illusion*,
20). This may hinder genuine maturity
and growth.

Yet in his latest writings Freud does not
presume to pronounce on the truth or
falsehood of these 'illusions'. Illusions are
without foundation, but they are not false
delusions. 'To assess the truth-value of
religious doctrine does not lie within the
scope of the present enquiry. It is enough
for us that we have recognized them as . . .
illusions' (ibid., 29).

DIFFICULTIES ABOUT SOME OF
FREUD'S CLAIMS

It cannot be denied that many religious
people show signs of regression into
immature attitudes. Faith may serve as a
psychological crutch, as NIETZSCHE also

observed. However, it is not the case that this applies to all, or even perhaps to most, religious people, or that it begins to approach the stereotypical.

Dietrich Bonhoeffer insists that Christian people, for example, would never choose a religion of the cross to gain 'comfort'; it serves the reverse: the nurture of courage, affirmation of life, and living life to the full in the service of the other. MOLTMANN responds in the same way. The life of the Spirit, he asserts, is one of 'universal affirmation' to life; not of retreat or self-protection.

Second, speculation about a father-figure cuts both ways. It is well known that Freud had a damaged relationship with his own father. Might his own account of religion, on his own premises, have something to do with expelling 'the Father' from the realm of ontological truth-claims as a wish-fulfilment?

Third, a counter-reply would apply both to the second point and to Freud's entire theories. As he came to see at the close of his career, does wishing either for the truth or for the falsity or of religion, make any difference at all to its actual status as true or false? Does it offer a criterion about 'illusion'?

Fourth, the first point may be extended to emphasize the enormous variety of temperaments, psychological conditions, expectations, personal histories and ethnic histories of those who are 'religious'. Can all these diverse characterizations fit into the category of neurosis and obsession concerning which Freud speculates?

Fifth, Freud is too heavily influenced by the naturalistic bioneurological explanations and metaphors which he assimilated from Breuer, and subsequently only marginally modifies. Can the human mind be 'explained' exhaustively as a neurological cause–effect mechanism? Even if Freud at times seeks to go beyond the neuro-physiological to the genuinely psychological, how far does he succeed in recognizing the genuine agency of human persons as human persons?

SOME FURTHER ASSESSMENTS

Freud does not carefully compare alternative models of the nature of religion. His views remain selective and speculative. This does not detract from, or fail to recognize, the huge advance in understanding that Freud made possible, and on which others have built. It cannot be denied that human wishes and motivations are often disguised. Indeed religions, as we have noted, often agree on this point. Further, the dividing-line between 'child-like' and 'childish' is often misjudged in religion.

Alfred Adler (1870–1937) and JUNG (1875–1961) also offer very different accounts of the 'drives' and desires of human persons. Adler ascribes this not to the urges of the id which are in conflict with the superego, but to a striving for power. Neurosis arises from a sense of inferiority. Jung stresses even more strongly the interpretation of human 'wholeness', and offers a more constructive account of religion as furthering this integration.

As in our assessment of Nietzsche, we may acknowledge the contribution of both thinkers as 'masters of suspicion' in exposing abuses and manipulative strategies in some forms of religion. This has provoked such thinkers as Bonhoeffer and Moltmann to respond with sober critiques of inauthentic religion. Nevertheless, as Freud seemed to recognize in his latest writings, it falls beyond the scope of empirical sciences to offer a definitive verdict on the truth or falsity of religion as an ontological world-view. Freud's empirical observations remain valuable, but are certainly not an exhaustive account of 'religion'.

Although other schools of psychology and psychiatry have overtaken much of Freud's theory, the clock can never be put back behind his influential work, whatever the evaluation of details.

Constructive and sympathetic critiques of Freud's critique can be found in

Ricoeur's *Freud and Philosophy*, and Hans Küng, *Does God Exist?* (London: Collins/ Fount, 1980), 262–340; also Küng, *Freud and the Problem of God* (New Haven: Yale, 1979). Küng cites Freud's own 'modest' admission that he provides only 'some psychological foundation' to FEUERBACH'S materialist and anti-theistic theory of projection.

Küng comments, 'Freud took over from Feuerbach ... the essential arguments for his personal atheism (*Freud and the Problem of God*, 75). Küng adds, 'No conclusions can be drawn about the existence or non-existence of God'. Even if some religions may be illusions, 'it need not be' (ibid., 77). 'A real God may correspond to the wish for God' (ibid., 78).

Religion is more than a quest for the satisfaction of personal needs, and where 'religion' is understood mistakenly in this way, a critique of such religion is required. We have noted that in the case of Christian religion, Bonhoeffer and Moltmann, among others, have provided such incisive critiques. (*See also* EMPIRICISM; HERMENEUTICS; ONTOLOGY; SCIENCE.)

G

Gadamer, Hans-Georg
(1900–2002)

Together with RICOEUR Gadamer is one of the two most influential writers on HERMENEUTICS in the twentieth century. His importance for philosophy of religion is manifold, but three points deserve particular note.

First, like HEGEL and HEIDEGGER (under whom he studied) Gadamer insists that knowledge and understanding are rooted in time and history. Second, he distinguishes between technical 'reason' for functional tasks and 'wisdom' (*phronêsis*), which is generated by corporate historical experience and transmitted in terms of its effects within tradition. Third, he stands at the border between ENLIGHTENMENT RATIONALISM and POSTMODERNITY, viewing neither as adequate.

In his earlier writings Gadamer produced a number of studies of PLATO, in which he emphasized the productive importance of asking questions. This also shows the importance of DIALECTIC in the sense of conversation. Bare propositions may lend themselves to abuse as propaganda; 'the logic of question and answer' gives rise to exploratory discovery.

Gadamer's most widely read and influential work is *Truth and Method* ([1960];

Eng. 2nd edn (from Ger. 5th edn.), London: Sheed & Ward, 1989). He uses the word 'method' negatively and ironically to indicate that the method of 'science' from DESCARTES to the Enlightenment lays down criteria of rationality in advance of specific historical situations of enquiry in life, and thereby restricts and distorts dimensions of understanding that may surpass these criteria.

In part I of *Truth and Method* Gadamer compares the shallower individualistic 'Cartesian' or 'Enlightenment' rationalist tradition with deeper, community-orientated, historical understanding, from Roman times to Vico and beyond. Being immersed in a work of art or in play offers a richer paradigm within which the art or play 'speaks' as subject, unrestricted by the prior dictates of individual consciousness. 'Art cannot be defined as an OBJECT of aesthetic consciousness ... It is part of the event of being that occurs in presentation' (ibid., 116). 'Play draws him [the player] into ... a reality that surpasses him' (ibid., 109). Art, not the mind, becomes the active, transformative, 'SUBJECT'.

In part II Gadamer traces the 'prehistory' of hermeneutics in ROMANTICISM, SCHLEIERMACHER and Dilthey, and its blossoming in Heidegger. The key notion of the 'history of effects' of successive processes of understanding (German, *Wirkungsgeschichte*, often translated 'effective history') takes account of historical distance between different times, but also permits a partial 'fusion of horizons' between those of the person who seeks to understand (including his or her agenda of questions) and the horizons of that of which understanding is sought. This history of effects traces a relatively stable core of TRADITION.

In part III Gadamer explores the nature of language as that which is both inherited and transmitted as an ontological 'given' (as well as shaped and shaping) that is always on the move. It provides the 'universal' horizon within which historical and finite particular events, texts, objects or persons are understood.

It is widely recognized that Gadamer succeeds in calling into question a 'rationality' or RATIONALISM that is based on 'timeless' individualism, or individual subjective consciousness alone. He anticipates the post-modern emphasis on 'situatedness' and pluralism, but does not travel down a relativist road. He also emphasizes (against postmodernism) the stability and continuity of traditions as transmitters and filters of TRUTH.

Nevertheless, it is also recognized that in spite of the magisterial stature of his work, Gadamer leaves virtually all questions about criteria of truth to be worked out retrospectively or *post hoc* from case to case in ways that too readily evaporate. Further, Jürgen Habermas and others criticize his work for inadequate attention to social values and social interests.

Gadamer's major contribution is to raise questions that arise from the relation of history and tradition to human understanding, and to demonstrate that such questions are unavoidable. His work constitutes a turning-point (among others) in the history of ideas, and makes a fundamental contribution to philosophical hermeneutics.

al-Ghazali, Abu Hamid
(1058–1111)

Al-Ghazali was associated with the Baghdad centre of ISLAMIC PHILOSOPHY (*see* AL-KINDI and AL-FARABI). However, within this tradition he strongly opposed al-Farabi's belief in the eternity of the world, and any accommodation with the Plotinian and Neoplatonic notions of divine emanations. God created the universe out of nothing, and gave it its temporal beginning.

The eternity of the world, al-Ghazali maintained, was both contrary to the Qur'an and philosophically indefensible. He affirmed that POST-MORTAL EXISTENCE involved not only the immortality of the soul, but also the resurrection of the body. The titles of several of his works exemplify his strong reaction against privileging philosophy over revelation, e.g. *The Incoherence of the Philosophers*.

Not surprisingly, therefore, al-Ghazali attacked with no less force the claims of al-Farabi to grant this privilege of philosophy over religion. In positive terms he aimed to reverse this error in such works as *The Revival of the Religious Sciences* and in his autobiography *The Deliverance from Error*. TRUTH, for which he spent his life in life-long quest, remains a gift of divine grace.

The core of al-Ghazali's philosophical theology remains, in harmony with the Qur'an, his emphasis on divine sovereignty. He pressed this to its most radical limit, arguing that effects in the world spring not from mediate, efficient causes but directly from the will of Allah or God. This leads him into a formulation of OCCASIONALISM.

Al-Ghazali's quest for truth led him to resign from his post in Baghdad, to embark on the solitary life of the mystic. As a Sufi (the mystical strand within Islam), he wandered for some ten years through many centres of Islamic learning. Although in his last years he returned to teaching, he stressed especially divine grace and human fallibility. (*See also* MYSTICISM; NEOPLATONISM; PLOTINUS.)

God, arguments for the existence of

TWO KINDS OF ARGUMENTS

Broadly, arguments for the existence of God have rested on either or both of two different approaches. The COSMOLOGICAL ARGUMENT and TELEOLOGICAL ARGUMENT begin from our experience of the everyday world, and draw inferences from these data and observations to seek to establish the reasonableness of the belief that God exists. This is an A POSTERIORI argument. By contrast, the ONTOLOGICAL ARGUMENT for the existence of God begins from the very concept of God as God, and seeks to show that by internal logical NECESSITY this concept carries with it divine existence or Being. This is an A PRIORI argument.

These arguments may also be expressed in negative terms, and this may give them greater plausibility. The first approach postulates that the everyday world cannot constitute the ground of its own existence, unless we resort to the implausible hypothesis of an infinite chain of CONTINGENT or finite causes. The second approach postulates that if we conceive of God as God, the denial of God's existence results in logical self-contradiction.

CAN THE ARGUMENTS SERVE A PURPOSE IF THEY ARE NOT VALID?

The logical implications and complexities of these arguments have fascinated many thinkers who nevertheless remain unconvinced by them. They have even been turned on their head as disproofs of God's existence. The first approach, however, finds a place in ancient Greek philosophy, and in Jewish, Christian and Islamic THEISM.

A number of theologians who reject the logical validity of the arguments as 'proofs' nevertheless see value in them as

emphasizing the 'otherness' or TRANSCENDENCE of God. They underline the logical impropriety, for example, of asking such a question as 'Who made God?'

On the other hand, if 'God' is God, what kind of evidence might we expect to find for God's existence? KIERKEGAARD (1813–55) declared that to try to prove the existence of the God who addresses us is a 'shameless affront'. BUBER declared that next to the foolishness of denying God is the folly of trying to prove God. If God were logically demonstrable, would such a God be God?

TILLICH (1886–1965) argued that to ascribe 'existence' to God amounts to reducing God to a mere object of thought. Rather, God is 'Being-itself' (*Systematic Theology*, vol. 1, London: Nisbet, 1953, 261). Where the arguments fail most sharply, some believe, they help to exhibit the peculiar way in which God is elusive, transcendent, 'Other' and Beyond.

While the cosmological and other *a posteriori* arguments may fail because they risk embracing 'God' too closely within the chains of CAUSE and effect that characterize the world, this approach may nevertheless help to underline the historical and temporal dimensions of God's action within the world.

By contrast the ontological *a priori* argument may seem to fail because it risks perceiving God as a timeless abstraction of logic, divorced from the real world. Yet this approach nevertheless presupposes the unique 'otherness' of the God who transcends all phenomena within the world. 'God' is not the kind of Being who might be located' by means of space flight or theories of cosmology. This would be a logical mistake. It is perhaps what RYLE would call a 'category mistake'.

One reason why Buber, Jewish philosopher of religion, regards these arguments as misleading is that he understands God as a 'Thou' or 'You' who addresses us, while seeking to prove God's existence seems to turn God into an 'It', or passive OBJECT of thought. However, while many theists agree that 'God' cannot be logically demonstrable, the traditional arguments tend cumulatively to suggest that belief in God's existence is not irrational. At very least, it is no less reasonable a belief than ATHEISM or AGNOSTICISM.

A POSTERIORI ARGUMENTS FROM OUR EXPERIENCE OF THE WORLD

We often seek to draw inferences from everyday observations or experience to something which we infer from these (a posteriori). If on a walk, for example, we find a single glove on the ground, it is reasonable to infer 1) that a passer-by preceded us; and 2) that they dropped and lost a glove. Theists find many 'clues' within the world that point to divine agency, activity or Being.

In ancient Greek philosophy PLATO, (428–348 BCE) in Laws X, and ARISTOTLE (384–322 BCE), in Metaphysics XII, argued that the finitude or contingency of objects or events in the world (objects or events that might or might not have been) could not provide adequate grounds for the world's coming into being. An endless chain of contingent or finite causes, they argue, remains implausible. Similarly movement or change within the world points to a Being who is changeless, or the ground of change; to a Being who is 'necessary' rather than contingent.

Aristotle's approach was revived in ISLAMIC PHILOSOPHY by IBN SINA (Avicenna, 980–1037) among others, and in Christian thought most notably by Thomas AQUINAS (1225–74). Ibn Sina underlined the implausibility of an infinite chain of contingent causes, in contrast to the more reasonable explanation that behind all finite causes stood the One Necessary Being, who is neither caused nor contingent.

Thomas Aquinas declares, 'There are FIVE WAYS in which one can prove that there is a God' (Latin, quinque viis probari potest). Of these the first three argue a posteriori. 'The first way is based on change' (Latin, Prima via sumitur ex parte motus); the second on efficient cause (causae efficientis); and the third on the contrast between contingency (possible being) and necessity (ex possibili et necessario; Summa Theologiae, Ia, Qu. 2, art. 3, London: Blackfriars edn, 1963, vol. 2, 13–15).

'A thing in process of change cannot itself cause that same change' (ibid.). In the contrast between the potential and the actual 'a series of causes must ... stop somewhere' (ibid.). Strictly this 'second' way is accorded the term 'the cosmological argument', but all of the first three of the five ways are variant forms of it. God is God's own ground (see ASEITY).

DESCARTES (1596–1650) attempted a reformulation of the cosmological argument, although few would accept his distinctive view of cause. HUME (1711–76) questioned whether efficient causality could be established by empirical observation, and KANT viewed causality as a category in terms of which the human mind ordered the world. Hence neither Hume nor Kant accept the validity of this argument.

The fifth way of Thomas Aquinas represents a version of the teleological argument for the existence of God. Aquinas calls this the argument from the 'guided' nature of the world (gubernatione rerum), or from purposive or 'final' causes that presuppose a goal (ad finem).

In the eighteenth century the classic exponent was PALEY (1743–1805). However, since Paley's era, many argue that the combined force of KANT's Critique of Judgement, which ascribed 'order' to a projection of the human mind, of DARWIN (1809–82) and of biodevelopmental theories of EVOLUTION, transposed the debate into a new key.

AN A PRIORI ARGUMENT FROM THE LOGIC OF THE CONCEPT OF GOD

The ontological argument for the existence of God rests on purely logical (a priori) considerations, not on observations drawn from experience of the world (*a posteriori*) arguments. In *Proslogion* 2–4 ANSELM of Canterbury (1033–1109) declares that God is 'that than which no greater can be conceived' (Latin, *a liquid quo maius cogitari possit*). BARTH rightly emphasizes that this utterance occurs in the context of worship rather than of theoretical argument. Anselm continues: 'You alone, of all things, exist in the truest and greatest way' (Latin, *verissime et maxime esse*).

Nevertheless, Anselm begins to draw an inference from this paean of praise. The very notion of 'maximal greatness' in every respect must include existence in reality, since if 'God' were to exist only 'in the mind' this would not constitute maximal greatness. Over the centuries some have endorsed the argument, provided that it is applied uniquely to God alone. Others perceive a logical fallacy that confuses existence of a concept with existence of a reality.

Barth is typical of those theologians who perceive it not as an argument about God's existence, but as primarily underlining the transcendence or Otherness of the sovereign God in contrast to the world. For more detail see entries on cosmological, teleological and ontological arguments. (*See also* EMPIRICISM; LOGIC; POSSIBILITY; REASON; SYLLOGISM.)

God, concepts and 'attributes' of

This entry summarizes a number of key issues under this heading to provide a general perspective on, or overview of, this large subject. More specific and detailed problems that arise under each section are treated in other entries. Thus CONCEPTS of God may be differentiated in more detail under such headings and entries as PANTHEISM, DEISM and THEISM, and also TRANSCENDENCE and IMMANENCE. 'Attributes' of God include especially divine OMNIPOTENCE, OMNIPRESENCE and OMNISCIENCE as well as ETERNITY and IMMUTABILITY.

CONCEPTS OF GOD: GOD AS TRANSCENDENT AND IMMANENT

In theism the distinction between God and the created order finds expression in divine transcendence, namely the belief that God is 'Other', and 'Beyond' the world. Some, including KANT, argue that God is beyond human thought. Linked with this notion of transcendence as 'other' is the notion of God as holy and sovereign, but this takes us into the area of the 'attributes' of God. On the other hand, BARTH relates this divine transcendence to God's surpassing of all human definition and characterization. Only divine self-REVELATION allows human persons to have even analogical concepts of God.

ISLAMIC PHILOSOPHY especially emphasizes the prohibition of images or representations of God. In general Judaism and Christianity share this reserve on two grounds: first, God cannot be comprehended or objectified in this way (*see* OBJECTIFICATION); second, God created humankind to show forth God's image through holy human personhood. Many Christian theologians, notably Eberhard Jüngel (b. 1934), argue that the 'thinkability' or 'conceivability' of God turns ultimately on the enfleshment of God in Jesus Christ (*God as the Mystery of the World*, Edinburgh: T & T Clark, and Grand Rapids: Eerdmans, 1983, 105–225).

Yet if God is 'beyond' the world, God is also said to be near; indeed God is present 'within' the world, animating and sustaining it moment by moment. This view is known as that of divine IMMANENCE (God remains, or dwells, within the world). PIETISM, MYSTICISM and warm devotional religion perceive God as closer than human heart-beats.

CONCEPTS OF GOD: GOD IN RELATION TO THE WORLD

The main traditions of theism in Judaism, Christianity and Islam, therefore, place a dual emphasis upon the transcendence and immanence of God. For God is not to be equated with CREATION, even the whole of creation (as in pantheism); but God is not so far 'above' the world that God does not act within it (as in deism).

Deist concepts of God tended to flourish in the seventeenth and eighteenth centuries in conjunction with quasi-mechanistic models of the world. The world was viewed as if it were a machine that God had set in motion. To intervene in the workings (e.g. by 'miracles') might imply that God had created an imperfect machine that required repairs. Hence the deist picture is that of a God who watches the universe, as if from a distance, without taking further action within it.

Pantheistic concepts of God tend to flourish either in Eastern religions, especially Advaita Vedanta schools of Hinduism, or in conjunction with organic, non-mechanistic, models of the world. Thus SPINOZA (1632–77) argued that we may speak either of 'God' or of 'nature' (*Deus, sive Natura*), since either term denotes an infinite reality. J.G. Herder (1744–1803) and Johann W. Goethe (1749–1832), at the dawn of the Romantic era, when RATIONALISM had passed its zenith, stressed the organic, anti-mechanistic aspect of Spinoza's pantheism.

In contrast to pantheism, PANENTHEISM stresses that God is present and active in all created things, although God is also more than God's creation. PROCESS PHILOSOPHY offers one example of such thought, but such a notion is also expressed co-jointly by ancient Greek writers and the New Testament (Acts 17:28): 'In God we live and move and have our being.'

Even more fundamental, however, are the contrasts between monotheism and polytheism, and between theism and DUALISM. Theism has been defined as 'belief in one God, the Creator, who is infinite, self-existent, incorporeal, eternal ... perfect, omniscient and omnipotent' (H.P. Owen, *Concepts of Deity*, London: Macmillan, 1971, 1).

Thomas AQUINAS reflects the Hebrew–Christian–Islamic tradition when he asserts that to declare 'God is One' has practical consequences. To assert the Hebrew *Shema* from Deuteronomy 6:4, 'Hear, O Israel, the Lord our God is one God', carries three implications or corollaries. 'First, ... God is simple', i.e. 'to be God is to be this God'. 'Second ... God's perfection is unlimited', in contrast to polytheism, in which 'something belonging to one God would not belong to the other'. Third, the one God is 'the primary source of unity and order' (*Summa Theologiae*, Ia, Qu.11, art. 3). This coheres with the biblical emphasis upon the unity, coherence and integrity of life committed to one God as one Lord.

CONCEPTS OF GOD: GOD AS A HUMAN PROJECTION?

No less fundamental a question concerns the basis of human concepts of God. FEUERBACH (1804–72) believed that Christian theology masked the true human origin and nature of belief in God. With HEGEL, he saw philosophy as a critical advance upon religion, which dealt with images rather than critical concepts. 'Consciousness of God is self-consciousness ... Anthropology [is] the mystery of theology' (*Essence of Christianity* [1854], New York: Harper, 1957, 12, 336). Human consciousness projects outwards and upwards 'the infinity of consciousness' to hypostatize or objectify a God-figure as if 'out there' (ibid., 2, 3).

As Hans Küng observes, this is the first instance of a 'planned' ATHEISM (*Does God Exist?* London: Collins/Fount, 1980, 192–216). It confuses claims about the force of wishing with truth-claims. Yet Feuerbach laid the foundation for Karl Marx (1818–83) and his account of 'God'.

Marx reinterpreted Feuerbach's critique of religion in social and political terms. The basic origins of concepts of God and the practice of religions lay in socio-economic conditions. Against

Feuerbach, Marx dismissed the primacy of 'consciousness', and replaced it by the primacy of social and economic conditions, especially of labour, exchange-value and power. Religion provides a 'moral sanction' for oppression of the poor. Because of its other-worldly and illusory prospect of eternal 'reward', it serves to sedate the masses: 'It is the opium of the people' (*Collected Works*, vol. 3, New York: Lawrence & Wishart, 1975, 175). Marx, like NIETZSCHE, ascribes the genesis or promotion of 'God' to vested interests of power and control.

Marx correctly perceived the importance of social forces as against mere theory or abstract ideas. However, as with Nietzsche's analysis, the observation that many abuse religion for purposes of class interest or for socio-economic power does not invalidate authentic theistic belief as such. Marx's views of history, economics and religion fall short through monolithic generalization. (For a fuller critique, see MARXIST CRITIQUES OF RELIGION.)

FREUD (1856–1939) perceived the origins of concepts of God to lie in the projection upwards and outwards of the inner conflicts of neurosis within the human mind. The conflict between the drive to fulfil personal gratification (especially sexual drives) and the repression of these drives by society and moral conventions can be softened by projecting them 'upwards' onto a 'God' of judgement and grace. This 'God' is both judge and comforting father. Especially the projection of a perfect, affirming father-figure enables human persons to cope with these inner conflicts through this illusory device of projection and externalization.

A closer study of FREUD exposes the limitations and speculative nature of some of his theories of the human mind. He also confuses (like Feuerbach) what wish-fulfilment may project with issues of TRUTH. Can 'wishing' in itself make what is wished for either true or false?

CONCEPTS OF GOD: 'NON-REALISM' OR REVELATION?

More recently the English philosopher of religion CUPITT has offered a 'non-realist' view of God, which shares with Feuerbach and with Freud the notion that 'God ... and his attributes are a kind of projection' (*Taking leave of God*, London: SCM, 1980, 85). 'I do not suppose God to be an objectified individual over and above the religious requirement' (ibid., 87). His main difference from Feuerbach and Freud is that the projection is generated by being 'religious', even if God is not 'there'. There is 'nothing beyond' human beings (A. Freemen, *Faith in Doubt: Non-Realism and Christian Belief*, London: Mowbray, 1993, 7).

Nevertheless, all the major theistic traditions claim not that God is 'reached' by sheer intellectual effort alone, but that God initiates a relationship with humankind by choosing to disclose divine presence and action. Revelation unveils what would otherwise remain unknowable, as divine gift. This may occur through sacred writings, events in the world, disclosure-situations, or, for Christians, through Jesus Christ. Islam stresses the inspired gift of the Qur'an; Judaism, the Hebrew scriptures; Christians also stress the role of the Bible.

It has been suggested that a 'god' who waits to be demonstrated by human reasoning from the nature of the world (A POSTERIORI), or a conceptual 'god' who emerges from purely axiomatic reasoning (A PRIORI) would not be God (*see* GOD, ARGUMENTS FOR THE EXISTENCE OF). KIERKEGAARD, BUBER and Barth take this view. Barth further argues that a truly sovereign God who is 'Other' chooses where, when and how to disclose and to communicate God's own Being and nature. Such a God, he argues, has more authenticity as God than any projection from human consciousness.

More precisely, PANNENBERG (b. 1928) insists that otherness and universality belong so inextricably to the concept of God that 'the term "God" ... serves to interpret what is encountered in it ... The situation is expressed as encounter with Another ... The word "God" is used for this Other' (*Systematic Theology*, vol. 1, Edinburgh: T & T Clark, 1991, 67).

Pannenberg concedes that part of this 'Otherness' consists in 'the unity and totality' entailed in the concept of God. 'If the word [God] is like a blank face to us, it reminds us by its very strangeness of the lack of meaning in modern life, in which the theme of life's unity and totality is missing' (ibid., 71). However, he understands the concept of God as implying a 'totality' that confronts and addresses humanity as 'Other', not merely as an extension of human consciousness.

'ATTRIBUTES' OF GOD? PERFECT, GOOD, INFINITE, ETERNAL, ONE

Our use of inverted commas signals reserve but not outright rejection of the conventional use of the term 'attributes' to denote features of distinguishing characteristics of God, especially those that are inseparable from, or internal to, God's own nature as God. The problem about the word derives from its use by ARIS-TOTLE to denote the properties of objects understood as categories of space, time and relation. God, however, is not an 'object'; still less an object in space and time. Only when we exclude inapplicable static and objectifying overtones can the term properly be applied to God.

Thomas AQUINAS follows his section on the 'FIVE WAYS' (on the existence of God) by expounding God's nature as (Latin) 'simplex', i.e. 'simple' in the sense of transcending all 'classes' (*genera*) of beings, and manifesting 'perfection simple and single' (*perfectio ... in uno simplici*: *Summa Theologiae*, Ia, Qu. 3, arts. 6 and 7). Further, 'the perfections of everything exist in God ... He lacks no excellence of any sort' (ibid., Qu. 4, art. 2). Aquinas notes that here he follows 'Averroes', i.e. the Islamic philosopher IBN RUSHD.

Indeed, 'God alone is good by nature', *bonus per suam essentiam*; ibid., Qu. 6, art. 3).

The notion that God is *infinitus* (Latin) may be translated as 'God is infinite' or as 'God is unlimited'. Following Aristotle, Aquinas considers several objections to this assertion. How can the summit of perfection be 'limitless'?

This introduces what today we might call the logical grammar of the assertion that the infinity of God is internal to God's nature as God. In an obvious sense, everything other than God derives from God. God is *infinitus* in the sense of ASEITY. God is also *infinitus* in the sense that God possesses unlimited power. This will be noted further in the next section (but *see* the entry on OMNIPOTENCE).

'Infinity' finds expression in the temporal dimension through language about God as eternal. However, 'calling God eternal does not imply his being measured by something extrinsic' (ibid., Qu. 10, art. 2). God has neither beginning nor end, and is not capable of decay into nonexistence (ibid., art. 4). Yet eternity is more than 'human' time stretched out indefinitely at both 'ends'. BOETHIUS offers the classic model when he insists that eternity belongs to God, since time is a property of the created order.

Boethius conceived of eternity as 'the complete possession all at once [Latin, *totum simul*] of an illimitable life'. Past, present and future are grasped simultaneously. This is a metaphorical way of accommodating the limits of human concepts and conceivability, for is there no succession, apart from within the created world order? In Hebrew–Christian theology God is living and purposive.

Time, Aquinas asserts, is a measure of change; but he also argues (in opposition to serious questioning today) that God is incapable of change. In Aquinas's view, eternity measures not time but existence itself. Like Boethius, he sees it as gathering together past, present and future. Such a view of the logic of 'eternal' is controversial, but has the merit of distinguishing it from the time God has created, and by which God is not conditioned. Nevertheless, it is not without problems, and it tends to predetermine how Thomas Aquinas approaches the related problem of divine omniscience (see further on ETERNITY.)

The belief that God is one also derives, as we have noted, from God's nature as God. 'To be God is to be this God' (ibid., Qu. 11, art. 3). In the modern era, Pannenberg convincingly relates this to the dual use of *Elohim*, 'God', and *YHWH*, '*this* God' (i.e. as a proper name) in the Hebrew scriptures.

THE SO-CALLED METAPHYSICAL ATTRIBUTES OF GOD

Traditionally in philosophy of religion the Almighty-ness or omnipotence of God, God's presence throughout the created order, or omnipresence, and God's full and complete knowledge of what can be known, divine omniscience, constitute the 'metaphysical attributes' of God. Aquinas expounds God's existence 'in everything ... everywhere' following his exposition of God as infinite (ibid., Qu. 8).

The logical complexities of these concepts are so great that we reserve detailed discussion for the entries on omniscience, omnipotence and omnipresence. If there are no logical constraints upon their scope, these terms result in self-contradiction. For example, would it enhance the 'almighty' power of the omnipotent God to assert that God can lie; or that God can divide odd numbers into two sets of integers; that God can change what occurred in the past; or that God can make a stone so big that God is unable to lift it?

It is not part of the logical grammar of divine omnipotence to claim that God can perform logical contradictions, can perform self-contradictory acts, or can act in ways contrary to God's own nature as loving, wise and good. Hence Peter Geach and Gijsbert van den Brink insist that 'Almighty-ness' is a preferable term.

SWINBURNE retains the traditional term, but insists that it denotes 'an ability to bring about any (logically possible) state of affairs' (*The Coherence of Theism*, Oxford: Clarendon, 1977 and 1987, 150).

When all has been said, however, a key factor is that God may choose to limit divine powers as a sovereign act of renunciation prompted by self-giving love. Barth and MOLTMANN underline this point. Any resultant self-chosen constraint is then not a denial of omnipotence but an expression of it.

The logical complexity of omniscience becomes most problematic when it is applied to divine knowledge of a future that has not yet occurred. Is anything 'there' yet, of which God can (logically can) have knowledge?

If we answer in the affirmative we seem to risk presupposing DETERMINISM. If God knows that I will choose a given commodity or course of action, how can I be free to choose another? AUGUSTINE responds by insisting that my choice would still be 'freely mine', even if God knows it and it is destined to occur. Aquinas distinguishes between the CONTINGENT NECESSITY of a state of affairs, and the logical necessity of a proposition that describes the state of affairs. RYLE suggests that a phrase such as 'It was to be' simply confuses the 'participant' logic of an agent with the retrospective logic of an 'observer' (*Dilemmas*, Cambridge: CUP, 1954, 15–35).

Swinburne eases the problem by applying the same logic to omniscience as that which he applied to omnipotence. Omniscience, he urges, is not 'knowledge of everything true, but (very roughly) ... knowledge of everything true which it is logically possible to know' (*The Coherence of Theism*, 175). 'P. is omniscient if he knows about everything except those future states ... which are not physically necessitated by anything in the past' (ibid.).

Indeed, in Swinburne's view, even God would not be truly free to make chosen sovereign decisions and decrees if the nature of every future decree were transparent at every point. Hence biblical passages use analogical language about God's change of purpose (e.g. Gen. 18: Ex. 32), especially in relation to human intercession or human repentance. Swinburne urges an 'attenuated sense' of the term 'omniscient'. HARTSHORNE adopts a similar approach, but PLANTINGA takes a different path (see the entry on omniscience).

Omnipresence as a concept shares some of the logical problems discussed under 'omnipotence'. Also placed elsewhere is the issue of the 'personhood' of God. Is such a term as 'supra-personal' perhaps less misleading, or would this lose more than it might gain? (See also ANALOGY; LOGIC; METAPHYSICS; SELF.)

God, transcendence of

See TRANSCENDENCE.

grace

In the biblical writings the Hebrew *chen* and Greek *charis* denote respectively loving kindness and gracious, unmerited love-gift. As biblical theology develops, it becomes clear that this means not simply a gift of love separable from God, but God's gift of God's own SELF.

In certain technical debates, for example that between AUGUSTINE (354–430) and Pelagius (c. 360–c. 420) prevenient grace came to be seen as God's granting of a power or capacity to respond to God's love and salvation. In AQUINAS and in Roman Catholic theology it became almost reified as an infused power.

Since the active presence of God ultimately has this effect, this view simply shifts the emphasis in Christian theology. However, 'divine grace is best understood as a mode of God's action towards, or relatedness to, the creature, and not as some kind of substance that God imparts to the creature' (Colin Gunton, *God and Freedom*, Edinburgh: T & T Clark, 1995, 126). In debates about grace and FREEDOM, it is more helpful to ask how divine action relates to human freedom, than to speculate about the nature of some reified quality.

H

Hartshorne, Charles (1897–2000)

An American philosopher, Hartshorne exercised wide influence as a distinctive thinker who combined a rational defence of THEISM with an advocacy of PROCESS PHILOSOPHY and the notion of God as 'always becoming', rather than as 'Being'. He was educated at Harvard, and taught at the University of Chicago, Emory and Texas University at Austin. He was influenced by WHITEHEAD (1861–1947) and by C.S. Peirce (1839–1914), whose *Collected Papers* he co-edited.

Hartshorne is probably most widely known on both sides of the Atlantic for his logical defence of the ONTOLOGICAL ARGUMENT for the existence of God, together with those of MALCOLM and PLANTINGA. Yet he also regarded the three classical arguments for the existence of GOD as mutually reinforcing one another, like strands of a rope. Further, he expounds a distinctive view of God, sometimes called a 'neo-classical' view.

GOD AS 'ALWAYS BECOMING': THE 'DI-POLAR' APPROACH TO DIVINE PERFECTION

Alongside his defence of the ontological argument, Hartshorne also expounds a distinctive view of God as 'di-polar': God is ABSOLUTE, but this alone does not do

justice to God's 'perfection'. 'Theism', he argues, tends to stress IMMUTABILITY and ETERNITY over against change and TIME; activity and sovereignty over against the capacity to experience and to respond. But 'perfection' embraces both sides of these di-polar contrasts.

Like MOLTMANN, Hartshorne believed that there is a sense in which God co-suffers with the world, but as a necessary entailment of divine 'perfection'. To restrict God to eternal 'Being', rather than to 'always becoming', is to reduce divine perfection. God is involved in the lack of symmetry between the past that has been actualized and the future that remains POSSIBILITY.

This points not to PANTHEISM, but to PANENTHEISM. OMNISCIENCE denotes the capacity to know what is 'knowable'. God's permanent 'being' consists in faithful, steadfast goodness exhibited through 'everlasting becoming'.

THE DEFENCE OF THE SECOND FORM OF THE ONTOLOGICAL ARGUMENT

Hartshorne addresses the nature of NECESSITY in the second formulation of ANSELM'S argument. He concedes that Anselm did not have at his disposal the resources of modern LOGIC. However, Anselm's second formulation states that

God's necessary existence is so self-evident that to deny it constitutes a contradiction. By MODAL LOGIC Hartshorne sharpens the negation: it is necessarily not true that 'God exists necessarily' strictly implies that God does not exist. Hence either 'God exists necessarily', *or* 'it is necessary that God does not exist'. However, the proposition 'God does not exist' cannot be a necessary proposition (i.e. it is not 'necessary' that God does not exist). The remaining unexcluded logical alternative is that 'God exists necessarily'.

The value of the ontological argument, Hartshorne concludes, is to show that it makes no sense to predicate 'possible existence' of God, while it is false to assert that God's existence is of necessity not possible. Hence 'God exists necessarily' may be accepted as the only remaining option. This coheres with Hartshorne's logic of perfection. (*See also* GOD, CONCEPTS AND ATTRIBUTES OF.)

Hegel, Georg Wilhelm Friedrich (1770–1831)

Hegel's dissatisfaction with KANT (1724–1804), especially with the status that Kant accorded to REASON, gave rise to a complex and highly original system of thought. Hegel rejected Kant's separation of the rational from the universal or ABSOLUTE. The rational, for Hegel, is 'the real' in its wholeness and universality.

Hegel's influence is seen mainly in his exposition of 'historical' reason, or, in other words, the notion of reason as a developmental process simultaneously anchored in processes of history but also exhibited in the dialectical process of LOGIC.

Yet Hegel's influence is also seen in his differences from those whom he opposed, or who opposed him. He opposed Kant's notion that reason yielded only an 'ordering' or regulative principle, which, in effect, operated only in terms of experience of the phenomenal, or CONTINGENT, world. He opposed Kant and FICHTE'S

identification of the absolute with the moral categorical imperative, rather than with reason or mind (German, *Geist,* also Spirit).

Hegel equally opposed SCHELLING's beginning with human consciousness. This Hegel sees as too subjective for a unified theory of reality. He also attacked SCHLEIERMACHER'S giving central privilege to the immediate sense of absolute dependence upon God. This he saw as giving hostages to Romanticist 'feeling' as against the rigour of conceptual thought.

No less, however, KIERKEGAARD attacked Hegel's emphasis upon a universal ONTOLOGY as impossible, except in logic alone. He also attacked Hegel's tendency to replace religious faith by conceptual philosophical thought. FEUERBACH and Marx replaced Hegel's notion of Absolute Spirit or Absolute Mind (*Geist*), with the notion of humanity (Feuerbach), or with the socio-economic forces of history (Marx: *see* MARXIST CRITIQUE OF RELIGION).

PHENOMENOLOGICAL, HISTORICAL AND DIALECTICAL REASON

Hegel's attempt to offer a unified ontology, or theory of reality, can be understood most readily in the context of his two parallel notions of development: historical and logical. At the level of history, Absolute Reality unfolds its nature not only through individual entities or persons, but through mental, social and political phenomena. Hegel shared this starting-point in part with Schelling in the early period of their collaboration. Their common question concerned the emergence of consciousness. Self becomes self-aware in relation to what is not-self.

In his *The Phenomenology of Mind* (1807) Hegel uses Mind or Spirit (*Geist*) to denote the finite human being as an inter-subjective (or related-to-an-other) reality. Ultimate reality is God as absolute Spirit, and also as *telos,* or End. God (the

Absolute) is the *telos* of the process of rational self-awareness as this unfolds itself through the 'ladder' of historical development and logical DIALECTIC.

The *Phenomenology of Mind* and the *Science of Logic* (1812–16) focus respectively on the historical and logical aspects of Hegel's system.

The term 'phenomenology' in the first title (from Greek *phainomai*, I appear) underlines that Mind or Spirit first appears in finite form in the contingent, historical or phenomenological world. This is partly also Kant's phenomenological world, ordered by categories, but is at the same time in process, as moving beyond the very confines that Kant proposed as A PRIORI categories of the mind.

Through historical and logical TRANS-CENDENCE beyond a prior constraint and finitude, the logical idea becomes transcended as the Universal Principle of Reason, in which only 'the Whole' is 'Reality'. As a wholeness, as a completed All, Reason is Reality, and Reality is Reason.

If nature were absolute, this would be a reductive 'naturalism'. If individual consciousness were absolute (as in Schelling) this would be SUBJECTIVISM. If the moral imperative were absolute (as in Kant and Fichte), this would be moralism. However, the 'objective IDEALISM' of objective logic exhibited as the spiritual, historical and developmental principle of historical reason does lead on to reason as absolute reality.

However, 'historical reason' as such takes account of the radical historical finitude or 'situatedness' of human minds within the phenomenological ascent or 'ladder' of dialectic. These 'placings' within history give rise to a dialectical process of differentiation, or even opposition. Thus Hegel presses further the logical resources first proposed by FICHTE and Schelling of moving from 'thesis' to 'antithesis', and thence (in the light of this awareness of 'the other') to a synthesis which takes thought 'higher'. Dialectic

thus entails both opposition, negation, or separation (antithesis) and mediation (synthesis) that is a negation of negation. The process 'raises' (German, *erheben*) the finite and 'sublates' or assimilates it (*aufheben*) into what is 'higher'.

HEGEL AND RELIGION

From the standpoint of the Christian theist, Hegel's system is simultaneously an attack on religious faith (as KIERKE-GAARD judged it to be) and yet also a vindication of a Trinitarian philosophical theology of history.

On one side, Hegel drew a contrast (already hinted at by Kant) between the simpler, less critical ways of representing God and religion among the devout through uncritical 'representations' (*Vor-stellungen*), and a more rigorous, critical use of the 'concept' (*Begriff*) in philosophical reflection. Philosophy is 'higher' than religion.

The former (*Vorstellungen*) include images, MYTHS and stories. They relate to the mode of 'immediacy' of awareness of God advocated by Schleiermacher, which Hegel explicitly attacks as primitive and uncritical. The processes of historical and logical development lead to an entirely rational and conceptual differentiation between finite modes of expression, in an attempt to reach beyond them through a rigorous application of conceptual thought. D.F. Strauss (1808–74) would later apply this contrast to biblical 'myth' with disastrously negative consequences for religion.

On the other side, however, Hegel believed that a Christian doctrine of the Trinity entirely cohered with his philosophy of history, logic and reason. The 'thesis' of creation and the religion of Judaism (God the Father) became 'negated' in the 'antithesis' of the incarnation and the cross (God the Son). The cross, in a dialectical sense, was the 'death' of God. Resurrection and Pentecost, however, now (historically and logically) begin the New Age of freedom (the Spirit of

God). The particularism of Judaism becomes universalized.

These two respective attitudes toward religion are less contradictory than might appear. For Hegel writes, 'In *thinking*, I lift myself up into the Absolute ... I am infinite consciousness while I remain at the same time finite self-consciousness ... It is in myself and for myself that this conflict and this conciliation take place' (*Lectures on the Philosophy of Religion* [1832], Eng. 3 vols., London: Kegan Paul, 1895; vol. 1, 63–4 (my italics)). Religion moves from feeling (*Gefühl*) through representation (*Vorstellung*) to concept (*Begriff*) and thinking (*Denken*) or knowledge (*Wissen*) (ibid., vol. 1, 155–99).

Similarly, within the divine life of God, the Absolute as Spirit encounters the truth of historical, finite otherness in the incarnation of God the Son and the cross. Thence God becomes the immanent and transcendent Spirit; the Spirit proceeds from God to work both within the finite world and beyond the finite as Universal Reality in relation to history-as-a-Whole. The key principle is teleology.

FURTHER INFLUENCE

Too often credit (or blame) for a developmental view of the world and of religion is given to the particular versions of biological evolution associated with DARWIN or ethical evolution associated with SPENCER. However, Hegel's complex exposition of historical reason and historical dialectic reaches beyond the nineteenth century (in materialist form in Karl Marx) to our own era.

In the 1950s the understandable attention given to 'the particular case' in British and Anglo-American ANALYTICAL PHILOSOPHY did not find Hegel congenial as a dialogue partner (apart from J. N. Findlay's work). Nevertheless Hegel remains a powerful influence upon European philosophy and modern Christian theology. His emphasis on 'historical situatedness' is presupposed in discussions of POSTMODERNITY and even in gender studies.

We do not have space to note the legacy of Hegel's political and social philosophy, and we have already alluded to his impact on Strauss, and by way of reaction, on Kierkegaard and in a different direction on FEUERBACH. At the beginning of the twentieth century Hegelian thought was represented in England partly by BRADLEY (1846–1924) and in America partly by Josiah Royce (1855–1916). In Christian theology the panoramic scope of Hegel's thought and his respect for the rational find powerful resonances especially in the work of PANNENBERG. (*See also* IDEALISM; IMMANENCE; OBJECTIVISM; THEISM.)

Heidegger, Martin (1889–1976)

LIFE, WRITINGS AND PERIODS OF THOUGHT

Heidegger taught at Freiburg before becoming Professor of Philosophy at Marburg from 1923, where his colleague as Professor of New Testament was BULTMANN. He subsequently returned to Freiburg, one year after the publication of his most famous work *Being and Time* (1927). Initially he supported Hitler when he was Rector of Freiburg University (1933–4; cf. *The Self-Assertion of the German University*, 1933). However, with the occurrence of more radical political developments he withdrew from the University, and worked in relative seclusion in the Black Forest.

Heidegger's work initially focused on the notion of human situatedness in time, place and history, for which he regularly used the term *Dasein*, Being-there. Understanding and interpretation proceed from within the temporal and practical horizons that bound the 'world' of *Dasein*. This perspective is traced through his magisterial *Being and Time* (*Sein und Zeit*).

This work was originally intended as merely the first stage toward a philosophy of Being, i.e. an ONTOLOGY that drew its roots from existential givenness in human life and in time. Although he rejected Edmund Husserl's concern with 'essences',

Heidegger was heavily influenced by his phenomenology, which featured prominently in *Being and Time*. However, how was he to move from *Dasein* (Being-there) in time to a genuine ontology of Being (*Sein*)?

Heidegger began to wrestle with preliminary problems in *What is Metaphysics?* (1929) and *Kant and the Problem of Metaphysics* (1929). Nevertheless, he became increasingly convinced that philosophical thought, as such, had become trapped in the DUALISM of the Platonic tradition. From PLATO to HEGEL philosophers were obsessed with 'CONCEPTS'. Yet this generated only a self-constructed illusion whereby 'technical' conceptual moves only served to hide a tragic human 'fallenness' out of 'Being'. Western philosophical language had fallen into a malaise of circularity and atomistic fragmentation.

The more fruitful way forward was through the creative poets, who transcended 'concepts'. The turning-point (*Kehre*) came with *Hölderlin and the Essence of Poetry* (1936), *On the Essence of Truth* (1947), *What is Thinking* (English also as *Discourse on Thinking* (1954)) and especially *On the Way towards Language* (*Unberwegs zur Sprache*, 1959).

THE 'EXISTENTIALIST' PERIOD OF 'BEING AND TIME'

Heidegger's greatest contributions were 1) to explore a non-substantival, non-objective mode of conceptual expression for the human in contrast to the language of objects and properties more appropriate to things; and 2) to explore the horizon of time (and 'temporality' as the basis for the possibility of time) as a fundamental dimension of human 'existence' and of the way of understanding this existence.

Heidegger thus anticipates post-modern and gender-related notions of human 'situatedness'. He began not with Being (*Sein*) but with existential Being-there (*Dasein*). Further, 'Time needs to be explicated ... as the horizon for the

understanding of Being, and in terms of temporality as the Being of *Dasein*, . . .' (*Being and Time*, Eng., Oxford: Blackwell, 1962, 39). 'Being cannot be grasped except by taking time into consideration' (ibid., 40).

In practice this means suspending ontological questions about being while we focus first on 'ONTIC' enquiring about concrete 'existents' in time; i.e. beings, especially human beings, not their being. This is the 'mode of Being' that characterizes the human. This requires the existential analytic of *Dasein* (ibid., 34).

This leads to an exploration of philosophical HERMENEUTICS. 'Meaning' is a projected 'upon which' in terms of which we understand an entity or mode of existence as what it is, through anticipating (as far as possible) a provisional and preliminary 'seeing-beforehand' (*Vorsicht*), or pre-conception (*Vorgriff*), or 'pre-understanding' (*Vorverständnis*; ibid., 191–3).

Several features mark the difference between the language of objects (categories) and that of the human being (*existentialia*). The latter (*Existenz*) does not have 'properties', but possibility. Moreover, objects can be replicated; but *Dasein* as human-being is in each case 'mineness' (*Jemeinigkeit*), an 'I' (ibid., 68). In biblical studies Bultmann draws on this analysis to show (rightly) that 'body' and 'soul' are not 'components' which humankind 'have', but what they are, in the given modes of their existence.

The 'world' of the human self is not merely physical or geographical, but is defined and bounded by given human interests, concerns and horizons of understanding. Important experiences that relate to engagement with TRUTH include dread and confrontation by death. A new depth, taking us beyond KIERKEGAARD, is given to 'SUBJECTIVITY' and to the distinction between OBJECTIVITY and objectivism.

In terms of a philosophy of religion a number of older questions are placed in a

new light. For example, *Dasein* is characterized by potentiality-for-Being (*Sein-
können*). Yet humankind begins from the
situation into which they were born (or
'thrown-ness', *Geworfenheit*, ibid., 74).
Bultmann exploits a correlation between
the existentialist notion that who a person
'is' derives from their 'thrown-ness' into
the world and their own subsequent
decisions. This is related to 'bondage' in
the Epistles of Paul, while the 'possibility'
or 'potentiality' that lies ahead is related to
'freedom in the Spirit'.

POETRY AND ART IN HEIDEGGER'S
LATER WORKS

Many philosophers have little time for his
works after 1936, although in Germany
and among theologians they remain influential, and contribute to the philosophy of
art. Heidegger believed that the Western
language-tradition had become flawed,
and had sunk to little more than a
technical, technological or instrumental
vehicle of pragmatic communication. In
short, 'we have fallen out of Being' (*Sein:
Introduction to Metaphysics*, New Haven:
Yale, 1959, 36-7). He accepts
NIETZSCHE's analysis of 'evaporating reality' and cultural crisis: 'the transformation of men into a mass ... suspicion of
everything free and creative' (ibid., 38).

The wonder of 'Being' has become
stifled by 'dreary technological frenzy':
by 'gadgetry' in America and by 'regimen-
tation' in Russian Marxism. The result is
'the standardization of man, the pre-
eminence of the mediocre' (ibid., 42). This
is largely due to the 'chasm' left by Plato's
dualism. Christianity settled down in it:
'Nietzsche was right in saying that Christianity is Platonism for the people' (ibid.,
106).

Heidegger sought wholeness in place of
dualism and fragmentation. Perhaps only
art and poetry can bring 'a new coming-
to-speech' of this Whole. Whereas 'aesthetics' divides 'concepts' of beauty (still
within the realm of Ideas) from sensuous
representations of beauty (still within the

CONTINGENT order), authentic art reaches
back pre-conceptually to enact the whole
work as an event in time. In summary,
poetry and art may be '*eventful*'. This
discloses Being not as a static entity
(*Seiendheit*), but as dynamic being-as-
event (*Anwesen*).

Heidegger explores a number of examples of eventful art. Van Gogh's painting of
a peasant's boots, far from atomizing
'concepts', brings together-into-one the
'world' of the peasant: 'her slow trudge
through the ... furrows of the field swept
by raw wind ... the silent call of the earth
... uncomplaining anxiety as to the
certainty of bread' ('The Origin of the
Work of Art', in *Poetry, Language and
Thought*, New York: Harper & Row,
1971, 33-4).

Whether this is 'philosophy' remains a
matter of controversy. However, Heidegger has gone some way to show the
potential circularity of some Western
philosophical 'concepts'. For philosophy
of religion, the themes of 'disclosure' or
REVELATION, of conceptual schemes
appropriate to the human and the personal, of 'possibility', of non-dualistic
wholeness, and of eventfulness-in-time,
offer resources for further exploration.
(*See also* EXISTENTIALISM; POSSIBILITY;
POSTMODERNITY; PRAGMATISM.)

hermeneutics

Hermeneutics denotes much more than
'rules for the interpretation of texts', even
though it first emerged in this form in the
ancient world and the pre-modern period.
Philosophically the subject enquires into
what conditions pertain for the understanding of 'what is other'; that is, of what
lies beyond 'my' world of immediate
concerns.

The term 'hermeneutics' seems to have
been used first by J.C. Dannhauer in his
Hermeneutica Sacra (1654). As a method
of interpreting texts, the subject goes back
to first-century rabbinic thought, and to
the interpretation of Homer by STOIC

thinkers. SCHLEIERMACHER (1768–1834) extended its scope to found it as a discipline of the modern university. It explored the nature of human understanding. Wilhelm Dilthey (1833–1911) used the term to denote the understanding of 'lived experience' (*Erlebnis*). He sought to replace HEGEL's emphasis on Mind or Spirit (*Geist*) by a more concrete concern for 'life' (*Leben*). The importance of 'life' and 'history' for all understanding clearly emerges in the work of GADAMER.

Anticipating Gadamer, Dilthey attacks ENLIGHTENMENT, RATIONALISM and EMPIRICISM with the comment: 'No real blood runs in the veins of the knowing subject that LOCKE, HUME and KANT constructed' (*Gesammelte Schriftem*, vol. 5, Leipzig: Teubner, 1962, 4). Dilthey's application of hermeneutics to social institutions paves the way for its place in sociology.

Schleiermacher asserts, 'Hermeneutics is part of the art of thinking' (*Hermeneutics*, Eng. Missoula: Scholar Press, 1977, 97). All understanding is rooted in the concrete diversity of life. It requires a 'divinatory' pole (*divinatorische*, denoting more, but not less than 'intuitive'), and a comparative or rationally critical pole (ibid., 150). He called these the 'feminine' and 'masculine' poles, which were complementary for hermeneutics.

Schleiermacher was perhaps the first fully to appreciate that understanding is not simply a matter of the human 'subject' mastering some passive 'object' of knowledge, but of inter-subjective, interpersonal, listening and evaluating. It is like seeking an empathy between two friends. Understanding should not be reduced to 'how I see it'. To understand one must step 'out of one's own frame of mind' to engage with 'the other' (ibid., 42, 109).

Both Schleiermacher and Dilthey stress the distinctive character of understanding (*Verstehen*) as against mere 'knowledge', since (for Dilthey) the former entails 'empathy' (*Einverständnis*) or 're-living' (*nacherleben*) the life-experience (*Erlebnis*) of 'the other'.

THE LATER TWENTIETH CENTURY

GADAMER (1900–2001), however, attacks both of these thinkers for placing too much weight on the 'SUBJECTIVITY' of human consciousness. This subjectivity can be 'a distorting mirror' (*Truth and Method*, 2nd rev. Eng. edn, London: Sheed & Ward, 1989, 276). Gadamer insists that the historical conditioning of traditions surround both the one who seeks to understand and that of which understanding is sought, and that these demand prior exploration, or 'pre-understanding' (*Vorverständnis*) and 'pre-judgements' (*Vorurteile*). He uses such analogies as the active impact of a work of art, a game, or a festival, to clarify his point.

RICOEUR (b. 1913) takes a mediating position between Schleiermacher and Dilthey on one side, and Gadamer on the other. He convincingly criticizes Gadamer for collapsing the 'critical' or 'explanatory' axis wholly into that of 'understanding'. His own hermeneutics revolve around the twin principles of 'a hermeneutics of suspicion' (which depends primarily but not exclusively on 'explanation') and a 'hermeneutic of retrieval' (which primarily depends on 'understanding').

Ricoeur states, 'Hermeneutics seems to me to be animated by … double motivation: willingness to suspect, willingness to listen; vow of rigour, vow of obedience … Doing away with idols … to listen to symbols' (*Freud and Philosophy. An Essay on Interpretation*, New Haven: Yale, 1970, 27).

Under the term 'radical hermeneutics' the discipline has entered into full engagement with POSTMODERNITY. However, more interpersonal and more traditional studies continue. These are bound together in a common recognition of the limitations of Enlightenment rationalism and empiricism, the importance of community, traditions and history, and the dimension of the inter-subjective or interpersonal. Emilio Betti, another late twen-

tieth-century exponent, insists that hermeneutics nurtures tolerance and the capacity
to listen *to* 'the other' in mutuality and
reciprocity.

Hick, John Harwood (b. 1922)

LIFE AND THOUGHT

John Hick took degrees in law and
philosophy at Hull and Edinburgh, and
undertook research at Oxford under H.H.
Price. He trained for Presbyterian ministry
at Cambridge, where he was influenced by
H.H. Farmer. Born in Yorkshire, he taught
in England at the universities of Cambridge and Birmingham, and in the USA at
Cornell, Princeton Theological Seminary
and Claremont Graduate School, California.

Hick's first book, *Faith and Knowledge*
(London: Macmillan, 1957) recognizes
ambiguity in the world, and attributes
theistic or non-theistic belief to experiencing the world in different ways. More
strictly, a cognitive decision is based on
whether we 'see' the world as the creation
of a good God, or whether we 'see' it as a
chance product of material forces. This
ambiguity generates more than one possible way of seeing the world. However, it
results, in Hick's view (following KANT)
from God's respect for human freedom.

Traces of the influence of Kant and
SCHLEIERMACHER, as well as WITTGEN-
STEIN on 'seeing ... as ...', can be
detected here. He writes, 'In each case
we discover and live in terms of a
particular aspect of our environment
through an appropriate act of interpretation ... [However,] the theistic believer
cannot explain *how* he knows the divine
presence to be mediated through his
human experience' (ibid. 118).

Hick's most widely read book, *Evil and
the God of Love* (London: Macmillan, 1st
edn 1966; 2nd edn 1977), also draws on
Schleiermacher's account of human fallenness and human development, although
Hick more especially emphasizes the
influence of Irenaeus (see below).

Since the 1970s Hick has become
increasingly involved in controversial
issues about Christianity, pluralism and a
THEISM which, while respecting the role of
Jesus Christ, also rejects any hint of
Christocentric or Christogically exclusive
theism.

Again, there is a link with his earlier
works. In *Faith and Knowledge* he writes,
'In making a Christological study of the
central data that God has revealed himself to men in Christ, we are not asking
which, if any, of the various Christological theories erected upon it is correct'
(p. 220).

Hick's book *Evil and the God of Love*
embodies a doctrine of universal salvation,
which is developed in *Death and Eternal
Life* (1976). However, he goes further in
his controversial work (ed.) *The Myth of
God Incarnate* (1977), in *God has Many
Names* (1980) and in *An Interpretation of
Religion* (1989).

Hick also produced a brief textbook on
philosophy of religion under the title:
Philosophy of Religion (Englewood Cliffs,
NJ: Prentice-Hall, 1963) with subsequent
revisions. This remains a clear and useful
introduction to the subject. We shall
focus, however, on the book that has
played the most influential role in this
subject.

EVIL AND THE GOD OF LOVE

Hick's central argument is that the problem of EVIL is best addressed not by
following AUGUSTINE and Thomas
AQUINAS who look back to some 'mythological' event of the past, the fall of
humankind, to explain the origins of evil.
Looking forward to the future, however,
to the ultimate goal for which the experience of evil may be a necessary condition,
provides a better way. This good goal or
end consists in a fuller relationship with
God.

Hick cites examples in human life
where the experience of opposition, disappointment, frustration or suffering can
contribute to the process of maturing

character. He borrows from the poet John Keats the allusion to life as 'the vale of soul-making' (2nd edn, 259, esp. n. 1; also 253–61). He is content to describe his new starting-point as 'an Irenaean theodicy', or as 'soul-making' theodicy (see J. Hick, 'An Irenaean Theodicy', in S. T. Davis (ed.) *Encountering Evil*, Edinburgh: T & T Clark, 1981, 39–68, for an exposition, critique and reply; also *Evil and the God of Love*, 2nd edn, 259).

This coheres with Hick's account of the development of humanity from a state of naïve innocence, which included an unself-conscious immaturity, through a difficult learning process, which entailed pain, to an ultimate goal of maturity and relationship with God.

However, this does not fit easily with the Augustinian and traditionally orthodox notion of humanity prior to the Fall as fully in relationship with God ('original righteousness') followed by a fall into a state of alienation and sin. Hick rejects a 'historical' reading of the Genesis account, which he regards as 'MYTH'; ready-made goodness is a contradiction in terms.

Hick appeals to what he calls 'another and better way', namely not the 'majority report' of the Augustinian tradition, but 'the minority report' of the Irenaean tradition' (*Evil and the God of Love*, 2nd edn, 253). This 'better' picture allows for evolutionary development: 'Man is in process of becoming the perfected being whom God is seeking to create' (ibid., 256).

The parental analogy is suggested in which God, like a parent, delights in humanity, but does not merely desire for humans 'unalloyed pleasure at the expense of their growth in such even greater values as moral integrity, unselfishness, compassion, courage, . . . capacity for love' (ibid., 258). 'This world must be a place of soul-making' (ibid., 259). Hick insists that humankind begins not with 'original righteousness', but with a lack of cognitive awareness of God as God, to which he gives the name 'epistemic distance'.

AN 'ALTERNATIVE STRAND OF CHRISTIAN THINKING'?

Hick presents his approach as an 'alternative strand of Christian thinking', built on the 'minority report' of the nature and story of humanity ('An Irenaean Theodicy', 41). He claims to follow a two-stage distinction in Irenaeus (120–202) between humanity as created in the 'image' (Hebrew, *tselem*; Greek, *eikōn*) of God, and the goal of entry into God's 'likeness' (Hebrew, *demûth*; Greek, *homoiōsis*).

Irenaeus distinguished 'image of God' as intelligence from 'likeness to God' as moral holiness or goodness. Crucially he writes that God could not give moral perfection to humankind 'as the latter was only recently created' (Irenaeus, *Against Heresies*, IV: 38: 2). At first humankind was 'infantile', because 'not exercised in discipline' (ibid., IV: 39: 1).

Schleiermacher's theology hinges upon a direct, immediate consciousness of dependence upon God. Yet this emerges in the context of development through fallenness and guilt. The Fall is part of a process leading to salvation. His critics have characterized it satirically as a fall 'upwards'. In Schleiermacher's view sin is what 'has arrested the free development of the God-consciousness' (*The Christian Faith*, 2nd edn, Edinburgh: T & T Clark, 1989, sec. 66, 271).

Without doubt Hick's emphasis on goal and futurity brings fresh perspective to the problem of evil and complements some of the emphases of the Augustinian–Thomist approach. Hick also strenuously criticizes the privative account of evil as absence of good in the 'major' tradition, even if we may hesitate to dismiss it (with Hick) as no more than 'a semantic conjuring trick' akin to describing a glass of water as half full rather than as half empty (*Evil and the God of Love*, 2nd edn, 38–58).

Nevertheless, Hick may at times overstate what he perceives as deficiencies in Augustine, including the extent of alien influences upon him and his use of the

principle of PLENITUDE. Hick's insistence
that this 'aesthetic' approach is utilitarian
has been turned on its head by his critics.
Thus David Griffin attacks 'the utility of
soul making' as presupposing God as
inflicting pain in order to produce creatures who accord with God's own goals,
i.e. treating persons as means not as ends
('*Critique*' in Davis, ed., *Encountering
Evils*, 53–55).

Hick's counter-reply is to underline
that everything is for the ultimate welfare
of humankind. Yet other critics ask
whether the proportion of experience of
evil is necessary for this end, and whether
the argument could be sustained without
the presupposition of a doctrine of universal salvation.

Hick may perhaps also overstate his
differences from Augustine and Aquinas.
In the end it is difficult to avoid seeing
Hick's critique of Augustine's FREE-WILL
DEFENCE as weakening his own case.
Hick, it might be argued, has enriched
the traditional approach with fresh strands
of arguments, and placed question-marks
against certain traditional assumptions.
While the emphasis differs, we need not
perhaps regard Hick's approach as a
fundamental 'alternative' rather than as a
modification and supplement.

Hindu philosophy

The philosophical traditions of Hinduism
address major issues of ONTOLOGY
(including the respective claims of MON-
ISM, DUALISM and the nature of ultimate
reality), EPISTEMOLOGY (including the
nature of perception), philosophy of language and the nature of inner SELFHOOD.
They also concern the practical issue of
'release' (*moksha*) from a cycle of rebirth
and reincarnation (*samsara*).

In spite of very wide differences of
'viewpoint' or philosophical emphasis, the
astika (Hindu) schools of philosophy find
their common roots in the Vedas (*c.* 1500–
800 BCE), which have the status of sacred
scripture (śruti). The Nastika schools

accord less status to the Vedas, but are
generally BUDDHIST or Jainist.

EARLY SOURCES FOR
PHILOSOPHICAL REFLECTION

The Vedas embody four collections of
texts: the *Rig-Veda*, *Sama-Veda*, *Yajur-
Veda* and *Athavna-Veda*. Although early
Vedic hymns address gods and goddesses
and Vedic material includes rules about
sacrifices, from around 800 BCE philosophical reflection begins to understand
these not in explicitly polytheist terms,
but either as symbolic representations of
ultimate reality, or (in other traditions) as
aspects of a supreme Being.

The foundation texts for later philosophical reflections are especially the Upani-
šads (*c.* 800–500 BCE). These 108 Sanskrit
texts count as Vedic scripture, but are
primarily philosophical treatises concerning especially the relation between *ātman*
(true, inner, Self) and *brahman*, ultimate
reality. 'What is *brahman?*' remains a
central question, which provides a point
of departure for later philosophical traditions.

The Vedanta ('end of the Veda') focus
particularly on *ātman–brahman* in terms
of the question about 'liberation' or
'release'. These reflections are later developed in two directions by the two most
significant Hindu philosophers of the
medieval age. ŚAṄKĀRĀ (*c.* 788–820)
interprets *brahman* along the lines of a
'monist', 'anti-dualist' philosophy
(Advaita Vedanta); RĀMĀNUJA (*c.* 1017–
1137) develops the theme of the Vedanta
in terms of a (clearly) 'modified' monism
(Visista-advaita Vedanta).

The *Bhagavad Gita* ('Song of God'),
emerging initially from around the third
century BCE but perhaps edited over some
five centuries, is a short philosophical
dialogue in poetic form, also on the theme
of liberation (*moksha*) of the true Self
(*ātman*). The divine figure of Krishna,
disguised as a charioteer, urges Prince
Arjuna to seek liberation by deeds of
selfless action and by religious devotion.

Although this has the status of post-scriptural sacred tradition (*smrti*), in practice it is treated as scripture (*śruti*), and is regarded as REVELATION.

Again, the two schools that follow Śankārā and Rāmānuja respectively adopt a different emphasis on the basis of the same source-text. Śankārā, whose philosophical concern lies with an eventual identification of the SELF with *brahman*, stresses self-less deeds as the path that leads on to liberation. Rāmānuja, whose philosophy allows for a more characterizable Supreme Being, emphasizes the path of religious devotion.

MONIST ONTOLOGY (ADVAITA VEDANTA) AND MODIFIED MONISM (VISISTA-ADVAITA VEDANTA)

The metaphysical question 'What is *brahman*?' remains foundational for numerous less basic philosophical viewpoints and religious practices. If *brahman* is viewed, with Śankārā and the Advaita Vedanta or monist tradition, as a virtually uncharacterizable Ultimate Reality with which the true inner Self (*ātman*) may be united, two consequences then follow.

First, Ultimate Reality is an impersonal ABSOLUTE, with no personal defining qualities. It may be perceived as 'undifferentiated consciousness' (*nirguna brahma*). 'Difference' within the Absolute is an 'illusion' (*avidyā*; sometimes also *māyā*). Second, the way to find liberation from the pain and fragmentation of earthly existence, rebirth and reincarnation is through the identity of the self with *brahman*. This may come about, in due time, by attaining the 'knowledge' (*vidyā*) that overcomes ignorance and sees illusion as illusion or ignorance (*avidyā*) or deception (*māyā*).

In this tradition, passion, emotion and strong desire nurture illusion. For example, a fearful concern for the self may lead to the misperception of a harmless rope as a harmful snake. By contrast, careful, disciplined, dispassionate habits of mental concentration and of disengagement from desire and passion, prepare the way for liberation in which the Self becomes identified with *brahman*. In Advaita Vedanta an appeal is made to the aphorism 'You are that' (*Tat Tvam Asi*) for the identification of the self with *brahman* (in the *Chandogya Upaniśad*).

By contrast, the strongly 'modified monism' (Visista-advaita) that finds notable expression in Rāmānuja accepts that differentiation and distinction need not be illusory. The early distinctions between different gods and goddesses in the Vedic hymns need not be understood in a polytheistic way. They may (to reapply Ninian Smart's term) come to express a 'refracted' THEISM; a theism that perceives God to have many characterizable faces or aspects, even if none characterizes God alone or fully.

In most theistic religions, anthropomorphic imagery is used to represent certain aspects of the character of God, even if these are duly qualified, in turn, either by negation or by other images. If, in monism, ultimate reality is 'All', in modified monism God may be, in one sense, all-pervasive, but as in PANENTHEISM rather than PANTHEISM. Moreover, rebirth may be release into the heavenly realm, rather than release into absorption in the All.

Issues about boundaries of identity are complex. For example, some view the figure of Krishna in the *Bhagavad Gita* as an incarnation of the deity Vishnu. Shiva is a destroyer god in Bhakti (devotional) Hinduism. Hinduism has retained a sacrificial system from earliest times, and numerous 'representations' of deities. In philosophical terms these may be regarded either as instrumentally useful but ontologically illusory (broadly, Advaita Vedanta and Śankārā) or as provisional, fragmentary, anthropomorphic and symbolic (very broadly, Visista-advaita and Rāmānuja).

When we survey the spectrum of 'schools' in Hindu philosophy, it emerges that Śankārā, and Rāmānuja do not constitute opposite ends of the spectrum. 'Radical' or 'Pure' monism (Sudhadvaita-vada) goes further than Śaṅkārā; dualist (Dvaitavada) ontology (in Madhva) makes a more clear-cut differentiation than does Rāmānuja.

PHILOSOPHICAL SCHOOLS AND DEVELOPING TRADITIONS

Śaṅkārā offers some attempt to mediate between the two main traditions by a complex use of the contrast between appearance and reality. At a 'lower' level of knowledge, the level of mere appearance, religious devotion to gods or a God has a certain relative validity. Nevertheless, 'higher' knowledge reveals that both the notion of God and religious devotion fall under the category of illusion (māyā). Brahman is revealed as undifferentiated Reality with whom the ātman is identical and united as One, but perceived to be so only in a state of avidyā. Cognitive or conceptual discourse may obscure this insight.

In contrast to notions in the early Vedic hymns of release and rebirth into a heavenly realm of gods and ancestors, in this tradition 'release' (moksha) does not mean rebirth into a new kind of existence but escape from the cycle of existence and reincarnation altogether, to become undifferentiated ātman/brahman. Universal, ultimate, Reality has embraced the Self as itself.

A third tradition, alongside those of Śaṅkārā and Rāmānuja, emerges in the philosophy of MADHVA (c.1238–c.1317). Madhva is said to have founded the school of Dvaita Vedanta. Although technically this denotes a dualist ontology, it is 'dualist' in the sense that Madhva asserts an absolute difference between God (īśvara) and human souls (jīva). This is not the difference between creator and a created order. As 'souls', humankind coexists as a second eternal principle. Nevertheless, it supports 'devotion' (bhakti) to a God who is transcendent by virtue of 'difference' (bheda).

As we noted, however, a fourth position stands even nearer to absolute monism than Śaṅkārā. Vallabhācārya (1479–1531), the last of the 'classical' Vedanta philosophers, promoted a 'pure monism' or 'pure non-dualism' (Sudhadvaita). Yet even so, he was more ready to speak of a Supreme Being than was Śaṅkārā.

As traditions of Hindu philosophy developed, there emerged a number of 'schools', which differed not only in where they placed the emphasis, but also in their specific range of interests or agendas. It has become conventional to identify six of these as the main schools, and usually they are categorized as three pairs.

The Nyāya school, or the 'Logic' school, reflects an earlier era in which philosophical reflection grew out of oral debate. It is concerned with method, or method of proof, but still serves the liberating goal of practical 'knowledge' (juana or vidyā). It addresses the agenda identified below as epistemology, including the nature of perception. Linked as the other of a pair is the Vaisesika, or Atomist, school. This is concerned to identify irreducible constituents within the world that account for difference. 'Distinction' (viśesas) or distinctive characterization and its criteria, possibility and grounds provide the main, but not exclusive, agenda. The nature of CAUSALITY forms part of this agenda.

A third school, Sāṇkhya or the 'Enumerationist' school, conceives of a self-sufficient universe, which leaves no need or room for God. The school is ancient and explicitly atheistic. It 'enumerates' the facts of the world or reality to explain components and categories. It is paired with the school of Yoga, which is arguably (the issue is disputed) not atheistic. Yoga explores disciplines of the body and the mind, with the aim of disengaging from distraction and attaining a disclosure of the essence of the soul (paruṣa).

Of the remaining two schools, Mimāmsa is the 'Exegesis' school, concerned with Vedic texts and their significance for life and devotion. The traditions of the school with which it is paired, the Vedanta, have already been explored in some measure (above) with reference to the Upaniśads and the different ontologies of monism and qualified monism focused by the themes of *brahman* and *ātman*. This continues to be an important, major, tradition. Trevor Ling, among others, calls it 'the most influential' for modern Hindu philosophy.

EPISTEMOLOGY, PHILOSOPHY OF LANGUAGE AND PHILOSOPHIES OF THE SELF

Hindu philosophy gives particular consideration to three sources of knowledge: perception, inference and first-hand verbal testimony. Perception may begin with sense-perception. However, most philosophical traditions recognize the contribution of mental or intuitive perception, while some include the heightened perception that may arise through mystical contemplation or ascetic techniques.

Inference utilizes A POSTERIORI argument when direct perception is excluded. Some perceptions may invite inferences about what is currently not perceived, in the way that ARISTOTLE in Greek tradition and AQUINAS in Christian tradition drew inferences from observed occurrences or phenomena in the world. Some schools of philosophy elaborate SYLLOGISMS for valid inference. These include a five-term syllogism where two of the terms formulate positive and negative examples, analogies or applications.

First-hand testimony may include the testimony of sacred writings on the basis of their status as revelation. A problem may arise here, however, in relation to classical claims that the Vedic texts are timeless and without human authors.

In the period of the fifth century Bhaṛtṛhari formulated a kind of philosophy of language. It includes, but goes beyond, questions of grammar. In positive terms he argues that COGNITIVE awareness of CONCEPTS depends on prior use of language. More questionably, he insists that the basis of language is 'natural', drawing on innate ideas, rather than resting upon convention.

The Schools of Mimāṃsa (Exegesis school) and (in part) Nyāya (Logic school) formulated what amounts to criteria for the currency of meaning. Words convey meaning not only as words but also in terms of what Saussure, in the modern era (1913), would call 'syntagmatic relations'. 'Tusk' derives its meaning-currency partly from its contextual juxtaposition to 'elephant', and so on. The term 'syntactic relations' comes near to 'syntagmatic relations', with even a rudimentary hint of what in the modern era would be called linguistic 'competence', or, in John Searle, 'Background'.

Questions relating to the self include debates about the stability or illusion of personal identity. Is it the same self who sleeps, dreams, wakes and reflects on the self? If someone is ill, is 'the self' ill? Is the self 'subject' of all experience, or witness of all experience, or both? Does the self provide grounds for differentiated identity, or is the self a manifestation of a universal consciousness? Does the same 'self' experience reincarnation in successive modes of existence, as different as the existence of human persons, animals, demons or angels?

This brings us back full circle to the discussion of the relation between *ātman* and *brahman*. Assessments of selfhood are bound up with ontologies: with monism with modified monism, with pure monism or with an eternal dualism. Similarly, the respective evaluations of appearance, illusion, deception and reality also serve as a major part of the framework for this debate.

COMPARISONS WITH INDEPENDENT PARALLELS OR RESONANCES IN WESTERN PHILOSOPHY

It is widely accepted that Eastern philosophies repay study not only for their own sake, but also because they often formulate issues that resonate with possible parallels in Western philosophies, from an independent and often unexpected angle. Another 'viewpoint' may throw fresh light upon both sides.

Although we may briefly mention Parmenides and Democritus on ontology, an outstanding example comes from PLATO (428–348 BCE), especially in the *Phaedo*. Plato writes: 'The body (Greek, *to sôma*) fills us with passions and fears (*epithymôn kai phobon*) ... It makes it impossible for us to think ... We must be free of the body to behold the actual reality with the eye of the soul apart from the body (*he psyche ... chôris tou sômatos*) (*Phaedo*, 66, c and e).

We noted above, by way of comparison, the passage in the *Chandogya Upaniśad* that desire and fear could nurture illusion (for example in misperceiving a rope as a snake), while the soul or inner, true self (*ātman*) belongs to the realm of *brahman*, or changeless, ultimate Reality. Release (*moksha*) from the body and from the cycle of rebirth and reincarnation into any 'body' is sought by disciplines of the mind and by 'knowledge'. Even the maxim of SOCRATES (470–399 BCE), that 'virtue is knowledge' has a loose resonance.

Arguably, even if less closely, philosophical debates about ontology, including cosmic atomism and the nature of Being or Reality, find some parallels. Thales of Miletus (*c.* 624–546 BCE) and Democritus (*c.* 460–370 BCE) formulate an atomism that offers resonances with the school of Vaiśeṣika, the Atomist school. Parmenides of Elea (fl. *c.* 510–492 BCE) argued that ultimate Reality is Being, while 'coming into being' is illusory, on the ground that we can assert 'that it is', while to try to assert 'that it is not' presupposes or entails a self-contradiction from which 'none can learn'.

Bhartṛhari's question concerning whether language is 'natural', or based on convention, is the main subject in Plato's *Cratylus*. Further, if we move from ancient Greek philosophy to the modern period, the debate about monism continues in SPINOZA (1632–77), while the distinction between *Appearance and Reality* provides the title of a major work by BRADLEY (1846–1924).

It would be misleading to see global philosophy as sustaining a broadly EMPIRICAL tradition even when we have exempted such 'minority' writers as Plato, Kant, Hegel and Bradley. Eastern traditions convey a different impression, as well as different methods and different approaches. (*See also* ANTHRO-MORPHISM; ATHEISM; EMPRICISM; LANGUAGE IN RELIGION; METAPHYSICS; MYSTICISM; NĀGĀRJUNA; NISHIDA; NISHITANI; SYMBOL.)

Hobbes, Thomas (1588–1679)

An English philosopher, educated at Oxford, Hobbes made his most influential contributions to political philosophy, especially through his work *Leviathan* (1651). This grew out of the earlier disputes between Royalists and Parliamentarians prior to the Civil War.

In relation to philosophy of religion, however, Hobbes also promoted a strongly materialist view of the world and humankind. Mental phenomena are epiphenomenal. The idea of spirit or soul, Hobbes asserted, is self-contradictory, as if one were to postulate the existence of 'immaterial material'.

The world and humankind are governed, Hobbes believed, by causal forces. Humankind is moved by appetites and passions. It is ignorance of second causes, Hobbes asserted, that gives rise to notions of 'RELIGION', together with the effects of fear and superstition. However, some argue that in spite of his critique of 'popular' religion, Hobbes merely found no place for 'God' within philosophy, but was not committed to an explicit ATHE-ISM. This issue remains disputed.

ETHICS can be formulated only in terms of the pursuit of self-gratification and heightened vitality. Nevertheless, Hobbes concedes that an anarchy in which 'might is right' would be destructive. This is the context of his well-known dictum that in the distant past, before the rise of 'civilization', humankind lived lives that were 'solitary, poor, nasty, brutish, and short'.

A social contract is needed whereby 'natural' powers to seize goods from others are replaced by a voluntary contract to subordinate personal power to a governing body, preferably a monarch. Thereby 'order' may be achieved, and provide a framework to constrain human appetites. This 'sovereign power' is the 'soul' of Leviathan, the state, that is a 'mortal God'. (*See also* CAUSE, MATERIALISM.)

Hume, David (1711–76)

Hume is the most radical and thoroughgoing of the major British empiricists, following on the empirical traditions of LOCKE (1632–1704) and BERKELEY (1685–1753), but differing from both. He differs from Locke on the powers and scope of REASON, and from Berkeley on the latter's 'immaterialist' ONTOLOGY.

Although he called his *Treatise of Human Nature* (1739–40) 'sceptical', Hume was too cautious in refraining from going beyond firm data to be called a 'sceptic' in the epistemological or fullest technical sense of the term. This is not to deny that he had a sceptical cast of mind.

A Scottish philosopher and historical writer, Hume was born and educated in Edinburgh. He served as a librarian and administrator rather than as a professional teacher of philosophy. His central philosophical theme was that we cannot go beyond 'experience'. He published *A Treatise of Human Nature* at around the early age of twenty-eight, to which he appended the sub-title 'Being an Attempt to Introduce the Experimental Method of Reasoning into Moral Subjects'. He

respected and admired natural science, including the work of NEWTON.

Hume's other works included *An Enquiry Concerning Human Understanding* (1748), *The Natural History of Religion* and (published after his death) *Dialogues Concerning Natural Religion* (1778). He also produced a six-volume history of England. He confessed to 'an aversion to everything but the pursuits of philosophy and general learning'.

The *Enquiry Concerning Human Understanding* is largely a re-working of the *Treatise*. The *Treatise* 'fell dead-born from the press without ... excit[ing] a murmur', and Hume was convinced that this was because of its presentation rather than its content. However, *The Treatise*, book I still stands in its own right, and book I, part 2 does not appear in the *Enquiry*.

SENSATIONS, PERCEPTIONS, IMPRESSIONS, AND SELF, IN THE *TREATISE* AND *ENQUIRIES*

Hume begins both the *Treatise* and the *Enquiries* by distinguishing between 'different species of philosophy'. The methods of 'natural' philosophy (i.e. science) tell us most about 'the objects of our senses'; speculative philosophy is 'uncertain and chimerical'; 'scepticism ... is subversive of speculation' (*Enquiries*, 3rd edn, ed. P.H. Nidditch, Oxford: Clarendon, 1975, sect. I, para. 8). Sense-data enter the mind as 'impressions' of sensation. Impressions are 'all our more lively perceptions' (sect. II, para. 12). The 'less lively' are 'Thoughts' or 'Ideas' (ibid.). The core of Hume's empiricist argument is 'that nothing can ever be present to the mind but an image or perception ... the senses are the only inlets' (ibid., sect. XII, pt I, para. 118).

This leads to inferences about the SELF. 'The mind has never anything present to it but the perceptions, and cannot possibly reach any experience of their connexion with objects' (ibid., para. 119). Hence Hume concludes that the 'self' is no more than a bundle of perceptions.

Even causality cannot be 'observed', only constant conjunction; while 'reasoning' A PRIORI provides no knowledge of cause and effect (ibid., sect. IV, pt I, paras. 23–6). Hume acknowledges that in practice daily life depends on assumptions about causality, space and time, and the independent existence of the external world, but these things are not empirically demonstrable, and no other avenue of demonstration is available.

DIALOGUES CONCERNING NATURAL RELIGION, AND 'OF MIRACLES' IN ENQUIRIES

Hume admits in his essay on MIRACLES that 'he could not let alone' issues of RELIGION, even though he did not assent to any version of received religion. He did not believe, in effect, in miracles, or in special REVELATION, or in POST-MORTAL EXISTENCE. 'God' remained for him 'a variable, an enigma, an inexplicable mystery'. The explicit aim of 'Of Miracles', however, was 'to silence ... bigotry and superstition'. (*Enquiries*, sect. X, pt I, para. 86; cf. paras. 87–101).

Indeed in *The Natural History of Religion* (1757) Hume expresses the view that 'monotheism' encourages intolerance. Sometimes more popular religion, he claims, by contrast remains more polytheistic and more tolerant beneath its official formularies. Hume's target is not so much 'religion' as 'organized' religion.

The *Dialogues* were completed before 1761, but waited seventeen years for publication. Hume preferred 'to live quietly'. The characters in the *Dialogues* are based on Cicero. 'Demea' is an exponent of orthodox RATIONALISM; 'Cleanthes' defends teleology and philosophical theism; 'Philo' probably represents a viewpoint similar to Hume's own.

Demea claims that by abandoning the A PRIORI ideas of rationalism, Philo and Cleanthes are selling out to SCEPTICISM, (*Dialogues*, pt I). Cleanthes appeals to observation of the world for inferences to the existence of design (ibid., pts II, III).

Philo questions whether Cleanthes rests too much on 'ANTHROPOMORPHISM' (ibid., pt IV). As the *Dialogues* proceed Demea appeals, in vain, for some rational foundation (e.g. pt VI); while Philo insists upon the lack of 'data' on which any system may be built (pt VII).

Part IX raises the question of a divine nature, and X–XI provide Hume's classic discussion of the problem of EVIL. Hume's cautious 'scepticism' emerges: there simply is not enough firm evidence to establish an argument from design, although he cannot utterly exclude it; the problem of evil generates as many counter-arguments against design on the part of a good God as whatever 'evidence' Cleanthes may try to cite in its support.

Evil is real: it 'embitters the life of every living being. The stronger prey on the weaker and keep them in perpetual terror' (ibid., pt X, 62). Hume observes: 'Epicurus' old questions are yet unanswered. Is [God] willing to prevent evil, but not able? Then he is impotent. Is he able, but not willing? Then he is malevolent. Is he both able and willing? Whence, then, is evil?' (ibid., 66).

In his essay 'Of Miracles' Hume is sceptical about the degree of genuine evidence offered in support of miracles in Judaeo-Christian tradition. He is overtly sceptical about evidence for the resurrection of Jesus Christ as the foundation of Christian faith.

However, this merges into a second line of argument. Since we are considering not regularities within the world but, by definition, virtually unique effects alleged to be caused by a clearly unique Agent, it is difficult, if not impossible, to conceive of what might count as adequate evidence, even if it existed. We have no experimental analogies which would allow induction from experience.

Yet the whole of Hume's work concerns what may be based upon empiricist criteria alone. The question about religion boils down to the argument: granted that there is no revelation, what kind of natural religion can built upon 'experience' since this is mediated solely through the senses and 'perception'? On the basis of Hume's EPIS-TEMOLOGY, then, it is scarcely surprising that an undogmatic, cautious, scepticism ensues. (*See also* BELIEF; CAUSE; EMPIRICISM; SCIENCE AND RELIGION; TELEOLOGICAL ARGUMENT.)

I

Ibn Rushd (Averroes) (1126–98)

Averroes is the medieval Latin name for the Arabic form transliterated as Ibn Rushd. He represents the greatest figure of Arabic or ISLAMIC PHILOSOPHY in the context of its late Spanish school. He was born in Cordoba, and served as lawyer, physician, judge and diplomat in Cordoba and Seville. In his philosophical writing he produced an extensive range of commentaries on texts of ARISTOTLE and a reply to AL-GHAZALI'S attack on the privileging of philosophy over revelation and religion. He entitled the latter *The Incoherence of the Incoherence*.

Whereas in modern philosophical thought it is customary to note substantial differences between PLATO and Aristotle, like AL-FARABI, Ibn Rushd drew on both traditions almost as if they were one. Like IBN SINA (Avicenna), he sometimes drew on PLOTINUS and NEOPLATONISM, but he preferred Aristotle's idea of the eternity of the world to Ibn Sina's scheme of emanations flowing from the First Cause, Prime Mover, God or Allah. Plotinian MYSTICISM also features in positive terms.

If al-Farabi was known among Arabic philosophers as 'the Second Teacher', and Ibn Sina as the 'third Aristotle', Ibn Rushd became widely known as 'the Commentator' (i.e. on Aristotle). Some of his commentaries are short paraphrases; others are detailed exegetical expositions. He also wrote a commentary on Plato's *Republic*, again seeking synthesis or integration between Aristotelian and Platonic perspectives.

A significant point of resonance between Plato, Aristotle, Ibn Rushd and the Christian philosophy of AUGUSTINE and Thomas AQUINAS is their common emphasis on the 'ordered' nature of the universe as an organic, rational, purposive hierarchy embodying differentiations of form or levels of being.

As for al-Farabi and Ibn Sina, such beliefs as the eternity of the world and the superiority of philosophical thought invited tension with the Qur'an. Hence Ibn Rushd postulated a HERMENEUTICS of sacred texts adapted to varying capacities of their readers. Philosophical minds could 'see' more than others in the Qur'an. He supports this by his philosophy of intelligence and of language. Not surprisingly, it appears that around 1195, three years before his death, a conservative reaction provoked his retirement. Nevertheless he remains a highly influential figure for medieval philosophy in the West. (*See also* EVIL; LANGUAGE IN RELIGION; PLENITUDE.)

Ibn Sina (Avicenna), Abu 'Ali al-Husayn (980–1037)

Ibn Sina (the Arabic form of the name known widely in the West as Avicenna) was born in Persia, showed early brilliance of mind, and became vizier and physician to several sultans. He formulated a system of philosophy that reflects, but does not merely replicate, his careful reading of ARISTOTLE. Of all the medieval thinkers of ISLAMIC PHILOSOPHY, his is the most detailed, complex and probably, influential work. The translation of his writings from Arabic to Latin had a huge impact on the revival of Aristotelian philosophy on the twelfth- and thirteenth-century West (*see* Thomas AQUINAS).

If AL-FARABI was often called 'the Second Teacher' in the Arab world (after Aristotle as 'the First Teacher'), Ibn Sina was widely known as the 'Third Aristotle', even if his philosophy did not merely replicate Aristotle's. He was also influenced by PLOTINUS and NEOPLATONSIM, as well as by al-Farabi's work on Aristotle.

Much of Ibn Sina's work was in the area of medicine. He was entirely familiar with the writings of Galen, and his work *The Canon of Medicine* attempted a synthesis of Greek and Arabic medical traditions expounded as a coherent 'science'.

Ibn Sina wrestles with the central problems of philosophy: with God and Being (ONTOLOGY); the nature of knowledge (EPISTEMOLOGY); CAUSATION; EVIL; CREATION and LOGIC. Some argue that his distinctive development of Aristotle's distinction between ACTUALITY and POSSIBILITY even anticipates the more modern contrast between essence and EXISTENCE.

REASON opens the way to travel through various levels of understanding, and ultimately may lead to God. Ibn Sina develops Aristotle's contrast between 'passive' knowledge (the reception of data through the senses and 'active' knowledge (relating data to construct ideas and concepts) into four elements: perception through the senses; retention and memory; imagination and evaluation. In effect, he allows for empirical and rationalist theories of knowledge supported by understanding and judgement.

The subtlety of Ibn Sina's distinctions between UNIVERSALS and particulars, between possibility and existence, between the NECESSARY and CONTINGENT served to stimulate the high SCHOLASTICISM of the West in the twelfth and thirteenth centuries. It is likely that this influence was felt in the University of Paris and perhaps Oxford in the thirteenth century.

Possible beings, Ibn Sina argued, required a CAUSE that determines whether they exist. God, however, is uncaused and, in the sense suggested by this contrast and context, a 'necessary' Being. This is not to be confused with the merely conceptual necessity of Plato's Forms. God is pure Intelligence, who is perfectly good and transcendent. Arguably Ibn Sina's concession to the notion of 'emanations' serves to underline divine TRANSCENDENCE, although it is difficult to reconcile with the Qur'an (or with Hebrew–Christian scripture). Doubtless Ibn Sina would reply that every level of being is derived from the One Being, God or Allah.

Although he denied bodily RESURRECTION, Ibn Sina argued for the immortality of the SOUL. A virtuous soul has actualized its possibility, and therefore continues to exist in this form. Ibn Sina remains closer to al-Farabi than to AL-KINDI or certainly AL-GHAZALI in his estimate of the privileged role of philosophy. It is scarcely surprising that al-Ghazali attacked his work as moving too far from Islam and the Qur'an. (*See also* EMPRICISM; POSTMORTAL EXISTENCE; RATIONALISM). For further details see L.C. Goodman, *Avicenna* (London: Routledge, 1992).

idealism

Traditionally in philosophy the term denotes the school of thought that regards the mind and ideas as more primarily constitutive of reality than the material or empirical world. Leibniz (1646–1716) may have been the first to use the term as a philosophical designation, which he applied to PLATO's thought.

One predictable problem arises from the different contrasts in relation to which the term idealism is used. When idealism stands in contrast to the phenomena of the material or CONTINGENT, Plato is rightly seen as an idealist. However, if idealism is allied with NOMINALISM against REALISM, the term would cease to apply to Plato, since in a broad sense he may also be regarded as a realist.

In British philosophy, LOCKE (1632–1704) and more radically BERKELEY (1685–1753) regard the sense data that is empirically perceived as objects of reflection as, in effect, constituting 'ideas'. Thus their EMPIRICISM turns out to be compatible with, even to imply, idealism. Locke was both an empiricist and an 'epistemological idealist'. For Berkeley, however, all perception took the form of ideas: 'To exist is to be perceived.' He termed his own idealism 'immaterialism'. Hence he might be thought of as ontologically 'an immaterialist idealist'.

In German philosophy, idealism becomes more dominant, following KANT'S emphasis (1724–1804) on the activity of the mind in shaping what we perceive through COGNITION and a structuring through the CATEGORIES that the mind brings to bear in order to understand and to 'order' perception and understanding. Although he produced a 'Refutation of Idealism', Kant's postulating a reality external to the mind still remains a presupposition required by the mind. Kant is sometimes called a 'transcendental idealist'.

The three most distinctive and characteristic German idealists are FICHTE (1762–1814) HEGEL (1770–1831), and SCHELLING (1775–1854). Fichte dispensed with Kant's 'things-in-themselves' to propose a more radical idealism than that of Kant. Fichte's *Attempt at a Critique of All*

Revelation (1792) and his work on the nature of philosophy (1794) expounded an idealism in which 'reality' is grounded in the SELF and self-consciousness. Schelling called this system, therefore, 'subjective idealism'.

In spite of Fichte's influence on Schelling, the latter sought to ground his system of idealism in a philosophy of nature (1797). This seemed to Schelling to be a more 'objective idealism'. Nevertheless, Schelling's version of idealism changed quickly, repeatedly, and radically, to the consternation of Hegel, who had been his collaborator in early years. Hegel criticized his lack of conceptual rigour and pantheist leanings, in which, by dissolving conceptual differentiations, he created 'a night in which all cows are black'.

HEGEL sought to ground his own idealist system in history and LOGIC. The ABSOLUTE, or absolute Idea, or 'God', manifests itself through a double DIALECTIC of history and of logic. There is also a dialectic between the finite and the Whole. Yet it was precisely Hegel's identification of the Absolute with Mind or Spirit (German, *Geist*) that provoked the reaction of the 'left-wing' 'young' Helegians, FEUERBACH (1804–72), Strauss, and Marx (1818–83) to replace 'Spirit' by humankind or by material, socio-economic forces. Hegel is sometimes described as an 'absolute idealist'.

In England, BRADLEY (1846–1924) drew a contrast between the self-contradictions that constitute 'appearance', and 'Reality', which comprises an all-inclusive totality, or the absolute (*Appearance and Reality*, 1893). 'Only the Whole is Real'; 'the Real is the rational'. He has been called 'the English Hegel'. Sometimes he is also classed (with Hegel and Royce) as an 'Absolute Idealist'.

In America Josiah Royce (1855–1916) combined aspects of Hegel's idealism with a pragmatic view of history and communities. He held to the notion of 'ultimacy' in the sense of unsurpassability, and saw ideas as the moving dynamic of history. In theory, much rests on the premises of Hegel's idealism. Yet Royce's notions of progress as instantiated in community and 'interpretation' may suggest that 'pragmatic idealism' might be a more revealing classification than 'absolute' idealism.

Over-easy labels are often seductive rather than constructive, tempting readers towards a simplistic pigeon-holing of thinkers. Nevertheless, to qualify different versions of idealism (after Plato) as epistemological (Locke), immaterialist (Berkeley), transcendental (Kant), subjective (Fichte), objective (Schelling in his early–middle period), absolute (Hegel and Bradley) and pragmatic (Royce), serves to convey the major point that idealism is not a single philosophy, but a network of loosely interrelated systems. (*See also* EPISTEMOLOGY; MATERIALISM; OBJECTIVITY; ONTOLOGY; PANTHEISM; SUBJECTIVITY.)

identity

See SELF.

ideological criticism

In MARXIST traditions the term 'ideology' is used pejoratively to denote systems of ideas or BELIEFS, or a 'false consciousness' that serves to perpetuate and to underpin capitalist attitudes and values. In the social sciences it is used more generally (either pejoratively or neutrally) to denote systems of belief that are consciously or unconsciously invoked to underpin particular political or social structures, institutions and practices.

Hence ideological criticism denotes the epistemological and hermeneutical process of bringing these beliefs and the dynamics of their application to the surface. 'De-ideologization' belongs to the family of processes that includes DEMYTHOLOGIZING (BULTMANN); demystifying (Roland Barthes, DERRIDA), deconstructing (Derrida), 'emancipatory critique' (Habermas) and 'criticism of ideology' (T. Eagleton) as the exposure of deceptive or false beliefs drawn from society.

In relation to EPISTEMOLOGY, ideological criticism (often written as the German *Ideologiekritik*) assumes that rational reflection is never value-neutral but always guided by 'interest'. NIETZSCHE regarded this 'interest' as a manipulative power-interest; Habermas accepts a broader notion. In HERMENEUTICS it has become a tool used in the critical reading of sacred texts. (*See also* FREUD'S CRITIQUE OF RELIGION; REASON.)

immanence

In philosophy of religion this term is most characteristically applied to GOD in contrast to divine TRANSCENDENCE. More strictly, in THEISM (especially in Judaism, Christianity and Islam) it complements divine transcendence. It moves in the direction of PANTHEISM, or more accurately PANENTHEISM, but is not to be identified with pantheism. It denotes God's presence and action within the world and in the world order, in contrast to notions of divine action 'from beyond' or 'without'.

In a secondary sense immanence may be used more narrowly as a term in Kantian philosophy to denote what lies entirely within the limits of possible experience. Here 'immanent' stands in contrast not with transcendent but with transcendental. Also in SCHOLASTIC PHILOSOPHY 'immanent action' denotes that action the effects of which do not reach 'beyond' the subject or agent of the action.

Normally, however, immanence refers to divine presence and agency within the world, and often, but not always, goes hand-in-hand with a mystical, pietist, or modified pantheist approach to God. Fundamentally it denotes the nearness or indwelling of God, especially as animating an organic universe in OMNIPRESENCE.

Theism holds together divine transcendence and divine immanence. For God is 'beyond' the world and any CONTINGENT network of causes within the world, yet God is also 'within' the

world working through such causal net-
works. Expressed most sharply, a truly
transcendent God remains free to choose
to be immanent within God's world,
whereas a wholly immanent God would
be caught up in determined patterns
imposed by the world. (*See also* DEISM;
GOD, CONCEPTS AND 'ATTRIBUTES' OF;
MYSTICISM; PIETISM; TRANSCENDENTAL
PHILOSOPHY.)

immortality of the soul

See POST-MORTAL EXISTENCE OF THE SELF;
SOUL.

immutability of God

If the immutability of God is defined as the
assertion that 'God cannot change', in
what sense are we using the word
'change'? When the sacred texts of Judaism, Christianity and Islam speak of God
as 'unchanging', the emphasis seems to fall
first of all upon God's never-ending, ever-
ready, presence, and God's faithfulness to
remain consistent with God's self-REVELA-
TION and character.

ARGUMENTS FROM 'PERFECTION'?
PLATO, BOETHIUS AND AQUINAS

PLATO (428–348 BCE) draws a sharp line
between the realm of appearance, change
and imperfection and that of Ideas or
Forms, perfection and God. On this basis
to say that God could change would
logically imply that we locate God in the
CONTINGENT, empirical, imperfect world
of change, rather than to ascribe to God
the changeless perfection that characterizes the realm of Ideas or perfect
essences.

BOETHIUS (*c.* 480–525) and AUGUS-
TINE (354–430) recognized that TIME
belongs to the created order as part of
that which God has created. Hence God
cannot be conditioned by time, but is
characterized by ETERNITY as the very
condition and ground for time. If God is
'beyond' time, how can God undergo
change?

AQUINAS grounded the immutability of
God in his doctrine that God is 'simple'
and 'perfect' (*Summa Theologiae*, Ia, Qu.
3 and 4). The currency of divine 'simplicity' is that 'God *is*' (ibid., Qu. 3, art. 4).
Change would add to, or subtract from,
this Being, and render it 'becoming'.
Further, God 'lacks nothing of the mode
of ... perfection' (ibid., Qu. 4, art. 1).
Change would imply either movement
from 'less than perfect' or to 'less than
perfect'.

SWINBURNE'S 'STRONG' AND 'WEAK'
IMMUTABILITY

In contemporary discussion, however, it is
customary to distinguish, with SWIN-
BURNE, between the 'weaker' sense of
'cannot change in character', and 'stronger' sense of being, in effect, disengaged
from time, or temporal succession, on the
basis of 'divine timelessness' (Swinburne,
The Coherence of Theism, Oxford: Clarendon, 1977, 212–15).

Swinburne argues that if God 'fixed his
intentions "from all eternity", he would be
a very lifeless thing, not a person who
reacts to man with sympathy ... pardon or
chastening because he chooses there and
then' (ibid., 214). 'The God of ... Judaism, Islam and Christianity ... is a God in
continual interaction' with human persons
(ibid.).

PANNENBERG similarly insists that the
unity and eternity of God represents one
of two dimensions: God is 'intrinsically
differentiated unity' (*Systematic Theology*,
3 vols.; vol. 1, Edinburgh: T & T Clark,
1991, 405). Pannenberg endorses BARTH's
emphasis upon 'order and succession' in
the life of God. Barth called for 'a revision
of the traditional opposing of time to
eternity. Eternity does not mean timelessness' (ibid., 407).

MOLTMANN goes further. He speaks of
God's 'giving himself', even 'serving', and
choosing to participate in the world's grief
and redemption in 'the history of God' (cf.
The Trinity and the Kingdom of God,
London: SCM, 1981, 33, 35, and through-

out). 'God empties himself in creation, in presentation and redemption ... God's history with the world is played out ... in the changing efficaces of the divine Persons' (*Experiences in Theology*, London: SCM, 2000, 310, 311).

Many Thomist theologians will not wish to go as far as Moltmann. Further, those Islamic thinkers (*see* ISLAMIC PHILOSOPHY) who also retain a more Aristotelian approach will also tend towards a 'hard' concept of immutability alongside a strong doctrine of the providential will of Allah operative within the world. In HINDU PHILOSOPHY the Advaita Vedanta tradition of ŚANKĀRĀ would reject any notion of 'self-differentiation' within, let alone differentiation from, *brahman* as Ultimate Reality. 'Change' would be illusory.

PROCESS PHILOSOPHY: WHITEHEAD AND HARTSHORNE

In the distinctive perspective of PROCESS PHILOSOPHY God is 'always becoming'. HARTSHORNE (1897–2000) argues that the notion of God as ABSOLUTE tells only half of the story. God is temporal as well as eternal, world-inclusive as well as transcendent. The 'maximal greatness' of Perfection may be what it is at different times. As 'di-polar', God is both absolute and relative to change. (*See also* EMPRICISM; GOD, CONCEPT AND ATTRIBUTES OF; OMNIPOTENCE; OMNISCIENCE; TRANSCENDENCE.).

incommensurability

The term derives from the philosophy of science, notably from the earlier work of Thomas S. Kuhn (1922–96). In 1962 Kuhn published *The Structure of Scientific Revolutions* (2nd edn, Chicago: University of Chicago Press, 1970). He interpreted the history of science not as a single linear development of observation and ideas, but as a series of scientific traditions shaped and moulded in terms of the prevailing or dominant 'paradigm' of the era.

Kuhn's work embodied the fundamental insight that the history of science is not merely the history of a set of value-neutral observations of unselected, raw, value-neutral data, but includes a social dimension that reflects the conceptual expectations of scientists. These conceptual expectations or conceptual frames change particularly at the nodal points of scientific 'revolution' or 'paradigm-shift'.

The most familiar 'revolutions' include the transition from a pre-modern geocentric concept of the universe after Copernicus (1473–1543) noted that data appear differently in accordance with the position of the observer, and after Galileo (1564–1642) noted that the sun, not the earth, is the centre of the solar system. Stars are perceived as other suns, and the relation between motion and force is explored. Similarly, the work of NEWTON (1642–1727) on gravity and motion provided the overriding model or paradigm of gravity, mass and movement until Albert Einstein (1879–1955) demonstrated pioneering work on the relativity of space and time.

Einstein moved beyond the Newtonian concept of an 'absolute' space and time, and postulated their interdependence and theoretical unity. The energy of any mass is the product of the mass multiplied by the square of the speed of light ($E=mc^2$). Mass increases as an object approaches the velocity of light, while time slows as velocity increases.

This 'special theory of relativity' (dating from 1905–7) also demonstrates that an event appears differently from within different systems. For example, within an inertial system measurements and even clock-time will become different from how they appear under conditions of extreme velocity. The General Theory of Relativity (1916) relates gravitational forces to space–time 'curvature'.

None of this suggests that Newtonian physics is 'wrong' for everyday observations of space, time, gravity and motion. We still use Newton's assumptions (or 'paradigm') daily. However, Einstein's 'paradigm' overtakes it when more sophisticated theories are addressed about the nature of the universe.

Kuhn points out that there is no value-neutral external criterion of reference by which to adjudicate between such different paradigms. For the applicability of each paradigm largely depends on the nature of the system or agenda for which it is called into play.

RADICAL AND MODERATE UNDERSTANDINGS OF INCOMMENSURABILITY: MISAPPLICATIONS?

Kuhn's work has often been misinterpreted in theology. It is often taken to imply that self-contained 'conceptual schemes' can operate side by side without any reference at all to a common rationality, on the basis of their 'incommensurability'.

To be sure, Kuhn argued that different paradigms in science 'work in different worlds' (ibid., 134). However, Kuhn himself disowned the more radical relativistic and anti-rational implications that some draw from his work. He advises caution about its applications in his 1970 'Postscript' to the second edition of his work of 1962, and more emphatically in his work *The Essential Tension* (1977).

RORTY takes up Kuhn's notions of incommensurability and paradigms to argue that philosophical debate rests not on rational adjudication, but on a PRAGMATISM of 'nudging old problems aside' (*Contingency, Irony and Solidarity*, Cambridge: CUP, 1989, 264). Yet Rorty seems to allude only to Kuhn's earlier work, and it may be doubted whether Kuhn's work as a whole provides currency for Rorty's post-modern pragmatism. To replace argument by rhetoric does not strictly derive from Kuhn.

Donald Davidson utilizes the argument from inter-translatability between the texts of diverse cultural communities to show that the radical version of incommensurability will not hold water. Even if words and vocabulary have different conceptual currency, there are ways of understanding and overcoming these differences ('On the Very Idea of a Conceptual Scheme' in Davidson, *Truth and Interpretation*, Oxford: Clarendon, 1984, 183–98).

A spectrum of philosophical thinkers take up a variety of standpoints on these issues. Paul Feyerabend is probably more relativistic than the earlier Kuhn. H. Sankey reviews the range of responses in *The Incommensurability Thesis* (Sydney: Averbury Press, 1994). However, whatever the pragmatic and relativist overtones, Kuhn succeeds in showing the conditioning of scientific advances by the agenda of scientific communities and the illusion of entirely value-free knowledge. 'Secular' approaches are often no more value-free than 'religious' ones.

instantiation

Instantiation denotes providing instances, especially of a property or class. Some books on a desk may instantiate the property of being red or blue.

RUSSELL (1872–1970) in effect confirms KANT's response to DESCARTES that in the context of the ONTOLOGICAL ARGUMENT 'existence' is not a predicate. 'Existence' is more strictly thought of as providing instances of that of which the word is predicated, i.e. by instantiation. In the ontological argument is 'Being' instantiated?

The broader context is Russell's work on logical form, which allows 'exist' to be bracketed in such a form as 'For all x, x is y'. Instantiation is expressed in logical notation through the use of a QUANTIFIER.

Instantiation need not be tied to reformulations in LOGIC. Instantiation may clarify more general or abstract debate, such as claims for the principle of FALSIFIABILITY or the status of UNIVERSALS. WITTGENSTEIN'S explanation of 'Now I understand ...' as 'Now I know how to go on ...' (in a mathematical rule or formula) is not wholly unlike recognizing the role of instantiation as a criterion of understanding.

'Ireanaean' theodicy

See HICK.

Islamic philosophy

The foundations of Islamic thought cannot be separated from the work of the Prophet (Muhammad) and the sacred texts of the Qur'an (broadly 610–32; sometimes in older works the Arabic word is Anglicized as the 'Koran'). More details can be found under entries for leading Islamic philosophers, including AL-KINDI, (c. 813–c. 871); AL-FARABI, (875–950); IBN SINA (Avicenna, 980–1037); AL-GHAZALI (1058–1111); and IBN RUSHD (Averroes, 1126–98).

The great Islamic philosophers thus belong to the period from the ninth to the twelfth centuries, when Islamic influence and culture flourished from Central Asia to parts of Spain and North Africa. It would be a mistake to limit 'medieval philosophy' to such Christian Western thinkers as ANSELM, Thomas AQUINAS, DUNS SCOTUS and WILLIAM OF OCKHAM. Indeed it was Islamic and Arabic philosophy that rescued ancient Greek philosophy, especially Aristotelianism and NEOPLATONISM, from decline and obscurity.

Works by ARISTOTLE and Porphyry had been translated into Syriac by the school of Edessa in Mesopotamia, but more significantly these were translated, in turn, into Arabic, including some books by PLOTINUS mistakenly attributed also to Aristotle. Thus the 'revived' Aristotle represented an Aristotle who also embodied Platonic and Neoplatonic elements.

FOUNDING THINKERS

Al-Kindi held a position in the court of Baghdad and is widely regarded as the first great Arabic or Islamic philosopher. He emphasized the coherence of REVELATION and reason, and stressed the TRANSCENDENCE of God as the ABSOLUTE. Less clearly, there is a correlation, if not identification, of Allah as described in the Qur'an with the Supreme Being of Aristotle, and the One of Neoplatonism.

Al-Kindi attempted to combine the Neoplatonic philosophy of emanations with the Islamic (and Jewish and Christian) doctrine that creation arises by the sole initiation of the divine will, from nothing. He also expounded a broadly Aristotelian theory of the nature of human knowledge.

AL-FARABI moved more clearly in the direction of Aristotle, except for his retention and development of the Neoplatonic and Plotinian notion of emanations. He could accommodate the Islamic emphasis on divine transcendence by postulating that reality flows continually out of the One Source of perfection.

If there are rudimentary anticipations of modern PROCESS PHILOSOPHY in this one simple aspect, it might be suggested also that in placing philosophy, or at least the rigour of logic, above religious reflection, al-Farabi anticipated HEGEL on this issue. Those who are without philosophy understand truth only through symbols, in contrast to the strict logical demonstration that rational philosophical thought can offer. Al-Farabi also expounded PLATO's *Republic*, perceiving the role of philosophical thought for politics and society.

THE HEIGHT OF THE MOVEMENT

Abu 'Ali Ibn Sina (Avicenna) was born in Persia, and is often regarded as the greatest of the medieval Islamic philosophers, in spite of the high reputation of al-Farabi. His is the most detailed, complex and extensive account of the nature of God and Being (i.e. ONTOLOGY). He also worked out an EPISTEMOLOGY, or theory of knowledge, which coheres with this. Reason embraces sense-perception, memory or retention, imagination, and evaluation, estimation or judgement.

Ibn Sina also develops Aristotle's distinctions between the actual and the possible – almost, some have agreed, as if to hint at the more modern contrast between EXISTENCE and essence. A 'NECESSARY' entity exists by virtue of its essence. The existence of possible beings implies the existence of a Necessary Being who is God (see COSMOLOGICAL ARGUMENT for the existence of God; and FIVE WAYS of Thomas Aquinas). God is, in effect, Aristotle's Unmoved Mover.

In combining this Aristotelian perspective with Islamic theology Ibn Sina arrives at an ontology in which all events that occur do so necessarily. God remains beyond this kind of necessity as Ground of all (see ASEITY).

Al-Ghazali, however, considered that Ibn Sina, and still more seriously al-Farabi, had assigned too privileged a place to philosophy over Islamic theology. In particular he rejected any attempt to defend the notion of the ETERNITY of the world as both philosophically self-contradictory and contrary to the Qur'an. Further, Ibn Sina's notion of explaining 'necessity' in terms of causal relations of POSSIBILITY or ACTUALITY violated the notion of God's universal causative will (see OCCASIONALISM). Almost anticipating HUME, but in a different context, al-Ghazali questions the very status of philosophical assumptions about CAUSE.

SOUTHERN SPAIN

The Islamic culture of southern Spain also provided a Western centre for Arabic philosophy. Among these philosophers Ibn Rushd (Averroes) was the most significant. He wrote a series of commentaries on Aristotle. He attempted to disentangle a more authentic understanding of Aristotle from the lenses of Neo-platonism and theological motivations, which had clouded some of the work of his predecessors in Arabic philosophy.

Ibn Rushd attended to the issues that impinged from Islamic theology by formulating a hermeneutical theory of 'levels of interpretation' of the Qur'an (see HERMENEUTICS). He therefore remains the closest to Aristotle of all the great medieval Arabic or Islamic philosophers, taking up especially Aristotle's notion of the intellect in De Anima, book III.

INFLUENCE

It is to these Islamic and Arabic philosophers that the Jewish and Christian philosophers of the Middle Ages (e.g. MAIMONIDES, 1135–1204; ALBERT THE GREAT, c.1200–80; and Thomas AQUINAS, 1225–74) owe the climate of interest in Aristotle that their earlier translations had nurtured. Arabic texts were translated into Latin in Spain in the twelfth and thirteenth centuries.

Other directions of Islamic philosophy during this period take their points of departure from concerns about medicine, science and LOGIC in ancient Greek philosophy, or in a different direction exploration of MYSTICISM, often related to the traditions of Neoplatonism and Plotinus.

The main thrust, however, runs parallel with some of the later Christian philosophical concerns of Aquinas. Can the sacred texts of the faith be reformulated in ways that accord with some of the conceptual issues of Greek philosophy, especially with reason and wisdom as these feature in Aristotle? These centuries yield the golden age of Islamic and Arabic philosophy. (For a useful introduction, see Oliver Leaman, Brief Introduction to Islamic Philosophy, Oxford: Blackwell, 1999.)

J

Jaspers, Karl Theodor
(1883–1969)

Jaspers graduated as a doctor of medicine at Heidelberg in 1909; practised psychiatry and lectured in psychology; and became Professor of Philosophy at Heidelberg in 1921. He was deprived of his chair during Hitler's years of power (1937–45), after which he was reinstated. He regarded his three-volume *Philosophy* (1932) as his major work, and wrote on NIETZSCHE, DESCARTES, MYTH, TRANSCENDENCE, guilt and FREEDOM.

Although he was unwilling to accept the description 'existentialist', Jaspers began with the human situation. As a medical psychiatrist and academic psychologist, he was well aware that a human person could be considered as an empirical entity within the world, about whom observations could be made. However, he explored the distinctive nature of human consciousness (*Bewusstsein*), and most especially and characteristically how human finite incompleteness points to a transcendent 'beyond'.

More technically, the human subject, as empirical subject open to observation, as logical subject who thinks, and as agent who experiences freedom, yields 'modes of encompassing'. Jaspers respectively designates these as (1) *Dasein* (Being-there,

empirical subject); (2) consciousness as being (*Bewusstsein überhaupt*); and (3) *Geist* (Mind or Spirit). All these are 'IMMANENT' modes. However, beyond these basic experiences of givenness or situatedness within the world, lies the possibility of a transcendent mode.

While he distanced himself from HEIDEGGER, Jaspers wrote: 'Existential philosophy has to keep consciousness free for possibility' (*Philosophy* [1932], Chicago: University of Chicago Press, 1969, vol. 2, 342). Truth, for Jaspers is never static: 'Truth is not a property, but something that is present as *we* search for it' (ibid., vol. 1, 37).

Life involves 'struggling and suffering ... I cannot avoid guilt ... I must die'. Jaspers calls these 'boundary situations' (ibid., vol. 2, 178). Because such situations confront the human subject with 'an indeterminate possibility, I must search for being if I want to find my real self' (ibid., vol. 1, 45). The 'object-like' conventions and standardizations of the empirical world and repressive traditions of religion or other value-systems peel away as I face 'truth' in the authentic mode 'for me'. Here the transcendent impinges on the immanent with authenticity.

Jaspers distinguishes between rigid, fixed, dogmatic forms of religious expression and 'the cipher [or symbol] that allows men's boundless yearning for the real presence of God to be satisfied in an instant so to speak ... God remains inevocably hidden' (*Philosophical Faith and Revelation*, New York: Harper & Row, 1967, 341). Authentic revelation of truth and authentic faith will never take away human freedom.

A positive view of 'God' or 'religion', therefore, is held together with a pluriform view of truth and a multi-valent, or many-level, account of language. This and other features are noted under the entry on EXISTENTIALISM. In his later works Jaspers applies some of these issues to politics, where he defends 'freedom and the rights of man'. The English title *The Future of Mankind* (1961) first appeared as a work in German as *Die Atombombe und die Zukunft des Menschen* (1958). (*See also* EMPIRICISM; IMMANENCE.)

Jewish philosophy

Jewish philosophy has taken a variety of forms, ancient, medieval and modern, but in general has sought to integrate insights into the human, or into the relation between God and the world drawn from Jewish sacred writings, traditions and experiences, with wider systems of rational thought and philosophy.

Among key Jewish philosophers who still retain considerable influence MAIMO-NIDES (1135–1204) holds together the TRANSCENDENCE and perfection of God with issues arising from the problem of EVIL, the use of ANTHROPOMORPHISM and ANALOGY in Hebrew scripture (the Christian Old Testament), debates about the nature of CREATION and the ETERNITY of the world, and issues of providence and human FREEDOM.

In more recent years BUBER (1878–1965) and LEVINAS (1906–95) have explored the distinctively personal dimension of human SELFHOOD, and the nature of God as the God who addresses humankind as 'Thou', and who gives 'without utility' as well as in other ways.

ANCIENT PHILOSOPHY: THE WRITINGS OF PHILO

PHILO of Alexandria (*c.* 20 BCE – 50 CE) was a well-informed intellectual, who led the embassy to the Roman emperor Gaius on behalf of the Jews of Alexandria. Modern estimates of him are divided. Yet without doubt he held together genuine loyalty to the traditions of Hebrew scripture with a firm desire to help the educated Graeco-Roman world of his day to perceive the rational coherence and value of these traditions for life.

In order to facilitate this task of establishing the rational credibility of Jewish thought about God and the world, Philo drew upon a variety of Greek philosophical sources. He drew upon PLATO's notions of the eternal and of Ideas: upon STOIC views of the world, especially their method of allegorical readings of classic foundation-texts; and even on Pythagorean notions of the world, including theories of numbers.

This is not simply, as some have claimed, the undisciplined ransacking of sources by an eclectic polymath, but an attempt to draw on a variety of conceptual and logical tools to expound Hebrew–Jewish texts and traditions in the most rational and intelligible light.

It is no longer customary to draw a sharp dividing-line between 'Palestinian' and 'Hellenistic' Judaism, not only because of difficulties of terminology, but also because Martin Hengel and other scholars have demonstrated the fluidity of this line. Nevertheless, Philo has a very different approach from that of pharisaic and rabbinic Judaism, which flowered in the Mishnah and later in the Jerusalem and Babylonian Talmuds.

A good example of Philo's work on LANGUAGE IN RELIGION and HERMENEU-TICS is his treatment of anthropomorphisms in the early chapters of Genesis. As a transcendent, spiritual Being, God did not 'walk' in the Garden of Eden; indeed even tilling the ground has a secondary meaning in the cultivation of virtue.

The book of Exodus and the legislative material in Leviticus, Numbers and Deuteronomy, reveal Moses as the supreme philosopher before Plato. His directions are not, as they may appear, trivial comments about animal sacrifices, but underlying axioms for a healthy life of wisdom (see entry on Philo for details).

EARLY MEDIEVAL JEWISH PHILOSOPHIES

In the early medieval period al-Favvumi Saadiah Gaon (882–942) brought together REASON, TRADITION and experience, to establish a systematic Jewish philosophy. These themes are expounded in his work *The Book of Beliefs and Convictions* (longer title, *Critically Chosen Beliefs and Convictions*).

Saadiah attacked SCEPTICISM as self-defeating and parasitic upon BELIEF about the scope of experience and knowledge. Hence reason, sense-experience and tradition constitute valid bases for an EPISTE-MOLOGY. He convincingly expounds, long before a modern awareness of historicality and historical reason, the continuity of a tradition handed on by a people over time.

These treatises also defend the unity and incorporeality of God, a doctrine of creation, human freedom and the phenomenon of evil in terms of trials or tests of character.

Saadiah also undertook careful biblical exegesis based on both Hebrew lexicography and SEMANTICS, and accorded this a role in his philosophy. The multiform character of the scriptures, which combine political, intellectual, aesthetic, erotic, procreative and moral goods, reveals that human well-being lies in no single 'good' alone, but on this rich diversity of gifts of God. It was in the context of his work in Baghdad that Saadiah came to bear the title 'Gaon' (Hebrew, 'Eminence').

Judaism in medieval Muslim Spain collaborated with ISLAMIC PHILOSOPHY and its agenda to a remarkable degree. Solomon Ibn Gabirol (c. 1021–57) wrote in both Hebrew and Arabic, and explored NEOPLATONISM as his broad philosophical frame. Thomas AQUINAS and DUNS SCOTUS were aware of his work *Source of Life (Fons Vitae)*, written in Arabic.

The importance of Ibn Gabirol's philosophy is as an example of minimalist Judaism. Indeed, so broadly does it share, through Neoplatonist themes, a common agenda for philosophical discussion in Jewish, Christian and Islamic traditions, that for several centuries it was assumed to be either Muslim or Christian. It stands in clear contrast to Saadiah.

Abraham Ibn Daud (c. 1110–80) also wrote in Spain, and in Arabic. He drew on the METAPHYSICS of Islamic philosophy, especially of IBN SINA (980–1037), but at the same time emphasized, with Saadiah Gaon, the distinctive continuity of Israelite and Jewish tradition. Yet again, however, the influence of Neoplatonism also makes itself felt.

THE LATER MIDDLE AGES: JEWISH RATIONALISM AND MAIMONIDES

Here only the most general outline of the thought of Maimonides is offered, since a separate entry on him offers more detail. Abraham Ibn Daud is usually perceived as paving the way for Maimonides.

Maimonides' *Guide of the Perplexed* stands in the tradition of Philo as facilitating a reconciliation between loyalty to the Hebrew scriptures and later rabbinic (Talmudic) traditions, and the search for rational coherence, integrity, credibility and intelligibility.

Above all, in the tradition of Philo in the context of his own day, Maimonides draws not only on Greek philosophy but also on Islamic philosophy, and even on a composite synthesis of ARISTOTLE and Neoplatonism.

That God is transcendent and perfect is not undermined by biblical anthropomorphism. These are accommodations to our human understanding. Thus, by the twelfth century, issues of cultural relativism were being explored, as Philo had anticipated more broadly. The philosophy of Maimonides became widely known, not least by LEIBNIZ (1646–1716) and SPINOZA (1632–77). It represents the tradition of Jewish RATIONALISM.

Within the later pre-modern period, mention must also be made of Levi ben Gerson, usually known by his Latin name as Gersonides (1288–1344). Although much of his work was on scriptural texts, his main philosophical work, *The Wars of the Lord*, owed more to Plato than to Genesis for its understanding of creation.

Maimonides and IBN RUSHD (Averroes) were probably the two greatest influences upon Gersonides' thought. Philosophy not only supplemented scriptural REVELATION; it was coextensive with it. Indeed he was less critically aware than Maimonides of the limits of human reason. Gersonides provided so extreme an example of Jewish rationalism that he provoked reactions against it.

THE MODERN PERIOD

The modern period reveals a hugely wide range of interests, agenda, positions and outlooks among Jewish philosophers. MENDELSSOHN (1729–86) followed the rationalism of Leibniz and Wolff. He defended and developed the arguments for the existence of GOD. His philosophy is discussed under a separate entry.

With Paul Natorp (1854–1924), COHEN (1842–1918) led the Marburg school of Neo-Kantian philosophy, which influenced thought about 'constructs' and about 'models' in the natural sciences.

Franz Rosenzweig (1886–1929) and Martin BUBER are sometimes known as Jewish existentialist philosophers, but their approaches differ, except in their shared rejection of IDEALISM.

Rosenzweig wrote on HEGEL (*Hegel and the State*, 1920) with reference to his political philosophy. His work *The Star of Redemption* (1921) proposes that the 'givens' of human experience are God, the self and the world. Divine revelation takes the form of a 'presence' rather than statements in sacred texts.

Buber's *I and Thou* (1923) is a profound, if brief, exposition of the distinctive dimension of interpersonal address and personhood. The SELF is SUBJECT, not merely OBJECT; and God is always subject. His subsequent works, including *Between Man and Man* (1947) and *Eclipse of God* (1952), make profound contributions to the interface between philosophy and RELIGION. Buber is discussed under a separate entry.

Mordecai Kaplan (1881–1983) is an example of a philosophical thinker who saw the essence of Jewish identity more in terms of patterns of social life than in religious beliefs. Abraham Joshua Heschel (1907–72) has been an influential figure in American Jewish philosophical theology. Levinas offers profound philosophical reflection on human relationality to 'the Other', especially in relation to transcendental questions about the self in *Otherwise than Being* (1981).

No single theme has dominated the modern period, except perhaps what it is to be human and to have a certain identity. Yet most of these philosophers have placed their questions within a firm framework of THEISM and Jewish tradition. (*See also* EXISTENTIALSIM; REASON; SELF.)

Jung, Carl Gustav (1875–1961)

Jung is regarded as one of three major founders of psychoanalytical theory, with FREUD (1856–1939) and Adler. However, he broke with Freud in 1913, not least because of his more positive evaluation of RELIGION and broader understanding of the drives generated by the unconscious. Jung stressed the 'collective' unconscious as the repository of the archetypes and SYMBOLS that are buried within it, but nevertheless transmitted.

He rejected Freud's negative view of symbols.

A native of Switzerland, Jung graduated in medicine from Basle, and became Professor of Psychiatry at Zürich. He believed that archetypal patterns and symbols precede the formulation of ideas and CONCEPTS. Like RICOEUR (b. 1913), he argued that symbols give rise to thought, rather than express thought.

SYMBOLS AND ARCHETYPES

Symbols also combine 'double meanings', in the way that interactive METAPHOR also brings together two or more worlds. Integration, rather than fragmentation, is a positive concern of Jung's 'analytical psychology'. This drive towards wholeness influenced TILLICH (1886–1965), together with Jung's estimate of symbol as pre-conceptual.

Symbols allow us to explore beyond the finite horizons of thought to rise towards the Ultimate. Jung writes, 'Because there are innumerable things beyond the range of human understanding, we constantly use symbolic terms to represent concepts that we can't define or fully comprehend' (Man and his Symbols, New York: Doubledays, 1971, 21).

In Jung's view the SELF is not autonomous. It has been created by what flows from the past history of the human race, including the archetypal patterns and imagery that cross the boundaries of times and cultures. Often the self's own past needs to be recalled to integrate unbalanced fragmentation. One example would be the recovery and positive reassimilation of the 'Shadow' side of a personality that has been neglected or repressed.

JUNG ON RELIGION

In contrast to Freud, who saw religion as a projection outwards and upwards of inner neurotic conflicts, Jung regarded religion positively, as a force for good. Also unlike Freud, he did not attempt to press scientific method into a theology or anti-theology. Empirical method, he insisted, cannot pronounce upon whether religious BELIEF is true, although it can note its life-enhancing effects.

Religion is 'one of the earliest and most universal expressions of the human mind' (Collected Works, 20 vols., Princeton: Princeton University Press, 1953–78, vol. 11, 5). Hence no serious psychology can avoid noting its importance for so many. The human psyche, in fact, is 'natively religious' (naturaliter religiosa)' (ibid., vol. 12, 13). Humankind needs 'that which the living religions of every age have given' (Modern Man in Search of a Soul, New York: Harcourt Brace, 1933, 229).

Religions, no less, provide the pre-conceptual, pre-cognitive symbols that serve to heal the rift between consciousness and the unconscious, or between divided parts of the mind. Archetypal models include, for example, the image of the stone or rock, 'eternally the same', which may be found in 'God' or in other religious sources.

Jung's method stands in sharp contrast to that of Freud, especially in acknowledging the limits of empirical method. He contributes an enriching awareness of 'depth' in the dimension of the human self, and of the healing potential for reintegration through that which lies beyond the instrumental concepts of science and technology. (See also AUNTONOMY; EMPRICISM; SCIENCE AND RELIGION.)

K

Kant, Immanuel (1724–1804)

Kant's CRITICAL PHILOSOPHY forms a watershed in the history of philosophy. He moved beyond both EMPIRICISM and RATIONALISM, by expounding a TRANSCENDENTAL PHILOSOPHY. He was born in Königsberg in Prussia, and taught at Königsberg University.

Kant was influenced by the rationalism of LEIBNIZ (1646–1716) but appreciated serious difficulties which Leibniz had identified. Similarly, he respected the work of HUME (1711–76) in the empiricist tradition, but was even more dissatisfied with some of the sceptical inferences that had to be drawn from Hume's conclusions (see SCEPTICSIM). Hume awoke him 'from his dogmatic slumber'.

The three great *Critiques* of Kant were all written in his mature years: *The Critique of Pure Reason* (1781); *The Critique of Practical Reason* (1788); and *The Critique of Judgement* (1790). The first critique is often published in two columns: the original 1781 edition as the 'A' editions: and the revisions that led to the second main edition of 1787 as 'B' material. In between these Kant wrote a defence of his claims, *Prolegomena to any Future Metaphysics* (1783) in which he identified as his central issue 'whether such a thing as METAPHYSICS is possible at all'.

This also strikes the keynote of transcendental philosophy. Whereas traditional EPISTEMOLOGY asks, 'How do we know?' and 'What do we know?', transcendental philosophy asks: 'What are the grounds and conditions for the very POSSIBILITY of knowledge?'

Kant also stressed the notion of AUTONOMY. He defined the ENLIGHTENMENT as 'man's exodus from his self-incurred tutelage' to a position of FREEDOM where persons are 'to use your own understanding'. Freedom was a pre-condition for the moral ABSOLUTE expounded in his *Critique of Practical Reason*.

CRITIQUE OF PURE REASON: THE ANALYTIC, SYNTHETIC AND TRANSCENDENTAL

Kant agreed with Hume that some things seem neither to be analytical truths A PRIORI, nor synthetic, empirical truths A POSTERIORI. 'CAUSE', for example, cannot strictly be observed; only constant conjunction. Yet it is hardly *a priori*, since its denial is not self-contradictory. Are these things, then, partly 'synthetic' truths, and partly *a priori* truths? How could this be?

It would not be acceptable, Kant argued, simply to postulate that synthetic *a priori* truths (both) are metaphysical truths. The issue is more complex. There are transcendental conditions: grounds or conditions for the POSSIBILITY of experiencing the world as we experience it. They express conditions for understanding the phenomenal world.

Kant subdivided three conditions between correlations and types of understanding. Thus synthetic *a priori* truths within the empirical realm provide conditions necessary for inferential or discursive thought. This was called 'the transcendental analytic'. Propositions within the 'metaphysical' realm provide conditions necessary for regulative reason and understanding in ordering the world. This is 'the transcendental dialectic'.

We experience the world as we experience it because these regulative concepts and regulative 'ordering' are constitutive of the experience construed by our minds. Kant identified certain 'antinomies of reason' that illustrate what is at issue.

One antinomy is 'the beginning of time', or 'the edge of space'. How can we conceive of the edge of space or the beginning of time without being seduced into letting our 'edge of space' fence off 'more space' beyond it, or seduced into asking, 'What was going on "before" time began?'

The antinomy, paradox or self-contradiction arises because it is our *minds* that insist upon ordering the world in spatio-temporal CATEGORIES. We cannot be otherwise. C.E.M. Joad once offered the over-simple but useful analogy of seeing a blue world through blue spectacles. Since we cannot remove the spectacles, we cannot know whether the world is 'really' blue; indeed, it is hardly possible to respond to the question.

The Critique of Pure Reason, then, shows the limits of reason. In Kant's view, it is an essentially regulative, ordering vehicle. Antinomies emerge when we try to push it beyond this function. Reasoning about God yields the antinomy that God is either 'outside' the world as First Cause and Absolute, or inside the world as acting within it. Kant saw these as irreconcilable.

CRITIQUE OF PRACTICAL REASON AND OTHER WORKS

In the period between the first and second *Critiques* Kant produced *Groundwork of the Metaphysics of Morals* (1785), in preparation for his *Critique of Practical Reason* in 1788. Kant had been educated in the tradition of PIETISM and high moral duty, and it was in the realm of the moral imperative that he found the Absolute that offered a framework for his notions of 'God, freedom and immortality'.

Kant regarded his *Critique of Pure Reason* as parallel with the 'Copernican Revolution'. In relation to OBJECTS in the empirical world, and to REASON in the traditions of RATIONALISM, there was no longer any self-contained world, comparable with a pre-Copernican world-view. This 'pre-Copernican' perspective treated objects as 'things-in-themselves' (*Dinge an sich*).

Only in the realm of ETHICS, Kant argued in his *Critique of Practical Reason*, do we leave the realm of the relative for the Absolute, unconditioned 'Categorical Imperative' of moral duty. This goes further in *The Metaphysics of Morals* (1797). The 'absolute', apart from the categorical imperative itself, is 'the absolutely good will'. This is the autonomous will of 'deontological' ethics, or an ethic of duty.

Kant permitted the moral dimension to enter the realm of metaphysics because he viewed the ideas of God, freedom and immortality as POSTULATES of practical reason. The virtuous person, he believed, deserves happiness, and only God can resolve the disharmonies that appear to conflict with such an expectation.

In *Religion Within the Limits of Reason Alone* (1793) it becomes clear how far Kant's view of God differs from what he calls that of 'ecclesial' religion and 'divinity schools'. God is not a personal agent who acts within the world. PRAYER is merely self-adaptation and mediation, without the hope of changing states of affairs. That would be 'ecclesial', not 'rational' prayer; indeed it would be 'superstition'. This coheres with *The Critique of Judgement (Urteilskraft)*. The 'ordering' of the mind regulates the subjective as aesthetics, and the logical or objective as teleology. But these are how the world appears in 'our' experience. There is no 'experience' that rests wholly upon what is 'given'; experience also embodies within it what the mind brings to it as categories of understanding and 'order'. Hence Kant's third *Critique* did much to undermine the TELEOLOGICAL ARGUMENT, even if Kant himself still respected it.

SOME EFFECTS OF KANT'S LEGACY

We cannot put the clock back to the pre-Kantian era. SCHLEIERMACHER recognized that Kant's philosophy required new thinking in theology. For the philosophy of religion Kant raises complex questions about 'experience'. Can we separate what we think that we experience from how our minds order and interpret that experience?

Reason also plays an ambivalent role in Kant. On one side, Kant opens up the importance of transcendental questions. These have to be asked. Yet is there the difficulty that in the end Kant holds to a regulative and thereby 'instrumental' role for reason, not much different from HUME'S, except for the purposes that it serves?

Finally, 'God' is squeezed into a role that performs what suits Kant's philosophical system, including an implausible notion of providing a backstop for expectations about the reward due to the 'good will'. Kant concedes that his philosophical God is hardly the God of the 'divinity school', let alone the God of most religious believers. (*See also* DUALISM; GOD, ARGUMENTS FOR THE EXISTENCE OF.)

Kierkegaard, Søren Aabye
(1813–1855)

Kierkegaard is credited with being, in effect, the father of EXISTENTIALISM. This arises from his emphasis on the individual in contrast to convention; on will and decision, in contrast to abstract REASON; and on 'SUBJECTIVITY' in the sense of venturing one's own stake in TRUTH, in contrast to objective content (*see* OBJECTIVITY). In the context of RELIGION, radicals lay claim to appeal to his attack on mere orthodox BELIEF, while pietists no less appeal to his emphasis on personal commitment rather than rational argument.

LIFE AND WRITINGS

Born and educated in Copenhagen, Kierkegaard grew up under the influence of a domineering father, who encouraged him to read theology in preparation for ordination. When this authority-figure became guilty of a serious moral lapse, Kierkegaard determined to disengage himself from all second-hand inherited values, and to live life and seek truth for himself. Yet he found no fulfilment in moral decline, and by his own independent decision resumed theological studies.

A crisis of personal confidence led Kierkegaard to break off his engagement to be married, precipitating a parallel withdrawal from initial pastoral ministry. He perceived this as following a path of obedience to God's will which transcended the ethical obligations of promises. In *Fear and Trembling* (1843) he invoked the story of Abraham's 'sacrifice' of Isaac in Genesis 22 as a supposed model. The command to slay the son through whom divine promise would be fulfilled seemed to contradict both ethics and logic, but still demanded obedience in face of all this.

Kierkegaard eventually retreated into a measure of isolation from society and from the Danish Church. He saw suffering and obedience as his Christian vocation, believing that whereas HEGEL and other thinkers talked about Christianity, his own work was to live it.

All this profoundly affected the style, method and content of Kierkegaard's many writings. To provoke decision rather than shallow assent to ideas he attacked his own work under pseudonyms (*Point of View for my Work as an Author*, Princeton: Princeton University Press, 1941). He called this 'indirect' communication in continuity with Socratic irony and the subversive parables of Jesus. He also wrote from the contrasting angles of a shallow 'aesthetic stage' which centred on passing pleasure, a deeper 'ethical' stage, and a 'religious' stage that moved beyond, and even 'suspended' the ethical. Transformative decisions change life, and they lie beyond general rules.

THE INDIVIDUAL AND 'SUBJECTIVITY'

Kierkegaard rejects the way of searching for truth by following the crowd. 'The most ruinous evasion of all is to be hidden in the crowd ... to get away from hearing God's voice as an individual' (*Purity of Heart is to Will One Thing*, London: Collins, 1961, 163). In Christian theism this approach is taken up by BARTH and BULTMANN, and in atheistic versions of existentialism by Camus and SARTRE.

In his satirical *Attack on 'Christendom'* Kierkegaard insists that 'Christianity has been abolished by expansion'. 'These millions of name-Christians' are merely those who passively assent to the rites and doctrines of the Danish state Church: 'God ... cannot discover that He has been hoaxed, that there is not one single Christian' (*Attack on 'Christendom'*, Oxford: OUP, 1940, 127). If a person can pay the priest's fee for burial 'there is no help for him – he is a Christian' (ibid., 197).

However, all this has little to do with 'truth'. For 'subjectivity is truth' (*Concluding Unscientific Postscript* [1846], Princeton: Princeton University Press, 1941, 306). 'Subjectivity' does not mean the unfounded personal opinions of subjectivism, nor does it denote introspection. It is how and when an individual stakes his or her life on something in first-person decision. It is not

being 'dulled into a third person' by mere passive assent to what is 'objectively' described (*Journals*, Princeton: Princeton University Press, 1938, 533).

'The objective accent falls on WHAT is said; the subjective accent on HOW it is said ... Thus subjectivity becomes the truth' (*Concluding Unscientific Postscript*, 181; Kierkegaard's capitals).

REJECTION OF EQUATING TRUTH WITH A RATIONAL SYSTEM OF IDEAS

Kierkegaard passionately rejected the IDEALISM of Hegel. Hegel, in effect, identified thought with reality. In Kierkegaard's view this approach contained several flaws. First, it presupposed some detached, world-surveying viewpoint from which 'the whole' could be constructed as a system. Second, it substituted mere passive assent to a system of ideas for genuinely participatory and self-transformative engagement with truth. Thereby, third, it elevated intellect or reason above will and decision. Everything remains purely speculative, without existential, concrete involvement.

Hegel portrayed history-as-a-whole as Absolute Idea in a process of self-manifestation. Kierkegaard diagnosed this as 'world-historical absent-mindedness': Hegel has forgotten what it is to be human. 'I should be as willing as the next man to fall down in worship before the System, if only I could set eyes on it' (*Concluding Unscientific Postscript*, 97). Kierkegaard observes drily that he might have been persuaded if the truth could be 'viewed eternally, divinely, theocentrically ... [But] I am only a poor, existing, human being' (ibid., 190).

A system of mere logical concepts is indeed possible. However, Kierkegaard continues 'an existential system is impossible' (ibid., 107). If humankind is grounded, located, and conditioned by 'existence', we cannot assume that thought and reality are coextensive. Deceit generates such a view.

FURTHER CONSEQUENCES FOR PHILOSOPHY OF RELIGION

Clearly Kierkegaard's critique of thought and reason suggests the fruitlessness of arguments for the existence of GOD. Indeed, to use them is 'a shameless affront'.

Further, faith is seen in voluntarist terms as a matter of decision, will or existential commitment and venture. Kierkegaard's critics accuse him of FIDEISM, i.e. of separating the truth of religion from wider issues of rationality and truth.

While his emphasis on the individual encourages active engagement and accountability rather than passive assent to conventional beliefs, Kierkegaard has underestimated the part played by the Church or communities of shared beliefs in maintaining and supporting TRADITIONS through TIME. Hence although his *Journals* record moments of Christian joy and assurance of faith, more often he was tortured by doubt in his lonely, self-chosen isolation from fellow believers.

All the same, Barth recognized in Kierkegaard's writings a prophetic witness to the TRANSCENDENCE of God and to human finitude. Concrete human existence is creaturely. Barth's aphorism that one cannot say 'God' by saying 'humankind' in a loud voice reflects this resonance with Kierkegaard.

Kierkegaard insisted that he did not wish to found a 'school', but to leave only the epitaph 'That Individual'. Nevertheless, he deeply influenced Christian and anti-theist existentialists, pietists who agreed about faith as decision and venture, radicals who attacked Church orthodoxy or belief-systems of 'Christendom', Barthian theologians who stressed transcendence and REVELATION, and the Bultmann school, which combined Lutheran pietism with historical SCEPTICISM.

Among nineteenth-century theological thinkers, Kierkegaard is widely regarded as the third major alternative to SCHLEIERMACHER or to Hegel. Yet since his works were written in Danish, he remained little known outside Denmark until Barth drew attention to his writings especially in his second edition of his *Romans* (1922).

al-Kindi Abu Yusuf Ya'qub Ibn Ishaq (*c.* 813–*c.* 871)

The first of the great Islamic philosophers of the classical period, al-Kindi, constitutes a bridge between Greek, especially Aristotelian, philosophy and Islam. In the court of Baghdad he served as tutor to the son of the caliph. He strongly advocated the importance of REASON, and urged the compatibility between Islamic faith based on the Qur'an and the philosophical concepts of ARISTOTLE and the drive towards a coherent Arabic 'science'.

Initially al-Kindi inherited access to Aristotle in part through Syrian translations, which had included some works of PLOTINUS as if these were parts of the writings of Aristotle, although some texts were already in Arabic. Up to 250 works have been accredited to him, but some 200 have been lost. In his work *On First Philosophy*, he argues that knowledge of the First Truth and First Cause constitutes the central and most blessed and noble part of philosophical inquiry.

In contrast to many later Islamic philosophers, al-Kindi stressed the finite and CONTINGENT nature of the universe. God is ABSOLUTE and transcendent. God created the universe from nothing (*ex nihilo*), and in due course the universe would perish. Also in contrast to those of his successors who would privilege philosophy over revelation (notably AL-FARABI), al-Kindi stressed the importance of the Qur'an and its responsible interpretation. However, the Qur'an's witness to Allah is compatible with Aristotle's Uncaused Cause or Prime Mover, and more broadly with the 'One' of NEOPLATONISM.

Al-Kindi develops an ontological account of Aristotle's CATEGORIES of form, matter, motion, place and time, as primary substances of the created world, i.e. categories of 'what is'. He also utilizes Aristotle's distinction between 'passive' intellect, in which the mind receives impressions of sense-data through the senses, and 'active' intellect, in which the mind relates such data coherently to form ideas and concepts. He also produced *The Metaphysics* in Arabic, and wrote on astronomy, astrology, mathematics, music and politics A useful resource is G.M. Atiyeh, *Al Kindi: The Philosophy of the Arabs* (Islamabad: Islamic Research Institute, 1967). (*See also* AQUINAS, GOD, CONCEPTS AND 'ATTRIBUTES' OF; ISLAMIC PHILOSOPHY; TRANSCENDENCE.)

language-games

The term 'language-game' was used by WITTGENSTEIN from 1932 onwards. It underlines that using language is an action or activity, and that language operates with constitutive 'rules', namely the constraining regularities of logical grammar.

In the *Philosophical Investigations* (Oxford: Blackwell, 1967) Wittgenstein writes: 'The term "language-*game*" (*Sprachspiel*) is meant to bring into prominence the fact that the *speaking* of language is part of an activity (*Tätigkeit*), or of a form of life (*Lebensform*)' (sect. 23). A language-game is a 'whole, consisting of language and the actions into which it is woven' (ibid., sect. 7).

The grounding of language in life and communal behaviour suggests that problems arise when questions are asked in the abstract '*outside* a particular language-game' (ibid., sect. 47). Sometimes Wittgenstein invents or compares model language-games for exploratory purposes, for example that of 'Wittgenstein's Builders' (ibid., sect. 2). The term may have originated from Wittgenstein's uses of analogies from chess. The point here is not the shape of the chess-piece, but the rules that define how the piece operates (ibid., sect. 31). (*See also* LANGUAGE IN RELIGION; SPEECH ACTS.)

language in religion

Whether language about God has genuine communicative currency, and if so, how it acquires it, belongs to those core issues that lie at the heart of the philosophy of religion. It ranks in importance alongside arguments for the existence of GOD, and the problem and nature of EVIL.

VARIETY OF OBJECTIONS TO THE GENUINE CURRENCY OF LANGUAGE IN RELIGION

(1) Some argue that 'religious language' bears no relation to the currency of language in ordinary life, since its function is merely expressive or commendatory. It may serve to express feelings of reverence, awe, or wonder, or commend religious attitudes appropriate to finite, created beings. However, it allegedly fails to communicate truth about events or states of affairs. In more technical terms, it is non-cognitive and expressive rather than COGNITIVE.

This objection will be examined more closely below. It was advocated, for example, by the Cambridge philosopher R. B. Braithwaite in his work *An Empiricist's View of the Nature of Religious Belief* (1955). Well-known examples of religious claims that may often lack cognitive context include, for example, 'God is on our side'; 'We shall overcome'. NIETZSCHE argued at the end of the nineteenth century that such uses of language were often manipulative: 'The salvation of the soul', he observed, may express a feeling of self-satisfaction: 'The world revolves around me' (*The Antichrist*, in *Complete Works*, London: Allen & Unwin, 1909–13, vol. 16, 186, aphorism 43).

(2) The view that language in religion is without cognitive truth-content receives added force when questions are raised about criteria to determine what truths, events or states of affairs it communicates.

The most widely known objection from this angle is that formulated by AYER (1910–89) in his *Language, Truth and Logic* (1st edn, 1939; 2nd edn, London: Gollancz, 1946). His view, known as LOGICAL POSITIVISM, and building on the POSITIVISM of the VIENNA CIRCLE, centres on the maxim that the meaning of a proposition must be verified (or verifiable in principle, 2nd edn) by observation or experience, unless it is logically true as an ANALYTIC STATEMENT.

While propositions of mathematics may be 'true' in this analytic sense, and propositions of sciences or of most everyday life are open to verifiability by observations of the states of affairs to which they refer, the language of religion and ethics falls into neither area. It is 'non-sense': because it is unverifiable, it remains without truth-content. 'God loves the world' or 'it is wrong to steal' merely express attitudes on the part of speakers.

(3) A more nuanced and more convincing version of this approach appeals to the principle of FALSIFICATION or falsifiability, utilizing the insights of Karl Popper (1902–94) on falsifiability in science, e.g. in *The Logic of Scientific Discovery* (Germ. 1934; Eng. 1959). What would it take to demonstrate the falsity of a proposition? Does the presence of horrendous evils in the world count as a criterion that invalidates, or demonstrates as false, the proposition 'God loves the world'? If someone asserts 'God is on our side' whatever may be discovered about the moral claims of the other side, does the proposition count as 'true'?

In philosophy of religion the so-called parable of the invisible gardener (used by John Wisdom and Antony Flew) illustrates the point. If two people disagree about whether a less wild patch of the jungle has actually been tended as a garden by a gardener, they can wait and observe whether such a gardener ever comes. However, if such a person never appears, and one of the two asserts that the gardener may nevertheless be invisible, a process of tests to falsify the claim may be set in motion. The gardener cannot be heard, and leaves no traces of bodily presence. If the 'believer' insists that the gardener must be invisible, inaudible, intangible and odourless, what remains of the original proposition? It has died the 'death of a thousand qualifications', it may be argued.

(4) Many argue that the operational currency or logical grammar is so different in 'religious language' from that of 'ordinary' language that such language functions only within an 'insider' group that uses highly coded linguistic concepts. WITTGENSTEIN observes: 'You can't hear God speaking to someone else (That is a grammatical remark).' (i.e. it is about the logical currency of 'hearing' God), (*Zettel*, Germ. Eng. Oxford: Blackwell, 1967, sect. 717).

Wittgenstein himself, however, recognizes that there are 'overlappings and over-crossings' that provide bridges between uses of the same word even when logical currency varies. There is some link between 'hearing'

God and hearing sound-waves, even if this requires conceptual exploration of the different roles performed by the word in different settings or in different 'surroundings'. The orientation of much of the debate about language in religion turns on this problem. Its recognition, however, leads to a general preference to speak not of 'religious language' (a term popular in the 1950's), but of how language is used in religion or in religious contexts.

TRADITIONAL WAYS OF ADDRESSING THE PROBLEM: ANALOGY

The sacred writings of Judaism, Christianity and Islam all warn against constructing images of God. This is not only because humankind as such is intended to exhibit the divine image of wisdom and goodness, but also because God is beyond ready or exact compare with persons or objects within the world. Exodus 3:13, 14 reflects reluctance to offer any easy characterization of God: 'I will be what I will be' (Hebrew uses future or 'imperfect'; 'I am' comes from the Greek translation of the Hebrew).

Much language about God uses the way of negation (VIA NEGATIVA): God is 'immortal', 'immutable', 'infinite' (*see* concepts and 'attributes' of GOD). Thomas AQUINAS observes: 'It seems that no word (Latin, *nomen*) can be used literally of God (*dicatur de Deo proprie*)', for 'every word used of God is taken from our speech about creatures'. Nevertheless 'such words are used metaphorically (Latin, *metaphorice*) of God, as when we call him a "rock"' (*Summa Theolgiae*, Ia, Qu. 13, art. 3 Blackfriars edn, 1964, vol. 3, 57).

Aquinas conceded that metaphorical uses do not represent a perfect correspondence or match. Nevertheless, they are not used 'equivocally' (*aequivoce*), as if ambiguous and unrelated to the ordinary uses of words (ibid., art. 5). 'It is impossible to predicate anything univo-

cally (*univoce*) of God', i.e. as if the meaning were identical with ordinary language. 'No word when used of God means the same as when it is used of a creature' (ibid.). He concludes: 'Words are used neither univocally nor purely equivocally of God and creatures, but analogically' (ibid.).

In what sense and on what basis religious believers use ANALOGY in talk of God, however, remains highly controversial. Thomas Aquinas finds the basis in a theological doctrine concerning 'the perfections that flow from God to creatures' (ibid., art. 9). Thus there is a genuine 'analogy of being' (*analogia entis*) between 'wise' or 'good' as applied to finite human persons and as these terms are applied to God. From the viewpoint of humanity, the use of analogy may therefore work 'upwards' to God (*via eminentiae*).

This view has been the dominant approach in Roman Catholic thought and in Neo-Thomism. However, many Protestant theologians, most distinctively BARTH, hold that this presupposes an appeal to NATURAL THEOLOGY, as if analogy of being were a 'given' apart from divine REVELATION. It would depend, Barth argues, on some inherent 'likeness' between God and humankind, when in actuality the initial gift of 'the image of God' has become corrupted and distorted by human sin and alienation.

Advocates of the view of Aquinas insist that an appeal to 'the analogy of proportion' (especially in Cajetan) allows sufficiently for the reality of a mixture of match and mismatch in his use of analogy in talk of God.

Within the Protestant tradition, however, some argue for a greater distance between God and humankind on philosophical grounds (following KANT); while others argue for this on theological grounds (following Calvin and Barth). Kant (1724–1804) believed that 'God' lies beyond the realm of human conceptual thought. God cannot be grasped by finite human minds. 'Religion within the limits of reason' (to use Kant's term) would hesitate to place too much weight on analogy, since it drifts towards ANTHROPOMORPHISM.

Barth does not reject every ground for the use of analogy, but rejects any notion of an 'analogy of being' (*analogia entis*). Rather, he urges, when humankind responds to God's revelation in faith, part of this response entails understanding and hearing God on the basis of 'an analogy of faith' (*analogia fidei*). Hence in the end Barth relies also on the use of analogy for the currency of language in religion, but on a different basis from that of Aquinas.

One reason why Barth pursues his causes so relentlessly stems from his reluctance to apply the term 'person' to God, preferring to speak of the divine 'mode of being' (*Seinsweise*; he rejects the German, *Person*). However, in the tradition of the Orthodox Church John Zizoulas places emphasis on 'person' as the CONCEPT that can most properly be applied on the basis of analogy both to God and to human persons. The distinctiveness, if not uniqueness, of 'person' adds force to this view (*see also* SELF).

An incisive, positive, and critical evaluation of the issues on Aquinas and Barth is offered in Alan J. Torrance, *Persons in Communion* (Edinburgh: T & T Clark, 1996). Since nothing of positive content could be conveyed exclusively though the *via negativa* (what God is not), while the danger of projecting human constructs 'onto' God remains (as Kant insisted) James Ross described the use of analogy as a middle way between anthropomorphism and AGNOSTICISM.

OTHER TRADITIONAL RESOURCES: SYMBOL, MYTH AND METAPHOR

TILLICH (1886–1965) insisted on the unique importance of SYMBOL for language that seeks to convey truth about God. Drawing especially on JUNG (1875–1961), Tillich urges that symbol reaches through to the depths of the pre-conscious and unconscious in humankind, and

escapes the peril of cognitive concepts in attempting to define 'God' in terms of some prior conceptual grid, or system constructed by human thought, which cannot reach, let alone encapsulate, God.

In addition to the depth psychology of Jung, Tillich shares with the existentialist philosopher and psychiatrist JASPERS (1883–1969) the view that MYTH and symbol, unlike conceptual thought, help to bridge and to integrate the levels of conscious and unconscious in humankind with healing and revelatory effects.

God, Tillich declares, 'is being-itself ... Nothing else can be said about God as God which is not symbolic' (*Systematic Theology*, vol. 1, London: Nisbet, 1953, 365). Thus he rejects such a cognitive proposition, even in an analogical sense, as 'God exists' or 'God is the highest being'. When applied to God, superlatives become diminutives. They place him on the level of other beings while elevating him above all of them (ibid., 261).

By contrast, 'symbols ... point beyond themselves'. Further, a symbol 'participates in' that to which it points (unlike a mere sign), and 'opens up levels of reality which otherwise are closed to us ... a level of reality which cannot be reached in any other way' (*Dynamics of Faith*, London: Allen & Unwin, 1957, 42). Symbols 'open up hidden depths of our own being' (ibid., 43). Thereby they are 'double-edged', revealing both God and the hidden depths of the human self.

Symbol, Tillich explains, is akin in these respects to art, poetry, pictures and to 'myths', which operate in the same way but by telling a story or narrative. 'Myths are symbols of faith combined in stories about divine–human encounters' (ibid., 49). Although the 'Ultimate' is beyond time and space, myth points to divine reality by using stories set within time and space. Hence myths inevitably demand critique and reformation, since they merely 'point' to the Beyond. Thus Tillich agrees with BULTMANN that myth demands DEMYTHOLOGIZING, but not in terms of merely descriptive concepts or propositions.

Jung, Jaspers and Tillich rightly underline the power of symbol and myth to reshape human perceptions, to involve the self in a participating way (not as a mere spectator) and to resonate with patterns or longings often buried deep within the self. However, they are insufficiently rigorous about criteria, which may establish whether certain symbols and myths convey truth or merely reflect projected human values, longings or aspirations.

The endowment of an ordinary object with symbolic power may in some surroundings be constructive. A wreath of poppies may have symbolic resonance in remembering and honouring those who fell in war on behalf of their country. On the other hand, there are cases of mental illness and instability where a person may perceive such an ordinary object as a table or a random drawing as a personal threat. What criteria distinguish the two cases? Tillich argues that symbols grow and die in a corporate context, but does this take us beyond mere descriptive PRAGMATISM?

Symbols belong to the constructive resources for the effective use of language in religion, but also require the kind of safeguards discussed in the entry on analogy and especially in MODELS AND QUALIFIERS and RAMSEY. Similarly, neither Jung nor Tillich adequately explores issues of conceptual grammar (*see* above, and the entry on Wittgenstein).

Myth also brings problems into the discussion. This is chiefly because the very term 'myth' is regularly used in quite different, even contradictory, ways (*see* the entries on myth, demythologizing and Bultmann). Sometimes it is used to denote a sequence of analogies or symbols presented in narrative form. Sometimes it is associated with a 'pre-scientific' worldview. Sometimes it functions in contrast to description, report or history-embedded narrative. Unless it is beyond question how the term is being used, the word 'myth' causes many more problems than it

solves, and could be abandoned without undue loss.

METAPHORS are sometimes used as substitutes for what might be said in other ways. These are generally 'dead' metaphors, which perform little more than illustrative, didactic or rhetorical functions. As Max Black and RICOEUR rightly show, creative metaphor, in an important rather than trivial sense, depends on interaction between words or concepts drawn from different domains of speech and understanding.

The metaphor 'The Lord is my Shepherd' produces an interaction between the whole SEMANTIC field of what it was to be a shepherd in the ancient Near East and the different semantic field of how human persons experience the providential activity and presence of God. When Jesus warns Nicodemus of the need to be 'born again' (Jn 3:3–7; which may also be translated 'born from above'), the semantic domain of a mother giving birth to a child interacts with the role of new beginnings in mature life. Like symbol, metaphors function with more creative power and resonance than analogy alone. However, for that very reason attention must be paid to criteria for their appropriate use.

A MORE RECENT PROPOSAL: IAN RAMSEY ON MODELS AND QUALIFIERS

Ramsey attempted to refine the issues discussed above by proposing that language in religion employs 'models drawn from everyday life and the empirical world, but in conjunction with "qualifiers" which ensure that their employment carries with it a distinctive logic appropriate to religion' (*Religious Language*, London: SCM, 1957). This God is 'cause' (model) but 'first' (qualifier) cause of the universe. God is 'wise' (model), but 'infinitely' (qualifier) wise (ibid. 61–6).

Ramsey saw the use of a logic that is 'odd, peculiar, and unusual' as setting in motion a creative experience such as that of which we might say 'light dawns' or 'the penny drops'; the language 'comes alive' in a situation of 'disclosure' (ibid., 19–21). It is like suddenly 'seeing' the shape presented by an enigmatic puzzle-picture as a *Gestalt*, or whole (ibid., 24).

The model ensures that religious belief has an 'empirical place'. The qualifier functions like a logical operator (ibid., 54–6). Ramsey is prepared to attribute to God such an everyday term as 'purpose', but qualifies it as 'eternal purpose' (ibid., 75–89).

Although he does not fully stipulate criteria for 'seeing' when religious believers perceive a *Gestalt* (he acknowledges e.g. that we may 'see' a 'face' in a cliff), Ramsey nevertheless offers some broad guidelines that go further than most, including Tillich, for example in the use of symbols.

Critical rational reflection does not demand the elimination or reduction of symbols. The reverse is the case. We may use symbols of God and of divine activity provided that these symbols are also qualified by other complementary symbols. Symbols of judgement may lead to distortion and potential error unless these are complemented by symbols of tender care, love, compassion and grace. Especially in his later writings, Ramsey emphasizes the need for a wide repertoire of linguistic models and tools, citing Wittgenstein's emphasis upon the multi-functional resources of language in action. The Christian hymn 'Crown him!' is acceptable because it qualifies a sequence of models by their very variety. 'The Virgin's Son' is 'mystic rose ... the Root ... the Babe' as well as victorious warrior (*Christian Discourse*, Oxford: OUP, 1975, 19).

BRIEF RECONSIDERATION OF NON-THEISTIC OBJECTIONS

We noted above the formulation of Ayer's principles of verification and subsequently verifiability, on the grounds of which he dismissed the language of religion and ethics as 'non-sense'. For Ayer such language is merely 'emotive', just as for R. B. Braithwaite it is merely the language of approval and recommendation. The language of religion is neither that of straightforward empirical statement nor that of formally internal analytic statement.

Within a decade of Ayer's writing, however, philosophers were beginning to ask what category Ayer's own principle of verifiability fell into. It is not an empirical assertion, but it is not a self-evident internal analytical statement of formal LOGIC. As the 1950s progressed, it became increasingly clear that Ayer simply presented a positivist world-view (i.e. that only the data that comes through the five physical sense constitutes 'reality'), but presented this world-view as a theory of language. H. J. Paton called it 'positivism in linguistic dress' (*The Modern Predicament*, London: Allen & Unwin, 1955, 42).

The principle of falsification carries more weight. However, it tends to overlook the point (emphasized by Wittgenstein in *On Certainty*) that belief-systems are more like a 'nest of propositions' than a series of isolated or independent verifiable or falsifiable belief-statements. The question, Wittgenstein observes, then becomes how many twigs can be removed before the nest as such collapses and disintegrates (*On Certainty*, sects. 142–4). The principle of falsification has its uses, but not as a comprehensive criterion for the truth of a belief-system and the currency of all of its language.

OTHER RECENTLY EXPLORED LINGUISTIC RESOURCES

Much of this present subject may be explored under such separate headings as analogy, falsification, logical positivism, Ramsey and so on. However, three more important topics must be mentioned for an overview of the subject as a whole.

(1) Count-generation, or 'counting x as y': Stuart C. Brown (*Do Religious Claims Make Sense?* London: SCM, 1969)

and more especially WOLTERSTORFF (*Divine Discourse*, Cambridge: CUP, 1995) attack the preoccupation with single words and a single object of reference as the key to meaning, rather than asking (with the later Wittgenstein) what role multiple references might play. To use an example from Wolterstorff, a human agent may perform action 'A' (moving an indicator button) in order to perform action 'B' (communicating that he or she is about to turn left or right). To press the button of the indicator counts as the conveying of information and warning about the decision to turn. It 'counts as signalling for a turn' (*Divine Discourse*, 79).

Religious contexts provide inexhaustible examples of such count-generation. To read a command in Jewish, Christian or Islamic sacred texts is frequently for a believer to count the words as a command of God or Allah. Wolterstorff alludes to the parallel of 'deputized discourse', in which what a secretary writes, with due authorization, counts as the words of an executive or director.

(2) HERMENEUTICS (exploring the relation between understanding and language) emerged from earlier writers, but has come into greater prominence in the context of language in religion and philosophy of religion more recently. It is considered under a separate entry in this volume.

(3) SPEECH-ACT theory is also reserved for a separate entry, but the comments (above) from Wolterstorff presuppose this approach, as, in effect, the work of the later Wittgenstein does in embryo. Such utterances as 'I promise', 'I repent', 'I confess', or even perhaps 'I believe', do not function to inform God or others of what they might already know, but to perform acts of promising, repentance, confession, or affirmation of belief. (*See also* EMPRISCISM; EXISTENTIALISM.)

Leibniz, Gottfried Wilhelm
(1646–1716)

Leibniz was born in Leipzig, and educated at Leipzig, Jena and Altdorf. During his lifetime he was best known for his innovative contributions to mathematics. He and NEWTON (1642–1727) independently discovered the infinitesimal calculus, although each was convinced that the other had plagiarized his work.

In addition to his work in mathematics, LOGIC and philosophy, Leibniz contributed to law, historical enquiry, natural science and politics, and served as a diplomat and librarian in the court of Hanover.

In the context of philosophy of religion, Leibniz's most original and distinctive work was his ONTOLOGY, coupled with the optimistic response to the problem of EVIL that God had created our world order as 'the best of possible worlds'. He also explored the nature of CREATION and issues of continuity, identity and change. He published his *Theodicy* in 1710.

ONTOLOGY: BODY, SUBSTANCE AND 'MONADS'

Leibniz's ontology is extraordinarily complex. Initially much of his concern arose from dissatisfaction with the legacy of DESCARTES (1596–1650) that 'bodies' have extension. If bodies had extension, such extension must be infinitely divisible, and 'units' of reality never defined or identified.

If the 'units of one', or 'monads', of reality are the smallest 'indivisible' (atomic) units of an ontology, they cannot by definition be spatial, or extended in space. For if they were, they would not be indivisible atoms.

Leibniz turned, rather, to the notion of monads as units of 'force'. Against Descartes, he argued that force was not generated merely by quantity of movement (mass x velocity), but mass x the square of velocity.

As non-spatial units, monads do not interact directly with one another: 'Monads have no windows' (*Monadology*, sect. 7). Nevertheless, they have a capacity for quasi-perception, or 'apperception'. 'Minute perceptions' are perceptions of which a monad is unaware. Yet this perception allows for the possibility of a monad's 'mirroring' another monad. Further, to a greater or lesser degree, a monad may mirror the nature of reality as a quasi-microcosm of the universe.

Why is such a complex ontology necessary? This emerges partly through logicical rigour: Descartes' notion of 'extension', for example, results in self-contradiction, unless the world were to have no stable continuum. This introduces the two 'labyrinths' of confusion out of which Leibniz seeks to escape to coherence.

'The labyrinth of the continuum' is the first. Leibniz seeks to explain individualism without losing the notion of a stable ontological continuum. As length, area and volume, the continuum of the world is infinitely divisible. But if monads (unlike 'extensions' in Descartes) are not inert but active, and do not collapse into endless assimilation ('monads have no windows'), we seem to arrive at an ontology that provides a ground for both continuity and change. His monadology appears to solve the problem of 'the continuum'.

Second, how can an ordered plurality of monads find room for CONTINGENCY and FREEDOM? For 'identity' rests upon continuity over time in which subsequent states are caused by preceding states that occur within the existence and activity of the monad.

Leibniz's central concern remains that of logic. As in later logical atomism, he held that the truth-value of all propositions is the sum of the truth of all elementary propositions. But how is it possible that, given action and change, some propositions are true that might have been false?

Leibniz's ontology also rests on considerations from mathematics. For his notion of infinite analysis suggests that such analysis cannot be exhaustive and final. Hence, if it is not final, there is room for contingency, freedom and POSSIBILITY, alongside stability and continuity. The 'labyrinth of freedom' has also been very carefully addressed.

GOD AND THEODICY: NECESSITY, POSSIBILITY AND CREATION

Leibniz endorsed the value of the ONTOLOGICAL ARGUMENT and the COSMOLOGICAL ARGUMENT for the existence of God. Since God 'is without limits, without negation ... without contradiction', it is valid to define God as including 'all perfections' (*Monadology*, sect. 45). The ground for the existence of contingent objects or events in the world lies outside themselves, and points to the existence of a 'necessary Being' (ibid.). Without God, there would even be 'nothing ... possible' (ibid., sect. 43).

God created the world by free choice, because God chose to create the best of all possible worlds. Evil exists in this world, but since it is 'the best possible', evil must be necessary to a 'best possible' world. Without the possibility of evil, it would not be the best possible.

Leibniz coined the word 'THEODICY' to describe this vindication of 'a sufficient reason' for God's creation of this world, even in the face of evil. The interplay of possibility and necessity is rational, and is based upon 'the Principle of Sufficient Reason'. The contrary (or logical denial) of a contingent event does not entail contradiction. The Fall of Adam is in this respect not 'necessary'. On the other hand, the contrary (logical denial) of a necessary proposition or event does result in a contradiction. Its affirmation is true 'in all possible worlds'. At one level 'the best possible world' is thus necessarily the best possible.

Yet Leibniz is equally insistent on God's freedom to choose whether or what God creates. Here, again, his infinitesimal calculus offers a way forward. For since an infinity of 'possible worlds' is in view, what can be asserted about infinity remains incapable of the 'closure' of necessity.

Many will be dazzled, if not intimidated, by the complexity and subtlety of Leibniz's thought. It may appear esoteric because it seeks a unified understanding of a large spread of interlocking areas, from mathematics and METAPHYSICS to physics and theology. He remains in the rationalist tradition of Descartes and SPINOZA, but his innovative thought is in part provoked by his awareness of where both thinkers fall short and commit fallacies that need to be rectified. (*See also* GOD, ARGUMENTS FOR THE EXISTENCE OF; RATIONALISM; REASON; TRUTH.)

Levinas, Emmanuel (1906–1995)

Born in Lithuania, Levinas subsequently settled in France. He, with others, introduced some of HEIDEGGER's themes into French philosophy. However, more significant is his own creative work as a Jewish philosopher, drawing on the thought of Franz Rosenzweig and BUBER. Many of his themes resonate also with the Catholic and 'human' existentialist themes of MARCEL (1889–1973).

In *Totality and Infinity* (Pittsburgh: Duquesne University Press, 1969) Levinas develops the I–Thou theme (of Buber and Marcel) in terms of a face-to-face relation as a foundation for an ethical way of life. Having suffered grievously under the Nazis as a Jew in France in the war years, Levinas offers a critique of the dehumanizing way of violence. In contrast to the assertion of self or of oppressive regimes, it is 'the Other' who places my demands and self-interests in question (*see* the discussion of 'availability' in the entry on Marcel).

Such 'human' qualities as 'the face', 'the home', 'hospitality', 'patience' and even the work of 'carers' say more about 'being human' than abstract philosophical systems. Much of this springs from reflection on classical rabbinic biblical interpretation. This looks to Hebrew Wisdom rather than to Greek REASON.

Levinas (with Bonhoeffer and MOLTMANN) gives the lie to NIETZSCHE's misunderstanding of 'religion' as world-denying. 'Love of life' includes working, thinking, eating and drinking. 'To enjoy without utility ... gratuitously ... this is the human' (ibid., 133).

In *Otherwise Than Being* (1981), Levinas holds together a dialectic of responsibility between retaining self-identity and sacrificing the self for the sake of the Other. However, he never moves beyond the concreteness of *Totality and Infinity*. For example, to be open to the Other manifests itself in such modes of humanness as giving hospitality. (*See also* JEWISH PHILOSOPHY.)

liberal theology

Strictly, it is necessary to distinguish between the technical use of the term in modern Christian theology in the academic world and a wider, popular, less rigorous understanding of the term, which is more widespread.

In Christian theology the era of liberalism flourished from the last two decades of the nineteenth century to the first quarter of the twentieth century. Adolf Harnack represents the peak of this movement. He portrays Jesus as a teacher who taught a minimal core of 'basic' truths: the fatherhood of God, the brotherhood of humankind and the infinite value of the human soul. He viewed Christian doctrine as a movement towards complication which arose when Christianity moved onto Greek soil.

The key characteristics of liberal protestant Christianity around 1890–1925 were that Christian truth is 'teaching', rather than proclamation of a saving event; the basic, core teaching is 'timeless'; doctrine is secondary; and, where it is disputed, largely dispensable. There is relatively little about the proclamation of the cross as an atonement for human sin.

More broadly, however, 'liberal theology' is also used to denote a means of holding together theology with changes in culture or in world-views. It is often associated with particular respect for intellectual integrity and honesty, especially in relation to the claims of other branches of knowledge. It is in principle tolerant, although some would claim not always so in political practice.

In this sense 'liberal theology' may be applied also to religions outside Christianity to denote willingness to change with the times, retaining only certain identifiable 'core' truths. This stands in contrast with 'orthodox' or 'conservative' attitudes, which retain traditional doctrines, sacred writings, creeds and practices, as far as possible virtually as they stand. It stands at the opposite end of the spectrum to 'fundamentalism'. The more strictly defined liberalism of Harnack and the period 1890–1925 should be distinguished from this wider use.

Especially with the rise of POSTMODERNITY, liberalism is now to be defined equally in contrast to radicalism as to conservative orthodoxy. Liberalism retains a confidence in human REASON which, for different reasons, radicals and conservatives do not. CUPITT insists that 'Radicals', of whom he is one, are far from 'Liberal'. (*See also* BULTMANN; HERMENEUTICS; JEWISH PHILOSOPHY; NATURAL THEOLOGY; REVELATION; SCHLEIERMACHER.)

linguistic philosophy

See ANALYTICAL PHILOSOPHY.

Locke, John (1632–1704)

Locke was born in Somerset, in England, and educated at Christ Church, Oxford. His early philosophical influences included most especially DESCARTES. He wrote on political philosophy, publishing *The Letter on Toleration* (1689) and *Two Treatises on Government* (also 1689). However, his major work, which was twenty years in the writing, was *An Essay Concerning Human Understanding* (1690).

This is widely thought of as a foundation text of English EMPIRICISM, but it has been rightly argued (for example by D.J. O'Connor and by WOLTERSTORFF) that while books I–III expound an empiricist EPISTEMOLOGY, book IV expounds reasonable BELIEF, with a focus upon REASON and reasonableness. Wolterstorff observes: 'Locke's main aim in Book IV was to offer a theory of entitled (i.e. permitted; responsible) belief' (*John Locke and the Ethics of belief*, Cambridge: CUP, 1996, xv).

Locke also wrote constructively on the relation between reason and Christian BELIEF. He attacked both SCEPTICISM and intolerant dogmatism alike. He published his *Reasonableness of Christianity* (1695), and concluded book IV of *An Essay Concerning Human Understanding* with chapters on faith and reason, 'enthusiasm' and related topics.

In 'Of Enthusiasm' he observed that intensity of conviction, or 'firmness of persuasion', is no proof that a proposition or belief is 'from God': 'St Paul believed that he did well and that he had a call to it when he persecuted the Christians' (*Essay*, IV: 19: 12). Locke also published a sane exegetical work, *A Paraphrase and Notes on the Epistles of St Paul to the Galatians, 1 & 2 Corinthians, Romans, and Ephesians* (published after his death, in 1707). His *Miracles* also appeared late (1716).

THE PURPOSE OF LOCKE'S *ESSAY CONCERNING HUMAN UNDERSTANDING*

Locke's *Essay* is clearly divided into four books, each a series of chapters which are divided, in turn, into sections. Book I begins with his 'Introduction'. He writes, 'My purpose [is] to inquire into the original [origins], certainty, and extent of *human knowledge*, together with the grounds and degrees of *belief, opinion and assent*' (*Essay*, I: 1: 1). In particular this entails searching out 'the bounds between opinion and knowledge' (ibid., 3).

This is no mere theoretical exercise. To know 'the *powers* of our own minds', and no less also their limits, provides 'a cure of scepticism' (ibid., 6). In his preface, 'Epistle to the Reader', he points out that an understanding in advance of what lies beyond the scope of our minds will disarm premature scepticism, while to appreciate such limits equally closes the door against undue dogmatism. Locke, as Wolterstorff implies, provides in this respect a model for the value of such reflection in the context of religious belief.

REJECTION OF 'INNATE IDEAS'

The remaining chapters of Book I successfully attack the notion of 'innate ideas' inherited from Descartes and other rationalists. First, 'universal consent proves nothing innate' (ibid., 2:3). Children need to learn what many philosophers regarded as 'innate' (ibid., 5). 'Moral rules need a Proof; *ergo* not innate' (ibid., 3:4). Ideas are 'not born with children' (ibid., 4:2).

SOURCES OF KNOWLEDGE: 'IDEAS' AND PRIMARY AND SECONDARY QUALITIES

Book II is entitled 'Of Ideas'. An 'Idea is the Object of Thinking' (ibid., II: 1: 1). 'All Ideas come from Sensation or Reflection' (ibid., 2). Perceptions arise through the senses as perceptions 'of things'; but as soon as we identify these as 'yellow, white ... soft, hard' these become 'sources of the ideas we have, depending wholly upon our senses' (ibid., 3). The view that '*experience*' is the source of knowledge (ibid., 2) is empiricism. However, for Locke and BERKELEY the 'how' also implies IDEALISM.

'Experience' is sub-divided into 'two ... fountains of knowledge' namely 'external ... objects' of the world of the senses, and 'reflection' within ourselves (ibid.). When the mind reflects upon the ideas which it perceives, 'simple' ideas may be combined together to form 'complex' ideas (ibid., 3: 1, 2; 4: 1–5; II: 6 and II: 7).

This leads to Locke's distinction between primary and secondary qualities. 'Primary qualities' are 'utterly inseparable' from their sources: 'solidity, extension, figure, mobility' (ibid., 8:9). Secondary qualities 'produce various sensations in us ... colours, sounds, tastes' (ibid., 10). It was left to Berkeley (1685–1753) to subsume both categories into the single class of immaterial ideas. Locke suggests that with powerful microscopes 'colour' might disappear; but not extension.

As in much pre-Kantian empiricist epistemology, Locke construes the mind as passive in the process of necessary sense-perceptions and ideas, on the analogy of a blank sheet of paper (*tabula rasa*). Once the data has been received, reflection may process the raw data.

PERSONAL IDENTITY AND LANGUAGE

Towards the end of book II Locke considers the problem of personal identity (ibid., 27). The identity of 'man', like that of animals or vegetables, is seen in its 'organized body' (ibid., 6). But in the case of 'personal' identity, 'consciousness makes personal identity' (ibid., 10). If the 'soul' of a prince entered the body of a cobbler, a distinction between public perception of bodily identity and introspective perception of inner identity would become unavoidable (ibid., 15). Yet the issue of identity turns in the end on the 'justice of reward and punishment' (ibid., 18:19).

The same strongly modified DUALISM charaterizes Locke's philosophy of language (ibid., III: 1–11). 'Words' serve as 'sensible marks of ideas' (ibid., 2: 1). Locke holds an 'ideational' view of language, as against a purely REFERENTIAL or functional view. Words represent reality; but through the medium of the ideas that enter the mind, which words then identify by means of stable signs, or semiotic markers. They 'signify ... the ideas that are in the mind of the speaker' (ibid., 11).

Today all the criticisms that are brought against referential and representational theories of meaning would apply to Locke's account of language. 'Ideas' merely insert a 'middle' term within a theory of reference. His view of language is also 'expressive', which covers only a segment of the ways in which language is used, with the implication that language may also fall short of 'prior' thought (ibid., 10, 11). RORTY, especially, attacks this 'representationalist' view.

KNOWLEDGE, OPINION AND 'ENTITLED' BELIEF

Recent interpretations of Locke have acknowledged that book IV is different in tone and stance from books I–III. However, they are less inclined to dismiss its value than were earlier interpreters. Indeed, Wolterstorff reached the conclusion that book IV, especially its second half, held a depth that addressed or generated 'the making of the modern mind' (*John Locke*, xii).

The heart of the matter, for Wolterstorff, is 'the interweaving of the language of rationality with the language of obligation ... What we ought to believe has something intimate to do with reasons, and/or reasoning, and/or Reason' (ibid., xiii). 'Locke was the first to develop with profundity and defend the thesis that we are all responsible for our believings, and that ... reason must be one's guide' (ibid., xiv). Book IV offers 'a theory of entitled ... belief' (ibid., xv).

Locke recognizes that 'reason' has different significations (*Essay*, IV: 17: 1). We need reason 'for the enlargement of our knowledge, and regulating our assent' (ibid., 2). The 'SYLLOGISM' may be a restrictive tool, inhibiting enlargement (ibid., 4–7). Reason is 'the discovery of CERTAINTY ... by DEDUCTION', whereas 'faith ... is the assent to any proposition ... upon the credit of the proposer, as coming from God' (ibid., 18:2). Nevertheless, 'revelation cannot be admitted against the clear evidence of reason' (ibid., 5). Faith may also concern things 'above reason' (ibid., 7).

'Enthusiasm' in the sense of 'I believe because it is impossible', or zeal for the irrational, is as morally disturbing as undue scepticism or undue dogmatism. 'Boundaries ... between faith and reason' are necessary to contradict enthusiasm and the intolerance that 'divides mankind' (ibid., 11). 'Enthusiasm' nourishes 'groundless opinion' by unprepared minds, and enthusiasts fancy this as 'illumination from the Spirit of God' (ibid., 19:6). Irrational impulses are deemed to be 'a call or direction from heaven' (ibid.).

The problem about all this is that it arises from a disproportionate undervaluing of 'evidence'. 'God, when he makes prophet, does not unmake the man ... *Reason must be our last judge and guide in everything*' (Locke's italics, ibid., 19:14).

Wolterstorff finds Locke's greatest originality at the point at which he addresses PLATO's questions about the respective roles of *doxa*, opinion and *epistemē*, or knowledge (*Republic*, bk VI; cf. Wolterstorff, *John Locke*, 218–26). An intellectual inheritance may not rank as 'certain knowledge', but it is not worthless. In many cases, argumentation becomes more important than demonstration (ibid., 223).

Doxa is of use, provided that is regulated. 'Regulated opinion' has its place in life. 'Governance is a central theme in Locke's epistemology' (ibid., 238). In particular, Locke, Wolterstorff concludes, suggests that 'When we are obligated to do our best in the governance of *beliefs*, then too we are to listen to the voice of Reason' (ibid., 241). This entails a critique and control of the SELF. (*See also* PIETISM.)

logic

Traditionally, formal logic attempts to provide a system for determining valid inferences from one proposition or propositions to others, based upon the relations between the propositions. One of the earliest formulations was ARISTOTLE's system of propositions and the SYLLO-GISM, but this remains a sub-area within modern logic, which nowadays plays a less prominent role than in earlier centuries. LEIBNIZ (1646–1716) saw the need for a logical notation that transformed sentences into logical propositions, and which exposed their logical form.

The logic of the relations between propositions, or propositional calculus, remains only one of several areas of modern logic. It failed to distinguish adequately between different types of predicates. With the development of existential and universal QUANTIFIERS, a second area of predicate calculus emerged as a refinement of basic propositional logic.

The third area, and third stage of development, was the formulation of a systematic logic of classes. Leonhard Euler (1707–83) represented class relations by means of diagrams, including the now well-known distinctions between 'A' propositions of universal affirmation, 'E', of universal negation, 'I', of existential (or particular) affirmation, and 'O', of existential (or particular) negation.

The foundation of a modern logic of classes came more fully with George Boole (1815–64) and his algebraic logic of classes; with John Venn (1834–1923); with C. S. Peirce (1839–1914); with Georg Cantor (1845–1918); with G. Peano (1858–1932); and especially with Friedrich Gottlob Frege (1848–1925), RUSSELL (1872–1970) and Alonzo Church (1903–95).

A fourth main area is that of MODAL LOGIC. Clarence I. Lewis (1883–1964), an American pragmatic philosopher and logician, moved beyond a logic of assertion to that of POSSIBILITY, impossibility and logical NECESSITY. More recently HARTSHORNE and PLANTINGA have utilized modal logic to address the claims of the ONTOLOGICAL ARGUMENT for the existence of God and (in Plantinga's case) also the problem of EVIL.

PROPOSITIONAL LOGIC (PROPOSITIONAL CALCULUS)

Sentences that find variable expression in different natural languages need to be expressed as propositions of logic. This logical form may now become apparent. These are represented by the signs or symbols of logical notation. Conventionally p, q, and r are used to denote prepositional variables.

Propositions are then qualified by connectives, to begin to form a calculus, or system. The most basic are four: 'and', 'or', 'not' and 'if ..., then ...' Conjunctions are represented by '.'; disjunction usually by 'v'; negation by '∼'; and conditional implication by '→' or by '⊃'. These four types of logical connectives are examples of 'logical constants'.

In his earlier work WITTGENSTEIN saw the origins and basis of logical necessity in the determinacy of the relations between elementary propositions: 'A proposition is a truth-function of elementary propositions' (*Tractatus*, London: Routledge, 1961, 5; cf. 5–11). On this basis he constructed 'truth-tables'. 'If all true elementary propositions are given, the result is a complete description of the world' (ibid., 3.24).

If 'p' and 'q' represent elementary propositions which may be combined to produce the 'complex' proposition 'p.q', the following truth-table could be produced to indicate the truth-value 'true' (T) or 'false' (F) under each combination of propositions:

'p' 'q'	'$p . q$'	'$p \vee q$' (exclusive
T T	T	F disjunction, i.e.
T F	F	T either one or
F T	F	T the other, but
F F	F	F not both)

PREDICATE LOGIC (PREDICATE CALCULUS)

Here we move beyond relations between propositions as a whole to distinguish between types of predication within them. In this notation x, y, and z usually represent the subject of a sentence transposed into a general propositional form. A capital letter often represents the predicate. Thus 'Fx' may represent 'the man is French'; 'Gx' may denote 'God is good'. The purpose of the existential quantification '(Ex)' or '($\exists x$)' to denote 'for some x', or 'for at least one x' is explained in the entry on quantifiers, alongside the universal quantifier (x) 'for all x'.

Russell showed that through the use of quantifiers it was possible to avoid the self-contradictory implication that statements about the non-existence of 'a round square', or about attributes predicated of 'the present King of France' assumed the reality of what the propositions denied or described.

In logical translation 'a round square does not exist' could be reformulated as 'it is false to assert that an x exists which is such that "round" and "square" can be predicated of it simultaneously'. In symbolic notation this might take some such form as: ~ (Ex) (Fx.Gx)...'

LOGICAL GRAMMAR OR 'INFORMAL' LOGIC

Wittgenstein recognized that part of the genius of Russell was to probe behind natural language to identify an underlying logical form. Yet in his later work his own explorations reveal an increasing preference for returning to uses of language in settings in life to explore the 'logical grammar' of concepts without the cast-iron fetters of logical calculus.

This gave rise in due time to a recognition of the explorations of 'informal logic' as a more flexible tool for examining the almost infinite variations of an ever-moving language in ordinary life. The logical grammar of 'hearing God speak', for example, owes more useful explanation to Wittgenstein's 'grammatical' question: 'why cannot we hear God speak to someone else?' than all the apparatus of modern formal logic.

Although the two tasks are not the same, there remains an overlap. RYLE (1900–76) explored the 'logical grammar' of issues about the mind–body relationship and of long-standing paradoxes. STRAWSON (b. 1919) argues that informal logic can often take us further than formal logic (*Introduction to Logical Theory*, 1952).

Yet, while the logic of classes relates most closely to set theory in mathematics, Hartshorne and Plantinga have drawn constructively on modal logic to illuminate 'necessity' in the ontological argument, and 'possible worlds' in the problem of evil. (*See also* BELIEF; REASON.)

logical grammar

See LOGIC.

logical positivism

POSITIVISM denotes primarily a commitment to an empiricist or natural-scientific world-view, and a rejection of METAPHYSICS. Logical positivism seeks to harness a theory of LOGIC and language that will support and strengthen these views.

The movement broadly originated in Austria and Germany in the 1920s, centring on the VIENNA CIRCLE, which was led by Moritz Schlick, Rudolf Carnap and others. In England the movement was represented especially by AYER (1910–89), whose *Language, Truth and Logic* ([1936] 2nd edn, 1946) reached a very wide audience. It is regarded as a classic of logical positivism. Ayer's edited volume *Logical Positivism* (1959) contains a selection of relevant essays.

The heart of the philosophical doctrine is that all propositions, to be true-or-false rather than 'non-sense', must be verifiable by empirical observation and empirical evidence, with the exception of ANALYTIC STATEMENTS, or the propositions of formal logic. In his second edition Ayer modified this criterion to that of 'verification in principle', i.e. capable of being verified if a hypothetical observer could gain such evidence in principle rather than necessarily in practice.

It became steadily recognized that the linguistic dimension was merely a quasi-disguise for positivism in linguistic dress. By what criterion was the principle of verification true-or-false, since it was neither a descriptive, verifiable proposition, nor a proposition of formal logic? Moreover, to dismiss all propositions of RELIGION, ETHICS and metaphysics as mere 'emotive' expressions of approval or disapproval, or of preference or distaste (let alone as 'non-sense') failed to do justice to the complexity of life.

In spite of RORTY's postmodernist, pragmatic claims about 'justification' and 'ethnocentric' criteria, few regard murder, theft or rape as merely 'less preferable' forms of behaviour than others, about which more could not be 'said' with operative meaning-currency. (*See also* EMPIRICISM; FALSIFICATION; LANGUAGE IN RELIGION; POSTMODERNISM; PRAGMATISM. The longer of these articles contain more details.)

logical syllogism

See SYLLOGISM.

Lyotard, Jean-François (b. 1924)

Together with DERRIDA (b. 1930) and FOUCAULT (1926–84), Lyotard is widely known as one of the leading French philosophical exponents of POSTMODERNISM. His definition of the postmodern is one of the most frequently quoted: 'I define *postmodern* as incredulity towards metanarratives' (*The Postmodern Condition*, Minneapolis: University of Minnesota, 1984, xxiv).

Lyotard uses the term 'metanarrative' to denote any 'grand' narrative of METAPHYSICS, of theology, or of religions that purports to offer an overall understanding of the 'local' or particular narratives of individual persons or of specific social groups. In his view, any attempt to offer trans-contextual criteria of meaning and truth is based on illusion, naïvety or self-deception.

This calls for a radical reappraisal of philosophy, ETHICS, liberal or totalitarian politics and religious truth-claims that speak beyond a severely limited context. Indeed, he transposes the task of philosophy as that of bearing witness to fragmentation, discontinuity and heterogeneity in a postmodern era, which has 'seen through' the pretensions of modernity to overlook these discontinuities.

Foucault's emphasis upon the discontinuities of history offers a case study of such an approach in philosophy. Further, Derrida's attempt to eliminate 'closure' in all but everyday texts resonates with Lyotard's emphasis on the non-representational character of literature and art.

The emphasis on the 'local' (or radically relative) is reflected in the American postmodernism of RORTY (b. 1931), except that American postmodernity is more progressive, optimistic and pragmatic. Rorty perceives himself as 'splitting the difference' between Habermas's 'universal pragmatics' and Lyotard's antipathy towards all 'theory' ('Habermas and Lyotard on Postmodernity' in R. Bernstein, ed., *Habermas and Modernity*, Cambridge: Polity Press, 1985, 161, 174). (*See also* PRAGMATISM; TRUTH.)

M

Madhva (c. 1238–c. 1317)

Madhva's work in HINDU PHILOSOPHY is characterized by a so-called dualist emphasis within the Vedic tradition (Dvaita Vedanta). His 'DUALISM' is usually set in contrast with the MONISM or 'non-dualist system' of ŚAṄKĀRĀ (c. 788–820), the Advaita Vedanta school. Indeed, in Hindu legend Madhva was an incarnation of Vāya, sent to destroy the monist philosophy of Śaṅkārā and Śaṅkārā's appeal to 'illusion' (māyā), seen as a Buddhist commandeering of Hinduism.

Madhva also differs from RĀMĀNUJA's 'qualified monism' (Visista-advaita), even though Rāmānuja rejects Śaṅkārā's appeal to māyā as a way of explaining 'differences' or 'differentiation'. Rāmānuja did not assimilate the world or the individual SELF into a single, uncharacterizable, ultimate Reality. However, Madhva asserts an absolute difference between God (īśvara) and human souls (jīva), which goes far beyond Rāmānuja's 'qualified' or 'modified' monism.

Like Śaṅkārā and Rāmānuja, Madhva wrote commentaries on the Brahma-Sūtras and on the Bhagavad Gita. His writings consciously oppose Śaṅkārā and Rāmānuja. The created order of souls and bodies remains dependent upon a self-existing, independent reality (brahman). (See also BUDDHIST PHILOSOPHY; ONTOLOGY; PANENTHEISM; PANTHEISM; THEISM.)

Maimonides, Moses (1135–1204)

Maimonides (Rabbi Moses ben Maimon) is known especially for his work Guide of the Perplexed. Broadly in the tradition of PHILO of Alexandria, it facilitates a rational understanding of the Hebrew scriptures and rabbinic TRADITIONS that permits the perplexed enquirer to retain a loyalty to the traditions with rational integrity.

As in Philo, a wide range of conceptual tools are drawn from Greek philosophy, but also in the twelfth century from ISLAMIC PHILOSOPHY. Some Islamic thinkers had used Arabic texts that filtered ARISTOTLE through NEOPLATONISM, and Maimonides also incorporated Neoplatonic elements within his own thought. His Guide of the Perplexed was written in Arabic.

Although he was born in Cordoba in 1135 Maimonides was forced to flee to Cairo, where he served as physician to the vizier of Saladin. In addition to medical treatises, he wrote his Commentary on the Mishnah. In parallel with Philo on the laws of Moses, Maimonides sought wider rational purposes behind more particularist rabbinic legislation.

Maimonides defends a doctrine of divine CREATION against the contentions of AL-FARABI and others that the world is eternal. He also attacks OCCASIONALISM on the ground that it implies an irrational understanding of CAUSES within the world. Like Philo, he uses allegorical interpretations of the sacred texts if or when they seem unduly irrational or inconsistent, and translates ANTHROPOMORPHISM into more acceptable conceptual expressions.

Symbolic interpretation is utilized to the utmost to facilitate the notion of God as perfect, simple, immutable and transcendent. The philosophy of Maimonides was respected by LEIBNIZ, and as an example of Jewish rationalist philosophy is still widely influential. (*See also* CONCEPT; ETERNITY; JEWISH PHILOSOPHY; MENDELSSOHN; RATIONALISM; TRANSCENDENCE.)

Malcolm, Norman (1911–90)

Malcolm was an American philosopher, who taught for most of his life at Cornell University. However, from 1938 to 1940 he received a Harvard fellowship and worked closely with WITTGENSTEIN in Cambridge. In philosophy of religion his thought is significant in three main areas.

First, Malcolm's interpretation of Wittgenstein offers a valuable resource in its own right for understanding the latter's approach to language and to the logical currency or 'grammar' of CONCEPTS. His *Ludwig Wittgenstein. A Memoir* (1958) singles out examples of Wittgenstein's understanding of how language is embedded in contexts in life. His essay 'Wittgenstein's Philosophical Investigations' (1954) and another long article on Wittgenstein (in Paul Edwards, ed., *The Encyclopedia of Philosophy*, 8 vols., New York: Macmillan, 1967, vol. 8, 327–40) remain important sources, as well as his more recent *Nothing is Hidden* (1986).

Second, like Wittgenstein, Malcolm worked on the logical grammar of consciousness, mind, BELIEF and related concepts. He opposed both a dualist account of mind and body and also a behaviourist account of SELFHOOD. His *Dreaming* (1958) and work on consciousness and memory (in *Knowledge and Certainty*, 1963 and *Memory and Mind*, 1976) explore selfhood and philosophy of mind. Malcolm places some question-marks against cruder behaviourist or materialist explanations. Third, most widely known in philosophy of religion is his sympathetic attempt to reformulate the ONTOLOGIAL ARGUMENT for the existence of God. He employs arguments from the nature of logical NECESSITY to reply to some of its critics. This work, together with that of PLANTINGA, should make us hesitate to yield too hastily to those who dismiss the argument as a mere logical trick. (*See also* BEHAVIOURISM; DUALISM; LANGUAGE IN RELIGION; LOGIC.)

Marcel, Gabriel (1889–1973)

Born in Paris, Marcel was raised by an agnostic father and (after his mother's death when he was aged four) an aunt, also agnostic, whom his father married. He described his childhood as a 'desert universe', made all the worse by being subjected to a 'dehumanizing' demand for academic achievement.

Just as KIERKEGAARD sought personal authenticity beyond the imposed demands of his early life, so Marcel sought a humanity, humanness and personal value-system that nurtured respect, love and openness to 'the Other'. In 1929 Marcel became a convert to Roman Catholicism. Nevertheless he did not follow the Neo-Thomist philosophy of many Catholic theologians. The cognitive, intellectual, and inferential, in his eyes, touched only the surface of human life.

Music, art and spiritual 'availability' (*disponibilité*) to fellow human beings were fundamental in Marcel's life. In the

Socratic tradition he saw philosophy as a continuous quest for practical wisdom, not as resourcing a system of speculative REASON.

Like that of DOSTOEVSKY and BUBER, Marcel's philosophy might be called the human face of EXISTENTIALISM. 'Availability' to 'the Other' entails recognizing that human persons are more than case studies, numbers on a file, or mere OBJECTS of study in the empirical world. Human persons become a focus for the dignity and sacredness of Being. Their capacity to trust, to hope and to love constitutes part of their identity as human beings.

In his work *Being and Having* (1935), Marcel associates the aspect of 'having' with objects, objectification (treating persons or art as 'objects'), I–It relationships (like Buber) and abstraction. By contrast, 'Being' is associated with presence, mystery, I–Thou relationships and participation. The drive to 'possess' stems from a desire to control. However, this in turn depersonalizes the one whom (nowadays) we might call 'consumer-driven'. True personhood retains a sense of wonder, and permits 'availability' to the other. Marcel, some might suggest, paves the way for the thought of LEVINAS (1906–95).

Love, reverence and communion all presuppose fidelity (*Creative Fidelity*, 1940). Since Being (ONTOLOGY) is rooted in mystery, it is not illogical to speak of the disclosure of Being (*The Mystery of Being*, 1950). Yet humankind constantly trivializes the richness of Being and humanness in its preoccupation with objects and possessions (*The Decline of Wisdom*, 1954; and *The Existential Background of Human Dignity*, 1964).

Marxist critique of religion

Karl Marx (1818–83) stands alongside FEUERBACH (1804–72) and FREUD (1856–1939) as one of the three most significant advocates of a theory of religion in which they view 'God' as a human projection and human construct. Religion, they argue, is not based on an encounter with a transcendent or 'objective' personal God (*see* OBJECT; TRANSCENDENCE). It is not the effect of divine REVELATION.

Marx proposes, rather, that projected beliefs about God come to be utilized by a ruling or 'establishment' class to promote submissive contentment, or at least acquiescence, on the part of the oppressed masses. Religion is the 'opium' of the people. The short *Communist Manifesto* (1847), written jointly by Marx and Friedrich Engels (1820–95) included as its last line the well-known slogan: 'Workers of all countries unite' (*Communist Manifesto*, London: Penguin, 1967, 121). The proletariat must throw off their chains, including capitalism and religion.

If this is the primary focus of relevance to philosophy of religion, there is also a second one. Marx regarded the material conditions of production as a more fundamental force for change and authenticity in the process of human history than 'ideas'. Ideas, including theologies and philosophical IDEALISM, often embody MYTHS that perpetuate and replicate elitist establishment attitudes.

Exchange-value for labour, economics and social class constitute the bedrock of what is foundational for life and action, thought and (above all) political action. Later Marx would write: 'The philosophers have only *interpreted* the world in various ways; the point is to *change* it' ('Eleventh Thesis on Feuerbach' [1845], in *Early Writings*, London: Pelican, 1975, 423; further also in *The German Ideology* (1845–6).

WRITINGS

Marx's Paris manuscripts from his earlier period reflect a humanism that later became more militant. All the same Marx asserts, 'Atheism is humanism mediated ... through the suppression of religion; communism is humanism mediated ... through the suppression of private property' (*Economics and Philosophic Manuscripts*

[1832], 1844). Private property, he declared, divides one person from another.

Marx published *The Holy Family* in 1845, jointly written with Friedrich Engels. They assess 'the young Hegelians', attacking the inadequacy of their social philosophy as insufficiently radical. In *The German Ideology* Marx criticizes Feuerbach for seeking to address the human situation in terms of thought rather than action. In his 'Theses on Feuerbach' (the famous Eleventh Thesis is cited above) Marx made his point less emphatically; here he distances Feuerbach's ideas from German socialism but retains Feuerbach's materialist account of the world and reality. In 1847 he produced the short *Communist Manifesto* to prepare the ground for the hoped-for revolution in France of 1848.

Marx's classic work is *Capital* (*Das Kapital*, 3 vols, 1867, 1885, 1895). This expounds a view of history in which the exploitation of the working class leads to 'expropriating the expropriators' through revolution. The dehumanizing competitiveness of capitalism is first replaced by state socialism; then looks toward an eschatology of genuine communism in which each will give according to ability and receive according to need.

PHILOSOPHICAL ROOTS: RELATION TO HEGEL AND TO THE 'YOUNG' HEGELIANS

Although he was not a 'professional' philosopher in the sense of teaching philosophy, Marx's younger years were spent in an atmosphere in which HEGEL's philosophy and politics dominated intellectual discussion. In place of Hegel's ABSOLUTE as *Geist* (Mind or Spirit) unfolding itself in the dialectical concrete expression of history and of LOGIC, the so-called left-wing 'young' Hegelians ('left', 'centre' and 'right' seem to have been coined by D. F. Strauss) postulated a driving-force of material causes.

These Hegelians included Feuerbach, D. F. Strauss (1808–74) and Bruno Bauer

(1809–82). With Marx, these all rejected the notion that either 'God' or idealism constituted the true ground for the temporal and CONTINGENT changes of and within history. As we note in the Feuerbach entry (above), Feuerbach moved from thoughts about 'God' to a critical appraisal of 'REASON', and finally reached his 'last thought' which focused everything on humankind. He postulated as 'infinite' human consciousness, which projected outwards and upwards an 'infinite' God.

Marx disputed whether 'consciousness' sufficiently addressed the problems bequeathed by Hegel. Although Hegel was politically conservative, Marx argued that the 'young' Hegelians failed to see how socially radical were the implications of Hegel's work on historical and temporal change. He addressed these issues in *The Holy Family*. The key forces were *social and economic*. The politics of working-class movements in Britain, France and Germany offered a more accurate and focused vision of forces for change.

Such economic forces were more powerful and more significant than 'human consciousness', which still left the issues too much in the realm of 'ideas'. Ideas could distort and disguise the realities of class, exploitation, labour, price and value, and oppression and freedom. Even Hegel had intended his philosophy to perform an 'emancipating' function for society. Marx promoted a philosophy of action.

MARXIST PHILOSOPHIES OF HISTORY

At the beginning of *The Communist Manifesto* Marx and Engels assert: 'The history of all hitherto existing society is the history of class struggles. Freeman and slave, patrician and plebeian, lord and serf, guild-master and journeyman, in a word, oppressor and oppressed, stood in constant opposition to one another, carried on ... a fight' (ibid., 79). Each struggle ended either in 'common ruin' or in 'a revolutionary re-constitution' (ibid.).

The next few pages of *The Communist Manifesto* (80–94) sum up in the shortest compass the philosophy of history that is set out more fully elsewhere. The classical age of oligarchy gave way to the feudal society of the Middle Ages, establishing 'new classes, new conditions of oppression' (ibid., 80). The industrial era established in its place the opposition between capital and labour; between property-owning bourgeoisie and the oppressed class of the proletariat.

As capitalists seek to exploit larger and larger world markets, the plight of the oppressed workers deteriorates. This can be halted only by class struggle issuing in revolution. However, it was Engels rather than Marx who explicitly used the term 'dialectical MATERIALISM', and made primary use of the logical and historical structure of thesis, antithesis and synthesis.

Some insist that Hegel himself made little or no use of the thesis-antithesis-synthesis triad. However, Hegel's notion of a process in history or logic reaching a 'nodal' point at which change may be marked or identified, and a 'higher' position on the ladder of dialectic 'sublating' (or assimilating) a lower stage into itself with effects for change, comes very close to such a formulation (*see* the entry on Hegel for his explicit German terms). This is not to ignore earlier versions in FICHTE.

If Engels believed that this formula applied to every level of reality, Marx was more certain than Engels that processes of history were determined by historical NECESSITY. Hence Marx could propose a communist eschatology. Only when the conflict with capitalism had ushered in the era of state socialism, which involved constraints on behalf of the masses, could history eventually lead on to a non-coercive end of true communism, when each would choose to give according to ability; each would receive only according to need; and all goods would be shared.

CRITIQUES OF RELIGION IN MARX AND IN MARXISM

Marx did not follow Feuerbach in all things, but in many. As Nicholas Lash observes, he followed him especially in the 'inversions' of traditional accounts of cause and effect, or the primary and secondary. Thus Marx writes, '*Man makes religion*, religion does not make man' (*Early Writings*, 244; cf. Lash, *A Matter of Hope: A Theologian's Reflections on the Thought of Karl Marx*, London: Darton, Longman & Todd, 1981, 156–68). Religion 'is the opium of the people. The abolition of religion as the *illusory* happiness of the people is the demand for their *real* happiness' (*Early Writings*, 244).

Marx's most practical objection to 'religion' was that by illusory promises of 'reward' for acquiescence and obedience, institutional faith blocked the way to action on the part of the masses towards their liberation from oppression by social, political, and violent revolution. Religion encouraged respect for the 'order' of the establishment powers, disguising their role as oppressors.

After 1919, Russian Marxism flourished as a system under Vladimir Lenin (1870–1924) and under Stalin (1879–1953). Lenin underlined even more forcefully materialist features in Marx, but sat loose to his notion of 'dialectic'. The constraints and even repressions of state socialism, which Marx had regarded as penultimate in the progress of history, became virtually absolutized.

Lenin transposed Marx's more compassionate concern that religion might tranquilize the oppressed into a more aggressive attack on bourgeois religion as 'ideology' serving as an anodyne dispensing opium produced by the oppressors for the oppressed. Religion, Lenin insists, is not an 'intellectual' question; it is a tool of class struggle manipulated by the bourgeois oppressors. Thus he comes nearer to the kind of anti-religious critique offered by NIETZSCHE than perhaps Marx himself does. The ATHEISM of Lenin and Stalin becomes more militant.

SOME FURTHER ASSESSMENTS

As Helmut Gollwitzer observes, Marxist criticisms of religion may well apply to certain examples of the phenomenon of religion in the empirical life of faith-communities or churches. However, on what grounds can this critique be applied as a universal explanation of all religion at all times? (*The Christian Faith and the Marxist Criticism of Religion*, Edinburgh: St Andrews, 1970, 28). The reply is similar to that addressed to Nietzsche: the origins of religion should not be defined in terms of the reasons for abuses of religion.

Yet the practical concern for the dignity of humankind is common ground between Marx (and, to a lesser extent, later Marxist regimes) and most world religions. Marx's refusal to identify a human person as a mere unit of production does strike a genuine chord with the ETHICS of the great theistic faiths. Whether, however, the regimes that have been founded on Marxism have also shared that vision in practice may be doubted.

Indeed, the respective roles of human sin in Marxist and in religious systems may be compared with profit. It is not merely generated by social inequity. Hence even in the era of state socialism constraint, law and governmental control becomes even more necessary. The collapse of such mechanism in post-communist states illustrates the point further. Religion sees the issue as one of the need to transform the whole person as a human person.

Most serious for philosophies of religion is Lenin's disparagement of religion as lying beyond intellectual matters. If reason, ideas and intellect are subordinated to the power of the merely social, economic and historical, we reach what has been called 'the paradox of materialism'. If this view of the world has not even arisen from 'conscious' reflections, but is merely the result of brute forces

beyond human conscious reflection, on what ground may we reach any rational decision about the supposed validity of materialism? Presumably the brain registers not rational evaluation, but the effects of neuro-physical forces. A materialist world-view 'cannot be demonstrated' (Hans Küng, *Does God Exist?* London: Collins/Fount, 1980, 244).

Philosophical reflection cannot be reduced to the effects of mere social conditioning. This would border on the radical edge of POSTMODERNITY except for the fact that Marxism makes universal claims about TRUTH. It offers neither the rational evaluations of religions and philosophies nor the relativizing pluralism of post-modern devaluations of rationality. In a largely post-Marxist world, it appears to have the worst of both worlds.

Nevertheless, the Marxist recognition that interpretation of the world remains less than the ultimate need for its transformation yields an insight which, again, offers common ground with most religions. In the Christian tradition the theology of MOLTMANN makes considerate use of this fundamental insight. Yet in historical reality, the world still awaits the promised fulfilment of the transformation once offered by Marxist systems.

materialism

Materialism denotes an ONTOLOGY in which it is postulated or inferred that only material entities exist. It stands in contrast to IDEALISM and to DUALISM, as well as to more subtle and complex ontologies which allow room for, or allow for interaction with, non-material realities.

Materialism is closely allied with BEHAVIOURISM (a psychological version of materialism) and POSITIVISM (a version of materialism based on a world-view arrived at by restricting all enquiry to scientific or empirical method alone). Arguably, positivism and behaviourism are subcategories within materialism. Some writers distinguished materialism as answering the question 'Of what is reality composed?' from a form of 'materialism' that yields a wider version of ontology.

ANCIENT AND PRE-MODERN PERIODS: EAST AND WEST

In Greek philosophy Democritus (460–370 BCE) held that the ultimate constituents of reality were simple, solid, material atoms. These atoms (smallest indivisible units) were thought to be in motion, and capable of combination to form larger objects. Since these atoms differ only quantitatively, it is not entirely clear how Democritus accounts for qualitative difference, except that 'fire' or 'fire atoms' make possible the emergence of 'life'. Consciousness, perception and sensation are at bottom physical experiences, and no survival of a being after death is conceivable.

Epicurus (341–270 BCE) was influenced by Democritus. His insistence on 'factual evidence' anticipates in some measure later empirical evidentialism. His ontology of atoms is similar to that of Democritus. The two principles of efficient causality are that the atoms are in motion, and that chance may lead them to collide or to connect together. This random feature provides the sense of freedom human persons have, while 'mind' is merely a term to denote finer, faster-moving atoms.

In Roman philosophy Lucretius (c. 99–55 BCE) stands in this same 'atomic' tradition. Since matter and space are infinite, atoms of matter are of an infinite number. The emergence of an ordered pattern of atoms led to the beginning of our world by natural causes.

In Eastern philosophy, Chang Tsai (1020–77) took up the two dualist principles of Chinese Confucianism, *yin* and *yang*, but understood both principles as powers of material force. It is material forces that provide the balance of material reality. This is a narrower understanding of *yin–yang* dualism than is found generally in Chinese philosophy, although for the most part these principles are models of material objects as forces.

Two major issues emerge from Graeco-Roman materialism which anticipate modern thought. First, how may we account for any supposed 'threshold' that leads to mind, cognition, or consciousness? Or is consciousness a mere complexity of the physical? If so, what is rationality? Second, does materialism in this period rest on a pre-scientific evidentialism? If so, is it not a circular theory to construct an ontology that derives from taking cognizance of strictly material evidence only?

MODERN DEBATES: SOME ISSUES

Much of the subject matter under discussion may be found in fuller detail under such entries as behaviourism, positivism, SELF, SCIENCE AND RELIGION and HOBBES. Hobbes (1588–1679), however, has been described with justice as less an explicit materialist than a cautious sceptic with a materialist cast of mind. He did indeed reject the concept of 'SOUL' or 'spirit' as a self-contradiction, on the basis that this seemed to imply 'an immaterial material'. Humankind is governed by physical appetites and passions (*see* SCEPTICISM).

Yet Hobbes acknowledged that even if REASON is more like instrumental 'computation' than a broader rationality, this capacity to compute presupposed not simply physical impulses but 'ideas, which are taken up into language'. The very language about 'what we can conceive' betrays his possible awareness that a thoroughgoing materialism leaves no grounds on which to promote thought and argument that is other than arbitrary. Hobbes remained ambivalent on this matter.

The eighteenth-century French materialists, especially Julien Offroy de La Mettrie (1709–51) and the encyclopaedists Denis Diderot (1713–84) and Paul-Henri d'Holbach (1723–89) take us into a different world. Their premise is that indicated by the title of the well-known work by La Mettrie, *Man the Machine* (1747). Mechanistic models provided the key to their view of the self and their ontology. In the case of human beings, all is accounted for, including consciousness, by physiological processes. Speech consists in physical sounds, which may generate 'images' within the brain.

In relation to La Mettrie, Diderot is a more moderate materialist; but d'Holbach is an even more radical one. Diderot's conception of matter bordered upon ascribing to it supra-material properties to account for consciousness. D'Holbach insisted that the whole world is a machine, an autonomous system of material particles that required no 'machinist'. 'Knowledge' is derived from sensation.

Increasingly in the nineteenth and twentieth centuries materialism may seem to stand or fall with developments in empirical science. The challenge of evolutionary themes is discussed under separate entries. So also is emergence of behaviourism as a purely functional account of the human mind in terms of internal observation. Sometimes this is associated with 'epiphenomenalism', the view that mind is merely 'thrown up' when organisms reach a given level of physiological complexity. With the rise of modern science, materialism tends to take the form of positivism.

After Einstein, on one side it may be argued that matter is more complex than writers formerly realized, and may be interrelated with other properties to account for consciousness. On the other side, the former, naïve, view of value-neutral observation and innocent 'evidentialism' is hardly still viable.

At all events, we seem to be left with the 'paradox' formulated by Arthur O. Lovejoy (1873–1962) about rationality and consciousness. If 'reason' is a matter of physical processes, on what rational basis can I argue for an ontology that reduces reason to manipulating or 'computing' counters purely on the basis of physical impulses? Can a materialist genuinely philosophize on a rational basis?

Lovejoy concluded that, 'non-physical particulars' are indispensable means to any knowledge of physical realities. Without these, to speak of rational argument verges on paradox.

Yet from simpler versions of positivism there has emerged a more sophisticated 'physicalism'. Sceptics view it as merely a version of epiphenomenalism, but some writers (notably J. J. C. Smart and Daniel Dennett) explore parallels between human consciousness and the mechanical and electronic processes of information technology. Are these computation, or rational processes? Is 'reason' (to take up the point from Hobbes) no more than a sophisticated version of 'computation', which can be simulated by machine?

The debate on religion and science throws up issues about 'levels' of explanation and understanding. For example, how does what is displayed on an oscilloscope relate to the appreciation of the form, purpose, design and mood of a musical performance? This entry on materialism now merges into issues explored under several other entries, especially that on science and religion as well as on the TELEOLOGICAL ARGUMENT and on self. (*See also* DARWIN; EMPIRICISM; EVOLUTION; LOGICAL POSITIVISM; MARXIST CRITIQUE OF RELIGION; VIENNA CIRCLE.)

Mendelssohn, Moses (1729–86)

Mendelssohn is perhaps the first major Jewish philosopher of the modern period to follow very broadly in the rationalist tradition of Maimonides (1135–1204). In his *Morning Hours,* or *Lectures on the Existence of God* (1785) he endorsed and defended the ONTOLOGICAL ARGUMENT and the TELEOLOGICAL ARGUMENT for the existence of God.

Mendelssohn drew especially upon the philosophies of LEIBNIZ (1646–1716) and Christian Wolff (1679–1754). Both of these thinkers stood in the rationalist tradition associated with DESCARTES. In his 'Phaedo', or *Concerning the Immortality of the Soul* (1767) he attempted to deduce the immortality of the soul from its nature, in effect as an A PRIORI argument.

In tune with much eighteenth-century thought, Mendelssohn argued for individual freedom of thought as well as political freedom, and urged that Judaism did not demand acceptance of certain dogmas. He insisted that Judaism is to be defined not as a set of doctrines but as a set of practices. In religious terms, Judaism is an aspect of a universal religion of REASON.

Understandably, Mendelssohn is often considered to be 'the' Jewish philosopher of ENLIGHTENMENT RATIONALISM. (*See also* JEWISH PHILOSOPHY; PHILO.)

metaphor

Metaphor may sometimes be used as an illustrative or aesthetic device, but this is only of secondary significance for philosophy or for the use of LANGUAGE IN RELIGION. The constructive and creative use of metaphor is neither ornamental, nor didactic, nor illustrative. It is not a mere substitute for what may be known or communicated by non-metaphysical language. Fundamentally it draws upon SYMBOL; and more especially it operates by interaction. It extends non-metaphysical linguistic resources by drawing on two or more SEMANTIC domains interactively.

Max Black is probably the classic exponent of the interactive theory. He writes: 'A memorable metaphor has the power to bring two separate domains into COGNITIVE and emotional relation by using language directly appropriate for the one as a lens for seeing the other' (*Models and Metaphors*, Ithaca, NY: Cornell, 1962, 236).

RICOEUR (b. 1913) endorses this account, and agrees that like a good theoretical model it provides 'a way of seeing things differently by changing our language about the subject of our investigations. This ... proceeds from the construction of a heuristic fiction' by

transposing the characteristics of the exploratory fiction 'to reality itself' (*Interpretation Theory*, Fort Worth: Texas Christian University Press, 1976, 67; also in *The Rule of Metaphor*, London: Routledge, 1978, 6).

ARISTOTLE (384–322 BCE) laid the foundation for this understanding in the *Poetics*. *Poiēsis* (making) uses interactions between *mimēsis* (a description of reality) and *mythos* (plot). It stands on the border between persuasive rhetoric and poetics. Metaphor is 'giving the thing a name that belongs to something else' (*Poetics*, 1457B, 6–9).

Above all, metaphor is not wooden and static, but entails a movement (Greek, *phora*) from current usage. Ricoeur insists that Aristotle anticipates an interactive (rather than merely substitutionary) theory: it is 'to see two things in one' (*The Rule of Metaphor*, 24).

In the mid-twentieth century Owen Barfield (1947) and Philip Wheelwright (1954) called attention to the 'tensive' power of metaphor to stretch language through 'double language'. Barfield compared the creative use of legal fiction in law to cover new or exceptional cases. Black (1955, 1962), Ricoeur (1976, 1978), Mary Hesse (1966) and Janet Martin Soskice (1985) show conclusively that metaphor has power not only to extend language creatively, but also to communicate cognitive truth, including truths of science.

This demonstrates the value of metaphor as a serious resource for language in religion. It combines the capacity to involve those who speak and are addressed as participants with the power to convey cognitive truth beyond more conventional or pre-established frontiers of conventional language.

The problems of metaphor include the overuse of 'dead' metaphor when its creative power and original contexts have become lost from view. Then, as NIETZSCHE, Barthes and DERRIDA point out, they can become reservoirs for the transmission of uncritical mythologies. (*See also* MODELS AND QUALIFIERS; MYTH; RAMSEY.)

metaphysics

In ARISTOTLE the treatise from which 'metaphysics' accidentally derived its name addressed 'large' philosophical questions. These included the nature of potentiality and ACTUALITY, of becoming and being, and of causality and substance. It was consciously 'general'. Today the term usually denotes the exploration of ONTOLOGY, ultimate reality or reasons why such explorations may or may not be undertaken.

The accidental origin of this meaning came from fact that in the classification of Aristotle's works in the first century BCE (by Andronicus of Rhodes), the treatise in question follows 'after' (Greek, *meta*) the work entitled *Physics*. 'Meta' does not denote 'beyond' physics, except in the sense of coming next in a list.

In practice, the word 'metaphysics' is often reserved for 'systems' that seek to address the nature of reality. It embraces both ontology (the nature of reality) and EPISTEMOLOGY (how or whether we have knowledge of what we seek to know), since to ask whether we are in a position to know any reality beyond that of the empirical is itself a metaphysical question. Positivists reject metaphysics as meaningless, but many argue that this rejection is itself an instance of a metaphysical assertion. (*See also* ABSOLUTE EMPRICISM; CAUSE, POSITIVISM.)

Mill, John Stuart (1806–73)

Born in London, Mill was an English empiricist thinker, known chiefly for his 'qualitative' version of utilitarian ETHICS. However, in addition to *Utilitarianism* (1863), he wrote on LOGIC and on political philosophy. He defended freedoms in *On Liberty* (1859) and his political theory in *On Representative Government* (1861).

Although initially he favoured and sought to refine the utilitarian ethics of Jeremy Bentham (1784–1832), Mill became disenchanted with Bentham's quasi-materialist refusal to distinguish between physical and spiritual pleasure. He advocated a qualitative distinction between types of pleasure in seeking to promote the greatest happiness of the greatest number.

If pleasure or happiness is defined in terms of moral improvement, it becomes both a duty and a political right to seek the greatest happiness of the greatest number. Even a measure of self-sacrifice may be required, in contrast to the egoistic hedonism of Bentham. Mill appears to have believed in the existence of a cosmic designer, but not necessarily in the personal God of THEISM. All of our ideas, he believed, derive from sense-experience. (*See also* EMPRICISM; GOD, CONCEPTS AND 'ATTRIBUTES' OF; MATERIALISM.)

miracles

In ancient texts and modern thought the term tends often to focus upon that which produces wonder, awe or insight. Nevertheless especially in the biblical texts criteria for the miraculous may include issues of agency and for what purpose the miracle was performed.

Generally the ultimate CAUSE is attributed to God, but this may leave open attributions of second, or mediate, causes which answer the question 'How?' As indicated under the entry SCIENCE AND RELIGION, in theology or religions a miraculous event relates to the question 'Why?' more readily than to the scientific or empirical question 'How?'

Accounts or stories of miracles occur in many religious traditions. They are associated with Moses, Elijah, Buddha, Jesus Christ and the Prophet Muhammad.

Although it is widely assumed that miracles are invoked to generate faith or BELIEF, many of the sacred texts, including biblical Judaeo-Christian texts, regard miracles as precisely not performed to fulfil this function. In the Gospel of John 'seeking a sign' (Greek, *semeion*) is discouraged, although if faith discerns a miracle, faith is duly strengthened.

In the Christian tradition, however, in this single respect the RESURRECTION of Jesus Christ provides an untypical counter-example. The resurrection is seen as a divine vindication and corroboration of the identity and effective work of Christ, and evidence is adduced for its occurrence (1 Cor. 15:1–11; also by inference, 15:12–34).

MIRACLES AND 'LAWS OF NATURE'

AUGUSTINE (354–430) was aware that miracles could be perceived as disrupting the regularities of nature. Yet he saw both the natural order (i.e. its 'orderedness') and miracles as expressions of the will and decree of God. Hence he concluded that miracles were not 'against' nature (*contra naturam*) but only conflicting with our knowledge of the operations of nature. 'We give the name "nature" to the usual common course of nature ... but against the supreme laws of nature, which is beyond knowledge ... God never acts, any more than he acts against himself' (*Reply to Faustus the Manichaean*, 26: 3).

Thomas AQUINAS (1225–74) defines 'miracle' as that which is 'sometimes done by God outside the usual order assigned to things ... because we are astonished (*admiramus*) ... when we see an effect without knowing the cause' (*Summa Contra Gentiles*, III, 101). 'God alone can work miracles' (ibid., 102). For only the Creator can initiate 'what is not in its [nature's] capacity to perform'. Miracles are thus 'beyond' the natural order, but not 'against' it.

HUME (1711–76) defines 'miracle' quite differently: 'A miracle is a violation of the laws of nature.' Hence, since 'unalterable experience established these laws', arguments against miracles are as conclusive as any argument from experience can be ('Of

Miracles', *Enquiries Concerning Human Understanding*, 3rd edn, Oxford: Clarendon, 1975, sect. X, pt 1, para. 90). The 'uniform experience' e.g. that dead men do not come to life 'amounts to a *proof*, from the nature of the fact' (ibid.). 'No testimony is sufficient to establish a miracle unless its falsehood would be more miraculous' (ibid., para. 91).

Nevertheless, Alastair McKinnon writes, 'The idea of suspension of natural law is self-contradictory ... If we substitute the expression "the actual course of events", *miracle* would be defined as "an event involving the suspension of the actual course of events"' ('"Miracle" and "Paradox"', *American Philosophical Quarterly*, 4, 1967, 309; also cited by R. Swinburne, *The Concept of Miracle*, London: Macmillan, 1970, 20).

SWINBURNE develops this further. After considering detailed examples of statistical 'laws' in the context of quantum theory, Einstein's equations of general relativity and Kepler on planetary motion, he comments, 'One must distinguish between a formula being a law *and* a formula being (universally) true or being a law which holds without exception' (*The Concept of Miracle*, 28).

John Polkinghorne offers parallel observations. 'Science simply tells us that these events are against normal expectation ... The theological question is: does it make sense to suppose that God has acted in a new way? ... In unprecedented circumstances, God can do unexpected things ... The laws of nature do not change ... yet the consequences of these laws can change ... when one moves into a new regime' (*Quarks, Chaos, and Christianity*, London: Triangle, 1994, 82).

Polkinghorne, distinguished as both a physicist and a theologian, concludes: 'Miracles are only credible as acts of the faithful God if they represent new possibilities occurring because experience has entered some new regime' (ibid., 88). Hence he finds the resurrection of Jesus

Christ credible because (for Christians) it signals the beginning of a new reality in God's dealings with the world.

MIRACLES AND DIVINE CREATIVITY

Miracles, then, are perhaps not best defined simply as that which evokes 'wonder', although this has been a traditional entailment of the concept If they do evoke wonder, this is within the framework of divine action as a signal of newness, purpose or 'beyondness'. In theistic traditions the nature of an authentic miracle will be to serve and to advance the purposes of God in accordance with the nature of God. 'Idle' portents may be suspected as such by theists as by antitheists.

From very different angles of approach A. Boyce Gibson and PANNENBERG attack the positivist assumption that any unique, once-occurring, event is somehow excluded by 'experience', as Hume tends to imply. Gibson writes: 'The dogma that nothing that happens only once, or for the first time ... can ever be caused, or a cause' is a Humean dogma that limits creative agency (*Theism and Empiricism*, London: SCM, 1970, 149). Can nothing new ever happen for the first time?

PANNENBERG points out that a mechanistic, positivist model of the universe as a closed system no longer reflects the more recent advances of the natural sciences, on one side, and inhibits 'the freedom of God', on the other. The 'biblical belief in God as the Creator ... finds in the incalculability and CONTINGENCY of each event an expression of the freedom of the Creator' (*Systematic Theology*, vol. 2, Edinburgh: T & T Clark, 1994, 46). (*See also* CREATION; EMPRICISM; IMMANENCE; OMNIPOTENCE; POSITIVISM; THEISM.)

modal logic

Traditionally Western logic explicates the conditions of valid inference, especially what may be inferred by DEDUCTION from propositions. A SYLLOGISM offers an inferential form that works from a premise to a conclusion through a logical relation to a middle term, which must be common (without change of meaning) to two of the propositions of the syllogism. Propositional calculus works with such operators or logical constants as those of conjunction (and); disjunction (either ... or ...); negation (not), and material implication (if ... then ...).

Modal logic builds on this foundation, but develops it to include finer distinctions of logical NECESSITY, logical POSSIBILITY, and different levels of implication. It investigates the validity not only of such propositions as 'If ... then ...' but also 'It is possible that ...'. In philosophy of religion, MALCOLM, HARTSHORNE and PLANTINGA utilize modal logic to clarify the logical force of the ONTOLOGICAL ARGUMENT and (in Plantinga's work) also formulations of the problem of EVIL. In ETHICS modal logic is sometimes used to formulate the possibilities and necessities of logic in DEONTOLOGY, or deontic logic.

In addition to the notation used in basic propositional calculus, for example, $p \vee q$ (for 'either p is the case or (alternatively) q is the case', or '$\sim p$' (it is not the case that 'p'), modal logic uses the symbol '$\Box$' to express necessity ('$\Box p$' denotes 'p is necessarily true') and the notation '$\Diamond$' to express possibility ('$\Diamond p$' denotes 'p is possibly true'). If 'p' is necessarily true, it may be said to be true in 'all possible worlds'. Thus in the example considered under COUNTERFACTUALS, 'America' might be smaller than 'England' in a possible world, but this could not be literally so.

'Possible worlds' may be said to help to clarify the logic of possible hypotheses, counterfactuals or projected scenarios, although some reject this claim. The American philosopher Clarence I. Lewis (1883–1964) urged the pragmatic value of interpretative structures, and formulated eight systems of modal logic with a view to distinguishing 'strict' implication from other levels of implication.

models and qualifiers

This phrase is associated especially with the work of RAMSEY. Ramsey aimed to enter into constructive dialogue, especially at Oxford, with empiricists and logical positivists concerning the currency of LANGUAGE IN RELIGION.

Models provide 'object language', which permits 'an empirical placing of theological phrases' (Ramsey, *Religious Language*, London: SCM, 1957, 19–48). These provide points of engagement between ordinary language and disclosure of the divine.

However, models would mislead us about God if they are not duly 'qualified'. Thus the 'models' of cause, wisdom, goodness and purpose need to be used in speaking of God's action as Creator, or of God's character as pure love, or of God's purposive designs. All the same, each needs to have an appropriate 'qualifier' attached to it: first cause; infinitely wise; infinitely good; eternal purpose (ibid., 49–89).

The biblical writings exhibit this logic. Thus Jesus uses the model of 'birth', but also explains to Nicodemus the distinctive logic with which 'birth' is used (Jn 3:1–10). Jesus is 'living [i.e. running] water' (Jn 4:10), but needs to explain to the woman of Samaria that it is not the kind of water that can be made available in a bucket (Jn 4:11–15). WITTGENSTEIN observes that logical grammar is distinctive when the model of 'hearing' God speak is used.

In Neo-Kantian philosophy the notion of construing scientific states of affairs through the use of models was explored by Heinrich Hertz (1857–94). In more recent work the heuristic or exploratory function of theoretical models and analogues in science has helped to break down a simplistic contrast between 'facts' and frameworks of interpretation. N.R.

Campbell developed a philosophy of models in science in *Physics, the Elements* (1920), and Max Black, Mary Hesse and Ron Harré have undertaken further logical explorations of models in the philosophy of science.

The upshot of this work is to demonstrate the value of models not only for exploration but also to convey COGNITIVE truth. Yet in both science and RELIGION, models also convey negative resonances that need to be discarded. In Ramsey's terms, all models require some kind of qualifier. (*See also* EMPRICISM; LOGICAL POSITIVISM; METAPHOR; MYTH; SCIENCE AND RELIGION; SYMBOL.)

Moltmann, Jürgen (b. 1926)

Born in Hamburg, Moltmann was conscripted into the German armed forces in 1943 at the age of seventeen. He saw his city destroyed by allied bombing, and many horrors of war. In February 1945 he was taken prisoner of war, and it was only in the prison camps that he learned of the further Nazi horrors of Auschwitz, Belsen and the Jewish Holocaust.

This, Moltmann writes, was 'the death of all my mainstays', producing a sense of 'daily humiliation'. With little or no church background, he came upon the Psalms that spoke of God as with those of 'broken heart'. He perceived God as not the lofty God of 'THEISM' in love with his own glory, but as a co-suffering God on 'his side of the barbed wire'. Moltmann declares, 'A God who cannot suffer cannot love either' (*The Trinity and the Kingdom of God* [1980], London: SCM, 1981, 38).

(1) In philosophy of religion this presents an influential but not altogether traditional view of God. 'A God who is eternally in love with himself … is a monster' (*Experiences of God*, [1979], London: SCM, 1980, 16). Rather, God shares in the suffering of the cross of Jesus Christ, and no human suffering 'is shut off from God'.

(2) Knowledge of God is not to be determined on the basis of 'what is', i.e. from a 'static' theism. In common with the Marxist philosopher Ernst Bloch, Moltmann stresses hope, but also promise. 'From first to last ... Christianity is hope, is forward-looking and forward moving ... transforming the present' (*Theology of Hope* [1964], London: SCM, 1967, 16). Against NIETZSCHE'S 'God is dead', Moltmann distinguishes between divine absence and divine hiddenness in the present. Future promise will enact 'a conquest of the deadlines of death' (ibid., 211).

(3) Moltmann seeks to address the problem of EVIL in terms of a 'post-Auschwitz' theology of God. 'Even Auschwitz is taken up into the grief of the Father, the surrender of the Son, and the power of the Spirit' (*The Crucified God* [1972], London: SCM, 1974, 278). 'Unless it apprehends the pain of the negative, Christian hope can never be realistic and liberating' (ibid., 55). He draws on the 'negative dialectic' of Adorno on Jewish–Christian and Marxist–Christian dialogue, and on a theology of God who genuinely 'feels' and 'suffers' by God's own choice. (*See also* ANTHROPO-MORPHISM; GOD, CONCEPTS AND 'ATTRIBUTES' OF; OMNISCIENCE; EVIL.)

monism

The term stands in contrast to DUALISM and to pluralism and very broadly denotes the view that all reality is a unity, or single 'substance' (Greek, *monos*, alone, i.e. the only entity within a class). Christian Wolff (1679–1754) appears to have coined the term to describe systems of thought that rejected a dualism of mind and body as two different entities, and sought to resolve them into one.

Parmenides (fl. 515–492 BCE), SPINOZA (1632–77) and BRADLEY (1846–1924) offer landmark examples of thoroughgoing monists. On the other hand, although LEIBNIZ (1646–1716) postulated 'units' of force without extension ('monads'), since these are all of one kind some have characterized Leibniz's philosophy as a relative or 'attributive' monism.

In practice the term is capable of too many applications to be very useful. In the context of discussion specifically about God, little can be said about monism that is not more constructively debated under such headings as PANTHEISM or PANENTHEISM. For examples of monism in Eastern thought, see also HINDU PHILO-SPHY, and especially ŚANKĀRĀ.

moral argument for the existence of God

This approach does not rank in comparable importance alongside the other three main arguments for the existence of God (*see* GOD, ARGUMENTS FOR THE EXISTENCE OF), namely the ONTOLOGICAL, COSMOLOGICAL and TELEOLOGICAL ARGUMENTS for the existence of God. Philosophically it emerges with full seriousness most specifically with KANT, (1724–1804), whose critique sought to demonstrate the limits of 'pure' REASON. Pure reason, for Kant (as for HUME) could not address transcendental questions, which went beyond CONTIN-GENT or finite phenomena within the world.

IMMANUEL KANT: GOD AS A 'POSTULATE' OF PRACTICAL REASON

Kant argued that only the absolute moral imperative (the 'categorical imperative' of moral obligation) in terms of 'practical reason' could relate to such unconditional notions as 'God'. Rather than pointing directly to God, absolute moral imperative presupposes a correlation between the good will, or virtue, and human happiness or the reward of worthiness, which only God or a Supreme Being could ensure.

This is not, however, a formal argument either A PRIORI or A POSTERIORI, since if it were it would relapse into the realm of theoretical reason. Kant has already exposed the limits and inadequacy of such theoretical reason to establish the existence of God. More succinctly, the very notion of 'the highest good' (*summum bonum*) presupposes 'God' and human freedom. God, freedom and immortality are 'POSTULATES' of 'Practical Reason' (*Critique of Practical Reason*, 1788, bk II, ch. 2). A 'postulate' is a demand or claim that is neither axiomatic nor strictly demonstrable.

In Kant's *Critique of Practical Reason* it is far from clear that 'God' denotes anything other than a supposedly absolute moral law, exempt from the contingencies of the empirical and phenomenal world. Kant's 'God' is hardly personal, and in *Religion Within the Limits of Reason* he criticizes as 'superstitious' the view of PRAYER that assumes governmental or providential responses to prayer within the world. 'Freedom', 'immortality' and 'God' are 'postulates' for the following reasons.

Freedom is a postulate because the achievement of the highest good is, in Kant's view, 'the necessary object' of the good will that is shaped by absolute moral law. In turn, the good will, which is wholly good, presupposes the possibility of 'infinite progress' in goodness or in holiness, yet this also presupposes 'an infinitely enduring existence and personality of the same rational being'.

This is the immortality of the soul (ibid.). However, the notion of 'happiness proportional to that morality' must also postulate the existence of God. What Kant calls 'the supreme cause of nature' is to be 'presupposed for the highest good'. To assume the existence of God is 'morally necessary' (ibid.).

At times Kant seems explicitly to concede that the existence of God is no more than a 'need' for his account of duty and moral imperative. Even in his high ethical account of human persons and the good will as 'ends', not means, he adds that even God cannot have 'ends' higher than the 'end' of a human person.

The force of Kant's argument seems to operate more successfully at a popular intuitive level. Is everything, including moral obligation and 'God', exhaustively explained in terms of the relativities and contingencies of the everyday empirical world? Is all morality and religion no more than a behavioural response to the variable challenges of natural environment or human society?

THE COUNTER-ARGUMENT: DIFFERENT ACCOUNTS OF MORAL OBLIGATION

Kant's approach depends on an absolute notion of moral obligation as that which transcends the contingent and variable. However, the history of ethics reveals numerous theories that account for moral obligation in other ways.

(1) HOBBES (1588–1679) held to a theory of psychological hedonism, namely that all human persons experience a compulsion to gratify their own desires. However, since society itself brings benefits, a half-conscious social contract subordinates these desires to a societal power (e.g. a king), who will hold the ring in face of competing interests, and restrain society from breakdown into anarchy.

(2) HUME (1711–76) argued that 'reason is and ought only to be the slave of the passions', and everything is directed towards the achievement of pleasure and the avoidance of pain. Sub-categories of pleasure and pain are woven into a supposed system of ethics or utility, complicated by the pleasure of social approval and the pain of social disapproval. This version of hedonism arises naturally from within the world and embodies no absolute.

(3) Jeremy Bentham (1748–1832) and MILL (1806–73) equated 'morality' with the principle of 'the greatest happiness' of the greatest number. Bentham more empirically spoke of degrees of pleasure and pain. Mill

introduced a more complex and less reductive criterion of 'higher' or 'lower' pleasure: 'It is better to be a Socrates dissatisfied than a pig satisfied.' For some this remains firmly within behavioural utilitarianism; for others this seems to open the door for the kind of value-system that might suggest a 'beyond', such as in principle religion and God. Mill himself had sympathy for the existence of some kind of 'limited' deity.

(4) NIETZSCHE (1844–1900) accounted for 'morality' largely in terms of self-interest and 'will to power'. His view of ethics is that the approval of society or power generates all the manipulative and instrumental strategies that serve the self. The notion of absolute moral obligation is part of the deception and illusion manipulated by some to control others.

(5) AYER (1910–89) and RORTY (b. 1931) sought to redefine moral goodness in terms of a vocabulary of approval or disapproval by a group within society. There can be no talk of absolute moral imperatives.

CAN THE ARGUMENT BE REINSTATED? RASHDALL AND OWEN

In *The Moral Argument for Christian Theism* (London: Allen & Unwin, 1965) H. P. Owen attacks naturalistic explanations for the experience of moral obligation. It is impossible to derive an evaluative moral 'ought' from merely naturalistic factors or to treat a good conscience as a gratified wish. Against AYER and others he insists that morality is irreducible, and not a mere matter of corporate or individual approval or disapproval. Is it enough to say that the Nazi Holocaust is merely a matter for 'disapproval', rather than a violation of moral values?

Naturalistic theories, Owen argues, depend on restricting 'morality' to acts rather than to will and habituated character. He agrees with Kant, that will and

persons are the focus of moral issues. This requires more than 'AUTONOMY', mere self-regulation. He sees a sense of the moral as a 'sign' that points beyond itself to God (ibid., 43–6). The logical currency of 'obedience' in Judaism, Christianity and Islam becomes illusory on the basis of naturalistic theories (ibid., 54–60).

Owen does not endorse Kant's formulation in terms of 'postulates' and presuppositions. Nevertheless, he agrees with Kant that in principle goodness and good character point beyond mere contingencies and relativities in human life.

At the beginning of the twentieth century Hastings Rashdall (1858–1924) insisted similarly that there is something 'unconditional' about duty or moral law (*The Theory of Good and Evil*, 2 vols., Oxford: Clarendon, 1907). We cannot dismiss 'value' as the mere interest of a specific group. Otherwise, what are we to make of the stable tradition of virtues as qualities of a good character from PLATO onwards? If it is not 'unconditional', it is not 'morality'.

Today there is more widespread scepticism about 'morality'. Arguments that moral codes reflect the interests and conventions of societies and are variable have gained ground. Nevertheless the view that often in the past the word 'moral' has been overextended may not necessarily imply that all INSTANTIATIONS of moral character and moral virtue are merely contingent and without universal grounding. This belief would not inevitably lead to a belief in the existence of God. It might, however, seem to imply a source of value beyond the merely contingent in the everyday life of societies. (*See also* EMPIRICSIM; ETHICS; TRANSCENDENCE.)

mysticism

The term broadly denotes a feeling of immediacy and oneness with God (or with Ultimate Reality) on the part of the SELF. In extreme forms of mysticism, the self almost seems to merge with God; in more traditional forms, the self experiences a oneness of communion which appears to dissolve the 'objectified' nature of a SUBJECT–OBJECT mode of knowing or perceiving.

One problem about the term is that it may denote, especially for those who use it pejoratively, a heightened psychological state induced by self-hypnosis or other manipulative techniques. A low sugar content in the blood, induced by fasting, may facilitate self-generated visions or hallucinations. On the other hand, an ethical and devotional self-forgetfulness in contemplation of the Other who becomes also One may denote a spiritual mysticism of authentic experience. German distinguishes clearly between these two uses by reserving the word *Mysticismus* for the first and *Mystik* for the second.

Some insist that the core of mystical experience remains the same whatever the context. Yet there are differences between Hindu, Christian and other traditions of mysticism that deserve note.

HINDU AND BUDDHIST MYSTICISM

The Upaniṣads embody mystical approaches in HINDU PHILOSOPHY and religion, especially in the later interpretations of the MONIST school of Advaita Vedanta and ŚAṄKĀRĀ (788–820). The goal of knowledge is to attain liberation or release (*moksha*) from individual identity and all that entails bodily life, rebirth or reincarnation, in order to become (or be shown to be) One undifferentiated consciousness as Ultimate Reality/Self (*brāhman–ātman*).

Śaṅkārā can readily quote ancient Upaniṣads to support this. 'All Brāhman is ... myself within the heart ... smaller than a mustard seed ... greater than the earth ... the sky' (*Chándogya Upaniṣad* 3:14); 'The Self is to be described by "No, no"' (*Brhadāranyaka Upaniṣad* III:9:26). 'Thou art woman, thou art man ... Thou art the thunder-cloud, the seas ... infinite ...' (*Śvetāśvetara Upaniṣad* IV:3:4).

It is well known that RĀMĀNUJA (*c.* 1017–1137) drew on the *Upaniṣad* for a 'qualified' non-dualism (Viśistā-advaita Vedanta), which tended towards a more theistic direction. Ultimate Reality, he taught, is not 'undifferentiated consciousness' (*nirguna brāhma*). Religious devotion (*bhakti*) looks beyond the self. Nevertheless in the *Bhagavad Gita*, *bhakti* serves alongside 'freedom from the thought of an "I"' (18:62). Even Rāmānuja teaches a 'qualified monism'.

In traditions in which bodily existence, rebirth, and reincarnation look towards 'release', a mystical colouring is inevitable. Yet for many it is 'not yet', and its degree and significance varies within traditions in Hinduism.

In BUDDHIST PHILOSOPHY an emphasis upon 'emptiness' may reflect a parallel ambivalence. NĀGĀRJUNA (*c.* 150–200) expounds psychological and ontological emptiness, but a mystical interpretation has to be qualified by his concern for LOGIC at the 'conditional' level, even though he renounces conceptual thought at the 'final' level. Nāgārjuna rejects the validity or applicability of assertion or denial of Ultimate Reality.

CHRISTIAN MYSTICISM

Again, much depends upon the scope of the term. This is a case where DEFINITION by means of examples can assist us. The classic mystics include PSEUDO-DIONYSIUS (*c.* 500), Bernard of Clairvaux (1091–1153), Hildegarde of Bingen (1098–1179), Meister ECKHART (1260–1327), Julian of Norwich (1342– *c.* 1413), the author of *The Cloud of Unknowing* (*c.* 1350–95); Teresa of Avila (1515–82); John of the Cross (1542–91) and Jacob Boehme (1575–1624).

In *The Divine Names*, Pseudo-Dionysius urges that God is beyond all understanding, and can be apprehended, if at all, only through indirect, non-conceptual SYMBOLS. The beauty and light of God prompts love and yearning for union with God (ibid., 4). In his *Mystical Theology* he uses the VIA NEGATIVA because God is beyond assertion and denial. The conceptual is derived from God, but God is above and beyond conceptual thought. God's love enfolds all.

Unlike the monism of Hindu mysticism, Pseudo-Dionysius draws both on a quasi-monist NEOPLATONISM, but also upon a Christian version of Platonism that retains notions of hierarchy and order. He speaks of 'a holy order' (*The Celestial Hierarchy*, III: 1).

Bernard of Clairvaux is usually described as 'mystic', but he also exercised a fine theological mind. Meister Johannes Eckhart speaks more characteristically as a mystic: the soul attains 'emptiness', which 'gives birth to God'. Eckhart's 'desert' becomes in John of the Cross a 'night of the senses' and 'dark night of the spirit', which disengage the soul from the world to be filled with love for God and union with God.

Although Adolf Deissmann wrote of Paul the Apostle as a mystic, more recent Pauline research is virtually unanimous in rejecting this understanding of 'being-in-Christ'. The phrase primarily refers in Paul to a shared solidarity of status especially denoting that of being 'raised with Christ'. Paul uses the phrase in a number of ways.

JEWISH MYSTICISM

The roots of Jewish mysticism may be traced to prophetic experiences of being overwhelmed by God (Is. 6:1–6) and the notion of the sh^ekinah (presence or glory of God). Some trace potentially mystical elements in PHILO's assimilation of Hellenistic thought,.but Philo is too 'rationalist' to merit the term 'mystic'. The period of mysticism, in the narrower sense, emerges in the medieval *kabbala*, especially in the *Zohar*. Poetic literature also speaks of spiritual love, for example in Judah Halevi (*c.* 1095–1143).

PHILOSOPHICAL SIGNIFICANCE

This varies from tradition to tradition. The major traditions of Hindu mysticism

are underpinned by a monist ONTOLOGY, whether 'qualified' or not. Many traditions seek to overcome the subject–object split in knowing or in relationality. Here, however, it is not exclusively a property of mysticism to share with BUBER an understanding of God as 'Thou'.

Some, like William Alston, explore the heightened perceptions of mysticism as part of an EPISTEMOLOGY. Yet the mainspring seems to remain a longing for union with God (or Ultimate Reality) in which 'knowledge' differs from 'REASON'. Generalization is impossible. Perhaps in the end, the enhancement of awareness to which most mystics lay claim must be balanced against the claim of LOCKE that reason needs to retain a 'control' or 'governance' for 'entitled' BELIEF. (*See* DUALISM; PANENTHEISM; PANTHEISM; RELIGION; THEISM.)

myth

Strictly the term denotes stories or narratives told about God or divine beings, narrated in a communal setting as of permanent or repeated significance, and believed to be true within the community in question. Each of these terms carries weight: narrative, deity, community, truth-status and community. However, the term retains little of this strict definition in popular usage, and is used in a variety of ways, some contradictory with others, even among philosophers and theologians.

First, the widespread popular application to polytheistic myths of the ancient oriental, Greek and Roman worlds should not mislead us. Although in the modern West (and elsewhere) 'myth' is used here in contrast to 'TRUTH', these stories are called 'myths' because they were *once* believed to be true among the communities within which they first emerged. The modern use of 'myth' to denote what is not true has little to do with the more serious, technical, use of the term (*see* M. Eliade, *Myths, Dreams and Mysteries*, 1960).

Second, myth applies to divine actions portrayed in narrative form. This stands in contrast to such categories as legends, which may apply to human heroes. Only a minority of writers regard myth as necessarily polytheistic. Most include monotheistic RELIGION and THEISM (e.g. John Knox, *Myth and Truth*, 1964 and 1966). This narrative form of myth is what permits both a personal and self-involving dimension, which draws the hearers or readers in; but at the risk of an objectifying tendency, that is, the risk of looking like pseudo-scientific or pseudo-explanatory description or report.

Third, this last characteristic has given rise to proposals about DEMYTHOLOGIZING sacred texts, most notably BULTMANN'S proposals to demythologize the New Testament. In effect, they seek to transpose all hints of description and report into modes of language that proclaim, address and challenge the reader to existential response.

On this basis, 'myths' of CREATION, of the RESURRECTION or of the gift of the Holy Spirit 'coming down' serve, it is argued, not to make truth-claims about states of affairs, but to call readers (respectively) to responsible stewardship, to new life and to liberation from past bondage into the 'futurity' of new possibilities represented by the Holy Spirit.

Fourth, David F. Strauss (1808–74) defined myth as 'the expression of an idea in the form of a historical account' (*Life of Jesus*, [1835–6], Philadelphia: Fortress, 1972, 148). He drew on HEGEL's contrast between the rigorous critical concept used by philosophy (*Begriff*) and the supposedly uncritical methods of 'representations' (*Vorstellungen*) used in religion. The

task of the interpreter, Strauss argues, was to 'de-historicize the supernatural'.

This provides a bridge between two of Bultmann's understandings of myth: that of a primitive, pre-scientific world-view, and that of a false 'OBJECTIFICATION' or descriptive report that needs to be 'de-objectified'. However, this cannot hide the contradictions in Bultmann's account of myth.

If myth merely denotes ANALOGY, we cannot demythologize at all. If 'myth' denotes the pseudo-scientific explanatory hypothesis of a primitive world-view, is this really how 'myth' operates, if at all, in the New Testament? How do either of these relate to the need to restore an existential thrust to the language of sacred texts without destroying their simultaneous claims about the truth of certain states of affairs? (see the entry on Bultmann).

On top of all this, PANNENBERG (b. 1928) identifies a fifth problem. Myth usually relates to what is repeated, especially to cyclical views of time and of ritual. However, the biblical writings of Hebrew–Christian theology stress the novel, the unique, the purposive, the linear. Only in a non-mythic sense does the repetition in liturgical celebration of these unique events occur.

We cannot put the clock back to dispense with the word 'myth'. However, extreme caution is needed in assessing whether or when the word is applicable in Jewish, Christian or Islamic contexts. At best, myth denotes a sacred narrative which through its symbolic resonances invites participation and self-involvement on the part of a community for whom the narrative is true. (*See also* EXISTENTIALISM; TRUTH.)

N

Nāgārjuna (c. 150–200)

Born in South India, Nāgārjuna became
the greatest and most influential dialecti-
cian in Mahayana Buddhism, and perhaps
in BUDDHIST PHILOSOPHY. He founded
the *Mādhyamika* school and exercised
deep influence over the development of
Buddhism in South and East Asia.

At the heart of Nāgārjuna's philosophy
stood a distinctive understanding of the
Middle Way of the Buddha as 'emptiness'
of all things. One of his two most important
writings is 'The Fundamental Verses on the
Middle Way' (*Mūlanadhyamakārikā
Prajnā*). The other is 'The Septuagint on
Emptiness' (*Śunyātasapatati*).

The silence invited by emptiness shows
itself perhaps most readily by restraint
from possible answers to a metaphysical
question, namely to withhold 'yes', 'no',
'both' and 'neither'. Silence avoids the
self-contradictory paradox of SCEPTICISM,
but allows a sceptical restraint from
assertions or denials that may be out of
place.

Nāgārjuna aimed to follow valid
LOGIC, but for his teaching also to cohere
with good Buddhist teaching and practice.
It has been said that Mādhyamika Buddhism is a particular Buddhist 'yogic form
of moral and intellectual purification'
(Christian Lindtner). An ineffable Ultimate

Reality lies hidden behind ordinary experience and conceptual description. Only
enlightenment makes it accessible to faith.

The practice of 'wisdom' (*prajnā*)
therefore remains important, and for
Nāgārjuna this also presupposes faith.
Compassion coheres with Buddhist doctrinal teaching (*dharma*) on opposing evil
and promoting good.

Nirvana is both a psychological state in
which passions and karma (*karma kleśāt-
makam*) disappear, together with suffering. But nirvana also ontological space: all
things have departed to leave 'emptiness'.
The use of dialectic is fundamental to
Nāgārjuna's philosophy. (*See also* HINDU
PHILOSOPHY; METAPHYSICS; MYSTICISM;
ONTOLOGY.)

natural theology

Natural theology seeks to establish TRUTH
about God through the natural resources
of human reason, in contrast to revelation
by means of such special sources as sacred
writings and ecclesial traditions. Such
resources of human reasoning are in
principle available to all human beings
without regard to time or place.

Depending on how broadly or narrowly
the term is defined, different thinkers may
be cited as advocates or exponents of
natural theology. Some suggest that PLATO

(*c*. 428–348 BCE) argues for divine reason on the basis of general rational principles. ARISTOTLE (384–322 BCE) offers a more explicit natural theology: 'God is perfect ... is One ... Therefore the firmament that God sets in motion is one.' That is to say, reason discerns a divinely grounded 'orderedness' of unity and diversity in the world.

BROADER UNDERSTANDINGS OF THE TERM: THE ROLE OF REASON

If natural theology is defined very broadly simply to allow for strong continuity between philosophical reasoning and divine revelation, then a number of 'borderline' examples might be included. Clement of Alexandria (*c*. 150–215) saw philosophy as a positive testament to the Greeks to prepare them for the Gospel, just as the law prepared the Jews. Yet he acknowledged that philosophical reasoning remains incomplete without the gift of faith, and further revelation.

In ISLAMIC PHILOSOPHY, IBN RUSHD (Averroes, 1126–98) built upon Aristotle's notion of the 'ordered' nature of the universe as a rational, purposive hierarchy of differentiation and unity. AL-FARABI and IBN SINA also urged the superior value of philosophical thought, but retained the religious conviction that reason cohered with the revelation of the Qur'an.

Thomas AQUINAS (*c*. 1225–74) believed that in principle philosophical reasoning could establish the existence of God. However, human blindness prevents this reasoning from giving such knowledge equally to all. 'Natural reason is common to the good and the bad ... Knowledge of God, however, belongs only to the good' (*Summa Theologiae*, Ia, Qu.12, art. 12). 'God is known to the natural reason through the images of his effects', but 'by grace we have a more perfect knowledge of God than we have by natural reason' (ibid., art. 13). Indeed, if God's existence may be apprehended through reason, knowledge of God's nature and character depends upon revelation.

EXAMPLES OF NATURAL THEOLOGY IN A FULLER SENSE OF THE TERM

A more specific and inclusive natural theology emerged in the seventeenth and eighteenth centuries. PALEY (1743–1805) argued for the existence of God on the basis of observations of evidence of design in the world. Paley's famous analogy of finding a watch on a heath features as a classic exposition of the TELEOLOGICAL ARGUMENT for the existence of God. The titles of two of his works, *Evidences of Christianity* (1794) and *Natural Theology* (1802) underline the aim and assumption of these writings.

The most extreme reliance on human reason and rejection of a need for 'special' revelation emerged in English DEISM. Reason is the only valid instrument through which God's existence and nature can be known. Any appeal to special sacred writings or traditions would compromise the universality of the Creator-God whose creation left no room for a need for special interventions of providence or the miraculous. Arguably the deists believed that anything else would also compromise the sovereignty of God.

THE BARTH–BRUNNER DEBATE

BARTH (1886–1968) is the most outspoken opponent of natural theology in modern times. Barth believed that natural theology compromises the sovereignty of God in a different way. God chooses when, where and how God will make himself known (*Church Dogmatics* I: 2, Edinburgh, T & T Clark, 1956, sects. 13–19). God 'speaks', 'where and when God by this activating, ratifying ... the word of the Bible and preaching lets it become true' (ibid., I: 1, sect. 4, 120).

Barth's specific attack on natural theology was written in 1934, a year after Hitler became Chancellor of Germany. His Swiss colleague Emil Brunner had attempted a tentative defence of a 'soft', or minimal, version of a natural theology.

Barth rejected this, and entitled his short work *Nein!* (*No!.*) Barth's chief contention was that human fallenness had left no 'point of contact' between sinful, alienated, humanity and the 'wholly other' transcendent God. He wrote his work in Rome, where he attributed a vacillating papacy in the face of Nazism to a failure to adopt the motto 'Christ alone; scripture alone'. These phrases became the badge of the 'confessing' German Church in the face of this same pressure.

Emil Brunner argued that if human sin had damaged the image of God in humankind, the Fall had not totally destroyed it. Citing Irenaeus, Brunner drew a contrast between the 'formal' image of God (including reason), which was left almost intact, and the 'material' image (that of moral character), which was seriously damaged. Moreover, if there were no 'point of contact', how could repentance be possible, let alone the possibility of moral action? Repentance and the benefit of such divine ordinances as the state and marriage were signs of 'general grace'. Humankind retains a capacity to respond to God.

Barth dismissed such arguments as blurring the distinction between the TRANSCENDENCE of God and God's freedom to determine when or where to address humankind, on one side, and the extent of human fallenness and blindness, on the other. Nevertheless this response should not be equated with a crude FIDEISM, as some philosophers of religion have in effect suggested (H.J. Paton, *The Modern Predicament*, London: Allen & Unwin, 1955, 47–58). Paton even attributes Barth's approach to 'his zeal for religion' (ibid., 57) when Barth has strong reservations about applying the very word 'religion' to the Christian faith.

LEVELS OF DISCUSSION

The debate is more complex than a short article can convey. There are quite different reasons for unease with natural theology. Some theists, atheists and agnostics simply agree that in practice it is unsuccessful. Others argue that the 'infinite qualitative difference' between God as transcendent Ground of the Universe, and finite, CONTINGENT phenomena within the world, would not lead us to expect easy success for 'natural theology'. Yet a third group subject the capacities of human reason to radical criticism, whether from the viewpoint of conservative theology, from the perspective of PIETISM, or in the light of secular or theistic POSTMODERNISM. (*See also* AGNOSTICISM; ATHEISM; ONTOLOGICAL ARGUMENT; THEISM.)

necessity, the necessary

Necessity may be attributed to a proposition when the denial of this proposition results in a logical contradiction. In MODAL LOGIC this is sometimes expressed by asserting that the proposition '*p*' is true, and its denial '~*p*' is false, in all possible worlds. The early WITTGENSTEIN wrestled with the nature of necessity in his work on the philosophy of LOGIC, especially on relations between propositions and on logical constants.

In addition to this meaning in logic, especially in MODAL LOGIC, the term 'necessary' may also be applied to conditions or CAUSES. Whereas in logic, necessity may stand in contrast to CONTINGENCY, in the sphere of causality, necessary cause stands in contrast to sufficient cause.

LEIBNIZ (1646–1716) wrestled with highly complex relations between necessity and POSSIBILITY. God is necessarily morally perfect, Leibniz maintained, since to deny this is to contradict what is entailed in God's being 'God'. Hence it seems that of necessity God chose to create 'the best possible world'. The world is actual by necessity. But how, then, can God's creative action be God's free choice? Leibniz invokes his infinitesimal logical calculus. Since there is an infinite number of 'possible' worlds, it is not possible for this range of options to reach closure by necessity. This allows a space for free choice.

This invites reflection upon whether we are obliged to conceive of necessity in more than one way. PLANTINGA and HARTSHORNE elucidate this approach in their respective expositions of the ONTO-LOGICAL ARGUMENT; and Plantinga also in his work on the problem of EVIL.

Neoplatonism

Neoplatonism represents a modification of aspects of PLATO's thought (428–348 BCE), but bridges Plato's DUALISM between a higher order of Ideas and the lower realm of empirical, material objects in the world by postulating a chain of intermediate beings between the highest and lowest in a unified order.

Above Plato's realm of eternal Ideas is 'the One', who is perfect, immutable, simple, and in effect 'God'. 'The One', or 'God', is wholly transcendent. From the One there flow emanations in the form of a hierarchy of intermediate beings, who mediate from the power of the One through a series of levels down to the lowest, namely to the material world. The whole hierarchy constitutes a unified and unifying 'order', without compromising divine TRANSCENDENCE.

The earliest roots of Neoplatonism began to grow shortly after Plato's death, but the first flourishing of Neoplatonic philosophy occurs with PLOTINUS (205–70) and his pupil, Porphyry (c. 233–304). Porphyry transcribed the classic source, Plotinus's *Enneads*, after the latter's death.

Prior to Plotinus, PHILO of Alexandria (c. 20 BCE–50 CE) anticipated Neoplatonic themes. Thus he regarded the God of Judaism as fully transcendent, but found scriptural precedent for the notion of divine agencies as mediators or intermediaries, from Moses to the figure of Wisdom and the Divine Word (or *Logos*).

In the hierarchy postulated by Plotinus 'the One' stands above even thought or mind, but *Nous* ('the Mind', 'Intelligence')

is the highest emanation, next below 'the One'. As the chain unfolds we reach the level of the 'World-Soul' (also found in STOICISM), and finally the material world itself. This eternal process of 'outflow', radiating-generation, or emanation, provides structure and unity to reality and the world. Matter does not exist as an end in itself, but as a vehicle for 'soul'. Plotinus includes a mystical dimension in his thinking and reflection.

Porphyry emphasizes this mystical element, stressing the preparation of the soul for union with 'the One'. He compiled a diagrammatic 'tree' of a hierarchy of levels reaching through five 'species', down to matter. More readily than Plotinus, but perhaps closer to Plato, he saw 'matter' as a source of evil. Porphyry exercised a wide influence, and AUGUSTINE and BOETHIUS were attracted to aspects of his thought in their earlier years.

A second major development was the Syrian school of Iamblichus (c. 245–325). A complex and elaborate 'chain of being' was postulated with admixtures of quasi-polytheistic Graeco-Roman divinities and components from magic. A 'Baghdad school' (c. 832) emerged after several centuries in Syria, which translated the Greek writings of Plotinus, Porphyry, Plato and ARISTOTLE into Arabic, sometimes as seen through Neoplatonic eyes. This made some impact on medieval ISLAMIC PHILOSOPHY, including AL-FARABI, IBN SINA, IBN RUSHD and others.

Finally, a minor revival of Neoplatonism occurred in an Athenian school of the fifth and sixth centuries, but the school was closed in 529. The broader influence of ideas continued in other forms, however, through the period of the Renaissance to the Cambridge Platonists. (*See also* JEWISH PHILOSOPHY; MYSTICISM.)

Newton, (Sir) Isaac (1642–1727)

Newton worked out in his *Mathematical Principles of Natural Philosophy* (1687) a formulation of the mechanics of motion and theory of universal gravity. His findings remain fundamental for modern physics, even if they have been partially overtaken by post-Einsteinian formulations in relation to specific contexts and purposes within the discipline. 'Newtonian mechanics' remains a foundational contribution.

Newton was educated at Cambridge, became an eminent physicist, mathematician and public figure, and was a close friend of LOCKE (1632–1704). Newton and LEIBNIZ (1646–1716) seem to have discovered infinitesimal or differential calculus independently. Each, however, accused the other of plagiarizing his work, and their rivalry extended to several areas of sharp disagreement.

One strength of Newton's work was his care to distinguish between clearly established results in sciences and speculative hypotheses or conjectures. He also made advances in optics and in the composition of light.

Newton was in broad terms a theist, and saw the unified system of motion, force, gravity and mass not as excluding the agency of God, but, rather, as a divinely created order. On the other hand, his work had the effect of encouraging the typical eighteenth-century model of the universe as a machine, which held sway until the rise of ROMANTICISM invited a more organic model of understanding. Further, as Leibniz anticipated, although Newton's most creative work was widely celebrated and in due time vindicated, his notion of time and space as absolutes could not be sustained.

Newton's three laws of motion (especially the first) are claimed by many to undermine the 'kinetological' version of the COSMOLOGICAL ARGUMENT. Every body continues in a state of rest or of uniform motion unless forces intervene to change this. Others dispute whether this disrupts the argument. (*See also* ENLIGHTENMENT; FIVE WAYS; SCIENCE AND RELIGION; THEISM; TIME.)

Nietzsche, Friedrich Wilhelm
(1844–1900)

Born in Röcken, Prussia, Nietzsche studied at Leipzig, and became professor at Basle in 1870. His first book was *The Birth of Tragedy* (1872). In 1879 he resigned from his Chair because of poor health, and from 1879 to 1889 produced numerous writings, including *The Gay Science* (1882), *Thus Spake Zarathustra* (1883–5), *Beyond Good and Evil* (1886) and *Twilight of the Idols* (1889). In 1889 his mental health collapsed, and he did not recover before his death eleven years later. However, during this period his most aggressively anti-theistic book was published, namely *The Antichrist* (1895).

EARLY WORK: THE REBIRTH OF DIONYSIAN TRAGEDY

From the start, Nietzsche sought in Schopenhauer and in ancient Greek tragedy and pre-Socratic philosophy a principle of the affirmation of life. A basic 'driving' force is not the same as a 'directing' force. He developed this theme further in *The Gay Science*.

Driving force can be seen as raw energy in Euripides' tragedy *The Bacchae*. The figure of Pentheus represents the 'Apollonian' principle of restraint, harmony, rationality and moderation. Through ARISTOTLE's LOGIC and ETHICS of 'the mean', this had been largely associated with the spirit of ancient Greece. However, Euripides portrays the Bacchae, the female worshippers of Bacchus or Dionysius, as 'Dionysian': life-affirming, exotic, frenzied celebrants for whom life is not restraint and rationality, but assertion, joy and self-will.

Nietzsche identified himself with the Dionysian, although he concedes that this drive may be focused or harnessed by Apollonian direction or instrumental reason. These two principles reflect Schopenhauer's contrast between will and representation.

From his student days at Leipzig until their friendship ended in 1879 over Nietzsche's cultural and political critique of him, Nietzsche's emphasis on affirmation, life and driving force also drew vitality from Richard Wagner's operas and Wagner's use of mythic sources. By 1879 Nietzsche was far more radical than Wagner. In Nietzsche's view, Wagner helped to prop up the cultural degeneration that Nietzsche wished to abolish altogether. It should be leading, he believed, through new birth, to nihilism. He termed this 'philosophy with a hammer'.

LATER MIDDLE PERIOD: *THE GAY SCIENCE* (1882), *BEYOND GOOD AND EVIL* (1886), AND *THE TWILIGHT OF THE IDOLS* (1889)

Both *The Gay Science* and *Thus Spake Zarathustra* look ahead to the end of nihilism, which will follow upon the declaration that 'God is dead'. During this period Nietzsche not only increasingly emphasizes 'will' over rational systems, but identifies systems of Western philosophy and RELIGION as 'fictions' and 'lies'. Thoughts are the shadows of our feelings, 'always darker emptier, and simpler' (*The Gay Science*).

In *Beyond Good and Evil* Nietzsche distinguishes between a 'master' morality of self-assertion and a 'slave' morality rooted in resentment and the desire for compensatory rewards. The 'master' morality is worked out in due course in terms of the *Will to Power*. These two principles are associated with proportionate drives and directions in different peoples and cultures.

Addressing the culture of his day and the traditions of Western philosophy and religions Nietzsche calls for a 're-valuation of all values'. Religion, and in particular Christianity, tend towards a servile 'negation' that diminishes humankind. It is against this background that Bonhoeffer and especially MOLTMANN portray an authentic Christianity as 'Universal Affirmation' (the subtitle of Moltmann's *The Spirit of Life*, London: SCM, 1992).

Nietzsche insists that 'Nothing is "given" as real except our world of desires and passions ... We can rise or sink to no other "reality" than the reality of our drives ... Thinking is only the relationship of these drives to one another' (*Beyond Good and Evil*, London: Penguin, 1973 and 1990, sect. 36). If one insisted on an 'intelligible' account of this, 'it would be "will to power" and nothing else' (ibid.). 'It is the rulers who determine the concept "good"' (ibid., sect. 260).

LAST PERIOD: FURTHER CRITIQUES OF LANGUAGE AND RELIGION

'All that exists consists of interpretation (*The Will to Power*, vol. 2, aphorism 493, Nietzsche's italics (in *The Complete Works*, 18 vols., London: Allen & Unwin, 1909–13, vol. 15)). If this is so, Nietzsche concludes, 'We shall never be rid of God, so long as we still believe in grammar' (*The Twilight of the Idols*, in ibid., vol. 16, 22, aphorism 5). This is why he must 'philosophize with a hammer'.

In *The Antichrist* Nietzsche presses what today we should call an anti-theistic 'ideological critique' of LANGUAGE IN RELIGION. He writes, 'The "salvation of the soul" – in plain English "the world revolves around me"' (ibid., 186, aphorism 43). 'A priest or a pope not only errs, but actually lies with every word that he utters' (ibid., 177, aphorism 38). 'Supreme axiom: "God forgiveth him that repenteth" – in plain English, "him that submitteth himself to the priest"' (ibid., 161, aphorism 26).

Nietzsche has now moved beyond 'atheistic EXISTENTIALISM' to an ideological critique of language which prepares the way for the post-modern suspicion of Roland Barthes, FOUCAULT and DERRIDA. Nevertheless, in the hands of such theological writers as Bonhoeffer and Moltmann this becomes not a critique that unmasks all THEISM as illusory, but a selective filter that exposes the illusory, self-deceptive nature of those inauthentic forms of religion that are motivated by self-assertion and a will-to-power.

Just as Nietzsche's early *The Birth of Tragedy* brought to our attention the important contrast in Greek thought between the Apollonian and Dionysian, but also involved dubious classical philological scholarship, so also *The Antichrist* brings to our attention a sharp critical tool to distinguish inauthentic religion from authentic religious truth, but is open to the criticism of the very kind of generalizing and mythologizing that it seeks to undermine. (*See also* ATHEISM; POSTMODERNISM.)

Nishida, Kitārō (1870–1945)

Nishida has been described as the foremost Japanese philosopher of the twentieth century. His importance for the philosophy of religion derives from his being probably the first philosophical exponent of Buddhist traditions to engage in a distinctive and original way with the problems of Western philosophy.

Nishida explores Zen not only in traditional Eastern ways, but more especially through terms and concepts drawn from Western thought. Basically he seeks to move behind the SUBJECT–OBJECT split of Western EPISTEMOLOGY and the series of disjunctions to which he believes this split leads. This includes the DUALISM of PLATO; the Kantian legacy of a split between fact and value (which permeates BULTMANN's theology); and the split between individual and universal, with which LEIBNIZ wrestled.

Among Western philosophers on whom Nishida drew more positively were William James (1842–1910) and BERGSON (1859–1941), and his explorations of Neo-Kantianism combined positive dialogue with critique. He is known as the founding father of the Kyoto School of modern Japanese philosophy. (*See also* BUDDHIST PHILOSOPHY; HEIDEGGER; HINDU PHILOSOPHY; MONISM; NISHITANI; VIA NEGATIVA.)

Nishitani, Keiji (1900–90)

If NISHIDA was the founder of the Kyoto school of modern Japanese philosophy, Nishitani is regarded as the leading thinker of its second generation. Like Nishida, he also draws upon both Zen thinkers and concepts, and also on mystical and existentialist philosophers of the Western tradition.

Western mystical influences include Meister ECKHART, while Western existentialist writers include DOSTOEVSKY (1821–81), NIETZSCHE (1844–1900) and HEIDEGGER (1889–1976). The influence of Zen thinkers embraces both Chinese and Japanese traditions. With these conceptual resources Nishitani explores the problem of nihilism. At bottom the SELF is 'nothingness' (*nihil*, or *mu*); but of such a nature that an exploration of nothingness can become 'fertile'. The underlying concepts build upon a LOGIC of 'affirmation in negation', alongside 'nothingness'.

Nishitani published *Religion and Nothingness* in 1962. There are certain resonances here and there with Heidegger's 'Dialogue on Language between a Japanese and an Inquirer' in his *On the Way to Language* (New York: Harper & Row [1959], 1971, 1–54). Heidegger ('the Inquirer') attributes operative language to 'the call of Being' (ibid., 5), in contrast to the Western dualist seduction of 'photographic OBJECTIFICATION' (ibid., 17). 'We must leave the sphere of the subject–object relation behind us' (ibid., 40) 'The farewell of all "It is" comes to pass' (ibid., 54). There are also parallels with his *Gelassenheit* (1959; Eng., *Discourse on Thinking*, 1966). (*See also* BUDDHIST PHILOSOPHY; DUALISM; EXISTENTIALISM; MONISM; MYSTICISM; ŚAṄKĀRĀ; VIA NEGATIVA.)

nominalism

The term refers especially to the intense debate in the medieval period about the ontological status of UNIVERSALS, or of language about essences, in contrast to language about particular objects or states of affairs. The term stands in contrast to REALISM and to CONCEPTUALISM. Nominalists argue that language about universal concepts is no more than a linguistic or SEMANTIC construction (Latin, *nomen*, name). It does not denote an independent extra-linguistic reality, as realists claim. WILLIAM OF OCKHAM (*c*. 1287–*c*. 1349) is often regarded as the most thoroughgoing nominalist. Ockham conceded that language that denoted particular objects, qualities or events referred beyond itself to the external world. Even within particulars, however, denotative signs are absolute or univocal (*see* ANALOGY); connotative signs represent qualities in a derivative or secondary sense.

However, in appearing to refer to abstract essences or universals, language may serve to bestow 'a name' (Latin, *nomen*) without guaranteeing any object of reference beyond language itself. The formulation of the 'general' is a feature of the mind and of language, rather than of something beyond the mind or beyond language.

After the medieval period, nominalism in modified forms is closely associated with a number of philosophers who urge a suspicion of language. HOBBES (1588–1679) warned his readers of 'phantasms' which language might suggest. In modern philosophy Nelson Goodman (b. 1906) explored extensionality, synonymy, and inductive reasoning, and concluded that 'universals' are nothing more than an aggregate of particular assertions categorized extensionally, i.e. by extension. A 'pure' universal, then, can be no more than a linguistic construction.

Willard Quine (b. 1908) addresses a similar range of problems, and his thought is perhaps too complex to permit easy classification as a nominalist. However, his distinction between meaning and reference, his rejection of A PRIORI knowledge and his FALLIBILISM (the view that each belief in a system is revisable) point in this direction. (*See also* LANGUAGE IN RELIGION; ONTOLOGY.)

non-realism

The term, especially in British thought, often denotes a particular set of views associated with the 'middle' period of CUPITT's writings, especially in his *Taking Leave of God* (1980) and *The Sea of Faith* (1st edn, 1984; 2nd edn, 1994). 'For us God is no longer a distinct person ... God is the religious requirement personified, and his attributes are a kind of projection of its main features as we experience them' (*Taking Leave of God*, London: SCM, 1980 and New York: Crossroad, 1981, 85). God is not to be objectified as 'out there'.

Following BBC broadcast television talks under the title *The Sea of Faith*, a loose 'Sea of Faith Network' was established by Cupitt's sympathizers. The key points were expressed in Cupitt's three themes during the period 1980–6, namely 'internalizing' (God is the sum of our values within); de-objectifying (God is not 'out there'); and 'autonomy' (religion must grow out of immature 'dependency' upon God). 'God is the sum of all our values, representing this ideal ... mythologically' (*The Sea of Faith*, London: BBC, 1984, 269).

Several small books followed in the same vein. Anthony Freeman, for example, argued that 'God' is a human construction in his *God in Us* (1993). A more thoughtful approach from this angle is David Hart, *Faith in Doubt: Non-Realism and Christian Belief* (1993).

Cupitt acknowledges affinities with Eastern philosophies, especially with Zen Buddhism. NISHIDA (1870–1945) explores experience prior to any SUBJECT–OBJECT split. In Advaita Vedanta (non-dualist) HINDU PHILOSOPHY Śaṅkārā argues that the SELF is separated from *brāhman* (undifferentiated Ultimate Reality) only by illusion (*māyā*). This Ultimate Reality cannot be characterized.

A broader use of the term non-realism also occurs to denote its contrast with classical REALISM. However, the more usual term for this would be NOMINALISM, together with the mediating approach of CONCEPTUALISM. (*See also* ATHEISM; BUDDHIST PHILOSOPHY; FEUERBACH; NISHITANI; THEISM.)

numinous

The term broadly denotes the sense of reverential awe that a finite or creaturely human person experiences in the presence of God, the transcendent, or the sacred. It signifies a dimension of religious experience that surpasses the rational, conceptual or ethical, especially in terms of a sense of awesome wonder and self-awareness as merely creative, finite and vulnerable.

The content of the term is best understood by consulting the work of OTTO (1869–1937), who made extensive use of this term. The numinous, he urges, includes both the element of godly fear and trembling in the presence of the Other (*mysterium tremendum*) and the fascination of the holy love that draws the worshipper to participate in the mystery of the numinous (*mysterium fascinosum*). (*See also* TRANSCENDENCE.)

object, objectivism, objectivity, objectification

The definition of each of these terms bristles with problems, mainly because changes of context shift the meaning of each. Further, each of these four terms carries a largely different meaning from the other three, or at least from some others. In very broad terms, for example, 'objectivity' tends to carry with it overtones of approval; 'objectivism' and 'objectification' frequently, but not always, imply an inadequate, distorting, or reductive use of language.

Further complications arise from variations in a universe of discourse. In EPISTEMOLOGY we may speak of a knowing SUBJECT having knowledge of a known object. In a rationalist or empiricist pre-Kantian scheme, the subject is active, and knows a passive object.

CAN A PERSON BE AN 'OBJECT'?

In a universe of discourse that concerns God or persons such thinkers as BUBER (1878–1965), LEVINAS (1906–95) and others insist that the 'I–Thou' language of interpersonal address regards 'the Other' as more than an 'object', or an 'it'. To reduce the personal 'Thou', 'You' or 'God' to the status of an epistemological 'object' is to reduce their personhood and their own active agency by objectification.

BULTMANN (1884–1976) has the constructive aim, whatever its failings in execution, of seeking to 'de-objectify' language that treats God as an object. REVELATION, he claims, is not primarily '*about* God'; but 'address *from* God'.

To demythologize is to translate a vocabulary and conceptual grammar that appears to speak of God as an entity in which objective CATEGORIES inhere into a conceptual scheme more appropriate to interpersonal activity. MYTH, he claims, reduces everything to description and report. A better, less 'objective', mode of discourse is borrowed from existentialist thinkers, especially from HEIDEGGER.

One problem with Bultmann's proposals is his failure, among other things, to note that often existential or self-involving language operates on the presupposition that certain states of affairs are true (*see* PERFORMATIVE UTTERANCES).

OBJECTIVISM OR OBJECTIVITY?

'Objectivism' is often used to denote the use of language which the language users consider to be value-neutral or 'objective', but which others consider to be no less value-laden than other language-uses. One side will consider that its language embodies commendable objectivity; the other side may doubt whether 'dispassionate' language does more than claim to be objective, and may denounce pseudo-objectivity as objectivism. A notorious example is the language of the natural sciences. Those who regard it as straightforward value-neutral description of the world will be inclined to call it 'objective', and view it as satisfying conditions for objectivity. Those who regard the propositions of natural science as heavily dependent upon the particular CONTINGENT conditions of time, place, resources, agenda, and the histories of scientific communities may speak of certain pretensions to value-neutrality as objectivism.

Just as LOCKE (1632–1704) argued that mere intensity of conviction is no guarantee in itself of CERTAINTY, so others insist that disengagement from emotion or personal involvement is, equally, no guarantee of TRUTH either. There is, for example, no adequate warrant for assuming that a 'secular' world-view is any more 'objective' than a religious one.

OBJECT (*OBJEKT*) AND 'OBJECT' (*GEGENSTAND*) IN THEOLOGY

Indeed, if God is 'the Subject who is never Object' since God is not at the beck and call of human scrutiny, revelation and theology, BARTH claims, are 'objective' in the sense that this method of enquiry has to be in accordance with the nature of the 'object' of enquiry.

German makes a distinction between two senses of 'object'. Barth's *Church Dogmatics* speaks repeatedly of '*Gott als Subjekt*', but hardly anywhere, if at all, of '*Gott als Objekt*'. All the same, faith (and sometimes enquiry) is directed towards *Gegenstand* ('object' in a sense yet to be explained), and theology is characterized by *Gegenständlichkeit* (objectivity). 'As knowledge, it [faith] is the orientation of man to God as an object (*Gegenstand*)'. (*Church Dogmatics*, II: 1, Edinburgh: T & T Clark, 1957, sect. 25, 13). God is

not an '*Objekt*', for God is 'non-objective, invisible, ineffable, incomprehensible'. Yet as One who 'stands over against' (*Gegenständlichkeit*) our own human acts of COGNITION, God may be called *Gegenstand*, 'Object' (ibid., 186–7).

Barth asserts, 'God is known by God, and by God alone' (ibid., sect. 27, 179). In other words, God is not the 'passive' object of anyone else's scrutiny, other than through the medium of God's own active self-disclosure in acts of REVELATION. These acts of disclosure primarily take the form of address. Barth and Bultmann hold this in common.

BEHIND THE SUBJECT–OBJECT SPLIT?

From KANT (1724–1804) onwards the previously more clear-cut contrast between subject and object in rationalist and empiricist epistemology becomes less sharp. No longer does a pure Cartesian subject look out at pure 'objects'; for in Kant there are no 'pure' objects, unshaped by the regulative or orderly principle of REASON or the human mind.

A number of diverse thinkers, ranging from the subjective IDEALISM of SCHELLING (1775–1854) to the Hindu philosophical MONISM of ŚAṄKĀRĀ (788–820), seek to reach behind the subject–object split. Śaṅkārā argues that the distinction is ultimately illusory (*māyā*), even if it is operative at a lower, everyday level. TILLICH (1886–1965) also understands God to be 'Being-itself' prior to any distinction between subject and object.

The complexities of the debates that stem from these varied contexts and standpoints should encourage caution before we use such terms as 'objective' or 'objectivity' in any over-easy, supposedly context-free, way. (*See also* DEMYTHOLOGIZATION; EMPIRICISM; EXISTENTIALISM; HINDU PHILOSOPHY; INCOMMENSURABILITY; MARCEL; MYSTICISM; NĀGĀRJUNA; SCIENCE AND RELIGION; VIA NEGATIVA.)

occasionalism

Two versions of occasionalism have emerged. The more general version ascribes all CAUSES to God alone. This effectively eliminates causal agency from human persons, and causal efficacy from objects or states of affairs within the finite world. God is directly responsible for all events.

A more specific version concerns causation within the SELF. It questions any causal relation between mind (or SOUL) and body.

Nicolas Malebranche (1638–1715) combined these two versions. According to him, on every occasion when the mind or soul consents to, or wills, a movement of the body, God causally initiates such a movement, since the mind alone cannot. Human will provides occasions for divine causal action.

Malebranche brought together two contexts of thought. A French philosopher, he developed further the DUALISM of mind and body inherited from his fellow-countryman DESCARTES (1596–1650). RYLE (1900–76) attacked and satirized this dualism of mind and body as that of 'the ghost in the machine'.

As a Catholic priest, Malebranche interpreted the sovereignty of God in as radical a way as possible, in conjunction with divine OMNIPRESENCE (in *The Search after Truth*, 1674).

In the seventeenth and early eighteenth centuries occasionalism seemed to some to address both problems of causation and of the mind–body relationship in an era when matter was often understood as passive and inert, under a mechanistic rather than organic model (*see* RATIONAL-ISM). For some theists, it also seemed to pay honour to the sovereignty of God.

In our era, however, occasionalism has widely fallen from favour, in part because of a deeper understanding of psychosomatic interaction within the self. Further, more careful accounts of divine sover-

eignty make us hesitate to resort to such generalized theories. Peter Geach and Gijsbart van den Brink, for example, argue that 'Almighty' does better justice to biblical and theistic traditions than 'omnipotent' (*Almighty God*, Kampen: Pharos, 1993). (*See also* DEISM; EVIL; GOD, CONCEPTS AND 'ATTRIBUTES' OF; ISLAMIC PHILOSOPHY; OMNIPOTENCE OF GOD; THEISM.)

omnipotence of God

The 'metaphysical attributes' of God, if this term is suitably qualified, are discussed in very broad terms under GOD, CONCEPTS AND 'ATTRIBUTES' OF. However, the logical grammar (*see* LOGIC) of divine omnipotence is so complex that the subject invites more attention under this separate heading.

Theists usually presuppose that God sustains the created order by an animating all-powerful providence. BARTH speaks of God's holding humankind 'from the abyss of non-being'. Moreover, if God invites trust, God, it is affirmed, has the almighty resources to act in ways that justify such trust. It is assumed that God has power to fulfil God's promises.

For Thomas AQUINAS God's almighty power puts 'into execution what [God's] will commands and what knowledge directs ... All confess that God is omnipotent; but it seems difficult to explain in what this omnipotence precisely consists' (*Summa Theologiae*, Ia, Qu. 25, arts. 2 and 3).

Aquinas cites Luke 1:37, 'No word shall be impossible with God', but acknowledges that issues about logical and CONTINGENT POSSIBILITY and NECESSITY may yield possible contradictions if 'omnipotence' is not qualified. His answer is that 'whatever implies a contradiction' cannot be a word; more broadly, 'the omnipotence of God does not take away from things their impossibility and necessity' (ibid., art. 3).

OMNIPOTENCE AND PARADOX:
POWER TO PERFORM SELF-
CONTRADICTORY ACTS?

In the modern era several models of self-contradiction have been used on both sides of the debate to demonstrate the coherence or incoherence of divine 'omnipotence'. J. L. Mackie appeals to some traditional paradoxes to argue for its incoherence: Can God make a stone that is so big that God cannot lift it? An assertion negates God's power to lift the stone; a denial negates God's power to make the stone.

A series of examples turns on acts of logical impossibility: Can God divide odd numbers in half in such a way that the result is a set of integers? Can God change the past, as if the past never was? Can God do EVIL or tell falsehoods, given that God is necessarily good?

Thomas Aquinas sees no contradiction in these supposed paradoxes on the ground that to do what is logically impossible is not an act of power at all, but an irrational, self-contradictory scenario. If God were conceived of as performing it, God would be an irrational, self-contradictory being; but God is not an irrational, self-contradictory being. Hence omnipotence must denote ability to do whatever is in accord with God's own nature. Thus to tell a falsehood or to retract a promise would not spring from omnipotence, but would entail logical contradiction if God is necessarily good.

One counter-reply would be to argue that if these acts are contingent rather than necessary, *logical* contradiction is avoided. A person can make an object that he or she cannot lift. However, the point of the argument concerns the applicability of the concept of God, for whom goodness and power (however qualified by ANALOGY or by MODELS AND QUALIFIERS) remain necessary characteristics.

PLANTINGA also qualifies the concept of omnipotence by arguing that omnipotence itself need not be a necessary quality of an omnipotent being. God may choose to limit and to contain divine power in the interests of goodness and love, and such a choice is itself an act of omnipotent, sovereign, free will.

To attribute unqualified logical necessity to 'omnipotence' questions the concept from a different angle by eroding the sovereignty of divine free choice. As a well-known writer on MODAL LOGIC Plantinga distinguishes between necessary propositions, which are indeed logically necessary, and supposedly necessary qualities or things, to which the application of logical necessity is more problematic.

In spite of the insistence of DESCARTES that God can transcend what is logically impossible, most writers accept that 'a logically impossible action is not an action ... It is no objection to A's omnipotence that he cannot make a square or circle' (Richard Swinburne, *The Coherence of Theism*, Oxford: Clarendon, 1977 and 1986, 149). Omnipotence denotes 'an ability to bring about any (logically possible) state of affairs' (ibid., 150).

This, SWINBURNE persuasively argues, excludes both logical contradictions and that which God could not do without contradicting God's own nature as God, for example, make a thing equal to himself.

OMNIPOTENCE AND ALMIGHTINESS:
'POWER OVER', OR 'POWER FOR'?

Although Swinburne and Plantinga are content to retain the term 'omnipotent' derived from Aquinas and the mainly Latin tradition of theology, Peter Geach and Gijsbert van den Brink insist that we should go behind the Latin term *omnipotens* to the Greek term from which it derives, namely *pantokrator*, the Almighty One. This New Testament term denotes 'the capacity for, not the exercise of, power' (van den Brink, *Almighty God*, Kampen: Kok Pharos, 1993, 47). '*Omnipotens* is to be found in the sphere of "having power over"'; but there are other ways of understanding 'power' also.

In an analysis of the logical grammar of the concept van den Brink distinguishes between power as authority, power as 'back-up' and power as capacity. PLATO, the STOICS and the New Testament all underline 'the sustaining power of the divine providence' (ibid., 51). 'The Almighty One' underlines God's 'capacity as Father and creator' (ibid., 57). However, this does not denote 'all power' in an exclusive sense, as if God left no power for others, since God's power sustains and enables creation.

The logic of power embraces a family of concepts in which 'almighty' more readily denotes an enabling power that springs from love than 'power over' that may sometimes suggest domination, oppression or taking power from the other.

This coheres more readily with Paul the Apostle's redefinition of power as the power of the cross, which is of a different order from 'worldly' power (1 Cor. 1:18–25). Indeed, if love seeks the best possible for 'the other', divine love, to be effective, presupposes 'power for'. Almightiness is that quality by virtue of which divine goodness and love brings about what God 'wants to bring about' (ibid., 271).

'The biblical notion of divine almightiness' does better justice to theological tradition and to conceptual analysis than 'the philosophical notion of divine omnipotence' (ibid., 274). MOLTMANN (b. 1926) expresses the same reservations about 'THEISM' as too often understood: 'A God who is eternally only in love with himself, and therefore without any concern for others, is a monster, an idol ... God himself has gone through the experience of Christ's cross' (*Experiences of God*, Philadelphia: Fortress, 1980, 16).

OMNIPOTENCE, INFINITY, CREATION AND 'PERFECTION'

BOETHIUS (c. 480–525) wrote that God is such that nothing greater than God is even conceivable (see *The Consolation of Philosophy*, 3: 10). This naturally leads on to the formulations about maximal greatness and perfection formulated by ANSELM (1033–1109) in *Proslogion* 2–4, which have now become foundational for discussions of the ONTOLOGICAL ARGUMENT for the existence of God. Like Aquinas, DUNS SCOTUS (c. 1266–1308) also noted that this maximal greatness must remain logically without contradiction.

How does this approach in terms of 'perfect being' cohere with the claims of van den Brink, Moltmann and others about differences between biblical and philosophical perspectives? Perhaps a complementary comparison will suggest that each approach constructively serves to qualify the others.

PANNENBERG (b. 1928) seeks to hold a view that does justice to both approaches. He writes as both a systematic and philosophical theologian. Pannenberg relates omnipotence not simply or primarily to 'perfection', but to infinity, creativity and holiness. Infinity, as HEGEL noted, denotes in the first place that which is not finite. In other words, whereas the finite is defined and sustained by something else, the infinite is its own Ground (*see* ASEITY). The meaning 'without end' (in the context of temporality) remains secondary to this.

Like van den Brink and Moltmann, Pannenberg recognizes that 'the abstract idea of unlimited power' may too easily lead to a 'one sided ... excessive omnipotence of tyranny' (*Systematic Theology*, vol. 1, Edinburgh: T & T Clark, 1991, 416). God's power is 'for' a goal, since 'only as the Creator can God be almighty' (ibid.). CREATION, RESURRECTION and salvation constitute such goals of almighty power. He includes resurrection, for 'only the Creator can awaken the dead' (ibid., 417).

Holiness expresses an awesome dimension of divine almighty power, for it leads to destruction or to salvation. Further, the God of theism is not the deist God who watches the world without intervening within it or reshaping it from within. Only a positivist 'closed system' could suggest that the almighty God could never act in its world with novelty and surprise to do 'new things'.

Nevertheless, coherence and rationality are also sustained by divine providence as characterizing the created order. Thus God acts with consistency, without self-contradiction, but in the Christian tradition this leaves room for God's almighty acts in the incarnation and resurrection of Jesus Christ. This instantiates divine omnipotence as a creative power for good, within this tradition.

In the Islamic tradition IBN SINA and IBN RUSHD hold to the idea of God as a perfect Being. However, they also seek to qualify what this entails, and express caution about the nature and scope of the knowledge that might be involved in divine OMNISCIENCE. There are parallels concerning the logical paradoxes or puzzles raised respectively by the concepts of omnipotence and omniscience. (*See also* ABSOLUTE; ISLAMIC PHILOSOPHY; OMNIPRESENCE; POSITIVISM; TRANSCENDENCE.)

omnipresence of God

Theists reject the sense in which God is 'present everywhere' in PANTHEISM on the ground that God is not to be identified exhaustively with the 'All' of creation. They also reject the view of SPINOZA that, like matter, God has indefinite 'extension' on the ground that Spinoza's attribution of both Spirit and matter to God depersonalizes and decharacterizes God, who is intelligent will. God is not a spatial entity who merely 'extends' God's Being.

Nevertheless, the omnipresence of God is firmly rooted in the tradition of the Hebrew scriptures, or the Christian Old Testament. 'Where can I flee from your presence? If I ascend to heaven, you are there; if I make my bed in Sheol you are there. If I take the wings of the morning and settle in the farthest limits of the sea, even there your hand shall lead me' (Ps.

139:7–10). '"Do not I fill heaven and earth"? says the Lord' (Jer. 23:24).

Just as OMNIPOTENCE denotes the capacity of not being limited in power except in terms of what may constitute self-contradictory acts or acts contrary to God's own nature, so also omnipresence denotes a total lack of any limitation that might supposedly be imposed by spatial distance or any other possible property of space. Thus the attempt of the prophet Jonah to flee from God's presence by taking ship to a distant location becomes an object of satire (Jon. 1:1–3). The satirist also notes that, apparently unaware of the contradiction, Jonah exclaims equally: 'I worship the God of heaven, who made the sea' (1:9).

In very different ways BARTH, TILLICH, MOLTMANN and PANNENBERG all explore ways in which divine omnipresence may be understood for religious faith. For Tillich, God is the Ground of Being, or Being-itself, not merely 'a Being'. God is therefore 'the depth of reason', i.e. the transcendental Ground of reason and rationality itself 'which precedes reason and is manifest through it' (*Systematic Theology*, vol. 1, London: Nisbet, 1953, 88; cf. also 227). He also expounds Psalm 139 in *The Shaking of the Foundations*.

In a more existential way Moltmann explains how even 'the experience of misery and forsakenness can build up into an experience of God ... God's presence in the dark night of the soul: "If I make my bed in hell, behold, Thou art there"' (Ps. 139, cited above). God is not confined to 'religions' or to 'churches'. God is present in the cross of Christ, in suffering and death; even in the suffering and death of Auschwitz (*Experiences of God*, Philadelphia: Fortress, 1980, 7–17). 'Nothing is shut off from God' (ibid., 16; cf. *The Crucified God*, London: SCM, 1974).

Pannenberg relates the concept of God's omnipresence to that of God's OMNISCIENCE and to God's enabling power, love and salvation. 'Those who would flee from the presence of God have nowhere to hide. The creature of God has no real reason to flee from him (Ps. 139:13–16) ... [God's] remembrance of them is a comfort to the righteous' (*Systematic Theology*, vol. 1, Edinburgh: T & T Clark, 1990, 379).

All the same, there are two persistent philosophical problems about the concept of divine omnipresence. The first arises in relation to the theist's claim that God is a person. Even if we call attention to the analogical use of 'person' by asserting that God is 'personal', but not 'a person', does this fully address the problem of how a personal agent can be omnipresent? Second, AQUINAS addresses the objection: 'One cannot be both in everything and above everything' (*Summa Theologiae*, Ia, Qu. 8, art. 1).

Aquinas responds to both problems by asserting that God's existence or presence 'in everything' (*in omnibus*) denotes not being part of a universal substance or accident (*pars essentiae vel sicut accidens*), but as 'an agent is present to that in which its action is taking place'. 'God is active in everything' (*Deus operantur in omnibus*) (ibid.).

To be present 'everywhere', Aquinas continues, is not to be understood as 'dimensional' space, but as universal activity and agency. Omnipresence relates to the unlimited scope of God's 'operative power' (ibid., art. 3). Although objections have been brought against the medieval formulations of Aquinas, SWINBURNE defends their broad thrust in outline against some of these criticisms (*The Coherence of Theism*, Oxford: Clarendon 1977, 1986, 97–125).

A philosophical discussion of 'attributes' remains valuable, but the concept of omnipresence permits its logical grammar and currency to emerge most clearly in the kinds of contexts identified by Moltmann and Pannenberg. The concept plays an active role in the traditions of Judaism, Christianity and Islam. In Hinduism, depending on what sub-tradition we are exploring, it may move sometimes

toward a qualified pantheism. (*See also* ANALOGY; EXISTENTIALISM; LOGIC; THEISM; TRANSCENDENCE.)

omniscience of God

Philosophically this concept abounds in complexities and difficulties. Yet most major theistic sacred writings and traditions ascribe a quality broadly of 'knowing all things' to GOD. Psalm 139, common to Jewish and Christian tradition, embodies within its detailed ascription of OMNIPRESENCE to God the words: 'Thou knowest when I sit down and when I rise up'; no one can hide from divine awareness (verses 2 and 13–16).

The Qur'an in Islamic tradition exclaims: 'Peace be to Allah, to whom belongs all that the earth contains ... He is the Wise One, the All-Knowing. He has knowledge of all that goes into the earth and ... all that comes down from heaven' (Surah. 34). In the New Testament 'God ... searches the heart', which is the seat of pre-conscious desires (Rom. 8:27).

DIFFICULTIES OF THE CONCEPT OF DIVINE OMNISCIENCE

One major problem arises from the necessary difference of kind and degree between 'knowledge' as ascribed to God and human knowledge. 'Our experience of awareness and knowledge ... can give us only a feeble hint of what is meant when we speak of God's knowledge' (Pannenberg, *Systematic Theology*, Edinburgh: T & T Clark, vol. 1, 1990, 380). This is difficult enough; but to speak of knowledge of 'everything' is totally beyond ANALOGY with human experience.

Perhaps the only hint of a human experience that resonates with the concept is that of a retrospective view of 'the whole' which has been explored in different ways by Wilhem Dilthey (1833–1911), HEGEL (1770–1831) and PANNENBERG (b. 1928). Dilthey argued that only at the end of life, when an individual can look back, can a fuller 'understanding' (*Verstehen*) emerge of what at the time is more fragmentary. Pannenberg appeals to the eschatological content of the RESURRECTION event of Jesus Christ as strictly an 'end event' in order to propose a provisional understanding of the 'wholeness' of a 'universal history' which is yet in process.

A second problem arises from whether 'knowledge' necessarily affects the agent or one who knows. However, if the created order 'contributes' to divine experience, how does this cohere with the 'prior' ASEITY of God, or with what has been termed divine IMMUTABILITY?

A third difficulty has preoccupied philosophers and theologians over the centuries, especially since AUGUSTINE (354–430) and BOETHIUS (c. 480–525/6). Does the notion that God knows the future, as well as the past and the present, necessarily yield a determinist view of both human decision and even the divine will? Augustine, Boethius, Thomas AQUINAS (1225–74), and more recently PLANTINGA, J. L. Mackie and SWINBURNE (b. 1934) debate this issue as one of major importance.

Within this debate several different components are involved. For example, can knowledge of the future be said to be knowledge as such, if the future does not yet exist and remains subject to retrospective or present knowledge only at a later point in time? Does the necessary truth of propositions concerning the future on the part of an omniscient Being presuppose or entail that consequent predictability must exclude the freedom of human agents to generate this future? If the world order is 'in time', but God creates the temporality that is the condition for time, can we disengage divine prescience from God's knowledge of the whole as the vantage-point of eternity? These issues invite consideration here.

DOES 'CERTAIN' KNOWLEDGE OF THE FUTURE YIELD DETERMINISM?

Boethius acknowledges that he has become initially 'confused' because it seems difficult both to assert 'God foreknows all things' and at the same time to assert 'there is FREE WILL'. God's foreknowledge cannot allow a flexibility which might permit the possibility of 'mistaken' foreknowledge, for this would not be *foreknowledge*. Yet, if this is so, 'there is no freedom ... The divine mind, foreseeing without error, binds ... to actual occurrence' (*On the Consolation of Philosophy*, sect. 3).

On further reflection, however, 'Wisdom' (or 'Lady Philosophy') provides a counter-reply. 'Foreknowledge is not *the cause* of any necessity for future events' (ibid., sect. 4, my italics). The free decisions of agents will these occurrences. The reason why there is no conflict arises from the different viewpoints of God who is eternal, and of human reflection, which conceives of a temporal future, which it seeks to impose on the God who is unconditioned by time.

The traditional 'solution' runs as follows: in eternity, or in the eternal realm, God's knowledge surveys the whole of created reality in a simultaneous vision of what in time would constitute 'past', 'present' and 'future' modes of occurrence. Hence Boethius suggests that 'foreknowledge' (*praeventia*) might better be called 'providence' (*proventia*). Thus within the CONTINGENT, temporal world order, willed actions and events are willed freely. However, the very same act or event 'when it is related to divine knowledge is necessary' (ibid., sect. 6). In summary, neither God nor God's knowledge exists in time.

If the factor of temporal succession is removed, it would not occur to us to argue, 'If I know that this paperweight is a gift from my colleague, my colleague's gift was not fully given but was determined by necessity.' However, if God created time as well as space along with the whole created order, how can it be valid to apply to God a logic in which 'God knows x' at $Time_1$ or at $Time_2$? Omniscience, therefore, does not exclude the contingency of events, nor freedom of will.

The approach of Boethius finds echoes in ANSELM, in Thomas Aquinas, and in LEIBNIZ. Currently it retains resonances also in the writings of Paul Helm and Eleonore Stump, although Helm is more cautious about 'simultaneousness' than Stump (Helm, *Eternal God*, Oxford: Clarendon, 1988, 23–40; cf. 109–70).

Thomas Aquinas begins a broader discussion of God's knowledge with the assertion that 'God has knowledge (*scientia*)', and has it 'in the perfect way' (*in Deo perfectissime est scientia*: *Summa Theologiae*, Ia, Qu. 14, art. 1). Paul exclaims, 'O the depth of the riches of the wisdom and knowledge of God' (Rom. 11:33).

On the more specific question of free, contingent events, Aquinas also argues that what God knows in eternity is known not in temporal terms as past, or future, but in terms of the wholeness of eternity. He distinguishes two different senses of 'NECESSARY'. One is applied to propositions; the other, to 'things' (*de re vel de dicto*). 'The statement, "*A thing known by God is*" is necessary'. On the other hand we may apply the word to a thing: this might suggest that whatever God knows is a necessary thing. Only this second application would entail the view that there is no free will (ibid., art. 13).

IN WHAT SENSE 'KNOWLEDGE OF THE FUTURE'?

Swinburne and Keith Ward do not accept that 'knowledge of the future' necessitates this disjunction between time and eternity. Both writers argue that 'knowing everything' is no more an absolutist, unqualified concept than 'power to do anything' turns out to be in a parallel study of OMNIPOTENCE. Under the entry on omnipotence it becomes clear that it gains nothing for the concept to include within it the supposed capacity to perform self-contradictory acts. In Swinburne's words, omnipotence denotes 'not ... the ability to do anything, but (roughly) ... the ability to do anything logically possible' (*The Coherence of Theism*, Oxford: Clarendon, 1977, 1986, 175).

Swinburne develops an account of omniscience 'along similar lines, not as knowledge of everything true but (very roughly) as knowledge of everything true which it is logically possible to know' (ibid.). In practice, this includes all those future events that are predictable by exact physical or causal necessity or by divine decree or promise, but not those events concerning which God chooses to permit created agents to make free choices of will.

Even God, Swinburne urges, may will to preserve room to make free choices of God's own; and in this case 'which free choices he will make and what will result' will lie outside the limits of divine omniscience (ibid., 176). Thus in the example of Abraham's intercession for Sodom (Gen. 18) or the intercession of Moses for Israel (Ex. 32) God chooses to leave room for God's own changes of plan. Similarly, 'God often makes, as well as absolute promises ... conditional promises ... Yet there would be *no need for a conditional promise* if God already knew how men would act' (ibid., 1).

Keith Ward makes a parallel distinction. 'An omniscient being, if it is temporal, can know for certain whatever in the future it determines ... but not absolutely everything. If this is a limit on omniscience, it is logically unavailable for any temporal being' (*Rational Theology and the Creativity of God*, Oxford: Clarendon, 1982, 131).

Paul Helm takes the very different view that 'only timeless eternity prevents the degeneracy of divine omniscience and divine immutability into the idea of a God who changes with the changing world and who is surprised by what he discovered ... Divine timeless eternity does not commit one to logical determinism' (*Eternal God*, 142). It is clear that the scope and logical grammar of omniscience is bound up closely with the logical relation between CREATION, TIME and ETERNITY and our understanding of them.

Plantinga provides a critique of Nelson Pike's view that divine foreknowledge would eliminate freedom by applying a MODAL LOGIC of 'possible worlds', as he does in addressing the problem of EVIL (*God, Freedom and Evil*, New York: Harper, 1974, 66–72). He begins by distinguishing different applications of 'necessary', and expounds the notion of 'essentially omniscient'. The issue turns not on what God knows, but on God's knowing 'true propositions' from the vantage-point of 'possible' worlds.

'MIDDLE KNOWLEDGE', FREE WILL AND PREDICTABILITY

Luis de Molina (1535–1600), a SCHOLAS-TIC Spanish Jesuit philosopher, attempted to hold together predestination or DETER-MINISM and a compatible freedom of the will through a concept of 'middle knowledge' (*scientia media*). Molina postulated that divine omniscience included within its scope knowledge of how contingent created beings would respond under different circumstances. God knows what human persons will freely choose to do. If God knows how a person would freely act through God's 'middle knowledge', God may create such a person with a range of choices or options in place, and yet also have knowledge of future events that would (both necessarily and conditionally) occur.

How far this takes us is doubtful, and only a minority of thinkers appear to endorse or to develop this approach. However, without its scholastic framework, it looks back to Augustine's view that God knows how human persons will freely choose. Augustine asks: 'Why do you think our free will is opposed to God's foreknowledge? ... If you knew in advance that such and such a man would sin, there would be no necessity for him to sin' (*On Free Will*, III: 4: 10).

Augustine argues that it is not specifically divine foreknowledge that supposedly raises the problem, but whether sheer 'predictability' (on the assumption that it is accurate and certain) imposes a deterministic view of the human will.

In the modern debate this issue is explored further under the entry on the FREE-WILL DEFENCE. J. L. Mackie and Antony Flew insist that God could have created beings who would always freely choose to do the right. However, what kind of predictability would this be? It has been suggested that if a group of friends predicted with certainty that Mary would marry John, and in fact they became married, this would in no way imply any lack of freedom in this mutual decision. However, this case suggests only that freedom is sometimes or often compatible with predictability.

Mackie and Flew demand a narrower definition of freedom which applies only to choices that can always be predicted. Mackie is willing to shift his ground, but as John Hick urges, his modified arguments do not fully address what a human nature would entail that is capable of resisting temptation and affirming goodnes. (Hick, *Evil and the God of Love*, 2nd edn, London: Macmillan, 1977, 268–1).

THE CONTROVERSIAL STATUS OF THE CONCEPT AND ITS REFORMULATIONS

In comparison with exploring the logic of omnipotence, the concept of omniscience seems to yield more problems than constructive insights and reformulations. Even if we remain unconvinced by his conclusions, Norman Pike's reservations about arguments of the form 'If it is true that God knows at Time$_1$ ...' may be justified. On the other hand, a God who is locked into the 'timeless' realm 'above' or beyond created time may seem closer to PLATO than to the dynamic, purposive, active God of the Hebrew scriptures and Christian Old Testament, even if Helm addresses some of these issues.

In classical THEISM, especially among many Catholic philosophical theologians, the traditional uses of the term (with varied nuances from Augustine, Boethius and Aquinas) retain widespread currency. This is not least because they cohere with the concept of God as 'perfect', impassible and immutable.

In modern Protestant circles, however, many questions have been raised about 'impassibility' and 'immutability', for example by MOLTMANN among others. In the PROCESS PHILOSOPHY of WHITE-HEAD and HARTSHORNE divine knowledge does have an 'effect' upon the Being of God. In some thinkers three factors lead to a near-abandonment of the traditional term, or at least the traditional sense of the term. Emil Brunner (1889–1966) places the concept in the context of personal encounter rather than of perfection and eternity. Hence he tends to reapply the term to denote God's unfailing love, through which God fully understands the created other. Gustav Aulén (1879–1977) defines it as 'love's sovereign and penetrating eye'.

The view that since it is not yet actual, the future may not necessarily 'count' as an object of divine knowledge at least deserves some consideration. Still more central is Swinburne's modification of the scope of the concept on the basis of parallels with the exclusion of logical contradiction from the notion of omnipotence. Whether the larger boundaries of the concept suggested from Boethius to Helm are tenable will depend upon our conclusions about the nature of eternity, and the relation between God, eternity and time. These complex issues demand an exploration of a large family of concepts, such as eternity, immutability, omnipotence, TRANSCENDENCE, creation, time, aseity, FREE-WILL DEFENCE; GOD, CONCEPTS AND 'ATTRIBUTES' OF.

ontic enquiry

Ontic enquiry is to be distinguished from ONTOLOGY or ontological enquiry. While ontology concerns reality or 'Being' (in HEIDEGGER, German, *Sein*), ontic questions concern 'existents' or 'entities' (in Heidegger, *das Seiende*). This distinction is observed in the tradition of German EXISTENTIALISM and Heidegger (1889–1976).

On the other hand Willard van Orman Quine (b. 1908) and some other American writers speak of 'ontic theories' as little different from metaphysical systems. The use of 'ontic' here, however, permits a plurality of such systems. (*See also* METAPHYSICS.)

ontological argument for the existence of God

AN ARGUMENT FROM THE CONCEPT OF GOD

The ontological argument begins A PRIORI from a concept of God, in contrast to the COSMOLOGICAL ARGUMENT for the existence of God, which begins with our experience of the world and constitutes an A POSTERIORI argument. This contrast is explained in this context under GOD, ARGUMENTS FOR THE EXISTENCE OF, and more broadly in the entries on A PRIORI and A POSTERIORI.

A CONFESSIONAL ACKNOWLEDGEMENT OF DIVINE TRANSCENDENCE?

Many theologians point out that in the first formulation of the ontological argument by ANSELM (1033–1109) in *Proslogion* 2–4 the 'argument' emerges as a paean of praise that God is who God is, rather than strictly as a rational argument. BARTH (1886–1968) insists on this in his book on Anselm's formulation, *Fides Quaerens Intellectum* (1931).

Faith (*fides*), in seeking understanding (*intellectum*) of God, perceives the wholly Other or transcendent nature of God in contrast to the CONTINGENT, creaturely and finite status of the world and of all objects within it. God alone holds the world 'from the abyss of non-being'. If Barth is correct, the ontological argument has value not primarily as an 'argument', but as an expression of a believing acknowledgement that the Being of God is of a different order from that of the contingent world (*see* TRANSCENDENCE).

DEBATES OVER THE LOGICAL STATUS OF THE ARGUMENT

By contrast, many philosophers continue to perceive the argument as an intriguing exercise in LOGIC, or (in Plantinga's view) especially of MODAL LOGIC (the logic of POSSIBILITY). It is perhaps no accident that after Anselm those philosophers who held a particular interest in pure mathematics were more inclined than others to accord it logical seriousness as an *a priori* argument, notably DESCARTES (1596–1650) and LEIBNIZ (1646–1716).

Although KANT (1724–1804) and RUSSELL (1872–1970) advanced devastating logical arguments against it, in the twentieth century HARTSHORNE, MALCOLM and Plantinga have defended reformulations of it.

ANSELM'S TWO DISTINCT FORMULATIONS

Anselm begins *Proslogion* chapter 2 with praise: 'O Lord, you give understanding to faith ... We believe that you are that than which nothing greater (*nihil maius*) can be conceived (*cogitari possit*)'. He then alludes to the utterance of 'the fool who says "there is no God"' (Ps. 14:1), to argue that if he genuinely understands who God is, the fool would not utter a self-contradictory statement, since if God were not to embrace existence, God would be 'less' than the 'greatest' or 'maximal' Being. For to exist in actuality (*in re*) is 'greater' (*maius*) than to exist exclusively in the mind (*in intellectu*), as a mere concept

The monk Gaunilo replied that such reasoning is patently absurd. He could readily conceive of an island with all the 'greatest' possible attributes of an island (more trees, rivers, mountains, springs, sand, grass than any other) without this in the least affecting the issue of whether such an island actually existed.

Anselm, however, has a counter-reply. At this point praise turns into argument also. The concept of 'greatest', or (in

Plantinga's more helpful translation) 'maximally great', does not make sense if it is applied to such contingent objects as islands: size, number of trees, lengths and numbers of rivers are not entities to which it is intelligible to apply 'maximal greatness'.

It is precisely because 'maximal greatness' applies uniquely to God as non-contingent, omniscient, almighty and perfect in wisdom, goodness and love that the transparent force of the argument emerges. Hence Anselm seeks to show the irrelevance of Gaunilo's reply. Some additional paragraphs to *Proslogion* 4 declare that anything in principle may be 'conceived not to be' except God, whose order of Being is unique. Anselm replies explicitly to Gaunilo in his *Liber Apologeticus pro Insipiente*. However, is this argument convincing or circular?

DID THOMAS AQUINAS REJECT THE ARGUMENT?

The attitude of Thomas AQUINAS (1225–74) is controversial. In *Summa Theologiae* (Ia, Qu. 2) he seems to argue that God's existence can only be inferred from effects that God brings about (Rom. 1:20). HICK, Plantinga and most modern philosophers see Aquinas as rejecting the ontological argument. On the other hand, a minority see the argument as implicit in Aquinas's fourth way, from degrees of Being (*see* FIVE WAYS of Aquinas, and E. J. Butterworth, *The Identity of Anselm's Proslogion Argument for the Existence of God with the Via Quarta of Thomas Aquinas*, Lampeter: Mellen, 1990).

RE-FORMULATION BY DESCARTES: DOES THIS GIVE THE GAME AWAY?

Descartes, not least in view of his interest in pure mathematics, was concerned with 'certainty' and 'certain' knowledge. In his *Meditations* V he states that it is 'certain' that 'I find no less the idea of God ... the idea of a supremely perfect Being in me than that of any figure or number ...

Eternal existence pertains to this nature.' He continues: 'I clearly see that existence can no more be separated from the essence of God' than can a triangle have three angles other than together being equal to two right angles. Similarly, 'mountain' carries with it logically and conceptually the idea of 'valley'.

Critics of the logic of the ontological argument believe that in his effort to defend the argument Descartes has let the cat out of the bag. He is explicitly recognizing that the argument is merely an ANALYTIC STATEMENT or proposition. It belongs to that class of statements the truth of which is arrived at merely by DEFINITION. These are of the class: 'all bachelors are unmarried'; '2 + 2 = 4'; 'the angles of a triangle add up to 180°'; 'water boils at 100° C'. This 'TRUTH' is independent of what specific bachelors say, or what calculations I make, or how well I draw triangles, or what kettle and heater I use.

The relation between analytic statements and PREDICATES has now been brought out into the open. Is 'existence' a predicate of that to which analytical A PRIORI truth has been ascribed? Are 'unmarried' and 'exist' the same kind of predicate to ascribe to bachelors?

If we define an orange analytically, do the statements 'it is coloured orange' and 'it is sticky' lead on along the same analytical level to 'it exists'? The argument backfires, as Kant perceived, by demonstrating that it addresses not 'existence', but the logic of CONCEPTS alone.

KANT'S CRITIQUE: EXISTENCE NOT A PREDICATE

Kant re-examined the traditional logical model subject/predicate (as discussed under ARISTOTLE); for example, the typical logical form: 'The grass' (subject) ...'is green' (predicate). He then argued that the ontological argument could hold only if 'existence' is regarded as a predicate, or a property or attribute to be ascribed to God or other entities alongside such properties

or qualities as 'is wise', 'is good', 'is loving' (or in the case of objects, 'is green', 'is white', 'is heavy'). We simply do not say: 'Look! This hammer is heavy and it exists.'

Kant insists: 'Being is evidently not a real predicate ... that can be added to the concept of a thing.' A hundred dollars that exist are not 'greater' than a hundred that might or might not exist. Hence the denial of the existence of God is not logically self-contradictory. 'Existence' does not 'add' one more quality of the same kind to others already listed.

DEVELOPMENT OF KANT'S CRITIQUE: RUSSELL ON 'INSTANTIATION'

Russell clinched Kant's argument that 'existence' is not a predicate by arguing that existence is best thought of in terms providing instances, i.e. as INSTANTIATION. A triangle adds up to 180°, and it is instantiated 'there' on the blackboard. The ontological argument raises the logical question: is the concept of the 'greatest' Being instantiated or not?

This insight is linked with Russell's work on the logical form that 'brackets' instantiation or existence, usually expressed in the form: 'For all x, x is y.' Such a complex rewriting of a logical form permits us to ascribe meaning to a proposition which may be true-or-false without smuggling in the presupposition of its truth. The often-repeated example in logic is: 'the present King of France is ...'. Instantiation is often expressed by logicians through the logical notation known as the use of a QUANTIFIER.

THE ARGUMENT AS A 'DISPROOF' OF GOD'S EXISTENCE

In the 1950s J. N. Findlay attempted an ingenious logical argument that turned the traditional argument on its head. His argument has three stages: (1) the ontological argument portrays God as One whose non-existence is unthinkable, i.e. as a logically NECESSARY Being. However, (2) what is logically necessary is true merely by analytical definition, and cannot be said to exist or not to exist contingently (i.e. it does not 'make a difference' outside the realm of conceptual logic). Hence, (3) to claim that 'God exists' (other than as a concept) is self-contradictory.

A. G. A. Rainer, among others, claims, however, that Findlay confuses the 'necessity' of God with the 'necessity' of what we assert about God. What is logically necessary applies to assertions, not to the Being of God. The very same confusion that besets many formulations of the ontological argument, he concludes, lead to the failure of the attempt to turn it into a disproof of the existence of God.

FURTHER TWENTIETH-CENTURY DEBATE: HARTSHORNE, MALCOLM AND PLANTINGA

Hartshorne sets out a detailed argument in which he deploys modal logic in defence of the ontological argument. In effect he argues that while Kant and Russell may counter Anselm's first formulation, their work on predication (or instantiation) still leaves Anselm's second formulation intact.

Hartshorne argues that, first, God's necessary existence is so undeniably self-evident that to deny it constitutes a self-contradiction. Second, it is necessarily not true that 'God exists necessarily' strictly implies that God does not exist. Hence, third, either: 'God exists necessarily'; or: 'it is necessary that God does not exist'. But 'God does not exist' cannot be a necessary proposition.

Hartshorne also provides a further modal argument. If God is the absolute maximum, God will be the absolute maximum in each time. This entails a PANENTHEISM, in which God's almightiness and perfection embrace the whole world, including both necessary Being and contingent existence.

For a fuller discussion see the entry on Hartshorne. His logical analysis in the context of dynamic PROCESS PHILOSPHY is valuable in restoring a possible relation between the ontological argument, divine action and history. Yet critics will continue to urge that it contains elements of circularity. His arguments can be found in *The Logic of Perfection* (La Salle: Open Court, 1962).

Malcolm and Plantinga also subject the negative evaluations to rigorous logical scrutiny. It is inconceivable that 'God' might not have existed, or 'God' would be less than God. Hence if God does not exist, this denial must be a necessary proposition. However, it cannot be shown that the denial of God's existence is logically necessary. We face the dilemma: either logically necessary' or (exclusive alternative) the denial of the logically necessary. This may be expressed in logical notation: $Nq \lor \sim Nq$). This formulation appears to exclude such denial (*see* the entries on logic and modal logic).

Plantinga extends the modal logic of Hartshorne and of Malcolm to argue that 'maximal greatness' is not just 'possibly' instantiated, but instatiated or exemplified in actuality. For it is not the case that to ascribe omnipotence, omniscience and perfect goodness to God is no more than a logically necessary proposition. Logical necessity does not exhaust the multiform sense in which we may speak of God as a 'NECESSARY' Being (Plantinga, *The Nature of Necessity*, Oxford: Clarendon, 1974).

The debate about the logical status of the ontological argument continues. Although many dismiss it as merely confusing the concept of God with the existence of God, it would be over-hasty to set aside either the conceptual significance identified by Barth, or the logical complexities that continue to occupy the application of modal logic (the logic of 'possibility') on the part of such rigorous logicians as Hartshorne, Malcolm and Plantinga.

ontology

Ontology denotes the study of being, or of what-is (from Greek, *ta onta*, the articular neuter plural participle, the things that actually exist, the things that are). As such it features alongside EPISTEMOLOGY, ETHICS and LOGIC as part of the core of traditional philosophy. As a technical philosophical term, the word seems to have originated during the seventeenth century. It is used by LEIBNIZ (1646–1716) and by Christian Wolff (1679–1754).

Initially the term was used interchangeably with METAPHYSICS, while some regarded ontology as a subdivision within metaphysics. Strictly, the latter is more accurate, since metaphysics may include questions of epistemology, but the two terms are now often used synonymously.

In the modern era HEIDEGGER (1889–1976) chastised the Western philosophical tradition for having 'long fallen out of Being *(Sein)' (An Introduction to Metaphysics*, New Haven: Yale, 1959, 37). He sought to address the question, 'How does it stand with Being' (*Wie steht es um das Sein?* ibid., 32). In different words, 'Why are these entities *(Seienden)* rather than nothing?' (ibid., 1, 2, 12, 22). This is 'the most fundamental of questions' (ibid., 6).

Yet Heidegger himself, in effect, gives up the attempt, and attributes blame for our inability to answer these questions to PLATO'S DUALISM of appearance and reality. He concedes that genuine ontology emerged in pre-Socratic philosophy (e.g. in Parmenides), and today, it occurs if at all in poets, art, and in Eastern non-dualist philosophies.

Heidegger is too sweeping. DUNS SCOTUS (*c.* 1266–1308) believed that the task of intellectual enquiry was to examine Being *(realitas)*, even if not in Heidegger's unusual sense of the term. WILLIAM OF OCKHAM (*c.* 1287–1349) based his SEMANTICS on substances and qualities. Leibniz explored the 'sufficient reason' for everything in the world; a world constituted by 'monads', namely irreducible ontological units which make up reality.

In his early period KANT addressed ontology as including the difference between spiritual and material beings.

HEGEL (1770–1831) formulates an entire system of an ontology of the ABSOLUTE as this unfolds in history and in logic. MATERIALISM, PANTHEISM, DEISM, MONISM and THEISM are all ontologies. (*See also* HINDU PHILOSOPHY.)

ordinary language

See ANALYTICAL PHILOSOPHY; AUSTIN; OXFORD PHILOSOPHY.

ostensive definition

It is often assumed that people learn language by pointing to the object to which a word refers, and uttering the sound used to denote it. This is the method of ostensive definition: a person points to an object and utters the sound that denotes it in a language. The reason for the plausibility of this account is, first, that it may seem to work with everyday physical or natural objects ('this is bread'; 'this is a tree'); second, it is widely used in teaching a *second* language to someone who already grasps how language is to be interpreted.

WITTGENSTEIN argues that this method can work within strictly limited confines. A builder may point to slabs, pillars, blocks, or beams, and call out their names (*Philosophical Investigations*, Oxford: Blackwell, 1967, sects. 2–6). However, this model in which 'naming something is like attaching a label to a thing' (ibid., sect. 15) falls down for wider and more complex (indeed many) examples.

If I point to two apples, and say 'two apples', how do I point to 'two', and what is to stop someone understanding 'two' as a name for this group to which I point? 'Ostensive definition can be variously interpreted in *every* case' (ibid., sect. 28). This method presupposes an understanding of how language operates. 'Point to a piece of paper. – And now point to its shape – now to its number (that sounds queer). How did you do it?' (ibid., sect. 33). It is like pointing to a chess-piece, as if the physical properties were what defined it, rather than how it moves in accordance with rules (ibid., sects. 30–50).

In philosophy of religion this suggests that a failure to identify 'God' or other religious realities in this way is entirely unsurprising, and no indicator of their lack of intelligibility or truth. Ostensive definition performs a severely limited role whether in ordinary or in religious uses of language. Like the referential theory of meaning, its application is valid only within limits.

Otto, Rudolf (1869–1937)

Otto's most widely known work is *Das Heilige* (Ger., 1917; 25th edn, 1936; Eng., *The Idea of the Holy*, Oxford: OUP, 1923). The central theme of this book is an exploration of the NUMINOUS – the feeling of awe and wonder that takes hold of a worshipper before God or before the sacred. Otto was influenced by KANT and by Neo-Kantian philosophy, and wrote extensively on the philosophy of religion.

One component of the experience of the numinous lay in 'fear of God' or 'godly fear' in a sense that surpasses a bare psychological fear of objects. In 'primitive' religions, into which Otto also undertook research, the numinous may be perceived as that which causes the worshipper to tremble or to stand aghast. In 'higher' religions this may take the form of mystic awe, which may invite some such religious or liturgical response as prostration before God.

The Hebrew scriptures, or Christian Old Testament, reflect this in Isaiah's vision of Isaiah 6:1–5: 'I saw the Lord ... High and lofty ... Seraphs were in attendance ... and said, "Holy, holy, holy, is the Lord of hosts ..." The pivots of the thresholds shook ... I said, "Woe is me! I am lost ... My eyes have seen the King, the Lord of hosts."' Similarly, the book of Exodus portrays God as a consuming fire.

While chapters 4–5 of *The Idea of the Holy* expound this theme of fearsome awe at the presence of 'the Other', chapter 6 expresses the complementary principle of being drawn by holy love. The mystery of the numinous or holy embraces both *mysterium tremendum*, the 'Beyond' who invites reverential fear, and *mysterium fascinosum*, the fascination or enchantment of a holy love beyond compare.

Otto describes the wholeness of this dual experience as 'a strange harmony of contrasts' that reaches far beyond merely rational explanation. The numinous cannot be explained exhaustively in rational or ethical terms. Religion cannot be reduced to the level of a mere BELIEF-system or system of ETHICS or values. Divine holiness is not simply 'moral' holiness, but also 'majesty' holiness.

In Pauline language, 'What no eye has seen nor ear heard nor the human heart conceived ... God has prepared for those who love him' (1 Cor. 2:9). With Kant and TILLICH, Otto saw experience of 'the holy' and 'the Beyond' as transcending human concepts in a sense of wonder. (*See also* GOD, CONCEPTS AND 'ATTRIBUTES' OF; OMNIPOTENCE; TRANSCENDENCE; VIA NEGATIVA.)

Oxford philosophy

The term is seldom used today, except to denote a particular period in the history of philosophy at Oxford, namely from around the late 1930s to about 1960. Especially in the 1950s it denoted a style and method of philosophy largely but not exclusively associated with RYLE (1900–76) and several of his Oxford colleagues. In his autobiographical essay Ryle recalls that in that period his 'chief ... interest in linguistic matters focussed on such dictions as were (or ... were not) in breach of "logical syntax".' He explored especially 'the trouble-makers and the paradox-generators' ('Autobiographical', in O.P. Wood and G. Pitcher, eds, *Ryle*, London: Macmillan, 1970, 14).

Some used the term approvingly to denote that area of thought which asks the most rigorous and searching questions about 'logical grammar' (ibid., 7). Others used the term more pejoratively, to denote a kind of philosophy that seemed always to be 'tuning up' rather than playing the tune. Although Ryle's approach was different from that of AUSTIN (1911–60), Austin's careful linguistic analysis also dominated Oxford philosophy up to 1960, and probably also comes under this term. A turning-point was reached in the broader concerns of STRAWSON (b. 1919), who used the term 'descriptive METAPHYSICS' of some of his own work. (*See also* LANGUAGE IN RELIGION; LOGIC.)

P

Paley, William (1743–1805)

Paley was educated, and taught, at Cambridge, and then served in the Church of England ministry, becoming Archdeacon of Carlisle. His published works include *The Principles of Moral and Political Knowledge* (1785); *Evidences of Christianity* (1794); and *Natural Theology* (1802).

Apart from his work in ETHICS and moral philosophy, Paley's contributions to philosophy of religion left their mark in two main areas. First, he was a major advocate of NATURAL THEOLOGY. He had a high regard for the capacity of human reason to draw theistic inferences A POSTERIORI from the natural world. Nevertheless, he also believed in the necessity of REVELATION in the scriptures for a grasp of specific doctrines of the Christian faith.

Second, Paley's name is closely associated with the TELEOLOGICAL ARGUMENT for the existence of God. He coined the well-known analogy of finding a watch during a walk on heathland. Even if it were broken or damaged, the watch would provide evidence of design. Its machinery would point to the originating agency of a designer.

Problems in Paley's work were in part anticipated by HUME (1711–76), but it was the implications of the theory of EVOLUTION through chance and random change formulated by DARWIN (1809–82) that blunted Paley's argument. Reformulations of the argument that address evolutionary theory have been offered by TENNANT and SWINBURNE, among others. (*See also* SCIENCE AND RELIGION; THEISM.)

panentheism

The term stands in contrast with PANTHEISM. If pantheism identifies God with the whole of reality, panentheism denotes the belief that the reality of the world and the whole created order does not exhaust the reality of God without remainder. Yet it also holds in common with pantheism that God's presence and active agency permeates the world, actively sustaining it in every part. It expresses the OMNIPRESENCE of God as immanent in the world.

Panentheism is still more sharply to be distinguished from DEISM, which tends to exaggerate a one-sided emphasis on divine TRANSCENDENCE in such a way as to make God remote from the world and from daily life. Panentheism stresses first and foremost divine IMMANENCE, but without excluding divine transcendence.

HARTSHORNE explicitly insisted that God is an eternal, world-inclusive and conscious Being, but also holds to panentheism, stressing that 'God is in all' (Greek, *pan+en+theos*), while excluding all notions of any identity between God and the world. He rejected any idea that 'God is all' (pantheism). Following WHITEHEAD (1861–1947) he held an organic view of the universe, in which God is understood in terms of constant creativity: 'God is not before, but with, all creation' (*Process and Reality*, 1929).

Against DECARTES, HUME and KANT, Whitehead and Hartshorne evolved a PROCESS PHILOSOPHY in which God is involved in the world's 'becoming'. The STOICS tended towards a blend of panentheism and pantheism, depending on individual schools and writers. The Acts of the Apostles ascribes to Paul the use of a panentheistic quotation from the Stoics (perhaps Epimenides): 'In him [God] we live and move and have our being' (Acts 17:28).

Pannenberg, Wolfhart (b. 1928)

Pannenberg is one of the most eminent Christian theologians of the late twentieth century. Of his numerous publications his three-volume *Systematic Theology* (Germ., 1988, 1991, 1993; Eng., Edinburgh: T & T Clark, 1991, 1994, 1998) constitutes a magisterial climax. He has written on almost every aspect of theology, including theological method, with rigour and precision.

Pannenberg's broadest impact on the philosophy of religion has been twofold. First, he vindicates the role of REASON and rationality, in theology and religion without dispensing with the equal necessity for REVELATION. Second, he approaches the issues of meaning in terms of the widest possible horizons of history.

On faith and reason Pannenberg declares, 'An otherwise unconvincing message cannot attain the power to convince simply by appealing to the Holy Spirit ... Argumentation and the operation of the Spirit are not in competition with each other. In trusting the Spirit, Paul [the

Apostle] in no way spared himself thinking and enquiry' (*Basic Questions in Theology*, London: SCM, vol. 2, 1971, 34–5).

On meaning, Pannenberg argues that a retrospective 'looking back' often communicates more than our attempts to understand the meanings of events and utterances while we are in the process of living through them. Hence he is sympathetic with the work of HEGEL on history as a universal horizon of wholeness (*Basic Questions*, vol. 3, 1973, 201). In theological terms this invites special emphasis on the RESURRECTION of Jesus Christ as an aspect of the 'End' provisionally breaking into history.

This short entry cannot do justice to the power, coherence and complexity of Pannenberg's theology, but simply aims to identify two of the points at which its relevance to the philosophy of religion is most far-reaching. Pannenberg also published *Theology and the Philosophy of Science* (Philadelphia: Westminster, 1976) and *Metaphysics and the Idea of God* (Edinburgh: T & T Clark, 1990).

pantheism

The term embraces a variety of different views bound together by a common belief that God and all that exists are identical. Crudely, word history suggests that shorthand: 'God is all' (Greek, *pan*, all; *theos*, God). However, this does not entail the belief that each individual part of the universe (or of nature) is 'God'. Rather, 'God' is the full totality of all existent things.

Pantheism may be said to stand in some kind of contrast to each of the following six terms. It stands in contrast to ATHEISM (although some dispute this: *see* SPINOZA); to POLYTHEISM (the belief that there are many gods); to DEISM (the view that God created the world but does not intervene in it, and is not immanent within it); to THEISM and to monotheism (the belief in one God, who is distinct from the created world, both transcendent beyond it and immanent within it).

The finest distinction, but an essential one, is between pantheism and PANENTHE-ISM, the belief that God is *in* (Greek, *en*) all created things. The analogy has been suggested of a saturated sponge: liquid might permeate the whole sponge, but is not to be identified with the sponge. Different writers among the ancient STOICS ranged on a spectrum between pantheism and panentheism.

The most fundamental distinction within pantheistic thought is that between *religious* pantheism, which stresses such an intense awareness of divine presence that it places too much emphasis upon divine immanence at the expense of divine transcendence, and philosophical panthe-ism, which arises out of MONISM, i.e. the philosophical world-view that everything is a unity; that all is One.

WESTERN EXAMPLES OF PANTHEISM: IN THE ANCIENT WORLD

Whether Parmenides of Elea (fl. 510–492 BCE) should be characterized as a panthe-ist or as a monist is open to debate. He argued for the unity of all things, espe-cially for the unity of being and thought. The material and CONTINGENT is mere appearance behind which thought is con-stant and invariable. The 'paradoxes' identified by his student Zeno of Elea (490–30 BCE) were formulated to try to defend this position.

STOIC PHILOSOPHY in the Graeco-Roman world included different strands of thought, but in general assimilated the early Stoic view that the world is ordered by its own 'world-spirit' or 'world-soul' which permeates it with the rational and the good. By contrast, Paul the Apostle dissociates the transcendent (as well as immanent) 'Spirit who comes forth from God' (i.e. from the beyond) (Greek, *to pneuma to ek tou theou*, out from God) from 'the spirit of the world' (world-spirit) (Greek, *to pneuma tou kosmou*, 1 Cor. 2:12).

Some regard NEOPLATONISM as pantheistic because everything derives from God's own Being rather than merely from God's agency and action. However, the fundamental belief that what proceeds from God does so through emanations or intermediate degrees of Being also assumes a transcendence on the part of God which does not cohere with thoroughgoing pantheism.

Similarly, while some identify mystical PIETISM with religious pantheism, a rever-ential and mystical feeling that 'God is all' tends to reflect an existential attitude rather than a metaphysical statement of pantheism. In practice, this stands nearer to panentheism.

WESTERN EXAMPLES OF PANTHEISM: THE MODERN WORLD

The classic representative of pantheism in the West is Spinoza (1632–77). Although a Jewish philosopher, Spinoza was excom-municated from the synagogue in 1656 after being accused of atheism. More strictly, he held to a philosophical mon-ism.

Since God is 'absolutely infinite being', God is coextensive with the whole of reality. Yet it is equally the case that if there is only one 'substance', this sub-stance is the whole of reality. God and substance are the same, namely the Whole. The respective goals of philosophy and religion are therefore the same.

One of Spinoza's most notorious max-ims was that on this basis we may speak either of 'God' or of 'nature' (*Deus, sive Natura*) without denoting different enti-ties or realities. Either term denotes infinite reality, which is One.

This identification invited the charge of 'naturalism' on the basis that Spinoza could hardly claim to believe in the personal God of theism. Nevertheless, Spinoza had been brought up with a knowledge of the Hebrew scriptures and rabbinic writings, and could claim that he took as his starting-point the Jewish belief in the unity of God ('Hear, Israel, the Lord is One') and also in God's infinity. Indeed, he had also been given the designation 'God-intoxicated'. Spinoza endorsed two principles about God: 'God necessarily exists' (Latin, *Deus necessario existit*); and 'that God is one' (*Deus esse unicum*).

The formula *Deus, sive Natura* (either 'God' or 'Nature') derived in part from Spinoza's deep concern to resolve the DUALISM bequeathed by DESCARTES, his older near-contemporary (1596–1650). If substance–God–nature is All, either principle can be formulated as a Whole; not as a component of a duality. God is not a mind excluded from the realm of substance or matter; nor is God an incomplete will striving for something 'more'.

This, in turn, provides a basis for ETHICS. Ethics arises not from seeking to accord with God's 'desire', for God is complete and without lack. However, finite human persons are to aim to transcend the limits of the partial; 'to live under the aspect of eternity', or the Whole. It was in part Spinoza's crusade against the constraints of the partial in religions, and his defence of secular 'freedoms', that contributed to his highly controversial status as a thinker during his lifetime.

Without question Spinoza left an uneasy balance between belief in an impersonal God who is All and a naturalistic monism which leaves no room for a personal, characterizable God who may act in freedom. On one side, he reflects the emphasis on the unity and infinity of God found in Judaism; on the other side he draws on the confused ONTOLOGY of Parmenides and the paradoxes of Zeno, and offers an unconvincing resolution of the dualism of Descartes.

Not surprisingly after his death the 'Pantheism Controversy' (*Pantheismusstreit*) erupted concerning whether Spinoza's 'pantheism' was a thin disguise for atheism or whether it offered a viable conception of God.

In 1785 Friedrich H. Jacobi published an attack on Spinoza's pantheism as deterministic and rationalistic monism,

and accused Lessing of holding to such a view. By contrast J.G. Herder (1744–1803) and Johann W. Goethe (1749–1832) urged that, to the contrary, Spinoza offered an anti-mechanistic, organic view of God and nature. In Goethe's words, he acknowledged 'the highest reality... Being *is* God'. He was to be praised as '*theissimum*', thoroughly theist.

Some view HEGEL (1770–1831) as a pantheist, since he identified the 'All' as Absolute Divine Spirit (*Geist*) unfolding its Being in and through historical and logical DIALECTIC. However, in the light of the part played by CONCEPTS and by differentiation in Hegel's philosophy, his thought is too complex to suggest more than leanings towards a qualified pantheism.

BRADLEY (1846–1924), the 'English Hegelian', may more readily be called a pantheist. He argues that change and differentiation are mere unreal appearance, and that only the Whole is real (*Appearance and Reality*, 1893). The whole is the ABSOLUTE.

Josiah Royce (1855–1916), the 'American Hegelian', was no more pantheist than was Hegel. He did indeed stress the reality of the Whole, against the fragmentary (*The Conception of God*, 1897). But history moves toward a single 'community of interpretation', not an undifferential Absolute.

PANTHEISM IN THE EAST

Whereas in the West, pantheism has never obtained a clear foothold because of the difficulty of treading a path between theism and naturalism, pantheism lies deep within the roots of Hindu traditions. The early Upaniṣads (*c.* 700 BCE) identify the divine with inner human consciousness or the inner self. In the Advaita (non-dualist) Vedanta, *brāhman* is impersonal divine being and consciousness.

Even so, within schools of the Vedanta, Dvaita Vedanta conceives of the *brāhman* as being characterizable qualities (*saguna*), while Advaita Vedanta sees *brāhman* as without such qualities (*nirguna*).

The Indian Hindu philosopher ŚAṄ-
KĀRĀ (788–820) defended the pantheistic
monism of the Advaita Vedanta against
the dualism of some Buddhist traditions.
The self (*ātman*) is undifferentiated consciousness. *Avidyā*, illusory perception, is
not unlike what Bradley terms 'appearance': it is how we perceive individual
particulars and differentiation, but this
masks the total reality of undifferentiated
consciousness, *nirguna brāhma*, which is
the All in reality.

RĀMĀNUJA (*c.* 1017–1137) modified
the teachings of Śaṅkārā by a 'qualified
monism' (Visista-advaita). Difference is
more than appearance or illusion (*avidyā*).
Brāhman is not to be identified with the
All, but is its origin and animating centre.
There are affinities here with the quasi-
pantheist 'world-soul' of Stoic philosophy,
and the extent of 'reality' remains ambivalent. Bhakti devotional Hinduism derives
from the Visista-advaita tradition. It has
been described as both 'emanationist' and
'relativist' pantheism or monism.

Some traditions of Chinese philosophy
stand in contrast to those of Indian Hindu
philosophy in stressing an explicitly dualist world-view. The most striking example
is the *yin–yang* tradition of Taoism, in
which the *yin* is said to denote the
feminine, weak or destructive and the
yang the masculine, strong or constructive. Some sub-traditions also propose a
'rotation of dominance' between the two
principles, but this is far from pantheism
and monism.

Nāgārjuna (*c.* 150–200), an Indian
Mahayana Buddhist, held to the unity
and non-duality of the Absolute on the
basis of the relativity of change and
unreality of matter. (For a fuller account
of Buddhist thought, however, *see* under
BUDDHIST PHILOSOPHY.)

ISLAMIC PHILOSOPHY normally stresses
the TRANSCENDENCE of God. However,
occasionalist views of divine action can
lend themselves to a relativist, or modified,
pantheism. Perhaps only the mystical
tradition of Sufism within Islam can be

said to lean towards pantheism, with its
emphasis on the 'unity of Being'. All
mystical traditions tend in this direction,
but most would claim to represent
panentheism rather than pantheism. (*See
also* EXISTENTIALISM; HINDU PHILOSO-
PHY; IMMANENCE; JEWISH PHILOSOPHY;
METAPHYSICS; MYSTICISM; OCCASIONAL-
ISM.)

performative utterances

This term is especially associated with
AUSTIN (1911–60). Although he introduced the term in 1946 in 'Other Minds'
(in *Philosophical Papers*, 1961, 44–84),
Austin's main exposition of the subject
occurs in his 1955 lectures later published
under the title *How to Do Things with
Words* (Oxford: OUP, 1962).

Performatives are distinguished from
statements, which are 'true' or 'false'.
Rather, performative utterances enact
actions either 'operatively' and effectively
or 'without effect' as null and void (ibid.,
10–11). Given that 'I baptize ...' is a
performative utterance, we do not speak
of a baptism as 'true' or 'false', but as
'valid' (if appropriate) or 'inoperative' (if
it merely 'went through the motions'). If,
Austin suggests, the officiating minister
says, 'I baptize this infant 2704' rather
than 'I baptize this infant John', is the
baptism operative or void (ibid., 35)?

Austin makes a distinctive point when
he insists that a conventional procedure
must normally be assumed. I cannot say
'My seconds will call on you ...' with
performative effect if duelling is no longer
an accepted, conventional way of solving a
dispute. I can write, however, 'I give and
bequeath my house ...', as long as the
house is mine to bequeath, the house is
correctly identified and (for the act to take
place) I become deceased.

Performatives may also be sub-categorized into 'illocutions' (distinctively performative) and 'perlocutions' (performative
only in a causal or rhetorical sense). A
clear example of an illocutionary act

occurs in the first-person use of 'I promise', when I pledge myself to undertaking to carry out the promise. This is an act (i.e. of promise) performed 'in' the saying of it. Perlocutions occur when an act is performed 'by' the saying of an utterance, as when a speaker persuades another of something through words.

The former case reflects an 'asymmetry' of logical operation between first-person and third-person linguistic acts. 'I promise' commits me to action and makes a promise in a way that 'he promises' does not. The asymmetry between 'I believe' and 'he believes' provides a parallel example.

LANGUAGE IN RELIGION makes extensive use of performative utterances, especially in liturgy and worship. 'I repent', 'I believe', 'I praise', are acts of repentance, declarative acts of confession of faith; acclamations or acts of praise. They do not represent pieces of information addressed to an omniscient God.

In the era after Austin, the term 'speech acts' came to replace 'performatives', especially in the work of John Searle, WOLTERSTORFF, Terrence Tilley and others. However, even before Austin, WITTGENSTEIN had noted the logical asymmetry between 'I believe' and 'he believes'. He writes, 'If there were a verb meaning "to believe falsely", it would not have any significant first person present indicative' (*Philosophical Investigations*, Oxford: Blackwell, 1967, ii, 190). (*See also* BELIEF; SPEECH ACTS.)

persons, personal identity

See SELF.

Philo of Alexandria (Philo Judaeus, *c.* 20 BCE – *c.* 50 CE)

Philo's work combines loyalty to the Jewish scriptures (the Christian Old Testament) with the aim of utilizing Hellenistic and ancient Greek philosophy for the expression of his ideas. He produced the largest body of Jewish writings prior to the second century.

Philo represents Hellenistic or Alexandrian Jewish philosophical religious thought, rather than rabbinic Judaism. However, how representative even of diaspora Judaism he is has been disputed. E. Goodenough (*An Introduction to Philo Judaeus*, 1940) regards him as a representative figure of Hellenistic Judaism; H. A. Wolfson sees him as a system-builder (*Philo*, 2 vols., Cambridge, MA: Harvard, 1947); G. F. Moore sees him as Stoicizing Platonist (*Judaism*, 3 vols., Cambridge, MA: Harvard, 1927, vol. 1, 211).

In *Against Flaccus* and *Embassy to Gaius* Philo recounts his leadership of a five-man delegation to Rome to plead for the Jews on the occasion when the Roman prefect Flaccus imposed cult-images of the emperor onto the Jews of Alexandria. Civil unrest, disorder and massacre had resulted. However, all of his other near-forty treatises are either expository or philosophical APOLOGETICS.

EXPOSITORY WORKS

Nearly nine treatises offer allegorical interpretations of Genesis or the 'five books of Moses' (the Pentateuchal traditions from Genesis to Deuteronomy). Philo places his own philosophical interpretation on the biblical traditions of creation. The 'six days' of CREATION, for example, denote not duration but 'order'. Before the material world, the incorporeal world existed as an Idea in the mind of the Designer, as divine reason. Moses is portrayed as the first great philosopher. The laws of Exodus and Leviticus relate not to local issues about sacrifices, but enunciate cosmic ideas.

Allegorical interpretation as a vehicle for the removal of ANTHROPOMORPHISM was already a familiar tool to STOICS, who were embarrassed by the polytheism of Homer's writings, and reinterpreted conflicts among the gods as accounts of natural elements or abstract principles. Philo does not always utilize this allegorical method, but frequently resorts to it when he believes that the sacred text would seem crude or offensive to educated Hellenistic readers. Where possible, he expounded ideas about God and ETHICS by more straightforward exegesis of the text.

APOLOGETICS: GOD AND THE *LOGOS*

Philo draws on ideas from PLATO and Platonism, from Stoicism and from Neo-Pythagoreanism, to present ideas about God; the *Logos*, or divine Reason; and ethics. God is nameless, invisible and incomprehensible. Hence Moses' request for God's name elicits only 'I am that I am' (Ex. 3:14, where the Greek Septuagint version uses a present to translate the more dynamic Hebrew verb 'I will be'). God is a unity (*Allegorical Laws* 2: 2, 3); eternal (*Decalogue* 41: 64); perfect and omnipresent; and Father (*Of the Confusion of Languages* 63, 146).

The *Logos* is the agent of God in creation, the 'firstborn' (*protogonos*), eternally begotten (*Allegorical Laws* 1: 2: 5). From Platonism Philo draws the notion of the *Logos* as 'archetype' of creation. Since God is perfect and the world is material and CONTINGENT, the *Logos* acts as mediator between God and the world, and between God and humankind. The *Logos* is the bond that binds the universe together (cf. Col. 1:17, 'in Christ the universe coheres').

JEWISH AND GREEK SOURCES: ETHICS

Philo did not have to draw exclusively on Greek sources for these ideas. The Hebrew tradition of Wisdom as mediating divine agent is found in Proverbs, in the Wisdom of Solomon, and in other documents of Hellenistic Judaism. The tradition of a 'chosen people' relates closely for Philo to ethical obedience. However, this is often expressed less in biblical terms than in philosophical terms as subordination to Reason, although there is common ground in the appeal to 'virtue' between Plato and the Wisdom traditions of Judaism.

Moses legislates through constructive laws that coincide with philosophical Good. God can be known indirectly from nature, and this leaves no moral excuse for the folly of idolatry. Like the Wisdom of Solomon and Paul the Apostle, Philo draws on this 'homily' theme that idolatry leads to disorder, to vice and to inbuilt judgement (Wisd. 14, 22–31; cf. Rom. 1:18–32). Yet God is patient (Wisd. 15, 1–6; cf. Rom. 2:4–11).

Even if he selects at will from a multiplicity of philosophical sources, Philo stands in the tradition of those religious philosophers who have sought to expound the TRANSCENDENCE of God and the value of sacred texts through the medium of ideas and thought-forms which were the common currency of the day. His work is largely philosophical apologetics for a Hellenistic or heterodox Judaism.

pietism, Christian

The term is used in both a positive and a pejorative sense. Positively it denotes a warm, committed, religious devotion. In the eighteenth century when DEISM and RATIONALISM were at their height, an era (according to John Henry Newman) when 'love became cold', the Wesleyan revivals manifested a pietist counter-reaction. Pejoratively, the term also denotes an undue disparagement of REASON and critical reflection in favour of feeling and RELIGIOUS 'EXPERIENCE'.

Whereas deism and rationalism are often associated with more mechanistic views of the world order, pietism coheres more comfortably with an organic world-view, often with an emphasis on the indwelling of the Holy Spirit and divine IMMANENCE. In the nineteenth century its relation to ROMANTICISM was more than accidental. Both stressed first-hand creativity in contrast to wooden replication of routinized doctrines or practices.

A founding figure of pietism was Philipp Jakob Spener (1635–1705). His main emphasis included the study of the

Bible, the priesthood of all believers, practical discipleship, a simple style of life, and the superiority of love over argument. Spener was supported especially by August Francke (1663–1727), who added a further emphasis on the need to be 'born again' (*Wiedergeburt*).

In the eighteenth century, leading figures included Friedrich Oetinger (1702–1782) and Count Nicholas Ludwig von Zinzendorf (1700–60) in continental Europe. Because he insisted on greater critical engagement with philosophy (especially with KANT) and with biblical criticism, but retained a pietist warmth, SCHLEIERMACHER (1768–1834) called himself 'a Pietist of a higher order'. His religion had at its centre a relationship of utter dependence upon God, a sense of immediacy and a 'love of the Saviour' (*Heilandsliebe*), but he wrote important works of philosophy and HERMENEUTICS.

In England in the eighteenth century, pietism broadly took the form of the Methodism of John and Charles Wesley, which began a reform movement for revival within the Church of England. There are also parallels with quietism as a reform movement within the Catholic Church in the southern Mediterranean. The Wesleys were directly influenced by Zinzendorf.

Plantinga, Alvin (b. 1932)

Plantinga writes as a first-rank analytical philosopher who is also a robust and explicit theist. With WOLTERSTORFF and with SWINBURNE, he is among those who have made an exceptionally important impact upon the debate about the rationality of THEISM and about warrants for theistic belief.

Plantinga (with Wolterstorff) is closely associated with what has been called 'Reformed epistemology', which questions the validity of NATURAL THEOLOGY, but does not thereby withdraw from discussions about warrants for Christian BELIEF. He taught from 1963 to 1987 at Calvin College, Grand Rapids, and from 1982 at the University of Notre Dame.

Some dozen books from Plantinga's pen mainly explore different avenues surrounding EPISTEMOLOGY, FOUNDATIONALISM and warranted belief, but also the problem of EVIL, the nature of God and the ONTOLOGICAL ARGUMENT for the existence of God, drawing on conceptual and logical tools which include those of MODAL LOGIC and 'possible' worlds.

RATIONALITY AND WARRANTED BELIEF

Plantinga's earliest book-length publications were *Faith and Philosophy* (Grand Rapids: Eerdmans, 1964) and (ed.) *The Ontological Argument* (New York: Doubleday, 1965). However, the direction of his most creative thinking on epistemology and theistic belief began to take shape in his *God and Other Minds: A Study of the Rational* (Ithaca: Cornell, 1967; also 1990).

It is difficult to set out a conclusive demonstration of the existence of other minds, but most of us consider such a belief to be eminently rational, almost as a 'pragmatic' but nevertheless rational belief. Yet, Plantinga argues, there are scarcely fewer factors that may be regarded as suggesting 'rational' belief in God, even though, like belief in other minds, this belief does not rest upon conclusive demonstration. If belief in other minds is rational, is not theistic belief also no less rational?

This approach coheres with Plantinga's conclusions in *God, Freedom and Evil* (New York: Harper, 1974, and Grand Rapids: Eerdmans, 1978) and *The Nature of Necessity* (New York: OUP, 1974, rpr. 1990). The appeal to modal logic as a counter-reply to objections to the ontological argument, as well as to defences of the 'best possible world' in the context of the problem of evil, yield not a knockdown conclusive demonstration of the existence of God and theistic responses to evil, but sufficiently compelling arguments to justify calling such theistic belief rational. It is rational rather than irrational, and probable rather than implausible.

In 1984 Plantinga published, jointly with WOLTERSTORFF (b. 1932), *Faith and Rationality: Reason and Belief in God* (Notre Dame: University of Notre Dame). This emphasized the point, already implicit in their work, that in the tradition of 'Reformed epistemology' neither natural theology (in a rationalist tradition) nor evidentialism (in an empiricist tradition) could provide a 'basic' foundation as the basis of which the validity of theistic belief could be demonstrated.

Plantinga developed this theme in his three-volume exploration of warrants for beliefs. The first volume (first delivered as the 1987 Gifford Lectures in the University of Aberdeen) was published under the title *Warrant: the Current Debate* (New York: OUP, 1993). What might accord to 'belief' the status of 'knowledge'? Plantinga examines and rejects, in turn, foundationalism; 'internal' warrants relating to the person of the believer; the epistemology of Roderick Chisholm; and issues of evidence. None of these epistemological approaches can provide conclusive warrant for theistic belief.

In his second volume, *Warrant and Proper Function* (New York: OUP, 1994, based on the Wilde Lectures at Oxford in 1988), Plantinga develops this theme further. If even coherence provides no conclusive demonstration, we reach the conclusion that theism stands on its own feet as a 'basic' belief (or one that does not rest upon arguments of a different kind as a condition for regarding theism as a properly warranted belief). This leads to the argument of the third volume of the trilogy, *Warranted Christian Belief* (New York: OUP, 1999).

BASICALITY AND FOUNDATIONALISM

In his earlier and middle periods Plantinga rejects the 'classical foundationalism' of the twin pillars of DESCARTES and LOCKE.

In relation to theism, it also appears odd (and theologically questionable) to suggest that belief in God is logically dependent for its justification or validity on the truth of other propositions within a humanly constructed system of epistemology.

By contrast, Plantinga insists that since 'God as conceived in traditional Christianity, Judaism, and Islam: an almighty, wholly good, and loving person who has created the world and presently upholds it', it makes rational sense to claim that 'belief in such a being is properly basic' ('Reformed epistemology'). However, if this is true, the objections of such anti-theists as Antony Flew and RUSSELL that theistic belief is irrational or unreasonable because there is not enough 'evidence' become open to question.

Plantinga exposes the lack of grounds for a 'deontological' (ethical) assumption behind evidentialism that a believer has a 'duty' to restrict belief only to that which is based in conclusive evidence, especially in the extreme form promoted by W.K. Clifford. Further, what kind of world and everyday reality must be postulated if we insist upon the non-existence of God? Are human persons merely part of nature? What day-to-day realities that we accept as realities through the network of assumptions that we live by now have to be placed on one side as equally 'irrational'?

WITTGENSTEIN alludes to what forms 'the scaffolding of our thoughts' as the background against which we count certain beliefs as rational or irrational, and arguably there is a partial parallel with Plantinga's common-sense appeal to how we form other beliefs that serve as markers and boundaries for life as well as for thought.

Perhaps the most controversial issue arises from Plantinga's attempt to offer criteria for the 'basicality' of beliefs. He writes: 'A proposition P is properly basic for a person S if and only if P is either self-evident to S or incorrigible to 'S' (first expounded in 'The Reformed Objection to

Natural Theology', *Christian Scholar's Review*, 11, 1982, 187–98; also in Plantinga and Wolterstorff, eds., *Faith and Rationality*; and most recently formulated in A. Plantinga, *Warranted Christian Belief*, New York and Oxford: OUP, 1998, 35–5, 175–7 and 345–53). For some, both 'to S' and 'incorrigible' raise difficulties.

Few other philosophers of religion, however, have explored the very central issues of philosophy of religion and theistic belief with such innovation, incisiveness and robust engagement with all comers. It is scarcely surprising that many regard him as one of the two or three most influential thinkers in this area. (*See also* EMPIRICISM; REASON; SOLIPSISM; REVELATION.)

Plato (428–348 BCE)

Plato was born in Athens into a distinguished family, and came strongly under the influence of SOCRATES (470–399 BCE). His earlier thoughts of a political career were abandoned for the pursuit of philosophy after the death of Socrates.

The medium of Plato's extant writings is that of dialogue. In the earliest dialogues it is difficult to distinguish between the voice of Socrates, who plays a leading role in the dialogues, and Plato's own views. Steadily, however, a distinctive Platonic philosophy emerges as we move through the middle and late dialogues.

The most characteristic feature of Plato's thought is a DUALISM of appearance and reality, of change and permanence, of opinion and knowledge, of body and soul, and of earthly 'copies' or 'images' and Forms or 'Ideas' (Greek, *eidos*) of which the world of sense yields mere copies, shadows or imperfect imitations.

OPINION AND KNOWLEDGE: IMAGES AND FORMS

It is entirely understandable that as a disciple of SOCRATES, Plato should see the task of philosophy as that of distinguishing between mere opinion (Greek, *doxa*) and true knowledge (*epistēmē*). 'The philosopher is always in love with knowledge of the unchanging' (*Republic*, book VI). For 'opinion' changes with the changing world; but 'knowledge' cannot deviate from what is established as true.

It is less far-fetched than might seem to be the case at first sight to attribute to the respective sources of the changing and unchanging their belonging to two different worlds. Everything within our own CONTINGENT, empirical world of change and decay falls short of perfection. Thus every circle that is drawn in a school classroom falls short of perfect circularity. Yet all can conceive of a perfect circle, with its exact geometrical and mathematical qualities.

In book VII of *The Republic*, Plato portrays people who live in a cave, in which they can face only away from the mouth, with a fire at their backs: 'They see nothing of themselves but their own shadows, or one another's ... The only real things for them would be the shadows.' Plato then compares the changing, imperfect, time-conditioned world of appearances with a 'higher' world of reality outside the cave. Thus 'the real world' is outside the cave; the realm of appearances is that of copies, shadows and images.

In his own more distinctive philosophy, Plato identifies the perfect realm of Forms with Beauty, Goodness and Truth. Human persons and objects in the everyday world approximate towards these ideals (or Ideas) to a greater or lesser degree. Geometrical figures approximate to true circularity or triangularity; expressions of opinion approximate towards knowledge of TRUTH; those deemed more or less beautiful approximate to perfect beauty to varying degrees. TIME is a 'moving image' of ETERNITY.

In the *Timaeus* the eternal One, as eternal God, is characterized by changeless Being. The 'World-Soul' is characterized by a process of Becoming and change. (To what extent the Forms or 'Ideas' (*eidos*) are independently actually ontological entities seems to vary in different writings at different dates.)

SOCIAL ETHICS AND THE SOUL

The Socratic questions 'What is virtue?', 'What is justice?' develop into 'Why is justice what it is?'; 'Why is virtue what it is?' Plato's theory of Forms suggests that justice is what it is because it derives its character from Justice as an Ideal Form. The abstract defines the particular. Since philosophers are most skilled in handling abstract UNIVERSALS, philosopher-statesmen in principle would be the most suited to guide and to lead a 'just' society or state. Humanity is otherwise chained, like those in the cave, to illusory opinions.

Plato firmly believes that the body (*sôma*) and soul (*psychē*) belong as two distinct entities respectively to the two orders of the phenomenal world of the empirical, and the true world of the real. The SOUL awaits release from the body.

In the *Republic* and in *Phaedo* the soul is portrayed as unchanging. Yet in the *Phaedrus* and in *Laws*, the immortality of the soul is grounded in the soul's capacity for self-motion. The weight of the contrast shifts from body-as-changing and soul-as-changeless to the body's having only derived motion, and the soul's providing its own motion.

The *Laws* presents a social philosophy or social ETHICS. Legislation ensures the good of all citizens, and education is essential. Truth is closely related to virtue, which includes courage, self-control and justice. Justice, however, sometimes has a technical meaning, namely balance of the 'parts' of the soul. *Aretē*, virtue, is closely related to the ideal of harmony in an 'ordered' society, in which person fulfils his or her proper function.

From the viewpoint of philosophy of religion perhaps the most important feature about Plato is his influence upon subsequent thinkers, and the difference of the direction of his thought from that of ARISTOTLE. Their respective understandings of the relation between universals and particulars offers one of several examples.

The greatest difficulty of Plato's legacy is caused by his dualism. HEIDEGGER speaks of the 'chasm' that split Western philosophy, while NIETZSCHE parodies Christianity as 'Platonism for the people'. In some Western religion traces of a world-denying dualism have proved difficult to eradicate. Judaism, Christianity and Islam all insist upon the fundamental goodness of the material world. Even if some Eastern religions are closer at this precise point (their view of matter) to Plato, few Eastern philosophies move in a dualist, rather than a monist, direction.

Plato's influence has extended far and wide. Within Western philosophical traditions, the Alexandrians Clement and Origen, and the Neoplatonists, including PLOTINUS, reflect this influence in the ancient world. The Cambridge Platonists of the seventeenth century, including Ralph Cudworth (1617–1688) who was broadly Neoplatonic, but sought to defend rational THEISM against HOBBES and SPINOZA, begin a series of those whom Plato influenced in the modern world. (*See also* ABSOLUTE; CREATION; GOD, ARGUMENTS FOR THE EXISTENCE OF; GOD, CONCEPTS AND 'ATTRIBUTES' OF; IDEALISM; IMMUTABILITY; NEOPLATONISM; NOMINALISM; REALISM.)

plenitude, principle of

This principle is formulated in more than one way. In PLOTINUS (205–70) and in NEOPLATONISM the differentiation of Forms is seen in terms of a series of levels, which give the universe its necessarily diverse character. Plotinus observes that 'the One' (God) exhibits a fullness or plenitude of superabundant productivity which thus characterizes 'the best of all possible worlds'.

AUGUSTINE endorses this view of 'rankings' within the world as a concomitant aspect of its fullness bestowed by God as Creator. 'Animals are ranked above trees ... Humankind above cattle ... these are the gradations according to the order of nature' (*City of God*, XI: 16). A world without form would be mere changing flux and chaos. God's gift of creation actualizes conceptual possibilities concretely in the diversity of the world. Black and white, light and shadow, exhibit a 'ranking' (*ordinatio*) among created entities (ibid., XI: 23).

Without such differentiation, richness, fullness or plenitude would be diminished, just as the rich harmony of a harmonic triad or a polyphonic chord would be diminished if only one single note could be sung or played. 'Good' is even 'richer' against the background of what is 'other'.

Thomas AQUINAS (1225–74) develops the same principle. 'The perfection of the universe requires that there should be inequality in things, so that every grade of goodness may be realized' (*Summa Theologiae* I, Qu. 48, art. 2). Thus creation is the work of the whole Trinity, to whom belongs 'a kind of order' (ibid., Qu. 45, art 6). 'God *divided* the day from the night' (Gen. 1:4) (ibid., Qu. 47, art. 1). Aquinas explicitly quotes Augustine's appeal to the model of the Creator as Divine Artist (ibid., art. 2).

In Augustine and in Aquinas this principle serves to expound themes not only about God and creation, but also about the origins of EVIL. Unevenness, difference, and inequality, which are necessary to the fullness of a good creation, can be misused as a pretext or catalyst for possible evil.

In SPINOZA, LEIBNIZ and modern RATIONALISM the principle of plenitude was taken to suggest that every genuine possibility is actualized. Everything that could exist has come, or will come, to exist unless there is sufficient reason that it should not exist.

Plotinus (*c.* 205–270)

Plotinus is the founder and leading figure of NEOPLATONISM. His pupil Porphyry (*c.* 233–304) collected and edited his substantial range of writings under the title *Enneads* (i.e. nine tractates in six volumes). He combines elements from PLATO (428–348 BCE), ARISTOTLE (384–322 BCE) and the STOICS. Plato's realm of Ideas is presided over by 'the One', who is beyond human thought and conceptual characterization.

The highest emanation of 'the One' is *Nous* (mind, intelligence), which occupies the place of Plato's realm of forms. The second-level emanation is the 'world-soul' of the Stoics. This then yields the world itself, the material 'body' of the world-soul. Thus Plato's DUALISM has been bridged, but his fundamental contrast between the perfect Forms and the CONTINGENT, empirical world remains the structure of Plotinus' thought.

Humankind is seen as both longing for the eternal realm and trapped within the body of matter. In this respect Plotinus has failed to expel a dualism of mind and body, even though he perceived his system as a unity. (*See also* MONISM.)

positivism

The origins of the term lie in the work of French social theorists who wished to restrict methods on the study of economics, politics and human social life to the methods of empirical or natural sciences. The term was popularized by Auguste Comte (1798–1858).

It seems, however, that Claude Henri Saint-Simon (1760–1826) introduced the term prior to Comte, to denote broadly the same meaning. Both writers rejected as illegitimate what went beyond 'observational', evidential, empirical criteria. The attitudes, as well as the methods, of sciences were to be applied to human affairs.

In common with SPENCER (1820–1903), Comte placed his philosophy and

ETHICS within a materialist evolutionary framework. Societies necessarily pass through a metaphysical or theological stage, when extraneous causes are postulated for what is not yet scientifically understood. But they are on the way to a positive, scientific stage of valid explanations.

Comte's lectures on 'Positivism' were delivered in 1826. Over the next century other uses of 'positivism' emerged, included a use by SCHELLING quite different from Comte's. But by the 1920s the term resumed its tightly empiricist, evidential, observational dimensions with the emergence of the VIENNA CIRCLE and LOGICAL POSITIVISM. AYER's criterion of verification (or more strictly, verifiability) comes close to Comte's concerns, although without his evolutionary hypothesis. (*See also* BEHAVIOURISM; EMPIRICISM; MATERIALISM; METAPHYSICS; SCIENCE AND RELIGION.)

possibility

This term has a variety of technical nuances in philosophy, but perhaps three or four carry particular significance for philosophy of religion.

First, logical possibility must be distinguished from real, CONTINGENT, empirical or actual possibility. Often in the English language the weight of this distinction may be lost through the use of the innocent-looking word 'can'. 'Can God lie?' marks the issue of whether for God to lie would constitute a logical contradiction with God's nature or stated promise to be true and faithful. 'God cannot ...' frequently denotes logical, rather than actual, limitations, imposed by God's own decision to act self-consistently, or 'rationally'.

Second, ARISTOTLE (384–322 BCE) drew a fundamental distinction between 'substance' (*ousia*) as 'that which is', namely form, and potentiality, the power to become, which resides in matter. To actualize the possible or potential requires

a 'mover', or ultimately a Prime Mover. This gives rise to the kinetological argument in the FIVE WAYS of AQUINAS, and influenced the thought of the medieval Islamic philosophers.

Third, LEIBNIZ (1646–1716) argued that the eternal mind of God contains ideas of an infinite number of possible worlds that God might have created. In actualizing a world in creation, God chose 'the best possible world', which he created. These 'alternative' worlds are coherent in themselves as 'possible worlds', or possible totalities of finite things.

This principle has been explored and developed almost in a fourth sense in MODAL LOGIC. PLANTINGA (following Leibniz) uses it strikingly to explore the problem of EVIL. As Saul Kripke shows, 'possible worlds' may provide models for understanding problematic concepts. A logically NECESSARY TRUTH is true in all possible worlds. (*See also* ETERNITY; GOD, ARGUMENTS FOR THE EXISTENCE OF; ISLAMIC PHILOSOPHY; LOGIC; ONTOLOGICAL ARGUMENT.)

postmodernity, postmodernism

Postmodernity has been defined in a large variety of ways. Richard Bernstein calls it 'a rage against humanism and the ENLIGHTENMENT legacy' (Bernstein, ed., *Habermas and Modernity*, Cambridge: Polity Press, 1985, 1–34). Norman Denzin argues that it signals a loss of trust in the capacity of the SELF to control its destiny, with concomitant byproducts of 'anger, alienation, anxiety ... racism and sexism' (*Images of Postmodern Society*, London: Sage, 1991, vii).

Probably the most widely known, although perhaps not best understood, definition is that of the French postmodernist philosopher LYOTARD (b. 1924): 'I define *postmodern* as incredulity towards metanarratives' (*The Postmodern Condition*, Minneapolis: University of Minnesota, 1984, xxiv).

'Metanarratives' are 'narratives' of an overarching view that attempt to explain the meaning of other more 'local' narratives. Thus if Judaism, Christianity or Islam attempts to offer a 'grand' narrative of God's dealings with the world which provides a frame of reference for understanding 'local' (e.g. personal or community) stories of guilt, suffering, redemption, love, joy, folly or whatever, this falls under suspicion as an imperializing instrument for power that is in actuality no less 'local', but purports to be the story of the world, an ONTOLOGY or an EPISTEMOLOGY. The particularities of social forces 'throw' us (to borrow HEIDEGGER's word) into pre-given finite 'situatedness' within prior worlds of meaning. The epistemological SUBJECT of traditional philosophy is no longer an active, 'innocent', observer, but already a victim of the socio-economic forces and 'interests' that predetermine the limits of this human subject.

THE BACKGROUND TO
POSTMODERNITY: SUSPICION OF
THE SELF, KNOWLEDGE AND LOGIC
The earlier influence of the 'Masters of Suspicion' NIETZSCHE (1844–1900) and FREUD (1856–1939) will be apparent. Nietzsche saw most of the 'narrative' of RELIGION and philosophy as projection of disguised power-interests. The phenomenon of guilt and confession, for example, serves the interests of the priesthood to control the people. Marx (1818–83) shared such suspicion, but Marxism is itself a 'grand narrative' and 'metanarrative', and is therefore in that respect a child of 'modernity', not of postmodernity (see MARXIST CRITIQUE OF RELIGION).

Freud played his part in diminishing the epistemological role of the human subject. The human agent is not 'innocent', but brings illusion and self-deception to the epistemological task. The self is, rather, a 'role' within a mechanistic system of 'forces'.

Heidegger (1889–1976) plays a less direct role than Nietzsche and Freud.

Nevertheless, he urges the radical historical finitude of human beings as *Dasein*, being-there, where prior forces of history have 'thrown' them. Their horizons are shaped by the place in which history has placed them, and by the practical concerns of the projects that lie to hand.

Although in other cultural contexts the dating of the rise of postmodernity may be different, for philosophy and religion the work of Roland Barthes (1915–80) in the 1950s and of DERRIDA (b. 1930) and FOUCAULT (1926–84) in the 1960s marks a turning-point away from 'modernity'. No less than three of Derrida's major works were published in 1967: *Of Grammatology*, *Writing and Difference* and *Speech and Phenomena*.

Derrida explicitly recognizes the influence of Nietzsche, Freud and Heidegger as three of his four main sources, adding also Husserl. The attack on the primacy of human consciousness and thought as subject to deception, manipulation and distortion, and as radically historically conditioned, seemed to demolish not only the rationalist, subject-centred epistemology of DESCARTES, but also the CRITICAL PHILOSOPHY of KANT. Both Descartes and Kant stand, in different ways, as models of high 'modernity'.

In place of the 'Speaking Subject', Derrida fills the stage with the shifting sign-system in which the human person becomes less an active agent or subject than a role. Even the traditional distinction or differentiations of LOGIC are 'deconstructed' in a process of 'de-centring' the word as 'presence'. Language is placed 'under erasure'.

THE 'MYTHOLOGY' OF GRAND
NARRATIVES AND FRAGMENTATION
INTO PLURALITY
Derrida shares Nietzsche's view that Western METAPHYSICS rests upon treating 'a mobile army of METAPHORS' as a definitive body of TRUTH. In practice, it is an illusion that needs to be exposed as MYTH. There is no stable world-view that may claim any

privilege over others. The whole tradition of Western philosophy must be dismantled and 're-read' in the light of historical and social relativity. Derrida expounds this theme in 'White Mythology: Metaphor in the Text of Philosophy' in his *Margins of Philosophy* (New York and London: Harvester Wheatsheaf, 1982).

To Barthes and Derrida must be added the name of Foucault. He also displaced the human subject from the central role that it played in humanism and in modernity since the Enlightenment. Systems of thought are CONTINGENT, and relative to a changing history of social situatedness. The works of Foucault are discussed in the entry under his name.

In the entries on PRAGMATISM and RORTY, the focus on the pluralist, local and 'ethnocentric' emerges clearly, especially in the work of Rorty (b. 1931). Postmodernity finds a fertile soil in America, where a pragmatic tradition which elevates 'effects', 'success', 'progress' and 'flourishing' is linked with consumerist notions of free-market pluralism and choice by consumer preference.

American postmodernity is altogether more optimistic than that of France, for it appears to cohere with progressivism and to remove potential conflicts between local sub-traditions by making none 'more "right"' than others.

Nevertheless in the entry on pragmatism, more sinister implications concerning pseudo-tolerance come to light. Once truth is 'made' rather than discovered, what cannot be done in the name of socially constructed truth? There is also a false appeal to the notion of INCOMMEN-SURABILITY, which has a special meaning in the philosophy of science not wholly compatible with Rorty's appeal to the earlier work of Kuhn.

It now becomes clear in what sense David Harvey's characterization of postmodernity is accurate. He perceives it as a reaction against 'the standardization of knowledge' generated by a naïve privileging of science; but, in turn, replaced by

'fragmentation, indeterminacy and intense distrust of all universal or "totalizing" discourse' (*The Condition of Postmodernity*, Oxford: Blackwell, 1989, 9).

Harvey also links this mood with the recovery of pragmatism, and with Foucault's emphasis on discontinuities in history. Further, there is a tendency to see all reality not only as socially constructed, but as virtual reality constructed by arbitrary, distorting or manipulative uses of signs. Such a philosophy (if philosophy it is) coheres well with the era of computer simulation and programmed 'worlds'.

Naturalistic versions of postmodernity verge on replacing philosophy and epistemology by the study of social history, including studies of class, race and gender. Does 'rationality' transcend these boundaries, or is it constructed by them? Religious versions of the post-modern may readily collapse into FIDEISM. This may generate an illusory sense of freedom from pressure to argue for reasonable BELIEF, but a heavy price has to be paid. (*See also* RATIONALISM; REASON; SCIENCE AND RELIGION.)

post-mortal existence of the self

Philosophical arguments about the post-mortal existence of the SELF are usually considered under the heading 'the immortality of the SOUL'. However, on one side anti-theist writers such as Antony Flew question the possibility of the post-mortal survival of the self on the ground that 'soul' is a meaningless designation of the self. On the other side, many theologians in the Jewish, Christian and Islamic traditions insist that these traditions await not the immortality of the soul but the RESURRECTION of the self into a fuller, transformed mode of existence.

In several Eastern traditions the hope of what event or change will occur at death may take the form of release (*moksha*) of the self from a repeated cycle of existence and reincarnation into either yet another form of existence, or release from 'existence' altogether. The Advaita (non-dualist) Vedanta tradition of HINDU PHILOSOPHY represented by Śaṅkārā looks for the explicit assimilation of the self (*ātman*) into *brāhman*, or Ultimate Reality, which has been hidden by illusion (*māyā*). This might not be conveyed entirely easily by language about the 'soul' (although *see* the entry on the SOUL).

In Western traditions, especially those of Judaeo-Christian thought, two philosophical problems may be distinguished from each other. First, the issue of post-mortal existence raises the problem of credibility. How can we believe in that which (by definition) lies beyond the boundaries of evidences drawn from daily life? Second, can the notion of such existence retain intelligibility? What does it mean to speak of post-mortal existence?

The incisive objections of Antony Flew bring these two together. He writes, 'Unless I am my soul, the immortality of my soul will not be my immortality; and the news of the immortality of my soul would be of no more concern to me than the news that my appendix would be preserved eternally in a bottle' (Flew, 'Death', in A. Flew and A. MacIntyre, eds., *New Essays in Philosophical Theology*, London: SCM, 1955, 270).

THE CREDIBILITY OF THE NOTION: WHAT KIND OF EVIDENCE WOULD COUNT?

The objection that once a self is dissolved in death nothing can count as evidence of the survival is, at best, double-edged. For some, death is 'not an event in life' (Wittgenstein, *Tractatus*, 6–4311). In other words we do not live to 'experience' death (only the process of dying); we simply reach an end. If death destroys the self, no evidence of its survival can exist A PRIORI.

Nevertheless, this argument can be turned on its head to yield the opposite conclusion. If even the possibility of empirical this-worldly evidence is

excluded *a priori*, why should the absence of such evidence be said to confirm or to strengthen disbelief in post-mortal existence? It is as much up to the sceptic as to the believer to specify what kind of evidence would support their view. It may be argued that the denial of post-mortal existence is neither verifiable nor falsifiable (*see* AYER, FALSIFIABILITY; LOGICAL POSITIVISM; SCEPTICISM).

Admittedly some (notably Paul Badham) appeal to evidence of a quasi-empirical kind in terms of 'near-death' experiences. Such evidence is often anecdotal, but is also often replicated. People report an experience of lying on their death-beds when they perceive themselves as somehow leaving the body, looking at it as if from above or from elsewhere, and eventually 'returning'.

Even if such accounts can be corroborated, however, would this be a strictly post-mortal experience? On the admission of many who appeal to it, it is often described as 'near'-death experience. Within the framework of a theology of resurrection, this would, at best, not be resurrection but mere restoration to continuing life in an earthly, this-worldly, body. Such narratives as the 'raising' of Lazarus in John 11:1–44 do not recount resurrection, but a parable of resurrection, since Lazarus in the narrative returns to life under this-worldly conditions, presumably to 'die' again in due course.

The Christian tradition, especially the Pauline writings, couple the probability of belief in the resurrection of the dead with the nature of belief in the Creator God and divine promise. Logically, Paul argues, belief in the God who has the power to design modes of being for every kind of environment entails the view that such a God would readily have the power and resourcefulness to create modes of being appropriate to a post-mortal resurrection order of being (1 Corinthians 15:35–49). For Paul, the credibility and intelligibility of belief in the resurrection of the dead hinges on whether 'some people have

[knowledge or] no knowledge of *God*
(15:34).

In earliest pre-Pauline Christian traditions (1 Cor. 15:3–5, well before 51 CE)
the transmissions of a corporate testimony
to the death, burial and resurrection of
Christ were perceived to be the fundamental basis for belief in the resurrection
of the dead, alongside belief in the God
who performs promise.

Among sophisticated modern theologians who expound this dual logic, special
mention may be made of MOLTMANN (b.
1926) and PANNENBERG (b. 1928).
Although some theologians had relegated
the tradition of the empty tomb to later
sources, Pannenberg largely re-established
its fundamental importance for the credibility of the earliest Christian preaching,
while Moltmann established the basic
importance of hope and promise as key
theological themes.

THE INTELLIGIBILITY OF POST-MORTAL TRANSFORMATION AND CONTINUATION OF THE SELF

H.H. Price explored the intelligibility of
the notion of post-mortal existence
through a common-sense appeal to the
role of imagination. If only physical modes
of existence are intelligible, how do we
come to imagine and to 'image' what
might be beyond sense-perception? ('Survival and the Idea of Another World',
*Proceedings of the Society for Psychical
Research*, 50, 1953, 1–25).

We experience concepts that may perform the 'same function as sense-perception performs now by providing us with
objects about which we could have
thoughts, emotions, wishes'. The notion
that we are 'alive' only in the body
confuses 'life' with 'bodily experiences'.
Is it more logically compelling to conceive
of all experience as 'body-dependent'
rather than as 'mind-dependent'?

The biggest question raised by the
present subject, however, concerns continuity of the identity of the self if the self
survives after death. Many have been
distracted by unconvincing or flawed
accounts of personal identity.

PLATO (428–348 BCE) saw the 'soul' as
the seat of permanence, and the body as
bound up with change. Hence stability or
continuity of identity remain dependent
on the soul, while such bodily conditions
as illness, ageing, damage or loss of body-
parts are irrelevant to the identity of the
self.

SOCRATES believed that the unity and
ETERNITY of the soul entail its immortal,
infinitely extended existence. On the other
hand, the STOICS associated the soul with
universal REASON, which is not a fully
personal identity.

LOCKE (1632–1704) attempted to compare notions of personal identity that
depend respectively on the criterion of
'the same body' and the criterion of
'internal memory'. His parable of the
cobbler-prince, in which each awakes in
the body of the other, appears to favour
the criterion of memory, demonstrated
through patterns of action which draw
on this memory. However, Locke fails to
solve the problem, and even he has
hesitations about both 'solutions'.

RICOEUR (b. 1913) more convincingly
calls attention to the categories of responsibility, entitlement and accountability. A
young man may begin to invest for a
personal pension. However radically his
character or physical appearance may
change, it is he who is entitled to draw
the pension that results from his sustained
agency. This entirely coheres with Christian eschatology, in which destiny is
closely related to earlier attitudes and
action.

Equally to the point, in contrast to the
philosophical traditions from Plato to
Locke, since SCHLEIERMACHER, HEGEL
and SCHELLING, selfhood has been seen
increasingly as a matter of intersubjectiv-
ity, i.e. how the self relates to an Other.
This coheres well with the notion of a
resurrection community rather than a lone
surviving 'soul', or absorption into the
'All'. It allows for an understanding of

personal identity in a transformed mode of existence in encounter with others.

While memory does not adequately sustain such continuity in abstraction from these inter-subjective factors (for example accountability), as a presupposition for COGNITION rather than mere perception, this concept has a part to play. Thus, against HUME's notion that the self is a mere bundle of perceptions, C.A. Campbell points out that we do not construe the striking of a clock at nine o'clock as merely a nine-fold replication of the single chime that would signify one o'clock. The self, by its very nature, embraces continuity and succession.

It is thus not self-contradictory to conceive of a continuity of personal identity that reaches through death to a transformed and different mode of existence, which nevertheless remains the 'same' self. Indeed Paul the Apostle brings together judgement, resurrection and forgiveness of past sin with the infinite resourcefulness of God as Creator of diversity and difference (1 Corinthians 15).

In philosophical terms these considerations serve to elucidate the coherence and intelligibility of belief in the post-mortal survival and transformation of the self. Whether such ideas are also *credible* is closely liked with a view of the nature of God and of the currency of divine 'promise'. It may be acknowledged that the mere wish for post-mortal existence is not an argument for its basis.

EASTERN THOUGHT: RELEASE (*MOKSHA*), NIRVANA, OR RE-INCARNATION?

The hope concerning what change may occur at or after death takes a variety of forms in different Eastern traditions. Sub-traditions within both Hindu philosophy and BUDDHIST PHILOSOPHY also vary respectively. All the same, a core belief in most Eastern philosophies associates suffering and pain with existence in the material body, and hopes for some form of release (*moksha*) from the body, or even for release from any differentiated identity on the part of the self. Such hopes may be found in certain traditions of thought in both Hindu and Buddhist philosophies.

In the non-dualist Advaita Vedanta school of Śaṅkārā the self (*ātman*), which is separated from the All of Ultimate Reality (*brāhman*) only by illusion (*māyā*) looks for full assimilation into undifferentiated consciousness (*nirguna brāhma*). By contrast, in MADHVA's dualist (Dvaita) Vedanta tradition release (*moksha*) may be into a heavenly realm of bliss, an abode of happy souls (*jīva*).

In Buddhist and Zen traditions the nature of nirvana also takes different forms. In early Buddhist thought and often in more popular thought it denotes a state of 'awakening' or 'enlightenment' into unclouded perception, but in NĀGĀRJUNA (*c.* 150–200) any attempt to define a return to reality can be expressed only in terms of negation.

Some concepts of *karma* are linked with a 'timeless' ONTOLOGY with the result that in principle cycles of reincarnation might be endless, like the turning of a wheel. On the other hand, some traditions imply that this cycle is without beginning but not necessarily without end. This carrying forward of the consequences of good and bad actions into the next mode of existence (*karma*) is a characteristically Indian mode of thought.

It is arguable that this stands as far as possible conceptually from the Christian connection of 'internal logical grammar' in which justification by pure GRACE and resurrection by divine favour belong together to the discourse of sheer unmerited gift. (*See also* DUALISM; SCIENCE AND RELIGION; ZEN; ZOROASTRIANISM.)

postulate

The term generally denotes a proposition which is laid down as the starting-point of an argument or an enquiry. It is weaker than an AXIOM, but is laid down as working a BELIEF. It does not require demonstration for the purposes of the exploration that follows.

ARISTOTLE (384–322 BCE) identified a family of terms that may initiate debate in different ways: axiom, hypothesis, DEFINITION, postulate. He viewed postulates as capable of demonstration, but as not requiring demonstration within the enquiry that they initiate as postulates. KANT (1724–1804) used the term more loosely. Postulates, he argued, are not necessarily capable of demonstration, but are not laid down without good reason. For Kant, God, freedom and immortality are 'postulates' of practical reason. This takes us close to the original Latin behind the English word as conveying some such meaning as 'requirement' or 'demand'.

pragmatism

Pragmatism denotes the BELIEF that 'TRUTH' is validated or justified in so far as it proves to be useful in relation to the criteria of a community or communities. 'Results' determine what is counted as true.

This unavoidably relativizes what is accepted as true, since what counts as 'useful', 'successful' or productive is likely to vary over time. Since it will also vary from community to community, one of its major advocates, RORTY (b. 1931) prefers to speak of 'local' criteria rather than 'relativism'.

In practice, advocates of pragmatism prefer not to use the words 'true' and 'false' except in certain contexts. For the recognition that what an earlier generation regarded as 'true' may be overtaken by new agendas and new criteria of usefulness may be said to render the earlier view 'obsolete' rather than 'false'.

As a philosophical tradition pragmatism remains distinctively rooted in American philosophy. It traces its roots especially to Charles S. Peirce (1839–1914), William James (1842–1910) and John Dewey (1859–1952). Recent exponents

of American pragmatism include Hilary Putnam and especially Rorty. Robert Corrington relates the movement to a distinctive American HERMENEUTIC of 'effects' in contrast to 'givens'.

THE PRAGMATISM OF PEIRCE, JAMES AND DEWEY

The earlier work of Peirce reflects a different emphasis from his later work. He introduced the term 'pragmatism' in 1878 primarily as a theory which defined meaning in terms of practical consequences. In a later essay, 'What Pragmatism Is' (*The Monist*, 15, 1905, 161–81, rpr. in *Collected Papers of Charles Sanders Peirce*, 6 vols., Cambridge, MA: Harvard, 1931–5, vol. 5) he shifted the emphasis to a philosophy of action.

The earlier work on meaning depicted meaning in terms of what, so to speak, it might buy as cash-currency. There are no 'givens' except linguistic signs and human behaviour. In his later work Peirce expresses concern about how his work has been understood, and makes it clear that (*pace* Rorty) his 'pragmaticism' (as he now calls it) does not replace all questions of EPISTEMOLOGY, but expands them.

It was largely through James that the pragmatism of Peirce became known to a wider public, although Peirce held strong reservations about the version of pragmatism promoted by James. This reservation lay behind his renaming his own thought 'pragmaticism'. James's major work was *The Principles of Psychology* (1890); but his essay 'The Will to Believe' (1897) stresses the need to take risks in matters of BELIEF, and his *Varieties of Religious Experience* appeared in 1901–2.

James's *Pragmatism* (1907) conceded that, in effect, pragmatism 'makes' rather than 'discovers' TRUTH. 'Truth ... *becomes* true; it is *made* true by events.' 'Reality' is 'malleable', for humankind shapes it in terms of what proves to be the case, or proves to be true. 'The true is the name of whatever proves itself to be good in the way of belief' (*Pragmatism* and the Meaning of Truth, Cambridge, MA: Harvard, 1975, 42). Such claims were highly controversial and met with strong protest at the time, especially from British thinkers.

Dewey addressed a range of issues and areas in philosophy, but all in relation to human life and activity. He was interested in the progress of the sciences, and his concerns combined a background of naturalism, progressivism and instrumentalism or functionalism. Rorty observes, 'Dewey anticipated Habermas by claiming that there is nothing to the notion of OBJECTIVITY save that of inter-subjective arrgreement' (Truth and Progress, Cambridge: CUP, 1998, 6–7). Rorty sums up Dewey's view of truth as: 'Truth as what works is the theory of truth it now pays us to have' (ibid., 305).

Dewey's The Theory of Inquiry (1938) well reflects the American culture of the era of progressivism, optimism and consumerism. Inquiry addresses practical problems of science, politics and ETHICS, and serves to create satisfaction, advantages, goods and solutions. Older 'theories' of truth were distractions from the business of practical 'progress' and 'success'.

POSTMODERN NEOPRAGMATISM: RICHARD RORTY

Rorty traces bridges between James and Dewey and his own thinking through Wilfrid Sellars (1912–89) and Hilary Putnam (b. 1926). Sellars attacked what he called 'the myth of the given', and promoted a naturalism that bordered on a linguistic version of BEHAVIOURISM. Rorty states, 'Sellars' attack on the Myth of the Given seemed to me to render doubtful the assumptions behind most of modern philosophy' (Philosophy and the Mirror of Nature, Princeton: Princeton University Press, 1979, xiii).

Putnam also queries whether traditional notions of 'warranted assertible truth-claims' can be sustained. Truth, in the end, can denote only inter-subjective consensus on the part of communities.

Unfortunately Rorty's Philosophy and the Mirror of Nature lists a very large number of 'allies' who, in his own particular 'reading' of them, lead cumulatively to his own view: WITTGENSTEIN, HEIDEGGER, Sellars, Quine, Davidson, RYLE, MALCOLM and Kuhn, as well as Peirce, James, Dewey and Putnam. Much depends on how these thinkers are 'read'.

The final two chapters of this work question the viability of epistemology as 'a way of knowing'; all that we can hope for is to use philosophy (he uses the term 'hermeneutics' in a particular way) as 'a way of coping' (ibid., 356).

Rorty attacks 'representational' views of language, and reformulates truth as an issue of 'justification', or more strictly as what a democratic liberal society or local ('ethnocentric') community accepts as a justification. Theories of truth that involve METAPHYSICS, ONTOLOGY or trans-contextual epistemology are candidates for the 'rubbish-disposal projects' of American pragmatism (Truth and Progress: Philosophical Papers, Cambridge: CUP, vol. 3, 1998, 10).

With NIETZSCHE, Rorty believes that 'what is believed to be true' has the 'highest importance'; while 'what is true' remains a matter of indifference (Nietzsche, The Antichrist, London: Penguin, 1990, aphorisms 13, 23). For 'justification is always relative to an audience' (Truth and Progress, 4). 'Truth is not a goal of inquiry' (ibid., 6). Ethics now becomes a matter of raw consequentialism; in the end, of "preference'.

Rorty's engagement with the postmodern emerges most clearly in his recognition that if 'communities' have become the arbiters of what counts as 'true', this varies from community to community. Hence he combines pragmatism with an emphasis on the 'local', or 'ethnocentric'. 'I have tried to sketch the connections between antirepresentationalism, ethnocentrism, and the virtues of the socio-political culture of the liberal democracies' (Objectivity, Relativity and Truth, Cambridge: CUP, 1991, 16). All of this, he adds, stands in continuity with Dewey.

Space prohibits counter-arguments here, although we may wonder whether Rorty's grand programme of 'rubbish-disposal' may look in twenty years' time like the proposals of AYER about removing 'nonsense' twenty years after *Language, Truth and Logic.*

Much stems from the particular culture of 'success', 'winners' and consumerism, in some strands of liberal American culture. Ironically what appears to be a tolerant pluralism has no ethical structures to avoid 'preferences' in which in the strongest community 'might is right'. As Christopher Norris and Cornel West point out, under the pluralist surface lies a potentially authoritarian philosophy, which permits whatever a 'strong' group wishes to be defined as 'truth and progress'. (*See also* POSTMODERNITY.)

prayer

PRAYER AS ADDRESS: VARIED TYPES OF ADDRESS

In the broadest sense of the term, prayer is indispensable in religions that conceive of God in personal (or supra-personal) terms, especially in Judaism, Christianity and Islam. For, to borrow BUBER's language, if a relationship with God is conceived of as an I–Thou or I–You relationship (not merely as an I–It relationship) address from God to human persons and address from human persons to God take centre-stage in a personal relationship with God.

Address to God may take numerous forms: praise, confession, worship, adoration, thanksgiving, confession, lament, complaint; request and intercession represent only two of ten selected modes of address. Prayer in its highest sense is prompted not only by desires for benefit or blessings, but by desire for God as God. In many sacred writings this desire is ascribed to the action of God's own Spirit, who brings this desire to prayerful speech (e.g. Rom. 8:15; Gal. 4:6).

Logically, however, if it is the Spirit of God who prompts prayer, the desires that are articulated include especially God's own desires for the world, implanted in the human heart by God's Spirit. Hence prayer cannot but include the expression of a loving and caring concern for others and for the world, which we call inter-cessory prayer on their behalf.

Those religions that give a serious place to human fallenness and sin necessarily recognize the role not only of confession or acts of repentance, but also a longing for a higher and better state. The Hebrew–Jewish Psalms express such longing repeatedly: 'As a deer longs for flowing streams, so my soul longs for you, O God' (Ps. 42:1).

PRAYER AS 'THERAPEUTIC MEDITATION' OR AS 'SHARING GOD'S PROVIDENTIAL ACTION'?

Philosophical questions arise when we begin to ask whether the expression of such longings constitutes more than religious or therapeutic self-adjustment through thought or thought and language. KANT saw prayer as 'conversing ... really with oneself' if this denotes the prayer of 'purely rational faith' (*reiner Vernunftglaube* (*Religion within the Limits of Reason*, Eng., New York, 1960, 185). This understanding of prayer he saw as rationally acceptable. However, he viewed the 'churchly faith (*Kirchen-glaube*)' view of prayer, in which prayer was thought to invite changes of states of affairs within the world, as a 'super-stitious illusion'.

In Kant's philosophical system this view is entailed by his belief that God does not act 'within' the supposed causal network of events that we call 'the world'. Indeed the very notion of CAUSE and effect is a merely regulative principle in terms of which the human mind seeks to understand the world as 'ordered'. D.Z. Phillips stresses the importance of self-adjustment in prayer (*The Concept of Prayer*, London: Routledge, 1965, 63, 64).

If Kant is right, however, the constantly recurring address 'Thou' or 'You' becomes a merely fictive device for focusing meditation and self-adjustment. Vincent Brümmer argues that its use would be not only illusory but also logically self-contradictory and a denial of much religious experience (*What Are we Doing When we Pray? A Philosophical Enquiry*, London: SCM, 1984, 16–28). What is at issue, Brümmer argues, is quite simply whether it makes sense to conceive of God as a personal agent.

Several of Brümmer's works explicitly argue for this view of divine personal agency (e.g. *Speaking of a Personal God*, Cambridge: CUP, 1992; *The Model of Love*, Cambridge: CUP, 1993). It is no accident that for Kant notions of God turn on issues of reason and law, whereas Brümmer sees love as standing at the heart of a mutual, reciprocal relationship between God and humankind. Hence prayer not only expresses the adoration and desires of love, but also leads to events that enhance its experience.

God chooses to act, Brümmer argues, within a context of mutual concern, of which the very act of asking provides evidence. Indeed, 'intercession is a prayer in which the person who prays both asks God to act on behalf of the [other] person … and *also* makes himself available as a secondary cause through whom God could act in answering the prayer' (*What Are we Doing When we Pray?* 57). Prayer is sharing God's providential action within the world.

WHY PRAY TO AN OMNISCIENT, ALL-WISE, ALL-LOVING GOD?

If God already knows the needs of humankind, and if God already wills the best for humankind, why is prayer necessary or appropriate? Is it not self-contradictory to call God omniscient and to tell God of our needs? Is it not an affront to ask God to act in goodness when God is already all-loving? If God is all-wise and all-good, will not God give without our asking? Edgar Brightman voiced the criticism that petition may seem to imply that we request God to 'improve'.

First, some kinds of prayers may perhaps fall into this category. These are the kinds of prayers discussed below under ethical objections and the problem of manipulative prayers.

Second, if God inspires the articulation of prayer and longing through God's own Spirit, as Brümmer argues (above) prayer may be understood as a co-sharing in seeking the good of the world (*What Are we Doing When we Pray*, chs. 5–7, 60–113). If, then, God seeks 'the best possible for the world', 'the best possible' is not a fixed A PRIORI quantity. In Brightman's words, 'The best possible when men pray is better than the best possible when men do not pray' (*A Philosophy of Religion*, London: Skeffington, n.d., 236).

Hence human self-involvement and shared concern for God's reign and for the well-being of others becomes a necessary constituent in what God wills as 'the best'. Brightman alludes to the role of 'a praying community who sighs and yearns with the yearning compassion of the heart of his (and our) world' (ibid., 237). This lies behind injunctions to pray in all the great theistic religions. God's Spirit places a 'divine discontent' within, which prayer articulates (cf. Rom. 8:15–16, 22–7).

ETHICAL OBJECTIONS TO PETITIONARY AND INTERCESSORY PRAYER

It has long been urged that prayer may be used to try to impose subjective notions of good and evil, prompted by self-interest, onto the governance of the world. HOBBES (1588–1679) declared, 'Every man calleth that which pleaseth "good"; and that "evil" which displeaseth him' (*Human Nature*, 1650, VII: 3). More sharply, NIETZSCHE (1844–1900) saw religion, including prayer, as a manipulative device employed to secure power: 'The "salvation of the soul" in plain English [German] "the world revolves around me"' (*The*

Antichrist, in *Complete Works*, 18 vols., London: Allen & Unwin, 1909–13, vol. 16, 186, aphorism 43). God, it is argued, is transposed into a means to achieve the ends of one who prays.

It is easier to apply this criticism to certain petitionary prayers for the self than to intercessory prayers for others. Nevertheless, even prayer for others can be 'loaded' to serve either self-interest or fallible misjudgements, and in triumphalist religion prayer for power, money, possessions – 'success' in various forms – has occurred from the Magical Papyri of the ancient Hellenistic mystery religions to sectarian religions (often associated with commercial media) today.

A prayer is selfish, however, only if, in Brightman's phrase, 'it seeks to take a benefit from another or to exclude another from a benefit'. Ethical objections do not address authentic prayer, prompted by God or by desires implanted by God's Spirit. They address only the abuse of prayer for self-centred or manipulative ends. It may be that this criticism implies a warning against undue specificity in precisely defining in human terms what we seek from God.

Finally, the claim that placing issues in the hands of God weakens moral effort runs counter to the public findings of the varied phenomena of religions. To claim, for example, that Jesus, Paul the Apostle, AUGUSTINE or Luther diminished moral effort because they placed everything in the hands of God runs counter to the transparent facts of the matter. Examples could be multiplied from other religions also.

PRAYER AND DIVINE ACTION IN THE WORLD

We noted above that Kant dismissed 'ecclesial prayer' (i.e. that which churchpeople 'superstitiously' think will contribute change within the world) because his view of God as 'outside' the world could not accommodate it. 'Rational' prayer, Kant believed, consisted primarily in self-adjustment through meditation. We noted

issues of logic, personhood and address which such a view bypasses or contradicts.

The issue turns on different understandings of divine action. Keith Ward convincingly argues that even as Creator of a billion galaxies whose reality we cannot fully grasp, God nevertheless relates to humans 'by knowledge, feeling and will … by complete empathy' and also through divine action (*Divine Action*, London: Collins, 1990, 155). The vastness of the universe and the mysterious TRANSCENDENCE of God, far from disengaging divine action from the world, suggest that such a transcendent, intricate mind comprehends every detail of the created universe (cf. Mt. 6:25–32).

The notion that God acts in the world only by 'suspending' so-called laws of nature rests on a mechanistic model of the universe as a 'closed' system. Keith Ward examines the inadequacy and dated status of such an approach in his chapter 'The Death of a Closed Universe' (*Divine Action*, ch. 5). Technical scientific support that defends notions concerning the plasticity of a post-Newtonian, post-Einsteinian universe can be found in Arthur R. Peacocke, *Creation and the World of Science* (Oxford: Clarendon, 1979).

If 'laws of nature' are prescriptive rather than descriptive, as Boyce Gibson observes, 'Nothing that ever happens only once or for the first time … can ever be caused or a cause' (*Theism and Empiricism*, London: SCM, 1970, 149). PANNENBERG applies this principle to the event of the RESURRECTION of Jesus Christ, which is normally held to be definitive for Christian belief. Even the classical premodern theologians (e.g. Augustine and Thomas AQUINAS) insisted that divine action within the world is not 'contrary to nature' (*contra naturam*) but utilizes natural regularities to work 'through nature' (*per naturam*).

PRAYER AND SPEECH-ACTS

The personal dimension of I–Thou address provides the overarching context in which prayer may be understood as embracing a multitude of functions, e.g. praise, thanksgiving, confession, petition, intercession, meditation, lament, expressions of longing. The problem of divine OMNISCIENCE not only involves problems and counter-replies identified above, but is also seen in a new light when the concept of SPEECH ACTS is applied to many (not to all) functions and types of prayer.

In such an example as 'I confess . . .' or 'I repent . . .' the utterance does not serve to inform God of what God may already know. It constitutes an act of confession, or an act of repentance. More profoundly, it may be compared with how the utterance 'I love you' usually serves not to inform the addressee about an attitude or emotion, but as an act of love. Hence to reply 'I know that already' is to demonstrate that the force of the utterance has been misunderstood. Frequently it invites reciprocal linguistic action: 'And I love you'.

To portray prayer as a communicative act in many (but not in all) contexts is thereby to be reminded that the 'therapeutic meditation' approach does not embrace all valid forms of prayer. On the other hand, as Phillips reminds us, self-involvement and self-adjustment constitute an important part of distinctive logical grammar of prayer. It is not simply 'asking for things'.

Most of the philosophical difficulties of this subject relate not to God-inspired or to Spirit-inspired prayer, but to abuses or misuses of prayer merely for personal enhancement or even for manipulatory purposes. Above all, in the major theistic religions it constitutes a co-sharing and co-desiring for God's will for the world, as well as adoration and the expression of acts of devotion and love.

CAN THE EFFICACY OF PRAYER BE TESTED EMPIRICALLY?

Brümmer, among others, demonstrates why we cannot expect to be able to apply either the principle of verification or the

principle of FALSIFICATION as empirical or 'scientific' tests for the efficacy of prayer. He writes: 'The only claim that would be open to falsification would be the claim that God *invariably* grants whatever we ask' (*What Are we Doing When we Pray*, 5). However, prayer is misunderstood if it is viewed mechanistically, almost as a matter of cause and effect.

The very attempt to test it in this way would presuppose that it is thought of as a manipulative device in which God responds, in effect, to human wishes and control. However, all that has been said about prayer suggests the very reverse of this. Prayer involves the self in a shared, co-operative vision for the good of the whole of God's creation. A mechanistic view would obstruct, and detract from, the role of God's freedom, goodness, sovereignty and love.

predicate, predication

'Predicate' denotes what is asserted of a SUBJECT. The proposition 'God is good' predicates 'good' of God. In the formal LOGIC of categorical propositions, the logical form 'S is P' (subject is predicate) allow the variables of sentences to be expressed as the logical form of a proposition.

In the context of other systems of logical notion, the symbol 'F' may be predicated of the variables x or y. (Fx.Fy) might represent 'Paul is good, and Seneca is good'. 'Predicate calculus' in formal logic moves beyond propositional logic to include QUANTIFIERS, connectives or other logical constants and functions or relations. (*See also* SYLLOGISM.)

process philosophy

If process philosophy is defined simply as a philosophical approach which emphasizes 'becoming' and change rather than 'being', it might appear that Heraclitus (*c.* 540–425 BCE) and perhaps HEGEL (1770–1831) are process philosophers.

Yet, with additional themes in modern thought, such an emphasis upon change and event rather than upon states of affairs and OBJECTS does provide a common thread through various examples of process thought. Typically, WHITEHEAD (1861–1947) and HARTSHORNE (1897–2000) are core figures of this philosophy. Such thinkers as BERGSON (1859–1941), Lloyd Morgan (1852–1936) and perhaps John Dewey (1859–1952) stand in a broader relation to the movement.

WHITEHEAD, BERGSON and HARTSHORNE are discussed in fuller detail in the entries under their respective names. Morgan saw the organic life of the world as 'emergent'. 'Emergents' appear through discontinuities in process of EVOLUTION. Following the model of Whitehead he sought to combine natural science and philosophy to formulate a notion of an ongoing cosmology in process.

Whitehead's 'event ONTOLOGY', expounded in his *Process and Reality* (1927), is perhaps the nearest to a classic text of process philosophy. Process thinkers tend to follow Whitehead in throwing their net widely to embrace all experience, including that of natural science as well as LOGIC and philosophy. In accordance with Bergson's *élan vital* and 'open' systems, process thinkers tend to reject a determinism that traces every event to an antecedent CAUSE.

Either misplaced abstraction or 'misplaced concretion' can lead respectively to a static ontology or to a materialist worldview. While process philosophy rejects materialist ontology, 'God' is not usually identified with the personal, transcendent God of classical THEISM. Certainly God is not unilaterally sovereign, as if to deny some reciprocal interaction between God and the world. Nevertheless, there are important differences within the process approach. Whereas in Whitehead, 'God' tends to be a limiting boundary to limitless possibilities, in Hartshorne we come closer to the God of THEISM, except that in the DIALECTIC of becoming and perfection there is no room for a 'hard' doctrine of divine IMMUTABILITY.

One strength of process philosophy is a simultaneous desire to reconcile contradictions and apparently conflicting arguments or inferences from evidence, while at the same time avoiding 'timeless' abstraction. In philosophy of religion, probably the most creative and constructive of the Process philosophers for reformulating concepts of GOD remains Hartshorne. (*See also* MATRERIALISM; OMNIPOTENCE; OMNISCIENCE; SCIENCE AND RELIGION; TELEOLOGICAL ARGUMENT; TRANSCENDENCE.)

Pseudo-Dionysius (*c.* 500)

The author of the writings traditionally attributed to Dionysius the Areopagite (convert of Paul, cf. Acts 17:34) is unknown, even if the traditional ascription to Dionysius was accepted until the modern era. The writings combine NEOPLATONISM and MYSTICISM, with a strong appeal to the VIA NEGATIVA in LANGUAGE IN RELIGION.

The four treatises and ten letters that are extant present a view of the world and of mystical perfection, and emphasize divine TRANSCENDENCE. God is beyond human language and beyond conceptual thought. Nevertheless, God is light that is shed upon the All, and love that enfolds all.

The *via negativa*, or way of negation, ensures that God, the First Cause, is not reduced to the status of 'a being' among other beings. However, Christian scripture also reveals positive insights, and Pseudo-Dionysius combines the *via negativa* with pre-conceptual MYSTICAL theology.

Within the world there is ordered ranking and conceptual distinction. However, light and love, rather than conceptual knowledge, lead beyond the world to God. Order and hierarchy within the world reflect a 'celestial hierarchy' that is a 'holy order' (*The Celestial Hierarchy*, III: 1): seraphim, cherubim, dominions, powers, archangels and angels.

The Christian Platonism of Pseudo-Dionysius influenced John of Damascus,

ALBERT the Great, Thomas AQUINAS and Peter Lombard, while his hierarchies find resonances in Dante and in Milton. Unity and order are derived from God, but knowledge of God is reached through negation of all that is less than God and by mystical understanding (Pseudo-Dionysius, *The Mystical Theology*).

quantifiers

Quantifiers are logical operators in the formal LOGIC of predicate calculus. An existential quantifier serves to indicate that a proposition of formal logic states something about 'at least one thing'. A universal quantifier serves to indicate that the proposition states something about 'everything', or more strictly, about everything that is instantiated by the entity within the proposition that the quantifier 'binds'.

Traditional formal logic frequently distinguished between universal assertions or universal denials and particular assertions and particular denials. These are Euler's well-known 'A' and 'E' logical classes of propositions respectively ('All philosophers are theists' and 'No philosopher is a theist') and also respectively 'I' and 'O' propositions ('Some philosophers are theists' and 'It is not the case that some philosophers are theists').

If the logical variable ('philosophers') is represented by the logical symbol x, and the predicate ('is/are theist') is denoted by T, the existential quantifier may be symbolized by (Ex) or $(\exists x)$ to signify 'for some philosophers' or 'for at least one philosopher'. The logical notation would then read (Ex) $(x\text{T})$. Its negation would read: (Ex) $(\sim x\text{T})$. The universal quantifier is usually denoted simply as (x). Thus (x) $(x\text{T})$ states the logical form of 'for all philosophers, philosophers are theists', or 'All philosophers are theists.' The logical form of its denial is (x) $(\sim x\text{T})$.

This introduction of quantification develops propositional calculus into predicate calculus by recognizing that predication is not all of one kind. By also serving to 'bracket out' the issue of existence from the central proposition, RUSSELL (1872–1970) developed this logical device to limit the logical scope of terms in such examples as 'a round square does not exist' (i.e. it is false to assert that an x exists which is such that 'round' and 'square' can be predicated of it simultaneously). Russell applies this further in his theory of definite descriptions (e.g. 'The present King of France is ...'). For a critique of Russell on descriptions, *see* the entry on STRAWSON. (*See also* INSTANTIATION and further details under RUSSELL.)

R

Rāmānuja (c. 1017–1137)

Together with Śaṅkārā (788–820), Rāmānuja remains one of the two most influential thinkers of HINDU PHILOSOPHY of his
era. In contrast to Śaṅkārā's exposition
and defence of 'non-dualist' MONISM (the
Avaita Vedanta school), Rāmānuja
expounds and defends a 'qualified monism' (Viśistādvaita, or Viśista-advaita
Vedanta). This permits a more theistic
version of ONTOLOGY than is possible
within Śaṅkārā's system.

OPPOSITION TO MONISM AND TO
ŚAṄKĀRĀ'S METHOD OF DEFENDING
IT

Both Rāmānuja and Śaṅkārā remain
within the tradition of Hindu sacred
scripture (śruti), namely the Vedic texts,
including the Upaniṣads. However, actual
and potential ambiguities and ambiva-
lences in these sacred texts permit wide
divergences of philosophical interpretation and 're-reading'. Hence Rāmānuja
strenuously opposes the monist view of
brahman that Śaṅkārā expounds on the
basis of these texts, and founds a very
different tradition of interpretation.

Rāmānuja opposes Śaṅkārā's ontology
in which Ultimate Reality is uncharacterizable as 'undifferentiated consciousness'
(nirguna brāhma). Liberation or 'release'

(moksha) is not finally dependent on the
absorption of the true, inner, SELF (ātman)
into the All by sheer identification with it.

Against Śaṅkārā, Rāmānuja insists that
the phenomenon of 'difference' (bheda) or
'differentiation' does not necessarily arise
from 'illusion' (māyā). 'Knowledge'
(vidyā) reveals more than the negative
property of 'superimposing' (adhyāsa)
misleading perceptions onto genuine ones.

RĀMĀNUJA'S COMMENTARY ON THE
BRAHMA-SŪTRAS

Among the nine or more of Rāmānuja's
writings the Sribhāṣya, his commentary on
the Brahma-Sūtras of Badarayana, is generally recognized as among the most
important, together with the Gitā-Bhāṣya,
his commentary on the Bhagavad Gita,
and the Vedārthasangraha, his commentary on the Upaniṣads. (On these terms,
see the entry on Hindu philosophy.)

The Sūtras embody succinct aphorisms,
which can yield a diversity of interpretations. Prior to the work of Rāmānuja,
Śaṅkārā's commentary supported the tradition that brāhman, or Ultimate Reality,
is absolute Oneness, Spirit or consciousness, beside which, and within which,
'difference' was either illusory, or at best,
part of a provisional, non-ultimate, phenomenal world. The external world
belongs to this provisional order, but the

spiritual self in humankind may become identified with *brāhman*.

Rāmānuja denies neither the reality of the world nor the reality of the individuality of SELF. He questions the notion of an all-pervasive impersonal monism that excludes a theistic God. He promotes an understanding of the second aphorism of the *Brahma-Sūtra* that interprets it to mean that *brāhman* is 'the supreme Person who is ruler of all, whose nature is antagonistic to all evil; whose purposes come true, who possesses infinite ... qualities such as knowledge ... who is omniscient, omnipotent, supremely merciful'.

COMMENTARIES ON THE UPANIṢADS AND ON THE BHAGAVAD GITA

Rāmānuja's commentary on the Upaniṣads, the *Vedārthasangraha*, is more explicit. In the *Śvetāśvetara Upaniṣad*, monism is 'modified' because *brāhman* is genuinely differentiated by INSTANTIATION respectively in the empirical SUBJECT (*bhoktṛ*), the objective world (*bhogya*), and the power of initiating agency or CAUSATION (*preritṛ*).

Since all of these instantiate *brāhman*, Rāmānuja does not fully abandon monism, in contrast, for example, to the Dvaita (dualist) tradition of MADHVA (*c.* 1238–1317). Yet it is a carefully qualified or modified monism (Visista-advaita), in contrast to 'monism' (Advaita Vedanta) or the 'pure' or 'radical' monism (Sudhadvaita) of Vallabhācārya (1479–1531).

Matter in all its forms constitutes, in effect, 'the body' of God. In accordance with most Vedic traditions, individual 'souls' are 'eternal' (*nitya*), and may experience successive stages of reincarnation. The status of non-sentient matter is less clear, but 'release' (*moksha*) is more akin to a heavenly mode of being than to Śaṅkārā's notions of absorption into, and identity with, *brahman*.

In his commentary on the *Bhagavad Gita*, Rāmānuja stresses the path of religious devotion (*bhakti*), where Śaṅkārā

had emphasized the role of 'selfless deeds'. There is a sense in which it is possible to speak of 'the will of God'. *Bhakti* requires meditation on God, not ecstatic states which bypass consciousness on the part of the self.

Although he stressed ceremonial duties in religion less explicitly than may characterize much Hindu thought today, Rāmānuja's philosophy coheres more readily with such practices than a number of other older philosophical traditions. It has been suggested that his philosophy, more than most in Hindu traditions, offers a foundation that coheres with 'devotional theism'. (*See also* ABSOLUTE; BUDDHIST PHILOSOPHY; DUALISM; GOD, CONCEPTS AND 'ATTRIBUTES' OF; OBJECTIVITY; OMNIPOTENCE; OMNIPRESENCE; OMNISCIENCE; PANENTHEISM; PANTHEISM; THEISM.)

Ramsey, Ian Thomas
(1915–72)

Ramsey, born in Bolton in England, taught at Oxford and Cambridge, and became professor at Oxford in 1951, and also Canon Theologian of Leicester Cathedral. His aim at Oxford was to engage in constructive dialogue initially with logical positivists and their demands for empirical criteria of meaning, and later with a broader linguistic philosophical movement, while demonstrating the intelligibility of LANGUAGE IN RELIGION concerning the God who is beyond the empirical world.

Ramsey's book *Religious Language* bore the subtitle *An Empirical Placing of Theological Phrases* (London: SCM, 1957). Religious language utilizes everyday 'object language', but through the use of 'strange qualifications' is extended and modified in such a way that it communicates disclosures of God (ibid., 19–48). By means of interaction between the two universes of discourses a 'disclosure situation' may occur of the kind of which we say 'the penny drops', 'the ice breaks', 'it came alive' (ibid., 23). It is like the experience of 'seeing' components 'as' a *Gestalt* (ibid., 24). This approach anticipated some insights of RICOEUR (b. 1913). A central chapter expounds 'MODELS AND QUALIFIERS' (ibid., 49–89). Thus we may apply 'cause' to God as a model of divine creation; but must qualify this as '*first*' cause (ibid., 61–5). God is 'wise' (model), but '*infinitely*' wise (qualifier) or 'infinitely good' (ibid., 65–71). 'Purpose', applied to God, is '*eternal* purpose'. The remainder of this work explores this principle in biblical and theological or doctrinal language.

In 1966 Ramsey became Bishop of Durham, the year in which he gave the lectures *Models for Divine Activity* (London: SCM, 1973). While Bishop of Durham he continued to explore language and models (*Words about God*, London: SCM, 1971) as well as work on religion and science. His unstinting hard work as bishop and academic may have contributed to a premature death in October 1972 (cf. David Edwards, *Ian Ramsey*, Oxford: OUP, 1973; and Jerry H. Gill, *Ian Ramsey: To Speak Responsibly to God*, London: Allen & Unwin, 1976). (*See also* ANALYTICAL PHILOSOPHY; AYER; EMPIRICISM; GOD, CONCEPTS AND 'ATTRIBUTES' OF; LOGICAL POSITIVISM; MYTH.)

rationalism

Loosely and broadly rationalism denotes the view that human REASON constitutes the major arbiter or court of appeal (or at very least, a major arbiter) for determining whether a given system of beliefs or set of propositions is true or false. However, this broad definition is of little value until we specify to what it stands in contrast.

In philosophy of religion this may be in contrast to EMPIRICISM (to the criterion of sense-experience); to REVELATION (to divine self-disclosure as gift); to TRADITIONS (to inherited systems of BELIEF); or to post-ENLIGHTENMENT concerns about history, life and inter-subjective

SELFHOOD; or, yet differently again, to POSTMODERNITY.

In the history of ideas a fundamental philosophical contrast can be drawn between the rationalism of DESCARTES (1596–1650), and more broadly of SPINOZA (1632–77) and LEIBNIZ (1646–1716), and the empiricism of LOCKE (1632–1704), BERKELEY (1685–1753) and HUME (1711–76). The former stress A PRIORI deductive reasoning; the latter, A POSTERIORI inferences from experience and observation. However, Locke also stresses 'reason' and 'reasonableness' as a major criterion in contrast to sheer feeling, while Hume explores 'instrumental' reason as 'the slave of the passions'.

RATIONALISM IN CONTRAST TO EMPIRICISM

From the thought of Descartes flow two types of rationalism. First, as a distinguished mathematician, he sought 'clear and distinct' ideas, which were certain. By contrast, sense-experience (experience mediated to the mind through the five senses of sight, hearing, touch, taste and smell) appeared to be 'obscured and confused'; it is fallible and capable of deception (*see* CERTAINTY AND DOUBT).

Second, Descartes employed the methodological tool of doubt in order to peel away those inherited assumptions drawn from history and tradition that were less certain, upon closer scrutiny, than many assumed. At least 'once in a life-time', we must 'demolish everything and start again right from the foundations', in order that 'these remain nothing but what is certain indubitable' (*Meditations*, La Salle: Open Court, 1901, II, 31).

After all has been stripped away, Descartes cannot doubt that he exists as a 'thinking being' (*cogito ergo sum*, ibid., II). Hence the rationalism of Descartes stands in contrast equally to empiricism (sense-experience) and to inherited value-systems and traditions. On the other hand, as GADAMER points out, the 'ideas' Descartes submits to this method of doubt do not include 'God' and moral values: a point that is often overlooked in discussions of his thought. Gadamer urges that this method is largely appropriate to the sciences. In the eighteenth century this EPISTEMOLOGICAL device (i.e. a way of exploring the foundations of knowledge) overstepped the boundaries of a theory of knowledge to become, in effect, a worldview, often associated with DEISM or even anti-religious attitudes. It came to elevate individual AUTONOMY over against either revelation or the supposedly privileged knowledge derived from doctrines or from inherited institutions.

KANT AND ENLIGHTENMENT
RATIONALISM

KANT (1724–1804) provided a classic definition of what is meant by the 'Enlightenment' (*Aufklärung*). It is 'man's exodus from his self-incurred tutelage. Tutelage is the inability to use one's understanding without the guidance of another person ... "Have the courage to use your own understanding": this is the motto of the Enlightenment'. In due course such a spirit, whether in terms of reason (Voltaire) or feeling (Rousseau) nurtured the sense of individual free thought and autonomy that was related in ethics and politics to the French Revolution (1789).

Whether Kant himself can or should be called a rationalist is debatable. On one side he rejected Hume's account of sense-experience, and wrote: 'Philosophical knowledge is *knowledge gained by reason from concepts*' (*Critique of Pure Reason*, 1781). On the other hand his notion of reason as a mere 'rule, prescribing a regress', or 'a regulative principle', reduces its nature and scope substantially from that assumed by Descartes, Leibniz and most pre-Kantian writers.

In place of the rationalism of Descartes, Spinoza and Leibniz, ENLIGHTENMENT rationalism emerged as more sceptical and critical. We need only compare the

work of the Deists, Matthew Tindal (1653–1733) and John Toland (1670–1722), and the philosophical and social critiques of Voltaire (1694–1778). Voltaire waged war against intolerance in the name of humanism, but also tended in the direction of a relativistic individualism and non-mechanist view of the world.

LOCKE, REASONABLENESS AND THE
FRAMEWORK OF HUMAN LIFE

Locke remained an empiricist, but on matters of the justification of belief firmly stressed that 'entitlement' to believe depends on the 'reasonableness' of what is believed. Reason and argument test claims to truth; not mere intensity of conviction or rhetoric. As a theist who wrote a commentary on Paul's Epistles, he is not far from the multiple Anglican criteria of scripture, reason and tradition or common sense, and can be called 'rationalist' only in a moderate and relative sense in promoting a concern for 'reasonableness'.

In 1960 Gadamer published his seminal work *Truth and Method* (2nd Eng. ed., 1989) on HERMENEUTICS. In this work a further nuance emerges in understanding 'rationalism'. Gadamer pointed out that while the major stream of philosophy followed Descartes until the end of the nineteenth century in stressing reason, LOGIC, individual consciousness, DEDUCTIVE REASONING, abstraction and knowledge, a minority tradition sought to recover the kind of insights represented by Giambattista Vico (1668–1744). Vico stressed the importance of history, life, community experience, inherited value, traditions and wisdom.

Hermeneutics acknowledges the role of reason, but regards Enlightenment rationalism as individualistic, abstract and shallow. It overlooks questions of time and history, which HEGEL, Dilthey and others raised. Even appeals to 'AUTHORITY', Gadamer asserts, are not a matter of 'tutelage' (in the pejorative sense in Kant), but of making a rational and reasonable assumption that 'others may know more than I' about what I seek to understand.

This entirely healthy insight had begun to gain some recognition when it was overtaken, and given a new direction, by postmodernity. Here 'reason' became subordinated to historical situatedness. Issues of race, class, gender, culture and historical era that shape the frame within which reason operates become more important than reason itself.

Philosophical claims concerning rational reflection now risk assimilation into a sociology of knowledge, and even philosophy of religion would risk becoming sociology of religion if all claims for the validity of rational reflection were subordinated to social and historical forces. In post-modern approaches 'rational' tends to become a devalued term, as against its overvalued role in Enlightenment rationalism.

Rationalism, it appears, is a slippery word, the very diverse meanings and assessments of which need to be carefully distinguished, especially in the light of different contexts of thought. (*See also* EPISTEMOLOGY; THEISM.)

rationality

See REASON.

realism, critical realism

The slippery term 'realism' has at least two or three different contexts of thought that shape its meaning differently. Its classical meaning stands in contrast to NOMINALISM, and belongs primarily but not exclusively to the period of philosophy from PLATO to medieval SCHOLASTICISM.

The point at issue in this first context concerns the status of 'UNIVERSALS', i.e. concepts, ideas or definitions that seek to identify essences rather than depending for their meaning directly on particular objects, events or cases. Are such universals anything more than mental, logical, semantic or conceptual constructions of the human mind? Do they convey genuine reality (Latin, *res*, a thing) that exists

independently of the human mind, i.e. in the external world?

PLATO (428–348 BCE) assumes the truth of realism in his doctrine of Ideas. Ideas that enter the mind are like shadows or images cast on the wall of a cave by an external reality outside the mind (*Republic*, bk VII). The real world is outside the cave. The universal and abstract provides the perfect Forms of which human representations in language or in art are mere copies, which fall short of the original and ABSOLUTE.

A plausible example comes from geometry. A perfect circle transcends any particular approximation to a perfect circle that might be drawn in everyday life or even by an architect. A beautiful person or beautiful object approximates in terms of degree to the perfect beauty of the Ideal Form of Beauty that constitutes the universal.

Few philosophers, however, have held such an unqualified realism. From ARISTOTLE to ABELARD a series of modified versions of realism have been formulated (*see* CONCEPTUALISM). Some role must be accorded to ways in which human ideas and concepts shape and construe what we perceive. The climax of this line of thought occurs in KANT (1724–1804), who understood the CATEGORIES of our understanding as regulative mechanisms of the mind that ordered and shape thought and experience. This becomes radicalized partly in FICHTE and fully in non-realist POSTMODERNISM.

With the dawn of the modern period, several other contexts of thought have served to redefine realism, although generally with shared features. If the contrast between realism and nominalism turns largely on the status of language about universals, the contrast between realism and IDEALISM turns on the status of ideas in EPISTEMOLOGY, or theories of knowledge. Idealism (as a broad term) proposes that material objects as we perceive them do not exist but are derived from our consciousness of them.

This epistemological idealism generated a counter-reactive realism at the
beginning of the twentieth century among
such thinkers as G.E. Moore, RUSSELL and
William James. Moore's 'Refutation of
Idealism' (1903) represented what has
been called 'Common-Sense Realism' or
'the New Realism'. An OBJECT of knowledge, Moore urged, does not depend upon
a SUBJECT–object relation of knowledge.
Such concepts or ideas as BRADLEY's claim
that 'time is unreal' is undermined by our
habit of always taking breakfast 'before'
lunch, both in logic and in reality.

Idealists were quick to point out that
the 'raw' object of perception, or 'raw'
sensation, was not a series of pre-shaped
'objects', but a bare sense-datum awaiting
interpretation. There is nothing 'common
sense' about thoroughgoing realism that
minimizes or evaporates the role of the
'ordering' of sense-data or 'experience' by
the mind. (*See* the entry on CONCEPTUAL-
ISM, where it is suggested that intermediate positions may be more akin with
'common sense').

The related term 'CRITICAL REALISM' is
no less slippery. The term properly denotes
the belief that there is more to reality than
what we perceive or know. In one sense it
reflects a commonsense acceptance of the
view that for finite beings epistemology is
unlikely to be necessarily co-extensive
with ONTOLOGY. Further, as a small step
in the direction of conceptualism, it
suggests that some general terms (for
example 'society') denote more than the
particulars that contribute to it (in this
example, individual persons). In theology
there is a danger that the term is becoming
overextended (like 'FOUNDATIONALISM'
and 'praxis'). (*See also* CUPITT; BERKELEY;
DUNS SCOTUS; HEGEL; LOGIC; NON-REA-
LISM; SCHELLING; SEMANTICS.)

reason, reasonableness

Reason and rationality should not be
confused with the philosophical movements of RATIONALISM or Enlightenment

rationalism. Even the word 'reason' carries multiple meanings. 'Reason' is often
used to denote the capacity to pass from
premises to logical conclusions. KANT
(1724–1804) sets this discursive or inferential reason in contrast to human understanding and judgement.

THEORETICAL AND 'PRACTICAL' REASON

The distinction between 'theoretical' reason and 'practical' reason is explicit in
KANT, but has an earlier history which
reaches back to ARISTOTLE (384–322
BCE). It also features implicitly in the
Judaeo-Christian biblical writings. On
one side, positively, reason cannot and
should not be equated with wisdom
(Hebrew *chokmah*; Greek, *phronēsis* and
sophia). A person may be skilled in LOGIC,
but lack wisdom and judgement in daily
life. On the other side, this paves the way
for a purely instrumental role for reason.
HUME (1711–76) accords to it the status
of being the 'slave of the passions'.

This instrumental use is conveyed by
the narrow Greek term *technē*, which
stands in contrast to *phronēsis*. In modern
philosophy this distinction is explored by
GADAMER (1900–2002) in HERMENEUTICS
and by Alasdair MacIntyre (b. 1929) in
moral philosophy and 'virtue' ETHICS.

HISTORICAL REASON

A turning-point is reached not only with
Kant, but no less with HEGEL (1770–1831).
Reason is not 'instrumental' for Hegel, but
explains the nature of reality. This in itself
is not the turning point, for it reaffirms a
theme of ancient philosophy. More to the
point, reason manifests itself as historical
reason within finite human life. Its nature
and operation are conditioned by its
situatedness in the historical flow of life,
in which social and cultural factors shape
its capacities and its horizons.

Ironically, Hegel's elevation of reason,
side by side with his recognition of
'historicality' (how human thinking is
radically conditioned by one's place within

history) led to a devaluation of reason by the 'left-wing' Hegelians, and paved the way for a radical underestimate of the capacities of reason in many examples of POSTMODERNISM. Radical post-modern thinkers tend to place more emphasis on the constitutive and regulative power of social, political, gender-generated and economic forces. In extreme form, traditional philosophy is almost replaced by a quasi-causal sociology.

'REASONABLENESS', RATIONALITY AND REASON: LOCKE

Nevertheless, the importance of human rationality and criteria of 'reasonableness' surface repeatedly in the histories of philosophy and RELIGION, and in philosophy of religion. A hugely important, but often unduly neglected, figure in this context is LOCKE (1632–1704). WOLTERSTORFF has drawn attention to this in his *John Locke and the Ethics of Belief* (1996).

Towards the end of book IV of his *Essay Concerning Human Understanding* (1690), Locke points out that mere intensity of conviction is no criterion for the TRUTH of a BELIEF. Prior to his conversion, Paul the Apostle was passionately convinced of the need to stamp out the emerging Christian community (ibid., IV: 19: 2).

Locke recognized that 'reason' has multiple meanings (ibid., IV: 17: 1). In a purely logical, inferential, sense, and tied to the 'SYLLOGISM', reason may prove to be restrictive by appearing to confine all 'knowledge' to that smaller segment of utterly 'certain', demonstrable truths of rationalism (ibid., 4–7). On the other hand, used as a critical, regulative tool to permit exploration within critical limits, we need reason 'for the enlargement of our knowledge and regulating our assent' (ibid., 2).

Reason, Locke argued, is of major importance in resisting both SCEPTICISM and undue dogmatism, as well as religious 'enthusiasm'. 'Boundaries ... between

faith and reason' are needed to contradict uncontrolled 'enthusiasm' and intolerance that 'divides mankind' (ibid., 18: 11). Locke defines 'enthusiasm' in religion as 'zeal for the irrational', when 'groundless opinion' is fancied to be 'illumination from the Spirit of God' (ibid., 19: 6). A rational understanding of what it is 'reasonable' to expect to know also addresses some false assumptions behind scepticism – for scepticism often arises when inflated claims to knowledge cannot be sustained.

REASON AND TRADITION

Wolterstorff points out that Locke sustained a broader view of the relation between inherited TRADITION and critical reason than did DESCARTES (1596–1650). Descartes approached the issue of the need for certain, demonstrable knowledge most especially in the natural sciences. Hence the tradition of rationalism in a narrower sense may be traced loosely from Descartes through LEIBNIZ to the Enlightenment thinkers of the late seventeenth and eighteenth centuries, including the deists and the French Encyclopaedists.

Descartes himself does not fully advocate the AUTONOMY that characterized Enlightenment attitudes and Kant. Nevertheless, in spite of his THEISM, his methodological individualism made way for it. On the other side, by contrast, Hegel's emphasis on historical processes disengaged issues about reason from this 'timeless' individualism centred on the SUBJECT of the knowledge.

Gadamer insists that it is entirely reasonable and rational to give due regard to tradition and to inherited knowledge. To pretend to strip away the tested beliefs of others is mere impoverishment, since reason itself, as Locke affirmed, could act as a critical filter for 'reasonable' (rather than wholly demonstrable) belief. It is widely recognized today that even in the natural sciences the part played by communities and social resources cannot be ignored.

REASON AND FAITH

Expressed in these terms, Locke and Gadamer provide a wider framework and context for understanding the relation between reason and faith than the more 'two-storey' model towards which even Thomas AQUINAS (1225–74) is in danger of veering. On the other hand, Aquinas expresses the view common to Judaism, Christian theology and ISLAMIC PHILOSO-PHY when he distinguishes between truths accessible to humankind only through REVELATION (especially in scriptural texts) and truths about the existence of God, which cohere with 'natural reason' (*Summa Contra Gentiles*, I, 2, 11; and *Summa Theologiae*, Ia, Qu. 12, arts. 1–13).

Aquinas concludes: 'God is known to the natural reason through the images of his effects ... Knowledge of God in his essence is a gift of grace ... Human knowledge by the revelation of grace' (*Summa Theologiae*, Ia, Qu. 12, art. 13). Further issues are discussed under NATURAL THEOLOGY. (*See also* CERTAINTY AND DOUBT; DEISM; IBN SINA; AL-FARABI; AL-KINDI.)

referential theories of meaning

In its simplest form this theory proposes that the meaning of words lies in the OBJECTS to which they refer. Words operate like labels for their referents, or objects of reference. Ryle dubbed it the 'Fido'-Fido theory: 'Fido' denotes the dog, Fido.

The theory has been advocated with various levels of complexity and nuances of LOGIC: by RUSSELL ('The Philosophy of Logical Atomism', rpr. in *Logic and Knowledge*, 1956); by Rudolf Carnap, (*The Logical Syntax of Language*, 1934); and in a particular 'logical' version by the early WITTGENSTEIN (in the *Tractatus*, 1921).

One major problem is that this theory gives privilege to the word, rather than the

sentence, statement, or longer stretches of language – as the basic unit of meaning. A second problem arises from the fact that it may work well (or appears to do so) only in certain segments of language. In his later work Wittgenstein observes that if 'naming something is like attaching a label to a thing', this may work for nouns such as 'table', 'chair', or 'bread', but what about exclamations, abstractions, or mathematical formulae (*Philosophical Investigations*, Oxford: Blackwell, 1957, sects. 15, 27; broadly sects. 1–49)? Third, 'One has already to know ... something in order to be capable of asking a thing's name' (ibid., sect. 30).

Wittgenstein's last point is that the satisfactory operation of referential meaning presupposes a more sophisticated prior level of linguistic competency, from which it is a derivation (*see* OSTENSIVE DEFINITION).

In philosophy of religion, two opposite misunderstandings are to be avoided. One is the assumption that if a word such as 'God' is not at once clear in meaning as an 'object of reference', this by no means implies that there are no other ways of explaining the meaning. The second mis-take would be to eliminate all referential language and meaning. Reference to the external world has a necessary place in LANGUAGE IN RELIGION. But it does not provide a comprehensive theory of mean-ing. (*See also* RAMSEY.)

religion, religious experience

Until around the middle of the twentieth century a number of textbooks on the philosophy of religion began with a section under some such title as 'Defini-tions of Religion'. The complexity and difficulty of attempting such a task was recognized increasingly towards the end of the twentieth century. At least three difficulties have been noted in late moder-nity and in post-modern thought.

One factor has been a growing under-standing of diversity and pluralism, and a reaction against over-easy generalization. In philosophy the later work of WITT-GENSTEIN and ANALYTICAL PHILOSOPHY have encouraged this emphasis on particularity.

What common traits, if any, might be said to exist not only between the 'Abrahamic' traditions of Judaism, Christianity and Islam (which is not an impossible question to address), but also between these and Hinduism, Buddhism, Confucianism, Taoism, Sikhism, Shinto and tribal or aboriginal religions?

A second difficulty arises from the recognition that it is difficult to go as far as we need in terms of supposedly value-neutral knowledge, let alone value-neutral understanding. Hermeneutical approaches may help. However, too many older studies have failed to avoid prematurely assimilating 'the other' in religions to the horizons of the enquirer, whether those horizons have been those of modern secularism or of a specific religion. By way of example, we cite below the incisive criticisms against J. G. Frazer formulated by the later Wittgenstein.

Third, especially in post-modern thought the view that religions serve vested interests of social power has led some to substitute a sociological or 'ideological criticism' approach for more philosophical or theological approaches. We examine these critical approaches later in this entry, as well as in more detail under MARXIST CRITIQUE OF RELIGION, NIETZSCHE and FREUD'S CRITIQUE OF RELIGION. We begin with the first two problems.

DO ATTEMPTS TO FIND A COMMON 'DEFINITION OF RELIGION' FOUNDER ON THE PROBLEMS OF PLURALISM, DIVERSITY AND PARTICULARITY?

While in the three great 'Abrahamic' religions the relation between God and CREATION is paramount, in the Advaita Vedanta traditions within Hinduism, the created order of space and time is deemed

to be illusory (*māyā*). From this viewpoint, Judaism, Christianity and Islam might appear to verge on the dualistic. Further, ultimate reality in this Hindu tradition is beyond form, and therefore hardly personal or entirely theistic. Yet, again, traditions within Hinduism vary (*see* DUALISM).

Some strands within Hinduism, for example in parts of the *Bhagavad Gita*, perceive the divine as personal, all-good, and loving. While there may be suggestions of polytheism in some popular Hindu religious traditions, there is also a notion of a tripartite hierarchy of Brahma, the creator; Vishnu, the sustainer; and Shiva, the destroyer. Further, Sikhism tried to encourage common ground in the sixteenth century between Hindus and Muslims.

Buddhism appears also to be ambivalent about 'THEISM', not least because of its different traditions. Most Mahayana Buddhists believe that the '*dharma*-body' of the Buddha (the *dharmakaya*) is absolute reality. In this case such a tradition comes close to MONISM, or even arguably to a modified theism. Yet in some traditions the absence of a genuinely abiding self and the emphasis on a cycle of rebirth marks it off from much in the 'Abrahamic' religions.

HOW FAR CAN A 'PHENOMENOLOGY' OF RELIGION TAKE US?

If one signal of a general cultural and intellectual shift in the mid-twentieth century arose from suspicion of undue generalization, another emerged from the recognition that few definitions of religion from the nineteenth century onwards were genuinely value-neutral, in spite of some claims to the contrary.

Wittgenstein criticized Frazer's *The Golden Bough* for offering 'explanations' of the beliefs and practices of other cultures and other religions as if these were practised by 'men who think in a similar way to himself'. Frazer too readily 'explained' them in such a way as to make them seem 'stupidities', because he abstracted them from the life-context that made then intelligible ('Bemerkungen über Frazers *The Golden Bough*', *Synthese*, 17, 1967, 235–6). Even though he did not regard himself as 'religious', Wittgenstein accused Frazer of a 'narrowness of spiritual life' which flawed his supposedly value-neutral observations. In effect they form the agenda of a white, male, late nineteenth-century intellectual.

This criticism applies strikingly to those writers (many in vogue from around 1890 to 1939) who saw 'the origins and nature of religion' through the lenses of a nineteenth-century evolutionary progressivism. One well-known example is that of the evolutionary theory of E.B. Tylor, who held that all religion evolved from a primitive ANIMISM (*see also* ANTHROPOMORPHISM) and uncritical confusions between dreams and wakeful reality.

A third of George Galloway's textbook *The Philosophy of Religion* (1914) (200 of 600 pages) deals with 'the Nature and Development of Religion' from the 'tribal' stage of 'primitive man', viewed as analogues to infantile consciousness, to more 'developed' 'national' religions. Tylor's animism, spiritism, magic and hypotheses about pre-conscious needs all take their place in this story of supposed development.

What does such a genetic account, even if it were valid, tell us about the nature of 'religion'? It is impossible to bracket out issues of I–Thou relations and encounters, such as are discussed under BUBER, or the experience of the NUMINOUS 'Other', discussed under OTTO, and to persuade ourselves that thereby we arrive at a value-neutral 'phenomenology' of religion; that is, how it appears (Greek, *phainomai*) to a supposedly disengaged observer. If we define 'religion' solely in terms of what appears on the outside alone, we shall make the mistake identified by SCHLEIERMACHER in his *Speeches on Religion* (1799) of confusing 'religion' with religious practices alone.

It remains possible, and within philosophy of religion appropriate, to compare both theistic and anti-theistic accounts of religion, and to suspend final judgements about the truth-claims of each, without resorting to disguising the world-view of one culture as 'value-neutral' and another as 'primitive'. The world-view of mechanistic MATERIALISM may be equally value-laden as some claims of theism, as the entries on FEUERBACH, Marxism and Freud tend to confirm.

Nevertheless, if a phenomenological study of religion is informed by a hermeneutical awareness, it remains possible to gain an understanding of where certain emphases are placed in seeking to understand patterns of religious belief and practice. Indeed these three terms (belief, experience and practice) go a substantial way towards recovering the more constructive elements in a phenomenology and hermeneutic of religion.

'FEELING' OF DEPENDENCE? 'SENSE OF IMMEDIACY' OF RELATIONSHIP?

Schleiermacher addressed the nature of religion in his *Speeches on Religion* of 1799. Many, he urges his Berlin audience of 'cultured despisers' of religion, mistake 'the trappings' of religion for 'religion itself' (*On Religion: Speeches to its Cultured Despisers*, London: Kegan Paul, 1893, 1). 'No room remains for the eternal and holy Being that lies beyond the world' (ibid.).

To be sure, Schleiermacher expounds the psychological and anthropological aspects of religion in human life: 'the innermost springs of my being ... the highest' are unlocked (Speech I, ibid., 3). But 'the Nature of Religion' is far more than 'a way of thinking, a faith, [or] a way of acting' (Speech II, ibid., 27).

Religion is not 'craving for a mess of metaphysical and ethical crumbs' (ibid., 31). Because of its outward forms, it never appears 'pure'; yet it is 'a revelation of the Infinite in the finite' (ibid., 36). Culture and art are 'self-produced'; but religion is 'sense and taste for the Infinite' (ibid., 39). Because it entails an immediate experience of 'the Beyond', it cannot be confined within 'miserable systems' (ibid., 55). Rather, the Deity offers 'a foretaste of all love's forms' (ibid., 72).

In psychological and ontological terms, all pure religion is creative (Speech III, ibid., 119–46). Further, it transcends individual consciousness, promoting relationality between persons and between human persons and God (Speech IV, ibid., esp. 155–73). Here Schleiermacher reaches the heart of the matter. It is more, but not less, than a feeling (*Gefühl*) of absolute (*schlechthinig*) dependence (*Abhängigkeit*) on God. For *Gefühl* denotes not only 'feeling' (in a psychological sense) but also immediacy (in an ontological sense). This becomes clearer in his mature work *The Christian Faith*, of 1821, (esp. sects. 4, 12–18).

In the final speech (Speech V) Schleiermacher ascribes consciousness of God in some degree to all major religions, but insists that in the person of Jesus Christ this 'God-consciousness' was most fully instantiated. In *The Christian Faith* he repeats: religion is 'neither a knowing or a doing, but a modification of feeling or of immediate ... consciousness' (sect. 3, 5). He espouses a panentheistic PIETISM: God is 'in all that lives and moves, in all growth and change' (ibid., 36) (*see* PANENTHEISM).

CLAIMS FOR TRUTH, RATIONALITY AND COHERENCE?

Schleiermacher did not dismiss issues of truth and rationality. His emphasis on 'immediacy' was in part pietist, in part an attempt to respond to KANT's demands for transcendental foundations for any claim concerning ultimacy. Indeed, because he refused to surrender the critical and comparative pole of HERMENEUTICS, Schleiermacher described himself as a 'pietist of a higher order', i.e. one not content to rest on untested 'experience' or on 'feelings' alone.

HEGEL, however, responded dismissively to Schleiermacher's notion of religion. If religion is primarily an immediate sense of utter dependence on what lies beyond me, my dog, Hegel declared, is 'religious' to a remarkable degree. In Hegel's view, the 'representations' or 'imagery' (*Vorstellungen*) needed to be tested and supported by the more rigorous conceptual thought of philosophical enquiry (*Begriff*). Philosophy is 'higher' than religions for Hegel, but Christianity is perceived as absolute truth in pictorial form.

Such intellectualist understanding of religion, however, was vigorously attacked by KIERKEGAARD. A conceptual system or logical system, he urged, has nothing to do with a fully engaged human SUBJECTIVITY in which the SELF is at stake. It is a 'religion' only in name, as Kierkegaard makes clear in his satirical *Attack on 'Christendom'*.

Indeed, as John Henry Newman observed, the eighteenth century, the 'Age of Reason', was an age 'when love grew cold'. Formal religion, as a system of doctrine, or alternatively as a NATURAL THEOLOGY, invited the counter-reactions of pietism, in England especially in the form of Wesleyan Methodism, but elsewhere as revivalism or quietism.

In the history of religious thought this dual emphasis always coexisted. In the early centuries the Christian apologists Clement of Alexandria (*c.* 150–215) and Origen (*c.* 185–254) saw a profound kinship between the Christian religion and a Christian philosophical world-view. On the other hand Tertullian (*c.* 160–225) saw no necessary coherence between Christianity and human reason. The religion of the cross was 'foolishness' to the sage.

Parallel divergences feature in the medieval period in Christianity and in Islam. Bernard of Clairvaux (1091–1153) believed that REVELATION received through grace, faith and love was primary. REASON merely served instrumentally to clarify what was already believed. Thomas

AQUINAS (1225–74) accorded a more significant role to reason. Knowledge of God's existence might be perceived through rational reflection, but the character of God and God's Being as Trinity could only be revealed by grace (see also FIVE WAYS.)

In the modern period similar tensions, or at least differences of emphasis, occur. In Protestant Christianity the existential approach of BULTMANN minimizes any role ascribed to systems of propositions, placing the whole weight on address, grace, existential challenge, faith and self-understanding rather than on history, states of affairs, description, report or coherence. This reflects one side of the dualism of Neo-Kantianism, the conceptual scheme of HEIDEGGER, and the anti-rational reaction of Kierkegaard.

By contrast PANNENBERG (b. 1928) insists that if religion speaks of God as Creator, theology has an intellectual obligation to engage with issues of universal truth and coherence. If divine action occurs in the world, this is not merely 'inward', but concerns the public domain. The very meaning of religious assertions depends on their wider interconnectedness with TRADITIONS, with open systems, and with the wholeness of truth.

The currency of religious belief, for Pannenberg, depends on distinguishing mere credulity from serious credibility. Faith would become mere credulity if there were not reasons to believe in the trustworthiness of that in which one trusts. Far from detracting from revelation and faith, this places them on a foundation that is not merely arbitrary. Theism seeks a coherent view of the world.

Here Pannenberg stands in the classical tradition of Origen, AUGUSTINE, Aquinas and many modern theologians. The tendency to oppose 'the religion of the heart' to rational argument and to philosophical world-views stems from a reaction (as in pietism) against an undue intellectualizing of religion, or from the anti-doctrinal reaction of liberal Protestantism.

PARALLEL DIFFERENCES OF EMPHASIS IN ISLAM, JUDAISM AND OTHER RELIGIONS?

ISLAMIC PHILOSOPHY and religion may be said to exhibit in their historical instantiations a broadly parallel duality of emphasis on reason and other aspects of religious faith and observance. AL-KINDI (c. 813 – c. 871), AL-FARABI (875–950), IBN SINA (Avicenna, 980–1037) and IBN RUSHD (Averroes, 1126–98) generate resonances with Augustine and especially with Thomas Aquinas in affirming a religious world-view that coheres with a religious philosophy and philosophical ONTOLOGY or METAPHYSICS.

On the other hand, AL-GHAZALI (1058–1111) attacked what he perceived as a tendency to assimilate genuine Islamic religion and observance into a philosophical world-view that seemed to owe more to ARISTOTLE than to the Qur'an. The titles of some of his works, such as The Self-Destruction of the Philosophers and The Incoherence of the Philosophers, reveal his outright condemnation of attempts to harmonize Islamic religion with a philosophical world-view that also drew on other sources.

Nevertheless, the radical monotheism of Islam and its reverence for the content of the Qur'an revealed through the Prophet Muhammad (570–632) ensure that cognitive truth-claims for its doctrines of God and the world lie at the heart of Islamic religion.

The sovereignty and TRANSCENDENCE of Allah (Arabic for 'God') and Islam's emphasis on divine OMNIPOTENCE and OMNISCIENCE (which led some Islamic thinkers into OCCASIONALISM) constitute core truth-claims of a rational nature, alongside such practical observances and practices as prayer, worship, almsgiving, fasting and pilgrimage.

Judaism also reflects both a concern for rational coherence and truth and no less an emphasis upon right practice (orthopraxy, rather than, more primarily, orthodoxy). To be sure, common religious practices undergird the world-wide unity of Judaism. Nevertheless, Judaism includes examples of religious philosophy. We need think only, by way of example, of PHILO of Alexandria (Philo Judaeus, *c.* 20 BCE–50 CE), and MAIMONIDES (1135–1204). Such thinkers do not obscure the emphasis on right practice, rather than only right belief, that marks several strands in Judaism.

Philo gives a cosmic and universal significance to Moses, to Jerusalem, to the Temple and to the Sabbath. The law of Moses functions to underline the 'orderedness' of the universe, and exhibits the coherence of the divine principle of reason in the world. Moses is no mere particularist legislator or prophet of a specific nation, but a philosopher for the world, a mediator between God and humankind (Deut. 5:5).

Philo saw Moses' ascent to Mount Sinai as an ascent into the divine realm (*Life of Moses* 1:158). He mediates in rational form the revelation of God, the 'I am', 'the One Who is'. As the embodiment of all knowledge and wisdom, Moses mediates, in effect, a world-view of religious philosophy. Philo is a system-builder. This aspect of this controversial figure is emphasized by H.A. Wolfson (*Philo*, 2 vols., Cambridge, MA: Harvard, 1947).

Others see Philo as an idiosyncratic borrower of ideas from a variety of sources (PLATO, the STOICS, Pythagorean thought, biblical exegesis often in highly allegorical forms). They question how far he represents first-century Alexandrian Judaism. Further, G.F. Moore argues that the 'unity and universality' of Judaism 'was not based on orthodoxy in theology but upon uniformity of observance' (*Judaism* [1927], 2 vols., Cambridge, MA: Harvard, 1966, vol. 1, 111).

Moore writes, 'Wherever a Jew went he found the same system of ... observance in effect ... the dietary laws ... forms of service ... prayers (*Shema'* and

Tefillah) ... religious ethics ... table blessings ...' (ibid., 110–12). Jewish monotheism was not reached 'by speculation on the unity of Being ... the metaphysical approach of ... philosophy' (ibid., 115).

Yet neither side should be overstated. The Wisdom literature of the Hebrew scriptures shares certain common agendas about the nature of God and of humankind with questions explored in Hellenistic philosophy, and the ritual observance of the Passover liturgy was based on theological corporate memory of the acts of God. The issue of a personal relationship with God was founded on a doctrine of the covenantal grace of God, and the Torah embodied revelation of God as well as required observances.

In most traditions of Hinduism and of BUDDHIST PHILOSOPHY, cognitive or propositional claims to rational truth take a less central place. However, they remain a backcloth to religious belief and practice. Indeed, in Eastern religions one fundamental distinction, namely that between 'appearance' and 'reality', has been prominent in certain eras of Western philosophy from Parmenides and the ancient Greeks to BRADLEY. Thus in the Advaita (non-dualist) Vedanta, space and time are regarded as ultimately illusory.

In broad terms, the rational, cognitive or intellectual aspect varies in weight not only from religion to religion, but, as we have seen, within the same religion. Christianity and Islam even find virtual replays of similar debates about the relation between revelation and philosophical world-views or rational coherence. We consider under a separate entry the nature of belief, including religious belief (*see also* those on reason, natural theology).

RELIGIOUS EXPERIENCE: ULTIMACY AND THE PENULTIMATE OR FINITE

SWINBURNE calls attention to the variety and diversity of what people count as 'religious experience', distinguishing five core examples (*The Existence of God*

[1979], Oxford: Clarendon Press, 1984, 249–53).

In a first group, an ordinary 'non-religious' object or event is 'seen as' an address by God, a sign from God, the handiwork of God, or as that which points to God. Wolterstorff illustrates in the context of SPEECH-ACT theory how the voice of a child could count as the voice of God in Augustine's experience of hearing the words, 'Take up and read.' This 'counted as' a divine command to read part of Paul's Epistle to the Romans (*Divine Discourse: Philosophical Reflection on the Claim that God Speaks*, Cambridge: CUP, 1995, 1–8 and 9–21).

In a second group divine address or divine encounter is mediated through some unusual object or event. Swinburne includes among 'unusual public objects' or events the resurrection appearances of Jesus, or (we might add) the burning bush in the revelation to Moses.

Swinburne's third and fourth groups include examples of various 'private' manifestations to individuals, for example Joseph's dream in Matthew 1:20–1, or the experiences of mystics which might include visual or auditory sensations. Finally, a fifth group need not involve any mediating object, event or sensation. A person may become aware of God, or become aware of some transcendent reality that impinges upon his or her life.

In the sacred writings of Judaism, Christianity and Islam, it is unnecessary to assume that such awareness need be induced by 'preparation' of a psychological kind. Contrary to the proposals of Feuerbach, Nietzsche and Freud, a prophet may receive a revelation that goes, in effect, against his or her expectations, hopes, wishes and interests.

Late twentieth-century research on the account of the conversion of the Apostle Paul suggests that the Christophany on the Damascus road, far from presupposing psychological preparation, came to him as a compulsion, against all his prior expectations and wishes.

Otto (1869–1937), a philosopher with Kantian sympathies, perceived both the rational and suprarational dimensions of religious experience, but believed that the latter had been too often neglected in favour of the former, as in DEISM. A 'non-rational numinous feeling', which is independent of theoretical reason or theoretical thought, lies at the heart of religion, even if rational reflection on the experience of the numinous follows.

The vision of the majestic holiness of God in Isaiah 6:1–10 provides a paradigm of such numinous experience as its peak: 'I saw the Lord, sitting on a throne, high and lofty, and the hem of his robe filled the temple. Seraphs were in attendance above him … they covered their faces … and said "Holy, holy, holy is the Lord of hosts …" And I said, "Woe is me! I am lost … My eyes have seen the King, the Lord of hosts".'

We must allow for the poetic imagery as the quasi-rational reflection on a pre-rational, intuitive, 'divinatory' experience of the kind that Otto termed '*Mysterium Tremendum*'; blank wonder at the wholly Other, who is both awesome in terror and infinitely attractive in grace. A person who encounters such majesty can only become prostrate before it.

Nevertheless, as Schleiermacher and TILLICH insist, the infinite can be revealed only through the finite (Schleiermacher); the ultimate, only through the penultimate (Tillich).

ACTION, PRACTICE AND RELIGIOUS INSTITUTIONS

Some writers have tried to equate religion with religious practices alone. Kant declared, 'Religion is (considered subjectively) the recognition of all our duties as divine commands.' Yet we observed Schleiermacher's response that religion is 'neither a knowing nor a doing but a modification of … immediate … consciousness' (*The Christian Faith*, 1989 edn, sect. 3, 5). Like Schleiermacher, Samuel Taylor Coleridge (1772–1834) also attacked fossilized, routinized, institutional religion. William Law earlier distinguished 'praying' from a routinized 'saying prayers'.

Nevertheless, most religions derive ethical implications from the nature of God for daily conduct. Moreover, creeds, rituals and repeated or 'routinized' patterns of worship, institutions and public conduct provide mechanisms for the preservation and transmission of continuity and often the 'corporate memory' of founding events in religion, especially in Judaism, Christianity and Islam.

In Judaism and in Christianity respectively the formulaic 'remembrance' of the founding events of the faith (the Passover and the Lord's death) provide one such key mechanism of corporate memory which nurtures the transmission of an identifiable belief-system and its concomitant practices.

Institutions within religion (synagogues, churches, mosques; liturgies; pilgrimages, fasting, dietary observances) provide systems of transmission that preserve identity and stability. Nevertheless, the springs of creativity (as Schleiermacher, Coleridge and Tillich insist) lie in the experiences of the Ultimate rather than the penultimate, even if the Ultimate is most often encountered through the penultimate.

When Nietzsche argues (or asserts) that religion is a manipulative device that merely serves human power-interests, this criticism usually falls first on the institutions of religion, and second on abuses of religion. Yet these institutions also serve not only to keep central the ethical values and obligations of religions, but also to nurture its corporate and communal dimensions. For the Abrahamic religions, God has redeemed 'a people'.

THE WHOLE PERSON IN ENCOUNTER
WITH THE BEYOND AS
TRANSCENDENT 'OTHER'

In the end, however, it is artificial to draw too clear a distinction between knowing or believing, feeling or experiencing, acting or observing, and self-transcendence or encounters with the Other, in religion. If God is perceived and worshipped as perfect love, practices of loving other human persons are hardly 'penultimate', but flow from this mutual reciprocity of loving 'the Other'.

The major religions, for the most part, perceive the Object of worship as both a Thou (Buber) and an Other (Otto). If 'God' or the Ultimate were merely a wish-fulfilment or extension of myself, the anti-theistic critiques of Feuerbach and Freud might be valid. However, encounter with the Other and address by the Other is perceived in the major religions as more than merely affirming: they are transformative. Among modern Christian theologians, BARTH, Bonhoeffer and MOLTMANN emphasize this aspect.

Such address and encounter, therefore, will inevitably result, in authentic religion, in what Bonhoeffer calls 'costly' discipleship. Religious practices such as almsgiving and intercessory prayer follow. To begin with the external phenomenology may risk missing the point behind the practices; on the other hand, this approach may serve as a reminder of the diversity of phenomena which lie before us. A hermeneutical approach will formulate a conversational DIALECTIC between the particular and the more universal in religion and religious experience. (*See also* ATHEISM; EXISTENTIALISM; GOD, CONCEPTS AND 'ATTRIBUTES' OF; HINDU PHILOSOPHY; ISLAMIC PHILOSOPHY; JEWISH PHILOSOPHY; POSTMODERNISM; PRAYER.)

resurrection

In terms of conceptual grammar and logical context, doctrines of the resurrection of the body (Greek, *sôma*, a broader term than the English) differs from the grammar and context of 'the immortality of the SOUL'. The latter doctrine is usually grounded in the capacity of an ETERNAL aspect or part of the SELF to survive death and to enter the eternal realm. Resurrection is conceptually grounded in a creative and transforming act of God which will change the whole self into a transformed mode of existence consonant with the holiness and glory of God.

Hope of future resurrection emerged in Jewish apocalyptic, although the Hebrew scriptures for the most part conceived of life after death as a bodiless existence in the shadow-land of She'ol. By the first century, however, pharisaic Judaism held to a notion of resurrection, although it appears that in that period the Sadducees did not believe in resurrection. Some pharisaic traditions believed in the literal reassembly of the parts of the body at the final resurrection.

In ZOROASTRIANISM the belief is found that in the final cosmic conflict Mazdā and the *spenta* powers will overcome evil, and souls will be brought back to earth from heaven and hell to enter their resurrected bodies. With those still living these will face a last judgement.

The resurrection of the body is a Qu'ranic doctrine in Islam, but while AL-GHAZALI (1058–1111) chastised philosophy for not allowing room for that doctrine, IBN SINA (Avicenna, 980–1037) argued that the soul is incorporeal and cannot be destroyed.

In Christian theology belief in the future resurrection of the body is paramount, at least in the New Testament and in major TRADITIONS. The doctrine is based on the belief that Jesus Christ was raised from the dead. First Corinthians 15:3–6 is a very early pre-Pauline formula, which also predates the writing of the accounts in the Gospels. Christian believers are said to be 'in Christ', and hence to derive the basis and pattern of their future resurrection from Christ's resurrection. Both events are explicitly described as acts of God, the creator of life (Rom. 8:11; 1 Cor. 15:38–57).

For this reason Christ's resurrection is called 'the firstfruits' (Greek, *aparche*) of the future resurrection (1 Cor. 15:20); i.e.

the first sample of that of which more is yet to come. The new resurrection mode of existence is raised in glory and power, and is fully transformed by the Spirit of God (Greek, *sôma pneumatikon*, 1 Cor. 15:44), and characterized by being 'in the image' (*eikon*, 1 Cor. 15:49) of Christ.

These issues are conceptual as well as theological. For Paul the Apostle is at pains to rest the argument for the credibility and intelligibility of the future resurrection upon belief in the creative power of God, not in the innate capacities of the 'soul'. If God can provide a diversity of 'modes of existence' for every type of environment in creation, can God not be trusted to provide a mode of being appropriate for the end-time (1 Cor. 15:33–44)?

The Greek word *sôma* denotes more than 'physical' body. The emphasis lies on a mode of being that is capable of communication, experience and self-identity in the public domain. Above all, it is capable of relating to others. This meaning in New Testament and Patristic Greek has moved beyond its empirical meaning in classical Greek and in PLATO, where the 'body' (*sôma*) is viewed as a restrictive tomb, rather than a communicative enhancement.

Just as in Islamic and Jewish traditions, there are divisions of opinion about immortality and bodily resurrection, so the 'official' doctrine of resurrection is declared in the Christian creeds, but has not found full expression in every Christian writer.

In HINDU PHILOSOPHY, since the ultimate goal is liberation from cycles of existence, we should not expect to find a comparable parallel with the resurrection of the body. (*See also* CREATION; ETERNITY; ISLAMIC PHILOSOPHY; JEWISH PHILOSOPHY; POST-MORTAL EXISTENCE; TRANSCENDENCE.)

revelation

It is not surprising that virtually every major RELIGION finds a necessary place for revelation. In traditional Jewish–Christian and Islamic THEISM, if God is transcendent and 'Other', it is not to be taken for granted that God is accessible to unaided human REASON. God is not necessarily an OBJECT to be 'discovered'. Further, if God is omnipotent or Almighty, it may be the case that God wills where and when God may be known. Many Eastern religious traditions are also rooted in appeals to scriptural texts as revelation.

REVELATION IN DIFFERENT
TRADITIONS

Within each of these three Western traditions, the relative emphasis placed upon the respective roles of revelation and reason has varied. In ISLAMIC PHILOSO-PHY, AL-KINDI and the predecessors of AL-FARABI viewed the Qur'an as paramount in authority and in its capacity as revelation, but al-Farabi (c. 875–950) argued that at very least knowledge of human nature came through reason ('aql).

Traditional Judaism looks back to the two major sources of revelation identified in the Hebrew scriptures: the gilluy shekinah, or manifestation of the glory of God by some wondrous revelatory act; and revelation through the gift of the law, the prophets and the writings. The law expresses revelation of the divine will through instruction and commandment; the prophetic utterances summon and promise; the Wisdom literature and other writings explore, lament, praise or perform varied SPEECH ACTS. As Judaism develops in history, MAIMONIDES (1135–1204) affirms the revelation of the sacred texts, but also the accommodation of scripture and TRADITION to the varied backgrounds of its recipients and to rational coherence.

In the Christian tradition Thomas AQUINAS (1225–74) argues that it is in principle possible to perceive that God exists through the right use of human reason, but to apprehend the nature or character of God presupposes and requires divine GRACE and the gift of revelation.

Many Protestant theologians accord less scope to NATURAL THEOLOGY, and insist that not least because of human fallenness, divine revelation is needed even to be aware that God exists. BARTH (1886–1968) lays stress on the revelatory Word of God as God's gift in a threefold form: the Word (proper) is the revelation of God through the person and work of Jesus Christ; the Word written is the word of sacred scripture; the Word proclaimed is the eventful communication of that word in preaching and other ways, as the Spirit of God actualizes it in communicative events.

In HINDU PHILOSOPHY and religion wide differences of 'viewpoint' find their common roots in the Vedas (c. 1500–800 BCE), which have the status of sacred scripture (śruti). The 108 Sanskrit texts of the Upaniṣads (c. 800–500 BCE) count also as Vedic scripture, even though their content has become more philosophical.

That these scriptures are regarded as revelation is confirmed by the fact that the Bhagavad Gita ('Song of God') is considered sacred tradition, a little 'below' Vedic scripture, but together with Vedanta is clearly also regarded as revelation.

MODES OF REVELATION

Arguably, if revelation is regarded as the self-disclosure of God to humankind, this self-disclosure proceeds from a free act of the divine will. It remains as free an act, and as much a free gift of loving self-expression as God's free act of CREATION.

In Hebrew, Christian and Islamic traditions, it is God who invites humankind to approach God's holy presence. Humanity may not force its way into this presence as of 'right'. Hence the divine communicative act is one of sovereign grace and initiative. This is simply an aspect of the 'coherence' of a theism which conceives of God as holy and transcendent as well as gracious.

Different thinkers have emphasized four different possible modes of revelation. Such writers as Oscar Cullmann and

PANNENBERG (b. 1928) have emphasized the unfolding of divine self-disclosure in history. Cullmann places the weight on 'sacred history' (*Heilsgeschichte*); Pannenberg, on a more 'public', universal history in the world. Others, notably Barth, stress the mystery of divine self-disclosure of address 'where and when God wills', although usually through the medium of Christ, scripture and proclamation.

Yet others urge the importance of viewing the communicative act, or speech act, of revelation as a process that necessarily entails human response, and remains otherwise merely formal; or in effect, empty. Hence BULTMANN (1884–1976) calls attention to the existential dimension of revelation.

Such an approach, with more equal balance on ONTOLOGY, was anticipated by John Calvin (1509–64), when he urged in his *Institutes* that God's revelation of God carries with it as a necessary corollary a simultaneous revelation of the nature of humankind. 'The knowledge of God and the knowledge of ourselves are bound together by a mutual tie' (*Institutes* I, 1, 3). Thus to disclose that God is Creator is thereby to disclose the creaturely, finite, dependent status of humankind as stewards of the world. To reveal Christ as Lord is to reveal the status of Christ's people as belonging to Christ in trust and obedience.

A fourth emphasis arises from the transmission of revelation that has been received. Catholic tradition in particular calls attention to the role of ecclesial structures and a delegated role in regulating the tradition as part of the wholeness of the process. Other Christian traditions also see the creeds and sacraments as ways of preserving corporate memory and continuity.

Within these aspects writers as diverse as SWINBURNE (b. 1934), and among conservative American writers Carl Henry, retain discussions about revelation as 'propositional' (Swinburne, *Revelation*, Oxford: Clarendon, 1991). Clearly scripture in the Judaeo-Christian tradition performs many more functions than description, and performs numerous speech acts. Address to God in poetic psalms, and working out the meaning of parables, belongs no less to revelation than 'teaching'. Yet behind this debate lies the valid recognition that revelation embodies cognitive TRUTH, ontology and references to states of affairs. (*See also* GOD, CONCEPTS AND 'ATTRIBUTES' OF; OMNIPOTENCE; TRANSCENDENCE.)

Ricoeur, Paul (b. 1913)

With GADAMER, Ricoeur is the most important thinker in philosophical HERMENEUTICS of the late twentieth century. Whereas Gadamer is concerned almost exclusively with 'understanding', Ricoeur pays equal attention to explanation (*Erklärung*) and understanding (*Verstehen*). These two dimensions of hermeneutics, the critical and the creative, entail respectively 'willingness to expose and to abolish idols' and 'willingness to listen with openness to symbolic and indirect language'.

Ricoeur was a student in Paris of MARCEL (1889–1973), from whom he learned the importance of interpersonal understanding. Persons are not OBJECTS, but presences. During the Second World War he became a prisoner of war in Germany, and used this period to study JASPERS, Edmund Husserl and HEIDEGGER. Heidegger's notion of 'possibility' became central for Ricoeur's notion of fictive narrative worlds of projected possibility and re-figuration.

FROM HUMAN WILL THROUGH SYMBOL TO HERMENEUTICS

Ricoeur's earliest works were on human will and finitude. This led to *The Symbolism of Evil* ([1960]; Eng., 1969) in which he examined symbols of guilt, burden and bondage as 'double-meaning expressions'. With Jaspers, he saw symbols as transempirical, creative and multi-layered: 'The symbol gives rise to thought.'

In 1965 Ricoeur explored FREUD's theory of psychoanalysis as an example (albeit a severely reductive one) of diagnostic, hermeneutical, readings of the 'texts' of the human psyche and its dreams. (Fr., *De l'interpretation: Essai sur Freud*; Eng., *Freud and Philosophy*, New Haven: Yale, 1970). An overlapping of multiple, intermixed signification requires interpretation that is both creative and critical.

'Hermeneutics seems to me to be animated by this double motivation: willingness to suspect, willingness to listen; vow of rigor, vow of obedience. In our time we have not finished doing away with *idols*, and we have barely begun to listen to *symbols*' (ibid., 27, Ricoeur's italics).

Both dimensions require inter-disciplinary inputs. Ricoeur draws on theories of METAPHOR, narrative theory, semiotics, structuralism, philosophy of language, philosophy of the will and of SELFHOOD. Progressively he moves from explanation of human will, through structuralism, to *The Conflict of Interpretations*, *The Rule of Metaphor*, *Time and Narrative* (3 vols., Eng. 1984–8), and *Oneself as Another* (1992).

METAPHOR, NARRATIVE, TIME AND SELFHOOD

'Conflicts' of interpretation cannot be avoided because interpretation is multiform, multi-layered and pluralist. Ricoeur rejects totalitarianism whether in philosophy or in hermeneutics or in politics. 'Metaphor' applies creative power to sentences in ways parallel to the power of symbols for words. Metaphors operate by interaction between two domains. 'Narrative' combines coherence with distension of a temporal nature.

Ricoeur draws on ARISTOTLE for the notion of the coherence of plot, but this is not merely static, logical coherence. Conversely, he takes up AUGUSTINE on distension or tensiveness in time, which entails a unity-in-difference of memory, attention and hope. Narratives do not simply

replicate or refer; they project 'possible worlds' of reconfiguration, and transcend the merely empirical.

A stable self is the human agent who holds together memory, attention and hope, and Ricoeur explores interpersonal selfhood and will in *Oneself as Another* (Chicago: University of Chicago Press, 1992). Echoing BUBER and Marcel, Ricoeur stresses the 'Otherness' of the Other, in relation to whom (not to which) 'the idea of myself appears profoundly transformed, due solely to my recognizing this Other' (ibid., 9).

Ricoeur thus rejects the total OBJECTIFICATION of the self in POSITIVISM or EMPIRICISM; he rejects the isolation of the individual self in the RATIONALISM of modernity; and he rejects the undervaluing of the self as active agent in POSTMODERNITY. In place of these more one-sided perspectives, he expounds a creative, interdisciplinary hermeneutic of selfhood, discourse and textuality. (*See also* LANGUAGE IN RELIGION; SYMBOL; TIME.)

Romanticism

The importance of this movement for philosophy of religion lies in its contribution towards displacing the largely mechanistic and rationalist world-view that dominated much of the eighteenth century. Romanticist thought emphasized not replication and mechanical models within a causal system, but personhood, creativity and human agency.

Whereas seventeenth-century RATIONALISM provided the soil in which DEISM could readily take root, Romanticism emphasized conditions in which PANTHEISM might be perceived as part of an organic world-view. Models of machines in science and engineering yielded some place to a greater emphasis on creative art and human agency.

In the seventeenth and eighteenth centuries 'romance' often carried negative connotations of fanciful imagination, sentimentality or melancholy. However, J. G.

Herder (1744–1803), Johann Schiller (1759–1805) and Friedrich von Schlegel (1772–1829) brought to German literature and poetry a new emphasis on individual creativity over against bland system. Freedom and struggle found expression in the theme of *Sturm and Drang* (storm and stress) in Germany from the 1780s.

LITERATURE

By the beginning of the nineteenth century, Romanticism was on the verge of becoming a widespread cultural phenomenon, spreading beyond literature, poetry and philosophy, to music, painting and religion. The great German Romantic poet Johann Wolfgang Goethe (1749–1832) perceived God 'within' the vibrancy of nature, but rejected a 'God' who was 'pushing it from outside'. 'In study of nature we are pantheists ... morally we are monotheists.'

In England William Blake (1757–1827) compared the free and creative life of the spirit close to rural land with the 'dark satanic mills' of routinized life under industrialization (1808). 'I will not reason and compare; my business is only to create' (1809). William Wordsworth wrote in 1798:

> Sweet is the lore which Nature brings;
> Our meddling intellect
> mis-shapes the beauteous forms of things –
> We murder to dissect ('Up, Up, my Friend, and Quit your Books').

George (Lord) Byron (1788–1824) became almost an international symbol of Romanticist colour, wit and melancholy. Humankind is 'half-dust, half deity, alike unfit to sink or soar'. Tension and passion replaces formalism and system.

MUSIC AND PAINTING

Ludwig van Beethoven (1770–1827) embodies the transition to Romanticism within his own work. The first two symphonies show the formal elegance of Haydn and Mozart. From 1801 there are hints of a new intensity, when love and the beginning of deafness came in the period of the Moonlight Sonata. The breakthrough occurs with the third symphony (the Eroica, 1804). Thereafter Beethoven's life of 'storm and stress' is never far below the surface of his music, reaching its climax (after the fifth, 1807) in the ninth symphony (1821). In 1812 he met Goethe, but each was disappointed with the other's manner.

Carl Weber (1726–1826) also made the transition only in his latest works from 1815; but Richard Wagner (1813–1883) was a romanticist in the fullest sense. His utilization of German folk lore and legends was to articulate tragedy, joy, conflict and psychic drama. He influenced Richard Strauss, Gustav Mahler and Anton Bruckner, but provoked also a reaction of abstract intellectualism and neo-classicism, seen perhaps in Stravinsky.

NIETZSCHE, one-time friend of Wagner, drew a contrast between the 'Apollonian' culture of order and control and the 'Dionysian' culture of freedom, creativity, self-assertion and emotional abandonment. Painting offers a world where contrasts between formalized order and more self-assertive expressions through bright colours and individualist angles of view may readily be perceived.

John Constable (1776–1837) began a new period only after 1811 (*Dedham Vale*, 1811, in bright sunlight; *Flatford Mill*, 1817; *Salisbury Cathedral*, 1823, with quasi-impressionist technique). Eugene Delacroix (1798–1863) was more clearly a French Romantic painter from 1822, expressing colours, force, passion, even violence.

PHILOSOPHY AND THEOLOGY

Philosophy, we noted, had already moved within the eighteenth century in some quarters. Thus Jean-Jacques Rousseau (1712–78) emphasized the place of human feeling over human REASON. If God were to be found, God was 'within myself'. Humanity needs 'no temples, no rites, no doctrines'. SCHELLING (1775–1854) taught at Jena and spent time with Schiller and Goethe, when Jena had become the centre of German Romanticism. (On Schelling's rapidly changing views, however, *see* the entry on him.)

SCHLEIERMACHER (1768–1834) emphasized both creativity and the emptiness of mere second-hand replication in religion (especially in the *Speeches*, 1799). He also expounded the immediacy of a sense of utter dependence upon God. He was strongly influenced by PIETISM and Romanticism, but also expressed firm reservations about aspects of Romanticism that were incompatible with authentic RELIGION.

In England, Samuel Taylor Coleridge (1772–1834) may be said to have respected reason and system too much to be classed as 'Romanticist'. Further, he distinguished carefully between pantheism and Trinitarian Christian faith. Yet he found a major creative theological vehicle in imagination. Coleridge the poet assisted Coleridge the theologian to bridge the split between SUBJECTIVE and OBJECTIVE through the creative use of imagination. (*See also* CAUSE; ENLIGHTENMENT.)

Rorty, Richard McKay (b. 1931)

Rorty combines American PRAGMATISM with radical POSTMODERNISM. He is well known as a public figure of pragmatic philosophy in the United States. His earlier work embraced linguistic philosophy (ed., *The Linguistic Turn*, 1967), but he became known especially for his attack upon representational views of language and also upon traditional EPISTEMOLOGY in his major work *Philosophy and the Mirror of Nature* (Princeton: Princeton University Press, 1979).

Rorty's attack on traditional epistemology and on 'privileged representations' takes us through the history of philosophy to 'forms of life' in WITTGENSTEIN, and to issues of analycity and justification in

Dewey, Quine and Sellars. The last two chapters trace the inevitable demise of epistemology, which is to be replaced by 'HERMENEUTICS', not as a new discipline but as 'another way of coping' (ibid., 356); not as a way of 'attaining truth' (ibid., 357).

After his *Contingency, Irony and Solidarity* (1989), Rorty produced three volumes of *Philosophical Papers* (Cambridge: CUP, 1991 and 1998) culminating in *Truth and Progress: Philosophical Papers*, (Cambridge: CUP, vol. 3, 1998; articles from 1992 to 1998). He endorses William James's verdict that 'the true' is 'only the expedient in the way of thinking' (ibid., 21). There is no task of 'getting reality right', because 'there is no Way the World Is' (ibid., 25). Justification of BELIEFS is always justification to a community, and what counts as this can be decided only in pragmatic and pluralist terms.

Inevitably Rorty has to anticipate the criticism that pragmatic theories of TRUTH are widely regarded as relativist. He accepts what lies behind this claim, but prefers to see it as a defence of the 'local' over against an illusory appeal to the trans-contextual or universal.

One common criticism is that ETHICS has now become grounded in sheer 'preference', and truth becomes the possession of 'the winners'. Rhetoric 'wins' over argument. This, however, exposes the post-modernist dilemma. Pluralism appears to be liberal and tolerant; but 'winners' are the strong rather than the good, the truthful or the right. An authoritarian appeal to tanks and dollars lies hidden under a rhetoric of the 'local' as arbiter. (*See also* REASON.)

Russell, Bertrand (Third Earl, 1872–1970)

Born in Monmouthshire, Russell was educated at Trinity College, Cambridge, where he then taught as Fellow and subsequently as lecturer in Philosophy until 1916. He produced his most influential work in those early years, from 1900 to about 1919, most notably on 'philosophical LOGIC' (a term which he coined) and on the foundations of mathematics as a logical system.

During this early period Russell taught Wittgenstein (1889–1951), and formulated the device of logical QUANTIFIERS as part of his Theory of Descriptions and his general disengagement of 'logical form' from the confusions generated by natural language. His work on mathematics focused also on logic and on issues of classes, in the context of which he formulated his theory of types.

Probably the most important published work (out of very many publications) is his *Principia Mathematica* (3 vols., 1910–13, written jointly with WHITEHEAD (1861–1947), but each as author of his own respective contributions). This is not to be confused with Russell's earlier *Principles of Mathematics* (1903). His theory of descriptions appeared in part (as an interim report) in 'On Denoting' (*Mind*, 1905, 479–93; also rpr. in R. C. Marsh, ed, *Logic and Knowledge*, London: Allen & Unwin, 1956); and his theory of types in 'Mathematical Logic as Based on the Theory of Types' (*American Journal of Mathematics*, 1908, also rpr. in Marsh, ed., *Logic and Knowledge*).

From 1916 onwards Russell's concern turned to political issues, including a leaflet on conscientious objection during the First World War (1916), election to Parliament in 1922, visits to China, Russia and the United States, and anti-nuclear demonstrations in the years after the Second World War. This absorbed much of his energy, although he continued to produce substantial works of philosophy. Some of these were addressed to a wider, more popular audience, and he became well known as a figure in public life.

LOGICAL FORM, DEFINITE DESCRIPTION, AND QUANTIFICATION

Russell firmly believed that the grammatical forms of everyday natural languages

often confuse us concerning the logical form of the propositions that they ambivalently express. Wittgenstein notes in the *Tractatus*, 'It was Russell who performed the service of showing that the apparent logical form of a proposition need not be its real one' (4.0031) (although F. Mauthner's work also explored this point before Russell).

Two examples among others seized Russell's attention. First, often the innocent-looking word 'is' functions differently at the level of formal logic from what may appear to be the case on the basis of its use in natural language. Its propositional functions may differ from its sentence function. Second, 'definite descriptions' may perform deceptive roles in natural sentences. Does the phrase 'The present King of France' refer to an entity (even if this entity does not exist)?

Everyday grammar might suggest that such expressions as 'the present King of France' or 'a round square' denote entities to which language refers, even if their 'existence' is negated. But this is as fallacious as Lewis Carroll's satirical parody about an entity called 'Nobody', who passed the messenger on the road, and therefore should have arrived first.

Russell proposed that the use of an existential quantifier should clarify the point that reference and denotation are not entailed by the strictly logical form of the proposition behind the sentence. An existential quantifier generates some such forms as 'For at least one x, there is an x such that x is F (King of France)'; or 'there is at least one x such that x is F (x is round) and x is G (x is square)'. The form $(\exists x)\,(Fx.Gx)$ is discussed under the entry on quantifiers. Strictly, the form would be a negation: $\sim (\exists x)\,(Fx.Gx)$.

LOGICAL ATOMISM, CLASSES IN MATHEMATICAL LOGIC AND RUSSELL'S DEVELOPMENTS

In his very earliest work Russell was influenced by BRADLEY (1846–1924) and other philosophical idealists, although

from the first he rejected Bradley's MON-
ISM. Russell's *Essay on the Foundations of
Geometry* (1897) reflects aspects of this
very early but short period. By around
1898 he was moving away from this
approach.

With G. E. Moore, Russell moved to a
realist position, which is reflected in part
in his *Critical Exposition of the Philosophy of Leibniz* (1900) and fully in his
Principles of Mathematics (1903). At this
stage Russell began to draw upon Peano's
symbolic logic, and argued that the whole
of pure mathematics rested upon the
foundations of logic, from which it could
be derived.

This raised issues, however, about
whether the whole of the logic of classes
could operate in this way, especially
questions about 'the class of all classes',
or more precisely, logical forms that
implied self-referential functions. Russell's
'mathematical logic as based on the
Theory of Types' (1908) sought to avoid
the paradoxes generated by their problems.

We may note that these two elaborate
theories (the theory of definite description
and the theory of types) appeared to be
necessary only because Russell understood
the whole of logic and language to be
referential, rather than only certain specific instances of language. Hence the later
Wittgenstein and subsequently especially
STRAWSON questioned the assumptions
that appeared to warrant these theories.

This position appeared plausible to
Russell because he retained the theory of
logical atomism as a comprehensive theory
of meaning when most others had perceived its limitations. It should also be
noted that in the *Tractatus* the 'atoms' that
made up elementary propositions were for
the early Wittgenstein purely logical entities, whereas for Russell they entailed more
than logic. It was Russell's preface to the
Tractatus, and Russell's influence, that led
many to interpret the *Tractatus* (against
Wittgenstein's intention) as a quasi-positi-
vist account of logic and language.

While Wittgenstein began to move in a
different direction during his 'middle'
period of around 1929–33, Russell
retained the same basic approach, but
extended its application to EPISTEMOLOGY
and to a wide range of questions. The
height of his innovative work appeared
(with Whitehead) in the three-volume
Principa Mathematica (1910–13), which
passed the basic theories that mathematics
is grounded in logic.

In 1914 Russell produced *Knowledge
of the External World*, which explored our
knowledge of material objects, and related
issues in physics to this problem. In 1916,
Russell's political writing led to his dis-
missal from Cambridge, although he
continued to work on the philosophy of
mind.

Russell's approach to the scope of
human knowledge and the nature of mind
very broadly reflects sympathy with HUME
and the empiricist tradition. However,
with increasing commitments to public
life and political issues, Russell's later
work commanded less influence than his
earlier writings on logic. In 1950 he
received the Nobel Prize for Literature,
and remained active in campaigning for
civil rights. (*See also* EMPIRICISM; IDEAL-
ISM; OSTENSIVE DEFINITION; POSITIVISM;
REALISM; REFERENTIAL THEORIES.)

Ryle, Gilbert (1900–76)

Ryle was educated at, and taught at,
Oxford, where for many years he was
recognized as a leading exponent of that
form of 'linguistic analysis' which sought
to disentangle and to elucidate conceptual
confusions and logical grammar. His most
important book was *The Concept of Mind*
(London: Hutchinson, 1949).

THE CONCEPT OF MIND AND THE 'GHOST IN THE MACHINE'

Ryle attacked the logical confusions that
he perceived to lie at the heart of language
about the body and the mind within the
philosophical tradition inherited from

DESCARTES (1596–1650). He wrote: 'I shall speak of it, with deliberate abusiveness, as "the dogma of the Ghost in the Machine" ... It is one big mistake ... a category mistake. It represents the facts of mental life as if they belonged to one logical type or category ... when they actually belong to another' (ibid., 17).

Ryle compares the conjoining of terms of different types that occurs in zeugma; for example, 'She came home in a flood of tears and a sedan chair' (ibid., 23). Hence, while he does not deny that 'there occur mental processes', Ryle insists that 'there occur mental processes' does not 'mean the same sort of thing' as 'there occur physical processes' (ibid.). It makes 'no sense' either to conjoin or to disjoin the two.

In logical terms, the conceptual grammar of 'exist' does not remain the same when this is predicated of minds as when it is predicated of bodies. It is as different, Ryle asserts, as the meaning of 'rising' when applied to a 'rising' tide and to 'rising' hopes (ibid., 24).

Descartes, Ryle insists, speaks as if mental and physical CAUSES and events constituted 'two collateral histories'. It is as if the body were an outer engine, controlled by an interior mini-engine called 'the mind'. But the mind is not an 'entity' within the body.

What is often presented as a Cartesian entity within or alongside the body is better viewed as an adverbial mode of ascribing a dispositional character to bodily behaviour. Ryle resists the implication that this makes him a behaviourist, although equally he is reluctant to dismiss BEHAVIOURISM as untenable. His major target is the presentation and formulation of language about the mind in such a way that it seems to constitute a mind–body DUALISM.

This 'dualism' rests upon a conceptual or logical confusion. The mental requires to be understood in terms of what can be observed in the public world. Some have used the term 'logical' behaviourist to denote this approach. At very least, mind and body are not independent entities. To assume this is to elevate an adverbial mode of behaviour (e.g. acting intelligently) into a 'thing' (e.g. called Intelligence, as if it were an entity rather than a quality).

DILEMMAS, PARADOXES AND CONFUSIONS

Among Ryle's other writings, *Dilemmas* (Cambridge: CUP, 1966), the Tarner Lectures for 1953, deserves special mention. Ryle considers a number of traditional paradoxes and apparent logical dilemmas, for which he offers a series of conceptual elucidations.

One very constructive example is that of Zeno's paradox of Achilles and the Tortoise. At the level of common sense, Achilles as the faster runner must overtake the tortoise. However, suppose that we calculate the distance that Achilles has to run to catch up with the tortoise, by the time Achilles has reached the marker, the tortoise has moved on ahead, however slowly. Mathematically, it seems Achilles can never catch up with tortoise, even though he whittles down the distance each time that a measurement is made.

Zeno believed that the paradox revealed the illusory nature of change. Ryle shows, by contrast, that the paradox rests upon confusing two different operations: 'We have to distinguish the question "How many portions have you cut *off* the object? " from the question, "How many portions have you cut it *into*?"' (ibid., 46). One is the logic of the observer; the other is the logic of the participant.

This provides an excellent model for unravelling some common misconceptions. In RELIGION, although Ryle does not attempt to explore this, it might be used to address the question of whether there is an 'intermediate state' or direct transformation into the divine presence, in Christian eschatology. The former may suggest the use of 'observer' logic; the latter is 'participant' logic.

Ryle equally constructively addresses the logical puzzle generated by such an utterance as 'It was to be'. The problem arises when we apply the logic of 'what is' to that to which has not occurred, about which certain BELIEFS are held in the present (ibid., 31–2).

In an autobiographical observation Ryle declares, 'My chief, though not sole, interest in linguistic matters focussed on such dictions as were (or ... were not) in breach of "logical syntax" ... and the paradox-generators' (O. P. Wood and G. Pitcher, eds., *Ryle*, London: Macmillan, 1970, 14). (*See also* LOGIC; SELF.)

S

Śaṅkārā (traditionally 788–820)

Śaṅkārā is probably the single most influential thinker in HINDU PHILOSOPHY, although the influence of RĀMĀNUJA (c. 1017–1137) is perhaps comparable. He wrote commentaries on the ten principal Upaniṣads, on the *Brahma-Sūtras* and the *Bhagavad Gita*. His main aim was to show that these Vedic scriptures taught or implied a monist ONTOLOGY.

In effect, Śaṅkārā stands as the founder and main representative of Advaita (non-dualist) Vedanta. These terms are explained in the entry on HINDU PHILOSOPHY, but a brief summary may also be outlined here.

Śaṅkārā intended his philosophy to be faithful to the Vedas (c. 1500–800 BCE) as Hindu scripture (śruti). Within this scriptural tradition also stand the Upaniṣads (c. 800–500 BCE), a collection of 108 Sanskrit sacred texts, which embody more explicitly philosophical reflection, or at least invite philosophical commentary.

Vedanta, 'the ends of the Veda', expounds how the inner, true SELF (ātman) may become one with Ultimate Reality (brāhman). Thereby the self attains 'release' (moksha) from painful and repetitive cycles of existence, rebirth and reincarnation (samsara). Advaita Vedanta is a non-dualist, monist philosophy within

the scriptural framework of the Vedic writings and the Upaniṣads.

The theme of *moksha* or liberation of the inner self is taken further in the *Bhagavad Gita*, or 'Song of God', which originates from the third century BCE onwards. The *Brahma-Sūtra* consists of four chapters of material expressed in terse aphorisms, which invite comments, interpretations and commentaries.

Śaṅkārā and the Adaita Vedanta tradition appeal to the aphorism in *Chandogya Upaniṣad* VIII: 8, 'That is the Self, the immortal ... Brāhman', and more especially to 'You are that' (*Tat Tvam Asi*). Freed from passion, strong desire and fear, the *ātman* may become identified with *brāhman* as undifferentiated Oneness, without 'difference' (*bheda*), as absolute, Ultimate Reality, no more to descend to 'existence' as an independent self. This indeed is *moksha*.

Nevertheless, philosophical reflection demands an answer to the question: why does differentiation appear to characterize everything that is perceived, if Ultimate Reality is one? Śaṅkārā expounds the principle that 'knowledge' (*vidyā*) begins to uncover 'appearance' as illusion (*māyā*) even if this includes practices of religious devotion. We may imagine that we perceive a dangerous snake when we are prompted by fear; but dispassionate knowledge will reveal that the illusory snake is a harmless rope.

Śaṅkārā's commentary on the *Brahma-Sūtra* also expounds the sole, exclusive reality of Absolute Spirit. The external world of objects is construed as 'reality' through lack of 'knowledge'. Perception does relate to good or bad action (*karma*), as the first aphorism of the *Brahma-Sūtra* seems to suggest.

Again, apparent contradiction need not be self-defeating. The ancient Vedic tradition embodied sharp debate of opposing viewpoints. As we note in the entry on Hindu philosophy, Śaṅkārā found a way of respecting religious devotion to a higher being, even if this found its place as a 'lower' level of knowledge. In 'higher' knowledge, anything beyond the oneness of *brahman* is *māyā*.

Such reasoning may not be entirely without parallel in modern Western philosophy. Both HEGEL (1770–1831) and KIERKEGAARD (1813–55), for all Kierkegaard's passionate opposition to Hegel as a mere theorist, expound a DIALECTIC which allows for 'levels' (Hegel), or 'stages' or 'viewpoints' (Kierkegaard). These offer frameworks within which what was acceptable within one might be denied in another. In Hegel's case, 'higher' philosophical concepts (*Begriff*) might undermine imagery (*Vorstellung*) that was acceptable in religion. In Kierkegaard, the 'stages', respectively, of the aesthetic, ethical and religious, might reveal truth-claims differently from different 'points of view'.

This must not seduce us into understanding Śaṅkārā's philosophy in Western terms. Śaṅkārā appeals to 'illusion' and 'superimposition' (*adhyāsa*). Śaṅkārā writes in his commentary on the *Brahma-Sūtras*: 'It is wrong to super-impose onto the subject (whose Self is intelligence, and which has for its sphere the notion of the "I") the object whose sphere is the notion of the "Not-I" ...' We should not 'superimpose' subject upon object or object upon subject, thereby confusing the Real with illusion or the Unreal. *Adhyāsa* entails a presentation of the attributes of one thing as if it were another. For example, mother-of-pearl may be misperceived by its being presented as silver (like the 'superimposition' of the snake-appearance onto the rope-reality).

The 'objective' world stems from such processes of superimposition. It has a practical function, and is (relatively) real for practical purposes. In actuality, or in metaphysical terms, however, only *brahman* has real existence as Ultimate Reality. The world of objects is unreal. Reincarnation denies any notion of a single creation, although a succession of rebirth and reabsorption into *brāhman* may appear to take place, but on the level of *māyā* or like a dream.

Śaṅkārā accepts the main widespread EPISTEMOLOGY of Hindu philosophy, except for one very major difference. The first three sources of knowledge in most Hindu philosophical traditions are perception, inference or A POSTERIORI reasoning, and word or testimony. The first is the primary mode of knowing. However, Śaṅkārā stresses the adequacy of the Vedic texts in such a way as to exclude inference from perception as an authentic path to the apprehension of reality.

Śaṅkārā also appears to accept a traditional view of *karma*. Acts of a prior incarnation may condition the range of good or evil, or scope of possibilities, for a self who is reborn into a world order. Yet in principle release, *moksha*, lies within the capacities of the self to attain, with due knowledge. (*See also* BUDDHIST PHILOSOPHY; DUALISM; MADHVA; METAPHYSICS; MONISM; MYSTICISM; PANTHEISM.)

Sartre, Jean-Paul (1905–1980)

Sartre was born in Paris, and studied in Paris and Freiburg. He was taken prisoner of war in the Second World War, and became a member of the resistance during the Nazi occupation of France. He is generally regarded as the most important of the French existentialists.

It is customary to divide Sartre's philosophy into two periods. In his earliest works he draws from Husserl and HEI-DEGGER a phenomenological analysis of human consciousness. Initially, in *The Transcendence of the Ego* (1936), his work is partly one of psychological analysis. His first novel, entitled *Nausea* (1938) and first story, 'The Wall' (1939) reflect his own partly autobiographical experiences of anguish, dread and the prospect of imminent death, which appear in JASPERS and Heidegger as existential 'Boundary Situations' and as 'Being-towards-Death' respectively.

The first-hand character of Sartre's quasi-autobiographical writing is more authentically 'existential' than Heidegger's treatise style. 'The Wall' recounts the extreme dread of military interrogation: 'The major... scanned the list ... You will be shot tomorrow morning.' 'There was a big puddle between his feet.' 'My life was closed, like a bag, yet everything inside it was unfinished' (rpr. in W. Kaufman, ed., *Existentialism from Dostoevsky to Sartre*, Cleveland: Meridian, 1956, 226, 232, 234).

The main themes in Sartre's major existentialist treatise *Being and Nothingness* (1943) are outlined in the entry on EXISTENTIALISM, including the contrast between 'OBJECTS' (being-in-itself, *être-en-soi*) and human being (being-for-itself, *être-pour-soi*). The latter is consciousness that is conscious of itself, and thereby aware of a kind of mobile freedom. The human battle is that of retaining the struggle against loss of freedom by becoming the 'object' of the constraints imposed by others.

'God' cannot fit into either category. If God is 'personal', God is not Being-in-itself; but Being-for-itself remains incomplete. 'God' does not exist, either in concepts or for reality.

The second period is one of Sartre's exploration of Marxism. At first these two may seem contradictory: existentialism is individualistic, Marxism is socio-economic, with a grand narrative of history. Nevertheless Sartre's analysis of the 'situatedness' of the human as 'given' by age, class, sex, race, war-or-peace and so on coheres with a Marxist interpretation of the human and of history as driven by socio-economic forces. Sartre attempted to reconcile existentialism and Marxism in his *Critique of Dialectical Reason* (1960). (*See also* MARXIST CRITIQUE OF RELIGION.)

scepticism

Scepticism assumes a variety of forms and different kinds of doubt. In broad terms, it denotes doubt about whether claims to human knowledge amount to more than mere opinion, or whether there can be grounds for assuming that human knowledge is reasonable, justifiable, or warranted. Radical scepticism demands suspension of BELIEF and judgement. Moderate scepticism denies the possibility of human CERTAINTY.

As a philosophical system, scepticism is usually attributed first to Pyrrho of Elis (*c.* 360–270 BCE). Pyrrho is reported as stating that it is impossible to know the nature of anything, not least because every proposition can be opposed by its contradictory. Therefore we must preserve suspension of judgement (Greek, *epochē*), and keep to an uncommitted silence (*aphasia*). Opinions merely reflect convention or chance.

It has been suggested that this attitude was prompted historically by a sense of disappointment or disillusion in the aftermath of the higher expectations nurtured by the philosophies of PLATO (428–348 BCE) and ARISTOTLE (384–322 BCE). The era marked the break-up of Greek city-states, and the beginnings of the STOIC call for fortitude and lack of passion or engagement (Greek, *ataraxia*) in the face of uncertainty. Times of cultural crisis and change nurture scepticism about the competing claims of assertions, possibly paralleled by some post-modernist strategies today.

Carneades (214–129 BCE) also anticipates elements in the SOPHISTS and POST-MODERNITY, by exalting a rhetoric of the 'plausible' against the possibility of arguments for the true or false. He used rhetoric to unmask alleged contradictions in theistic belief, and attacked 'justice' as a viable concept, in part by exploiting the limits of language.

Sextus Empiricus (third century CE) defended the scepticism of Pyrrho. He called attention to the variety and divergence of opinion found on many issues. He also viewed as illogical the process of constantly correcting and re-correcting corrigible beliefs. Whatever is asserted can with equal reason be denied.

In Western thought these sceptical formulations lay dormant, in general, until the Renaissance. Richard H. Popkin (*The History of Scepticism from Erasmus to Spinoza*, Berkeley: University of California Press, 1979) sets out issues during this period clearly. Pyrrho's works were rediscovered, and his arguments redeployed. Martin Luther's famous claim against Erasmus that scripture is 'clear' (Latin, *claritas*) meant in this context that they were sufficiently clear to counter the claim of Erasmus that divided opinions demanded lack of action (ibid., 1–41).

Michel Montaigne (1533–92) developed Pyrrhonian scepticism and an early theory of cultural relativism. For him many of the issues turned on the difficulty of formulating criteria for TRUTH.

In more moderate forms, HUME (1711–76) develops some of these themes, with particular reference to issues of CAUSE, probability and the SELF. Hume explicitly called himself a sceptic, but recognized that consistent sceptics would be diffident about their beliefs and their doubts. He uses sceptical arguments to attack dogmatism and to encourage cultural reform.

Two standard criticisms are made of scepticism. First, if sceptics deny the possibility of knowledge, how do I know that I cannot (with more exploration) know? Does this not entail a logical contradiction? Second, is not scepticism parasitic upon what it doubts? WITTGEN-STEIN observes that doubt comes 'after' certainty. (*See also* AGNOSTICISM; CORRIGIBILITY; LOCKE; REASON; SWINBURNE; WOLTERSTORFF.)

Schelling, Friedrich Wilhelm Joseph von (1775–1854)

Prior to 1794 Schelling began his earliest work on the nature and language of MYTH. However, in 1794 his interests turned to the philosophy of religion. His complex thought developed through several distinct phases, in general beginning with the 'subjective' IDEALISM of FICHTE, moving towards and through 'objective' Idealism which entailed an awareness of the ABSOLUTE in history, and finally arriving at a pre-conceptual view of God as the Ground of Being beyond SUBJECT–OBJECT distinctions. This had a strong influence on TILLICH.

Schelling's interest in art, nature, myth and creativity earned him in some quarters the title 'the philosopher of the Romantic movement'. He studied in Tübingen with HEGEL and Hölderlin, and became friends with Schiller, Goethe and Schlegel.

In early years Schelling co-edited a journal with Hegel, but there came a parting of the ways. Hegel eventually observed, 'Schelling carried on his philosophical education before the public, and signalled each fresh stage with a new book' (Hegel, *Sämtliche Werke*, rpr. Stuttgart: Frommann, 1965, vol. 19, 647; more loosely, W. Kaufmann, *Hegel*, London: Wiedenfeld & Nicholson, 1966, 279).

Schelling was concerned with how consciousness emerged as consciousness of the self. He found the key in the contrast or polarity between self and notself, or between self and Other. Encountering otherness is a precondition for understanding the self, as SCHLEIERMACHER urged in his HERMENEUTICS, followed by

Dilthey and recently RICOEUR. Against Fichte, Schelling saw 'nature' as part of this 'Other'.

For Schelling this is the transcendental ground for the possibility of understanding. However, in his *Philosophy of Art* (1803) he perceived all reality as also sharing an identity that eclipsed the subject–object contrasts of conceptual thought. This is what provoked Hegel's caustic criticism of a MONISM or PANTHEISM as like 'the night ... in which all cows are black'.

Schelling's view of God and nature now verged on the mystical, in contrast to Hegel's high regard for critical concepts and differentiation within the Whole. For Schelling, God is the outflowing, outspreading, self-giving ground of all that is. God is beyond the realm of conceptual thought. Hence LANGUAGE IN RELIGION needs myth and SYMBOL, which transcend concepts (against Hegel). (*See also* GOD, CONCEPTS AND 'ATTRIBUTES' OF; MYSTICISM; TRANSCENDENCE.)

Schleiermacher, Friedrich Daniel Ernst (1768–1834)

In older textbooks on philosophy of religion Schleiermacher is often portrayed as an advocate of defining RELIGION in terms of 'feeling'. This distorts his significance, and overlooks his main concerns.

Schleiermacher marks the beginning of 'modern' theology, not least because he was the first theologian seriously to seek to come to terms with the TRANSCENDENTAL PHILOSOPHY of KANT, especially Kant's *Critique of Pure Reason* (1781). Just as Kant sought grounds for the very possibility of thought, Schleiermacher explored the basis on which theology and religion were possible.

IMMEDIACY OF RELATION TO GOD AS FINITE TO INFINITE

Schleiermacher had been nurtured in a pietist tradition, and never lost the central pietist conviction that religion rested on

experience rather than doctrine, and on the consciousness of a personal relationship with God. However, from his days at the University of Halle he welcomed rigorous critical reflection, appropriate to 'PIETISM of a higher order'. He sustained both approaches throughout his life. As professor at the University of Berlin and also as pastor of Trinity Church, he published thirty volumes of works: ten volumes on philosophy; ten on theology; and ten of church sermons.

Prior to more recent translations of his work, Schleiermacher was credited with defining religion as a 'feeling of absolute dependence on God'. However, although he uses the word 'feeling' (H.R. Mackintosh's translation), as J. Macquarrie and others urge, this is not 'feeling' in a purely psychological sense.

Schleiermacher viewed this experience as an 'immediacy of awareness' (in a quasi-ontological sense) of 'being utterly dependent upon God' (German, *das Gefühl schechthinner Abhängigkeit*: *The Christian Faith* [1821–2], Eng. Edinburgh: T & T Clark, 1989, sect. 62, 261).

In his early *On Religion: Speeches to its Cultured Despisers* ([1799], Eng., New York: Harper, 1958) Schleiermacher made it clear that this addressed a transcendental issue, not a mere CONTINGENT mode of experience. The basis of piety is not 'craving for a mess of metaphysical and ethical crumbs' (ibid., 31). Religion is 'a sense and taste for the infinite' (ibid., 39).

Doctrines are derivative from experience. 'Ideas, principles, are all foreign to religion' (ibid., 46). Indeed, religion is ill-served by 'miserable love of system' (ibid., 55). This at once marks off Schleiermacher both from Kant and from HEGEL (1770–1831), who was Professor of Philosophy at Berlin while Schleiermacher was Professor of Theology.

THE FOUNDING OF MODERN HERMENEUTICS

Schleiermacher's distaste for system and his emphasis on the interpersonal and experimental led him to formulate the first 'modern' theory of HERMENEUTICS that did not transpose hermeneutics into a mere sub-discipline designed to serve or (worse) to justify some prior system of theology or of philosophical thought. He defined hermeneutics not as a 'theory of interpretation' but as 'the art of understanding'; it is not 'mechanical' (*Hermeneutics: The Handwritten Manuscripts*, Atlanta: Scholars Press, 1977, 175).

The subject matter to be understood embodies that which is 'strange' or 'other'; hence the person who seeks to understand needs a 'divinatory' (intuitive, person-to-person) capacity. Nevertheless, contrary to popular misunderstandings of him, Schleiermacher insists that a 'comparative' or 'critical' dimension is no less necessary. The first is 'the feminine strength in knowing people'; the second, the 'masculine' strength of classifying and criticizing: 'each needs the other' (ibid., 150–1). On Schleiermacher's development of 'the hermeneutical circle', see the entry on hermeneutics.

Hegel criticized Schleiermacher for an over-churchly, inadequately conceptual and critical approach to religion. Yet his influence remains. Some suggest that Schleiermacher, Hegel and KIERKEGAARD represent the three main nineteenth-century figures who have shaped three distinctive mind-sets in twentieth-century theology. (*See also* ONTOLOGY; PANENTHEISM; ROMANTICISM.)

scholasticism, scholastic philosophy

These terms allude to the period of the great schools of late medieval Western Europe, especially in the twelfth and thirteenth centuries. The Latin *scholasticus* denoted the master of a school, and would have included such figures as Peter ABELARD (1079–1142), Peter Lombard (1100–60) and Hugh of St Victor (1096–1141). The flowering of the movement came with Thomas AQUINAS (1225–74) and his magisterial *Summa Theologiae*.

Scholasticism included the major goal of exploring and demonstrating the coherence of faith-beliefs and the conclusions of rational enquiry within a single unified system. The method of Aquinas in the *Summa Theologiae* was to present a systematic, scientific treatise through questions, articles, objections, replies and counter-replies. This characterizes the method of scholastic philosophy.

Scholastic methods were applied to theology, philosophy and law, and drew on Greek philosophy, especially ARISTOTLE. In the seventeenth century scholasticism was too readily portrayed as a body of common doctrine. In content, it could embrace diverse views, but its unifying factor was its common method, especially disputation and commentary, and the common attempt to expound a coherent, rational, 'scientific', philosophical theology or view of God and the world.

From the schools of the twelfth century, often based in the great cathedrals, it was a short step to the founding of the earliest universities of the thirteenth and fourteenth centuries, including Paris and Oxford. BONAVENTURE (*c.* 1217–74), Professor of Theology at Paris, John DUNS SCOTUS (1266–1308) of the universities of Oxford and Paris, and WILLIAM of Ockham (*c.* 1287–1349) of Oxford may all be included among the great scholastic philosophers and theologians.

Typically William of Ockham retained and developed the scholastic concern with scientific system. *Scientia rationalis* included philosophy and logic; *scientia realis* included physics. The drive towards unified system lies behind his well-known 'principle of economy' (Ockham's razor) whereby multiplicity is not to be assumed unless it is unavoidable, i.e. rejected if 'without necessity'.

Schopenhauer, Arthur (1788–1860)

Schopenhauer's contribution to philosophy of religion, in contrast to his influence on the history of ideas, is difficult to calculate. Even in the nineteenth century, his impact on philosophy was not great. His influence was felt rather by Richard Wagner and Friedrich NIETZSCHE (1844–1900), and he explores distinctive affinities with Eastern thought.

Schopenhauer's major work was *The World as Will and Representation* (often translated *Idea*, but German *Die Welt als Wille und Vorstellung*, 1818, with a second volume in 1844). The world is perceived as will, or as will to live, in the form of an unconscious striving which finds expression in a multiplicity of INSTANTIATIONS.

The thinkers in Western philosophy whom Schopenhauer most respected were PLATO (428–348 BCE) and KANT (1724–1804), but he was perhaps the first modern Western philosopher to engage seriously with Eastern thought, especially Indian philosophy in the tradition of HINDU PHILOSOPHY and BUDDHIST PHILOSOPHY.

Although he looked to Kantian thought to try to find both metaphysical and empirical support for his concept of the world as will as it presents itself to the mind, Schopenhauer's pessimism about the struggle of existence, its pain and suffering, and the hope of 'salvation' in self-renunciation and denial of will owes perhaps more to resonances with themes found in Eastern philosophies (see EMPIRICISM; METAPHYSICS).

In the end, it remains unclear whether Schopenhauer's complex discussion of Kant genuinely saves his system from the status of a speculative world-view, although he wrestles seriously with how the mind construes its succession of perceptions and cognitions. For philosophy of religion the emergence of a notion of the unconscious prior to FREUD is significant, and his resonance with some themes of Eastern philosophical thought about bodily suffering and the discipline of renunciation for 'salvation' offers another unexpected facet in a Western thinker of the nineteenth century.

science and religion

In the earliest, pre-Socratic, period of Greek philosophy, principles of explanation for the world and its elements formed part of the study of philosophy. Thales (*c.* 624–546 BCE) held that everything was derived from water. Anaximander (610–547 BCE) ascribed the origins of the world to a boundless, moving material, out of which the world emerged by a 'separating' of opposite qualities.

ARISTOTLE (384–322 BCE) defined 'science' as 'demonstrated knowledge of the CAUSES of things'. However, 'cause' was sub-categorized into four kinds: efficient cause, material cause, formal cause and final cause. The first three, in effect, address a question about cause by answering 'how'; the fourth, by addressing the question 'Why?'

Two writers, among others, who are both established physicists and also theologians, insist that 'science is essentially asking, and answering, the question "How?" By what manner of means do things come about? RELIGION, essentially, is asking, and answering, the question "Why?" Is there in a meaning and purpose at work behind what is happening?' (John Polkinghorne, *Quarks, Chaos, and Christianity: Questions to Science and Religion*, London: Triangle, 1994; similarly, Ian G. Barbour, *Issues in Science and Religion*, London: SCM, 1966, 23–6).

The contrast is a useful one because it begins to explain how TRUTH in the natural sciences and truth in religion is often complementary, and need not be competitive; yet at the same time they are not compartmentalized as if they addressed different, self-contained segments of reality.

WHY DO CONFLICTS EXIST? FROM THE SIDE OF 'RELIGION'

On both sides there have been misperceptions that have generated confusions and unnecessary tension, even hostility. Galileo (1564–1642) was a devoted Catholic, and found no tension between his scientific advances and religious BELIEF. Yet the story of his persecution by the church of the day is notorious.

Galileo's work provided a firm conceptual basis for the view of Copernicus (1473–1543) that the universe is not geocentric; according to him the earth circled round the sun, and stars were perceived as other suns. To defensive church authorities of the time, this seemed to remove humankind from the centre of the universe as God's crowning creation above God's other creatures. They cited the sequence of creation in Genesis and the role of humankind in Psalm 8 and elsewhere.

In 1613 Galileo wrote to Castelli, 'In discussion of physical problems we ought to begin not from ... scriptural passages ... which may have some other meaning beneath their words.' Today virtually all biblical specialists would agree with Galileo's verdict. The Bible does speak of the unique dignity of humankind (especially Ps. 8:6–8; also quoted and endorsed in Heb. 2:6–8). But this has no explicit connection with any astronomical location. Religion and theology had tried to imperialize an area of knowledge that was not at issue in a responsible interpretation of scripture and tradition.

WHY DO CONFLICTS EXIST? FROM THE SIDE OF 'SCIENCE'

On the other side, conflict arises when scientists extend the scope of scientific methods to areas and issues beyond natural science. Even granted that, as most informed scientists and philosophers of science would agree today, it is more accurate to speak of scientific methods (plural) than of a single scientific method, these methods operate within the sphere of the natural phenomena under observation or exploration. They become overextended if their theoretical dependence upon empirical data is transposed into a metaphysical or ontological world-view. Empiricist method then becomes positivist ONTOLOGY.

A memorable example of the difference comes from comparing the approach of NEWTON (1642–1727) with that of the 'French Newton', Pierre Simon de Laplace (1749–1827).

Newton was not strictly 'orthodox' in terms of a Trinitarian Christian theology, but was firmly and devoutly theist. Yet in terms of scientific method he was rigorously empiricist. It was his rule 'to admit no more causes of natural things than are true and sufficient to explain them'. He used only scientific method, but held to a theist world-view, in which God had created the world and sustained the stability of its rational 'order' by divine providence.

Laplace believed that Newton was the greatest genius to live, and assimilated Newton's theories and methods as his model for science. He developed Newton's mechanics of planetary motion. Yet in some circles he is remembered more especially for his dialogue with Napoleon. Napoleon is said to have queried why Laplace did not mention the Creator in his large book on the universe. The famous (or infamous) reply was: 'I had no need of that hypothesis.'

This, in itself, might have been a legitimate reply if it were innocently on behalf of science. However, Laplace was articulating a broader world-view, namely that of the AUTONOMY of science and a view of the world as a self-sufficient, independent, impersonal mechanism. A mechanistic method had become an explicitly mechanistic and materialist world-view. Ian Barbour describes this as a 'reductionist' EPISTEMOLOGY (*Issues in Science and Religion*, 59). It led almost inevitably to Diderot and to La Mettrie's *Man the Machine* (*see* ENLIGHTENMENT).

'FACTS', INTERPRETATION AND LEVELS OF EXPLANATION

The notion that natural sciences work simply from observation of empirical facts tested by experiment and prediction tends to hold only for the simpler segment of 'schoolroom' science. As John Polkinghorne comments, it is 'not just *what* they [scientists] see but the *way* that they see it that counts' (*Quarks, Chaos and Christianity*, 5). He cites the example of the discovery of the planet Neptune as an unobserved inference from the behaviour of Uranus: there is 'a chosen point of view'; a desire not only to observe, but also to understand and to interpret.

In a series of detailed studies, Karl Heim shows that the outworn myth of the neutral scientific observer looking out onto a world of value-neutral 'objective' facts has been displaced by a widespread recognition of the relativity of the observer to what is observed. This is no longer a simple SUBJECT–OBJECT epistemological process.

Moreover, 'levels' of interpretation and explanation are involved. At one level, an acoustic scientist observes varying sound-wave patterns on an oscilloscope. At another level these may be 'observed' as variations of acoustic pitch and timbre. At what level, and by what kind of observer, do these become a Beethoven symphony or a Schubert quartet? Does empirical method suggest that they are only vibrations of varying wavelengths and wave-shapes? Does empirical enquiry provide a comprehensive account of the world? Is a painting no more than blobs of variable light-waves within the colour spectrum? The importance of 'levels of explanation' is explored by Polkinghorne in *The Way the World Is* (London: Triangle, 1983, 16–19).

Although the example may have become overworked, there are few more striking illustrations of the problematic status of 'fact' divorced from interpretation than that of quantum field theory established at Cambridge in the late 1920s by Paul Dirac. Questions about light formulated on the basis of assumptions about particles elicit 'answers' in terms of particles; questions couched in terms of waves produce answers about atomic or sub-atomic waves. An electron will behave sometimes like a wave; sometimes like a particle.

'If you have something like an electron, then if you know where it is, you can't know what it's doing; if you know what it's doing, you can't know where it is. That's Heisenberg's celebrated Uncertainty Principle in a nutshell' (Polkinghorne, *The Way the World Is*, 16–17). The 'unpicturable' world of electrons gives us 'some surprises', just as religious experience of God reflects both 'ordered' faithfulness and unpredicted surprise (ibid.). An over-simple account of value-neutral observation and predication is too narrow to fit the advances in physics and other sciences since the 1920s and more recently.

'THE CLOCKWORK UNIVERSE IS DEAD'

Whitehead makes similar points to those of Karl Heim. Supposedly stable foundations in physics, he comments, have been broken up. 'Time, space, matter, electricity ... all require interpretation.'

The biochemist A.R. Peacocke develops this principle with reference to biological sciences. Biology, he reflects, used to assume that 'law-like behaviour at the macro-level rests on statistical analysis at the micro-level' (*Creation and the World of Science*, Oxford: OUP, 1979). But now nature, supposedly simple in structure, is seen as 'multi-dimensional', including the sub-atomic; once it was regarded as mechanistic; now as interplay between chance and causal uniformity; once, with little novelty; now with 'dynamic newness' (ibid., 62).

Peacocke examines Jacques Monod's *Chance and Necessity*, and the implications of Einstein's theory of general relativity, and places these within a theistic framework (also further Peacocke, *God and the New Biology*, London: Dent, 1986). In his *Science and Providence* (London: SPCK, 1989) Polkinghorne defends the notion of divine action in the world in the context of modern physics. In course of argument he observes, 'The clockwork universe is dead' (ibid., 33). Natural science and theology have both travelled a long way since Laplace and La Mettrie.

We have left aside the challenge of the organic and developmental theories associated with Darwin (1809–82) and Spencer (1820–1903) since these are discussed under TELEOLOGICAL ARGUMENT, EVOLUTION and related entries.

However, a fundamental issue lies at the heart of theistic responses to Darwinian theories. We noted the responses of TENNANT and of W. R. Matthews that the very possibility of processes that could permit constructive adaptation supports, rather than undermines, the notion of a divine Designer, or of purpose in the world. 'Lucky accidents ... bewilderingly accumulate until the idea of purposiveness ... [becomes more] reasonable ... [than] groundless contingency' (Tennant, *Philosophical Theology*, 2 vols., Cambridge: CUP, 1930, vol. 2, 92–93).

SWINBURNE also incisively argues for the importance of this phenomenon of 'orderedness' as a principle of the universe with reference to multiple phenomena including electrons and positrons. Einstein confessed himself puzzled by the very fact that the world is 'understandable'. Polkinghorne builds up a case for the 'very special universe' that is needed to meet the emergence and sustaining of our carbon-based life. Its margin of brute possibility is around 'one in a trillion'. 'If the universe expands too quickly ... it will rapidly become too dilute for anything interesting to happen in it ... If it expands too slowly, it will re-collapse before anything interesting happens ... To make carbon in a star, three helium nuclei have to be made to stick together. This is tricky ... Also carbon is not enough; for life one needs a lot more elements' (*Quarks, Chaos, and Christianity*, 27, 29). The argument mounts up.

RELIGION, SCIENCE AND TECHNOLOGY

Many of the numerous epoch-making applications of science to practical ends raise issues for ETHICS, rather than more broadly for the philosophy of religion.

However, computer technology relates to the philosophy of mind, and more especially genetic engineering and embryology relate to questions about human SELFHOOD. In this area, technologies that alter a genetic cell affect only a life-span; but changes to a germ-line are irreversible because they reorder DNA sequences for subsequent generations.

The debate about therapeutic and reproductive cloning seems to cause problems about human identity, but only at a popular, not at an informed, scientific level. For a clone shares only genetic identity, of the same order as already pertains to an identical twin. Yet no responsible person ascribes the same 'identity' to both twins. In this respect, the debate clarifies a theistic view that 'persons' are more than their genetic inheritance, even if allowance is made for environmental influences also. Moreover, the long-term degenerative effects of a decreasing gene-pool would underline the importance of differentiation as a characteristic of humankind and the animal kingdom.

It is sometimes asked whether CREATION entails the possible role of co-creation for humankind in facilitating new departures in genetic developments. Here, however, the philosophical issue becomes an ethical one. Even if it is acceptable to conceive of humankind continuing creation by 'co-creation', is the risk of inadvertent mutation caused by genetic manipulation of a germ-line one that can be taken responsibly?

This area of biogenetics and medicine challenges those who define human persons merely as naturalistic mechanisms. For can we avoid the inference that these are moral decisions, not to be left to scientific and clinical interests alone? If we accept this moral dimension, however, we have already accepted the principle of 'levels of explanation' discussed above. The discussion of paradigms and INCOMMENSURABILITY by Kuhn and Feyerabend, even if we allow for possible overstatement in their earlier work, at very least serves to relate 'science' to human communities of scientists. (*See also* EMPIRICISM; FREUD'S CRITIQUE OF RELIGION; MATERIALISM; METAPHYSICS; POSITIVISM; THEISM.)

self, selfhood

From earliest times philosophers have noted a particular DIALECTIC or duality between continuity and change in the self. PLATO (428–348 BCE) addressed the problem by an over-neat DUALISM between the body (*sôma*), which belongs to the realm of change and decay, and 'the SOUL' (*hē psychē*), which belongs to the unchanging realm of eternal Forms or Ideas. These dualist perspectives persist, even though many recognize that they generate serious problems.

DUAL CRITERIA FOR PERSONAL IDENTITY? LOCKE ON THE SELF

LOCKE (1632–1704) did not subscribe to Plato's dualism as a world-view. Nevertheless, he recognized that identifying a person through their biological organization (today we might speak of fingerprints and even of DNA fingerprints) addresses only one aspect of human identity. At the level of humankind's participation in the biological animal kingdom, identity is perceived in an individual's 'organized body' (*Essay Concerning Human Understanding*, II: 27: 6). Locke declares, however, that if we are speaking of the identity of human persons *qua* persons (not just as men, or women) 'consciousness makes personal identity' (ibid., 10).

Locke expounds the hypothetical analogy of the body of a cobbler which becomes inhabited by the 'soul' of a prince. To the outside world, the identity of the new hybrid appears to be that of the cobbler; but in his heart of hearts, the prince knows by introspection that he is really the prince (ibid., 15). The 'inner' identity, however, defies, or seems to defy, the application of public criteria.

Yet, anticipating more recent discussions by thinkers such as RICOEUR, Locke rightly perceives that the most significant trans-subjective criterion of identity arises from responsibility and accountability on the part of *this* person (ibid., 18, 19).

A modern analogy would be that of contributing to a pension or superannuation fund. I may be almost unrecognizable at the age of eighty, from my snapshot at twenty-one. Yet if it is 'I' who contribute the pension payments, no matter how much accident, illness or misfortune may ravage my demeanour, it is 'I' who claim entitlement to receive superannuation payments after retirement. The experience of continuity through change is a legal and social reality.

NO CONTINUITY OF SELF-IDENTITY THROUGH CHANGE? HUME ON THE SELF

Does this stand philosophical scrutiny at a deeper level? Further, are we obligated to depend on Locke's distinction between 'body' and 'consciousness', let alone on any dualism of body and soul?

Hume (1711–76) was sceptical about the notion of a stable self. He enters into a critical discussion in his *Treatise of Human Nature* (1739: I: 4, esp. 'Of Personal Identity', sect. 6). Experience reveals, or seems to reveal, that as 'selves' we are simply a succession of perceptions: impressions, ideas, emotions, memories, hopes. We perceive only perceptions. We perceive no underlying structure that ties them together. We can never catch ourselves without a perception; but these are merely fleeting and successive.

Persons are 'nothing but a bundle or collection of different perceptions'; for perceptions are exhaustively all that we can perceive by introspection (ibid.). There is no 'invariable and uninterrupted' core of selfhood that we can observe. To ascribe 'identity' to what is constantly changing is both groundless and logically self-contradictory, or paradoxical.

THREE RESPONSES TO HUME'S CRITIQUE

Various strands of argument have been offered by those who dissent from Hume. First, identity and sameness are not synonyms for an 'unaltered' condition in all or in most contexts. If someone steals one of my books and damages it, and it is recovered by a search, I may logically identify it as 'the same' book, even if it has lost its cover or had ink splashed over the pages. WITTGENSTEIN and linguisticians have explored the multi-level meanings of 'the same'.

Second, in the psychology of moral action we distinguish between act, desire, wish, will, habit and character. It makes sense for someone to say 'I acted out of character,' or more sharply, 'I was not myself when I did that.' Character pre-supposes a continuity of habituated acts that is describable in terms of character-istics identifiable over TIME. Otherwise we could not write references endorsing someone's 'reliability' or 'loyalty'.

Third, C.A. Campbell appeals to a judgement theory of COGNITION. Percep-tion alone might suggest that when Big Ben strikes nine o'clock we 'perceive' it strike one o'clock nine times. In practice, however, we review our series of percep-tions to make cognitive judgements: 'the clock has struck nine' (*On Selfhood and Godhood*, London: Allen & Unwin, 1957, 76). This presupposes a continuity which binds together the series of perceptions through the agency of a stable selfhood. 'Activity implies a subject that is active' (ibid., 70).

Given that the self is 'distinguishable from its experiences', Campbell declares, 'we have no right to assume that the self manifests *all that it is* in the human experiences' (ibid., 108, Campbell's italics). Percepts lead on to judgements and to interpretations, which utilize frameworks of understanding built up over time (ibid., 36–94) The experience

of moral struggle and moral change presupposes 'the self-same being through-out its different experience' (ibid., 74 and 181–209).

A broader, highly sophisticated inter-disciplinary approach that takes account of agency, responsibility and inter-subjec-tivity is offered by Ricoeur, in *Oneself as Another* (Chicago: Chicago University Press, 1992).

DUALISM RESOLVED BY NATURALISTIC BEHAVIOURISM?

The traditional soul–body dualism asso-ciated with Plato, largely with AQUINAS, and with DESCARTES is vulnerable to criticism. RYLE has attacked it as the myth of the 'ghost in the machine'. Such criticisms, however, tend to relate more directly to the notion of dualist 'compo-nents' of the self than to a recognition that the self lives through two, or indeed multiple, dimensions as body, as a spiri-tual being, as a morally responsible agent and so on.

J. B. Watson's *Behaviour* (1914) and *Behaviourism* (1924) in theory present a method in psychology which excludes introspection. However, in B.F. Skinner and others 'radical behaviourism' becomes a naturalistic and materialistic account of the self. The self is a neurological machine without a higher level of explanation. This generates what has been called 'the para-dox of materialism'. If thought is merely a given level of complexity reached by random neurological processes, on what basis might materialism count as a 'rational' or 'reasonable' view of the self? (*See* BEHAVIOURISM; MATERIALISM; REASONABLENESS.)

Often the word 'person' is used in preference to 'self' to denote those dis-tinctive characteristics of being human which many in philosophy and religion have striven to designate by using the word 'soul', but which are perhaps better expressed through less reifying, substantial terminology.

THE GRAMMAR OF PERSONS IN EUROPEAN CONTINENTAL PHILOSOPHY

Two complementary approaches invite attention, one from the Continental tradition of EXISTENTIALISM or phenomenology; the other, from the British tradition of the analysis of logical grammar (*see* LOGIC).

Among existentialist thinkers MARCEL (1889–1973) stresses that human beings are not 'cases' or 'numbers', but persons worthy of respect as persons. Humanity, love and openness or 'availability' (*disponibilité*) to the 'other' enhances not only the humanness of the 'other', but also my own claim to be human. In *Being and Having* (1935) Marcel contrasts 'having' impersonal OBJECTS with 'being with' another person as a 'Thou', without any desire to 'possess' or to dominate.

Marcel reflects the thought of the Jewish philosopher BUBER (1878–1965), and paves the way for LEVINAS (1906–95). Buber distinguishes between the 'attitude' conveyed by regarding 'the Other' as 'Thou' and the attitude of 'I' towards an 'it': 'the combination I–Thou ... the combination I–it' (*I and Thou*, New York: Scribner, 1958, 3). Like Locke's 'man', persons may be regarded as 'objects to be observed' for scientific purposes. Yet persons are more than things. A person is one who addresses me as a 'Thou'. Until I discover this interpersonal dimension, I myself am not fully human.

Levinas also explores the face-to-face relation of human persons. While violence and force is dehumanizing, it is 'the Other' who makes me human by placing my own interests in question. Self-identity and self-sacrifice are to be held together in a dialectic of mutuality and responsibility, so that neither is 'gobbled up' by the other, which each nevertheless gives of the self to the other. Such qualities of life as home, hospitality, the face, patience, mark out 'personhood' in the human. Further themes of this kind are also developed by Ricoeur (b. 1913).

THE LOGIC OF PERSONS IN BRITISH PHILOSOPHY

In the logical tradition of British philosophy STRAWSON (b. 1919) discusses the status of language about persons in his work *Individuals* (London: Methuen, 1959). After discussing 'structural features of the conceptual scheme' concerning identification and individuation in the case of 'Bodies' which have proper names (ibid., 15–58), and their 'Sounds' (ibid., 59–86), Strawson considers 'Persons' (ibid., 87–134). The focus here is 'personal experience' dependent on a 'certain body' (ibid., 97).

Strawson concludes that the concept of person is 'primitive' in that '*both* predicates ascribing states of consciousness *and* predicates ascribing corporal characteristics, a physical situation ... are equally applicable to a single individual of that single type' (ibid., 102). Hume, Strawson observes, was mistaken in assuming that 'I' refers to a 'pure' SUBJECT: 'The concept of a person is logically prior to that of an individual consciousness. The concept of a person is not to be analyzed as that of an animated body or of an embodied anima' (ibid., 103).

Corporeal characteristics (M-predicates) and predicates that apply to persons (P-predicates) complement each other in describing persons. Hence 'is smiling', and 'is thinking', 'believes in God', all draw on a reservoir of personal language. Both axes are necessary for an understanding of the conceptual grammar in question. Even those who contemplate the possible logic of a 'post-mortal soul' can do so only on the basis of its continuity with the self 'as a *former* person' (ibid., 116).

DOES IDENTITY MATTER IN POST-MORTAL SURVIVAL?

Most philosophical and theological discussion in the West has focused on the intelligibility of, and criteria from, the continuity and extension of personal identity. Two approaches, among others, question the value of this focus. One arises from the work of Derek Parfit; the other from Eastern thought.

In modern Western philosophy Derek Parfit argues that 'identity is not what matters in survival' (*Reasons and Persons*, Oxford: Clarendon, 1984). Parfit sees no 'rational' explanation for why we should be exclusively concerned about 'our' survival and well-being rather than survivors who replaces us.

In Judaism, Christianity and Islam, the reason for a concern about identity lies in trust that it is the will of God or Allah to continue the care and love that the self has already enjoyed. It is bound up, in other words, not with egoism, but with a particular understanding of the God of THEISM.

In HINDU PHILOSOPHY the case is different. In the tradition of Advaita Vedanta, as mediated through Śaṅkārā (788–820), the very notion of differentiation as an individual self is a 'lower' understanding based on 'illusion' (*māyā*). Final release (*mokṣa*) from an unwelcome cycle of existence, rebirth and reincarnation takes the form of an awaited assimilation into undifferentiated consciousness. Then the inner self (*ātman*) becomes now explicitly and clearly one with an uncharacterizable Ultimate Reality (*brāhman*).

This stands in contrast to the traditions of the major Western religions. At worst, these suffer from undue individualism. At best, they look forward to a transformed mode of existence in the resurrection, which allows for both continuity of identity and the destiny of a community of persons. (*See also* POST-MORTAL EXISTENCE; RESURRECTION.)

self-involvement, the logic of

This phrase denotes existential involvement on the part of the SELF in language that commits the speaker or the addressee to certain attitudes or actions, or appoints them to a certain status or task, or involves them in some other way. Such language is more than 'flat' description.

Donald D. Evans (*The Logic of Self-Involvement*, London: SCM, 1963) explores the significance of PERFORMATIVE UTTERANCES in AUSTIN for LANGUAGE IN RELIGION, including Austin's categories of constatives, commissives, exercitives, behabitives and verdictives (ibid., 27–40). He applies these to biblical language about CREATION (ibid., 145–252).

The term 'self-involvement' has a distinct advantage over the more widely used parallel 'existential'. In the tradition of Anglo-American linguistic philosophy it is clear that for self-involving language to be effective, certain states of affairs are either presupposed or are true. Existential language in KIERKEGAARD, BULTMANN and European Continental philosophy all too often overlooks the necessary interaction between self-involvement, or SUBJECTIVITY, and questions about the TRUTH of those states of affairs on which the currency of this self-evolving dimension is often based. (*See also* EXISTENTIALISM; SPEECH ACTS; WOLTERSTORFF.)

self-transcendence

See TRANSCENDENCE.

semantics

Most specialists in this area accept the definition of semantics as 'the study of meaning' (John Lyons, *Semantics*, 2 vols., Cambridge: CUP, 1977, 1). Charles Morris proposed a threefold division between 'semantics' as the meaning of signs, 'syntactics' as a study of combinations of signs and 'pragmatics' as the 'uses and effects' of signs within human behaviour.

The distinction between semantics and syntactics is blurred and difficult to sustain, since signs in language draw their meaning-currency from their syntagmatic and paradigmatic relations with other signs, i.e. in conjunction with which they function (syntagmatic relations); and in place of which are they selected (paradigmatic relations).

The role of semiotics also overlaps with semantics. Both may include non-linguistic signs and sign-systems (flags, traffic lights, road signs), and both depend on a distinction between the sign-system or language-system (Saussure's *la langue*) and the particular selection and use of a sign from this repertoire to perform a communicative event (Saussure's *la parole*).

In practice, semantics often concerns relations of contrast, antithesis or semantic opposition, as well as the perceived scope of a semantic domain. The principle of contrast or 'difference' is often illustrated from kinship terms or colour-words, since the semantic scope may vary from language to language. If a language has no word for 'orange' as a colour, the semantic scope respectively of 'red' and 'yellow' will be extended.

Most works on semantics include, at least, discussions of classes (types and tokens); reference; denotation; semantic fields; opposition and contrast; synchronic and diachronic meaning; synonymy; grammatical ambiguity; and lexicography. (*See also* CONCEPTS; DEFINITION; LANGUAGE IN RELIGION; LOGIC; WITTGENSTEIN.)

skepticism

See SCEPTICISM.

Socrates (470–399 BCE)

Socrates, philosopher of Athens, perceived his mission as that of a midwife who facilitates the birth of TRUTH. His major method was to question unexamined assumptions, or common assumptions that had been insufficiently explored. The midwife metaphor may readily have been suggested by the occupation of his mother, Phaenarete.

Socrates wrote no treatise, but the early dialogues of PLATO (428–348 BCE) portray encounters between Socrates and his dialogue-partners. Plato's *Crito, Euthyphro, Ion, Protagoras,* and the *Apology* of Socrates are likely to have embodied Socratic teaching. His *Phaedo* recounts the trial and death of Socrates. Xenophon provides a further source.

Self-knowledge and the questioning of accepted opinion were two key emphases of Socrates. 'Know yourself' and 'virtue is knowledge' provide aphorisms that reflect the first. 'The unexamined life is not worth living' articulates the second. Alongside the midwife metaphor, which encouraged people to think for themselves, Socrates used a second image: he perceived himself as a gadfly to rouse the lazy 'horse' of Athens into critical self-examination and reflection.

Although he was accused of 'ATHEISM', Socrates rejected only the institutional and ANTHROPOMORPHIC gods and goddesses of Athens. According to Plato's *Euthyphro* and also Xenophon, he claimed to have experienced guidance from a divine voice. His view of ETHICS and virtue was high, although he believed that at bottom every human being seeks virtue, and that this is hindered only through ignorance. He dissented from Gorgias and many of the SOPHISTS in their view that ethical value and virtue is merely subjective.

Socrates's self-portrait in his dialogues as a perplexed enquirer is largely but not wholly an ironic device to provoke the dialogue-partner into active reflection and response. However, Socrates always remained suspicious of over-easy certainty. His methods of philosophizing remain a constructive legacy for all branches of philosophy, including philosophy of religion. Socrates, Jesus of Nazareth and KIERKEGAARD are all masters of 'indirect communication'.

solipsism

Solipsism denotes the belief that nothing exists outside one's own mind. It derives from the Latin *solus*, alone, and *ipse*, oneself. Only oneself exists. A 'softer' version of solipsism takes the form of the belief that there are no grounds for concluding that anything else exists outside one's own mind, even if the possibility cannot be excluded.

In his earlier writings WITTGENSTEIN (1889–1951) acknowledged that what the solipsist 'means' is understandable, even correct, primarily as a comment on the boundaries and limits of 'my' world.

In his later work Wittgenstein pointed out in his attack of 'private' language that the very concepts and understanding that are needed to formulate such a view presuppose a shared logical grammar of language through interaction with 'other minds'. Wittgenstein's critique of 'private' language is forceful and constructive, but assumes a special, technical use of 'private' which is often misunderstood. STRAWSON helpfully paraphrases 'private' as 'unteachable' (i.e. the grammar has been 'learned'). (*See also* LOGIC; PLANTINGA; SCEPTICISM; SELF.)

Sophists

The fifth-century Sophists included Protagoras (*c.* 490–420 BCE) and Gorgias (*c.* 483–380 BCE), who were categorized by their opponents as seeking fees for their philosophy and rhetoric, and as teaching epistemological relativism. Protagoras declared, 'Man is the measure of all things', especially in contrast to some supposed external standards imposed by the gods.

Although we must allow for coloured portrayal through the eyes of opponents, Aristophanes' contention that Sophists urged invalid argument through persuasive rhetoric finds corroboration in recent research in the 'Second Sophistic' movement of the first century. Clearly in the time of the Apostle Paul there were Sophist rhetoricians who gained status, applause and professional fees for aiming at pragmatic rhetorical success in the face of an implausible case, placing more value on 'winning' than 'TRUTH'.

This insight in recent research (e.g. in S. M. Pogaloff, *Logos and Sophia*, Atlanta: Scholars Press, 1992; more recently also works by Bruce Winter) explains much of Paul's simultaneous use of classical rhetorical forms and criticism of a pragmatic rhetoric of self-promotion (cf. 1 Cor. 2:1–5, and elsewhere). (*See also* EPISTEMOLOGY; PLATO; POSTMODERNITY; PRAGMATISM; RORTY.)

soul

Concepts of the soul vary from one religious tradition to another, and from one philosophical system to another. In some systems the term is almost synonymous with 'spirit'; in others, the term virtually overlaps with 'mind'. Some thinkers, including Thomas AQUINAS (1225–74), envisage the soul as existing independently of the body; other atheistic or empiricist thinkers reject both the credibility and intelligibility of the notion (for example, Antony Flew).

PLATO (428–348 BCE) held a dualist view of soul and body. The soul is the immaterial part of the human person. More than this, it is the essential part, the essence of the SELF, which constitutes the mental life of the self and survives the dissolution of the body.

Plato offers several arguments for the POST-MORTAL EXISTENCE of the soul. In *Phaedo* (78b) he postulates that the soul is 'simple', i.e. without parts. Entities that consist of parts suffer dissolution when the parts disintegrate into fragments, but in the soul of these are no 'parts' that can be separated. Hence the soul remains eternal.

Plato also ascribes to the soul or mind memories which appear to be innate ideas, but are better explained as surviving from a previous existence. If, however, there was a previous embodiment, it is reasonable to infer that there will also be a subsequent embodiment (*Phaedo*, 73a–78a; cf. *Meno*, 81b–86b). (This is close to the notion of reincarnation in Eastern religions, discussed below.)

ARISTOTLE (384–322 BCE) holds a different view, which finds its way in a radically modified and changed form, to elements in Aquinas. The soul, for Aristotle, is the 'form' of a being that defines or expresses the being's modes of behaviour in the public world. It is not dualistic, but verges on what in modern philosophy might be called a dispositional understanding of mind or character. Its nature is instantiated in bodily actions, and it cannot be separated from the body.

Thomas Aquinas was closer to Aristotle than to Plato's DUALISM, but insisted that (against Aristotle) the soul could survive separation from the body. However, since Aquinas also looked forward to the final RESURRECTION of the dead, this separation would be temporary rather than ultimate; at least until it received some 'body' or 'somatic' form.

The biblical writings of the Judaeo-Christian tradition, however, give almost minimal emphasis to 'the soul'. In Hebrew, the word *nephesh*, probably the nearest to 'soul', has a wide range of meanings, even meaning 'dead body' in one passage, and simply 'life' in many texts. The alternative, *ruach*, usually translated 'spirit', does not denote what Plato, Aristotle or Aquinas tend to mean by 'soul'. The nearest notion in the Hebrew Bible (Christian Old Testament) is a quasi-conscious 'thinned down' existence of She'ol, among the shades: a bloodless, 'reduced' existence.

In the New Testament, Jesus speaks of the need to fear God who can destroy the soul as well as the body, but the term *psychē* ('life' or 'soul') and *pneûma* (spirit) are used only rarely to denote a surviving entity. The major weight is placed upon a transforming and creative act of God in which the whole person will be raised by divine power in resurrection. The Greek *sôma* is used to denote an entity capable of full identity and communication, a public, inter-subjective, heavenly mode of being.

The patristic and medieval traditions became mixed, as Graeco-Roman thought affected the conceptual expression of future hope. The emphasis falls more upon an ultimate future destiny than upon immediate individual survival.

In Eastern religions the dominant themes take either of two forms. Some look to the law of Karma and reincarnation of the soul into a level of existence (often in this world) that reflects ethical conduct in this life. Others envisage the goal of full liberation from existence as a differentiated individual into assimilation with the All.

In HINDU PHILOSOPHY the Advaita Vedanta school, especially Śaṅkārā, stresses the Oneness of *ātman–brahman*. The apparent separation of the SELF is at bottom illusory, and the goal is to overcome this illusion, and to experience explicit assimilation into the One Ultimate reality.

In both Hindu and BUDDHIST PHILOSOPHY, particular sub-traditions vary in emphasis. However, a major emphasis in Buddhism is to find liberation from the cycle of death and rebirth, and to be released to nirvana. In most Buddhist traditions nirvana denotes 'nothingness', but in some it may come to signify a state of bliss. These two variations may have different implications concerning notions of a 'soul', but mostly a broader idea of the self provides adequate language for expression of what is at issue.

In practice, perhaps only those traditions that hold to some notion of an intermediate state, such as purgatory, may be seriously troubled about the precise nature of the soul as a metaphysical entity. For many religious traditions the term is used almost as an adverbial term to denote the continuity of the self who enters a mode of life after death. (*See also* ATHEISM; EMPIRICISM; ETERNITY; RYLE.)

speech acts

Speech-act theory focuses on the kinds of acts or actions that are performed in the uttering of language. The fundamental principles are expounded and instantiated in the entries on PERFORMATIVE UTTERANCES and AUSTIN.

Austin (1911–60) laid the groundwork for speech-act theory, but WITTGENSTEIN (1889–1951) had already noted the distinctive logic or function of certain first-person utterances such as 'We mourn ...' or 'I believe ...' (Wittgenstein, *Philosophical Investigations*, Oxford: Blackwell, 1967, II: ix, 189; x, 190).

'We mourn' constitutes an act of mourning, not a description of the inner mental states of the speakers. In religious worship or PRAYER, 'I repent' is not an attempt to inform God about an inner state that God presumably knows, but performs an act of repentance. In a solemn context of worship, 'I believe' (as in a creed) is as much an action as nailing one's colours to the mast in a naval battle.

Austin classified a variety of speech acts under five headings. 'I find you guilty' is an act of pronouncing a verdict, or a verdictive. In sports a verdictive may be expressed in shorthand form: 'Out!'; 'Off-side'; 'No ball'. Exercitives perform acts that set new states of affairs in motion: 'I appoint you ...'; 'I open this fête'; 'I name this ship ...'. Austin added commissives ('I promise to ...') and behabitives ('I apologize'; 'I thank'); and a 'weaker' form of constatives ('I make the point ...').

DEVELOPMENTS AFTER WITTGENSTEIN AND AUSTIN: JOHN SEARLE

John Searle (b. 1932) offers a more systematic and thorough theory of speech acts than does Austin. He reclassifies Austin's categories, replacing 'verdictives', for example, with 'declaratives', partly to facilitate a far-reaching and fruitful distinction between 'differences in the direction of fit between words and the world'. Speech acts that are performative or illocutionary are '*to get the world to match to the words*'. Descriptive propositions, by contrast, '*get the words ... to*

match the world' (Searle, *Expression and Meaning: Studies in the Theory of Speech Acts*, Cambridge: CUP, 1979, 3; his italics).

'Promising' in 'I promise to ...' constrains the speaker to act in certain ways, following the act of promising (given the conditions of sincerity, power to implement the words, and so forth). In RELIGION, a divine word of promise is transformative and creative, and may also be a free choice of God to constrain God's own 'raw' OMNIPOTENCE.

Searle distinguishes between illocutionary force and propositional content in logical notation. The basic form is '$F(p)$'. 'I promise not to come' takes the form '$F(\sim p)$'. Speech-act theory explores the nuances of 'F', the force of the action, in contrast to the concerns of more formal LOGIC with 'p'.

FURTHER DEVELOPMENTS AFTER SEARLE: WOLTERSTORFF AND OTHERS

Searle produced a series of volumes on this subject, and goes well beyond the core points outlined here. All the same, others focus on particular aspects. F. Recanati (*Meaning and Force*, Cambridge: CUP, 1987) explores issues of performative force. A large group of writers might be mentioned, including Vincent Brümmer (*Theology and Philosophical Inquiry*, London: Macmillan, 1981). However, the work of WOLTERSTORFF has important relevance for issues in the philosophy of religion, which is his special area of expertise.

Wolterstorff's earlier works, *Art in Action* (Grand Rapids: Eerdmans, 1980) and *Works and Worlds of Art* (Oxford: OUP, 1980), primarily address a theist or Christian approach to aesthetics and the philosophy of art. However, they also introduce his concept of 'count-generation', which is fundamental for his philosophy of speech acts. 'By performing one or another action with or on his work of art, the artist generates a variety of other

... actions' (*Art in Action*, 14). A sophisticated and convincing theory of count-generation emerges in *Works and Worlds of Art*.

In his later *Divine Discourse* (Cambridge: CUP, 1995) Wolterstorff offers a rationally coherent argument for the intelligibility of the notion that 'God speaks'. For certain speech acts may be performed by human deputies which are believed to 'count as' acts of promising, commanding, acquitting, or appointing, on the part of God. 'Speech-action theory opens up the possibility of a whole new way of thinking about God speaking' (ibid., 13).

Like Austin and Searle, Wolterstorff gives due allowance to institutional or personal stance as the background which operative speech acts presuppose (ibid., 35). In short, 'one locutionary act' may 'count as' more than one illocutionary act (ibid., 55).

The latest in a long line of studies (at the time of writing) is a constructive treatment by Richard S. Briggs (*Words in Action: Speech Act Theory and Biblical Interpretation*, Edinburgh: T & T Clark, 2001). Briggs shows that Austin and Searle may have paid too much attention to criteria derived from vocabulary, although he broadly endorses their approaches. He explores the institutional and contextual presuppositions of speech acts, and endorses Wolterstorff's notion of 'doing x to bring about y' (ibid., 9). Yet he establishes further clarifications and refinements. (*See also* LANGUAGE IN RELIGION; THEISM.)

Spencer, Herbert
(1820–1903)

Spencer was born in Derby, in England, and had little formal education in philosophy. He extended DARWIN's (1809–82) theory of EVOLUTION into an explanatory hypothesis for issues of philosophy, ETHICS and human life.

Evolution, he argued, provided an explanatory theory based on development from the simple to the ever more complex, culminating in consciousness and the adjustment of the SELF to its social environment. Adaptation to society yields the ethical goal of pleasure or happiness. Pain is a sign of maladjustment.

Spencer pressed a liberal political ethic to support free-market competitive capitalism, which was not unrelated to his aphorism 'the survival of the fittest'. He was greatly admired as a prophet of capitalism in late-nineteenth century America. Nevertheless, he was criticized in Britain for an over-simple view of evolution, and for over-pressing the claims of free-market economy against measured legislation for its control. (*See also* SCIENCE AND RELIGION.)

Spinoza, Baruch (Latin, Benedict, 1632–77)

Spinoza is most widely known as an exponent of MONISM or PANTHEISM. He follows the rationalist and mathematical method of DESCARTES (1596–1650), and was also influenced by HOBBES (1588–1679).

Although many refer to him as a 'Jewish' philosopher, Spinoza was Jewish only by birth and rabbinic or Talmudic education. He also read modern philosophy and other 'secular' subjects, and soon abandoned Jewish faith and practice. In 1656 he was excommunicated from the Jewish synagogue on a charge of ATHEISM. He changed his name from the Hebrew Baruch to the Latin equivalent, Benedict.

Spinoza's major exposition of his pantheistic philosophical system occurs in his major work *Ethics Demonstrated in a Geometrical Manner* (completed in 1675). He also wrote on biblical criticism as part of a plea for free thought and tolerance in his *Tractatus Theologica-politicus* (published anonymously in 1670). He lived most of his life partly in the area of Amsterdam, where his rejection of traditional THEISM caused huge hostility, and partly in The Hague.

SUBSTANCE, 'GOD', AND NATURE

At first sight it might appear contradictory that Spinoza received the two seemingly opposite designations of 'atheist' and 'the God-intoxicated man'. But the reasons for these dual labels are not difficult to explain.

Spinoza drew from Descartes the notion of 'substance' as an underlying ontological principle. However, if substance denotes that which has independent existence of itself, substance is coextensive with the whole of reality. Yet, since 'God' is infinite, God is also 'the whole of reality'. Hence, Spinoza concludes, we may speak equally either of God, or of nature (*'Deus, sive Natura'*) to denote the same single reality, the single Whole.

Many theists viewed this as 'naturalism', and hence as atheism. Spinoza saw it as remaining true to his Hebrew roots, in which, above all, God is 'One': a divine unity and a divine infinity. 'God is One' (*'Deus esse unicum'*), and 'God necessarily exists' (*'Deus necessario existit'*).

Spinoza's insistence on these formulae arose not least from his simultaneous respect for Descartes and utter rejection of Cartesian DUALISM. In particular, God is not a 'mind' to be excluded from the realm of substance or matter.

Through this monist METAPHYSICS and pantheist ONTOLOGY, Spinoza was able to formulate the ETHICS promised by the title of his work. The ethical goal is to transcend the limits of the partial. This explains, in turn, his passionate concern for freedom and tolerance. Lack of tolerance (which he experienced in person from others) was due to elevating partial knowledge into the status of a pretension to have grasped the Whole.

Yet the price for pantheist monism of this kind is that God remains uncharacterizable. God is neither personal nor transcendent. Thus after his death the 'pantheism controversy' (*Pantheismusstreit*) erupted concerning whether Spinoza's ontology was indeed 'atheistic'.

Friedrich Jacobi viewed it as a determinist, rationalist monism without God (1785); Johann W. Goethe and J.G. Herder praised the system as thoroughly theistic (*theissimum*).

EPISTEMOLOGY AND BIBLICAL CRITICISM

If the knowledge of the order of nature (*natura*) is thereby knowledge of God as the One Being, the human mind does not depend upon special REVELATION for this knowledge. Understanding, as Hobbes had suggested, comes when we see what we seek to know as a logical effect of its CAUSE. EPISTEMOLOGY is therefore linked with Spinoza's DETERMINISM as well as his RATIONALISM.

In addition to his ontology, Spinoza's passionate concern for tolerance and political liberalism led him to publish anonymously (for reasons of safety) on a historical and critical approach to the Bible, especially to the Pentateuch. He argued that the early documents reflect the intellectual limitations of the era, and that the Bible does not promote the intolerance that was often 'read' from it. His view of the state was broadly similar to that of Hobbes, but he did not live to complete his work on political philosophy.

In spite of his clear awareness of the problem, Spinoza does not explain with full adequacy his simultaneous emphasis upon determinism and his campaign for FREEDOM. Freedom seems at times in Spinoza to denote little more than a lack of awareness about what causes certain actions.

Stoicism, Stoics

The earliest traditions of Stoicism go back to Zeno of Citium (*c.* 333–262 BCE). The central theme is the rationality of the world, governed by the 'world-soul', its orderedness, and its unified wholeness. The order of the world is reasonable and immutable. This provides a foundation for an ETHICS of self-control in the light of

REASON. Well-being (Greek, *eudaimonia*) stems from rational action.

The creative power of the world is reasonable *logos*, but this divine principle is immanent rather than transcendent. It is probable that Paul the Apostle had this contrast in mind in 1 Corinthians 2:12: 'We have received not the spirit of the world (Greek, *to pneûma toû kosmou*) but the Spirit who proceeds forth from God (*to pneuma to ek toû Theoû*)', where *ek* conveys 'from' or 'out of' rather than 'of'.

Happiness or well-being lies in independence from all external distractions, including those of the passions (*pathe*). In contrast to THEISM, Stoicism promotes self-sufficiency, AUTONOMY and the achievement of one's own goals, set by the SELF. 'Value' is what accords with these self-determined goals. However, among the early Stoics, Cleanthes (*c.* 330–231 BCE) formulated the ethical goal, 'live harmoniously with nature' (Greek, *homologoumenos tē physei zēn: Stoic*, 3:12), which offered a less subjective or self-focused ethic.

The early school of Zeno (333–262 BCE), Cleanthes and Chrysippus (*c.* 280–206 BCE) declined, but Stoicism underwent revival in the period of the 'Middle' Stoa (*c.* 185–98 BCE). A fuller revival came with the Stoics of the imperial Roman period, and included Seneca (*c.* 4 BCE – 65 CE; almost the exact contemporary of Paul the Apostle); Musonius Rufus (*c.* 30–100); and Epictetus (*c.* 50–120).

Debates about affinities or differences in relation to the New Testament continue. There may be resonances about 'freedom from distraction' (1 Corinthians 7:29–31), but the early Christian emphasis upon the TRANSCENDENCE of God, and a more positive view of the body and human emotions mark fundamental differences. (*See also* IMMANENCE; PANTHEISM.)

Strawson, Peter Frederick

(b. 1919)

Strawson was born in London, and educated at Oxford. He taught at Oxford for many years, becoming Waynflete Professor of Metaphysical Philosophy in succession to RYLE (1900–76).

Strawson's writings have had considerable influence, especially in the areas of LOGIC, 'descriptive' METAPHYSICS and a distinctive exposition of the philosophy of KANT. He also contributed decisively to a change of philosophical climate at Oxford, moving from the 'linguistic philosophy' of AUSTIN to a more metaphysical, less 'formal' approach. In the context of philosophy of religion his work on individuation, persons and the SELF holds particular importance.

LOGIC AND LANGUAGE

An early influential paper 'On Referring' (1950) attacked RUSSELL's reformulation of definite descriptions in a logical form that entailed the use of existential QUANTIFIERS. Russell had translated ordinary language into formal logical propositions that would bracket out, by the use of the quantifier, whether or not the referent of the definite description was held to exist.

Thus 'The present King of France is ...' was translated as '(For at least one present King of France) (The present King of France is ...)' i.e. '(Ex) (Fx)'. Russell claimed that by this device, he had disengaged the definite description from acting as a referring expression. Strawson argued that Russell leaves insufficiently clear the contrast of function between sentences of natural language and what propositions or formal logical statements are made by uttering the sentence. In the natural language sentence, he concludes, the referring dimension is presupposed, even if it is not entailed formally.

The broader upshot of the debate was to raise the issue already in the air with the later work of WITTGENSTEIN about the relation between 'logical form' (or formalized propositions) and sentences in ordinary language. This theme is developed further in the latter part of Strawson's next book, *Introduction to Logical*

Theory (London: Methuen, 1952). In the first part he expounds the issues in formal logic, but then raises the fundamental question about how far strictly *formal* logic can take us in considering the complexities and nuances of natural languages as they are spoken and written. He is particularly concerned about the rigidity of logical constants, and the tendency to underplay the role of non-explicit presuppositions.

PERSONS: INDIVIDUATION AND KANTIAN PHILOSOPHY

Strawson's *Individuals* (London: Methuen, 1959) is perhaps his most influential work. The ability to re-identify particulars or persons over time presupposes that they are more than subjective constructs of the mind, and are also locatable in space. Partly drawing on a background from Kant, Strawson argues for the irreducibly 'primitive' concept of person as an entity of which bodily or material predicates ('M' predicates) and personal, consciousness-related or supra-material predicates ('P' predicates) are predicated simultaneously and interactively.

Strawson's third chapter, 'Persons', attacks both a Cartesian DUALISM of mental entities alongside bodies and a behaviourist or positivist reductionism. The grammar is not that of 'mind plus body', or 'body plus mind', but irreducibly of 'person'.

In *The Bounds of Sense* (1966) Strawson offers a constructive and sympathetic exposition of the thought of Kant (1724–1804), in particular of Kant's *Critique of Pure Reason*. He focuses especially on the transcendental issues raised by Kant, which Strawson himself formulates in a different and distinctive way. These transcendental questions are closely relevant to EPISTEMOLOGY in the philosophy of religion. (*See also* BEHAVIOURISM; POSITIVISM; TRANSCENDENTAL PHILOSOPHY.)

subject, subjectivity, subjectivism

It is of fundamental importance to distinguish between these three terms. 'Subject' usually denotes the active human agent as subject in a process of knowledge or interpersonal relation. 'Subjectivity' usually denotes the participatory stance of active engagement by a human agent or subject in which the 'I' becomes sharpened in a venture that may entail the staking of one's very life on the outcome. 'Subjectivism' denotes the unverified standpoint of a human agent or subject who makes a purely subjective judgement without serious grounding in public argument or in the public domain.

SUBJECTIVISM

This third use accords with popular, non-philosophical, usage, although the pejorative use of 'subjective' in philosophy of religion is well established and accepted. The term often denotes that for which a person claims truth or value merely on the basis of desire, hope or uncorroborated opinion.

Subjectivism may seek to dress up personal opinions as tested beliefs when they may reflect no more than preferences or personal attitudes of approval or disapproval. This may apply, for example, to ETHICS, systems of BELIEF, claims to TRUTH or EPISTEMOLOGY.

SUBJECTIVITY

'Subjectivity' denotes a dimension of human personhood that reaches the heart, or depths, of what is it to be a responsible human agent. In this context KIERKEGAARD (1813–55) declared, 'Subjectivity is TRUTH.' It is how we engage with truth, including wrestling, struggle and first-hand decision and commitment, that brings us face-to-face with 'truth'; not merely assenting to the 'right' answer as if the whole were a value-neutral objectivist abstraction of the intellect alone.

SUBJECT OF KNOWLEDGE AND SUBJECT AS PERSON

'Subject' falls into two distinct sub-categories within the notion of an active human subject seeking knowledge or relationship. Traditionally DESCARTES (1596–1650) isolates the human 'subject' in terms of individual human consciousness looking out from within to scrutinize a world of OBJECTS. This is the subject–object relation in rationalist and empiricist epistemology, or theories of knowledge. The thinker is the subject: what is thought about is the object.

In BUBER (1878–1965), MARCEL (1889–1973) and LEVINAS (1906–95), a concern is also expressed that the human subject does not become a mere object in the eyes of other human subjects. Because other subjects have the personal status of a 'Thou', their humanity and personhood can suffer reduction if they are objectified into a mere 'it'. This does not overlook the need for scientific or empirical observation of persons as 'objects' of inquiry on occasion. However, 'I–Thou' constitutes the fundamental dimensions of the subject-to-subject relation.

This gives rise to the constructive notion of inter-subjectivity. The human subject is not a mere individual mind, but contributes to a community of active, personal agents who share inter-subjectivity.

GOD AS 'SUBJECT'

BARTH (1886–1968) (with Buber) insists that 'God is always the *Subject*' who addresses humankind. God is not an 'object' to be demonstrated or 'proved'. Hence Buber observes that next to the foolishness of denying God is the folly of trying to 'prove' God. If God is active Subject, humanity, in the first place, it is argued, needs to place itself in the role of listener before that of explorer or scrutinizer. Such an approach is related closely to concepts of divine TRANSCENDENCE and REVELATION. On the other hand, many more thinkers see religious discourse as about God as well as from God.

Whatever our evaluation of subject, subjectivity and subjectivism, these three terms denote very different characteristics, and need to be identified within their appropriate contexts of discourse. They are not concerned, as one writer expresses it, with 'grubbing about in the depths of one's psyche'; and it is questionable simply 'to identify truth with objectivity and error with subjectivity' (James Brown, *Subject and Object in Modern Theology*, London: SCM, 1955, 13). Often there is a DIALECTIC in which 'control' on the side of subject or object depends on the issue. Many writers seek to move beyond a subject–object split, but not always with success. (*See also* EMPIRICISM; SELF; GOD, CONCEPTS AND 'ATTRIBUTES' OF; RATIONALISM.)

Swinburne, Richard (b. 1934)

Swinburne, Nolloth Professor of the Philosophy of Religion at Oxford, is one of the two or three most influential theistic philosophers of religion currently writing. Like PLANTINGA (b. 1932) and WOLTERSTORFF (b. 1932) in America, he combines a robust and explicit commitment to theistic BELIEF with incisive philosophical argument. He taught at the University of Hull (1963–72) and the University of Keele (1972–84) prior to his Oxford chair (to 2002).

MOST INFLUENTIAL WRITINGS

Among students of philosophy of religion Swinburne's three most influential books are probably *The Coherence of Theism*, (Oxford: Clarendon, 1977, rev. edn, 1993); *The Concept of Miracle* (London: Macmillan, 1971); and *The Existence of God* (Oxford: Clarendon, 1979, rev. edn, 1991). However, his *Faith and Reason* (Oxford: Clarendon, 1981) and *Revelation* (Oxford: Clarendon, 1991) are also widely read and used.

The titles indicate particular areas of substantial contributions to the philosophy of religion. In *The Concept of Miracle* Swinburne rejects the suggestion that MIRA-CLES disrupt the 'orderedness' of the natural world. He agrees (with Alastair McKinnon) that they are not suspensions of 'natural law', but only changes to a normally expected course of events (ibid., 20). Some 'laws' denote observations of customary events: these may be bypassed. But miracles would not suspend 'laws' in the sense of a law 'which holds without exception' (ibid., 28). Swinburne believes that there is good evidence for the miracle of the bodily RESURRECTION of Jesus Christ.

The title *The Coherence of Theism* sums up much of Swinburne's main philosophical agenda. He argues clearly and rigorously that even the problem of EVIL does not render THEISM incoherent. Many of the traditional arguments receive a new vitality under his treatment, and he consistently addresses counter-arguments such as those of Mackie against the FREE-WILL DEFENCE argument.

In *The Existence of God* Swinburne argues for the cumulative probability of the valid force of the three main arguments for the existence of God. On the TELEOLOGICAL ARGUMENT, he expounds a concept of 'order' or 'orderedness', which embraces both a 'spatial' and a 'temporal' order (ibid., 136). The former exhibits 'regularities of co-presence': the latter, 'regularities of succession'. Spatial order might include the very possibility of (for example) alphabetical lists, or right-angled corners; temporal order includes regularities in the behaviour of objects or events, such as those that give rise to descriptive 'laws' in natural science.

This mode of formulating teleology anticipates some of the difficulties put in the way of the notion of purpose or design by DARWIN's theory of EVOLUTION. For it applies to the very presence of order and to conditions for the emergence of ordered phenomena without stipulating 'how' the order is to emerge. This work stands in the tradition of W.R. Matthews and TENNANT (1866–1957).

Swinburne develops the argument to take account of the mass and movement of electrons and positrons, and issues of predictability in post-Einsteinian science. However, he also considers the cumulative force of such phenomena as consciousness, patterns of history and the nature of religious experience.

SOME FURTHER DISTINCTIVE CONTRIBUTIONS AND THEMES

Swinburne has devoted himself to promoting arguments for theism at all levels, not least for student audiences in universities and for student readers. However, it would be a mistake to perceive Swinburne as writing only or primarily at this level.

First, an important and distinctive area is Swinburne's conception of 'the philosophy of Christian doctrine'. This embraces philosophical theology as well as philosophy of religion. His book *The Christian God* (Oxford: Clarendon Press, 1994) represents constructive work this area, together with his *Responsibility and Atonement* (Oxford: Clarendon Press, 1989).

Second, Swinburne holds a deep respect for, and belief in, the 'orderedness' of the world, as we have noted above. This points to God as Creator and perceives the world as a rational expression to God's own 'rational' nature. Swinburne pays close attention to the phenomena in the light of modern science. This emerges in his *Space and Time* (London: Macmillan, 1968; 2nd edn, 1981), in his edited work *Space, Time, and Causality* (Dordrecht: Reidel, 1989) and in his edited volume *Miracles* (New York: Macmillan, 1989).

Swinburne's work not least addresses conditions for the coming into being of an ordered universe. With John Polkinghorne and others, he notes the narrow margins of 'viability' (within astronomy and physics) that allow for the very possibility of the creation and sustaining of our ordered world. As we have noted, this softens some of the claims put forward on behalf of evolutionary theory as a less relevant critique of purpose and design suggested by our world.

One reason for the wide influence of Swinburne's works may be their particular combination of philosophical rigour with clarity and a respect for common-sense rationality. In his chair at Oxford, he succeeded Basil Mitchell, whose writings were marked by similar qualities. (*See also* ETERNITY; GOD, ARGUMENTS FOR THE EXISTENCE OF; GOD, CONCEPTS AND 'ATTRIBUTES' OF; OMNISCIENCE; SCIENCE AND RELIGION.)

syllogism

In Western logic the syllogism is based upon three terms, of which the 'middle term' serves as a bridge occurring in two of the three propositions of the syllogism. Often it occurs in the major premise and the minor premise of the syllogism. A conclusion necessarily follows, as an inference of DEDUCTIVE REASONING.

ARISTOTLE (384–322 BCE) first formulated the syllogism as form of LOGIC 'in which, a certain thing being stated, something other than what is stated follows of necessity from being so' (*Prior Analytics*, 24B, 18). The terms must not change their meaning through implicit redefinition (ibid., 25B, 32–7).

The inference is 'NECESSARY' because if both the major premise is true and the minor premise is also true, the conclusion cannot of necessity be false.

The following standard example demonstrates the use of the 'middle' term (M), 'man'; the 'major' term (P), the predicate of the conclusion, 'is (are) mortal'; and the 'minor' term (S), the subject of the conclusion, 'Socrates':

Major premise:	'All men are mortal'	(M is P);
Minor premise:	'Socrates is a man'	(S is M);
Conclusion:	'Therefore Socrates is mortal'	(∴ S is P).

Since the middle term (M) may be either subject or predicate in each premise, this may yield four different 'figures' of the syllogism. Given that the three propositions may be of four different kinds ('A', 'E', 'I', 'O'), each figure contains 64 (4^3) types of syllogism. If the figures are four, the four figures together may formalize 256 combinations, or 'moods'.

The four designated 'A', 'E', 'I' and 'O' represent respectively propositions of universal affirmation ('all are ...'); of universal negation ('none are ...'; 'no ...'); particular affirmation ('some are ...'); and particular negation ('some are not ...' or 'it is not the case that some ...'). These four classes have been portrayed by Euler (1707–83) and John Venn (1834–1923) in diagrammatic forms. Inclusive circles, exclusive circles and overlapping circles are familiar features of these diagrams.

DEVELOPMENTS IN THE USE OF SYLLOGISM

Although the logic of syllogisms remains a subsidiary area within modern formal logic, after developments in the late nineteenth century the Aristotelian syllogism has tended to fade from prominence in modern logic.

In less formal philosophical discourse, however, syllogisms retain some place. Sometimes a formal syllogism may expose or sharpen a logical fallacy. Thus it is a weakness of the COSMOLOGICAL ARGUMENT for the existence of God that on a formal logical level its use of CAUSE is at best ambivalent, and at worst violates the rule about redefinition, as follows:

Major premise:	Every state of affairs has a cause	(M is P);
Minor premise:	The world is a state of affairs	(S is M);
Conclusion (Questionable):	Therefore the world has a cause (cause$_1$ or cause$_2$?)	(S is P$_1$/P$_2$).

Arguably, 'M' is thereby equally ambivalent; 'caused state of affairs' (by caused causes) may not be identical with 'causal state of affairs' (by an uncaused cause). The syllogism also occurs in HINDU PHILOSOPHY. Here the syllogism has five terms. Usually a positive and negative INSTANTIATION serve to give concrete substance to the abstract argument, even if the logical bridge is now broader than that of formal DEDUCTION and inference.

Even if the 'categorical syllogism' (discussed above) is supplemented by hypothetical and disjunctive syllogism (i.e. where the premises are hypothetical or the major premise yields a disjunction), this still fails to cover the numerous categories required by modern logic, let alone 'informal' logic. Hence the syllogisms has less importance today than in earlier times.

symbol, symbolism

In the context of RELIGION, symbols are linguistic or non-linguistic signs that are recognized as pointing beyond themselves to God, the Ultimate, or a transcendent reality. This meaning of 'symbol' differs from the use of the same term in formal LOGIC. In logic it generally denotes a fixed piece of logical notation which serves in place of variables in sentences, in order to distinguish between logical forms in propositions and variables in sentences of natural languages.

Symbols in religion feature prominently in the work of JUNG (1875–1961), JASPERS (1883–1969), TILLICH (1886–1965) and RICOEUR (b. 1913). In all of these writers they denote the pre-conceptual or pre-cognitive, usually as a vehicle to express or to communicate that which lies beyond the realm of conceptual, SUBJECT–OBJECT thinking.

SYMBOLS AS PRE-CONCEPTUAL AND INTEGRATIVE

Jung wrote, 'Because there are innumerable things beyond the range of human understanding, we constantly use symbolic terms to represent concepts that we

can't define' (*Man and his Symbols*, New York: Doubleday, 1971, 21). Jung himself believed that symbols are generated from archetypal patterns mediated through the collective unconscious of humankind.

Jung, Jaspers and Tillich all perceived a positive role in the use of symbols as vehicles of integration and wholeness. Whereas COGNITIVE CONCEPTS may seem to depend on differentiation between subject and object in EPISTEMOLOGY, symbols operate with an immediacy that integrates conscious and unconscious levels of the human mind, and resists the danger of elevating the fragmentary or partial to the status of a supposed wholeness.

By pointing beyond themselves, symbols invite supplementation by other complementary symbols. Jung and Ricoeur stress the 'double meanings' of symbols. Like METAPHORS, they operate at more than one level, often interactively. Thus while 'stone' or 'rock' is a permanent, lasting object at one level, at another level it may open up understanding of God as steadfast and ever present.

T. Todorov explores metaphorical and symbolic readings of biblical texts as 'allegorical' or double-meaning effects in *Symbolism and Interpretation* (1982) and *Theories of Symbol* (1984).

SYMBOLS AS VEHICLES OF CREATIVE POWER

Tillich also viewed symbol as metaphorical or 'figurative', and as rendering the 'invisible' and transcendent 'perceptible' especially by the human imagination. He adds: 'The third characteristic of the symbol is its innate power ... a power inherent within it that distinguishes it from a mere sign' ('The Religious Symbol', in S. Hook, ed., *Religious Experience and Truth*, Edinburgh: Oliver & Boyd, 1961, 3–11; also in F.W. Dillistone, ed., *Myth and Symbol*, London: SPCK, 1966, 15–34, quotation on 16).

'Every symbol is two-edged. It opens up reality, and it opens the soul ... It opens up hidden depths of our own being'

(*Theology of Culture*, New York: OUP Galaxy edn, 1964, 57). Here Tillich compares the revelatory power of a work of art – for example, a Rubens landscape painting. This power is enhanced by engaging the unconscious.

Ricoeur saw the necessity of HERME-NEUTICS to do away with 'idols' and to retrieve the power 'to listen with openness to symbols'. Symbols have not only revelatory power, but also creative and initiating power. 'The symbol gives rise to thought' (*Freud and Philosophy*, New Haven: Yale, 1970, 543).

CRITIQUE OF SYMBOLS

Ricoeur seems to have been more alert than Tillich to the problem that the enormous power of symbol may at times become distorted and destructive. Even our idols, Ricoeur insists, can be served by symbols. Hence 'the critique of idols remains the condition of the conquest of idols' (ibid.).

Without linguistic controls, a person who suffers from mental disorders may perceive almost any object as symbolic of some threat or self-affirmation, without warrant or due grounds. Hence the pre-conceptual immediacy of symbols must, in turn, be placed critically within a frame of reference that will test the validity of their interpretation.

To be fair to Tillich, he argues that symbols cannot be contrived at will, but grow and die in accordance with their perceived resonance. Nevertheless, this does not address the issue of their becoming distorted while they still have power, or of their gaining power in destructive contexts.

Armies have crushed victims under the spell of symbols, just as martyrs have faced death under their inspiration. Symbols operate with power, but they do not bypass questions of TRUTH. (*See also* CONCEPT; LANGUAGE IN RELIGION; MODELS AND QUALIFIERS; TRANSCENDENCE.)

T

teleological argument for the existence of God

THE NATURE OF THE ARGUMENT

Together with the COSMOLOGICAL ARGU-MENT and the ONTOLOGICAL ARGUMENT for the existence of God, this constitutes one of the three main traditional arguments, although some include the MORAL ARGUMENT as a fourth. The term 'tele-ological' is derived from Greek, *telos*, denoting 'end' or 'goal'. Hence it operates as an argument from the observation of design, purpose, or order in the world.

This is an A POSTERIORI argument from the nature of the world to the existence of an Intelligence, or intelligent Designer, who is usually identified as God. (On the broad differences between a posteriori and A PRIORI arguments, see GOD, ARGU-MENTS FOR THE EXISTENCE OF; and the entries on A POSTERIORI and A PRIORI.)

The simplest illustration of the argu-ment, and the most widely known, was suggested by PALEY (1743–1805). 'In crossing a heath ... I found a *watch* upon the ground ... When we came to inspect the watch, we perceive ... that its several parts are framed and put together for a purpose, e.g. that they are so formed and adjusted as to produce motion, and the motion so regulated as to point out the hour of the day.' Such examination yields an 'inevitable' inference, 'that the watch must have had a maker ... an artificer' (*Natural Theology, or Evidences of the Existence and Attributes of the Deity ...* 1802, ch. 1, sect. 2). Such phenomena as the complexity of the human eye similarly point to a divine creator and designer.

Clearly this argument is closely bound up with the approach of the cosmological argument. It derives from ARISTOTLE's distinctions between efficient, material, formal and final (purposive) CAUSE. It features in the FIVE WAYS of Thomas AQUINAS. 'The fifth way is based on the guidedness of nature (Latin, *ex guberna-tione rerum*). An orderedness of actions to an end (*propter finem*) is observed.' They tend towards 'a goal' (*finem*), just as an arrow is directed to a target by an archer. The One who orders and directs nature we call 'God' (*Summa Theologiae*, Ia, Qu. 2, art. 3).

WILLIAM PALEY'S FORMULATION

Paley wrote several works of APOLO-GETICS. He opens his *Natural Theology* (1802) with a comparison between finding and examining a stone, and finding and examining a watch. A stone is simply 'there' and suggests no particular inference about its nature and origin, at least for theology. The watch, however, contains a coiled elastic spring, and a flexible chain which conveys the motion initiated by the spring to wheels, cogs, a balance, and pointers. The sizes and shapes of components cause 'an equable and measured progression', and the whole yields an 'inference, ... [which] is inevitable, that the watch must have had a maker' (ibid., ch. 1, sect. 2).

It would not weaken the force of this inference if we had never seen a watch made; it would make no difference if we had never met a watchmaker. Even if the watch went wrong on occasion, this would not invalidate this inference. The design need not even be perfect for us to infer the work of the designer.

Such LOGIC applies to mechanisms that abound in nature, or in creation. Paley alluded to the complexities of animal and human life also on the analogy of mechanisms. The mechanism of the eye, he believed, was duly designed for the purpose of sight.

DEPENDENCE OF THE VALIDITY ON THE COSMOLOGICAL ARGUMENT?

Thomas Aquinas had attempted to trace both continuities and contrasts between these two arguments in his Five Ways. The first three ways turn on potentiality, efficient cause and CONTINGENCY, while the fifth concerns order, purpose and design. In as far as 'mind' presupposes direction and conscious will, some have traced the teleological argument back to Anaxagoras (c. 499–422 BCE) and more convincingly to PLATO (428–348 BCE) and ARISTOTLE (384–322 BCE).

Some, however, have called attention to the logical fallacy in versions of the cosmological argument that overlook the logical difference between caused causes and an uncaused cause. If this is applied to the teleological argument, the following attempt to formulate it as a SYLLOGISM exposes the problem:

Major premise:	a designed state of affairs requires an intelligent cause;
Minor premise:	the world is a designed state of affairs;
Conclusion:	therefore the world requires an intelligent cause.

However, the logic would remain valid only if the terms within the syllogism are defined consistently without any change of meaning (*see* the entries on Aristotle and syllogism). Otherwise the conclusion does not necessarily follow. Hence, it may be argued, the teleological argument is no more successful than the cosmological in this respect.

HUME (1711–76) in his posthumously published *The Dialogues Concerning Natural Religion* (1779) attacked a version of the teleological argument which virtually anticipated Paley's. The three characters of the 'Dialogue' include an anticipated 'Paley' ('Cleanthes'), an orthodox believer ('Demea') and a sceptic, probably close to Hume's own views ('Philo').

'Cleanthes' (the 'NATURAL THEOLOGY' believer) portrays the world as a machine the existence of which points *a posteriori* to God as its Designer. The orthodox theist 'Demea' has reservations about an argument to God in terms of 'probability'. This does not go far enough. 'Philo' points out that if 'Cleanthes' follows the logic of his analogies, a designed effect (e.g. a house) might simply suggest a plurality of designers. It does not require a single uncaused cause, who is other than finite.

Hume also anticipated later debates in questioning whether the analogy of the world as a 'mechanism' was any more than a subjective ANALOGY. Moreover, he claimed that causality cannot be observed empirically. What is observed is only constant conjunction of events (*see* the entry on CAUSE).

KANT (1724–1804) goes further. First, he views cause as a regulative category brought by the human mind to make sense of the world, rather than as a 'given' that independently constitutes the order of the world. The aesthetic judgement that perceives order and purpose in the world is not based on reason (German, *Vernunft*). Teleological interpretation emerges when we 'objectify', or treat as 'objective', the order which we project as a regulative principle of understanding (*Critique of Judgement*, 1790).

The teleological argument, for Kant, 'rests upon the cosmological proof, and the cosmological upon the ontological' (*Critique of Pure Reason* [1788], Eng., London: Macmillan, 1933, ch. 3, sect. 6).

Nevertheless Kant does not utterly reject the teleological argument. It 'always deserves to be mentioned with respect. It is the oldest, clearest, and the most accordant with the common reason of mankind' (ibid.). Teleology is indeed a constructive aspect of human judgement. It may not escape the rigours imposed by strictly logical argument. 'God' is not 'within' the world order. Nevertheless, it stimulates insight.

THE DARWINIAN LEGACY AND SCIENTIFIC EXPLANATION

DARWIN (1809–82) published *The Origins of Species* in 1859. While it is an overstatement to suggest that Darwin single-handedly exploded Paley's argument, the wider evolutionary movement of which Darwin's work became most widely known provided the most serious attack suffered by the teleological argument.

The developmental approach instantiated earlier in the philosophy of HEGEL (1770–1831) and his attention to TIME, and the later coining of the slogan 'the survival of the fittest' by SPENCER (1920–1903) in biology and even ETHICS, made a huge impact that emerged as the spirit of the times, namely nineteenth-century evolutionary progressivism. Darwin's work was one contributory factor among many.

Developmental METAPHORS associated with ROMANTICISM began to replace the mechanical metaphors of the eighteenth century with more organic ones. No longer could a merely static model of the world as 'designed machinery' hold sway.

Far from the eye being designed to give sight, it now seemed to be the case that because the eye developed in processes of EVOLUTION and adaptation, it was animals that could see that survived. In a competitive evolutionary world the Psalmist's expression of gratitude that God filled all things living with plenteousness became transposed into a minor key: what failed to be filled with plenteousness was no longer one of 'all things living'. As individuals, or more especially as a species, they became extinct.

Radically naturalistic theories of evolution propose that the illusion of design emerges only because blind mechanisms of natural selection, or (in more recent terms) genetic mutation, ensure the adaptation and survival of those whose functional capacities appear to be 'designed' (i.e. in fact 'fit') for the demands of a given environment. The development of the human brain and the emergence of tools, weapons and language for co-operative enterprise mark a decisive stage in this process.

It should not be assumed, however, that 'evolution' constitutes a single generalized theory. Darwinism specifically presents the view that species evolve biologically through chance variations and natural selection. This leads to Spencer's 'the survival of the fittest'. Darwin, however, used greater caution than Spencer, preferring to speak of 'modification'. He conceded that variations can occur either in constructive or in degenerative directions. If it develops the 'right' characteristics, a species flourishes and proliferates. Environments also change, for better or worse.

Darwin's theory did not become popular in his own day. Fellow biologists criticized his detailed POSTULATES about 'inheritance', and many rejected his materialist account of the world. Nevertheless, the principle of evolution as such took hold of many thinkers in the last quarter of the nineteenth century. More sophisticated versions of the theory have emerged with the more recent development of genetics.

The cosmological argument addresses 'explanation' and design at different levels. In terms of a 'First Cause' or 'Prime Mover' what is required is a universe that embodies the potentiality for design, however this goal of design is achieved. In terms of 'caused causes' the possibility that God as Designer may have determined to utilize genetic processes in order to produce 'human being' or other creatures 'as God wills' (1 Cor. 15:38) remains open and conceivable.

Evolutionary theory thus does not attempt to explain the origin of life, or even how the earliest forms of life came to exist. It is a descriptive science, when properly understood. It concerns the DIALECTIC between phenotypes (the observable characteristics of an organism resulting from how its 'geneotype' interacts variably with the environment) and *stenotopic* or 'constraining' ranges of *observable* tolerance in the face of environmental change. Genetic mutation gives rise to necessary variation, not least since if a gene-pool becomes too small and inbred, degeneration occurs.

None of this excludes the possibility of an intelligent Designer of the universe, unless it is assimilated within an already presupposed materialist world-view. Evolutionary theories do not exclude the possibility of purpose either within or beyond the universe.

FURTHER COUNTER ARGUMENT: F.R. TENNANT

TENNANT (1886–1957) believed that even if each of the main arguments contains logical flaws, their cumulative effect is to establish the probability and rationality of theistic belief. He addresses the impact of Darwinism on Paley's work and on the force of the teleological argument in his *Philosophical Theology* (2 vols., Cambridge: CUP, 1930). 'Gradualness of construction is in itself no proof of the absence of external design' (ibid., vol. 2, 84). The practical 'sting' of Darwinism lay in replacing 'mechanical' explanations for

processes in the world that eighteenth-century teleologists (Paley) had ascribed to God.

'The survival of the fittest presupposes the arrival of the fit', and Darwin shed no light on the originating source of variations (ibid., 85). Tennant moves the focus to the provision of necessary conditions for the possibility of processes which may well include progressive adaptations in organisms. What is at issue is 'the conspiration of innumerable causes to produce, by their united and reciprocal action, and to maintain, a general order of Nature' (ibid., 79).

To suggest a parallel: if, for example, it can be shown that a secondary agent arranged letters in alphabetical order, the more important question concerns the emergence of twenty-six letters which had the potentiality to provide an intelligible, purposive sign-system in English. The secondary question of how they are sorted does not explain the primary ground of their designed origin.

'The outcome of intelligent design lies not in particular cases of adaptedness in the world ... Lucky accidents and coincidences bewilderingly accumulate until the idea of purposiveness ... is applied to effect the substitution of reasonable, if alogical, probability for groundless contingency' (ibid., 79, 92, 93). Purposiveness, Tennant urges, already lies to hand as the most reasonable account of human conduct.

FURTHER COUNTER-ARGUMENTS: RICHARD SWINBURNE

SWINBURNE (b. 1934) also believes that the force of the three main arguments is cumulative, and also appeals to the notion of an 'ordered' universe. He distinguishes between 'spatial' and a 'temporal order' (*The Existence of God*, Oxford: OUP, 1979, 136). He describes the former in terms of 'regularities of co-presence' and the latter in terms of 'regularities of succession'. Spatial order would include such phenomena as an alphabetical order of names, or roads all at right angles to each other. Temporal order would include regularities of behaviour of objects or persons, such as the laws of gravity and motion identified by NEWTON. The universe manifests both kinds of order.

Paley's watch clearly illustrates spatial order, but so does the kind of regularity presupposed by evolutionary competition for survival. The very possibility of adaptation to a changing environment reflects 'great spatial order' and regularity. However, the teleological argument from temporal order is 'a much stronger one'. Regularities of succession are 'all-pervasive'. The universe might well have been chaotic, but it is not.

Against Kant, Swinburne argues that since this temporal order stretches back into the past and continues (however human agents 'interfere') into the future, such order and regularity 'exists independently of' human actions and mental construals.

This is not invalidated as a matter of 'order' even if specific case studies (e.g. of protons, electrons, positrons and quarks) may raise some less clear-cut issues about fundamentals or predictability in given instances. Thus, for example, 'all electrons have a mass of $\frac{1}{2}MeV/c^2$, a change of -1, a spin of $\frac{1}{2}$, etc.'. Positrons share these constants, except that they have a charge of $+1$.

Even if the teleological argument is not demonstrable by strict deductive *a posteriori* logic, this approach reflects 'a reaction to the world deeply embedded in the human consciousness'. Thomas Aquinas and Newton both express this positive human insight.

DYSTELEOLOGY AND COSMOLOGY

The prefix *dys-* derives from the Greek for 'hard' or 'bad', and 'dysteleology' is the identification of actual or alleged counterexamples to teleology. The most prominent are discussed in greater detail under EVIL, and include examples of apparent waste and destructiveness and the natural

world. The struggle for existence can be cruel and severe. Animal predators devour weaker species.

On the basis of many evolutionary theories, a species that may take more than a million years to evolve finally becomes extinct. There are too many 'rejects'. How are they part of a 'purpose'?

Hume pointed to the superabundance of stars and astronomical phenomena as challenging a providential account of the existence of humankind. However, such an anthropocentric account of divine purposes reflects neither biblical perspectives nor those of modern Christian theology nor Islamic theologies of God.

Many supposed examples of dysteleology, on closer examination, serve some ecological balance. It is well known that the elimination of certain bacteria or 'pests' will thereby open the door to more substantial threats which these had held in check. Indeed, ecology underlines the importance of the more general potentiality for 'order', emphasized by Tennant and Swinburne.

Exploration of the immensity of the cosmos reveals an 'order' which points far beyond the small horizons of humankind and beyond a teleology centred mistakenly on the welfare of our planet alone rather than God's delight in a larger creation.

The explosion of a hydrogen bomb is infinitesimally small compared with that of supernovae. Yet this unimaginable vastness and energy provides no counterargument to teleology. It makes the modifications to the pre-modern formulations of Aquinas and Paley undertaken by Tennant and Swinburne, and others all the more to the point.

The alternative hypothesis of contingent accident becomes (or seems to become) increasingly less probable when the extraordinarily narrow margins for the development of life in terms of the expansion/contraction of the universe and its cosmic forces of cold and heat are considered. The one lucky throw of the dice is more than lucky: it is almost too good to be true. (*See also* MATERIALISM; OBJECTIFICATION; SUBJECTIFICATION; SCIENCE AND RELIGION; THEISM.)

Tennant, Frederick R.
(1886–1957)

Tennant made a number of contributions to philosophy of religion and to Christian theology. Probably his most influential book was his two-volume *Philosophical Theology* (Cambridge: CUP, 1930). One purpose of this work was to argue that the principle of 'order' in the universe is such that DARWIN's evolutionary theory does not invalidate teleology, or the notion of divine purpose in the world.

Tennant writes, 'Gradualness of construction is in itself no proof of the absence of external design' (ibid., vol. 2, 84). 'The survival of the fittest presupposes the arrival of the fit' (ibid., 85). Tennant anticipates the work of such more recent thinkers as John Polkinghorne and Richard SWINBURNE. He asserts, 'Lucky accidents and coincidences bewilderingly accumulate until the idea of purposiveness' hardly seems less reasonable (ibid., 79, 92). Tennant's emphasis upon probability, induction and 'orderedness' in the light of modern science paves the way for more rigorous developments of this particular approach by SWINBURNE (b. 1934).

Tennant also wrote further on the philosophy of religion: *Miracle and its Philosophical Presuppositions* (1925); *The Philosophy of the Sciences* (1932); and *The Nature of Belief* (1943). His earlier work, however, was more especially in Christian theology: *The Origins and Propagation of Sin* (1902), and *The Concept of Sin* (1912). (*See also* EVOLUTION; SCIENCE AND RELIGION; TELEOLOGICAL ARGUMENT.)

theism

The term 'theism' emerged in the seventeenth century to denote belief in God, in contrast to ATHEISM, and also belief in the God who acts in the world, in contrast to DEISM. By the beginning of the eighteenth century it likewise came to stand in contrast to PANTHEISM, to denote belief in the God who transcends the world as its Ground 'Beyond' the world. The God of theism is not identical with the world or with some impersonal, amoral ABSOLUTE. The term derives from the Greek word *theos*, God.

Fundamentally, the God of theism is both transcendent and immanent. God is 'Other' than the world and the whole of the created order. Hence many theists (but far from all) expect that the COSMOLOGICAL ARGUMENT for the existence of God will fail, since if God were part of the causal chain in the CONTINGENT world, this Being would not be the 'God' of theism. Equally, the God of theism indwells the world and God's creation as immanent, animating and sustaining it. In contrast to deism, theism affirms BELIEF in divine action, providence and divine OMNIPRESENCE.

Theism also excludes polytheism, since it holds to the Being of One God, who is sovereign, eternal and almighty. The so-called attributes of omnipresence, OMNIPOTENCE and OMNISCIENCE are usually ascribed to God, except that the precise logical grammar of these terms is complex and not to be taken for granted.

Some Christian theologians distance themselves from 'theism' for specific reasons. Thus MOLTMANN (b. 1926) perceives the term as denoting too static and too 'invulnerable' a God to do justice to the God of the Bible. In the opposite direction, TILLICH (1886–1965) distanced himself from a God who is said to 'exist' and to be described by analogy with human qualities through superlatives. For him, God is 'Being-itself', the Ground of Being, or the God beyond 'God'.

Nevertheless the main traditions of Judaism, Christianity and Islam are broadly theist, even if we allow for these disclaimers. Although BARTH (1886–1968) called God 'Wholly Different' or 'Wholly Other', and had reservations about the application of 'person' rather than 'mode of Being' to God as Father, Son and Holy Spirit, in general Christian tradition from AUGUSTINE and Thomas AQUINAS conceives of God as a thinking, willing Being, who is 'person' in an analogical sense (Aquinas, *Summa Theologiae*, Ia, Qu. 13, arts. 1–12). 'The One who is' (*Qui est*) is the most appropriate name for God (*maxime proprium nomen Dei*: ibid., art. 2, 'Reply').

Whether some Hindu and other Eastern traditions are 'theist' depends on how broadly or narrowly we define the term (*see* BUDDHIST PHILOSOPHY). It is more important to define the major characteristics of theism than to debate what may be included at its edges. Judaism, Christianity and Islam are strongly theistic. Hinduism contains some quasi-theistic strands, although more generally some of its traditions tend towards pantheism. (*See also* GOD, CONCEPTS AND 'ATTRIBUTES' OF; IMMANENCE; LOGIC; PANENTHEISM; TRANSCENDENCE.)

theodicy

Derived from the conjunction of the two Greek words for 'God' and 'justice', theodicy denotes the task of deploying arguments that seek to defend the coherence of THEISM in the face of the problem of EVIL. If God is good, omnipotent and wise, and if evil is evil, how can divine action, or lack of action, be explained in the face of evil?

Prior to the ENLIGHTENMENT the emphasis tended to fall upon the coherence of BELIEF in the sovereignty and goodness of God among theists. Increasingly in the modern period the emphasis changed to that of defending theistic belief in the face of the reality of evil. 'Theodicy' applies especially to this second aspect.

The currency of the term today, however, has acquired pejorative as well as neutral overtones. Many writers express unease that the philosophical and logical debates about the grammar of OMNIPOTENCE, and

the FREE-WILL DEFENCE debate, should have become a dominant method of responding to the existential anguish of evil.

A classic expression of this unease is Terrence Tilley's work *The Evils of Theodicy* (Washington: Georgetown, 1991). Tilley seeks to recast the dialogue in terms of SPEECH ACTS rather than of arguments or propositions. Vincent Brümmer also pleads for timeliness in using traditional theodicy. It may be argued that polyphonic dialogue, as seen in the book of Job and in DOSTOEVSKY's *The Brothers Karamazov* offers a complementary approach to the problem of evil.

Both more existential approaches and the more traditional logical approaches have their place. Yet, as Tilley argues, care is required when some simply transplant the arguments of AUGUSTINE and AQUINAS into the guise of a post-Enlightenment 'theodicy'. (*See also* EXISTENTIALISM and a detailed discussion under EVIL.)

Tillich, Paul (1886–1965)

Tillich exercised considerable influence as a theologian, especially in the third quarter of the twentieth century in America. He lived and taught in Germany up to 1933, when he resigned his professorship at Frankfurt with Hitler's rise to power. He emigrated to the United States where he taught in New York, at Harvard Divinity School and at the University of Chicago.

Tillich saw himself as consciously standing *On the Boundary* (one of his book titles) between religion and culture, between theology and philosophy, between German and American traditions, between thought and art, and between sacred and the secular. He sought 'to mediate' between different BELIEFs and cultures.

METHOD AND ATTITUDE TO PHILOSOPHY

Tillich drew on the German traditions of philosophy to argue that 'every philosopher is a hidden theologian' (*Systematic Theology*, 3 vols., London: Nisbet, 1951, 1957, 1964, vol. 1, 29). He wrote 'from the point of view of a passionately loved and studied philosophy' (*The Protestant Era* [1948], Chicago: Chicago University Press, 1957, vii). He broadened the definition of 'religion' into whatever is of 'ultimate concern'.

Tillich perceived his work as that of an apologist, which he defined as providing an 'answering' theology, in contrast to a declarative theology. His major work, the three-volume *Systematic Theology*, is structured around a 'principle of correlation' between philosophical questions and theological 'answers'.

Questions about REASON suggest answers concerning REVELATION; and questions about being (ONTOLOGY) point to answers about God (vol. 1). Questions about concrete 'existence' invite answers relating to Christ (vol. 2). The ambiguities of life and questions about the meaning of history point respectively to 'answers' concerning the Spirit and the Kingdom of God (vol. 3).

On one side critics have challenged the degree of openness of the questions. Do they implicitly already contain the expected answers? On the opposite side, some theologians claim that the answers are too heavily pre-shaped by the questions to be fully Christian, or even 'theist'.

TILLICH'S DISTINCTIVE NOTION OF GOD BEYOND 'GOD'

Tillich argues that to seek to describe God by use of concepts is irretrievably reductionist, in the sense that it fails to do justice to the TRANSCENDENCE of God. God is not 'a being' who 'exists': God is Being-itself, or the Ground of Being. To ascribe 'existence' to God compromises divine ultimacy, and implies a CONTINGENT, finite status that is not God's.

However, there is a price for this. Although he concedes that we may speak of God through symbols, in the end Tillich is reluctant to identify 'God' in terms of a

theological content, rather than in formal terms as 'Ultimate Concern'. God is that which concerns us as Ultimate. What he terms 'the Protestant principle' forbids any assimilation of God as Ultimate, into such penultimate forms of religion as those of the scriptures, creeds, doctrines or other conceptual formulations.

This leads to an incisive and profound question. Does the religious believer genuinely encounter 'God' when he or she identifies 'God' with a limited concept of God, drawn, for example, from childhood, church, or Israel's early history? Conversely, has an unbeliever genuinely encountered and then rejected 'God' when he or she has merely examined the credibility of a concept of 'God' drawn from opinion, church or from a theological textbook?

On one side this underlines the participatory or existential dimension of theism. It should not be forgotten that Tillich's philosophical roots and training came from Germany, where HEIDEGGER's thought remained very influential from 1920s to the 1960s. On the other side, the notion of being willing to die for what is ultimate defines ultimacy only for this or that person. Possible confusions between the psychological and ontological reflect a partially parallel problem in SCHLEIERMACHER's appeal to the psycho-ontological *Gefühl* (more than 'feeling' alone).

TILLICH'S VIEW OF SYMBOL

Second in importance only to his view of God is Tillich's account of SYMBOL as the basis for thought and language about God as Ultimate. It is fundamental for Tillich that symbols reach beyond the sphere of CONCEPTS. 'Religious symbols' represent 'that which is unconditionally beyond the conceptual sphere'. Symbols represent the transcendent. 'They do not make God a part of the empirical world.'

Tillich drew heavily on the psychology of JUNG (1875–1961) for his view of symbol. Psychic forces both conscious and unconscious find integration and focus through symbols, which grow and die rather than being contrived by conceptual systems. Thus Tillich writes: 'Every symbol is two-edged. It opens up reality, and it opens the soul', i.e. 'hidden depths of our own being' (*Dynamics of Faith*, New York: Harper & Row, 1957, 43; also in *Theology of Culture*, 1959).

The emphasis on integration is constructive. Tillich reserves the term 'demonic' for whatever causes fragmentation, and then treats the part as if it were the whole; the penultimate as if it were ultimate. He finds biblical resonance with this in the principle: 'The Lord is One; and you shall love the Lord your God with all your heart and with all your soul ...'

Tillich successfully distinguishes between representational 'signs' and 'symbols' which, he argues, participate in that to which they point. Thus symbols of the sacred carry a penultimate sacred status. However, while he successfully expounds their power, does Tillich provide criteria for their TRUTH? Is his account of LANGUAGE IN RELIGION dependent on too specific a tradition of thought?

MAIN SIGNIFICANCE FOR
PHILOSOPHY OF RELIGION

Tillich presents some distinctive, even if controversial, themes. He broadens a possible definition of RELIGION, and seeks to promote dialogue between religion and twentieth-century culture. In particular his theme of 'God' beyond God promotes a powerful challenge to more conventional and sometimes shallow notions of God. His distinction between genuine ultimacy and the merely penultimate phenomena of religions clarifies distinctions between God and religions, although his critics argue that his way of achieving this pays too heavy a price which compromises THEISM and Christianity. His work on symbol contributes both insights and problems to discussions of language in religion. (*See also* CONCEPT; EXISTENTIALISM.)

time

A fundamental difference marks cyclical views of time, found most characteristically in Eastern philosophies and especially in HINDU PHILOSOPHY, and 'linear' views characteristic of Western THEISM that embody direction, dynamic purposiveness and teleological goal. However, in the West secular PRAGMATISM has also nurtured an optimistic social progressivism, in which human AUTONOMY is to carve out its own goals.

Traditions associated in the West with PLATO (428–348 BCE) tend to view the changes and differences wrought by time as a CONTINGENT 'moving image' of 'timeless' ETERNITY (formulated in Plato's *Timaeus*). Traditions of Eastern philosophy find a parallel expression in the Advaita Vedanta of ŚAṄKĀRĀ (788–820), although rather than viewing temporal or spatial differences as a mere 'image' or shadow of the real, Śaṅkārā attributes perception of differences to illusion (*māyā*).

CLOCK TIME, CREATED TIME AND
'HUMAN' TIME

Augustine (354–430) points out that temporal processes in the world give rise to distinguishing between memory, sight and expectation (or hope). WITTGENSTEIN (1889–1951) explains Augustine's puzzlement in attempting to answer the question 'What *is* time?' by showing that questions about time need to be contextualized in practical ways. Metaphors of flowing rivers of time give rise to fruitless and nonsensical questions (*Philosophical Investigations*, sect. 89–90). Augustine's more important point was that God created the universe with time (*cum tempore*) not in time (*in tempore*). Time was not a pre-existing medium into which God placed the world.

Einstein's theory of relativity assists our understanding of the interrelationship between space and time as co-jointly CATEGORIES of a space–time continuum. Literary theory and sociology, as well as theology, shed light on how we construe sequence, periodicy, tempo, duration and opportune time, in accordance with certain subjective controls that differentiate them from astronomical or 'clock-time' intervals.

A person in power has control over the diary of an employee in working hours. The shaping of 'human time' by commerce and industry is a concern of sociologists. 'Narrative time' is also different from merely succession in clock time. A narrator will use flashbacks or changes of narrative tempo to make a point that enhances the movement or tension of the plot. HEIDEGGER (1889–1976) sees 'temporality' (*Zeitlichkeit*) as the transcendental condition for the possibility of time and of such construals.

All of this makes more plausible the need to distinguish between time as it generates succession, duration and periodicy in the world and the possibility of different modes of expressing sequence, progression and novelty within a realm usually designated as eternal.

TIME AS GIVEN? OPPORTUNE TIMES AND THE GIFT OF TIME

In theism, God may be said to give the gift of time as opportunity; as an interval for promise, hope and faithfulness; as a resource for which humankind is accountable; or as sheer gift for enjoyment. This is as much part of the order of CREATION as spatial distance or spatial resource. In more philosophical terms, Heidegger rightly urges that time constitutes a horizon for hermeneutical understanding.

In modern Western philosophy J.E. Taggart (1866–1925) attempted a distinctive way of demonstrating the 'unreality' of time, as well as of matter and space. Nevertheless, it is arguable that his logical arguments bypass the multiform distinctions outlined above between different modes, levels and experiences of human time, and the 'givens' of sequence and duration, whatever the arbitrariness of periodicy and tempo.

A constructive interdisciplinary dialogue between philosophy, literary theory and issues of the SELF is required, and for example may be found in RICOEUR's, *Time and Narrative* (3 vols., Chicago: University of Chicago, 1984–8). (*See also* BRADLEY; HERMENEUTICS; SCIENCE AND RELIGION.)

tradition

This word has assumed increasing importance with the steady weakening of the privilege accorded to the model of thinking represented by ENLIGHTENMENT RATIONALISM, and often by versions of the so-called scientific world-view. A number of cultural factors have contributed to this shift, including the impact since the 1960s of philosophical HERMENEUTICS.

Many definitions of 'tradition' are heavily value-laden, on both sides of the debate. Negatively, when it is defined as 'customary sets of BELIEF of obscure origins but based upon convention', it appears that tradition belongs to the Socratic realm of mere 'opinion'. It is implied that we must employ the methodological doubt associated with DESCARTES (1596–1650) to regain a more solid foundation for knowledge.

On the other side, more positively some writers, notably the hermeneutical theorist GADAMER (1900–2002), define tradition differently, with different implications. Gadamer claims that the subjective consciousness of the individual alone is 'a distorting mirror'. To listen to what has been handed down and filtered through a succession of community experiences and community judgements is 'based not on the subjection and abdication of REASON, but on an act of acknowledgement ... and knowledge that the other is superior to oneself in judgement' (*Truth and Method*, London: Sheed & Ward, 2nd Eng. edn, 1989, 276).

In Gadamer's view, to value tradition for its cumulative wisdom is 'an act of reason itself' (ibid.). Nevertheless, he may be too optimistic in emphasizing the positive, tested content of tradition. Some people value tradition less for epistemological reasons than for its role in defining and locating their identity.

POSTMODERNITY, like the Enlightenment, tends to undervalue tradition, and to substitute discontinuities, or a 'local' PRAGMATISM. Traditions yield a positive resource, but are capable of perpetuating distortions and falsehoods, which persist not because they survive testing, but because they serve the interests of those who maintain them.

WITTGENSTEIN's emphasis on 'life' and community reminds us that 'every human being has parents', and that doubt comes 'after' CERTAINTY. To discard tradition simply because it is tradition is to impoverish our epistemological resources, and in a limited sense potential criteria of coherence. Nevertheless, an uncritical acceptance of tradition would not be 'an act of reason'. Traditions are fallible and corrigible, but often they are to be treated more seriously than as if they were never more than mere 'habit' or 'convention'. (*See also* AUTHORITY; CORRIGIBILITY; EPISTEMOLOGY; SCIENCE AND RELIGION; SUBJECTIVITY.)

transcendence

The term denotes that which surpasses or goes beyond (Latin, *transcendere*) human thought and human finitude. When applied to God, it denotes divine 'Otherness' or 'Beyondness', in contrast to divine IMMANENCE, which denotes God's indwelling presence within the world. The latter reaches its most exaggerated form in PANTHEISM. An exclusively transcendent God would be, in effect, the 'God' of DEISM.

'Transcendence' and its adjective, 'transcendent', should be distinguished from 'transcendental'. However, both terms carry the connotation of 'beyond human thought', since TRANSCENDENTAL PHILOSOPHY denotes the quest of KANT and others to explore the basis on which human thought is possible at all, together with the limits of thought. In SCHOLASTIC PHILOSOPHY the two terms become close, since here 'transcendental' denotes whatever lies beyond thought and definition by CATEGORIES or classes.

This feature leads to an understanding of the transcendence of God both in terms of God's 'Otherness' from the finite world and in terms of God's unique Being, as well as God's unique relation with the world. In religion and theology this is often expressed in terms of divine holiness.

One classic study produced by OTTO under the title *Das Heilige* (1917, Eng. *The Idea of the Holy*) expounds this in terms of the NUMINOUS which embodies the *mysterium tremendum et fascinoscum*. This is fathomless, holy mystery, which evokes creaturely awe.

In contrast to a more optimistic LIBERAL THEOLOGY in which God was perceived as primarily 'within' humanity and the world, existentialist approaches from KIERKEGAARD to the mid-twentieth century call attention to human finitude, and thereby to God's transcendence. In theology, BARTH (1886–1968) stands as a key figure who sought to re-establish the Otherness or Godhood of God, in contrast to earlier turn-of-the-century liberalism.

Barth expounds divine transcendence in many contexts, but especially in terms of the need for divine REVELATION or disclosure. God is free to choose whether to become 'knowable' or 'thinkable', as Eberhard Jüngel elaborates further. Barth writes: 'God is known through God, and through God alone' (*Church Dogmatics*, II: 1, sect. 27; Eng., Edinburgh, T & T Clark, 1957, 179).

Barth's comment occurs in his section on 'The Hiddenness of God'. God is known not by logical proof but 'in utter dependence, in pure discipleship ... in faith itself ...' (ibid., 183). This marks 'the limitation of our perception and ... thinking' (ibid., 184). God is 'incomprehensible and inexpressible ... not defined' (ibid., 186, 187). Only divine GRACE permits divine disclosure in times of divine choice.

Barth's emphasis in Continental Europe found a broad parallel in Reinhold Niebuhr (1892–1971) in the United States. Niebuhr saw the creatureliness and finitude of humankind (in contrast to God) expressed also morally in illusory human aspirations towards pride. He sought to recover the emphasis on divine transcendence found in the Hebrew scriptures (Christian Old Testament).

Both Niebuhr and TILLICH emphasized not only that God is 'beyond' the horizons of human thought and concepts, but also the notion of self-transcendence. Human freedom and creativity point to the possibility of lifting the self above and beyond merely routine, instrumental and material. Self-transcendence denotes the capacity of the self to reach 'beyond' to higher ideals and values.

Tillich speaks of the 'God beyond "God"'. 'The being of God cannot be understood as the existence of a being alongside others or above others ... When applied to God, superlatives become diminutives. They place him on the level of other beings while elevating him above all of them' (*Systematic Theology*, 3 vols., London: Nisbet, 1953, vol. 1, 261).

God is not 'a being', Tillich insists, but 'Being-itself' (ibid., 265). Every other statement about God has to make use not of CONCEPTS (which are inadequate) but of SYMBOLS, which point to what lies 'beyond' conceptual thought. This is the context in which we should understand Tillich's comment that 'it is as atheistic to affirm the existence of God as to deny it' (ibid., 263). If God is the Ground of Being, or 'Being-itself', this is 'more' than 'existence', which is an attribute of CONTINGENT objects in the world.

ISLAMIC PHILOSOPHY also stresses the transcendence of God, especially in its prohibition of representations of God. This feature is shared (alongside a doctrine of immanence) with most strands of mainline Jewish and Christian theology and religion.

In recent Christian theology PANNENBERG holds together a strong emphasis on divine transcendence with a recognition of divine immanence. Jesus, he argues, witnesses to this transcendence: 'He lets God be God over against himself' (*Systematic Theology*, 3 vols., Edinburgh: T & T Clark, 1994, vol. 2, 22). 'The contingency of the world ... has its basis in the omnipotent freedom of the divine creating' (ibid., 20). In Pannenberg's theology of the Trinity, such is God's transcendence that 'only the persons of the Son and the Spirit act directly in creation. The Father acts in the world only through the Son and the Spirit' (ibid., vol. 1, 328).

This draws upon the tradition of the Hebrew scriptures that God, as transcendent, acts upon and within the world primarily through such intermediaries as God's Word, God's Wisdom, and God's Spirit, viewed as mediating 'extensions' of God's action. (*See also* EXISTENTIALISM; GOD, CONCEPTS AND 'ATTRIBUTES' OF.)

transcendental philosophy

Transcendental philosophy asks such questions as: 'What conditions are necessary for the possibility of thought, reason, or knowledge?', rather than the more traditional questions: 'What do we know?' or 'How do we know?' That which is transcendental goes beyond 'experience' to what thought and experience presuppose as a necessary A PRIORI. It is not derived empirically.

KANT (1724–1804) in effect may be regarded as the founder of transcendental philosophy. 'Transcendental' denotes that which is presupposed by experience, but not derived from experience. This lies beyond the categories that regulate thought.

Such a distinction is already implied in ARISTOTLE and in medieval philosophy, for the transcendental is what lies beyond and above such classes or categories as characterize objects in the world. However, Kant (followed by FICHTE and HEGEL) postulates problems about the very possibility of knowledge and human reason. It was SCHLEIERMACHER's assimilation of this problem into theology that marks the beginning of 'modern' theology at the dawn of the nineteenth century.

Transcendental arguments are often deployed to combat SCEPTICISM by showing that what the sceptic doubts may constitute a precondition or presupposition for the intelligibility of the sceptic's formulation of the problem. In other words, the scepticism is parasitic upon what it presupposes as a transcendental. (*See also* EMPIRICISM.)

truth

The two oldest, traditional theories of truth hinge respectively on the correspondence between what is claimed to be true (usually in a proposition) and states of affairs in the world; and on the coherence between propositional claims to truth, and between such claims and other propositions which are accepted as true.

THE CORRESPONDENCE THEORY OF TRUTH

PLATO (428–348 BCE), ARISTOTLE (384–322 BCE) and Thomas AQUINAS (1225–74) held to a correspondence view of truth. In the *Sophist* Plato states that the proposition 'Theaetetus is sitting down' is true because 'Theaetetus is in fact sitting down'. The proposition 'Theaetetus is flying' is false because this is not the case (*Sophist*, 263 A, B).

Aristotle holds the same view. 'To say of what is that it is not ... is false, while to say of what is that it is ... is true'. Thomas Aquinas asserts, 'Truth is the correspondence (or more strictly, adequacy) between mind and the thing itself' (Latin, *veritas est adequatio rei et intellectus: Summa Theologiae*, Ia, Qu. 16, art. 1).

In modern philosophy it has been noted that this theory of truth tends to presuppose a REFERENTIAL theory of meaning. RUSSELL (1872–1970) consistently promoted a theory of reference, but also held to an empiricist view of the world, and deployed sophisticated devices of LOGIC to address those cases where this theory of truth and reference appeared to break down.

The early WITTGENSTEIN expounded this view in the *Tractatus* (1921). An 'elementary proposition' is true if it corresponds with a state of affairs: (*der Sachverhalt*). In the case of more complex propositions, 'a proposition is an expression of agreement and disagreement with truth-possibilities of elementary propositions' (*Tractatus*, 4.4).

The correspondence theory of truth places virtually all of its weight on the status of propositions rather than on the testimonies of persons. The initial problem is how we reach back to the states of affairs that the propositions depict, other than through the propositions (or the perceptions, observations or judgements that they formulate) that describe the states of affairs. In other words, can we escape a circularity which vitiates their application as criteria, even if it permits their function as replicated descriptions of the same state of affairs?

A second problem arises from asking whether all human language communicates or conveys truth in this way. In his later thought Wittgenstein came to see that he had given undue privilege to the descriptive propositions of natural science, alongside those logical propositions that are true by virtue of their status as ANALYTICAL STATEMENTS.

Third, the correspondence theory leaves aside issues of warrant on the part of human witnesses, and this becomes transparent in its neglect of community and history. Where is there room for a process of discovery and confirmation, not least as a corporate journey?

THE COHERENCE THEORY OF TRUTH

The coherence theory has the advantage of broadening a range of criteria of truth.

Coherence is required not only between the various propositions or truth-claims which together constitute a system of BELIEF, but also between what is claimed in these beliefs and what is generally accepted as true by others in other areas of thought. Thus the status of the person who makes the claim to truth is considered in the light of whether other people hold beliefs, or state truths, that are consistent with that of the person in question.

LEIBNIZ (1646–1716), SPINOZA (1632–77), HEGEL (1770–1831) and BRADLEY (1846–1924) promote versions of a coherence theory of truth. Since all of these stand in a broadly rationalist or idealist tradition, there is a tendency for all of them to seek to build systems of coherent ideas. Moreover just as empiricist attitudes engender questions about observing what 'corresponds' to 'facts', so rationalist assumptions tend to work with mathematical models of coherent systems.

A mathematical proposition is 'true' if it coheres with AXIOMS or other mathematical propositions within the system. It is scarcely surprising that Spinoza, Hegel and Bradley worked with notions of 'the Whole'. The partial is necessarily provisional and fragmentary, because, as KIERKEGAARD insisted, an incomplete system is not adequate as a system.

How do we know whether a test of coherence has reached widely enough? What resort is there when an apparently coherent and self-consistent set of truths is promoted, but runs up against a competing system of truths that is also self-consistent?

It is at this point that debate emerges over the so-called phenomenon of INCOMMENSURABILITY. Might it be that there is no ground from which the competing claims of the two systems can be assessed and arbitrated? In the entry on incommensurability it appears unlikely that no potential overlap can be identified, but this would still not be enough to satisfy the criteria of 'strong' coherentists.

The notion of incomplete systems, of competing systems and of incommensurability suggests a third possible approach to truth.

PRAGMATIC THEORIES OF TRUTH

If truth is in the process of evolving, and if the corporate body of human knowledge of truth is growing as history advances, can we say more than that a given set of propositions, or growing system of beliefs, can be tested for their effectiveness against competing claims relative to a given stage of history?

If the first model has affinities with EMPIRICISM, and the second with RATIONALISM, the third recognizes that truth is conditioned by the CONTINGENT advances of history, the radical historical finitude of human persons and the communal context of knowledge of truth and its usefulness for solving problems.

The maxim 'By their fruits you shall know them' (Mt. 7:16) seems initially to encourage such a practical approach. It recognizes the corrigible nature of knowledge and fallibilist aspects of the agenda. In the entry on PRAGMATISM, the approaches of C.S. Peirce, William James, John Dewey and RORTY (b. 1931) are noted.

Yet even a false belief can help someone to succeed or to come to terms with life, or to help them forward. Under pragmatism, the distinction emerged between a pragmatic theory of action and a pragmatic theory of truth. Peirce expressed reservations about the latter, even if Rorty replaced epistemological questions by strategies of 'coping'. It is difficult for RELIGIONS, especially THEISM, to accept the notion of purely 'local' or temporally and culturally relative criteria of truth, if it is believed that language about God (for example as Creator) makes universal truth-claims.

PERFORMATIVE, SEMANTIC AND EXISTENTIAL VIEWS OF TRUTH

Alfred Tarski urged that 'It is true that ...' adds nothing to the truth-content of a proposition, except at the level of meta-statement. Truth then becomes the subject matter of a statement about a sentence. It offers a semantic description of the role that the original proposition is to play.

More to the point, STRAWSON (b. 1919) argues that to say 'It is true' is to perform a SPEECH ACT of endorsement. The speaker 'stands behind' the proposition, in a commissive, self-involving stance. He or she adds their authority to it. They admit to a stake in it. This provides a bridge from truth-claims to belief, for it is the logic of creeds, confessions and testimony.

This comes close to what Kierkegaard (1813–55) called truth when he declared, 'SUBJECTIVITY is truth'. This is not the 'what' of a propositional truth-content, but staking one's life on the currency of that which is at issue in terms of 'how'. Hence Kierkegaard declares, 'Truth becomes untruth in this or that person's mouth' (*Concluding Unscientific Post-script*, Princeton: Princeton University Press, 1941, 181).

THE UNITY OF TRUTH? CONTEXTUAL ISSUES

PANNENBERG calls for the need to regain a sense of the unity and comprehensiveness of truth in theology ('What is Truth?' in *Basic Questions in Theology*, London: SCM, 1971, vol. 2, 1–27). Yet even he concedes that truth contingently 'proves itself anew' in life and history (ibid., 8).

Each theory of truth offers criteria relevant to different contexts in life, thought, history and experience. None is to be rejected on the ground that it fails to offer a comprehensive criterion of truth. Theories of language and meaning operate in a parallel way. A correspondence theory of truth has useful, but limited, currency, like the referential theory of meaning. Nevertheless, religion and theology do not operate with 'double' systems of truth. Rationality is conditioned by context, but not created by context. Hence an attention to context needs to be held together with the recognition that truth-claims are far more than of 'local' or 'semantic' status. (*See also* CORRIGIBILITY; EPISTEMOLOGY; FALLIBILISM; IDEALISM; PERFORMATIVE UTTERANCES; REASON.)

U

universals

The term 'Universals' denotes a class that embraces common shared features of the individuals or particulars that make up the class in question. The term, therefore, stands in contrast to 'particulars'. The main philosophical issue raised by 'universals' is their status. Are they linguistic constructions the reality of which depends solely on language or SEMANTICS? Or are they genuinely 'REAL' entities, on the basis of which the particulars are what they are?

The respective answers to these questions are denoted by the terms NOMINALISM (universals are construct of language), REALISM (the universals are realities) and CONCEPTUALISM (universals have a kind of reality in the mind, but not in the external world or elsewhere). (*See also* ABELARD; DUNS SCOTUS; PLATO; WILLIAM OF OCKHAM.)

via negationis, via negativa

The Latin phrases 'the way of negation' and 'the negative way' allude to the use of negation in LANGUAGE IN RELIGION to speak of God. The term emerged in JEWISH, Christian and ISLAMIC PHILOSO-PHY in the medieval period, for example in MAIMONIDES (1135–1204) and in Thomas AQUINAS (1225–74).

Aquinas considers the objection that no name (Latin, *nomen*) 'is applicable properly to God', since all are borrowed from prior use to denote 'creatures' (*Summa Theologiae*, Ia, Qu. 13, art. 3). Aquinas allows ANALOGY to function as an 'imperfect' match, but only language that asserts what God is not has genuinely accurate currency.

Thus 'negative language' may attribute to God infinity and immortality: God is neither finite nor mortal.

A second meaning emerges, however, of 'the way of negation', in broader contexts. In MYSTICISM writers often speak of self-emptying. John of the Cross (1542–91) speaks of 'the night of the soul' as part of this process. In HINDU PHILO-SOPHY any difference between SELF (*ātman*) and Ultimate Reality (*brāhman*) is negated in the non-dualist Advaita Vedanta of ŚAṄKĀRĀ.

A third strand of ontological and epistemological negation finds expression in some ancient and modern Buddhist traditions. NĀGĀRJUNA (*c.* 150–200) argued that nothing has a determinate nature. In modern BUDDHIST PHILOSO-PHY, NISHIDA (1870–1945) urges the role of negation prior to a SUBJECT–OBJECT split, while NISHITANI (1900–90) discusses nihilist perspectives in dialogue with Western thought.

It would be difficult to conceive of all language in religion as functioning negatively. For if we have no idea at all of the Being of whom we are negating certain attributes, the process of negation has no stable reference. Of whom is it being said that given qualities cannot be predicated? Thus Aquinas gives a necessary role to the *via negationis*, but not a comprehensive one. (*See also* EPISTEMOLOGY; MODELS AND QUALIFIERS; ONTOLOGY.)

Vienna circle

The Vienna circle published its manifesto in 1929, under the title 'The Scientific Conception of the World: The Vienna Circle' ('*Wissenschaftliche Weltanschauung: Der Wiener Kreis*'). Empirical method in natural science was extended into a 'world-view' or ONTOLOGY of the world. The main editorial name associated with this 1929 manifesto was Rudolf Carnap (1891–1970). He regarded the language of empirical science as the highest in a possible hierarchy of language.

The group of thinkers who became 'the Vienna circle' had already been organized less formally as what came to be called 'the Schlick circle' when it met under Moritz Schlick (1882–1936) in 1924. Schlick, rather than Carnap, therefore, is usually thought of as the founder of the Vienna circle.

Schlick was a physicist who anticipated AYER in formulating the criterion of verifiability. Friedrich Waismann (during this early period) was a member, and those who visited from abroad included Ayer, Willard van Orman Quine and Alfred Tarski.

The institutional structure was linked with the chair of the Philosophy of the Inductive Sciences in the University of Vienna, which was founded in the tradition of the work of Ernst Mach (1836–1916), who was both a physicist and a philosopher. (*See also* EMPIRICISM; FALSIFICATION; LOGICAL POSITIVISM; POSITIVISM; SCIENCE AND RELIGION.)

Weil, Simone (1909–1943)

Weil was born and educated in Paris, and qualified as a lecturer in philosophy in 1931. She lived a life of selfless devotion to others, which finds expression in her philosophical, mystical and autobiographical writings, published for the most part after her death.

For periods of time Weil abandoned her teaching to discover the experience of 'oppression' in heavy industry. Oppression, she concluded, is more than physical constraint: 'it crushes the spirit'. During the Spanish Civil War she undertook hospital service, sharing the painful horrors of war. In this situation she also encountered what she perceived as a deep experience of God, which redirected her thought.

In 1941 Simone Weil laboured in the fields of southern France, also studying Greek and HINDU PHILOSOPHY. She sought to work with the French Resistance, but was rejected on health grounds. In England she refused to eat more than the minimum allocation for her compatriots in Occupied France, and died in 1943, with near-starvation contributing to her death.

This background provides first-hand credibility to Weil's writings on 'the love of God and affliction' (French, *malheur*) and the problem of EVIL (for example, in

Waiting on God, London: Routledge, 1951, 63–78). 'God is not satisfied with finding his creation good; *he wants it to find itself good*.' 'We can be thankful for … fragility', which removes complacency, and for that 'intimate weakness' which under certain conditions makes it possible to be 'nailed to the very centre of the Cross' (*Gateway to God*, London: Collins, 1952 and 1974, 88).

Weil exudes a solemn mystical optimism. We may celebrate the beauty of the waves of the sea, even if the sea is no less beautiful because the gravity of the waves also wrecks ships. (*See also* MYSTICISM.)

Whitehead, Alfred North (1861–1947)

Whitehead was a leading thinker and probably in effect also founder of PROCESS PHILOSOPHY. This approach explores the importance of change, and especially of 'becoming' rather than 'being' as an ONTOLOGY. A British philosopher and mathematician, Whitehead was educated at Cambridge, and wrote his first book under the title *A Treatise on Universal Algebra* (1898).

It is helpful, as well as conventional, to distinguish between three periods in Whitehead's academic life, each of which represents new interests and new contexts.

In the decade from 1900–10, Whitehead worked collaboratively with his
former student RUSSELL (1872–1970).
They jointly published the innovative
Principia Mathematica (3 vols., 1910–
13), which provided a theoretical foundation of mathematics in LOGIC. This decisively contributed to the shaping of modern
logic.

In the second period (about 1910–24)
Whitehead's concerns moved on, away
from Russell's. He became professor at
Imperial College in the University of
London, where he combined an interest
in education for the less privileged with
work in natural science. He published *The
Concept of Nature* (1922) and completed
The Principle of Relativity (1924).

In 1924 Whitehead was invited to
become Professor of Philosophy at Harvard University, a post which he held until
retirement in 1937. This period saw the
publication of *Process and Reality* (1929),
Adventures of Ideas (1933) and *Nature
and Life* (1934). His *Essays in Science and
Philosophy* appeared in 1947.

Process and Reality challenges the
phase of philosophy that stretched from
DESCARTES to HUME. This period tried,
and failed, to base EPISTEMOLOGY upon a
static METAPHYSICS of substance. By contrast, Whitehead saw OBJECTS not as
'things' in their own right, but as having
action and effect. 'Objects' as static
abstractions divide 'the seamless coat of
the universe'. Objects have significance
only in their 'ingressive' relation to events.
This 'ingression' is complex, and prohibits
our conceiving of substance or objects as
defined in terms of a location, thereby
'bifurcating the universe'. Whitehead postulated a four-dimensional space–time
continuum ('the extensive continuum').

Since LEIBNIZ rejected the notion of
'monads' (atomic 'units of one') as spatial
entities and re-formulated their identity in
time of force, there are resonances
between the common dissatisfaction with
Descartes that Leibniz and Whitehead
shared. Yet there are differences, and

Whitehead calls his space–time events
'occasions'.

Adventures of Ideas paints more
broadly on a wider canvas. BELIEFS serve
to articulate aspirations, and thereby to
promote change. It brings to a more
popular readership a perspective motivated by issues of change, 'connexions',
creativity, process and temporality.

Whitehead thought of 'God' as the
Ground of occasions or events, but not as
Creator in the sense of a theistic doctrine.
As 'first event', God constitutes a principle
of limitation on otherwise boundless
possibilities. God is 'the Poet of the world
... leading it by the vision of TRUTH,
beauty, and goodness'. Arguably, Whitehead's ontology borders on MONISM, but a
distinctively 'eventful', not static, monism.
(*See also* BERGSON; HARTSHORNE; THE-
ISM; TIME.)

William of Ockham
(*c.* 1287–1349)

Born in Ockham in Surrey, William taught
at Oxford, London, Avignon and Munich
as a member of the Franciscan order. He
was a leading and very influential late
SCHOLASTIC thinker, who also defended
NOMINALISM.

William taught both Aristotelian LOGIC
and Christian theology, and was more
willing than many other scholastic thinkers to maintain a clear distinction
between the two disciplines and the
independence of theology. He is widely
known today for the principle of
'Ockham's razor', which resisted the
undue multiplication of explanatory
hypotheses beyond what was strictly
necessary. The gratuitous proliferation of
hypotheses merely clouded the issue:
'Multiplicity is not to be assumed without
necessity.'

Ockham carefully qualified his acceptance of nominalism. Only individual
particulars exist, since general designations are largely generated by language
and SEMANTICS. Nevertheless, a general

concept signifies all the entities within a class. He admits that regularities may typify real individual entities, to provide a foundation for the semantic use of UNIVERSALS.

William was critical of the traditional arguments for the existence of GOD. He based theology upon REVELATION. However, an order of nature coexists alongside an order of GRACE. William became involved in a theological confrontation between the head of his Franciscan order and Pope John XXII concerning the poverty of the church. Ahead of his time he stressed the right of people to choose their rulers, and stressed the freedom of all people to follow 'right reason'.

William's most sophisticated contributions were to logic, semantics and the philosophy of language. He wrote extensively on signification, connotation and other aspects of semantics. His work was discussed across the universities of Europe from the early fourteenth century.

Wittgenstein, Ludwig Josef Johann (1889–1951)

Wittgenstein remains one of the most creative philosophers of the twentieth century. His impact on the philosophy of religion concerns especially uses of LANGUAGE IN RELIGION, particularly the logical currency of language about believing, thinking, understanding and experiences of pain, love and joy. Such language, he observed, is rooted in the concrete situations in life shared by more than one person, or within a community.

It is fundamental to note key differences of approach between Wittgenstein's earlier and later writings. The *Notebooks 1914–1916* and especially the *Tractatus Logico-Philosophicus* (Germ. and Eng., London: Routledge, 1961) form the main earlier writings up to 1929; the later writings include *The Blue and Brown Books* (dictated 1933–35), especially *The Philosophical Investigations* (mainly 1936–49; Germ. and Eng., Oxford: Blackwell, 2nd

edn, 1967) and *On Certainty* (1950–1), alongside many other works. Some emerge from an arguably 'middle' period (1930–2).

From the standpont of philosophy of religion, the later writings explore the logical grammar of concepts in constructive ways, and some have appealed to them (almost certainly mistakenly) to support either a fideist view of language and TRUTH in RELIGION, or some modified version of INCOMMENSURABILITY. For the sake of accuracy in understanding Wittgenstein, however, we need to begin with the difficult early writings, even though some may prefer to move directly to the later works. The early works have also been misconstrued as implying a positivist view of the world, which is also to be questioned.

THE EARLY PERIOD AND ITS
WIDESPREAD MISINTERPRETATION
UNTIL THE 1960s

Wittgenstein was born in Vienna into a home where music and culture were valued. In his earliest years he specialized in mathematics and the sciences, and in 1908 undertook aeronautical research at the University of Manchester, in England. By 1912 his interests had moved from applied to pure mathematics, and he entered Trinity College, Cambridge, to study philosophical and mathematical logic under RUSSELL. With the outbreak of war he joined the Austrian army, writing his *Notebooks* on LOGIC, which he carried with him during his war service. This prepared the way for his widely famed *Tractatus*. His journey from engineering to mathematics, from philosophy to logic, from logic to the philosophy of logic reflects his drive to reach fundamentals behind phenomena in this period.

The *Tractatus* is written in the form of seven succinct logical propositions, the first six of which are subdivided into a series of assertions identified as subheadings by the use of decimal points. Just as KANT sought in his TRANSCENDENTAL

PHILOSOPHY to define the scope and limits of thought, Wittgenstein offered a critique of language in which 'the limits of my language mean the limits of my world' (*Tractatus*, 5.6).

The first three main propositions expound the function of language as portraying (or 'picturing') states of affairs. Thus

(1) 'The world is all that is the case.'
(2) 'What is the case – a fact – is the existence of states of affairs (Ger., *Sachverhalten*).'
(3) 'A logical picture of facts is a thought.'

Wittgenstein's biographers convincingly trace his exposition of 'the picture theory of language' to his early reading of a report in 1914 of a traffic accident in which 'the facts' were portrayed to a court by means of models (cars, dolls, roads, houses) in which the relations between the models represented the relations between the objects that were configured to represent a state of affairs.

The fourth main proposition of the *Tractatus* ('A thought is a proposition with a sense', *der sinvolle Satz*) expounds the principle of projection or representation whereby the states of affairs and corresponding constituents of proposition stand in a determinate relation to each other. He explores 'what was essential to depiction' (*Abbildung*, ibid., 4.016).

Yet Wittgenstein as mathematical logician knew that language also functions to formulate logical relations, and not only to describe states of affairs in the world. Descriptive, representational language portrays CONTINGENT states of affairs; formal or ANALYTIC STATEMENTS formulate NECESSARY, A PRIORI, logical relations independently of the world. The second kind of language does not 'say' (*sagen*) anything. Rather, it 'shows' something (*zeigen*). These must not be confused. 'What *can* be shown (*gezeigt*) *cannot* be said (*gesagt*)' (ibid., 4.1212).

Analytic statements have only one truth-possibility. They are true whatever states of affairs pertain in the world. Hence they lack 'sense' (*sind sinnlos*), even though they are not 'nonsense' (*unsinnig*). Thus leads on the famous concluding proposition of the *Tractatus*. 'The correct method in philolosophy would really be that of the following: to say nothing except what can be said, i.e. propositions of natural science' (ibid., 6.53). 'What we cannot speak about we must pass over in silence' (ibid., 7).

These sentences might be understood in a positivist, materialist or behaviourist sense, as in LOGICAL POSITIVISM or in the positivist philosophy of the VIENNA CIRCLE. Russell understood them in this way, viewing Wittgenstein's linguistic 'atoms' or simple elements of language as representations of units of the empirical world. However, Wittgenstein almost certainly viewed these as logical entities, which did not necessarily prescribe a positivist (or any) world-view.

After unsuccessful attempts to have the *Tractatus* published, Wittgenstein appears to have handed the manuscript to Russell 'to do as he liked with it'. Russell successfully secured its publication, but only with a preface of his own, which implies a line of interpretation reflecting Russell's own understanding of the work.

More recent research and the publication of letters from this period have led to reappraisals. Was the Wittgenstein who admired music and the writings of Tolstoy, KIERKEGAARD and DOSTOEVSKY, in whose childhood home Brahms, Ravel and other composers were welcome visitors, likely to have held a reductive and materialist world-view? 'What cannot be "said"' (it became increasingly evident) includes some of the deepest values of life. (See G.H. von Wright and N. Malcolm, *Ludwig Wittgenstein: A Memoir*, Oxford: OUP, 1966, 3, 21 (von Wright); 27, 40, 42, 52 (Malcolm); P. Engelmann, *Letters from Ludwig Wittgenstein*, Oxford: Blackwell, 1967; and esp. A. Janik and S. Toulmin, *Wittgenstein's Vienna*, London: Nicholson, 1973.)

This coheres with the Kantian legacy in the *Tractatus* which presupposes a contrast between 'facts' or states of affairs, which are located within human thought and language, and the 'beyond' of the world, which transcends conceptual thought but remains a source of value, ethics or even the presuppositions behind religion. These are not to be dismissed; but they lie beyond the limits of language, at least as Wittgenstein saw it in his earlier period.

FRESH QUESTIONS AND FRESH EXPLORATION: A 'MIDDLE' PERIOD?

For some years Wittgenstein seems to have considered that the *Tractatus* had solved the most burning problems of language and philosophical thought. During the period 1919 to 1929 he became, in turn, an elementary schoolmaster in Austria and a gardener to a monastery, and designed a house. In 1929, however, he returned to Cambridge as a Fellow of Trinity College. 'He put his whole soul into everything he did ... his life was a constant journey' (von Wright, op. cit., 20). 'He drove himself fiercely with absolute, relentless, honesty [and] ruthless integrity' (Malcolm, ibid., 27).

Works from 1929 to 1933 reveal a new, restless exploration of conceptual or logical problems and uses of language which did not easily fit into the dualist categories of the *Tractatus*. These include *Philosophische Bemerkungen* ([1929–30], Oxford: Blackwell, 1964) and *Philosophical Grammar* [1929, 34], Oxford: Blackwell, 1974).

There is a well-known story of an encounter with an Italian from Naples who made a vigorously derisive gesture with the comment, 'And what is the logical form of that?' What emerged at the end of this period (around 1933) was a fuller recognition of the infinitely complex, multi-layered texture of language in everyday life. Such language served to perform a variety of functions in a variety of ways.

THE LATER PERIOD: MULTIPLE FUNCTIONS OF LANGUAGE OBSERVED IN PRACTICE

Initially in the notes that were published under the title *The Blue and Brown Books*, and then more rigorously and in fuller detail and scope in the *Philosophical Investigations*, Wittgenstein exchanged an *a priori* theory of logic and language for a series of exploratory questions and observations arising from actually looking at how people use language in life. 'Don't say: "There *must* be ..." – but *look and see* whether there is ...' (ibid., sect. 66, his italics).

This has profound consequences for issues about language in religion, although this is not Wittgenstein's agenda at this point. Of any issue of intelligibility in language Wittgenstein sees its context in life (or form of life) which it serves as a crucial frame of reference. 'One learns the game by watching others play' (ibid., sect. 54). To imagine a language is to imagine a form of life (*Lebensform*, sect. 19).

The characteristic term 'LANGUAGE-GAME' is used especially to denote a whole, namely 'language and the actions into which it is woven' (ibid., sect. 7). Language performs a variety of actions like 'tools in a tool box ... a hammer, pliers, a saw, a screwdriver ... The functions of words are as diverse as the functions of these objects' (ibid., sect. 11).

Wittgenstein implicitly criticizes his own earlier work. In the *Blue Book* he attacks 'our craving for generality' and promotes 'the particular case' (*The Blue and Brown Books*, Oxford: Blackwell, 2nd edn, 1969, 18).

Wittgenstein also attacks 'a logic for a vacuum', as if our concern was almost 'an *ideal* language', rather than language in action (*Philosophical Investigations*, sect. 81). In daily life we learn to use language in given ways often 'by receiving a training' (ibid., sect. 86). A logic of abstraction may confuse us, because it is like an engine idling and disengaged from a specific task (ibid., sect. 88).

Thus the meaning of such a word as 'exact', for example, cannot be determined in the abstract; but only when we know whether we are talking of 'exact' distances in astronomy, or of 'exact' measurements in carpentry or joinery, or of 'exact' quantities in micro-sciences.

Wittgenstein therefore rejects the value of talking about 'essences': the essence of language, the essence of meaning, the essence of thought. 'The language-game in which they are to be applied is missing' (ibid., sect. 98). He speaks of 'turning our whole examination round', to destroy the seduction of 'the *preconceived idea* of crystalline purity' in logic and language (ibid., sect. 108).

In this context Wittgenstein utters one of his most widely known aphorisms: 'Philosophy is a battle against the bewitchment of our intelligence by means of language' (ibid., sect. 109). We should not be deceived by the surface grammar of language. This is like trying to explain chess by describing the physical properties of its pieces, rather than how they move on the board. 'A picture held us captive' (ibid., sect. 115).

In this later work we run our heads up against 'the limits of language' not on the basis of an *a priori* Kantian-type theory, but by a confusion which derives from failing to observe the multiform contexts in human life which give currency to diverse uses of language. It is in this sense that 'philosophy may in no way interfere with the actual use of language ... It leaves everything as it is' (ibid., sect. 124). It is not even the case that *all meaning* is 'use'; only in a 'large class of cases' (ibid., sect. 43).

EXPLORATIONS OF SPECIFIC USES OF LANGUAGE IN PHILOSOPHY

The remaining two-thirds of the *Philosophical Investigations* apply this approach mainly to particular uses of language that have generated confusions and lack of clarity in philosophy. Such examples concern the conceptual 'grammar' or logical

status of e.g. 'thinking', 'understanding', 'expecting', 'intending' and 'believing'. They also concern the role of communities within which language uses are shared, in contrast to the technical phenomenon of 'private language'. Wittgenstein uses this term in a technical sense which seems to have been misunderstood by AYER, among others. STRAWSON more convincingly calls it 'unteachable' language, for it is of a kind that never presupposed an inter-subjective or genuinely communicative use.

Some meanings derive simply from our shared status as human beings. Wittgenstein sometimes uses 'language game' to explore hypothetical language-situations involving, for example, dogs or aliens. An alien might be puzzled to hear humans uttering bleating noises and shaking up and down. Given an appropriate context, human beings would understand that as laughter. Conceptual grammar is grounded in communal life. One could say, 'I am in pain – Oh, it has gone away now'; but one could hardly say, 'I am in love – Oh, it has gone away now' (see Wittgenstein, *Zettel*, Oxford: Blackwell, 1967, sects. 53–68 and 504). Pain-language and love-language are grounded in specific human behaviour for their currency.

APPLICATIONS TO USES OF LANGUAGE IN RELIGION

Work on the conceptual grammar of BELIEF remains of constructive importance for philosophy of religion. 'If there were a verb meaning "to believe falsely" it could not have any significant first person present indicative' (*Philosophical Investigations* II: x: 190, 192). Hence when I say, 'I believe' I am making not simply a statement about a state of affairs, but also an act of endorsement, involvement, pledge or commitment. Thus it makes sense to say, 'He believes it but it is false', but to say, 'I believe it but it is false' is meaningless. Similarly, 'I repent' or 'We mourn' is a SPEECH ACT: it does not seek to 'inform' God or others about some inner state of mind (*see* further PERFORMATIVE UTTERANCES; AUSTIN).

A central achievement is to show by example that the logical currency of much language in religion is distinctive not because of some special vocabulary, but because of special uses to which ordinary vocabulary is put. Thus 'hearing' God has a different currency from 'hearing' sounds: 'You can't hear God speak to someone else' (*Zettel*, sect. 717). Hence it would be logical or conceptual nonsense to advise someone who lamented, 'I never hear God speak to me', by commenting 'Then buy a hearing-aid.' Impaired 'hearing' operates with a different logic in these two 'surroundings'.

This has given rise, however, to at least one possible misunderstanding. A few writers speak as if Wittgenstein saw all religion as playing 'the religious language-game' in contrast to a supposed 'language-game of science', or whatever. However, the very term 'language-game' is as complex, flexible and varied as the particularities of all human life. That is why Wittgenstein's work contributes to HERMENEUTICS, but does not justify a 'fideistic' or ghetto-like approach to language in religion. Religion is also part of human life, with varied traditions and currencies.

The varied bridges between language in religion and the language uses of the everyday world emerge in several ways. Most distinctively, the embedding of language in human life means the language-games in religion become intelligible by 'watching' how language is 'backed' by life in religions. Does the utterance 'I have freely received' gain currency in part through observing a generous lifestyle that matches the words? Wittgenstein's work by implication challenges the credibility of religious people by this approach. It is like a paper currency that has to be 'backed' by genuine wealth (explored further in the entry on belief).

Further, Wittgenstein sees varied language uses not as self-contained subsystems, but as 'a complicated network of similarities overlapping and criss-crossing', sometimes reflecting 'family resemblances' (*Philosophical Investigations*, sects. 66, 67). Wittgenstein's observations ring true to the language of primary religious texts. For example: Jesus of Nazareth discusses with Nicodemus the different logical grammar of being 'born' (Jn 3:3–7), and with a woman from Samaria the different grammars of 'drawing living [running] water' (Jn 4:31–4). (*See also* ANALOGY; BEHAVIOURISM; EMPIRICISM; FIDEISM; MATERIALISM; MODELS AND QUALIFIERS; POSITIVISM; RAMSEY.)

Wolterstorff, Nicholas (b. 1932)

Wolterstorff has made outstanding contributions to the philosophy of religion in the areas of METAPHYSICS, EPISTEMOLOGY and SPEECH-ACT theory. He has also written on aesthetics and the philosophy of art and on ethical and political issues. He is probably one of two or three most incisive contemporary philosophers of religion who writes from an explicitly theistic perspective.

Wolterstorff was educated in the Christian Reformed tradition of Dutch America at Calvin College, Grand Rapids, but then also studied at Harvard University. He has taught at Yale, at Calvin College, at the Free University of Amsterdam and from 1989 again at Yale, as Professor of Philosophical Theology.

METAPHYSICS AND AESTHETICS

During the period up to 1980, Wolterstorff's publications included *On Universals* (Chicago: University of Chicago Press, 1970), *Reason Within the Bounds of Religion* (Grand Rapids: Eerdmans, 1976, 2nd edn, 1984), *Works and Worlds of Art* (Oxford: OUP, 1980) and *Art in Action* (Grand Rapids: Eerdmans, 1980, 2nd edn, 1994).

Are UNIVERSALS 'real', and instantiated in particulars; or are they merely verbal or semantic constructs that engage with reality only at the level of the particular from whose shared properties they linguistically derive?

In a very broad sense Wolterstorff defends 'REALISM', in contrast to the view that the activity of the mind so decisively constructs 'the world' that, in effect, nothing is 'given'. Wolterstorff does not present a naïve OBJECTIVISM, as if the conceptual activity of the human SUBJECT were irrelevant; but he rejects the anti-realism that extends KANT'S TRANSCENDENTAL PHILOSOPHY into a forerunner of social constructionism.

This coheres with Wolterstorff's observations about art and epistemology. He expounds a philosophy of art which entails engaging 'in critique, in unmasking ... the institution of high art ...', so that works of art do not 'become surrogate gods' (*Art in Action*, 11 and 30). Works of art are often 'an expression of the *Weltanschauungen* of their makers' (ibid., 221). Art, however, *can* be representational; it can project depictions of the world.

This touches upon the theme that emerges centrally in Wolterstorff's work on speech acts: 'By performing one and another action with or on his work of art, the artist generates a variety of other, distinct, actions. Some of those ... are count-generated, some are causally generated' (ibid., 14), One action may 'count as' performing another: '*instruments* in the performance of generated actions' (ibid.).

The very capacity to distinguish between 'projecting a world' in art (or in literary narrative) and using 'descriptive' representational language, or between authorial or artistic commitments to portray states of affairs and authorial or artistic explorations of fictional 'possible' worlds, presupposes the possibility of reaching out beyond the mind to the 'given' world (*Works and Worlds of Art*, 222–39). The factual worlds may also be 'fictive' worlds, but these differ from 'possible' worlds.

'Count-generation' assumes a major role in the later work *Divine Discourse* (1995). However, in 1980 the main concern is to offer a Christian understanding of aesthetics and a model of the dynamics of creative art. The emphasis falls upon creativity, not mere replication; but a creativity that is more than mere self-expression. It carries those who contemplate it beyond the self of the artist to the divine creation. The world is 'created' in accord with God's own ideas ... full-bodied realities in their own right' (*Art in Action*, 31).

SPEECH-ACT THEORY

The two works that are fundamental and seminal for the philosophy of religion are both mainly from the Yale period: *Divine Discourse* (Cambridge: CUP, 1995), mainly on LANGUAGE IN RELIGION and speech acts; and *John Locke and the Ethics of Belief* (Cambridge: CUP, 1996) mainly on the epistemological issue of 'entitlement' to BELIEF, or 'reasonable' belief. This develops further, in the light of a new appreciation of LOCKE, the epistemology begun in the volume jointly edited with PLANTINGA, *Faith and Rationality* (Notre Dame: Notre Dame University Press, 1984).

In *Divine Discourse*, Wolterstorff observes, 'Contemporary speech-action theory opens up the possibility of a whole new way of thinking about God speaking: perhaps the attribution of speech to God by Jews, Christians and Muslims, should be understood as the attribution to God of *illocutionary actions*, leaving it open how God performs these actions' (ibid., 13).

Convincingly, Wolterstorff insists that promising, commanding and taking up a certain kind of narrative stance are no less fundamental (probably more so) than 'communicating or expressing knowledge' (ibid., 35). This may be perceived as 'from God' through 'Double Agency Discourse', in which human persons utter discourse as deputized appointees, like a secretary writing on behalf of the director or president.

The key point is that 'by way of a single locutionary act one may say different things to different addressees' (ibid., 55). This is where Wolterstorff reintroduces his notion of count-generation: one or more speech acts may count as the action of divine promise, divine appointment, divine forgiveness or a wide range of multi-level speech actions.

EPISTEMOLOGY

Wolterstorff's work on LOCKE gives a distinctive turn to his earlier discussions of FOUNDATIONALISM and 'Reformed epistemology' in *Reason within the Bounds of Religion*, in *Faith and Rationality* (with Plantinga) and a number of research articles. In the first of these, Wolterstorff had attributed an unqualified foundationalism to 'AQUINAS, DESCARTES, LEIBNIZ, BERKELEY, logical positivists – all of them and many more have been foundationalists' (*Reason within the Bounds*, 26). Such an approach he had attacked.

In the light of a fresh appraisal of Locke, Wolterstorff came to distinguish between the 'far more restricted' foundationalism of Descartes and the altogether more promising work of Locke on 'reasonable belief'. Locke represents a foundationalism, but a version with 'that depth for which I was looking' (*John Locke*, xi).

The centre of gravity of Locke's *Essay on Human Understanding* is not book II, but the often neglected book IV (although less neglected among recent commentators). Wolterstorff agrees with Locke's point that mere intensity of religious conviction offers no warrant for the truth of religious belief. Further, he retains the core of 'Reformed Epistemology', namely the belief that NATURAL THEOLOGY, or REASON without the aid of GRACE or revelatory discourse, is an inadequate foundation for religious belief. Yet Locke's careful, reasonable, balanced middle path on broad criteria of reasonableness avoids both evidentialism and 'hard' RATIONALISM, and this offers a sane way forward.

Since 1996, Wolterstorff has continued his concern for public ETHICS in *Religion in the Public Square* (with R. Audi; Rowman & Littlefield, 1997) and for epistemology in *Thomas Reid and the Story of Epistemology* (Cambridge: CUP, 2001). (*See also* AUSTIN; INSTANTIATION; LOGICAL POSITIVISM; PERFORMATIVE UTTERANCES; SEMANTICS; THEISM.)

Z

Zen philosophy

The term generally denotes a sub-tradition within Mahāyāna Buddhist thought in the form in which this developed in China and Japan after about the sixth century CE. Self-awakening and liberation remain prominent themes, together with perception unclouded by desire or undue distraction.

Since SUBJECT–OBJECT conceptual thought and over-neat 'definition' is regarded as obtrusive rather than illuminating, it is difficult to characterize Zen by a list of defining abstractions, rather than by more helpful INSTANTIATIONS. In modern thought NISHIDA (1870–1945) and NISHITANI (1900–90) offer bridges between Zen themes and Western concepts, while several Western philosophers have sought to interact with Zen. These include the later HEIDEGGER and CUPITT, among others.

One attempt to move beyond subject–object thinking is the use of the *koan* to provoke a different level of thought and perception. The *koan* intended to stimulate meditative or 'non-objective' reflection, namely the image of 'one hand clapping', is frequently cited by Western writers. (*See also* BUDDHIST PHILOSOPHY; MONISM; MYSTICISM; VIA NEGATIVA; more broadly, DUALISM; HINDU PHILOSOPHY; NĀGĀRJUNA.)

Zoroastrianism

Zoroastrianism was the major religion of ancient Iran (Persia) founded by Zoroaster or, in Iranian, Zarathustra. His date is contested: from 1400 BCE to as late as 500 BCE. Zoroastrianism suffered severe decline after the Muslim invasion of the seventh century, with virtually enforced conversion to Islam.

It is estimated that today a following of the order of 100,000 remain, of whom three-quarters are Parsis ('people from Persia') who had migrated from persecution to Western India.

The sacred scriptures of Zoroastrianism is the *Avesta*, of which the *Gāthās* are seen as containing the essential teaching of Zarathustra as the prophet. In summary, Zoroastrianism embodies a metaphysical DUALISM, in which Ahura Mazdā ('the Wise Lord'), or Ormadz, represents the force of righteousness; and the evil power is Ahriman, or Angra Mainyu. The righteous power is light, life, order, law and truth; the evil power is darkness, death, evil and falsehood.

Zoroaster, as the prophet, seeks the protection of Ahura Mazdā in the *Gāthās,* prays for victory, and gathers together a group of 'immortal holy ones', or disciples, to help forward the cause. The world is the theatre and cosmic arena of this cosmic struggle. After a current period of balance Ahura Mazdā will prevail, bringing in the judgement of the power of evil and the new kingdom. The words and deeds of the righteous are recorded in the Book of Life.

After earlier years in which some polytheistic assimilation seems to have taken place, Zoroastrians today affirm a form of monotheism, in spite of a dualist dimension, on the ground that they worship only Ahura Mazdā. Among specialists on this subject, John Hinnells stresses the increasing role of 'sweet reason' and liberal influence among modern adherents, not least through the influence of the philosophy of M.M. Dhalla (1875–1956), although he also concedes that other currents also influence the religion.

Zoroastrianism today is not a 'centralized' religion, and has developed in different directions. The conservative tradition has been sustained by Rustom Sanjana of Bombay, who emphasizes 'One God', and respect for the Prophet. J.J. Modi allows for some 'DEMYTHOLOGIZING' of the texts (as Hinnells describes it), but retains many elements in a moderate way. Yet others have stressed the rational and philosophical, sitting loose to the earlier core, and explaining away many texts and much ritual. Zoroastrianism is an identifiable but barely unified religion today, except for the common reference-point of the *Gāthās*, at least in principle.

Chronology

c. 1500–800 BCE	Era of the *Vedas*.
c. 800–500 BCE	Era of classical Vedanta and Upaniṣads
c. 600 BCE (?)	Zoroaster, (Zarathustra) founder of Persian religion, Zoroastrianism (?) Date contested from 1400–500 BCE
c. 624–546 BCE	Thales of Miletus, Greek philosopher
c. 551–479 BCE	Confucius, Chinese philosopher; in effect founder of Chinese philosophy
c. 550–470 BCE	'The Buddha': Siddhartha Gautama, 'Enlightened' founder-teacher of Buddhism
c. 550–470 BCE (?)	Mahāvira, 'Enlightened' founder-teacher of Jaina philosophy
c. 540–425 BCE	Heraclitus of Ephesus, Greek philosopher
fl. 515–492 BCE	Parmenides of Elea, Greek philosopher
c. 470–399 BCE	Socrates, Athenian philosopher
c. 428–348 BCE	Plato, Athenian philosopher
c. 384–22 BCE	Aristotle, Greek philosopher of Stagira and Athens
c. 341–270 BCE	Epicurus of Samos, Greek philosopher
c. 334–262 BCE	Zeno of Citium, Greek philosopher
c. 20 BCE – 50 CE	Philo of Alexandria, Jewish philosopher and biblical commentator
c. 30 CE	Approximate date of crucifixion of Jesus Christ

c. 150–200	Nāgārjuna, Buddhist philosopher, founder of the Madhyamaka school of Mahāyāna Buddhism
c. 185–254	Origen, Christian biblical and philosophical theologian
205–70	Plotinus, Neoplatonist thinker
354–430	Augustine, Christian theologian and philosopher
411	Augustine: *City of God*
c. 480–525	Boethius, Roman philosopher
622–32	The Prophet (Muhammad) and the texts of the Qur'an; capture of Mecca, 628
c. 788–820	Śaṅkārā, influential Hindu philosopher of non-dualist (Advaita) Vedanta tradition
c. 813–71	al-Kindi, Islamic philosopher and mathematician
875–950	al-Farabi, Islamic philosopher
882–942	Saadiah Gaon, Jewish philosopher
980–1037	Ibn Sina (Avicenna), Islamic philosopher
c. 1017–1137	Rāmānuja, Hindu philosopher of 'modified' Advaita Vedanta
1033–1109	Anselm of Canterbury, philosopher, theologian and archbishop
1058–1111	al-Ghazali, Islamic philosophical theologian
1079–1142	Peter Abelard, French theologian and philosopher
1126–98	Ibn Rushd (Averroes), Islamic scholar and philosopher
1135–1204	Moses Maimonides, Jewish religious philosopher
1200–80	Albertus Magnus, scholastic philosopher
c. 1238–1317 (?)	Mādhva, Hindu philosopher and theologian of Dvaita (dualist) Vedanta school
1260–1327	Meister Eckhart, German mystic
c. 1266–1308	Duns Scotus, Scottish theologian and philosopher
1287–1349	William of Ockham, English philosopher

1288–1344	Gersonides, Jewish philosopher and astronomer
1401–64	Nicholas of Cusa, German philosopher and church theologian
1465–1536	Erasmus of Rotterdam, European humanist
1483–1546	Martin Luther, German Reformation leader; *Ninety-five Theses*, 1517
1509–64	John Calvin: *Institutes of the Christian Religion*, 1536
1542–91	John of the Cross (Juan de Yepez y Alvarez), Spanish mystic
1588–1679	Thomas Hobbes, English philosopher
1596–1650	René Descartes, French rationalist philosopher and mathematician
1619	Jakob Boehme: *On the Principles of Christianity*
1624	Lord Herbert of Cherbury, deist: *On Truth*
1632–77	Baruch Spinoza, Dutch monist philosopher
1632–1704	John Locke, English empiricist philosopher
1641	René Descartes: *Mèditations*
1651	Thomas Hobbes: *Leviathan*
1663	Leibniz: *De principiis individui*
1670	Spinoza: *Tractatus theologico-politicus*
1685–1753	George Berkeley, Irish idealist and empiricist philosopher
1690	John Locke: *An Essay Concerning Human Understanding*
1695	John Locke: *The Reasonableness of Christianity*
1710	Leibniz: *Théodicée*
1711–76	David Hume, Scottish empiricist philosopher and historian
1714	Leibniz: *Monadology*
1724–1804	Immanuel Kant, German transcendental philosopher
1728	William Law: *A Serious Call to Devout and Holy Life*

1729–86	Moses Mendelssohn, German Jewish philosopher
1730	Matthew Tindal, deist: *Christianity as Old as the Creation*
1738	Voltaire introduces ideas of Isaac Newton to France
1739	David Hume: *A Treatise of Human Nature*
1748–53	David Hume: *Philosophical Essays Concerning Human Understanding*
1751–72	French 'Encyclopédie' published
1762–1814	Johann Gottlieb Fichte, German idealist philosopher
1768–1834	Friedrich Schleiermacher, German theologian, philosopher and founder of modern hermeneutics
1770–1831	Georg Wilhelm Friedrich Hegel, German idealist philosopher
1775–1854	Friedrich Wilhelm Joseph von Schelling, German philosopher
1779	David Hume: *Dialogues of Natural Religion* (posthumously)
1781	Kant: *Critique of Pure Reason*
1788	Kant: *Critique of Practical Reason*
1788–1860	Arthur Schopenhauer, German philosopher
1792	Fichte: *Versuch einer Kritik aller Offenbarung*
1793	Kant: *Religion Within the Limits of Pure Reason*
1798–1858	Auguste Comte, French positivist philosopher
1799	Schleiermacher: *On Religion: Speeches to its Cultured Despisers*
1800	Schelling: *System of Transcendental Idealism*
1804–72	Ludwig Feuerbach, German philosopher
1806–73	John Stuart Mill, English philosopher
1807	Hegel: *Phänomenologie des Geistes* (*Phenomenology of Mind/Spirit*)

1809–82   Charles Darwin, English naturalist and exponent of evolutionary theory.

1813–55   Søren Kierkegaard, Danish philosopher of existentialist outlook

1818–83   Karl Marx, German political philosopher and social theorist

1819   Schopenhauer: *Die Welt als Wille und Vorstellung (The World as Will and Idea)*

1820–1903   Herbert Spencer, English philosopher and evolutionary theorist

1821   Schleiermacher: *The Christian Faith*

1836–86   Ramakrishna, Hindu *guru* and teacher

1838   Auguste Comte: gives the basic social science of sociology its name

1839–1914   Charles S. Peirce, American philosopher and logician

1841   Ludwig Feuerbach: *Das Wesen des Christentums (The Essence of Christianity)*

1842–1910   William James, American philosopher and psychologist

1844–1900   Friedrich Nietzsche, German iconoclastic philosopher

1846–1924   F. H. Bradley, English Hegelian philosopher

1859   Charles Darwin: *On the Origin of Species by Natural Selection*

1859–1938   Edmund Husserl, Austrian philosopher

1859–1952   John Dewey, American philosopher of progressivist pragmatism

1861–1947   Alfred North Whitehead, English mathematician and philosopher

1870–1937   Alfred Adler, Austrian psychiatrist

1870–1945   Nishida Kitarō, Japanese philosopher and innovative thinker; founder of Kyoto school

1875–1961	C.G. Jung, Swiss psychiatrist and philosopher of symbol
1878–1965	Martin Buber, Austrian Jewish philosopher of personhood
1886–1929	Franz Rosenzweig, Jewish philosopher
1886–1957	Frederick R. Tennant, English philosophical theologian
1886–1965	Paul Tillich, German-American philosophical theologian and apologist
1889–1951	Ludwig Wittgenstein, Austrian and Cambridge philosopher
1889–1973	Gabriel Marcel, French Roman Catholic existentialist philosopher
1889–1976	Martin Heidegger, German philosopher of human existence
1893	F.H. Bradley: *Appearance and Reality*
1900	Sigmund Freud: *The Interpretation of Dreams*
1900–76	Gilbert Ryle, English philosopher of conceptual analysis.
1900–90	Nishitani Keiji, Japanese philosopher of Kyoto school, influenced by Zen and Western thought
1900–2002	Hans-Georg Gadamer, German philosopher and major hermeneutical thinker
1904–90	B.F. Skinner, American psychologist and behaviourist
1906–95	Emmanuel Levinas, Lithuanian-born Jewish philosopher of personhood
1907	William James: *Pragmatism*
1907–72	Abraham Joshua Heschel, Polish-American Jewish philosopher
1913–	Paul Ricoeur, French hermeneutical thinker and philosopher
1915–80	Roland Barthes, French philosopher and semiotic theorist
1919	Karl Barth: *Der Römerbrief* (*The Epistle to the Romans*, 2nd edition, 1921)

1923   Martin Buber: *I and Thou*

1927   Sigmund Freud: *The Future of an Illusion*

1927   Martin Heidegger: *Being and Time*

1929   The 'Vienna circle': Carnap, Schlick, *et al.*

1930–   Jacques Derrida, French philosopher and postmodern
                theorist of signs

1932–   Alvin Plantinga, American theistic philosopher and
                logician

1932–   Nicholas Wolterstorff, American theistic philosopher

1934–   Richard Swinburne, English theistic philosopher of religion

1936   A.J. Ayer: *Language, Truth and Logic*

1941   Rudolf Bultmann: 'New Testament and Mythology'

1950   Gilbert Ryle: *The Concept of Mind*

1953   Nishitani: *What is Religion?*

1953   Ludwig Wittgenstein: *Philosophical Investigations*
                (posthumously)

1953–64   Paul Tillich: *Systematic Theology* (3 volumes)

1959   P.F. Strawson: *Individuals*

1962   J.L. Austin, *How to do Things with Words*

1962–5   Second Vatican Council in Rome

1966   John Hick, *Evil and the God of Love* (2nd edition, 1977)

1966   Ian Ramsey, Oxford philosophical theologian, becomes
                Bishop of Durham

1967   Jacques Derrida: *Of Grammatology*, and *Writing and
                Difference*

1967   Alvin Plantinga: *God and Other Minds*

1969   John Searle: *Speech Acts*

1974   Emmanuel Levinas: *Otherwise than Being*

1977	Richard Swinburne: *The Coherence of Theism* (revised edition, 1991)
1979	Richard Rorty: *Philosophy and the Mirror of Nature*
1979	Richard Swinburne: *The Existence of God*
1984	Alvin Plantinga and Nicholas Wolterstorff: *Faith and Rationality*
1984–88	Paul Ricoeur: *Time and Narrative* (3 volumes)
1989	Revised English translation of Gadamer, *Truth and Method*
1994	Richard Swinburne: *The Christian God*
1995	Nicholas Wolterstorff: *Divine Discourse*
1998	Richard Rorty: *Truth and Progress*
1999	Alvin Plantinga, *Warranted Christian Belief*
2002	Death of Hans-Georg Gadamer (b. 1900)

Index of names